THE
HISTORY
HIGHWAY
3.0

THE
HISTORY
HIGHWAY
3.0

A GUIDE TO
INTERNET RESOURCES
Third Edition

Dennis A. Trinkle and Scott A. Merriman

Editors

M.E. Sharpe

Armonk, New York
London, England

Library of Congress Cataloging-in-Publication Data

Trinkle, Dennis A., 1968–
   The history highway 3.0 : a guide to internet resources / [edited by] Dennis A. Trinkle
and Scott A. Merriman.—3rd ed.
     p. cm.
   Rev. ed. of: The history highway 2000.
   Includes index.
   ISBN 0-7656-0903-7 (alk. paper) — ISBN 0-7656-0904-5 (pbk. : alk. paper)
     1. History—Computer network resources. 2. Internet. 3. History—Research.
4. History—Computer-assisted instruction. I. Merriman, Scott A., 1968–
II. History highway 2000. III. Title.

D16.117.T75 2002
025.06′9—dc21

2001049817

Printed in the United States of America

The paper used in this publication meets the minimum requirements of
American National Standard for Information Sciences
Permanence of Paper for Printed Library Materials,
ANSI Z 39.48-1984.

BM (c) 10 9 8 7 6 5 4 3 2 1
BM (p) 10 9 8 7 6 5 4 3 2 1

In Honor of Our Teachers and Mentors:

John Dittmer, John Schlotterbeck, Barbara Steinson, Frank Kafker, Neal Abraham, David Powell, David Sterling, Daniel Beaver, David Hamilton, and Robert Ireland.

Contents

Acknowledgments

The first edition of *The History Highway* was written more than five years ago. That the work is now entering its third and most ambitious incarnation is a testament to its value to students, instructors, and lovers of history. It is also a tribute to the many individuals who have contributed directly and indirectly to the project over the past five years. We cannot possibly thank everyone who has played a small or large role in the writing of this book, so we hope that you know that your efforts and support are recognized and appreciated.

Dennis A. Trinkle would like to thank the faculty, staff, and students of DePauw University for their many tangible and intangible contributions to *The History Highway*. DePauw is a lively learning community, and I want to thank President Robert Bottoms and Vice President Neal Abraham for their support and encouragement of my many activities. I also want to especially thank several faculty and staff colleagues who daily make my teaching, research, and work better and more successful: John Schlotterbeck, Barbara Steinson, John Dittmer, Julia Bruggemann, Glen Kuecker, Aaron Dzuibinskyi, Lou Miller, Sue Balter, Bob Hershberger, Carol Smith, Julianne Miranda, Dan Pfeifer, Scott Cooper, Ken Owen, and Bob Bruce. I would also like to thank the members of my other professional family—the American Association for History and Computing. In particular, my sincere appreciation is extended to Ken Dvorak, Charles Mackay, Jeffrey Barlow, Kelly Robison, Jessica Lacher-Feldman, Steve Hoffman, and Deborah Anderson. It is a genuine pleasure to work with so many creative and passionate teachers and scholars. Finally, but certainly not least, special thanks to my wife, Kristi, my brother, Keith, my mother, Gayle, and all the members of my extended family. Your constant energy and care are a great inspiration.

Scott A. Merriman would like to thank his family, friends, and teachers, both past and present, for their support and guidance. Special thanks to my wife, Jessie, for her assistance, both in this writing effort and many others. I would also like to recognize the History Department of the University of Kentucky, faculty, staff, and fellow graduate students alike, for their support and encouragement. Especially deserving of gratitude for serving as mentors are Robert Ireland, Eric Christianson, David Hamilton, and Robert Olson. My years at UK have been enriched by my friendships with Holly Grout, John Patrick Mullins, Tom Riley, Erin Shelor, Jules Sweet, and Jennifer Walton. In my larger travels, I have been ably assisted by many people, far too many to mention, and I would be remiss if I did not thank at least some of them here. I am truly grateful for my continuing friendships and professional relationships with Jeffrey Barlow, Rowly Brucken, Randal Horobik, Charles Mackay, Jen McGee, Kelly Robison, David Staley, Amy Staples, and Paul Wexler. I am thankful to my family for their perpetual support. Finally, for all those who have supported me, but who are not specifically mentioned, thanks!

Introduction

More than 60 percent of American households now report that they regularly access the Internet. This figure represents a stunning historical transformation. The number of Web pages is increasing so rapidly that no reliable estimate exists, though best guesses suggest more than a billion pages and climbing. The growth rate and proliferation are staggering and is historically unprecedented. Radio, television, and the telephone became part of American daily life at a comparatively glacial pace. Such dizzying expansion and alteration make the Internet a tremendously exciting phenomenon, but also unsettling and unwieldy. When we wrote the first edition of *The History Highway* in 1996, we lamented that tying to explore and sample the Internet was like trying to sip water from a fire hose. When *The History Highway 2000* appeared in 2000, the metaphor seemed even more apt. Today, the fire hose might be replaced by Niagara Falls. The pace of expansion and change is accelerating.

To novices and even seasoned users, the Information Superhighway can be information overload at its worst, often more intimidating and frustrating than exciting. For anyone interested in history, however, the Internet simply cannot be ignored. The resources are richer and more valuable than ever. There are nearly fifty thousand sites dedicated to the American Revolution alone. Students can find the complete texts of hundreds of thousands of books, work with previously inaccessible primary documents, and explore thousands of first-rate sites dedicated to historical topics. Publishers can advertise their wares, and professors can find enormous databases devoted to teaching suggestions, online versions of historical journals, and active scholarly discussions on a wide variety of research topics. The Internet is quite simply the most revolutionary storehouse of human knowledge in history.

For most of us, however, whether we are students, professors, librarians, editors, or just lovers of history, there are not enough hours in our already busy days to go chasing information down an infinite number of alleyways, no matter how useful or interesting that information might be. This is especially true for those of us who have never logged on to a computer network or who have only a basic acquaintance with the Internet. The aim of this book is to provide a general introduction to the skills and tools necessary to navigate the Information Superhighway and to offer detailed information about the thousands of quality resources that are out there and how to find them.

Part I is a short primer for those with little or no experience using the Internet. It discusses what exists and what you can do with it. It explains how to gain access to the Internet and outlines what types of software are necessary. There is also an important section on the manners and rules that govern the Internet— "netiquette," as seasoned users call it. A valuable new section on evaluating Internet resources has been added to the chapter as well.

Part II is the heart of the book. It lists thousands of sites that will appeal to anyone interested in history and that our specialist section authors have determined to be reliable and useful for the serious study of history. This section will allow you to avoid the helter-skelter databases, such as Yahoo!, Excite, and DogPile, that take you to information regardless of quality and utility. You will not find sites created by first graders in Indianapolis or by biased, ahistorical groups like the Holocaust Deniers of America. Bon Voyage!

THE
HISTORY
HIGHWAY
3.0

Part I

Getting Started

Chapter 1

The Basics

History of the Internet

Since this book is directed at those interested in history, it seems sensible to begin with a brief history of the Internet itself. The story of the Internet's origins is as varied, complex, and fascinating as the information the Net contains. Ironically, the Net began as the polar opposite of the publicly accessible network it has become. It grew out of the Cold War hysteria surrounding the Soviet launch of *Sputnik*, the first man-made satellite, in 1957. Amidst paranoia that the United States was losing the "science race," President Eisenhower created the Advanced Research Projects Agency (ARPA) within the Department of Defense to establish an American lead in science and technology applicable to the military. After helping the United States develop and launch its own satellite by 1959, the ARPA scientists turned much of their attention to computer networking and communications. Their goal was to find a successful way of linking universities, defense contractors, and military command centers to foster research and interaction, but also to sustain vital communications in case of nuclear attack. The network project was formally launched in 1969 by ARPA under a grant that connected four major computers at universities in the southwestern United States—UCLA, Stanford, the University of California, Santa Barbara, and the University of Utah. The network went online in December 1969. The age of computer networks was born.

In the early 1970s, it became clear to the initial developers of the ARPANET that the system was already stretching past its Cold War origins. Non-military research institutions were developing competing networks of communication, more and more users were going online, and new languages were being introduced all of which made communication difficult or impossible between networks. To resolve this problem, the Defense Advanced Research Projects Agency (which had replaced ARPA) launched the Internetting Project in 1973. The aim was to create a uniform communications language that would allow the hundreds of networks being formed to communicate and function as a single meganetwork. In an amazing display of scientific prowess comparable to the Apollo Program, this crucial step in the development of the Information Superhighway was accomplished in a single year when Robert Kahn and Vinton G. Cerf introduced the Transmission Control Protocol/ Internet Protocol (TCP/IP). This protocol (as the rules governing a computer language are termed) made possible the connection of all the various networks and computers then in existence and set the stage for the enormous expansion of the Internet.

Over the next decade, the Department of Defense realized the significance and potential of the Internet, and non-military organizations were gradually allowed to link with the ARPANET. Shortly after that, commercial providers like CompuServe began making the Internet accessible for those not connected to a university or research institution. The potential for profiting from the Internet fueled dramatic improvements in speed and ease of use.

The most significant step toward simplicity of use came with the introduction of the World Wide Web (WWW) which allows interactive graphics and audio to be accessed through the Internet. The WWW was the brainchild of Tim Berners-Lee of the European Laboratory for Particle Physics, who created a computer language called "hypertext" that made possible the interactive exchange of text and graphic images and allowed almost instantaneous connection (linking) to any item on the Internet. Berners-Lee was actually developing this revolutionary language as the Internet was expanding in the 1970s and 1980s, but it was only with the introduction of an easy-to-use Web browser (as the software for interacting with the Web is called) that the Web became widely accessible to the average person. That first browser—Mosaic—was made available to the public by the National Center for Supercomputing Applications at the University of Illinois, Urbana–Champaign in 1991. Three years later, Mosiac's creator, Marc Andreessen, introduced an even more sophisticated browser that allowed the interaction of sound, text, and images—Netscape Navigator. The next year Microsoft launched a browser of its own—Internet Explorer.

Today, there are many software options for exploring the Internet, and access can be purchased through thousands of national and local service providers. One need no longer be a military researcher or work at a university to "surf the Net." There are now more than one hundred million users logging onto the Internet from the United States alone. Tens of thousands of networks now are connected by TCP/IP, and the Internet forms a vast communication system which can legitimately be called an Information Superhighway.

Uses of the Internet

This section of Part I will explain the most useful features of the Internet for those interested in history. It will discuss sending and receiving e-mail, reading and posting messages to Usenet newsgroups and discussion lists, logging on to remote computers with Telnet, transferring files using the File Transfer Protocol, and browsing the WWW. The next section will discuss in greater detail the software packages that perform these tasks and explain exactly how to get online.

Sending and Receiving E-mail

E-mail (electronic mail) is the most popular feature of the Internet. It offers almost instantaneous communication with people all over the world. The Nora Ephron film *You've Got Mail* has made e-mail as widely known as the United States Post Office, and e-mail functions very similarly, allowing users to send and receive messages or computer files over the Internet. Rather than taking days or weeks to reach their destination, however, e-mail messages arrive in minutes or seconds. A professor in Indianapolis, Indiana, can correspond with a student in Delhi, India, in the blink of an eye. A publisher, editor, and author can exchange drafts of a history book they are preparing with no delay. And, e-mail does not involve the high costs of international postage, fax charges, or long-distance telephone premiums. E-mail is always part of the basic service arrangement provided with Internet access, and it is quite easy to use with the software packages discussed later.

A Note on E-mail Addresses

E-mail addresses are very similar to postal addresses. Like a postal address, an e-mail address provides specific information about where the message is to be sent along the Internet. For example, a friend's address might be something like

Gkuecker@depauw.edenvax.edu.

If you look at the end of the address, you will notice the .edu suffix. This means the e-mail message is going to an educational institution. In this case, it is DePauw University, as the second item indicates. Edenvax shows that the message is traveling along the Net to someone on a Vax computer designated as Eden at DePauw University. Finally, the address reveals that the recipient is your friend Glen Kuecker (Gkuecker). This is just like providing the name, street address, city, state, and zip code on regular mail.

The names that individual institutions choose for their Internet address vary widely, but to help make e-mail addresses a little easier to understand, all addresses in the United States are broken down into the computer equivalent of zip codes. We already noted that the .edu in the above message indicates that the recipient's account is at an educational institution. There used to be six key three-letter designations that provided a clue as to where your e-mail was going to or coming from. Seven additional designations have recently been approved. The thirteen designations are

Category	Meaning
.com	commercial organizations
.edu	educational institutions
.gov	government organizations (non-military)
.mil	military institutions
.net	network service providers
.org	miscellaneous providers and nonprofit organizations
.aero	air-transport industry
.biz	businesses
.coop	cooperatives
.info	unrestricted
.museum	museums
.name	individuals
.pro	accountants, lawyers, and physicians

A common naming system for American primary and secondary schools has also recently been introduced. This system uses the school name, the k12 designation, and the state where the school is located in the address. A typical address might read

KeithTrinkle@howe.k12.in.us.

This indicates that a student, teacher, or administrator at Howe High School in Indiana sent the e-mail. The k12.in.us will always be present in e-mail coming from a primary or secondary school.

These designations do not apply to e-mail addresses for accounts located outside the United States, but an equally simple system exists for identifying foreign messages. All mail going to or coming from foreign accounts ends with a two-letter country code. If you have a colleague in France, you might receive an e-mail message ending with .fr. You may receive an e-mail message from an editor in Canada ending in .ca. Or, if you met a historian with similar interests on that last trip through Tanzania, you might soon receive mail ending with .tz. These extensions are:

AF	Afghanistan
AL	Albania
DZ	Algeria
AS	American Samoa
AD	Andorra
AO	Angola
AI	Anguilla
AQ	Antarctica
AG	Antigua and Barbuda
AR	Argentina
AM	Armenia
AW	Aruba
AU	Australia
AT	Austria
AZ	Azerbaijan
BS	Bahamas
BH	Bahrain
BD	Bangladesh
BB	Barbados
BY	Belarus
BE	Belgium
BZ	Belize
BJ	Benin
BM	Bermuda
BT	Bhutan
BO	Bolivia
BA	Bosnia-Herzegovina
BW	Botswana
BV	Bouvet Island
BR	Brazil
IO	British Indian Ocean Territory
BN	Brunei Darussalam
BG	Bulgaria
BF	Burkina Faso
BI	Burundi
KH	Cambodia
CM	Cameroon
CA	Canada
CV	Cape Verde

KY	Cayman Islands
CF	Central African Republic
TD	Chad
CL	Chile
CN	China
CX	Christmas Island
CC	Cocos Islands
CO	Colombia
KM	Comoros
CG	Congo
CD	Congo, Democratic Republic
CK	Cook Islands
CR	Costa Rica
CI	Côte d'Ivoire
HR	Croatia
CU	Cuba
CY	Cyprus
CZ	Czech Republic
DK	Denmark
DJ	Djibouti
DM	Dominica
DO	Dominican Republic
TP	East Timor
EC	Ecuador
EG	Egypt
SV	El Salvador
GQ	Equatorial Guinea
ER	Eritrea
EE	Estonia
ET	Ethiopia
FK	Falkland Islands
FO	Faroe Islands
FJ	Fiji
FI	Finland
FR	France
GF	French Guiana
PF	French Polynesia
TF	French Southern Territories
GA	Gabon
GM	Gambia
GE	Georgia
DE	Germany

GH	Ghana
GI	Gibraltar
GB	Great Britain
GR	Greece
GL	Greenland
GD	Grenada
GP	Guadeloupe
GU	Guam
GT	Guatemala
GN	Guinea
GW	Guinea-Bissau
GY	Guyana
HT	Haiti
HM	Heard and McDonald Islands
HN	Honduras
HK	Hong Kong
HU	Hungary
IS	Iceland
IN	India
ID	Indonesia
IR	Iran
IQ	Iraq
IE	Ireland
IL	Israel
IT	Italy
JM	Jamaica
JP	Japan
JO	Jordan
KZ	Kazakhstan
KE	Kenya
KI	Kiribati
KP	Korea (North)
KR	Korea (South)
KW	Kuwait
KG	Kyrgyz Republic
LA	Lao People's Democratic Republic
LV	Latvia
LB	Lebanon
LS	Lesotho
LR	Liberia
LY	Libyan Arab Jamahiriya
LI	Liechtenstein

LT	Lithuania
LU	Luxembourg
MO	Macau
MK	Macedonia
MG	Madagascar
MW	Malawi
MY	Malaysia
MV	Maldives
ML	Mali
MT	Malta
MH	Marshall Islands
MQ	Martinique
MR	Mauritania
MU	Mauritius
YT	Mayotte
MX	Mexico
FM	Micronesia
MD	Moldova
MC	Monaco
MN	Mongolia
MS	Montserrat
MA	Morocco
MZ	Mozambique
MM	Myanmar
NA	Namibia
NR	Nauru
NP	Nepal
NL	Netherlands
AN	Netherlands Antilles
NT	Neutral Zone
NC	New Caledonia
NZ	New Zealand
NI	Nicaragua
NE	Niger
NG	Nigeria
NU	Niue
NF	Norfolk Island
MP	Northern Mariana Islands
NO	Norway
OM	Oman
PK	Pakistan
PW	Palau

PA	Panama
PG	Papua New Guinea
PY	Paraguay
PE	Peru
PH	Philippines
PN	Pitcairn
PL	Poland
PT	Portugal
PR	Puerto Rico
QA	Qatar
RE	Réunion
RO	Romania
RU	Russian Federation
RW	Rwanda
SH	Saint Helena
KN	Saint Kitts and Nevis
LC	Saint Lucia
PM	Saint Pierre and Miquelon
VC	Saint Vincent and the Grenadines
WS	Samoa
SM	San Marino
ST	São Tomé and Principe
SA	Saudi Arabia
SN	Senegal
SC	Seychelles
SL	Sierra Leone
SG	Singapore
SK	Slovakia
SI	Slovenia
SB	Solomon Islands
SO	Somalia
ZA	South Africa
ES	Spain
LK	Sri Lanka
SD	Sudan
SR	Suriname
SJ	Svalbard and Jan Mayen Islands
SZ	Swaziland
SE	Sweden
CH	Switzerland
SY	Syria
TW	Taiwan

TJ	Tajikistan
TZ	Tanzania
TH	Thailand
TG	Togo
TK	Tokelau
TO	Tonga
TT	Trinidad and Tobago
TN	Tunisia
TR	Turkey
TM	Turkmenistan
TC	Turks and Caicos Islands
TV	Tuvalu
UG	Uganda
UA	Ukraine
AE	United Arab Emirates
UK	United Kingdom
US	United States
UM	United States Minor Outlying Islands
UY	Uruguay
UZ	Uzbekistan
VU	Vanuatu
VA	Vatican City State
VE	Venezuela
VN	Vietnam
VG	Virgin Islands (British)
VI	Virgin Islands (U.S.)
WF	Wallis and Futuna Islands
EH	Western Sahara
YE	Yemen
YU	Yugoslavia
ZM	Zambia
ZW	Zimbabwe

A Note on E-mail Security

Because sending e-mail is so similar to sending a letter by postal service, many people forget that there is a major difference—federal laws discourage anyone from looking at (or intercepting) your mail, and sealed packaging provides a fairly reliable way to detect tampering. Unfortunately, e-mail is not protected in the same ways. As your electronic message passes through the Internet, it can be read, intercepted, and altered by many individuals.

Some security measures have been developed to protect e-mail just as an envelope secures letters. The latest versions of many programs that process e-mail now include the ability to encrypt messages. Encryption converts your e-mail into a complex code that must be deciphered by an e-mail program or Web browser that is designed to convert the encoded message back into regular text. The latest versions of Netscape, Internet Explorer, Eudora, and Pegasus include the ability to code and decode encrypted e-mail, but no e-mail program automatically converts a message into a secured code. If you want your messages or files encrypted, you will have to follow the directions provided with your e-mail package for doing it. If you purchase products and services over the Internet, you will also want to be certain that your account or credit card numbers are insured by some sort of encryption. Nevertheless, it is prudent to keep in mind that no security measure is completely reliable.

Reading and Posting Messages on Usenet Newsgroups

For anyone interested in history, Usenet newsgroups are another rewarding feature of the Internet. They are the electronic equivalent of the old New England town meetings at which anyone could pose a question or make an observation and others could respond to it. At present, there are more than ten thousand newsgroups dedicated to thousands of different topics, and many of these relate to history. Each is regulated by a moderator who, like the editor of a newspaper, sets the quality and tone of the posts. There are groups that regularly discuss the Holocaust, the American Revolution, historical publishing, library concerns, and cartography, just to mention a few areas.

The software that allows one to easily locate and participate in these newsgroups will be discussed later. Before passing on to the next topic, however, you should note that there are several clues to determining the content and nature of groups that will help down the road. Like e-mail addresses, the addresses of newsgroups provide some insight into the nature of the group. Take the newsgroup

alt.civilwar.

This address indicates that the group discusses the alternative topic—the Civil War. Each newsgroup will have a similar address revealing its type and topic. The following categories will aid in determining which of the more than ten thousand newsgroups are worth investigating:

Category	Meaning
alt.	alternative themes (Most groups relating to history carry the alt. designation)
comp.	computer related topics
misc.	miscellaneous themes
news.	posts about newsgroups
rec.	recreational topics
sci.	scientific discussions
soc.	social concerns
talk.	talk radio style format

Reading and Posting Messages on Discussion Lists

Discussion lists are a hybrid mixture of e-mail and newsgroups. With discussion lists, the posts and replies that anyone can access in newsgroups are sent by e-mail only to those who have subscribed to the list. As with most newsgroups, there is an editor who screens the posts before they are sent to subscribers, maintaining quality and decency. There are discussion lists that target students, professors, editors, publishers, librarians, and general readers. Almost any historical topic imaginable has a list devoted to it. How open the discussion lists are to subscribers is determined by the moderators. Some limit membership to those with a special interest, while others permit anyone who wishes to join. Chapter 2 discusses the lists focusing on history and explains their qualifications for subscription in more detail.

Chapter 2 will also provide more specific instructions on how to subscribe to each group. All discussion lists share a basic subscription format, however. To subscribe (or to unsubscribe), you simply send an e-mail message to the computer that receives and distributes the messages. This computer is called the listserver (or listserv) because it serves the list. For example, to send a message to a list discussing the history of dogs (H-Dog), you would send the e-mail message

Subscribe H-Dog yourfirstname yourlastname

to the e-mail address

Listserv@ucbeh.san.uc.edu.

The listserv would quickly acknowledge your registration as a member, and e-mail posts from the other list members would begin arriving in your box.

A Word of Warning about Discussion Lists

You should be careful to join only subscription lists that are truly of interest and be certain to read your e-mail several times a week. Most discussion lists are very active, sending out fifteen or more messages per day. If you get carried away at first, you may find yourself buried under an avalanche of several hundred e-mail posts awaiting your eager attention. So be careful to subscribe only to those lists that most interest you until you gain a feel for how much mail you are likely to receive.

Multi-User Virtual Environments

Unlike discussion lists, multi-user virtual environments (MUVEs) allow real-time conversations between participants anywhere in the world—that is, they can speak to each other at the same time as if on a conference telephone call. The most popular and widely known version of a multi-user environment is the chat room. There are now thousands of "rooms" on the Internet where people come together daily to discuss philosophy, politics, or the latest NBA game. Chat rooms are generally informal arenas. Another type of MUVE, the Multi-User Domain, Object Oriented, or MOO as they are commonly called, has been widely adopted for educational and serious use. MOOs allow the same real-time conversation of chat rooms, but the participants interact within a textually described world created by other participants. MOOs offer every user the opportunity to construct and describe the spaces and objects of this textual world.

Many universities and scholarly societies now sponsor MOOs that are open to the public. On some of these MOOs you can take a virtual class, engage in historical re-creations, or simply converse about historical issues. The MOOs related to history are discussed in more detail in Part II. A good directory to educational MOOs and to tutorials for those who would like more guidance can be found at: http://www.itp.berkeley.edu/~thorne/MOO.html.

Logging onto a Remote Computer with Telnet

Anyone who has ever used an electronic library catalog is familiar with the computerless screens and keyboards that allow patrons to access the library's catalog. These machines do not have their own microprocessors, but are linked to a central computer that shares information with all of the terminals connected to it. Telnet is a program offered by all Internet service providers that permits your home or office computer to act just like the terminals at the library. It enables you to temporarily connect to a remote computer and access its information as if it were on your own computer. Those interested in history will find Telnet particularly important because almost every major library in the world now allows Telnet access to its catalogs. You can do subject searches or find out which libraries possess a specific work you are looking for.

Transferring Files with File Transfer Protocol (FTP)

File Transfer Protocol (or FTP) is similar to Telnet. Like Telnet, it is a program that connects you to a remote computer. FTP does not allow you to read the material on the remote machine; rather, it actually allows you to copy the files or programs and transfer them to your own computer. You can use FTP to get a copy of the United States Constitution or to download (as retrieving information with FTP is called) a program that teaches you the history of the Vietnam War. Thousands of sites with downloadable files, programs, and historical information are out there waiting to be tapped. Many of the best and most useful FTP sites will be discussed in Part II.

As with Telnet, there are many packages that permit FTP access. For now, we will mention only that there are three main types of FTP access. There is anonymous FTP, identified FTP, and restricted FTP. Anonymous FTP allows you to connect to a computer and download information without identifying yourself. Identified FTP also allows you to copy materials, but it requires you to give your e-mail address and name, so that the sponsors of the site can maintain statistical information about the use of their site. Restricted FTP is used by some commercial and private institutions that only allow FTP for a fee or for authorized users. The sites mentioned in Part II specify which of these categories the sites fall into and explain how to gain access when a fee or password is required.

Browsing the WWW

For most computer users, time on the Internet will mean exploring the WWW and working with a Web browser (as the programs that allow access to the WWW are called). The Web is the most popular and fastest growing section of the Internet because it combines text, sound, and graphics to create multimedia sites. History buffs can find everything from an audio track of the *Battle Hymn of the Republic* to short film clips of JFK's assassination to a complete version of the French *Encyclopédie*. The most powerful Web browsers also perform all of the other Internet functions such as e-mail, Telnet, and FTP, so new users need only master one basic software package.

The Web and Web browser packages owe much of their popularity and potential to their multimedia format, but they also profit from their ability to link information. With the WWW, Web page developers can create links to any other page on the Web so that, when you use your mouse to point at a highlighted image or section of text and then click the correct mouse button, your computer can almost instantly bring up that information. Thus, a link on a home page (the first page of information that you see when you connect to a Web site) can connect you to any other site, just as a cross-reference in a textbook sends you to other related information. This makes the WWW an amazingly easy-to-use source of information or recreation (for those who become Web junkies).

Chapter 2 discusses the software that makes connecting to the Web possible, but as with e-mail, you will need to understand Web addresses to find information on the WWW. These addresses are called URLs—uniform resource locators—which is simply techno-talk for addresses. Every page on the Web has a unique URL. This makes it very easy to go directly to the information you need. They look something like this:

http://mcel.pacificu.edu/JAHC/JAHCiv2/index.html

Some addresses are longer than this. Some are shorter. All contain three basic parts. Looking from right to left, the first designation you notice is index.html. This tells you that you are retrieving a file called index in the html format. HTML (Hypertext Markup Language) is the standard language of the Web for saving multimedia information. Other possibilities include .gif and .jpeg, which indicate graphic image files; .avi and .wav, which indicate audio files; and .mov, which signals a movie. XML is a new markup protocol like HTML that also allows metatags or descriptive tags that describe the content without appearing on the page. Software can then do more sophisticated searches. Another common protocol is .asp. This means that the page is being created via a database. ASP refers to active server pages, which are a language for getting information from databases.

The middle part of the address, mcel.pacificu.edu/JAHC/JAHCiv2, is just like an e-mail address, specifying what network and computer stores the information so that your software package can find it on the Internet. The .edu extension tells you the information is at an educational institution; as with e-mail, there will always be a three-letter code revealing the type of institution that sponsors the site.

The http:// lets you know that the browser is using the Hypertext Transfer Protocol to get the information. This is the standard language that governs the transfer and sharing of information on the Web. If you were using your browser to Telnet or FTP, the http:// would be replaced by ftp:// or telnet:// and then the address, showing which function your computer is performing.

Of course, you can use the Internet and profit from the WWW without spending hours studying their technical background, history, and terms. The next chapter tells you how to get on the Internet and what software you need.

Chapter 2

Signing On

Getting on the Internet

Once upon a time, getting connected to the Internet was the hardest part of going online. In the early days, if you did not work for the military or a research institution, you were out of luck. The introduction of commercial providers in the 1980s made access easier to obtain, but it might cost you as much as a new car. Today, there are thousands of local and national Internet service providers, and the competition has made Internet access amazingly inexpensive. In most markets, you can now get almost unlimited access for $10 or $15 per month. For those fortunate enough to work for a library, college, university, or publisher, the price is often even better—free. Getting on the Internet has never been easier or less expensive.

Internet access is offered by three basic categories of service providers—corporate/institutional, national commercial, and local commercial providers. For those who work at companies or institutions offering Internet access to their employees, the best way to learn about your options is to speak directly to your system manager or computer support staff.

For those who do not have access to the Internet at work or school, there are several factors to consider in choosing a provider. Perhaps most important is finding a service that offers a local phone number or a toll-free number, so that you need not pay long distance charges for your Internet access. The attractiveness of the Internet vanishes quickly in the presence of a $400 phone bill. Fortunately, there are now so many service providers it is usually easy to find a provider that offers a local phone number in your area. Cable and satellite providers are also scurrying to offer other access options besides telephone connections.

The second consideration is the type of service you desire. Many national and local service providers in your city or state will offer almost unlimited access to the WWW, e-mail, FTP, and other basic services for very affordable rates ($5 to $20 a month). (Local service providers can be found by looking in your local phone book under "Internet Service Providers" or "World Wide Web Service Providers.") There are also several national service providers, such as America Online and CompuServe, which provide special services in addition to basic Internet access. These services include access to electronic versions of national newspapers, up-to-the-minute stock market reports, and special discussion lists and newsgroups available only to subscribers. Because these national service providers offer features you cannot find elsewhere, they are more expensive. The best way to decide if any of the national service providers feature packages you want.is to contact each of them directly, keeping a record of the benefits and limitations of each service.

The Hardware

Convenient use of the Internet and its many tools is governed by speed. The faster your computer can send and process information, the more pleasurable and productive your time on the Net will be. Thus, a simple rule of thumb guides the purchase of computer equipment for use on the Internet: Buy the best machine you can realistically afford. This does not mean to mortgage your house just to get better equipment. All new computers sold today are more than adequate for exploring the resources described in this book. For those with older computers, machines with the minimum configurations listed in Tables 2.1 and 2.2 will allow you to easily access the resources of the Internet. More memory (RAM), a faster processor, and a speedier modem will all enable you to interact with the Net more quickly, however. If you want to start with the basic system described below and gradually upgrade, make sure the first addition you make is more RAM. Upgrading from 32 megs to 64 or 128 megs of RAM or more will make the most noticeable difference in the performance of your computer. Improving your processor should be second and trading in your old modem should be done last. At present, the speed of phone lines restricts the effectiveness of modems, so you will get the least improvement in your system from the purchase of a faster modem.

The Software

While many educational institutions and the national service providers such as AOL and CompuServe offer their own software packages with directions and

Table 2.1

Windows-Based Configurations

Processor	486 or higher
RAM	32 MB with Windows 95, 98, or NT
Modem	28.8 KBS or faster recommended
Hard drive	35 MB free space recommended
Sound card and speakers	Recommended for multimedia
VGA monitor	Required
Network or dial-up connection	Required

Table 2.2

Apple Configurations

Processor	PowerPC with OS 7.6.1 or higher
RAM	24 MB or higher
Modem	28.8 kbs or faster recommended
Hard drive	35 MB free space recommended
Sound card and speakers	Required
VGA monitor	Required
Network or dial-up connection	Required

tutorials, those who choose local service providers can select the software they wish to use to access the Internet. Most local service providers will also give new users software needed to access the Internet along with detailed instructions. In principle, however, you can use any package you wish to connect to the Internet through a local provider. This section will present brief descriptions of some of the best packages and explain where to obtain them.

Web Browsers and E-mail Programs

Netscape Communicator and Microsoft Internet Explorer

The two powerhouse packages (Web browsers, as they are called) that most Internauts use are Netscape Communicator and Microsoft Internet Explorer.

They combine all the tools for accessing the Web, sending e-mail, Telnetting, and using FTP. Both can display the combinations of graphics and text that make the Internet a lively and exciting resource. They are simple to use, come with tutorials and a help feature, and are good choices for all users from novices to experts.

Netscape Communicator and Microsoft Internet Explorer also can both be downloaded on the Internet. You can download Netscape at the following address (please note, addresses are case sensitive):

http://www.netscape.com/computing/download/

Microsoft Internet Explorer can be downloaded at

http://www.microsoft.com/windows/ie/default.htm

Both Netscape and Internet Explorer are currently available free.

Eudora and Pegasus

Netscape and Internet Explorer perform all of the functions you need to explore the Internet, including e-mail. However, those who send and receive a lot of electronic correspondence, or who plan to send long files along with their messages, may prefer to use a package designed specifically to handle electronic mail. Qualcomm's Eudora and Pegasus are currently two of the best packages for handling e-mail that are available on the Internet at no cost to students, faculty, and staff. Both packages can send messages to lists of recipients, permit the use of special filters to sort and screen e-mail, allow secure protection of files, send files in addition to or along with text, and feature attractive graphic environments and menus that make them easy to use. Eudora is available via FTP at

http://www.eudora.com/

Pegasus is available via FTP at

http://www.pmail.com/

Netiquette and Copyright

Because electronic communication is still new, the rules governing online expression are still evolving. There are already, however, some basic courtesies that keep the free and open communication of the Internet polite and enjoyable.

With this goal in mind, here are some Netiquette hints that can keep you from accidentally offending someone.

General Netiquette

The most important thing to remember is that Internet communication is just like writing a letter. Electronic messages can be seen by many individuals other than the intended recipient. They can be forwarded to countless people. They can even be printed and posted in public areas. Thus, the golden rule of Internet communication should never be forgotten:

Never write anything you would not want a stranger to read.

It is also important to remember that e-mail is judged by the same standards as other written communication. Sometimes, the ease and speed of electronic communication lull users into forgetting to check grammar and spelling. This can lead to your e-mail being forwarded to thousands of individuals, and you do not want people all over the Internet laughing because you innocently asked if it was Vasco de Gama who circumcised the world with a forty-foot clipper.

There are also several special grammatical conventions that govern the Internet. One important rule is not TO WRITE EVERYTHING OUT IN CAPITAL LETTERS, to underline everything, *to italicize everything*, or **to put everything in bold**. Seasoned e-mail readers consider these the equivalent of shouting at the top of your lungs—the mark of a "newbie," or someone who has not yet learned to behave properly on the Internet.

Because e-mail lacks a convenient way to convey emotion through text, you will often encounter special symbols in e-mail correspondence. For example, a :) or :(is often put after a sentence to express happiness or sadness. A :0 may be added to express surprise. A :; may be inserted to indicate confusion, and history buffs who think they are Abe Lincoln may include a =|:-)= somewhere in their messages. These symbols add a bit of charm to Internet communication, but it is important to remember that they are only appropriate in informal correspondence. They also should not be overdone. Using too many emotive symbols is considered to be another mark of a newbie.

Rules for Newsgroup and Discussion List Posts

Besides the Netiquette governing general Internet communication, there are also some rules for those who wish to participate in newsgroups and discussion lists.

1. Before you make a post to a group or list, it is wise to follow the group's posts for a while. This will help you to know what has already been asked and what type of questions/statements are considered appropriate. Asking repetitive or uninformed questions can get you off to a bad start.

2. Think before you write. Do not send off emotional or ill-considered responses to posts. (This is called "flaming" in Internet parlance.) Take time to consider criticisms, sarcasms, and insults carefully. Remember the Internet is not an anonymous frontier, and online remarks can be just as hurtful to a person as any others.

3. Do not send private correspondence to groups or lists. If you just want to thank someone, send the message to the person directly. And be very careful in replying to a message. You do not want to accidentally tell several thousand readers about your date last night because you replied to the wrong address.

4. Do not post advertisements to groups or lists. This is considered extremely rude and intrusive, and it is the surest way to become the victim of vicious flaming. Internauts are being careful to avoid the spread of junk mail to the Internet.

Copyright

The question of copyright is an important one for students, teachers, librarians, publishers, and all those on the Internet. Everyone wants to know what the laws are governing copying and sharing information on the Internet, and lawyers and lawmakers are working to develop clear rules that govern electronic mediums. For now, the issues of copyright as they pertain to the Internet are still somewhat hazy, but there are some certainties that can guide your steps.

Most importantly, all online correspondence, files, and documents are handled like other written documents. They are automatically held to be copyrighted in the individual author's name. When an Internet item is copyrighted by some other party, the copyright holder generally identifies him or herself at the end of the document.

Students, teachers, and general users will be glad to know that a judge ruled in 1996 that Internet documents can be copied according to the fair use rules that govern printed sources. You can make personal copies of online documents and images, and you can incorporate them in instructional packages (if you are a student, teacher, or librarian) as long as the package is in no way intended to generate a profit. Other more precise rules governing copyright will undoubtedly be developed in the near future. For now, the safest course seems to be treating Internet sources just like other written documents.

Evaluation of Internet Content

Jessica Lacher-Feldman

It is often said that the WWW places the world on your desktop. From the comfort of your home, your office, a cybercafé, or any computer with Internet access, you can access vast amounts of valuable information. But how do you know as an information consumer what information is accurate, true, or legitimate?

Human history and educational experience give researchers an urge to rely on the accuracy of everything they see in print. The act of publishing lends a sense of legitimacy that is not necessarily justifiable. Simply because something has been published, whether online or in print, does not allow you to conclude that the work is accurate.

Traditionally, academic publishing involved a great deal of editorial control, and the distribution of scholarly works was greatly limited. Electronic publishing has leveled the playing field, making it much easier to produce and distribute works to a broad audience. A wealth of information exists on the WWW, information that can answer questions, further research, spark an interest, and put people in contact with others with similar interests and agendas on the other side of the world. But in terms of publishing to the WWW, we must ask if all Web resources are created equal.

The Web offers convenience, speed, and variety that are unprecedented. Many students and other information consumers view the Web as the first and only stop that needs to be made when doing any kind of research. This is a dangerous assumption. Researchers and others who use the Web who believe that "everything you need is on the Web" are invariably hindering their scholastic potential. That certainly is not to say that there is not a vast amount of very valuable information on the Web. Useful information can be found in the form of self-published articles and Web sites by historians and scholars. Course syllabi from other colleges and universities shed light on a particular subject and provide still more resources both in print and online. Web sites of archival repositories and other cultural institutions identify and describe their collections online, providing users with digital surrogates and context for some of their holdings. The WWW offers an incredible bounty of information, but as with any type of research, the user must exercise good judgment in evaluating its value, authority, verity, and validity.

Information literacy is a set of abilities that allows individuals to "recognize when information is needed" and to "locate, evaluate, and use effectively the needed information."[1] Information literacy is a critical skill in the era of the WWW. With the ease and access of the WWW, anyone with the ability to use an HTML editor and access to a bit of Web space can place any material at all on the Web. This accessibility can create numerous problems for researchers who fail to evaluate the information provided.

The History Highway 3.0 presents a broad range of history-related Web sites that have been evaluated and recommended by scholars in their respective fields. This text provides direction for information seekers that has been evaluated by respected scholars. The fallibility of any work concerned with the WWW remains that of the Web itself. In such a volatile environment, a site can disappear overnight, leaving frustrated researchers behind. Unless a Web site has been archived on a hard drive or CD-ROM, if it disappears, it could disappear permanently. Sites are constantly being added and deleted from the WWW. Sites that were once free might begin charging a fee for use, limiting access, or the search tool might change and interfere with previous work.

The speed, breadth, and availability of online resources have changed the way that libraries do business, as well as the way a researcher might approach a project. For many researchers, serendipitous browsing of library stacks has been replaced by surfing the Web. There is room in this world for both approaches, and it is certain that one approach is not better than the other.

Over the years, users have developed a degree of trust in regard to print sources. Editors review books and journals, and publishers are committed to printing and distributing these works. The process of publishing an article in an academic journal or a scholarly monograph through a commercial or university press is long and tedious. Copy editors carefully scrutinize these print materials. A panel of peers reviews and edits them long before the material is presented to the public. Then these print sources are often reviewed in other journals. These peer-reviewed sources are traditionally deemed reliable and accurate.

The WWW has democratized the distribution of information by offering a means to self-publish material without necessarily benefiting from scrutiny and peer review. Web sites are almost never reviewed or refereed, certainly not to the extent that scholarly print materials are. This freedom has opened up new opportunities to those with very specialized interests and a desire to make that information available to the world. At the same time, this information explosion has created a much greater need to learn to evaluate these online materials. The danger of finding faulty information on the WWW increases as additional sites are added. By taking a Web source at face value without first trying to verify the information and the source, users run the risk of perpetrating an untruth, not to mention the possibility of embarrassment. Many Web sites indicate on the index page that they are endorsed by a particular group or evaluating body. While this endorsement does not necessarily hold the same weight as a review in a scholarly journal, depending on the endorsing body, this information offers evidence of the validity and value of a Web site.

With the ability to do research online at any time from any place comes the responsibility to understand and evaluate online materials to make certain that these resources are accurate, unbiased, and of high quality. With practice and a few skills, it isn't difficult to become a good information consumer. You must develop critical thinking skills and an understanding of how to evaluate online sources—that is, you must gain a degree of information literacy. The ability to evaluate online resources when doing research is an extension of the ability to evaluate print sources and primary source materials. Drawing upon analytical skills and common sense, and incorporating some guidance from information professionals and others, the evaluating of online resources becomes a critical step in the research process.

There are several questions that you need to ask when viewing a site for the first time. First, look at the **content**. Are the title and the author of the site easily identified? Is the author credible? Does the author have experience and expertise on the subject? Does the site represent a specific group or organization that is clearly indicated? If a corporate entity or a political or religious body sponsors a site, there might be a hidden agenda, despite the organization's attempt to present clear and unbiased information. Clues to the kind of site are present in the URL. If the Web address ends with a .com, then it is a corporate site. A site with the .edu suffix is from an educational institution, probably a college or university. However, an .edu site such as www.ua.edu/~esmith.html should be considered a personal page that, although hosted by an educational site, may not be officially sanctioned by the college or university and therefore could be biased. Information on a site with the suffix .gov indicates a government Web site. The information on .gov sites and .edu sites is among the most reliable information on the WWW with relation to history and history-related sources.

When looking at the content, you must also seek out the **purpose** of the material. Does the material appear to be scholarly or popular? Who is the intended audience? Is it written for students, scholars, or peers? Also consider the **tone** of the material. Is it written in a comic or satirical fashion? As with print material, the researcher needs to be able to recognize the fundamental differences between a scholarly work and a nonscholarly work. A scholarly work is intended for a narrow audience and is usually serious in both content and the overall appearance of the work. Popular works are written for a broader audience and therefore have a broader appeal—the Web sites will have more graphics and color, and the topics will be broader and of a more popular interest. This is true of both Web and print materials. For example, compare these sites:

http://people.aol.com/people/index.html

and

http://mcel.pacificu.edu/JAHC/jahcindex.htm

The first site is full of images, bright colors, and blinking graphics. The second site is a sober white page with black and blue text. The second site, while it is full of valuable information, is not meant for as broad an audience as the first.

Other types of Web sites should be duly noted. The first is the general interest site or publication. These sites, while they do provide valuable information, are not geared toward the scholar or expert in a given field. Another type of site is the sensational site, which plays upon the gullibility and curiosity of its readers by using inflammatory language and humor.

Compare these two sites:

http://www.scientificamerican.com/

and

http://www.weeklyworldnews.com/index.cfm

While these may be obvious examples of the differences in types of online publications, comparing the style, content, and language serves as a useful exercise in understanding the broad range of publications. While we may never consider using the *Weekly World News* in a research project, information that is just as inaccurate and inflammatory exists in other, more subtle guises.

Even the simple question of the **date** and **edition** of material should be noted. You should also consider the **scope** of the material presented. Does the site intend to be narrow or broad in discussing the subject matter? If the creator omits important events, dates, or aspects of a particular issue, this would indicate a problem with the site. Does the site provide a list of related resources? Does this list appear to be complete or selective? Does the list appear biased in any way?

Also be aware of the **uniqueness** of a site. Is the material presented at this site available in print or elsewhere online? If the information on the site has been published elsewhere, that fact should be noted on the site. If the researcher is seeking out general information on a specific topic, is the Web site the best place to seek out this information?

Images on the Web provide historical evidence and valuable tools for research. Images of handwritten letters, photographs, art, and other materials can be extremely interesting and valuable to the historical researcher. But you should be aware that images can be altered in order to provide evidence to support a controversial belief. Such alterations have been especially common in sites created by hate groups, most notably Holocaust deniers, who proliferate on the WWW. Altered aerial photographs are presented as "evidence" that the Holocaust never happened. Because the WWW is so accessible, both to the end user and to the publisher or creator, it has become an easy way to publish materials that are subversive and perpetrate hate or falsehoods. Some Web sites are blatant in that regard, but others are very cleverly orchestrated to manipulate the user. This can be done with both images and text. Look for evidence of

bias by investigating the creator of the site and their agenda. This information may not be obvious to the user. Be aware that a legitimate nonprofit organization can have an .org Web site, but an .org site is not necessarily an indicator of reliable information.

When controversial information is presented to an audience in a slick and manipulative fashion, the novice researcher could easily be fooled. When using digitized surrogates of primary sources, including images of photographs, letters, or other correspondence, it is critical to take note of the Web address and trace its origin. Verify the source!

For example, the URL

http://rmc.library.cornell.edu/frenchrev/Lafayette/Images/Screen/2_11.JPG

is an image of a handwritten recipe for Martha Washington's lip salve, transcribed by Eleanor Parke Custis, adopted daughter of George and Martha Washington, for Natalie, Mathilde, Clementine, Oscar, and Edmond Lafayette, written December 17, 1824. By looking at the URL in its entirety, we can see that it is from a library at Cornell University, from a grouping related to the French Revolution and to Lafayette. We also know that this is a .jpg image. Without this URL, and just looking at the page, all we see is a digitized handwritten page, with no identifying information from the creator. Using a software program such as Adobe PhotoShop, the creator of a Web site could alter a photograph or a document with relative ease. While there is no great controversy about a recipe for lip salve, remember to look for a hidden agenda and for inconsistencies in an image itself.

Digitized primary sources in the form of online exhibits and collections have increased dramatically in the past few years. Libraries and archives are creating digital surrogates of collections and presenting this material on the WWW. These exhibits and digital collections are excellent opportunities to gain access to materials that, without the advent of the WWW and its graphics capabilities, would be nearly impossible to see. It is important to remember that these collections are made of digitized copies of the originals. Whether they are being accessed as preservation copies or from a location halfway across the world, you should look at the URL to determine where these images are from and how they are being used.

When researching on the WWW, you must always look for the **sources** used in creating a site. All of this information should be clearly stated, either on a bibliography page or on the index page of the site. Are there accurate and clear **citations**? Can you verify these citations? If this information is not readily available, this may indicate a problem. Check the **links** provided. Are the sites listed appropriate and useful? Is the site **current**? Are the links current? While a Web site that was mounted in 1996 may have the best information available online about a particular event, it is the responsibility of the researcher to verify this information and make certain that the site is the best possible source for the purpose.

When it comes to Web sites, **style** is not just a question of aesthetics but can often indicate if the creator of the site is skilled and serious about the information presented. An attractive Web site suggests to the researcher accuracy and authority, but this certainly is not always the case. In this information age, we must learn to be good *information consumers*. You should take note of the navigability, structure, and usability of the site. Is there search capability on the site? If not, how does the lack of a search function interfere with the functionality of the site? How does the writing style correspond to the information in the site and the site's intended audience? All of these factors should be noted when considering a Web site for use in research. All information is not created equal.

It is also essential to remember **copyright** and **fair use**. Copyright laws are complicated and confusing to everyone. Even if copyright information on the Web site is not made clear to the user, the material still falls under copyright law. While access may be free on the WWW, you must still adhere to copyright laws just as you would with print media.

When doing a search for online sources, it is very important to understand the **types of sources** you are looking for. A user doing historical research needs to seek out sites that are best suited for the project at hand, such as material presented by experts in the subject matter or cultural agencies that specialize in that particular area. While the Web site of a regional chamber of commerce might offer current demographics information, that may not be the best material to use when you are writing on the geographic area as it was in the mid-nineteenth century. Before you begin to search the Web, you must define your research and gain an understanding of what kinds of sites will be helpful. The sources need to match your purpose.

Searching the Web is a task that many have grown accustomed to and comfortable with in just the past few years. How do you know if you are doing an **effective search**? Use a good search engine such as google.com or northernlight.com, paying attention to its instructions on how to search effectively. It is useful to try the same search terms with several different search engines and compare your results.

When choosing a search engine, there are some important factors to consider:

- Is the interface clear and easy to use?
- How large is the database? (This should be evident on the main page of the engine.)
- How is the material indexed (by a machine, or by people)?
- How well do the search capabilities (Boolean searching, advanced searching) work?
- Are the results ranked?

You can also take advantage of workshops and instruction in your local academic or public library. Brief courses in online search skills are offered frequently at educational institutions. Don't hesitate to **ask a librarian** for advice and instruction with online searching. A few minutes spent receiving a few good tips can be extremely valuable, ultimately quite time-saving.

If you have a strong interest in a particular topic, it is a good idea to frequently check the Web for information on that topic. Some Web sites offer alerts to new sites in your particular area of interest.

If you keep a few basic principles in mind, developing the skills needed to evaluate online resources is not a difficult task. *The History Highway 3.0* has done some of this work for the researcher by providing online sources that have been scrutinized by scholars in their respective fields. As the WWW grows and changes, the researcher must be prepared to interpret and access the very best that the WWW has to offer without risking the use of inaccurate, subversive, or inappropriate information. By asking the right questions and approaching online research with a critical eye and an open mind, the history researcher can reap the bounty of the WWW.

Note

1. American Library Association, *Presidential Committee on Information Literacy: Final Report* (Chicago: American Library Association, 1989), available at http://www.ala.org/acrl/nili/ilit1st.html.

Part II

Internet Sites
for Historians

The history sites on the Internet present an astounding amount of information. No one could ever hope to examine and read everything that is now online. Of course, no one could ever read every book in the Library of Congress either. This is why the Library of Congress is meticulously organized and cataloged. When you need to find a book or fact, you can go to an index or turn to a librarian for assistance. There is no Internet librarian, but the subject-area specialists who have written the following sections offer the same guidance and assistance one gets from a knowledgeable librarian or seasoned teacher. Part II of *The History Highway 3.0* is designed to help you find specific information when you are looking for it and guide you to interesting and useful sites that are worth examining for pleasure or serious study.

As you read this guide, you will notice that the historical sites on the Internet have been created by a wide variety of people, ranging from history professors and students to publishers and history buffs. There is also a broad range of content on the Internet. Some sites are scholarly; others are more informal. Some are composed entirely of links to other sites. The resources described in *The History Highway 3.0* have been screened for quality, utility, and reliability. In an age of information superabundance, however, it is important that everyone become a skilled critic of electronic information. To help you make personal determinations about each site, whenever possible the names and sponsoring institutions or organizations are clearly indicated. The contributors have identified, with a checkmark (✓), the sites that they feel are exemplary. Nevertheless, we urge you not to assume that every argument or resource that you encounter on the following pages is credible or valid. Just as many excellent books contain some errors and misinterpretations and every library contains fallacious books, so some of the sites mentioned here contain a mixture.

Chapter 3

General History

Dennis A. Trinkle and Scott A. Merriman

A Walk Through Time

http://physics.nist.gov/GenInt/Time/time.html

A Walk Through Time is an interesting look at the history of timekeeping. Beginning with an explanation of various ancient calendar systems, the site then discusses early clocks such as sundials and waterclocks, modern time keeping methods, and time zones. The National Institute of Standards and Technology maintains the site.

ArchNet

http://archnet.asu.edu/

ArchNet is sponsored by the University of Connecticut and contains field reports, images, conference information, electronic exhibits, fieldwork opportunities, and more. It covers archaeology throughout the world, and the site is an excellent way to learn about field practices and the scholarship of historical archaeology.

Arctic Circle

http://www.lib.uconn.edu/ArcticCircle/index.html

Arctic Circle presents information on the history and culture of the Arctic regions. The site focuses on the people of the Arctic, but there is also much information on the natural resources and environment of the area. Norman Chance, a cultural and environmental anthropologist at the University of Connecticut, manages the site.

ArtServ: Art and Architecture

http://rubens.anu.edu.au/

ArtServ provides access to 16,000 images relating to the history of art and architecture around the world. The site is maintained by Michael Greenhalgh, Professor of Art History at the Australian National University.

Best Witches

http://www.rci.rutgers.edu/~jup/witches/

Best Witches contains information on witchcraft trials from around the world; some historical diaries, letters, and testimonials; and links to other sites of interest.

Bill Douglas Centre for the History of Cinema and Popular Culture

http://www.ex.ac.uk/bill.douglas/

This archive houses the Bill Douglas and Peter Jewell Collection at the University of Exeter, which contains over 60,000 items, including 25,000 books and thousands of films.

A College Web Index of Significant Historians and Philosophers

http://www.scholiast.org/history/histphil.html

This is a site with many links to significant historians and philosophers, including George Berkeley and Thomas Paine. It is the effort of Peter Ravn Rasmussen, a history doctoral student at the University of Copenhagen.

Eighteenth-Century Resources

http://andromeda.rutgers.edu/~jlynch/18th/

Eighteenth-Century Resources contains a wide variety of material on the eighteenth century, from electronic texts to calls for papers. There is a large collection of digitized primary sources and many links to other sites. These pages are the labor of love of Jack Lynch, an English professor at Rutgers University.

Galaxynet

http://www.galaxy.com/cgi-bin/dirlist?node=53033

Galaxynet is a large, searchable database of links to sites on all subjects. This address takes you to Galaxynet's list of links to history sites.

Great Books of Western Civilization

http://www.mercer.edu/gbk/index.html

This site is arranged around eight "great books" courses offered by Mercer University. Each section has a course description.

History Departments Around the World

http://chnm.gmu.edu/history/depts/

This is an alphabetical listing of links to history department home pages in the United States and foreign countries. It is managed and updated by the Center for History and New Media at George Mason University.

History of Money from Ancient Times to the Present Day

http://www.ex.ac.uk/~RDavies/arian/llyfr.html

This is an interesting collection of essays by Glyn and Roy Davies of the University of Exeter on a range of topics dealing with money and currency. The topics include: "Warfare and Financial History," "The Significance of Celtic Coinage," "The Third World and Debt in the Twentieth Century," and "Origins of Money and Banking."

History/Social Studies Web Site for K-12 Teachers

http://www.execpc.com/~dboals/boals.html

This is a large annotated metasite aimed at K-12 teachers and students. The site is maintained by Dennis Boals.

H-Net Home Page

http://h-net2.msu.edu/

H-Net is a project sponsored by the National Endowment for the Humanities to bring the humanities into the twenty-first century. H-Net's home page contains links to the more than one hundred discussion lists they sponsor, to the Web pages of each of those discussion lists, to their extensive book review project, and to hundreds of other resources for historians.

The Horus History Links

http://www.ucr.edu/h-gig/

Created and maintained by history faculty members at the University of California, Riverside, Horus History Links is one of the best general gateways to historical Web sites. The Horus project contains links to more than 1,000 sites, and it features excellent interactive graphics and a multimedia format.

HyperHistory Online Project

http://www.hyperhistory.com/

The HyperHistory Project attempts to present world history as a flowing, illustrated timeline. In ten-year increments, major figures and events are presented with clickable biographies and descriptions. The project is still under construction.

Maritime History on the Internet

http://ils.unc.edu/maritime/home.shtml

The Guide to Maritime History Web page provides general information on all aspects of maritime history, including ships, music, art, and nautical archaeology. Peter McCracken of the University of North Carolina, Chapel Hill's School of Information and Library Science maintains the pages.

Professional Cartoonists Index

http://www.cagle.com/teacher

This site offers the largest collection of newspaper editorial cartoons on the Web. Current cartoons from seventy-one newspaper editorial cartoonists are presented with the permission and participation of the creators, who include the top names in the field, such as Pulitzer Prize winners Michael Ramirez, Jeff MacNelly, Jim Borgman, Mike Luckovich, Steve Breen, Dick Locher, Jim Morin, and Mike Peters. Along with the cartoons is a rich network of resources for students and teachers, including lesson plans for using the editorial cartoons as a teaching tool in the social sciences, art, journalism, and English at all levels. The goal is to help teachers and students use cartoons for interactive learning.

Tennessee Technological University History Resources

http://www2.tntech.edu/history/

Created by the Department of History at Tennessee Technological University, this is a good general starting point for resources on the Internet, including Gopher resources and essays on why one should study history and what careers are available for historians.

University of Kansas History Resources

http://www.ukans.edu/history/VL/

This site, sponsored by the University of Kansas, is one of the oldest and largest collections of links to sites on all topics of history. It is an excellent starting point for research.

World Rulers

http://rulers.org/

World Rulers lists the past and present leaders of every state in the world. Birth and death dates are provided, as well as pictures for some. Monthly updates are posted.

Chapter 4

Ancient History

TammyJo Eckhart

Any attempt to use the Internet to discover all the sources concerning "ancient" cultures will prove frustrating at worst and annoying at best. Terms are inconsistently used not only on the Internet and WWW but also between institutions, professionals, and cataloging systems. Instead of just typing in the term "ancient," it may be wisest to try to determine what terms are used most often for the culture and time period you are interested in. If your interest is very new and you are unsure of the correct terminology, look for the general regional or cultural term and scan the results for hints as to the time period covered, or find a general site that gives an outline of the history of that place and people.

While most Web sites dealing with the ancient world are in English, knowledge of German, French, and Italian is also quite useful. Alternative languages for Web sites will be noted. All sources listed here are in English if you follow the given link.

Search Engines

Because the terminology can differ radically between sources and across periods and regions, the best search engines are the ones geared specifically toward early human culture. Subsections of each of these search engines will not be listed separately, since they are easily found at the main site.

The Ancient World Web

http://www.julen.net/ancient/

Designed and maintained by Julia A.M. Hayden, who earned a bachelor's degree in ancient studies and art history, then a master's in information design, this search engine provides a much wider range of cultures and periods than Argos (see below). However, the links are not peer-reviewed, and sites may be added fairly freely. Note that these include "alternative" views of, and modern uses of, the ancient world, though as separate categories. Any site found via this search engine therefore requires individual evaluation of its usefulness and accuracy; this is not a site for students without instructor guidance.

ArchNet: The WWW Virtual Library for Archeology

http://archnet.asu.edu/archnet/

This site has recently been moved from the University of Connecticut and is now maintained by and run from the Archeological Research Institute at Arizona State University, under the direct management of Destiny Crider. This search engine focuses on finding archaeology information based on region, subject, academic department, museums, journals, publishers, and news events concerning archaeology. Forums allow users to ask questions and share information. Internet Explorer works better than Netscape, but they are working on those access problems. The home page is also available in Catalan, Dutch, French, German, Italian, and Spanish.

Argos: Limited Area Search of the Ancient and Medieval Internet ✓

http://argos.evansville.edu/

Designed at the University of Evansville, Indiana, by Anthony F. Beavers and Hiten Sonpal during the summer of 1996, Argos is the first specialized search engine for Internet sources dealing with the ancient and medieval worlds. The search engine is updated and reviewed regularly by a board of academics that maintain indexes of sites relating to particular time periods, cultures, and topics. The range of cultures that can be found via Argos includes the traditional Near East, Greece, and Rome along with Egypt, India, and China. The board must approve any site requesting to be included in this engine.

General Sites

Beyond the specialized search engines, there are some more generalized Web sites that cover a wide range of cultures and time periods. Instead of listing rather specific sources, the sites below either give a large number of links or are unique in their offerings.

Ancient Civilizations Resources: ResiNets™ Data Sets

http://www.resinets.com/topics/ancient.htm

A ResiNets site that claims to be a better source of information about WWW resources dealing with the ancient world. It may not be "better," but it includes many links not easily found elsewhere. Created by Stan Nicotera, the site can be used freely in its online version and is available for purchase on CD.

Art History Resources on the Web

http://witcombe.sbc.edu/ARTHLinks.html

Chris Witcombe, professor of art history at Sweet Briar College in Virginia, in 1995 created an extensive metasite of online resources about art history around the world, from the prehistoric to the modern periods. The sections are chrono-logical as well as geographical and include often-overlooked regions such as Oceania and North America.

BUBL LINK

http://bubl.ac.uk/link/a/ancienthistory.htm

This is an index maintained by the Centre for Digital Library Research at the University of Strathclyde, Scotland, with the stated goal of promoting the use of information technology in education. Descriptions and links to a variety of Internet resources are listed by Web site title. The links range from Mesoamerica to Asia and include topic lists, subject bulletin boards, and a Latin dictionary and grammar text, as well as a section for today's news and events relating to any of the cultures covered.

Cindy Renfron: Culinary and Brewing History Links

http://members.aol.com/renfrowcm/links.html

An inclusive site from the well-respected author of books on the history of cooking. Provides links to many sites dealing with different aspects of food and drink in the ancient and medieval European worlds. Renfron's home page also provides a hands-on approach to learning about ancient food.

Costume History at The Costumer's Manifesto

http://www.costumes.org/pages/costhistpage.htm

Created and updated regularly by Tara Maginnis, professor of theater at the University of Alaska, Fairbanks, this amazing site provides a timeline of twenty-four periods of human clothing in the Western world, each with an explanation and images drawn primarily from the period in which they were fashionable.

There are also links to other sites dealing with historical clothing, modern costuming and clothing, and recommended books on the subject.

Encyclopedia Mythica

http://www.pantheon.org/mythica.html

Started in 1995 and still chiefly edited by Micha F. Lindemans, this is a searchable online encyclopedia that boasts over 5,700 entries. The Web site is organized into several areas: mythology, folklore, bestiary, heroes, an image gallery, and genealogy tables. Several parts of the site are under continuous construction. The site has a staff of specialists from around the world who focus on particular cultures or periods, but also gathers articles from anyone wishing to submit materials. While the bulk of the information covers the Greco-Roman world, there is a real attempt to include as many folktales and cultures as possible.

International Numismatic Commission

http://www.amnumsoc.org/inc/index.htm

The home page for the INC provides links to major collections and updates on legal changes relating to numismatics, as well as information about the organization itself. It can be accessed in both English and French.

Modern Western Civilizations

http://www.execulink.com/~bcox/hwm/index.htm

Do not be put off by the site's title; it has excellent links to the subjects of history, art, music, geography, psychology, and sociology for cultures around the world and throughout time. The extensive links are divided into dozens of categories including organizations, archives, architecture, and even employment resources, which are missing from many other metasites.

Mything Links: An Annotated and Illustrated Collection of Worldwide Links to Mythologies, Fairy Tales and Folklore, Sacred Arts and Traditions ✓

http://www.mythinglinks.org/

The stated audience of this metasite may be college students conducting research, but the searchable database of WWW links is amazing, and there is a section for instructors as well. The index is categorized by "themes," region, and culture. This Web site is designed and maintained by Professor Kathleen Jenks of the Mythological Studies Department of the Pacifica Graduate Institute in California.

OSSHE Historical and Cultural Atlas Resource

http://www.uoregon.edu/~atlas/

Developed at the University of Oregon in 1996, this site offers a variety of maps from Europe, the Middle East, North Africa, and North America throughout history. It is the continued effort of the Departments of History and Geography along with the New Media Center.

Papyrology Home Page

http://www.users.drew.edu/jmuccigr/papyrology/

Designed and maintained by John D. Muccigrosso, assistant professor at Drew University, this Web site offers links to papyri collections, images, journals, and professional societies, as well as other papyrology sites.

Research Institute for the Humanities: History

http://www.arts.cuhk.edu.hk/His.html

Excellent site by the Methodology Programme of the Research Institute for the Humanities (RIH), Faculty of Arts, The Chinese University of Hong Kong. Provides links based on topic and geographic and historic period, as well as to journals, archives, and museums. It offers rare links on Asian history.

Sites By Region

Ancient Africa

This section is based solely on location; it is not a commentary on cultural connections between the civilizations found on these Web sites. Aside from resources on Egypt, the selection for Africa is still very slim. Being specific about the people or nation or language group you are looking for will help when searching.

Africa: The Cradle of Civilization

http://library.thinkquest.org/C002739/AfricaSite/1Main.shtm

This site is part of ThinkQuest, an online project that presents the work of students and teachers from around the world on many subjects. The focus is on the earliest cultures of Africa prior to the "discovery" of the continent by Europeans. The site has great images, straightforward essays, and links to other resources about Africa.

African Timelines

http://www.cocc.edu/cagatucci/classes/hum211/timelines/htimeline.htm

Edited by Cora Agatucci, professor of English at Central Oregon Community College, this site has many links to specific periods and cultures as well as addressing some controversial topics confronting ancient history and African history today.

Building a Database of Ancient Egypt

http://members.bellatlantic.net/~easfour/

Ongoing project created in 1998 by Emad Asfour that hopes to provide an online collection of material finds from ancient Egypt. The format of each entry follows the scholarly process of collecting, analyzing, and interpreting each artifact, with the discoverers listing their institutions and qualifications for their work. Also has 3–D images of a few temples.

Egyptology.com

http://www.egyptology.com/

Full of links to other online resources about Egypt. The "alternative" sites are set aside from the mainstream and scholarly lists, a large gallery of images, and sections on select individual subjects. There is also a link to the journal *KMT*, where the site's creator, Greg Reeder, is a contributing editor.

Ancient Asia

As with Africa, the number of countries and the sparse remains of written evidence have left a considerable gap in resources on ancient Asia. It may be best to search for specific countries when looking for information about Asia, then trace the history backwards. Some unique sites and metasites are listed below.

Ancient History, Culture, and Art of Northern Asia

http://sati.archaeology.nsc.ru/virtual.htm

A unique site created and maintained by the Siberian Branch of the Russian Academy of Sciences, Institute of Archaeology and Ethnography, it has links to museums, other resources, and descriptions of projects the institute is involved with.

Ancient Korean History

http://violet.berkeley.edu/~korea/ancient.html

This is the only Web site devoted to the earliest history of Korea. It was the group project of a University of California, Berkeley history seminar in fall

1994. The site covers the mythical beginnings from 2333 B.C.E. to 661 C.E., when the peninsula was unified.

Asian Arts

http://www.asianart.com/

Regularly updated and searchable Web site that provides information about galleries, resources, books, and events related to art throughout Asian history. Also has a forum for questions and discussion.

China History

http://www.china-contact.com/www/history.html

Focuses on the dynasties of early China with introductory information about each period from 2200 B.C.E. to the twentieth century.

China WWW Virtual Library

http://sun.sino.uni-heidelberg.de/igcs/

Maintained and regularly updated by the Institute of Chinese Studies, Heidelberg University, this searchable site has links to a wide range of periods and topics and focuses on scholarly resources. Hanno Lecher edits it with a staff of scholars specializing in Chinese culture and history.

Harappa: Glimpses of South Asia before 1947

http://www.harappa.com/

A wonderfully visual site produced by Omar Khan; offers brief information and a multitude of images from the earliest civilizations of the Indus Valley region until India's independence from Great Britain in 1947.

History of China

http://www.chaos.umd.edu/history/welcome.html

Leon Poon's site is still the best one-stop source for information and links about the earliest civilizations of China. The basic information is legally copied from the *U.S. Army's Area Handbook on China.*

Ancient Europe

This section includes cultures throughout Europe with the exception of resources focused on Greece and Rome. More detailed information can be found searching by country or culture name.

ARGE: Archeological Resource Guide for Europe

http://odur.let.rug.nl/arge/

Originally created in 1994, this evolving virtual library of information on European archaeological sites is funded by the EC-SOCRATES and EC-INCO projects. Links are divided into geographic and thematic subjects. Currently the site can be viewed in either English or Dutch.

The Bronze Age in Europe

http://www.geocities.com/Athens/Crete/4162/

Indexed by region along with links to resources on metallurgy, this site is regularly updated by B. Sprenzel, a student of European archaeology at the University of Regensburg. It is more focused on prehistory than ARGE and available in English or German.

The Prehistoric Web Index of Ancient Sites in Europe

http://easyweb.easynet.co.uk/~aburnham/database/

A database of over 2,000 Web resources discussing megalithic sites as well as other archaeological sites in Europe. Indexed by geography and type of surviving structure.

Ancient Greco-Roman World

The greatest number of sites dealing with ancient history are dedicated to Greece and Rome, with a few that focus on other civilizations in the Mediterranean area.

Ancient Medicine/*Medicina Antiqua*

http://www.ea.pvt.k12.pa.us/medant/

The site is primarily in English though it does include essays in French, German, Latin, and Spanish. Sponsored by The Episcopal Academy, Merion, Pennsylvania, and maintained by Dr. Lee T. Pearcy, in consultation with the AM/MA Advisory Committee, the site offers history, essays, e-texts, and links to other Web resources about medicine in the ancient world. There is also information about the Society for Ancient Medicine, which is not limited to the study of the Greco-Roman world.

Classics and Mediterranean Archeology

http://rome.classics.lsa.umich.edu/welcome.html

Extensive, searchable Web site with one of the greatest sets of links to both the ancient Mediterranean world and the Near East. Includes Web pages, Internet groups and lists, academic departments, publications, organizations, teaching resources, maps, and much more. Maintained by Sebastian Heath of the Department of Classical Studies at the University of Michigan.

Diotima: Women and Gender in the Ancient World ✓

http://www.stoa.org/diotima/

This expanding Web site grew from its beginnings in 1995 under the guidance of Ross Scaife and Suzanne Bonefas to be the best single metasite on gender and women for the ancient Mediterranean world. It is peer-reviewed by a volunteer editorial board of scholars and frequently updated.

Electronic Resources for Classicists: The Second Generation

http://www.tlg.uci.edu/~tlg/index/resources.html

This metasite, maintained by Maria C. Pantelia of the University of California at Irvine, offers the most extensive listing of subjects and services available today. It is a must-save site for anyone serious about classics.

Interactive Ancient Mediterranean Project

http://iam.classics.unc.edu/

This provides wonderful maps and atlases as well as links to other map sites. It is a cooperative effort of the American Philological Association's Classical Atlas Project, the Departments of Classics and History at the University of North Carolina at Chapel Hill, and the UNC-CH Classics Department's Apollo Project.

The Perseus Digital Library

http://www.perseus.tufts.edu/

One of the standard Web sites linked to by any scholar interested in the ancient Mediterranean. While it offers many links and some translations, it is not a substitute for other sites that have more extensive online e-texts. However, the material here is current and frequently reviewed by the editor, Gregory Crane. It may take a bit of time to figure out navigation since its remodeling.

ROMARCH

http://acad.depauw.edu/romarch/

A metasite for art and archaeology of Italy and Rome from the earliest periods to late antiquity. It has a clickable map of the Roman Empire, as well as the traditional links to other Web sites for related materials. The site was started in 1995 by Pedar W. Foss at the University of Michigan, but is now housed at DePauw University. Happily, it will not link to commercial sites where antiquities may be illegally marketed.

Warfare in the Ancient World

http://www.fiu.edu/~eltonh/army.html

Designed by Hugh Elton of the Department of History, Florida International University, this site provides syllabi, bibliographies, links, and FAQ for military matters of the ancient Greco-Roman world from the Bronze Age to the Byzantine Empire.

Ancient Near East

After Greece and Rome, the Near East is the subject of the next largest collection of Internet historical resources found on the WWW today. As with Africa and Asia, being specific about the culture you are looking for will aid any search. Some of the most useful metasites and unique Web sites follow:

ABZU ✓

http://www.oi.uchicago.edu/OI/DEPT/RA/ABZU/ABZU.HTML

This guide to resources for the study of the ancient Near East available on the Internet, maintained by the Oriental Institute, is a clearinghouse for Internet sites, publications, institutions and museums, online discussion groups, and online texts concerning the ancient Near East.

Ancient Jewish History

http://www.us-israel.org/jsource/Judaism/jewhist.html

Part of the Jewish Virtual Library, an online encyclopedia created by the American-Israeli Cooperative Enterprise, this site has articles, links, and images about Jewish history. The site does have modern political undertones, but the ancient information is still quite valuable.

The Oriental Institute, University of Chicago

http://www.oi.uchicago.edu/OI/default.html

This Web source has evolved from humble beginnings in 1994 to an enormous collection of links to Web sites concerning the ancient Near East, e-texts available, catalogues of images, and publication lists, while still focusing on the Oriental Institute, its research, offerings, and running exhibits. The virtual museum shows us the layout before 1996, when the facilities were expanded and revised.

Ancient Western Hemisphere

Traditionally, when you think of the ancient peoples of the Western Hemisphere, the cultures of Central and South America are most likely to come to mind, and indeed the majority of WWW resources deal only with Mesoamerica. However, this section lists Internet sources dealing with ancient civilizations from the North Pole to the tip of Chile and Argentina.

Ancient Mesoamerican Civilizations

http://angelfire.com/ca/humanorigins/index.html

Designed by Kevin L. Callahan of the Department of Anthropology at the University of Minnesota, this site provides links and information about ancient writing, government, religion, and much more for the Maya, Mixtec, Zapotec, and Aztec cultures.

CMC: Life and Art of an Ancient Arctic People

http://www.civilisations.ca/archaeo/paleosq/peinteng.html

Part of the Canadian Museum of Civilization (CMC), this section of its Web site concerns an ancient culture that you may never think of: the Dorset. The site includes brief descriptions of Paleo-Eskimos and the Dorset along with images currently housed in the CMC. There is a suggested reading list as well, though no links to other WWW sources yet.

Mesoweb

http://www.mesoweb.com/

Directly linked with PARI (Pre-Columbian Art Research Institute), this site offers drawings, rubbings, timelines, maps, site reports, and essays on various topics for the Mesoamerican cultures. Several of the sections are interactive media or animation.

Resources
Geared Toward Teaching

All of these recommended sites focus on pedagogical issues. Some offer step-by-step lesson guides, links, and images to use in courses, while others are designed as a supplement to a class. None of these resources can replace the instructor's own knowledge and skills. This is the largest section on ancient history in *The History Highway 3.0* since it includes resources from around the world and targets students, teachers, researchers, and laypersons alike. Note that some of the civilizations discussed on these pages are not found elsewhere on the WWW at this time, so these sites may be the best online source for those cultures.

The Amazing Ancient World of Western Civilization: Act I

http://www.omnibusol.com/ancient.html

The first of a set of online for-credit history courses offered at Foothill College at Los Altos Hills, California, designed and taught by Konnilyn Feig. Professor Feig is a historian whose specialization is not ancient history; thus, the site is geared toward making the past interesting and useful for students and laypeople instead of only for experts in antiquity. The course begins with prehistory, looks at "nonwestern" cultures that preceded the better-known Greeks and Romans, spends considerable time on the Greco-Roman world, and finally lists online and offline resources for further exploration. The graphics are kinetic and might be fun for primary and secondary students.

Ancient World Resources for Elementary Teachers

http://www.rmc.edu/~gdaugher/elem.html

Associated with The Classical Association of the Middle West and South (CAMWS), this site has provided links to the best online resources for elementary education since Laura Gawlinski created it in 1998. Currently it is published by the Randolph-Macon College Department of Classics.

Classical Technology Center

http://ablemedia.com/ctcweb

Part of the AbleOne Education Network, this site provides free Internet and teaching materials created by classics teachers primarily for classics teachers. The site sponsors highlights, and recognizes other teaching resources for ancient studies by awarding the AbleMedia Bronze Chalice.

Classics Teachers Page

http://www.users.globalnet.co.uk/~loxias/teachers.htm

Andrew Wilson personally checks all of the links listed on this site. Includes information about contests, software, and organizations for classics instructors as well as links to other sites dealing with the ancient Greco-Roman world.

Exploring Ancient World Cultures

http://eawc.evansville.edu/index.htm

Edited by Anthony F. Beavers with the assistance of Patrick Thomas, Alison Griffith, Paul Halsall, Hiten Sonpal, and Bill Hemminger, this is a supplement for courses about the ancient world. Geared toward teachers and students, it provides images, e-texts, basic outlines, and links relating to the early civilizations of China, Islam, Egypt, Greece, India, medieval Europe, Rome, and the Near East. Started in 1997, the links are updated.

Gander Academy: Ancient Peoples/Archeology Theme Page

http://www.stemnet.nf.ca/CITE/peoples.htm

Jim Cornish, fifth-grade teacher at the Gander Academy in Newfoundland, Canada, has collected a unique list of resources exploring the Aztec, Anasazi, Maya, and Inca cultures as well as Chinese dynasties.

History/Social Studies For K-12 Teachers

http://www.execpc.com/~dboals/boals.html

Maintained by Dennis Boals, this offers links to a wide variety of WWW resources on ancient civilizations. Links are listed by period, topic, or location and include a guide to critical thinking as well as resources geared to parents, teachers, students, and even authors. Some updates are made each month.

Internet Ancient History Sourcebook

http://www.fordham.edu/halsall/ancient/asbook.html

The goal of this Web site, compiled and edited by Paul Halsall, is to provide e-texts for students and instructors to use along with visual and aural materials. These are provided along with recommended timelines and course outlines for instructors. An acknowledged limit of the site is that many of the translations used are well over seventy-five years old. For most secondary and college classes, these will be accurate enough, though certainly not for serious scholarly work.

The textual focus is on Greece, Egypt, Mesopotamia, Rome, and the beginnings of Christianity. Persia is also addressed, primarily in secondary and visual form. The links to other Internet history sourcebooks at the top of the page are very useful.

Latinteach

http://www.latinteach.com/

A forum where instructors of Latin meet to share resources, syllabi, and experiences in teaching Latin today. It is both a list you can subscribe to and a Web site of materials and links.

Mr. Donn's Ancient History

http://members.aol.com/donnandlee/index.html

Has lesson plans and resources for middle school units ranging from prehistory to the Renaissance and from around the globe. It also has clip art, fonts, games, and other materials to use in your own teaching. The "Daily Life" lessons are particularly interesting for younger students.

Mr. Dowling's Electronic Passport

http://www.mrdowling.com/

Geared toward middle school students, this site offers lessons and links for twenty-eight subjects ranging from prehistory to modern issues. Not only are the "facts" given, but basic concepts and methods of history are explained.

Online Classics Course Materials ✓

http://www.colleges.org/ctts/courses_frames.html

A searchable database of syllabi and related course materials used in classics and related subjects. Faculty are asked to help the collection grow by submitting their own syllabi. Created and maintained by the Classics, Teaching and Technology Subcommittee of the APA.

The Prehistoric Archeology of the Aegean

http://devlab.dartmouth.edu/history/bronze_age/

Currently a detailed set of twenty-nine lessons on the history of the prehistoric period based on the courses of Jeremy B. Rutter, Chairman of the Classics Department. Created at Dartmouth College in 1996, sadly this promising site has not been updated or expanded since summer 1997.

Rome Project

http://www.dalton.org/groups/rome/

Used at the private Dalton School in New York City, this Web site offers a large selection of materials and links designed to aid the study of ancient Rome. However, much of the information also includes Greek authors and images. The color maps and e-texts of selections from ancient works are particularly impressive.

Welcome to Jan's Corner

http://www.cmi.k12.il.us/~kempeja/

The Web site of a middle school teacher who focuses on ancient history. Jan Kempe's site has links to her own courses as well as to Web sites she has used to teach units from prehistory to the Middle Ages.

World Cultures and Geography: Ancient History

http://www.teachersfirst.com/cnt-wrld-ancient.htm

Part of TeachersFirst.com network, this regularly updated site allows primary and secondary teachers to find Internet, mass media, and traditional resources about aspects of the ancient world. Sponsored by the Network for Instructional TV, Inc., the site relies heavily on television projects, but it is clear from the wide range of materials and the topics and suggestions offered that the site is truly geared toward making the ancient world come alive to young minds. The "Professional Resources Matrix" addresses concerns about teaching, working with a variety of students, and developing as an instructor.

Chapter 5

Medieval History

Christopher A. Snyder

Because of the prevalence of Medieval Studies programs, curricula, and scholarship in academe, many of the Internet sites in this category are of an interdisciplinary nature and not solely historical.

The Aberdeen Bestiary Project

http://www.clues.abdn.ac.uk:8080/besttest/firstpag.html

The *Aberdeen Bestiary*, written and illuminated in England around 1200, is considered one of the best examples of its type. The entire manuscript has been digitized and placed online by a team at the Aberdeen University Library. The digitized version, displaying full-page images and detailed views of illustrations and other significant features, is complemented by a series of commentaries and a transcription and translation of the original Latin.

The American Academy of Research Historians of Medieval Spain

http://kuhttp.cc.ukans.edu/kansas/aarhms/mainpage.html

The American Academy of Medieval Historians, an affiliated society of the American Historical Association, sponsors sessions at both the AHA's annual meeting and at the International Congress of Medieval Studies. Its Web site, maintained by James W. Brodman of the University of Central Arkansas and

Lynn Nelson of the University of Kansas, offers translations of medieval charters, manuscript images, and book reviews.

Anglo-Saxon Charters on the WWW

http://www.trin.cam.ac.uk/chartwww/

An online collection of Anglo-Saxon charters, royal diplomas, episcopal confessions, and other early medieval documents. Maintained on behalf of the British Academy–Royal Historical Society Joint Committee on Anglo-Saxon Charters on a server at Trinity College, Cambridge.

Anglo-Saxon History: A Select Bibliography

http://www.wmich.edu/medieval/rawl/keynes1/index.html

Despite its name, this is an extensive bibliography of Anglo-Saxon history compiled by Simon Keynes and presented online by the Medieval Institute at Western Michigan University.

Antique and Medieval Atlas

http://www.roman-emperors.org/Index.htm

This site contains historical maps of Europe for every century from 1 C.E. to 1500 C.E. Maps are in color and clickable. Maintained by Christos Nüssli.

Argos: Limited Area Search of the Ancient and Medieval Internet

http://argos.evansville.edu/

Argos was the first peer-reviewed, limited area search engine (LASE) on the Web. Designed to cover the ancient and medieval worlds, quality is controlled by a system of hyperlinked Internet indexes managed by an editorial board. Designed by Anthony F. Beavers and Hiten Sonpal at the University of Evansville, Indiana.

Arthuriana: The Scholarly Journal of Arthurian Studies

http://dc.smu.edu/Arthuriana/

Arthuriana, the quarterly journal of the International Arthurian Society (North American Branch), covers many aspects of medieval history and literature. Its Internet site contains article abstracts, bibliographies, a timeline and illustrated gazetteer, and Arthurian links.

Arthurnet Links

http://web.clas.ufl.edu/users/jshoaf/Arthurnet.htm

The home page of Arthurnet, an Internet discussion group sponsored by the journal *Arthuriana* and located on the University of Florida server. Mostly a metasite with an excellent collection of links to Arthurian and medieval resources.

The Avalon Project

http://www.yale.edu/lawweb/avalon/medieval/medmenu.htm

A substantial online collection of medieval legal documents at Yale Law School.

Bede's World

http://www.bedesworld.co.uk/

The Museum of Early Medieval Northumbria at Jarrow sponsors a Web page for exploring the world of the Venerable Bede (673–735 C.E.) through his writings and related archaeological discoveries.

Beowulf Bibliography

http://spirit.lib.uconn.edu/Medieval/beowulf.html

This online bibliography by Robert Hasenfratz attempts to cover all scholarship relating to *Beowulf* published from 1979 through 1994, derived mostly from Hasenfratz's *Beowulf Scholarship: An Annotated Bibliography, 1979–1990*, Garland Medieval Bibliographies, 14 (New York: Garland, 1993).

Byzantium: Byzantine Studies on the Internet

http://www.fordham.edu/halsall/byzantium/

One of the most extensive online resources for Byzantine Studies. Contains texts, images, syllabi, conference information, essays, and bibliography. Maintained by Paul Halsall at Fordham University.

CAPITULUM: Research Group for Medieval Church History

http://www.jate.u-szeged.hu/~capitul/capiteng.htm

This Hungarian academic site features unique links to sites on the Crusades, medieval medicine, and more.

CELT: Corpus of Electronic Texts

http://www.ucc.ie/celt/index.html

The CELT Project at University College, Cork, is an online resource for contemporary and historical Irish documents in literature, history, and politics.

Celtic Art and Cultures

http://www.unc.edu/courses/art111/celtic/index.html

This site was developed as part of an art history course at University of North Carolina, Chapel Hill. Contains timelines, essays, links, and a remarkable collection of images of Hallstatt, La Tène, and medieval Celtic art.

Celtic Inscribed Stones Project

http://www.ucl.ac.uk/archaeology/cisp/database/

The Celtic Inscribed Stones Project is an online database that includes every non-Runic inscription raised on a stone monument within Celtic-speaking areas (Ireland, Scotland, Wales, Dumnonia, Brittany, and the Isle of Man) in the early Middle Ages (400–1000 C.E.). The database, maintained by the Department of History and the Institute of Archaeology at University College, London, contains over 1,200 inscriptions and is fully searchable.

Celtic Studies Bibliography

http://www.humnet.ucla.edu/humnet/celtic/csanabib.html

The Celtic Studies Association of North America (CSANA) sponsors this substantial online bibliography, which is fully searchable. Edited by Karen E. Burgess.

Centre for Medieval Studies, University of Toronto

http://www.chass.utoronto.ca/medieval/index.shtml

The Web site of one of the most prominent medieval studies centers in the world. In addition to information about programs and publications, this site has dozens of good links.

Diplomatarium Norvegicum

http://www.dokpro.uio.no/engelsk/about_dn.html

A searchable database of transcriptions of some 20,000 diplomas relating to Norway c. 1050 to 1590. Maintained by Bjørn Eithun, University of Oslo.

DScriptorium™

http://www.byu.edu/~hurlbut/dscriptorium/

This project, at Brigham Young University, is devoted to collecting, storing, and distributing digital images of medieval manuscripts. Maintained by Jesse Hurlbut.

Dumbarton Oaks Byzantine Studies

http://www.doaks.org/Byzantine.html

The Dumbarton Oaks Research Library and Collection, in Washington, D.C., has one of the best collections of Byzantine images, rare books, and research materials. The collection is searchable online.

Early Medieval Europe

http://www.blackwellpublishers.co.uk/asp/journal.asp?ref=0963–9462

The Web site of the journal *Early Medieval Europe* features searchable tables of contents, article abstracts, prospective author information, and online ordering of a sample paper copy. Hosted by Blackwell Publishers.

Early Medieval Maps

http://gate.henry-davis.com/MAPS/EMwebpages/EM1.html

A good collection of images of medieval maps and cartographic bibliography, sponsored by Henry Davis Consulting.

Early Medieval Resources for Britain, Ireland and Brittany

http://members.aol.com/michellezi/resources-index.html

This nonacademic site contains good chronologies, bibliographies, links, and translations of early Welsh poetry. Maintained by Michelle Ziegler.

Early Music Institute

http://www.music.indiana.edu/som/emi/

The Web site of the Early Music Institute, at the Indiana University School of Music, offers information about recordings and performances of medieval music as well as scholarly articles and bibliographies.

Epact: Scientific Instruments of Medieval and Renaissance Europe

http://www.mhs.ox.ac.uk/epact/

Epact is an electronic catalog of medieval and Renaissance scientific instruments—astrolabes, armillary spheres, sundials, quadrants, nocturnals, compendia, surveying instruments—from four European museums: the Museum of the History of Science in Oxford, the Istituto e Museo di Storia della Scienza in Florence, the British Museum in London, and the Museum Boerhaave in Leiden.

Essays in Medieval Studies

http://www.luc.edu/publications/medieval/

Essays in Medieval Studies: The Proceedings of the Illinois Medieval Association is available online. The general editor of the online version is Allen J. Frantzen.

Gregorian Chant Home Page

http://silvertone.princeton.edu/chant_html/

This site is full of links and resources supporting advanced research on Gregorian chant. Maintained at Princeton University by Peter Jeffery.

A Guide to Medieval and Renaissance Instruments

http://www.s-hamilton.k12.ia.us/antiqua/instrumt.html

A unique site featuring replicas of medieval and Renaissance instruments, including images, sound recordings, and bibliographies. Sponsored by the group Musica Antiqua, formed at Iowa State in 1967.

The Heroic Age

http://members.aol.com/heroicage1/homepage.html

The Heroic Age is a refereed online journal dedicated to the study of Northwestern Europe from the late Roman Empire to the advent of the Norman Empire. Issues include feature articles, essays, book and film reviews, archaeology news, historical biographies, and "Medievalia on the Web."

The Hilandar Research Library

http://www.cohums.ohio-state.edu/cmrs/rcmss/

The Hilandar Research Library at Ohio State University has the largest collection of medieval Slavic manuscripts on microform in the world. Its Web site features an online exhibition and links to medieval Slavic resources.

Hill Monastic Manuscript Library

http://www.hmml.org/

The Hill Monastic Manuscript Library at Saint John's University in Minnesota has several medieval manuscripts in its collection. At its Web site you can view images of these manuscripts, hear audio files of medieval music, and connect to related medieval sites.

The Historicity and Historicisation of Arthur

http://www.users.globalnet.co.uk/~tomgreen/arthur.htm

An online article by Thomas Green that examines the historical and archaeological evidence for King Arthur. Contains a good bibliography with links to other Internet resources.

The International Medieval Institute

http://www.leeds.ac.uk/imi/

The Web site of the International Medieval Institute contains information about its annual conference at Leeds, the published proceedings of the conference, and its *International Medieval Bibliography (IMB)*. Trustworthy links as well.

The Internet Medieval Sourcebook ✓

http://www.fordham.edu/halsall/sbook.html

One of the first and most extensive online collections of medieval texts, both excerpts and full texts. Though many are older English translations, the site also includes texts in French, Spanish, and Latin, as well as some secondary literature. Searchable, with texts listed under convenient categories as well as by author and title. Maintained at Fordham University by Paul Halsall.

The *Journal of Medieval History*

http://www.elsevier.co.jp/inca/publications/store/5/0/5/5/9/1/

The Web site of the *Journal of Medieval History (JMH)* features searchable tables of contents, prospective author information, and online ordering of a sample paper copy. Hosted by Elsevier Science.

The Labyrinth: Resources for Medieval Studies ✓

http://labyrinth.georgetown.edu/

One of the first and most highly acclaimed medieval Internet sites. In addition to its impressive collection of texts and images, the Labyrinth provides connections to databases, services, texts, and images on other servers around the world. The Labyrinth is sponsored by Georgetown University and is fully searchable.

Maps of Medieval Islam

http://ccat.sas.upenn.edu/~rs143/map.html

An online collection of color maps tracing the development of Islam in the Middle Ages. Part of Barbara R. von Schlegell's Islamic Religion course at the University of Pennsylvania.

Marginality and Community in Medieval Europe

http://www.kenyon.edu/projects/margin/margin.htm

Designed as a class project at Kenyon College, this site has good articles, bibliographies, and links to primary source documents.

Medieval Academic Discussion Groups

http://www.towson.edu/~duncan/acalists.html

Maintained by Edwin Duncan. Contains descriptions of the lists and subscription addresses.

Medieval Academy of America

http://www.medievalacademy.org/

The Medieval Academy's Web page has information about publications (including its journal *Speculum*), conferences, awards, and jobs for medievalists.

Medieval and Renaissance Europe: Primary Historical Documents

http://library.byu.edu/~rdh/eurodocs/medren.html

Part of the Primary Historical Documents project at Brigham Young University, this metasite has links to medieval manuscript facsimiles, original language texts, and English translations.

Medieval and Renaissance History

http://www.nyu.edu/gsas/dept/history/internet/geograph/europe/medieval/

Good metasite from the History Department at New York University.

Medieval Art and Architecture

http://www1.pitt.edu/~medart/index.html

Alison Stones of the University of Pittsburgh has a Web site that features images of medieval art and architecture as well as a useful glossary of terms.

Medieval Canon Law

http://www.maxwell.syr.edu/maxpages/faculty/penningk/

Ken Pennington's home page includes very useful essays, bibliographies, and texts concerning medieval canon law. Professor Pennington has also made available online his medieval course syllabi and information about the Medieval and Renaissance Studies program at Syracuse University.

Medieval English Towns

http://orb.rhodes.edu/encyclop/culture/towns/towns.html

Stephen Alsford's very useful site provides capsule histories of select English towns, primary sources, and links to other sites on medieval towns. Now part of the Online Reference Book (ORB) project.

Medieval History Lectures

http://www.ukans.edu/kansas/medieval/lecture_index.html

Lynn Nelson at the University of Kansas has made available online several of his undergraduate medieval history lectures.

The Medieval Institute at Western Michigan University

http://www.wmich.edu/medieval/index.html

The Medieval Institute at Western Michigan University was established in 1961 as a center for teaching and research in the history and culture of the Middle Ages. Its Web site has information about academic programs and its annual conference, the International Medieval Congress, the largest gathering of medievalists in the world.

Medieval Literary Resources

http://andromeda.rutgers.edu/~jlynch/Lit/medieval.html

An excellent metasite with links to primary sources (in several languages), modern criticism, academic sites, journals, and organizations for medievalists. Maintained by Jack Lynch at Rutgers University.

The Medieval Review

http://www.hti.umich.edu/b/bmr/tmr.html

This book review journal (formerly the *Bryn Mawr Medieval Review*, now published by Western Michigan University) is searchable and has put all of its reviews since 1993 online.

The Medieval Science Page

http://members.aol.com/McNelis/medsci_index.html

A metasite with links related to all aspects of medieval and Renaissance science. Edited by James McNelis.

Medieval Studies at UC-Davis

http://medieval.ucdavis.edu/

A good metasite, housed at the University of California at Davis, with lots of links to primary sources.

Medieval Sword Resource Site

http://www.aiusa.com/medsword/

This noncommercial site provides information of interest to students and collectors of medieval European swords and other edged weapons. Good bibliography.

The Medieval Technology Pages

http://scholar.chem.nyu.edu/technology.html

These pages offer scholarly discussion of medieval technological innovations, with timeline and bibliography. Maintained by Paul J. Gans at New York University.

The Middle English Collection

http://etext.virginia.edu/me.browse.html

The Middle English Collection at the Electronic Text Center, University of Virginia, includes everything from mystery plays to the works of Chaucer. Fully searchable.

The Mining Company Guide to Medieval Resources

http://historymedren.miningco.com/

This popular metasite/search engine has devoted a lot of effort to collecting medieval links. The sites represented are a mixed bag, but include online essays, scholarly journals, map collections, and images.

NetSERF ✓

http://www.netserf.org/

A metasite with over 1,000 medieval-related links, maintained by Beau Harbin. Also contains an excellent glossary of medieval terms and medieval-related news items.

Old English Pages

http://www.georgetown.edu/cball/oe/old_english.html

The most diverse and useful of the Old English Web sites, maintained by Cathy Ball at Georgetown University. Here are links to dependable history and language sites, plus information about software, courses, manuscript images, and even sound recordings (in Real Audio) of early English poetry.

Online-Bibliographies for Historians: Medieval History

http://www.geocities.com/history_guide/ebib/ebib-c08.html

A searchable metasite of links to online bibliographies dealing with medieval history and culture.

The Online Medieval and Classical Library (OMACL)

http://sunsite.berkeley.edu/OMACL/

English translations of more than thirty medieval and classical texts (not excerpts). Searchable, with links to other primary source collections. Housed at the University of California, Berkeley, and maintained by Douglas B. Killings.

ORB: Online Reference Book for Medieval Studies ✓

http://orb.rhodes.edu

This is an ambitious project to create an evolving online textbook for medieval studies. Contains links, primary sources and images, instructional materials, bibliographies, and original "encyclopedia" essays on over fifty medieval topics.

Peritia

http://www.ucc.ie/peritia/index.html

Peritia is the journal of the Medieval Academy of Ireland. Its Web site features contents and abstracts from past issues as well as related links. Maintained at University College, Cork.

The Pictish Arts Society

http://www.pictarts.demon.co.uk/

The official home page of the Pictish Arts Society, a charitable organization dedicated to the study and discussion of Pictish and Early Scottish history. The site includes contents of the society's journal and conferences, online book reviews, bibliography, and related links.

Plague and Public Health in Renaissance Europe

http://jefferson.village.virginia.edu/osheim/intro.html

A hypertext archive of narratives, medical consilia, governmental records, religious and spiritual writings, and images documenting epidemic disease in Western Europe between 1348 and 1530. Published by the Institute for Advanced Technology in the Humanities at the University of Virginia.

PSC Medieval Society

http://oz.plymouth.edu/~medsoc/links.html

The Plymouth State College Medieval Society has a links page with a significant number of both academic and nonacademic medieval sites.

Richard III Society

http://www.richardiii.net/

The Web site of the Richard III Society (London) is dedicated to the study of fifteenth-century England and to the scholarly reassessment of the much-maligned English king. It features essays, links, and information about the society's journal and conference. The North American branch also has an excellent Web site (http://www.r3.org/).

The Robin Hood Project

http://www.lib.rochester.edu/camelot/rh/rhhome.stm

The Robin Hood Project is designed to make available in electronic format a database of texts, images, bibliographies, and basic information about Robin Hood. The project is sponsored by the University of Rochester and is overseen by Alan Lupack.

ROMIOSINI: Hellenism in the Middle Ages

http://www.greece.org/Romiosini/

This site, sponsored by the Hellenic Electronic Center, includes essays, maps, genealogies, bibliographies, and photos of Byzantine churches and icons. Maintained by Professor Nikolaos Provatas and Yiannis Papadimas.

Russian and East European Studies

http://clover.slavic.pitt.edu/~djb/slavic.html

This metasite contains lots of good links to medieval Slavic resources, including online primary sources. Maintained by David J. Birnbaum at the University of Pittsburgh.

Secrets of the Norman Invasion

http://www.cablenet.net/pages/book/index.htm

This unique Web site features essays, primary sources, and aerial photographs relating to the landing of the Normans in England in 1066. Included are photographs of the Bayeaux Tapestry. Created by Nick Austin of The Landscape Channel (UK).

SUL Medieval Pages

http://www-sul.stanford.edu/depts/ssrg/medieval/medieval.html

This site at Stanford University Library is a good place for searches for bibliography and e-texts.

The Sutton Hoo Society

http://www.suttonhoo.org/

The Web page of the Sutton Hoo Society contains bibliography, maps, photos, and an interactive tour of the famous Anglo-Saxon royal burial.

The Texas Medieval Association

http://www.towson.edu/~duncan/tmahome.html

The home page of the Texas Medieval Association (TEMA) serves as a good medieval metasite as well as offering information about the organization and its conferences.

Thesaurus Musicarum Latinarum

http://www.music.indiana.edu/tml/start.html

The *Thesaurus Musicarum Latinarum* (TML) is an evolving online database of the entire corpus of Latin music theory written during the Middle Ages and the Renaissance. Sponsored by the Center for the History of Music Theory and Literature at Indiana University, Thomas J. Mathiesen, Director.

The Très Riches Heures du Duc de Berry

http://humanities.uchicago.edu/images/heures/heures.html

Online images of and background text to this early fifteenth-century "book of hours," considered by many to be the greatest example of late medieval manuscript illumination.

Viking Heritage

http://viking.hgo.se/Members/Members_area.html

A public history initiative launched by a group of Viking researchers, this fully searchable Swedish site offers information about Viking exhibits, images, and bibliography.

The Viking Home Page

http://www.control.chalmers.se/vikings/indexframe.html

A Swedish metasite with several good links to academic sites and texts. Maintained by Lars Jansson.

WEMSK: What Every Medievalist Should Know

http://www.artsci.wustl.edu/%7Esmcarey/WEMSK.html

An extensive and idiosyncratic collection of bibliographies for beginning medievalists. Created by James W. Marchand.

The World of Dante

http://www.iath.virginia.edu/dante/

A hypermedia project for the study of the *Inferno*, using VRML to search and navigate the text. Created by Deborah Parker and the Institute for Advanced Technology in the Humanities at the University of Virginia.

The World of the Vikings

http://www.pastforward.co.uk/vikings/

A Viking metasite with international links to museums, texts, ship images, and essays.

The WSU Anglo-Saxon Homepage

http://www.wsu.edu:8080/~hanly/oe/503.html

This home page for Michael Hanley's Old English course at Washington State University serves as a good Anglo-Saxon metasite with some images thrown in. Links to other Old English course Web pages.

The WWW Virtual Library History Index: Medieval Europe

http://www.msu.edu/~georgem1/history/medieval.htm

The Michigan State University Graduate Student Medieval and Renaissance Consortium maintains this extensive metasite.

Chapter 6

Renaissance and Reformation History

Julia Landweber

Metasites

Discoverers Web

http://www.win.tue.nl/cs/fm/engels/discovery/

Maintained by Dutch historian Andre Engels, the Discoverers Web is an enormously rich set of links to English-language Web sites about discovery and exploration. The site is especially strong on quality links for the Age of Discovery and European expansion.

European Renaissance and Reformation

http://www.execpc.com/~dboals/rena.html

This is an exceptionally comprehensive and well-chosen list of sites, annotated with an eye to K-12 teachers.

Medieval and Renaissance Europe: Primary Historical Documents

http://www.lib.byu.edu/~rdh/eurodocs/medren.html

A subset of the Eurodocs Web site, Medieval and Renaissance Europe offers huge numbers of links, mostly to primary historical documents.

Medieval, Renaissance, Reformation: Western Civilization, Act II

http://www.omnibusol.com/medieval.html

This site is a great compendium of links to topics ranging from Machiavelli, to the Black Death, to the Spanish Inquisition, and on through castles, cathedrals, medicine, food, drink, and more.

The Reformation

http://www.mun.ca/rels/hrollmann/reform/reform.html

This site links to a variety of texts, in original languages and in English translation, by Luther, Melanchthon, Calvin, Zwingli, Bullinger, the Mennonites, and Catholic reformer Saint Ignatius of Loyola. The site also includes a portrait gallery of Reformation figures.

Witchcraft Craze History

http://www.geocities.com/Athens/2962/witch.html

Privately maintained by a person with an academic background, this site contains a wide set of links to many areas of early modern witchcraft research. Also included are a précis of current scholarly views on the subject, a regularly updated list of academic publications, timelines of witch-hunts in Britain and on the Continent, and other resources.

Regular Sites

Bodleian Library Broadside Ballads

http://www.bodley.ox.ac.uk/ballads/ballads.htm

The Bodleian Library at the University of Oxford holds over 30,000 ballads and broadside sheets in several major collections, including many from the sixteenth and seventeenth centuries. The remarkable Broadside Ballads project makes digitized copies of the ballads and sheets available to the research community; these are easily searchable by subject, date, and words in the title or text. An especially thoughtful touch is the addition of sound files for the ballads that have scores. Copies may be downloaded for study and teaching purposes.

Centre for Reformation and Renaissance Studies

http://crrs.utoronto.ca/

The CRRS is a library and research center belonging to Victoria University in the University of Toronto, Canada. CRRS owns a strong collection of rare books on the topics of northern humanism, Reformation history, English drama, French literature, and confraternity studies. Its Erasmus collection is a particularly rich resource. The CRRS also hosts lectures and seminars and publishes Renaissance and Reformation texts in translation.

Columbus and the Age of Discovery

http://muweb.millersville.edu/~columbus/

A searchable database of over 1,100 text articles pertaining to Columbus and themes of discovery and encounter. The site, which was built by the History Department of Millersville University of Pennsylvania in conjunction with the U.S. Christopher Columbus Quincentenary Jubilee Commission of 1992, has unrestricted access.

The Columbus Navigation Homepage

http://www1.minn.net/~keithp/

This top-notch Web site, built by Keith A. Pickering, examines the history, navigation, and landfall of Christopher Columbus and more generally discusses fifteenth-century navigation and voyages of discovery. It is a wonderful site about early map-making and navigational tools, and would make an excellent teaching tool.

Creating French Culture

http://lcweb.loc.gov/exhibits/bnf/bnf0001.html

Creating French Culture is an exhibit of illuminated manuscripts from the collections of the Bibliothèque Nationale de France, first presented by the Library of Congress in 1995. The site traces the history of France from Charlemagne to Charles de Gaulle, but it has valuable highlights from the fifteenth through seventeenth centuries, including a focus on the Wars of

Religion, which make it a good site for the study of Renaissance and Reformation history.

The *Decameron* Web

http://www.brown.edu/Departments/Italian_Studies/dweb/dweb.shtml

In addition to the full text of Boccaccio's *Decameron* in its established critical English edition, the beautiful *Decameron* Web provides the reader with abundant background information on the literary, historical, and cultural context of the work, in the form of documents and images. The site, which is intended for college and high school teachers and students, is run by Massimo Riva, associate professor of Italian Studies at Brown University, and Michael Papio, assistant professor of Italian at the College of the Holy Cross.

Del's Dance Book

http://www.pbm.com/~lindahl/del/

Del's Dance Book is a guide to the Renaissance dance styles of Italy, Burgundy, France, and England. The site includes audio and sheet music files for many of these dances, as well as an extensive annotated bibliography, discography, and links to articles.

Digital Dante

http://dante.ilt.columbia.edu/

Digital Dante, an ongoing project of Columbia University, provides multimedia versions of Dante's works that can serve as research and teaching tools. The site contains, in comparative format, the complete text of *The Divine Comedy* in its original language and in two standard English translations, by Henry Wadsworth Longfellow and by Allen Mandelbaum, as well as teaching aids, image collections, and mentions of Dante in recent news and exhibits. Allen Mandelbaum also serves on the project steering committee.

Discovery and Reformation

http://www.wsu.edu/~dee/REFORM/

Discovery and Reformation is a cyberspace "research textbook" created by Richard Hooker of Washington State University. It is intended to be used as a resource for students who seek background material to enhance historical projects about the period of European discovery, the Reformation, and the Northern Renaissance. Resources include a historical text, an atlas, a glossary of terms, a collection of primary readings, and an image gallery. The site is an exciting portent for the rich future of online textbooks for serious student use.

The Electronic *Sixteenth Century Journal*

http://www2.truman.edu/escj/

This is the online version of the academic journal that is the scholarly hub of Renaissance, Reformation, and early modern European studies. The Web site offers recent tables of contents, information about the annual Sixteenth-Century Studies Conference, and links to related sites.

The Elizabethan Costuming Page

http://www.dnaco.net/~aleed/corsets/general.html

Drea Leed's site includes detailed instructions, illustrations, and historical information for designing a complete Elizabethan outfit. It is a terrific resource both for historical costume buffs and for those interested in making period clothing. A "Monthly Costume Feature" directs the reader to other excellent sites of interest. This site is very thorough and definitely worth a visit even if you're not a costumer.

Elizabethan Fencing and the Art of Defense

http://jan.ucc.nau.edu/~wew/fencing.html

The Elizabethan Fencing Web site is run by William Wilson, president of the Tattershall School of Defense and coach for the Fencing Club at Northern Arizona University. The site is dedicated to fifteenth- and sixteenth-century fencing. It includes information on period fencing masters, online instruction manuals, terminology, theatrical combat, and contemporary groups who take part in period fencing demonstrations.

EMWWeb: The Early Modern Warfare Website

http://www.ostwald.hispeed.com/EMWWeb/EMWebFrame.htm

Created by graduate student Jamel Ostwald, EMWWeb (pronounced "m web") is a promising new site for scholarly collaboration on all topics of early modern military history. It has several links to interesting early modern military materials, plus a thoughtful wish list of materials and ideas Ostwald is seeking from would-be collaborators. The site's goal is to "to encourage better communication among scholars researching military history in the early modern period."

Exploring Leonardo

http://www.mos.org/sln/Leonardo/LeoHomePage.html

This impressive teaching site, devoted to the study of Leonardo da Vinci as a scientist, is run by the Science Learning Network Staff at the Museum of Science in Boston. It is intended primarily for classroom use (grades four through eight). The site is appropriately graphics-rich, with sections on Leonardo as inventor, Leonardo's perspective, and Leonardo's strange ability to write in reverse. There are also a biography of the artist, four interactive exercises, and five lesson plans for hands-on classroom activities.

Florence Arts

http://www.arca.net/tourism/florence/arts.htm

Although run by a tourism board, this site has very rich links to the art, history, museums, and monuments of Florence, and everything else one would wish to know about the quintessential city of the Renaissance.

Florentine Renaissance Resources: Online *Catasto* of 1427

http://www.stg.brown.edu/projects/catasto/overview.html

This is an online version of the tax data for the city of Florence from 1427 to 1429, originally collected by historians David Herlihy and Christiane Klapisch-Zuber. The site has its own search engine that helps users find information for specific people, places, or topics.

The Folger Shakespeare Library

http://www.folger.edu/

This site provides information about the holdings and activities of the Folger Library in Washington, D.C., home to the world's largest collection of Shakespeare's printed works and a large collection of other rare Renaissance books and manuscripts. It also links to the Folger Institute (http://www.folger.edu/institute/nintro.cfm), the center for advanced study and research in the humanities sponsored by the Folger Shakespeare Library and a consortium of other universities.

The Galileo Project

http://es.rice.edu/ES/humsoc/Galileo/

The Galileo Project, run by Rice University, is a hypertext site on the life and work of Italian astronomer Galileo Galilei and the science of his time. It includes textual and pictorial information about his family, his contemporaries, and his career, a detailed timeline of his life, searchable maps, and links to other resources on the Web about Galileo. The site also includes Dava Sobel's English translations of all 124 surviving letters from Galileo's daughter Maria Celeste, made famous by Sobel in her recent book *Galileo's Daughter*. The existence of these letters online forms a remarkable new Internet source for the study of women in early modern Europe.

The Geometry of War

http://www.mhs.ox.ac.uk/geometry/title.htm

Presented by the Museum of the History of Science, Oxford, The Geometry of War is a virtual exhibition about the relationship between warfare and geometry from 1500 to 1750. The exhibition highlights how advances in early modern warfare and technology led to many new developments in practical mathematics, and vice versa.

The Internet Renaissance Band

http://www.csupomona.edu/~jcclark/emusic/

This site offers midi files of music from the Middle Ages and Renaissance, sequenced by Curtis Clark. The music is freely available for noncommercial purposes.

Iter: Gateway to the Middle Ages and the Renaissance

http://iter.library.utoronto.ca/iter/index.htm

Developed in part by the Renaissance Society of America, Iter is a nonprofit searchable database containing approximately 43,000 articles on Renaissance Europe, considered by Iter as the period from 1300 to 1700. To access the database, a paid subscription (available on an individual and group basis) is required. Free guest access allows entry to a sample subset of the database.

Le Poulet Gauche

http://www.lepg.org/index.html

Le Poulet Gauche, in its real-world incarnation, was a living history re-creation of a sixteenth-century tavern in Calais, France, which, before it went defunct, made twice-yearly appearances at Society for Creative Anachronism events in the United States. The Web site, which has kept the project alive, is an impressively detailed guide to the history, culture, religion, and daily life of sixteenth-century France as seen from the bottom up. This site is designed to be a resource for historical re-creation, and in the process it offers nonspecialist readers an unparalleled insight into life in Calais 400 years ago.

Life and Times of Martin Luther

http://www.reformation.org/luther.html

A good image-oriented synopsis of Martin Luther's career as a reformist, although written with a heavily anti-Catholic bias. The site also succinctly explains the origins of the Reformation.

Life in Elizabethan England: A Compendium of Common Knowledge

http://renaissance.dm.net/compendium/home.html

This attractive and intelligent site contains many fascinating details of historically correct information, presented in small, easily digestible chunks, about life in England during the reign of Elizabeth I (1558–1603). It is the work of Maggie Pierce Secara, a professional freelance writer and published poet.

The Lutheran Electronic Archive: Project Wittenberg

http://www.ctsfw.edu/etext/

Project Wittenberg is an online collection of documents by Martin Luther and related materials by other Lutheran scholars from the sixteenth through nineteenth centuries. The documents are posted both in their original languages and in English translation.

The Medici Archive Project

http://www.medici.org

The Medici Archive Project was founded in 1995 in order to develop the potential of the Medici Granducal Archive (1537–1743), housed in the Archivio di Stato in Florence. Grand Duke Cosimo I in 1569 established the archive of the Medici Grand Dukes, and today it holds nearly 3 million letters written to and by the Medici family from the sixteenth to the eighteenth century. The project's goals include documenting Jewish history, costume history, and textile history in the Medici Archive and also bringing the Archive's collections online.

Medieval and Early Modern Data Bank

http://www.scc.rutgers.edu/memdb/

The Medieval and Early Modern Data Bank is a project established at Rutgers University and codirected by Professors Rudolph M. Bell of Rutgers University and Martha C. Howell of Columbia University. Its aim is to provide scholars with an expanding library of information in electronic format on currency exchanges and prices in the medieval and early modern periods of European history.

Medieval and Renaissance Brewing Home Page

http://www.pbm.com/~lindahl/brewing.html

The Brewing Home Page is a collection of reference works and guides to medieval and Renaissance brewing. The Home Page also offers recipes for brewing your own period ale, and links to groups interested in the practice of brewing period ales.

Medieval and Renaissance Food Home Page

http://www.pbm.com/~lindahl/food.html

The Medieval and Renaissance Food site provides many articles and recipes to help you re-create period dishes dating before 1600. The site includes the texts of several Renaissance cookery books.

National Geographic Interactive Salem Witchcraft Trials

http://www.nationalgeographic.com/features/97/salem/index.html

The Salem Witchcraft Trials is a moderately interactive approach to understanding the seventeenth-century witchcraft trials in New England. The hook is to let you, the reader, "experience the proceedings first hand as you assume the identity of a town resident accused of sorcery." *National Geographic* designed the site with assistance from historian Richard Trask.

The Newberry Library Center for Renaissance Studies

http://www.newberry.org/nl/renaissance/L3rrenaissance.html

The Newberry Library houses a world-class collection of manuscripts and printed matter from the late medieval and Renaissance periods. The Center for Renaissance Studies, located at the library, offers programs at graduate and postdoctoral levels, including research training in paleography and other archival skills, workshops, and conferences.

New Historians of Early Modern France: Research in Progress

http://www.emory.edu/HISTORY/BEIK/index.htm

Run by early modern French historian William Beik and supported by the History Department of Emory University, this site provides a forum where graduate students and recent Ph.D.s can exchange information about research projects with others pursuing related investigations. The list is open to any topic in the social, cultural, or institutional history of France from the fifteenth to the eighteenth century, excluding the French Revolution.

Palladio's Italian Villas

http://www.boglewood.com/palladio/home.html

This site is devoted to one of the Italian Renaissance's most famous architects: Andrea Palladio (1508–1580). Palladio's villas are explored, explained, and shown. For the potential traveler, the site also provides maps and information about visiting five of Palladio's eighteen surviving villas.

Plague and Public Health in Renaissance Europe

http://jefferson.village.virginia.edu/osheim/intro.html

This site is a hypertext archive of medical consilia, governmental records, and religious writings documenting the arrival, impact, and handling of the bubonic plague in the three Italian towns of Florence, Pistoia, and Lucca in 1348.

Renaissance and Baroque Architecture: Architectural History 102

http://www.lib.virginia.edu/dic/colls/arh102/index.html

This site is built entirely of photographs taken by Professor C.W. Westfall and used in his survey course on Renaissance and Baroque Architecture at the University of Virginia's Department of Architectural History. Organized by topic, each section includes both images relating to that topic and images of comparative material. The site is intended for personal, noncommercial use by the public as well as by Dr. Westfall's students.

The Renaissance Society of America

http://www.r-s-a.org/

The Renaissance Society of America is the leading organization in the Americas for scholars dedicated to the study of the late medieval, Renaissance, and early modern periods. The home page describes the RSA's activities, membership, publications, and annual conference schedule and lists an online directory of all members of the RSA.

Renaissance Women Online

http://www.wwp.brown.edu/texts/rwoentry.html

Run by the Brown University Women Writers Project and funded by The Andrew W. Mellon Foundation, the RWO collection includes 100 Renaissance texts, accompanied by introductions to the historical context and topical essays on women's life and writing in the Renaissance. Access is by subscription only.

Rome Reborn: The Vatican Library and Renaissance Culture

http://www.ncsa.uiuc.edu/SDG/Experimental/vatican.exhibit/
Vatican.exhibit.html

The Library of Congress in Washington, D.C., originally presented this exhibit in 1993. Through a display of rare maps, manuscripts, and books possessed by the Vatican, Rome Reborn tells the story of the Vatican Library as "the intellectual driving force behind the emergence of Rome as a political and scholarly superpower during the Renaissance."

Seventeenth Century Women Poets

http://www.uni-koeln.de/phil-fak/englisch/kurse/17c/index.htm

This site, built by English professor Suzanne Webel, houses a very good collection of primary documents, secondary articles, and bibliographic materials for the study of seventeenth-century English women's writings.

Tudor England (1485–1603)

http://www.englishhistory.net/tudor.html

Tudor England is an enthusiast's guide to the Tudor family of England. This site contains fact-checked histories of the family members, many primary documents written by various Tudors, and an image gallery.

Tudor History

http://tudorhistory.org/

Tudor England is another enthusiast's guide to the Tudor family of England. The site also includes Tudor society, architecture, food (with recipes), maps, a chronology, and current events related to the Tudors, such as their appearances in recent literature and in theater and film productions.

Tyburn Tree: Public Execution in Early Modern England

http://www.unc.edu/~charliem/index.htm

The Tyburn Tree site contains documents, images, bibliographies, and transcripts of last words, focusing largely on hangings in London in the sixteenth, seventeenth, and eighteenth centuries. Zachary Lesser of Columbia University originally created it in 1995. Charlie Mitchell of the University of Colorado at Boulder has greatly expanded the original site and now maintains it.

The Virtual Renaissance

http://www.twingroves.district96.k12.il.us/Renaissance/VirtualRen.html

The Virtual Renaissance site was developed for gifted eighth-grade students by three teachers, Bonnie Panagakis, Chris Marszalek, and Linda Mazanek, at Twin Groves Junior High School of Buffalo Grove, Illinois, as part of the Fermilab LInC program. The intended use is within teaching units on Shakespeare and the Renaissance. It is a cleverly designed and moderately interactive site, with good information, good graphics, and links to a highly sophisticated range of other Web sites.

The Virtual Sistine Chapel

http://www.rm.astro.it/amendola/sistina.html

A short introduction to the chapel's construction is followed by a series of high-resolution images of Michelangelo's masterpieces.

Web Gallery of Art

http://gallery.euroweb.hu/

The Web Gallery of Art is an exceptional site for Renaissance and Reformation art history, presenting over 3,500 digital reproductions of European paintings and sculptures created between the years 1200 and 1700. Informative biographies are presented for the more significant artists, and commentaries accompany each high-resolution image. Guided tours and a good search engine are also available.

WebMuseum: La Renaissance

http://metalab.unc.edu/wm/paint/glo/renaissance/

The Renaissance WebMuseum is an excellent introduction to the artistic wealth of the period in Italy, the Netherlands, Germany, and France. High-quality images of famous and lesser-known artworks are paired with good explanations.

The Witchcraft Bibliography Project

http://www.hist.unt.edu/witch.htm

Periodically updated, the Witchcraft Bibliography Project is an enormously comprehensive compendium of scholarly books and articles published in many languages about witchcraft in early modern Europe. The project was begun by Professor Jeffrey Merrick, University of Wisconsin, Milwaukee, and is currently maintained and updated by Richard M. Golden, Chair of the Department of History, the University of North Texas (Denton, Texas). This Web site is an ideal place to start whether you are beginning research on the history of early modern witchcraft, or if you are brushing up on existing knowledge.

Witchcraft in Europe and America

http://www.witchcraft.psmedia.com

This exceptional Web site is edited by Mark Dimunation of Cornell University and Edward Peters of the University of Pennsylvania and produced in association with Cornell University and Primary Source Media. The site offers more than ninety-five important works on early modern witchcraft in Europe and America produced between 1440 and 1750, from Cornell University's rare books collection. Each book is available as a digital facsimile, and all texts are fully searchable by word, phrase, or concept. Access is by subscription, after an introductory trial period.

Women Philosophers of the Renaissance

http://www.geocities.com/Athens/Forum/9974/ren.html

This site consists of information on a few influential women thinkers of the Renaissance, including Catherine of Siena, Saint Teresa of Avila, Christine de Pisan, Julian of Norwich, and Birgitta of Sweden.

Chapter 7

African History

Kathryn L. Green

Metasites

Adminet: Africa

http://www.adminet.com/africa/

A rich French commercial site with links for Africa by country and by various topics: black culture, Arab resources, African art, culture, and African cooking.

African Studies Center, University of Pennsylvania

http://www.sas.upenn.edu/African_Studies/AS.html

This site is a major gateway for scholarly information on African Studies. Linkage sections include, among others, Africa Web Links and Feeds from Africa, country-specific links, black/African resources, K-12 resources for teachers, and multimedia and book links dealing with African Studies. It is maintained by Ali B. Ali-Dinar at the University of Pennsylvania.

Africa South of the Sahara ✓

http://www-sul.stanford.edu/depts/ssrg/africa/

This site, developed and maintained by Karen Fung of Stanford University, arose from the 1994 meeting of the African Studies Association Electronic Technology Group. This searchable site is the best starting point for finding links for the study of African history. There are hundreds of links under the Topics–History section, and links are also accessed through a separate Countries/Regions section. The site has a Breaking News section, which gives numerous links for current events. Fung keeps the site current and has forms to reply to her if broken links, incorrect URLs, or other inaccuracies are found on the site. She responds quickly to these notices.

An A-Z of African Studies on the Internet

http://www.lib.msu.edu/limb/a-z/az.html

http://docker.library.uwa.edu.au/~plimb/az.html

A gateway site developed by Dr. Peter Limb (Africana Bibliographer, Michigan State University, and online editor for H-Africa and H-SAfrica of the H-Net listserv group). Arranged alphabetically to link users to several hundred Web sites and listservs dealing with all topics related to the study of the African continent. A rich resource from which to begin a search.

Columbia University: African Studies Internet Resources

http://www.columbia.edu/cu/lweb/indiv/africa/cuvl/

An important gateway site for news, topical, and geographic Internet resources on Africa.

H-Net African Gateway

http://www.h-net.msu.edu/gateways/africa/

H-Net Humanities and Social Sciences Online is an interdisciplinary organization of scholars interested in the use of the Internet in teaching and research. One of its strongest components is the Africa section. From this URL gateway, users are taken to links with nine African Studies discussion listservs, to which thousands of scholars are subscribed. Of particular interest to historians of Africa are H-AfResearch, dedicated to the discussion of issues surrounding the use of primary sources in African humanities and social sciences research, and H-Africa, dedicated to discussion of Africa's history and culture and African Studies in general. Each of the listservs has a Web page with archived posted messages, discussion threads, links to related sites dealing with Africa, journals' tables of contents, special publishing ventures of the various lists, conference reports, and other materials. There are also lists on the gateway dedicated more specifically to topics regarding West Africa and South Africa.

University of Illinois Center for African Studies

http://wsi.cso.uiuc.edu/CAS/

This is a gateway with numerous links useful for historians and educators dealing with Africa. The site has information about the University of Illinois's African Studies academic programs, outreach activities, library services, study abroad, and other activities (conferences, lectures, and so on). In addition, there are links to African sites dealing with Information Sources, Art and Culture, Country Information, Electronic Journals and Books, Events and Opportunities, Governments and Intergovernmental Organizations, Human Rights, Libraries and Publishing, News, Outreach Centers, Research Links, Tourism and Weather, Web Guides and Portals. The site is managed by Professor Al Kagan.

General Sites

The Abyssinia Cyberspace Gateway

http://www.abyssiniacybergateway.net/acg.html

http://www.cs.indiana.edu/hyplan//dmulholl.acg.html

Contains multiple links, including photographs, general information, and mailing lists for Djibouti, Eritrea, Ethiopia, Somalia, and Somaliland. Most of the pages of the site date from 1996. Authored by Daniel Yacob.

Africa Action

http://www.africapolicy.org/

Africa Action, newly reorganized in March 2001, incorporates the American Committee on Africa, the Africa Fund, and the Africa Policy Information Center (APIC), with offices in New York and Washington, D.C. "Our objective is to provide accessible information and analysis in order to promote U.S. and international policies toward Africa that advance economic, political and social justice and the full spectrum of human rights." APIC produces documents on major issues in Africa in which the United States has an interest. The site contains APIC documents; full-text archives from 1995; selected APIC publications, surveys, and survey reports; and an Africa policy electronic distribution list with policy documents from various sources that are distributed to listmembers. It also has several policy/development links for African issues. Fully searchable, this is a very important site for more recent African history.

AfricaNews Online

http://www.allafrica.com/

This site has daily headline news from around the continent from over eighty African media organizations, various other news links, and a rich archive of past news stories. The site is searchable by region, country, and topic.

African History and Studies

http://www2.tntech.edu/history/african.html

This site, contributed by the History Department of Tennessee Technological University, is a page of links to over sixty-five Web sites on African history and studies, sites of some American universities with African Studies programs, and a few discussion lists and journals for African history.

African Internet Resources Relevant to Museums

http://www.icom.org/africom/africa1.htm

This page, authored by Andrew Roberts and produced by the International Committee for Documentation of the International Council of Museums, consists of links to Internet home pages of museums in Africa or with African collections, as well as related organizations on the Internet, African programs of international organizations on the Internet, African subject information relevant to museums on the Internet, and general interest African Internet resources relevant to museums. The page was produced in 1996, and some of the links are no longer extant.

African National Congress

http://www.anc.org.za/

The home page of the major antiapartheid resistance group and postapartheid political party, this is a deep site with links to the home pages of the first two postapartheid presidents and a very rich government information link that contains verbatim texts of legislation, commission reports (including the full text of the Truth and Reconciliation Commission report), conference documents, discussion documents, policy documents, notices, press statements, proclamations, regulations, reports, speeches, summits, and white papers. There is a complete section on the antiapartheid movement with historical documents. There are also links from the government information page to other South African Internet resources. The site is being constantly updated.

The African Studies Association (U.S.)

http://www.africanstudies.org

This home page for the African Studies Association of the United States gives all the pertinent information about the organization, as well as links to its journals, papers, and book publications in African Studies. This site is maintained by Ali B. Ali-Dinar of the University of Pennsylvania.

African Studies at Central Connecticut State University

http://www.ccsu.edu/Afstudy/

In addition to information on the university's program, the site contains full-text articles from the publication *Africa Update* and a gateway for a few online resources in African Studies.

Africa Research Central: A Clearinghouse of African Primary Sources

http://www.africa-research.org/

This site, developed by Susan Tschabrun and Kathryn Green, serves as a gateway to archives, libraries, and museums that have important collections of African primary sources, focusing on collections in Africa with links to those institutions with a Web presence in Europe and North America. The site is aimed at both researchers and repository professionals, seeking to bring these two professional groups together to facilitate research and to better preserve the primary sources—written, audio, photographic, and material culture—that are at risk in many areas of the continent. Some full-text documents and archival guides are available on the site. The site is updated through periodic questionnaires to African repositories and through user input. The site is bilingual in French and English and fully searchable by keyword, country, and institution type.

Afrique francophone

http://www.lehman.cuny.edu/depts/langlit/french/afrique.html

This is a site of assorted links to sites on and in francophone Africa, with a rating given to each site found at the bottom of the list of links. It contains some links for francophone Africa that are not commonly found on anglophone gateway sites. Site maintained by Thomas C. Spear, professor of French of Lehman College of the City University of New York.

Anglo-Boer War Database

http://www.uovs.ac.za/data/index/angloboer.asp

This site consists of a select bibliography compiled by E. Steyn and J. Prophet. It is searchable by author, title, keyword, categories, and format.

The Atlantic Slave Trade: Demographic Simulation

http://www.whc.neu.edu/afrintro.htm

http://www.whc.neu.edu/simulation/afrintro.html

This simulation was developed by Patrick Manning and Computer Science Department members of Northeastern University. Manning writes: "This simulation, in summarizing available information on slave trade—and combining it with what is known of normal human patterns of birth, death, and migration—has made it possible to offer a coherent picture of African and diaspora population in the era of slave trade. In exploring the simulation, you are invited to vary the demographic conditions and see their implications."

BBC World Service Online: Africa

http://news.bbc.co.uk/hi/english/world/africa/default.stm

This is an important site for recent African history, archived from November 1997 with a searchable database. Has audio and video files.

BBC World Service: The Story of Africa

http://www.bbc.co.uk/worldservice/africa/features/storyofafrica/

This Web site consists of twenty-four half-hour programs produced by the BBC World Service and broadcast between February and July 2001, telling the history of Africa from the origins of humankind to political independence from European colonialism. The site contains the audio programs as well as assorted video links. For those connecting through a modem, the download using RealPlayer is slow. The wait is worth it, though.

Center for Middle Eastern Studies, University of Texas, Austin

http://link.lanic.utexas.edu/menic/

This site has extensive topical and country-specific links for the African countries traditionally included under the "Middle East" rubric—Algeria, Egypt, Libya, Mauritania, Morocco, Sudan, and Tunisia—plus links to K-12 educational resources for teachers.

Central Oregon Community College Humanities 211

http://www.cocc.edu/cagatucci/classes/hum211/index.htm

This site is the home page for Cora Agatucci's interdisciplinary African humanities class at Central Oregon Community College. There are extensive and annotated links on topics regarding African literature, history, and film, and the site seems to be updated fairly frequently. It is a very good resource for teachers and students.

Eric Charry's Home Page

http://www.wesleyan.edu/~echarry/

Professor Charry, an ethnomusicologist of Mande and West African music, has created a site with good links for the history of West African music and instruments as well as world music sites. Sound, graphics, and videos illustrating some of his articles are also posted.

Clio en afrique: L'histoire africaine en language française

http://www.up.univ-mrs.fr/~wclio-af/accueil.html

French-language site of an African history bulletin of the Université de Provence. It is dedicated to African history in the French language. Each bulletin contains editorials, thematic articles, bibliographical studies, reviews, and conference notices. Some full-text articles and published papers are also presented.

Core Historical Literature of Agriculture

http://chla.library.cornell.edu/

Searchable full-text database of monographs maintained by the Cornell University Library. The search engine by keyword yields the number of matching pages per total pages in each of the resulting monographs.

COSATU: Congress of South African Trade Unions

http://www.cosatu.org.za/

This home page of COSATU is a good starting point for labor history in Africa and in South Africa in particular. The site has many links to other labor Internet resources, policy papers, documents, resolutions, submissions, and speeches of the organization.

Daily Mail & Guardian: The Teacher

http://www.teacher.co.za/

Site of the South African newspaper designed to highlight stories of interest to students, parents, and teachers. Archived and searchable.

Death in Ancient Egypt

http://www-oi.uchicago.edu/OI/DEPT/RA/ABZU/DEATH.HTML

"The developing family of documents under the general title of Death in Ancient Egypt has multiple purposes. First and foremost is to provide simple, clearly expressed, and factually accurate information on various aspects of ancient Egyptian civilization." The site contains many hypertext links to already-published Web materials on the topic as well as a bibliography, notes, suggestions for further reading, and resources used.

Demotic Texts Published on the WWW

http://www-oi.uchicago.edu/OI/DEPT/RA/ABZU/
DEMOTIC_WWW.HTML#Preface

Rich site on papyri of ancient Egypt in the Demotic language. The site, maintained by Charles E. Jones and Alexandra A. O'Brien, is "intended to be a constantly up-dated collection of the Demotic language material available on the WWW and is the beginning of a catalogue of all Egyptian language materials published on-line."

Detroit Institute of Arts: Ancient Egypt: Lesson Plans for Teachers

http://www.dia.org/education/egypt-teachers/art/index.html

Site oriented to elementary school teachers to assist in developing creative lesson plans for teaching about ancient Egypt. The site is divided into five topics: art, language arts, math and science, mummies, and social studies.

Egypt and the Ancient Near East: Web Resources for Young People and Teachers

http://www-oi.uchicago.edu/dept/ra/abzu/youth_resources.html

http://www-oi.uchicago.edu/OI/DEPT/RA/ABZU/
YOUTH_RESOURCES.HTML

This very rich site is a project and publication of the Research Archives of the Oriental Institute, Chicago. It contains extensive links dealing with ancient Egypt for students and for teachers. It is authored, edited, and maintained by Alexandra A. O'Brien.

Electronic African Bookworm

http://www.hanszell.co.uk/navtitle.htm

Developed by Hans Zell Publishing Consultants in Oxford. "The Electronic African Bookworm is a quick-access guide and pick-list to some of the best Internet sites on Africa, African and development studies, and on African publishing and the book trade. It also provides links to the home pages of African and Africanist journals, African newspapers, to Web sites of libraries in Africa and to some of the major Africana libraries in the countries of the North, as well as annotated listings of the major publishers (outside Africa) with African studies lists. Additional links cover a variety of resources for writers and editors, African literary and cultural journals, and a number of African literature sites. There is also a section on ICT and the Internet in Africa and electronic networks for development, with many useful Web sites featuring discussions and resource material on Internet infrastructure and connectivity in Africa." There are short descriptions for most of the links presented. The database is updated each month. It is also available in a print version.

Foreign Policy In Focus ✓

http://www.foreignpolicy-infocus.org/

Site of an international network of more than 650 policy analysts and advocates whose goal is to advance "a citizen-based foreign policy agenda." The site is searchable by region (Africa), topic, product, and media center. A crucial site for contemporary issues in Africa and their historical background.

Fourth World Documentation Project: Africa

http://www.cwis.org/africa.html

This site, a project of the Center for World Indigenous Studies, contains the full text of approximately twelve studies on various regions in Africa where indigenous peoples are at risk.

Historical Graphics: Political Cartoons, Photographs, and Advertising ✓

http://www.boondocksnet.com/gallery/index.html

Excellent site of political graphics presented by Jim Zwick. Of interest to the history of Africa are the pages Stereoscopic Visions of War and Empire, with material regarding the Congo Free State, and Kodak vs. the King, presenting photographic and witness testimony evidence used by the Congo Reform Association in its confrontation with King Leopold's rule over the Congo. The site also includes the full text of Mark Twain's "King Leopold's Soliloquy." An excellent resource for students and teachers.

Human Rights Watch Reports in Print

http://www.hrw.org/hrw/pubweb/

This site gives the full text of various Human Rights Watch reports on Africa by country, on the organization's analysis of U.S. policy in Africa, and on various African countries that have been deemed by this international organization to have human rights issues that need to be addressed.

IGC: Africa: Internet-Resources Collection

http://www.igc.org/igc/issues/africa/or.html

A collection of links to progressive Web sites dealing with issues relating to Africa.

Images of the Transatlantic Slave Trade

http://gropius.lib.virginia.edu/SlaveTrade/

Jerome S. Handler and Michael L. Tuite compiled this image database under sponsorship of the Virginia Foundation for the Humanities. The images are divided into ten categories: Maps; Africa: Society, Polity, Culture; Slave Capture and Coffles; Slave Sales on the Coast; Forts, Castles and Factories; Slaves Ships and the Middle Passage; European Written Accounts; New World Slave Sales; Enslaved Africans: Portraits and Accounts; and Newton Plantation Barbados. In addition to the arrangement by categories, the site is also searchable by keyword.

INCORE (Initiative on Conflict Resolution and Ethnicity) Guide to Internet Sources on Conflict and Ethnicity in Algeria ✓

http://www.incore.ulst.ac.uk/cds/countries/

http://www.incore.ulst.ac.uk/eds/countries/algeria.html

This is a must-see site for anyone interested in the history of recent African conflicts. It has a multitude of links for each of the following country pages: Algeria, Angola, Burundi, Côte d'Ivoire, Ethiopia, Eritrea, Liberia, Nigeria, Republic of the Congo, Rwanda, Sierra Leone, Sudan, Tanzania, and Uganda.

Each of the country pages cites relevant e-mail lists and newsgroups, news sources, (full text) articles and documents (though not available for every country), nongovernmental organizations, maps, and other sources.

Internet African History Sourcebook ✓

http://www.fordham.edu/halsall/africa/africasbook.html

This site is a subsite derived from three other Internet History Sourcebooks (Ancient, Medieval, and Modern) produced by Paul Halsall of the Fordham University History Department. "In addition to direct links to documents, links are made to a number of other Web resources." The African sourcebook contains materials on general African history (including documents and articles on debates in the Africanist communities), human origins, ancient Egypt and other ancient African societies, Greek and Roman Africa, Africa and Islam, Ethiopia and Christianity, slavery, European imperialism, modern Africa, gender and sexuality in modern Africa, and further resources on African history. The selected links on the site are noted as "2nd," linking "to a secondary article, review or discussion on a given topic"; "MEGA," linking "to one of the megasites which track Web resources"; and "WEB," "linking to a website focused on a specific issue." An important site for teachers of all age groups.

Italian Colonial History

http://www.geocities.com/historyweb_uk/

This site is an introduction to the 1911 Italian invasion in Libya and the resistance to the invasion, with bibliography, map, timeline, and photos.

The Kennedy Center African Odyssey Interactive

http://artsedge.kennedy-center.org/odyssey.html

"The purpose of African Odyssey Interactive (AOI) is to promote an ongoing exchange of ideas, information, and resources between artists, teachers and students of African arts and culture." The program focuses on culture, dance, music, textiles, storytelling, and theater, and the site has links to online resources for the study of African history and culture as well as teaching resources.

L'Afrique à Paris 7

http://www.sedet.jussieu.fr/sedet/Afrilab/Afrhome.htm

French-language site with good links to instruction at the Université de Paris 7, news, Internet links, current research projects, and a bibliography by country of completed studies. Most links are in the French language and give anglophone students access to sites not frequently linked to English-language gateway pages.

The Living Africa ✓

http://hyperion.advanced.org/16645/contents.html

This site is of interest for K-12 teachers in particular. It was completed in August of 1998 as part of the Thinkquest 98 contest in which students around the world collaborated in creating educational resources for the Internet community. This particular site was produced by three students from the United States, the Netherlands, and Côte d'Ivoire, and involved multiple text and photographic links about Africa, its peoples, its wildlife, and its lands. It also includes feedback forms for communicating with the authors. A search of the main Web site, http://www.thinkquest.org/library/, brings up over fifty resources on Africa submitted through various Thinkquest competitions over the years.

Mamluk Bibliography Home Page

http://www.lib.uchicago.edu/LibInfo/SourcesBySubject/MiddleEast/MamBib.html

This site is part of an ongoing project of the Middle East Documentation Center of the University of Chicago. The project is dedicated to compiling all research and discussion, scholarly and popular, germane to the Mamluk sultanate of Egypt and Syria. The bibliography is divided into nineteen categories and is searchable.

Museum of African Slavery

http://jhunix.hcf.jhu.edu/~plarson/smuseum/welcome.htm

The primary author of this site is Professor Pier M. Larson of The Johns Hopkins University. The site is designed for American primary and secondary school pupils and teachers interested in Atlantic slavery—that is, slavery both in Africa and the Americas. The site contains Works Progress Administration interviews, songs of enslaved Africans, and the personal account of Olaudah Equiano, an enslaved African. With many useful links and FAQ with links to answers or discussions of the questions themselves, the site is a work in progress. There were a few broken links on the days that this reviewer browsed the site.

Prélude: Database Relating to the Use of Traditional Medicinal Plants in Sub-Saharan Africa

http://pc4.sisc.ucl.ac.be/prelude/sommaire_ang.html

Part of the network PRÉLUDE (Programme for REsearch and Link between Universities for DEvelopment) started at the end of the 1980s that has thus far produced a databank of traditional veterinary medicine. A full explanation of the formation of the database, symbols used, and type of information presented is given in the summary pages.

Repositories of Primary Sources: Africa and the Near East

http://www.uidaho.edu/special-collections/africa-html

Prepared by T. Abraham of the University of Idaho, this site gives links to African archives that have Web sites as well as additional links to various archival and museum collection sites on the Web.

Resources for African Archaeology

http://archnet.asu.edu/archnet/regions/africa.php3

Site of the Archaeological Research Institute of Arizona State University, this has links to approximately thirty sites dealing with archaeology in Africa and the Middle East, though most deal with North and sub-Saharan African topics and digs.

South African Truth and Reconciliation Commission

http://www.truth.org.za/

This rich official site of the South African commission has a searchable database, amnesty hearings and decision transcripts, human rights violations submissions and transcripts, reparation and rehabilitation policies and updates, special hearings, media reports, legal background, links, and the official report of the commission. There is also a mailing list that users can join to receive reports whenever the site is updated.

South African War Virtual Library

http://www.bowlerhat.com.au/sawvl//

http://www.uq.net.au/~zzrwotto/

This rich site, authored by Robert Wotton, has photographs, a variety of links on military history and the Boer War, and a database searchable by subject for numerous issues on the history of this period in South African history. A very dense table of contents provides links, discussions, and articles on most of the major issues surrounding the war, including biographies of people on both sides.

United Nations High Commissioner for Refugees: Africa ✓

http://www.unhcr.ch/world/afri/afri.htm

This site gives country profiles for most African countries, and each profile has a series of links dealing with issues of interest in refugee studies and historical background on the conflict involved. A section for teachers links to discussions, articles, and sites on the history of asylum and various refugee issues. There are a multitude of links and descending levels on this site. A rich resource.

United Nations Reliefweb/IRIN (Integrated Regional Information Networks) ✓

http://www.reliefweb.int/IRIN

Part of the United Nations Office for the Coordination of Humanitarian Affairs. "Governments, aid workers, disaster specialists, members of the public receive regular reports on a wide array of political, economic and social issues affecting humanitarian efforts. Though essentially serving these groups, IRIN takes an increasingly broad view of what comprises 'humanitarianism' and seeks to cover the full range of humanitarian issues from the abuse of human rights to the environment." African coverage is divided into five regions: Central and East Africa, Great Lakes, Horn of Africa, West Africa, and Southern Africa. Special reports, specific news items, daily updates, and weekly digests are available in French, English, and Kiswahili for posting on the mailing lists and on the organization's Web site. The mailing lists and searchable Web site archives are very important for anyone interested in understanding contemporary Africa.

University of Chicago, Oriental Institute: Nubia Salvage Project and Exhibitions

http://www-oi.uchicago.edu/OI/PROJ/NUB/Nubia.html

This site has good historical introductions to the salvage project of ancient Nubia and two exhibitions (1987 and 1992) of the institute's museum based on the salvage expeditions. Many of the pieces from the UNESCO expedition are part of the institute's permanent collection, and this site includes photos of these objects, along with good historical introductions.

WoYaa!

http://www.woyaa.com/links/SOCIETY/HISTORY/

http://www.woyaa.com/

Alphabetical listing of numerous sites related to African and African diaspora history and society. There is a searchable database for the entire WoYaa! site with numerous thematic entries.

Yves Person: Samori: Une révolution dyula

http://www.Mande.net/histoire/yperson/

Full text of the seminal (French-language) three-volume work by the late French historian, Yves Person. A critical work for nineteenth-century history in western West Africa—the countries of Guinea, Sierra Leone, Liberia, Mali, Côte d'Ivoire, Burkina Faso, and Ghana. A second link is available as well for the popular, short treatment of Samori Touré by the ABC Editions series, *Collection Grandes Figures Africaines*.

Chapter 8

Asian History

Jeffrey G. Barlow

Many changes have been made to Asian Studies sites on the Internet, most of them for the better. However, too many sites still give no indication of when they were updated or who is primarily responsible for them, greatly reducing their scholarly authority.

Metasites

The Asian Studies WWW Monitor

http://coombs.anu.edu.au/asia-www-monitor.html

This site contains frequent updates on issues affecting the WWW in East Asia. It is a useful site for studying the WWW in Asia, as well as a point to begin many searches dealing with contemporary issues.

Asian Studies WWW-Virtual Library

http://vlib.org/AsianStudies.html

This is another important metasite. The Asian Studies WWW-Virtual Library at the Universita de Venenzia, relocated to Harvard, and then moved to the vlib.org servers. Sadly, this complex no longer gives good information on its standards and ratings, although it remains a very comprehensive gateway.

Guide to Online Bookstores in Asian Studies

http://www.ciolek.com/WWWVLPages/AsiaPages/VLBookshops.html

These shops have a strong Internet presence, including online ordering procedures in several cases.

Internet Resource for East Asian Studies: China

http://lark.cc.ukans.edu/~eastasia/linkcall.html

Geoff Wade, Research Officer at the Centre of Asian Studies, University of Hong Kong, has nominated this metasite at the University of Kansas at Lawrence. This is an astonishingly large and diverse site. Its many materials on using Asian languages on the Internet are particularly useful, as this is a key problem for Asianists on the WWW.

Library of Congress Experimental Search System

http://lcweb2.loc.gov/catalog/

More a general search engine than a metasite, this is the search engine of the Library of Congress, again nominated by Geoff Wade. This engine searches the enormous holdings of the library and has facilities for very sophisticated narrowly defined searches.

World Area Studies Resources

http://www.wcsu.ctstateu.edu/socialsci/area.html

This metasite, sponsored by Western Connecticut State University, is one of those surprising sites that appear to be largely the work of a single zealous individual, in this case, J. Bannister. It covers not only Asian Studies but many other areas as well and has won a number of awards.

The WWW Virtual Library (WWWVL) remains the place to begin for almost any search in Asian Studies. The change for 2001 in the WWWVL is that many of the important elements of the project are now on vlib.org servers rather than distributed among university sites, as was true in previous years.

WWWVL: Alphabetic Catalog

http://vlib.org/Home.html

The alphabetical catalog for the WWWVL is found at this site.

WWWVL: Asian Studies

http://coombs.anu.edu.au/WWWVL-AsianStudies.html

In Asian Studies, the grandest of the WWWVL sites is this metasite at the Australian National University (Coombs) maintained by Dr. T. Matthew Ciolek. The Coombs site is staggering in its extent and will lead the visitor to literally thousands of additional sites in every conceivable field of Asian Studies. An index of its importance is that every scholar I queried mentioned Coombs as an important site.

WWWVL: Regional Studies

http://vlib.org/Regional.html

This is the Virtual Library Regional Studies page of the WWW Virtual Library (WWWVL), a massive cataloging project in which experts in each field maintain that topic or division. Almost any search in any field should begin here, but particularly one in Asian History.

Area or Country Sites

East Asia

Asian-Pacific Economic Cooperation

http://www.apecsec.org.sg/

This is an area-wide site, also nominated by Geoff Wade, that is maintained by the organization for Asian-Pacific Economic Cooperation. It is a gigantic site with many free downloads of publications. This would be particularly useful for those working in recent history and in economic issues, of course.

Search Engines: Asia Databases

http://www.ciolek.com/SearchEngines.html#asia

The metasites listed above are a useful gateway into Asia on the Web, but subject area sites devoted to geographic areas or to individual countries are also very important. A good place to begin for country-specific search engines is here. For unknown reasons, the site now opens with a listing of search engines, likely to be very familiar to anyone desiring specific searches in the Asian Studies area. But if one scrolls down to "Simple Search Engines, Asia Databases," one encounters a wide variety of search engines for individual countries of Asia. Most are commercial sites, but as they contain search engines for sites specific to that country or culture, each is an important resource for that country and will presumably uncover materials not found in larger sites or search engines. The "Annotated Guide to WWW Search Engines," edited by Dr. Ciolek and now in three parts, is very useful.

China

European Association of Sinological Librarians

http://www.uni-kiel.de/easl/easl.html.

This very useful site is maintained by the European Association of Sinological Librarians. This site provides entry into a wide variety of collections and resources in Chinese studies.

Mao Zedong Internet Library

http://www.marx2mao.org//Mao/Index.html

This site, an extensive online archive of the works of Mao Zedong, is an example of the high degree of politicization of the Chinese Studies field, as well as an example of how scholars may benefit from it. This is a very useful site, but it seems to relocate frequently. You may have to search "Mao Zedong, works of" to turn it up in the future.

U.S. Embassy: China

http://www.usembassy-china.org.cn/

This is the new site of the U.S. embassy in Beijing and has many useful resources for the study of or travel to the Peoples Republic of China.

WWWVL Internet Guide to Chinese Studies

http://sun.sino.uni-heidelberg.de/netguide/netguide.htm

This site is maintained by Hanno Lecher at Heidelberg University. It links to a number of mirror sites, including one under construction in the United States.

Taiwan

Academia Sinica

http://www.sinica.edu.tw/

This is the site of the central scholarly institution in Taiwan, the Academia Sinica. Its site is a true treasure for Asian historians as it permits full text retrieval of 92 million characters of ancient Chinese texts.

Index of Taiwanese Organizations

http://www.taiwandc.org/index.html

This site provides an index of Taiwanese organizations. It is definitely slanted away from the Kuomintang, the party that ruled Taiwan for many decades.

Taiwan: Government

http://www.taiwan.com.au/Polieco/Taiwan/Government/index.html

This site contains a broader treatment of the government and politics of Taiwan than the one directly above. While its purposes are primarily commercial ones, it provides good information and is frequently updated.

WWWVL: Taiwan

http://peacock.tnjc.edu.tw/taiwan-wwwvl.html

This site is maintained at Tung Nan (Dong Nan) Institute of Technology in Taiwan. While this site was exhaustive, it has apparently not been updated since November 2000 and may be somewhat dated.

Japan

Japan Information Network

http://www.jinjapan.org/index.html

This is a metasite that focuses only on Japan. It has a very sophisticated (if annoyingly slow) search engine that will turn up both graphical and textual files. It has recently been updated and appears to be an extremely varied and well-maintained site with a wide range of resources.

Japan Policy Research Institute

http://www.jpri.org/

The Japan Policy Research Institute, begun by Chalmers Johnson, is a very active, rapidly growing site with a great deal of information relating to historical and contemporary issues affecting Japan and U.S.-Japanese relations. Many of its resources are now available only via passwords and membership.

Network Pacific Asia

http://law.rikkyo.ac.jp/npa/indx.htm

The Network Pacific Asia is an interesting site in Japanese Studies maintained at Rikkyo University in Tokyo. It provides entrée to a number of journals, book reviews, and so on, all of use to the scholar in this field. Like all too many sites on the WWW, however, there is no indication of when it was last updated.

US–Japan Technology Management Center

http://fuji.stanford.edu/

The U.S.–Japan Technology Management Center at Stanford University has long been one of the important centers for contemporary economic issues in Japanese studies. It also hosts many important sites, such as that of the Japanese Diet. The "J-Guide" accessible from this site is also the WWW Virtual Library for Japanese Studies.

Korea

WWW Virtual Library for Korean Studies

http://www.skas.org/

This site, formerly found at Duke University, is now maintained by the Society of Korean-American Scholars. It seems to serve organizational purposes as well as research ones, and its future bears watching.

Vietnam

Saigon Times

http://www.saigontimesweekly.saigonnet.vn/

This is the site of the *Saigon Times*, a weekly newsmagazine from Saigon. It has many useful resources, though it is annoyingly slow to load because of the extremely complex graphical interface.

Vietnam Online

http://www.vietnamonline.net/

This useful commercial site in Hanoi is a compilation of diverse databases, primarily commercial ones.

Vietnam Web

http://home.vnn.vn/index_e.html

Nominated by William S. Turley, a noted Vietnam specialist, this site is maintained by the Vietnamese government. It has, at this writing, some problems in trying to mix Vietnamese and English scripts. But it is a very useful gateway into a great deal of information in and about Vietnam.

WWW Virtual Library for Vietnam

http://coombs.anu.edu.au/WWWVLPages/VietPages/WWWVL-Vietnam.html

The WWW Virtual Library for Vietnam seems to be the most highly commercialized of the WWWVL portals.

Teaching the Vietnam War

The History of the ARVN

http://mcel.pacificu.edu/mcel/barlow/TR2/tianrong2/arvnhist.htm

This site, which I maintain, is one of the few with a statement by ARVN (Army of the Republic of Vietnam, Saigon) veterans.

Edwin E. Moïse's Vietnam War Bibliography

http://hubcap.clemson.edu/~eemoise/bibliography.html

A wonderful bibliography is maintained at this site by the scholar Edwin Moïse of Clemson. This site is an exemplar of what one scholar can do to assist others less knowledgeable in teaching a particular area.

Pacific University Asian Studies Resource Page

http://mcel.pacificu.edu/as/home/resources.html

I hope I can be pardoned here for mentioning one of my own sites, if only because it has some original materials in it: These pages contain many interviews with American veterans and have received considerable attention.

The Wars for Vietnam: 1945–1975

http://students.vassar.edu/~vietnam/

An excellent university site is this Vietnam War site at Vassar.

South Asia

WWW Virtual Library: India

http://webhead.com/WWWVL/India/

This is the WWW Virtual Library site for India.

WWW Virtual Library: South Asia

http://www.columbia.edu/cu/libraries/indiv/area/sarai/

This is the South Asian metasite for the WWW Virtual Library, found at the South Asia Resource Access on the Internet site (SARAI) at Columbia University, and maintained by David Magier. Of all the Virtual Library sites, this has one of the cleanest and most useful opening pages, from which one can move quickly to a wide range of specific materials.

Southeast Asia

Southeast Asia Guide

http://www.library.wisc.edu/guides/SEAsia/

Also nominated by Geoff Wade, the Southeast Asian site at the University of Wisconsin, Madison, is impressive. It is very easy to use in that the opening or splash page quickly opens to a wide variety of well-considered and carefully arrayed resources.

WWW Virtual Library: Southeast Asia

http://iias.leidenuniv.nl/wwwvl/southeast.html

This is the WWW Virtual Library for Southeast Asian Studies, hosted at the University of Leiden. Here one can find good portals for eleven different countries of this region.

Asian Art

Beijing Palace Museum

http://www.dpm.org.cn/C-english/C_english.htm

This is the site of the Beijing Palace Museum. As an Internet site, it rivals the site of the Palace Museum in Taipei and is far ahead of the Shanghai Museum site.

Jacques-Edouard Berger Foundation

http://www.bergerfoundation.ch

This site includes a wonderful trove of professionally produced photographs of Asian locations and Asian art.

National Palace Museum

http://www.npm.gov.tw/english/index-e.htm

This is the site of the National Palace Museum, Taiwan, which holds one of the great Chinese art collections of the world.

Shanghai Museum

http://www.sh.com/travel/museum/museum.htm

This is the site of the Shanghai Museum, one of the world's truly great museums of Chinese art and culture. Unfortunately, its Web pages are still in their infancy, but the site merits watching as it is bound to improve steadily.

WWW Virtual Library: Asian Art

http://www.nyu.edu/gsas/dept/fineart/html/chinese/index.html

This is the WWW Virtual Library for Asian art, hosted by the indefatigable Nixa Cura.

WWW Virtual Library: Museums and Exhibitions

http://vlmp.museophile.com/world.html#museums

This site provides a list of world museums on the Internet, indexed by country and region.

Philosophy and Religion

Chinese Philosophical e-Text Archive

http://www.wesleyan.edu/~sangle/etext/index.html

This site is the wonderful Chinese Philosophical e-Text project, which provides originals and translations of classical texts. It is based at Wesleyan University.

WWW Virtual Library: Religions

http://www.vlib.org/Religion.html

This site is the index for the WWW Virtual Library for Religions. However, this site is not highly developed for religions outside East Asia.

Buddhism

Buddhism in Europe

http://www.sunderland.ac.uk/~os0dwe/bs10.html

The site is hosted by Martin Baumann in the United Kingdom. It contains a wonderful series of links to English-language bibliography on Buddhism in Europe, although it has not been updated for several years.

Buddhist Palace

http://mcel.pacificu.edu/mcel/omm/

This site, maintained at Pacific University, is a very complex and interactive guide to Buddhism with an emphasis upon the Lotus Sutra. Fair disclosure requires that I mention that I had a hand in its creation. The site has garnered many favorable mentions from Buddhists.

Resources for the Study of East Asian Language

http://www.human.toyogakuen-u.ac.jp/~acmuller/index.html

This site, maintained by an individual enthusiast, Charles Muller, professor of East Asian Philosophy and Religion at Toyo Gakuen University, Chiba, opens into a number of Buddhist and Japanese resources. Professor Muller shows a degree of thoughtfulness too often lacking in Asian-related sites in that he provides links necessary to download useful software for viewing his site and other encoded ones. This site also contains the Electronic Buddhist Texts Initiative, a promising resource for scholars and students in this field.

Taoism/Daoism

WWW Virtual Library: Taoism

http://www.clas.ufl.edu/users/gthursby/taoism/

This is the WWW Virtual Library site for Taoism, the best entry point for this religion/philosophy.

Organizations

Asia Society

http://www.asiasociety.org/

This site is maintained by the Asia Society, which, according to its own Web pages, is America's leading institution dedicated to fostering an understanding of Asia and communication between Americans and the peoples of Asia and the Pacific. A nonprofit, nonpartisan educational institution, the Asia Society presents a wide range of programs, including major art exhibitions, performances, international corporate conferences, and contemporary affairs programs.

Association for Asian Studies

http://www.aasianst.org/

The Association for Asian Studies, with its many regional associations, is the leading professional organization for Asianists.

Miscellaneous and Much to be Discouraged

Asian Studies Papers

http://www.asianstudiespapers.com/

This is the site of a Web-based term paper factory specializing in Asian Studies. Anyone teaching in this area should become familiar with the papers sold here.

Explain to your students that the penalty for ordering from this site is a sanction known to the Chinese in earlier eras as "extinction through five generations."

Please note that a Web page with live links to all the sites mentioned above can be found at: http://mcel.pacificu.edu/MCEL/Barlow/research.html

Chapter 9

Australian and New Zealand History

Christine de Matos

Australia

General Sites and Indexes

Australian Council of Professional Historians Associations, Inc. (ACPHA)

http://www.historians.org.au/

The ACPHA is a national body representing professional historians in Australia. The site hosts links to the state representative professional historian bodies, as well as an extensive list of links to other Australian history-related Web sites. Current events in the field of history in Australia and the Pacific can be located in the What's On page.

Australian Heritage Bibliography

http://www.environment.gov.au/heritage/infores/HERA/index.html

Formerly known as HERA, this site contains a searchable bibliographic database about significant places in Australia's natural and cultural environment, produced by the Australian Heritage Commission. Full public access to the bibliography is available on the Web, but it is recommended that professional users use the subscription service for greater flexibility of searching and output.

Australian History on the Internet

http://www.nla.gov.au/oz/histsite.html

This is a high-quality index of Australian history Web sites provided by the National Library of Australia. It includes links to reference libraries, historical documents, online journals, resources at Australian universities, and current issues and debates.

Australian History Resources

http://sunsite.anu.edu.au/austudies/info/docs.html

This is a vast collection of links to various Internet sites dealing with Australian history, with an emphasis on primary sources. These links include major Australian archives, documents, e-journals, historical societies, and resources on Australia held in the United States.

Australian Literary and Historical Texts

http://setis.library.usyd.edu.au/ozlit/

This exciting Web project provides free online and fully text-searchable access to over a hundred Australian literary texts from the seventeenth to the early twentieth century. All texts included are out of copyright, and the collection ranges from a seventeenth-century Portuguese account of the discovery of Australia to Henry Handel Richardson's trilogy *The Fortunes of Richard Mahony*. A very valuable resource for researchers and educators. The site is developed and maintained by the Scholarly Electronic Text and Image Service (SETIS) at the University of Sydney Library.

Australian Periodical Publications 1840–1845

http://www.nla.gov.au/ferg/

Part of a project to preserve and provide access to selected publications (the Australian Cooperative Digitisation Project), this amazing site acts as a digital library of Australian journals published between 1840 and 1845. To access the titles, the Adobe Acrobat viewer is required.

Papers of Sir Joseph Banks

http://www.slnsw.gov.au/Banks/index.html

Sir Joseph Banks (1743–1820) was a naturalist who sailed with Captain James Cook on the *Endeavour* and was actively involved with Pacific exploration and early Australian colonial life. The State Library of New South Wales holds approximately 10,000 of Banks's manuscript pages, which include correspondence, reports, invoices and accounts, journals, and a small quantity of maps, charts, and watercolors. Indexed facsimiles of all these have been made available via this site, demonstrating the potential of the Internet to be a useful research tool for historians and researchers by making primary resources more accessible.

The Dismissal of the Whitlam Government 11 November 1975

http://vcepolitics.com/dismiss/intro.shtml

The dismissal of the Whitlam government (Australian Labor Party [ALP]) in 1975 remains the most controversial political event in Australian history. This site gives an overview of, and background to, these events, along with texts of some key documents. Key questions and issues for Australian politics arising from the dismissal are listed. A great resource is the sound archive, which includes "It's Time" (the 1972 ALP campaign theme), Whitlam's "Kerr's Cur" speech, and Malcolm Fraser's (Liberal Party) policy speech from November 1975. Some parts of this site are restricted to registered students only.

Documenting Democracy

http://www.foundingdocs.gov.au/

Developed as a cooperative project between eight Australian archives with the support of the National Council for the Centenary of Federation, this site aims to tell the story of the development of democracy in Australia through key documents. Particularly useful is the explanatory information supplied for each of the documents. The site can be explored in a number of ways, such as by document, by themes, or randomly. A text-only option is available if download time is a problem.

Gold 150

http://www.anmm.gov.au/gold150/gold150.htm

Gold 150 is a Web project sponsored by Sovereign Hill, the National Maritime Museum, the University of Ballarat, and the Australia Foundation to celebrate 150 years of Australian gold rush history. The site includes images, documents, essays, and guides to other sources on the gold rushes.

The Great War in Australia

http://www.pitt.edu/~novosel/aussi.htm

Part of the Great War Web site (http://www.pitt.edu/~novosel/ww1.htm), this page provides an exhaustive index of Web sites and other information related to Australian involvement in World War I.

History of Places in Australia

http://www.zades.com.au/ozindex/ozindex.html

This Web project is a continually expanding index to histories of cities, towns, suburbs, and other places in Australia.

Life on the Goldfields

http://www.slv.vic.gov.au/slv/exhibitions/goldfields/

This is a beautifully presented virtual exhibit by the State Library of Victoria. The story of life on the goldfields is told through images and extracts of documents (letters, diaries, newspapers, and books) created by those who participated in the gold rush era. Find out about the entertainment, mining techniques, and Australia's own rebellion on the goldfields, the *Eureka Stockade*.

Local Heroes: An Oral History of World War Two

http://www.localheroes.8m.com/

This site contains a large collection of interviews conducted and recorded by Year 10 High School History students in the Melbourne area (Victoria).

National Library of Australia's Federation Gateway

http://www.nla.gov.au/guides/federation/index.html

Links to resources on Australian Federation, both within the collection of the National Library and elsewhere, are provided on this site. Resources include electronic documents, databases, maps, images, film, and manuscripts.

Oral History Association of Australia

http://www.geocities.com/oha_australia/

Membership details, conferences, and links to other oral history Web sites can be found at this site.

Our House

http://www.heritage.gov.au/ourhouse/index.html

Our House is an online publication, edited by Susan Marsden and made available by the Australian Heritage Commission, detailing the history of Australian homes in text and images.

PictureAustralia

http://www.pictureaustralia.org/

The PictureAustralia database provides a central Web-based search point to locate images of Australian history and heritage held in a number of participating Australian cultural institutions. This is a wonderful and extremely useful Internet resource for anyone interested in Australia. Copyright information for commercial use of the images is available on the site.

Pictures of Health

http://www.tld.jcu.edu.au/hist/main.html

This site is attractively constructed and provides information on the history of health in Australia. It is organized in a module format designed for use by students and educators. Some of the interesting modules include the health of those who joined the Australian Imperial Force in the First World War (War's Cruel Scythe) and the health of Australians living in isolated areas (Fever).

Rare Maps Digitisation Project

http://www.nla.gov.au/mrsid/raremaps/

The National Library of Australia had provided online access to this collection of digitized rare maps of Australia. Netscape users may need to download the free MrSID Online Viewer to view the maps.

Teaching Heritage

http://www.teachingheritage.nsw.edu.au/index.html

Although this site is primarily aimed at teachers within the New South Wales secondary education system, its many valuable teaching ideas and resources concerning the teaching of heritage perspectives and issues may be of wider relevance. It makes the most of Internet technologies, with links to documents (that can be saved as Microsoft Word 97 files), other Web sites, and discussion forums you can *listen* to. The site is also linked to a database of items of significant heritage value in New South Wales, the State Heritage Inventory. The main problem that may be experienced on this very visual site is downloading time on slower machines.

Women in Politics in South Australia

http://www.slsa.sa.gov.au/int_pubs/women/index.html

South Australia was the first state in Australia (indeed, one of the first places in the world) to grant women's suffrage in 1894. This site, hosted by the State Library of South Australia and sponsored by the Women's Suffrage Centenary Steering Committee, looks at the role of women in politics in South Australia in historical context. Topics covered include women's suffrage, Federation, and key individuals.

Aboriginal and Torres Strait Islander History

Aboriginal Studies WWW Virtual Library

http://www.ciolek.com/WWWVL-Aboriginal.html

Part of the WWW Virtual Library, this site boasts a wide collection of links to Aboriginal Studies Internet sites.

Australian Institute of Aboriginal and Torres Strait Islander Studies

http://www.aiatsis.gov.au/

The institute's Web site provides information on indigenous research, seminars, and family history.

Frontier Online

http://www.abc.net.au/frontier/

This site was originally designed to accompany the Australian Broadcasting Corporation's (ABC) 1997 television series *Frontier*, so parts of the site are dated. However it remains active and valuable. Scripts of Internet discussions that have taken place on contemporary issues raised by the series, on topics such as treaties and reconciliation, are available. Educational resources and ideas for teachers and students are especially worthwhile.

The Hidden Histories

http://www.museum.vic.gov.au/Hidden_Histories/

The Hidden Histories Project, sponsored by the Museum Victoria and the Department of Education, Employment and Training (Victoria), aims to document the oral histories of Koorie communities and to increase the wider community's understanding of Koorie culture. The site is interactive, as questions can be asked about Koorie life and history and oral history interviews can be contributed to the site's collection. This project is very appropriate and useful for school communities.

Papers of Edward Koiki Mabo (1936–1992)

http://www.nla.gov.au/findaids/8822.html

Edward Koiki Mabo was an indigenous community leader and human rights activist who came to national prominence in Australia after his death in June 1992 as the successful principle plaintiff in the landmark High Court ruling on native land title. This decision challenged the 205–year-old legal doctrine of *terra nullius*. The National Library of Australia holds Mabo's papers, and this site is a guide to those papers. The site also includes some images and biographical information about Mabo.

Archives, Libraries, Museums, and Journals

AustraliaGenWeb

http://www.rootsweb.com/~auswgw/

A comprehensive entry point for resources on genealogy research in Australia.

Australian Journals OnLine

http://www.nla.gov.au/ajol/

The National Library of Australia maintains this database of electronic journals, magazines, and newsletters with Australian content.

Australian Libraries Gateway

http://www.nla.gov.au/libraries/

Find any library in Australia in this Web-based directory service, hosted by the National Library of Australia.

Australian and New Zealand Genealogy Pages

http://freepages.genealogy.rootsweb.com/~kemp/aust_genealogy.html

This site has links to genealogy societies, professional genealogists, libraries and archives, ship and passenger lists, and other genealogy records.

Australian Museum

http://www.austmus.gov.au/index.cfm

The Australian Museum has developed an extensive online guide to its collection and exhibits, including online search facilities.

Australian Museums and Galleries Online

http://amol.org.au/

Developed by the Heritage Collections Council, this site provides guides to the collections and other useful information on over 1,000 Australian museums and galleries. There are also resources for museum workers, including the *Open Museum Journal*.

Australian War Memorial

http://www.awm.gov.au/

Research on Australia's involvement in overseas conflicts necessitates a visit to the Australian War Memorial's Web site. It includes searchable databases on the memorial's vast collection (art, books, film, official records, private records, photographs, roll of honor, sound recordings), information about the Australia-Japan Research Project, current events, and an online journal, the *Journal of the Australian War Memorial*.

Directory of Archives in Australia

http://www.asap.unimelb.edu.au/asa/directory/

The Directory of Archives is a comprehensive database of information about archives in Australia developed by the Australian Society of Archivists, Inc., and the Australian Science Archives Project. The site can be browsed alphabetically or geographically or searched via keywords.

The Electronic Journal of Australian and New Zealand History

http://www.jcu.edu.au/aff/history/

This peer-reviewed forum is an initiative of the School of Humanities at James Cook University and the Tasmanian School of Nursing at the University of Tasmania.

Eras: School of Historical Studies Online Journal

http://www.arts.monash.edu.au/eras/

Eras is a fully refereed online journal for history/archaeology/theology postgraduate students produced by postgraduate students at Monash University in Melbourne, Australia. The journal also runs a discussion page for readers to provide feedback and debate on the published articles.

Journal of the Australian War Memorial

http://www.awm.gov.au/journal/

The *Journal* publishes current research on Australia's military history.

National Archives of Australia

http://www.naa.gov.au/

This is an essential starting point for historical research pertaining to the Australian Commonwealth government. The site has general information about the archives, an online database to search the collection, links to other archives, and notices of events and exhibits.

The National Archives of Ireland Transportation Records

http://www.nationalarchives.ie/search01.html

The National Archives of Ireland has developed this site to provide an online facility to search for the records of convicts sent from Ireland to Australia from 1788 to 1868.

National Library of Australia

http://www.nla.gov.au/

The National Library of Australia provides an exhaustive entry point to information on Australian history, both within its own collections and on the Internet. The library has developed a number of online databases to aid researchers, including the Register of Australian Archives and Manuscripts (RAAM) and Australian Journals OnLine (AJOL).

National Museum of Australia

http://www.nma.gov.au/

This site provides information on the newest large museum in Australia. It includes some "virtual tours" of regular exhibits and educational resources.

Register of Australian Archives and Manuscripts (RAAM)

http://www.nla.gov.au/raam/

The National Library of Australia provides this database. It allows researchers to search for nongovernment records held in Australian archival repositories. The RAAM database can be searched in a variety of ways, including keyword searches.

State and Territory Archives

http://www.aa.gov.au/AA_WWW/StateAs.html

This site lists the links to the various state and territory government archives in Australia.

New Zealand

General Sites and Indexes

GENEoNZ: New Zealand and Maori Genealogy

http://www.geocities.com/Heartland/Park/7572/nz.htm

Listed on this site is a huge range of sources and services for genealogy in New Zealand.

Historical Timeline

http://www.nzhcottawa.org/aboutnz/histtimeline.htm

The New Zealand High Commission in Ottawa provides this historical timeline from C.E. 1300 to 1999.

Land Ownership and Settlement Timeline

http://www.maf.govt.nz/MAFnet/schools/kits/ourland/timeline/httoc.htm

The Ministry of Agriculture and Forestry has developed this very comprehensive timeline of land ownership in New Zealand from pre-1840 to 1998. A useful resource for teachers and students.

New Zealand: Ancient and Modern History

http://www.enzed.com/hist.html

This site is part of the larger *eNZed* Web site, which provides links to information on New Zealand. It is a very comprehensive index, with everything from the arrival of the Maori to recent economic reforms.

New Zealand and the Great War

http://www.greatwar.org.nz/

The primary concern of this site is to give an overview of the social and cultural effects of World War I on New Zealand.

New Zealand Historic Places Trust

http://www.historic.org.nz/

Information concerning historic and culturally significant places in New Zealand can be found on this site.

New Zealand Society of Genealogists, Inc.

http://homepages.ihug.co.nz/~nzsg/

Genealogy news, school project resources, research collection services, and membership information can all be found on this Web site. Forms and charts for genealogists can be downloaded as Adobe PDF files.

NZHistory.net.nz

http://www.nzhistory.net.nz/index.html

The NZHistory site aims to be the "first port of call" for research on New Zealand's history. As well as links to Internet sites, it has a discussion forum and online quizzes to test your knowledge of New Zealand's history.

Treaty of Waitangi 1840

http://www.wcc.govt.nz/aboutnz/treaty.php3

Three versions of the Treaty of Waitangi can be found on this New Zealand government site (in Maori, English, and a modern English translation), as well as a summary of the treaty's history and images of the treaty (the latter two are hosted by the National Archives of New Zealand).

Archives, Libraries, Museums, and Journals

The Electronic Journal of Australian and New Zealand History

http://www.jcu.edu.au/aff/history/

This peer-reviewed forum is an initiative of the School of Humanities at James Cook University and the Tasmanian School of Nursing at the University of Tasmania.

The Museum of New Zealand

http://www.tepapa.govt.nz/default.html

The Museum of New Zealand/Te Papa Web site provides information about the museum's collections and activities.

National Archives of New Zealand

http://www.archives.govt.nz

The National Archives Web site contains information about the archives' holdings, government discussion papers, and links to other sites.

National Library of New Zealand

http://www.natlib.govt.nz/

This attractive site greets you with the sights and sounds of the Maori creation myth. It hosts information on the library's collections, catalogues, and digital resources. The home page also has a link to the Alexander Turnbull Library's online image database, Timeframe.

National Register of Archives and Manuscripts (NRAM)

http://www.nram.org.nz/

The NRAM site is a database that helps archivists and researchers locate archival collections held in museums, local government bodies, libraries, historical societies, community repositories, and in-house business, religious, and sporting archives throughout New Zealand. The New Zealand Society of Archivists funds the site.

New Zealand Museums Online

http://www.nzmuseums.co.nz/default.html

This site provides access to a database of information on museums in New Zealand that can be searched by a collection, region, or name.

Chapter 10

Canadian History

Tracy Penny Light

Metasites

Association for Canadian Studies in the United States

http://canada-acsus.plattsburgh.edu/index.htm

The Association for Canadian Studies in the United States (ACSUS), a multidisciplinary association of scholars, professionals, and institutions, is dedicated to improving understanding of Canada in the United States. Founded in 1971, ACSUS encourages creative and scholarly activity in Canadian Studies, facilitates the exchange of ideas among Canadianists in the United States, Canada, and other countries, enhances the teaching of Canada in the United States, and promotes Canada as an area of academic inquiry. This site offers a rich array of resources and links.

British Columbian History

http://www.freenet.vicoria.bc.ca/bchistory.html

This site is dedicated to tracking Internet and WWW resources for the study of British Columbian history specifically and Canadian history generally. The compilation is intended to be as comprehensive and broad as possible, rather than selective.

Canada's Digital Collections

http://collections.ic.gc.ca

Canada's Digital Collections showcases more than 400 Web sites celebrating Canada's history, geography, science, technology, and culture. These fascinating Web sites range from the treasures of federal institutions, such as the National Library, the National Archives, and the Museum of Civilization, to the local histories and way of life of Canadian communities. Canada's Digital Collections also features a growing set of online educational resources, such as curriculum units, classroom activities, quizzes, and games.

Canadian Archival Resources on the Internet

http://www.usask.ca/archives/menu.html

The purpose of this site is to provide a comprehensive list of links to Canadian archives and associated resources on the Internet. Created and maintained by Cheryl Avery, University of Saskatchewan Archives, and Steve Billinton, Archives of Ontario, the pages include links to individual repositories, multirepository databases, archival listservs, archival associations, educational opportunities, and other related sites. Links are generally limited to archival repositories, but museums and library special collections departments have been included when they contain reference to nonpublished materials.

Canadian History on the Web

http://members.home.net/dneylan/index.html

Compiled by Susan Neylan, an assistant professor in the Department of History at Wilfrid Laurier University, this site is a rich gateway to resources on Canadian history. This is probably one of the most comprehensive sets of links available for researching Canadian history on the Web.

Learning and Researching Canadian History

http://web.uvic.ca/hrd/history.learn-teach/learning.html

This is an excellent scholarly guide to some of the best resources for studying Canadian history. The site includes links to online images, documents, historical topic areas, and Canadian history databases. The site was designed by Hilary Street, under the direction of Stewart Arneil of the University of Victoria Language Centre. The content was initially vetted by John Lutz and Lorne Hammond of the University of Victoria History Department.

General Sites

Canadian History Portal

http://www.canadianhistory.ca

The Canadian History Portal was created by the Canadian Historical Association and Chinook Multimedia with assistance provided by the Millennium Bureau of Canada. The two purposes of the portal are to provide a reliable guide to materials on Canadian history in digital format and to create resources that will enhance the use of digital materials in teaching and learning about Canadian history. The site will assist Canadians and others to find the relevant information they seek on Canadian history while encouraging the development of best practice in the creation of new digital materials related to Canada. Currently, much of the site is still under construction, but a module on immigration and a women's history timeline are both available.

Canadian Institute for Historical Microreproductions

http://www.nlc-bnc.ca/cihm/cihm.htm

CIHM was established in 1978 to locate early printed Canadian materials (books, annuals, and periodicals), to preserve their content on microfilm, and to make the resulting collections available to libraries and archives in Canada and abroad. Sixty-six libraries in nine countries now own part or all of the CIHM Early Canadiana collection, including thirty-six Canadian institutions. The searchable database allows researchers to search for materials by keyword, title, author, and subject.

Canadian Women in History

http://www.niagara.com/~merrwill/

This Web site provides histories of Canadian women from various walks of life. Over forty biographies are now available. The site also includes trivia, a woman of the week, and links to related sites.

Early Canadiana Online

http://www.canadiana.org/eco/index.html

Early Canadiana Online (ECO) is a full-text, keyword searchable digital library based on the Canadian Institute for Historical Microreproductions collection of pre-1900 published Canadiana. The ECO pilot project included 3,100 books and pamphlets comprising 500,000 page images. New materials are added continuously to this collection, with many partners, such as the Champlain Society of Canada (thirty society publications) and the National Library of Canada (the Thwaites editions of the *Jesuit Relations* and online educational tools). These texts will remain available to all free of charge. Lesson plans for grades 7 through 12 and discussion topics in the college and university levels are also available in the collection. The Canadian Institute for Historical Microreproductions catalog can also be accessed through this site.

H-Canada

http://h-net.msu.edu/~canada

Sponsored by H-Net, this is the Web site of the H-Canada discussion list. The site contains information about the discussion list and allows one to subscribe. It also includes calls for papers, conference announcements, bibliographies, book reviews, articles, and links to related sites.

Historica

http://www.histori.ca/

This Web site is dedicated to the promotion of Canadian history and heritage. The site contains links to the *Canadian Encyclopedia* online, a valuable resource for information on a wide variety of Canadian topics, as well as links to the popular Heritage Minutes, information on the National Heritage Fairs, resources for teachers, online quizzes and games, a variety of links to Canadian sites of interest including a site of the month, and discussion forums.

The *Historical Atlas of Canada* Online Learning Project

http://mercator.geog.utoronto.ca/hacddp/page1.htm

The *Historical Atlas of Canada* Online Learning Project is under development in the Geography Department at the University of Toronto. The product features maps, graphs, and texts based on the highly acclaimed and successful *Historical Atlas of Canada*, redesigned for online and interactive viewing. To date, approximately 25 percent of the maps are available for viewing in this format.

The National Archives of Canada

http://www.archives.ca/08/08_e.html

The National Archives is a treasure house of the memory of Canada, caring for and sharing millions of documents of all kinds—films, maps, diaries, treaties, journals, art, government records, photographs, sound recordings, and more. Through its services to researchers and government, its exhibitions and other initiatives, the National Archives of Canada seeks to connect Canadians to the sources of these stories. Researchers can search the archival collection through its online research tool, ArchiviaNet.

The National Library of Canada

http://www.nlc-bnc.ca/index-e.html

The National Library's collections focus primarily on Canadiana, works in all subjects written by, about, or of interest to Canadians, published in Canada or abroad. From the main index site you can access the National Library's Digital Library of Canada (History), which contains links to a number of research guides and short overviews of historical topics, as well as Canadian Information by Subject, the library's information service, which provides links to information about Canada from Internet resources around the world. The subject arrangement is in the form of a "subject tree," based on the structure of the Dewey Decimal Classification system. This service is updated regularly and constantly developing and expanding. Be sure to check back often to see the latest additions.

Who Killed William Robinson? Race, Justice and Settling the Land: A Historical Whodunit

http://web.uvic.ca/historyu-robinson/

Created by Ruth Sandwell, postdoctoral fellow in history at the University of British Columbia, and Jon Lutz, assistant professor in history at the University of Victoria, this site includes a complete collection of historical documents relating to the death of William Robinson in 1868. Robinson, a settler of Salt Spring Island in the British colony of British Columbia, had arrived there a decade before his death as part of a contingent of black Americans fleeing persecution and slavery before the American Civil War. Visitors to this site can interpret the raw material to ask larger questions, like "how do we know what happened in the past?" The authors also provide links to interpretations of this case as well as a teacher's guide to using the site. This is an excellent site for anyone interested in practicing how to "do" history; its collection of documents also provides insight into this period of British Columbian history and the larger themes of race relations, criminal justice, and land settlement.

Chapter 11

European History

General European History
Patrick Callan and Dennis A. Trinkle

Andorra

http://www.sigma.net/fafhrd/andorra/history.html

This site provides a history of Andorra, the world's smallest nation, a 450–square-kilometer territory located between France and Spain. The site also links users to information about the area, people, and economy of Andorra.

Encyclopedia of the 1848 Revolutions

http://cscwww.cats.ohiou.edu/~Chastain

This is an exemplary site, showing how the international community of historians can collaborate in producing an innovative and challenging site, expanding historical awareness and understanding in a manner rarely encountered on the Internet. Hosted by James G. Chastain at Ohio University, it calls on over 170 extensive articles on the experience of the revolutions throughout Europe, from Ireland in the west to Russia in the east. The authors are specialists in their fields, and the net result is a top-quality resource.

Eurodocs

http://library.byu.edu/~rdh/eurodocs/

This is Brigham Young University's excellent collection of online primary historical documents from Western Europe, including selected transcriptions, facsimiles, and translations. The entries cover political, economic, social, and cultural history.

Modern History Sourcebook

http://www.fordham.edu/halsall/

One of the first and most extensive online collections of primary historical documents, both excerpts and full texts. Though many are older English translations, the site also includes texts in French, Spanish, and Latin, as well as some secondary literature. Searchable, with texts listed under convenient categories as well as by author and title. Maintained at Fordham University by Paul Halsall.

Olympics Through Time

http://www2.fhw.gr/projects/olympics/classical/

An interesting account of the Olympics of Hellenic antiquity, at the Foundation of the Hellenic World site, with a review of athleticism in prehistoric times, as well as a succinct outline of the revival of the Games in the late nineteenth century under the inspiration of Baron de Coubertain. The site has useful links to relevant sites dealing with the history of the Olympics, as well as complementary features on ancient history, including the Homeric Age and Mycenean Greece.

Royal Genealogical Data

http://www.dcs.hull.ac.uk/public/genealogy/royal/catalog.html

Royal Genealogical Data is a searchable database on European royalty from ancient times to the present.

WESSWeb

http://www.lib.virginia.edu/wess/

The WESSWeb site aims to provide specialists in Western European studies with professional information and data about ongoing and recent Western European research efforts.

WWW-VL History Links

http://www.ukans.edu/history/VL/

The WWW Virtual Library history section is a metaguide created by Lynn Nelson of the University of Kansas. It links to more than 4,000 history-related Web sites.

Yale Avalon Project

http://www.yale.edu/lawweb/avalon/avalon.htm

Sponsored by the Yale Law School, the Yale Avalon Project focuses primarily on American texts, but it also includes many topics of interest to Europeanists, including *The Communist Manifesto*, Franco-American diplomacy, Spanish-American diplomacy, Nazi-Soviet relations, and the Nuremberg Trials. Arranged by period from pre-eighteenth century through the twentieth century.

British History

Richard Wojtowicz

Metasites

Anglo-Saxon Charters

http://www.trin.cam.ac.uk/sdk13/chartwww/charthome.html

Web guide from Trinity College, from royal diplomas to wills of prominent clergy, laymen, and women.

Britannia

http://www.dalton.org/groups/rome/Britannia.html

Numerous sites on Britannia, the Roman name for Britain, from historical pages to related archaeological materials.

British Legal History

http://www.lgu.ac.uk/lawlinks/history.htm

Selected sites on the Web from the Department of Law, London Guildhall University.

History of the United Kingdom: Primary Documents

http://library.byu.edu:80/~rdh/eurodocs/uk.html

This site, from Brigham Young University, provides links to primary documents ranging from seventh/eighth-century Ruthwell Cross runic inscriptions through the Scotland Act of 1998.

Internet Modern History Sourcebook: Nineteenth-Century Britain

http://www.fordham.edu/halsall/mod/modsbook20.html

Nineteenth-Century Britain includes general topics, radicalism, liberal reform, social class, Ireland, Victorian sensibility, and Victorian literature sources.

Nineteenth Century Britain

http://www.fordham.edu/halsall/mod/modsbook3.html#Britain

Documents and information from various sites from the Fordham University Web pages.

Roman Britain

http://web.simmons.edu/~marrus/britain/index.html

Introductory Web guide to the Roman Conquest, combining archaeology with timelines and maps.

Royal Navy

http://www.royal-navy.mod.uk/static/content/211.html

History of the Royal Navy is available through pull-down menus.

The Victorian Age

http://www.jscc.cc.tn.us/users/libjscc/subdir/wh_vic.html

This site links to the Victorian Web Overview, Victoria Research Web, Victorian Web sites, Victorian Studies on the Web, SparkNotes, and the Napoleon Foundation.

The Voice of the Shuttle History Page: United Kingdom

http://vos.ucsb.edu/shuttle/history.html#uk

This site has resources on general British history, early Britain, medieval Britain, Renaissance Britain, seventeenth- to eighteenth-century Britain, nineteenth-century Britain, Ireland, Scotland, and Wales.

Content Sites

BBC Online: History

http://www.bbc.co.uk/history/

Although touching on some other areas of world history, this site gives valuable information on the history of Great Britain by topic, time, people, and place. A search facility assists in navigation. The Reading Room has several articles expanding on important figures and events.

Britannia: America's Gateway to the British Isles

http://britannia.com/history/

Features timelines, narrative histories, original source documents and important texts, biographies, maps, glossaries, reading lists, informative articles by guest writers, interviews, and more.

British History

http://www.british-history.com/

Links to short essays on Roman Britain, the medieval period, the Civil War, the Napoleonic period, and World War II.

The British Monarchy

http://www.royal.gov.uk/

This official government site provides information on the monarchy today, royal palaces, the royal collection, monarchy through the ages, links to other related sites, and a site search engine.

Concise History of the British Newspaper Since 1620

http://www.bl.uk/collections/newspaper/britnews.html

Short histories and images of newspapers from the seventeenth through the twentieth century.

Encyclopaedia of British History, 1700–1950

http://www.spartacus.schoolnet.co.uk/Britain.html

Educational Web site from *The Guardian* covering various aspects of British history, including the monarchy, emancipation of women, education, members of Parliament, political parties, prime ministers, industry and labor, World War I, socialism, religion, and society. No search engine.

Great Britain

http://www.bartleby.com/65/gr/GreatBri.html

A general survey of British history is part of this *Columbia Encyclopedia* entry.

History of the United Kingdom: Primary Documents

http://library.byu.edu:80/~rdh/eurodocs/uk.html

This site, from Brigham Young University, provides links to primary documents ranging from the seventh/eighth-century Ruthwell Cross runic inscriptions through the Scotland Act of 1998.

The Prehistoric Period

http://www.britannia.com/history/h20.html

Timelines, narrative histories, travels through history, biographies, historical maps, articles, and outside links for prehistoric Britain.

Roman Britain

http://www.britannia.com/history/romantime.html

From Julius Caesar's first invasion of Britain in 55 B.C.E. to independence from Rome in 410 C.E. with the Goth sacking of Rome. Links to other significant names and subjects of the period.

Roman Britain circa 400

http://www.vii.com/~cda/atlas/1.htm

Map and history of the Roman period with illustrations.

Early Middle Ages

Gildas's *Concerning the Ruin of Britain*

http://www.fordham.edu/halsall/source/gildas.html

Gildas: from *Concerning the Ruin of Britain* (De Excidio Britanniae).

Historia Brittonum by Nennius

http://www.fordham.edu/halsall/basis/nennius-full.html

Nennius: *Historia Brittonum* (History of the Britons).

William of Malmesbury's *Chronicle of the Kings of England*

http://www.fordham.edu/halsall/source/malmsbury-chronicle1.html

William of Malmesbury: *Chronicle of the Kings of England*, about the Anglo-Saxon kings.

Late Middle Ages

The Anglo-Saxon Chronicle

http://sunsite.berkeley.edu/OMACL/Anglo/

The Anglo-Saxon Chronicle based on the 1912 edition.

The History of William of Newburg

http://www.fordham.edu/halsall/basis/williamofnewburgh-intro.html

William of Newburgh: *History.*

Internet Medieval Sourcebook: Later Medieval England

http://www.fordham.edu/halsall/sbook1n.html#Later Medieval England

The Later Medieval England section in the *Internet Medieval Sourcebook* provides links to primary documents of the period, from "Documents of the Church of Salisbury in the Early 13th Century" to "The Ballad of Bosworth Field."

William the Conqueror

http://www.newadvent.org/cathen/15642c.htm

The article on William the Conqueror from *The Catholic Encyclopedia.*

The Tudor Era

The History of the Crown: The Tudors
http://www.royal.gov.uk./history/tudor.htm
The monarchy's official Web site describes each of the Tudor monarchs.

Life in Elizabethan England: A Compendium of Common Knowledge
http://renaissance.dm.net/compendium/index.html
Concise descriptions of everyday life in Elizabethan England from games to occupations to maps. Includes site search engine.

Tudor England, 1485–1603
http://www.englishhistory.net/tudor.html
Information on monarchs, relatives, citizens, Henry VIII's wives, images, primary sources, life in Tudor England, and genealogy. Includes a search engine.

The Stuarts

Charles II, James II, William III, and Anne
http://www.great-britain.co.uk/history/restore.htm
From James I to Anne. Summary of the monarchs' reigns and the Stuart period on two Web pages, including significant events. Accompanied by very small images.

The History of the Crown: The Stuarts
http://www.royal.gov.uk/history/stuart.htm
From James I to Anne. Some links to other names, events, and issues of the period.

Monarchs of England and Britian
http://www.britannia.com/history/h6f.html
The division Monarchs of England includes the Stuarts, and the category Monarchs of Britain covers Anne, last of the Stuarts.

Georgian Britain

The Hanoverian Period in England

http://www.britainexpress.com/History/Georgian_index.htm

Short essays on George I through George III, with reference to some dominant events, landscape gardens, country houses, canals and waterways, and architecture.

History of the World: Georgian Britain

http://www.lukemastin.com/history/georgian_britain.html

Timeline of the Georgian period from 1714 to 1836.

The Victorian Age

History in Focus: The Victorian Era

http://www.history.ac.uk/ihr/Focus/Victorians/index.html

Scans the Age of Victoria with short items on men and women, Ireland, asylums, law and order, politics, diaries, and ancestors. Also links to other items and sites about the period.

The Irish Famine, 1845–50

http://www.people.Virginia.EDU/~eas5e/Irish/Famine.html

This site offers a hypertext archive. Resources encompass images of the famine, famine reportage and commentary, and background materials. Slow loading.

Queen Victoria

http://www.royal.gov.uk./history/victoria.htm

Profile of Queen Victoria from the British monarchy's official Web site.

Victorian and Victorianism

http://landow.stg.brown.edu/victorian/vn/victor4.html

This site hyperlinks to essays on Queen Victoria, science and technology, religion, prevalent ideas, literature, and other areas.

Twentieth-Century Britain

The British Army Search Page

http://www.army.mod.uk/search/

Use of the search facility at this British Army Web site by entering, for example, "history" retrieves numerous useful short histories of various units and actions.

British Labour Party Election Manifesto, 1945

http://www.psr.keele.ac.uk/area/uk/man/lab45.htm

This site reproduces the Labour Party's postwar declaration "Let Us Face the Future: A Declaration of Labour Policy for the Consideration of the Nation."

The British War Blue Book

http://ibiblio.org/pha/bb/bb-preface.html

This site presents primary documents regarding British entry into World War II against Germany and Italy. Users have the choice of reading documents through the table of contents or downloading a Zip file of the entire book.

Winston Churchill's "Blood, Toil, Tears and Sweat" Speech

http://www.fordham.edu/halsall/mod/churchill-blood.html

Winston Churchill on Conservative Party Principles in 1946

http://www.fordham.edu/halsall/mod/1946churchill-conservatism.html

"Churchill made this speech to the Conservative Party Conference in 1946, after he had been replaced at British Prime minister by the Clement Atlee, whose Labour government was in the process of creating the modern British welfare state. Churchill rejects socialism, but not that he does not adopt a radical free market approach either."

Winston Churchill's "Their Finest Hour" Speech

http://www.fordham.edu/halsall/mod/1940churchill-finest.html

Winston Churchill's "We Shall Never Surrender" Speech

http://history.hanover.edu/courses/excerpts/111chur.html

History of the Royal Air Force

http://www.raf.mod.uk/history/index.html

RAF site with timelines, histories, and galleries.

The National Health Service Explained

http://www.nhs.uk/thenhsexplained/history_of_the_nhs.asp

History of the National Health Service from pre-1948 to 1997.

The Royal Navy

http://www.royal-navy.mod.uk/static/content/211.html

Naval history in both world wars and up to the present is available through pull-down menus.

G.R. Strauss on Nationalising Industries

http://www.fordham.edu/halsall/mod/1948–ironsteel-nationalisation.html

A speech by G.R. Strauss, Minister of Supply, on nationalizing the iron and steel industry in 1948.

World War I Remembered

http://news.bbc.co.uk/hi/english/special_report/1998/10/98/world_war_i/newsid_197000/197437.stm

The BBC's World War I Remembered site tells the story of the war mostly from the British perspective, covering some battles, people's reactions, the realities of war, background of the conflict, letters home, radio interviews, images, and newsreels.

Eastern European and Russian History
Alexander Zukas

Metasites

Armenian Embassy Web Site

http://www.armeniaemb.org/index.html

This site has a large collection of Armenian links on the Internet arranged alphabetically, without annotations. There are several history-related sites, dealing mainly with the Armenian Genocide of 1915–1916. Maintained by the Embassy of the Republic of Armenia, Washington, D.C.

A Belarus Miscellany (ABM)

http://misc.home.by/

A collection of links to resources from and about Belarus. Organized by subject and featuring a separate history links page, which in turn contains annotated links to onsite and external resources. Maintained by Peter Kasaty and hosted by University of Tennessee in Knoxville. Mirror site in Belarus.

Central Eurasia Project Resource Page

http://www.eurasianet.org/

This site focuses on Armenia, Azerbaijan, Tajikistan, Uzbekistan, Georgia, and Kyrgyzstan. Each of these Central Eurasian countries has a separate resource page, with links grouped according to subjects, with some history links, although the amount and quality of the material vary from country to country. Maintained by the Soros Foundation.

Cilicia.com

http://www.cilicia.com/

A large Armenian information site with extensive resources and outside links. Many of the history-related links are located on the Armenian Genocide page. External links are grouped together following the internal resources, and it is easy to distinguish one from another. Maintained by Raffi Kojian and hosted by Cilicia.com. Part of the Armenian Web Ring.

Faculty of History, Moscow State University

http://www.hist.msu.ru/Menu/index_english.htm

The site is still under construction, but it contains very useful links to materials not available from other metasites. Materials available include sites dedicated to the eight hundred and fiftieth anniversary of Moscow and to the two-hundredth anniversary of the birth of Alexander Pushkin. Maintained and hosted by the Faculty of History, Moscow State University.

F and P History

http://www.friends-partners.org/friends/history/opt-tables-unix-english-

This metasite provides links to resources in Russian, Soviet, and American history, as well as to historical documents, like the constitutions of the Russian Federation and the United States, and the 1867 Alaska treaty. Many of the links lead to Russian language resources. Hosted and maintained by Friends and Partners, a Russo-American citizens' organization.

Funet Russian Archive

http://www.funet.fi/pub/culture/russian/index.html

A links and resources site on Russia and the former Soviet Union. History-related links are located at Funet Russian Archive Index and Links, which is arranged alphabetically. The whole site itself is at its best in providing onsite historical resources. Maintained by and hosted by Finnish University and Research Network, Espoo, Finland.

History/Social Studies Web Site for K-12 Teachers

http://www.execpc.com/~dboals/boals.html

An important metasite in that it is virtually the only site to provide links to history resources that are specifically chosen for K-12 teachers. The Russian history area is large (sixty-six links), with links to general resources and resources of specific interest to schoolteachers. Maintained by Dennis Boals and hosted by Xplore Company.

Horus' History Links

http://www.ucr.edu/h-gig/horuslinks.html

This metasite maintained and hosted by the History Department, University of California, Riverside, gives an overview of sites relating to all geographical and thematic areas of historical study. The site is still under construction, but a large number of Russian history sites are already available.

H-RUSSIA WWW Links

http://h-net2.msu.edu/~russia/links/

A selection of links to Russian resources from H-Net. Some history materials are available from the Politics and Miscellaneous subject sections. Highlight: Russian Revolution page from the Military History section of the New York Public Library, with rare photographs of the early Soviet Union. Hosted by Michigan State University.

Illustrated History of Russia and the Former USSR

http://www.cs.toronto.edu/~mes/russia/history.html

This is a collection of links to sites dealing with artifacts, photographs, and other graphic material from the various periods in Russian history, from the era of Genghis Khan to the July 1996 presidential elections in Russia. Privately maintained by Mikhail Soutchanski and hosted by the Department of Computer Science at the University of Toronto.

Important Places

http://www.vwc.edu/wwwpages/dgraf/places.htm

A general metasite, organized by region, with links to Russia and the former Soviet Union, Central Europe, and the Balkans, among other regions. Related metasites with Russian links: e.g., Exhibits and Museums, Military History. Maintained by Professor Dan Graf and hosted by Virginia Wesleyan College.

Index of Resources for History

http://www.ukans.edu/history/VL/

A general metasite with worldwide links to sites devoted to history. Organized by subject and geographical area. Sites are neither annotated nor organized by subheadings. Highlight: a number of links to nineteenth-century maps of Russia and Central and Eastern Europe. Jointly maintained by the Department of

History of the University of Kansas and the Lehrstuhl für Ältere deutsche Literaturwissenschaft der Universität Regensburg; managed by Eric Marzo of Regensburg and Lynn Nelson of Kansas.

Institute of Baltic Studies

http://www.ibs.ee/

An Estonian site with links to resources on Estonia and other Baltic states. Organized by subject. History subject area is small, with both internal and external links listed together. Highlight: Department of History, University of Tartu site, with its Electronic Library of Estonian History page. Maintained and hosted by the Institute of Baltic Studies, Estonia.

Internet Resources for Russian Studies

http://src-h.slav.hokudai.ac.jp/link/index-e.html

Probably the best metasite for materials on Russia, the Commonwealth of Independent States, and the Baltic States. This is extremely well-organized geographically (by region and country) and by subject. All of the country pages have a history section, with history links on the Slavic and Baltic pages further subdivided chronologically. Many of the links on this metasite lead to resources compiled within the former Soviet Union, which cannot be found on other metasites. Most of the links are reliable in their connection. Maintained by Slavic Research Center, Hokkaido University, Japan.

Links Slavica

http://www.celtoslavica.de/links/links_slavica.html

A part of the larger CeltoSlavica site, this metasite deals with the various facets of Slavic life, including history of the Slavic countries and peoples. History links are scattered throughout the site, within areas dedicated to various countries. Maintained by CeltoSlavica and hosted by Geocities.

Medieval Russia: Medieval History Net Links

http://historymedren.miningco.com/msubrus.htm

A small but well-organized metasite on medieval Russian history. Links to chronologies of Russian history, overviews of Russian ruling houses and medieval Russian cities, and compilations of medieval Russian law. Equipped with its own search engine. Maintained by the Mining Company.

Military History

http://www.cfcsc.dnd.ca/links/milhist/index.html

This metasite provides links to internal and external resources in military history. Russian, Soviet, and East European resources are scattered throughout entries on various wars. Hosted and maintained by the Information Resource Center, Canadian Forces College, Toronto, Canada.

Orthodox Christian Resources on the Internet

http://www.hrweb.org/orthodox/

This well-designed metasite is unique in bringing together the links related to the Russian and other Slavic Orthodox churches. Arranged by subject. History page is small but very useful. Highlights: ERP Church History, a comprehensive history of the Orthodox Church, including the Russian church. Maintained by Catherine Hampton and hosted by The Human Rights Web.

REESWeb

http://www.ucis.pitt.edu/reesweb/

One of the oldest links sites dealing with Russia, the former Soviet Union, and Eastern Europe, this site has fallen into a state of disrepair, with many dead links. Highlight: ArcheoBiblioBase, which presents vital data about individual archival repositories in Russia and Ukraine and a structured bibliography of their finding aids. There also is a large number of national home pages. Maintained by the University of Pittsburgh.

Russia on the Web

http://www.valley.net:80/~transnat/index.html#Russia

A well-designed metasite with links to Russian sources. Organized by subject with a small History page. Many of the sites on this page can, however, be found on other larger metasites. Hosted by the Transnational Institute.

Russian and East European Network Information Center (REENIC)

http://reenic.utexas.edu/reenic.html

A large metasite with links to resources on Russia, the countries of the former Soviet Union, and Eastern Europe. Most country pages have a history subject listing, but these are not abundant in resources. The site is at its best as a starting point to other relevant metasites on the WWW. Maintained by the Center for Russian, East European, and Eurasian Studies at the University of Texas in Austin.

Russian History

http://www.departments.bucknell.edu/russian/history.html

A well-organized and well-maintained Russian metasite. The links are generally arranged in chronological order, although there are large thematic sections. A number of links lead to photographic and genealogical material, as well as Russian and Soviet historical documents. Maintained by Bucknell University, Lewisburg, Pennsylvania.

Russian History on the Internet

http://www.ucr.edu/history/seaman/

An information and links site on Russia and the Soviet Union. Contains a links page with some history-related links. Main strength is the photo archive of the Bolshevik leaders and the bibliography of the materials related to Russian history. Maintained by James Seaman, History Department, University of California, Riverside.

Russian History on the Web

http://www.russianhistory.org/

Launched by Marshall Poe of the School for Historical Studies at the Institute for Advanced Study, this valuable gateway provides academic researchers, educators, and students with a collection of critically evaluated Internet resources relevant to the study of Russian history. This selective, well-organized gateway offers an annotated index of high-quality information resources including metasites, guides, indexes, bibliographies, dissertations, scholarly articles, journals, maps, surveys, archives, professional organizations, research centers, discussion lists, primary texts, image databases, and much more.

The Russian Revolution

http://www.barnsdle.demon.co.uk/russ/rusrev.html

A fairly small but very useful metasite with particular emphasis on the February and October Revolutions of 1917 in Russia and the Russian Civil War. It also contains links to political parties, figures, and movements, images and maps, and critiques of the events in the years after 1917. Privately maintained by David Barnsdale.

Russophilia!

http://www.russophilia.com.au/flash.html

An excellent Russian links page from Adelaide in Australia. Arranged by subject, with a large and varied History and Social Sciences section. Major topics include the Romanov Dynasty, Soviet Russia, and regional histories, with many sites not listed in other metasites. Maintained by Rita Bogna.

The Society for Romanian Studies

http://www.huntington.edu/srs/

This site contains a large Romanian Studies Internet Gateway, with links to outside sites on Romania, organized by subject. While history is not one of those subjects, a significant number of history-related links can be found in the Scholarly Publications and Cities areas. Maintained by Paul E. Michelson and hosted by Huntington College, Huntington, Indiana.

Ukraine

http://www.physics.mcgill.ca/WWW/oleh/ukr-info.html

One of the oldest national sites on the former Soviet Union, dating back to at least 1994. History links are located in the Historical Items subsection of the General Information area. The section is small, but it contains links to a diverse range of materials. Maintained by Oleh Baran and hosted by the Physics Department of McGill University, Canada.

UNCG's Slavic Studies Trails

http://www.uncg.edu/~lixlpurc/russian.html

A collection of links to resources on and from Poland, Russia, and Ukraine. The Russian links are the most numerous and reliable, and some of them lead to history sites. This site is best used as a starting point to other larger and more history-oriented metasites. Maintained by the Department of German and Russian at the University of North Carolina, Greensboro.

The University of Kansas History Group

http://kuhttp.cc.ukans.edu/history/WWW_history_main.html

A part of the WWW Virtual Library, this site is an important starting point for research in history. Russian and East European resources are located in the Russia and Eastern Europe section, the Central Europe section, and in the sections on Slovakia and Romania. The links are not annotated. Maintained by the University of Kansas History Group under the auspices of the WWW Virtual Library and hosted by the University of Kansas.

World History Compass

http://www.worldhistorycompass.com/whlindex.htm#Europe Index

A large and important metasite with links to history materials throughout the world. Russian, former Soviet Union, and East European links are indexed under "Europe," where in turn they are indexed under separate countries. No annotations for sites are provided. Maintained by Schiller Computing, Stratford, Connecticut, and hosted by LexiConn Internet Services, Colchester, Connecticut.

Reference Sites

ArcheoBiblioBase

http://www.iisg.nl/~abb/

An important information source on federal and regional archives of the Russian Federation. The information for each archive includes name, address, phone number and e-mail, hours, outline of holdings, library facilities, and finding aids. Maintained by Patricia Kennedy Grimsted in collaboration with Rosarkhiv, the Federal Archival Service of Russia, and hosted by the International Institute of Social History, Amsterdam, Netherlands.

Armenian Research Center

http://www.umd.umich.edu/dept/armenian/

A U.S.-based resource site that deals with various aspects of Armenian history and culture. The most useful part of the site is a collection of bibliographies on Nagorno-Karabakh conflict and the Armenian Genocide, which constitute an important starting point in a study of these two topics. Maintained by the Center for Armenian Research and Publication and hosted by the University of Michigan, Dearborn.

Brokgaus Online

http://www.agama.com/bol/

The core material presently at this site is the *Brokgaus-Efron Encyclopedia* and the pre-Revolutionary dictionaries by Pavlenkov, Mikhelson, and Starchevskii.

The encyclopedia is a very important source of information on pre-Revolutionary Russia, a source that may not be readily available elsewhere. The site is in Russian, and a knowledge of the language, as well as a Russian-English keyboard, is needed to access the site. Compiled and maintained by Sergei Moskalev and jointly hosted by Agama WWW Server and Cityline Internet Service Providers (Moscow).

A Chronology of Russian History

http://www.departments.bucknell.edu/russian/chrono.html

A chronology of Russian history, this site is "divided into four arbitrary periods": Kievan-Appanage (860–1689), Imperial (1689–1916), Soviet (1917–1991), and post-Soviet (1991 to the present). "A fifth page displays related chronologies on specialized subjects."

The House of Romanov

http://www.departments.bucknell.edu/russian/facts/romanov.html

The detailed family tree of the Romanov tsars and emperors who ruled Russia between 1613 and 1917. The site appears to be under construction, and key figures in the dynasty will have links to more detailed information about themselves and their contribution. Maintained by Robert Beard and hosted by the Russian Studies Department, Bucknell University, Lewisburg, Pennsylvania.

The House of Rurik

http://www.departments.bucknell.edu/russian/facts/rurik.html

The detailed family tree of the Rurik Dynasty, Russia's first ruling dynasty descended from Viking princes. The site appears to be under construction, and key figures in the dynasty will have links to more detailed information about themselves and their contribution. Maintained by Robert Beard and hosted by the Russian Studies Department, Bucknell University, Lewisburg, Pennsylvania.

H-RUSSIA WWW Site

http://www.h-net.msu.edu/~russia/

H-RUSSIA, a member of H-NET, encourages scholarly discussion of Russian and Soviet history. Makes available diverse bibliographical, research, and teaching aids and features a review project. Maintained by H-NET Humanities and Social Sciences Online and hosted by Michigan State University.

Information about Lithuania

http://neris.mii.lt/homepage/liet1–1.html

An important reference site on Lithuania. Features a short outline of the country's history, with links to a cultural timeline and a list of rulers. The site also contains detailed information on the major urban centers in the country. Maintained by Danute Vanseviciene and hosted by Lithuania Academic and Research Network at the Institute of Mathematics and Informatics.

The Lost Churches of Kyiv

http://www.kiev.ua:8100/oldkiev/

This site is an important reference source on the churches in the Ukrainian capital destroyed during the Stalinist era. Each link leads to a separate page with the photograph of the church in question and a description of its history and the circumstances of its destruction. Maintained and hosted by the Global Ukraine ISP under the auspices of the Ukraine Online project.

Moldova: Important Events

http://www.timisoara.com/msoccer/eventsMOLDOVA.htm

A chronology of the history of Moldova, from Roman times (105 c.e.) to the present. Maintained and hosted by the Embassy of Moldova in Washington, D.C.

Political Leaders, 1945–2001

http://www.terra.es/personal2/monolith/00index.htm

A continually updated index of leaders of the countries in the world, from 1945 to the present day. Heads of states, prime ministers, and the leaders of ruling parties are featured. Some countries also have picture links.

Reference Sources: Russian History and Literature

http://www.lib.berkeley.edu/Collections/Slavic/russref.html

This online bibliography of reference material is extremely useful as a starting point in research on Russian and Soviet history and literary heritage. Sources listed include general guides, encyclopedias, serial reference publications, and guides to archival materials and émigré sources. Library of Congress classification numbers are provided. Maintained by Allan Urbanic and hosted by the Library of the University of California, Berkeley.

Romanov Dynasty WWW Encyclopedia (Russian Edition)

http://www.online.ru/sp/cominf/romanovs/index.rhtml

This site is based on the Dinastiia Romanovikh (The Romanov Dynasty) CD-ROM, published by the Cominfo Electronic Publishers of Moscow. Information is available by browsing tsars and famous individuals, or by using a chronology. Includes photographs of the artifacts connected with the dynasty. The site is available in Russian only, but an English version is under construction. Maintained by Cominfo Publishers, Moscow, and hosted by Russia Online.

Russian History

http://hulmer.allegheny.edu/history.html

A short chronology of Russian history, concentrating on the rulers of Russia, from early times to the Bolshevik Revolution of 1917. Hyperlinks to a glossary of related terms. Maintained by Kristen Magee and hosted by Allegheny College, Pennsylvania.

Russian Revolution in Dates

http://www.barnsdle.demon.co.uk/russ/datesr.html

A detailed chronology of the Russian Revolution, from Bloody Sunday in January 1905 to the death of Lenin in 1924. Privately maintained by David Barnsdale as a part of his Russian Revolution site.

Sites by T.F. Boettger

http://www.geocities.com/~tfboettger/

T.F. Boettger has a number of extensive sites dealing with Russian and Georgian nobility. Although still under construction, they are an important source of information about the members of the upper echelons of Russian and Georgian nobility and their descendants. Maintained by T.F. Boettger and hosted by GeoCities.

Soviet Leaders

http://artnet.net/~upstart/soviet.html

A chronology of Soviet leaders from Khrushchev to Gorbachev. Features a minute-by-minute chronology of the August 1991 coup, and the seventy-three slogans advanced by the Central Committee of the Communist Party of the

Soviet Union (CPSU) in celebration of the sixtieth anniversary of the October Revolution, among other items. Hosted by aNet Communications, Los Angeles, California.

Ukraine: History

http://www.hopenow.org.uk/HTML/History.htm

This site features a straightforward summary of Ukrainian history and a set of pages with information on various other aspects of Ukraine, including links to historical towns.

Online Exhibitions and Virtual Tours

The Alexander Palace Web Sites

http://www.alexanderpalace.org/

The palaces showcased include the Alexander Palace, the Great Catherine Palace of Tsarskoe Selo, and the Yelagin Palace of St. Petersburg. Each of the sites includes a virtual tour of the palace in question, its history, and its connection with the various members of the Romanov dynasty. Other exhibits showcased include the Romanov Jewels. Maintained by Alexander Palace Association and hosted by PalasArt Web Design and Hosting, Austin, Texas.

Alexander Rodchenko Museum Series Portfolios

http://photoarts.com/schickler/portfolios/rodchenko/

Alexander Rodchenko (1891–1956) was a consummate artist in all media; his painting, design work, and photography were fundamental to the founding of abstract art in Revolutionary Russia. From the historical point of view, the second portfolio is the most important, as it features portraits of famous Soviet artists, actors, and intellectuals in the 1920s and 1930s. Maintained by Howard Schlicker Fine Arts, New York, and hosted by PhotoArts.

Beyond the Pale: The History of Jews in Russia

http://www.friends-partners.org/partners/beyond-the-pale/

This site explores the history of Jews in Russia and the Soviet Union, from Jewish life during the Middle Ages to the resurgence of anti-Semitism in the post-Soviet period. Each section outlines the events, policies, and ideas, and is accompanied by images of artifacts, paintings, and photographs. English and

Russian versions available. Maintained by M.F. Miller and Matvey B. Palchuk; hosted by Friends and Partners.

The Chairman Smiles

http://www.iisg.nl/exhibitions/chairman/

An online exhibition of posters from the former Soviet Union, Cuba, and China. The Soviet section features thirty-three posters dating between 1919 and 1938. A brief introduction is given, followed by images of the posters. Each image contains an explanatory note, giving the author, translation of the slogan, and a brief historical background. Maintained and hosted by the International Institute of Social History, Amsterdam, Netherlands.

Estonia: Land, People, Culture

http://www.erm.ee/pysi/engpages/index.html

An online version of the permanent exhibition from the Estonian National Museum in Tallinn. The site covers all historical facets of Estonian life, including peasant life, holidays and festivities, and regional peculiarities, through tsarist, interwar, Soviet, and post-Soviet eras. Maintained and hosted by the Estonian National Museum, Tallinn, Estonia.

The Face of Russia

http://www.pbs.org/weta/faceofrussia/

An online companion to the acclaimed PBS series of the same name. This well-developed site includes an interactive timeline of Russian history and culture, a description of the series, and reference material. Maintained and hosted by the Public Broadcasting Service, Alexandria, Virginia.

The Jewels of the Romanovs

http://mfah.org/romanov/index.html

Based on an exhibition by the same name hosted by the Museum of Fine Arts, Houston, this Web site showcases images of jewels, costumes, paintings, icons, and religious artifacts of the Romanov dynasty from the eighteenth century to its fall in 1917. Maintained and hosted by the Museum of Fine Arts, Houston.

Moscow Kremlin 3W Guide

http://www.online.ru/sp/cominf/kremlin/kremlin.html

This site is a well-designed and well-developed online guide to the Kremlin, organized according to its architectural elements. Each area is described textually, with hyperlinks to important persons, buildings, and organizations connected with the Kremlin. The site is available in Russian and in English. Maintained by Cominfo Publishers, Moscow, and hosted by Russia Online.

Nicholas and Alexandra

http://www.nicholasandalexandra.com/

This online exhibition proceeds chronologically, from the youth and courtship of Nicholas II and Alexandra to their exile and execution in Yekaterinburg in 1918. The site also contains Russian maps of the period, a timeline, a list of the Romanov rulers, and related links. Hosted by Broughton International, an organizer and promoter of exhibitions, based in St. Petersburg, Florida.

Pictures of Russian History

http://metalab.unc.edu/sergei/Exs/His/His.html

A selection of illustrations completed by S. Ivanov from 1908 to 1913 for *Pictures of Russian History*, published in Moscow. The original work, in a series of albums, gives important insight into how the history of Russia was perceived in the Russian Empire at the beginning of the twentieth century.

Revelations from the Russian Archives

http://lcweb.loc.gov/exhibits/archives/

The documents presented in the exhibition come from the archives of the Communist Party of the Soviet Union and cover a wide range of chronological periods and themes, such as Lenin's attitudes, Stalin's purges, Chernobyl, and the changes in relations between the Soviet Union and the United States. Each page describes historical background of a given theme, then presents scanned images of illustrative documents relating to that theme and period, together with translations. Maintained and hosted by the Library of Congress.

The Romanovs: Their Empire, Their Books

http://www.nypl.org/research/chss/slv/exhibit/roman.html

This exhibit presents a selection of items from a collection of over 3,000 Romanov volumes acquired by the New York Public Library during the 1920s and 1930s, organized thematically according to six broad areas: Empire, War, Exploration, Work and Leisure, Culture, and Faith. Each area contains a short summary and one or two sample illustrations. Maintained by R. Davis and hosted by the New York Public Library.

Rudolf Abel: Legendary Soviet Spy

http://members.tripod.com/~RUDOLFABEL/

A biography of Rudolf Abel (real name William August Fisher) the legendary Soviet spy in Britain and the United States, where he was arrested in 1957 and freed in 1962 in exchange for U-2 pilot Gary Powers. Features an online exhibit of photographs and documents associated with Abel. Maintained by Alex Heft and hosted by Tripod, Inc.

Russian Art from the Hulmer Collection

http://hulmer.allegheny.edu/

An online exhibition of Russian religious art bequeathed to Allegheny College by Eric C. Hulmer. Maintained by Amelia Carr and hosted by Allegheny College, Pennsylvania.

The Russian Church and Native Alaskan Cultures

http://lcweb.loc.gov/exhibits/russian/s1a.html

This online exhibit includes scanned images of the lithographs, documents, and photographs that illustrate the relationship between the missionaries of the Russian Orthodox Church and the native peoples and cultures of Alaska and the Aleutian Islands between 1741 and 1915. Maintained and hosted by the Library of Congress.

Russian Empire, 1895–1910

http://cmp1.ucr.edu/exhibitions/russia/russia.html

A selection of photographs from Moscow, St. Petersburg, and Kiev dating from 1895 to 1910, which are part of the Keystone-Mast collection of some 900 stereoscopic images of Russia, housed at the California Museum of Photography. Maintained and hosted by the California Museum of Photography at the University of California, Riverside.

Russian Icons

http://www.auburn.edu/academic/liberal_arts/foreign/russian/icons/

A large collection of digitized images of Russian icons dating from the twelfth to the late seventeenth century. Maintained by George Mitrevski as a part of his resources page and hosted by Auburn University, Alabama.

Soviet War Photography

http://photoarts.com/schickler/exhibits/sovietwar/index2.html

A collection of thirty-three Soviet World War II photographs by the country's most noted master photographers of the time. Covers a wide range of topics, from the partisans gathering to thwart the Nazi advance into Belorussia to the subsequent war crimes trials at Nuremberg in 1946. Maintained by Howard Schlicker Fine Arts, New York, and hosted by PhotoArts.

Treasures of the Czars

http://www2.sptimes.com/Treasures/

An exhibition of the tsars' treasures that was mounted in 1995 at the Florida International Museum in St. Petersburg, Florida. The site contains the exhibits as well as historical information about the Rurik and Romanov dynasties, including an interactive timeline of the tsars and a detailed tour of the exhibition itself. Maintained and hosted by *St. Petersburg Times*, St. Petersburg, Florida, as a part of its Web site.

Yevgeni Khaldei

http://photoarts.com/schickler/exhibits/khaldei/exhibit/exhibit.html

A selection of the photographs of Yevgeni Khaldei, one of the most preeminent Soviet news photographers of the World War II era. The photographs include such famous images as the raising of the Soviet flag over the Reichstag, the portrait of Churchill, Truman, and Stalin seated at the Potsdam Conference, and the images of the Nuremberg Trials. Maintained by Howard Schlicker Fine Arts, New York, and hosted by PhotoArts.

Online Archives

The Armenian Genocide

http://www.cilicia.com/armo10.html

This site aims to provide documentary material concerning the massacres of Armenians in the Ottoman Empire in 1915–1916. Section I provides a summary of earlier Armenian history, section II summarizes events leading up to the genocide, section III briefly describes the massacres, and section IV discusses life after the atrocities. The site also contains the map of Armenia's border with Turkey as drawn by President Woodrow Wilson.

Armenian National Institute

http://www.armenian-genocide.org/

Armenian National Institute is an organization based in Washington, D.C. Its Web site has an extensive research area, which contains photographs, a selection of documents from American and British archives, statements from various official sources on the subject, and press coverage in the United States of the massacres between 1915 and 1920.

Cold War Document Library

http://cwihp.si.edu/cwihplib.nsf

An online collection of documents connected with the Cold War and the participation of various powers (e.g., Soviet Union, United States, and China) in it. Maintained and hosted by the Woodrow Wilson International Center for Scholars as a part of its Cold War International Project site.

The Development of the RSFSR

http://www.marxists.org/history/ussr/index.htm

A significant repository of the material relating to the establishment and the early days of the Soviet Union, in the form of the Russian Soviet Federative Socialist Republic (RSFSR). Contains Soviet documents on foreign policy, American-Soviet relations, the Constitution of the RSFSR, and photographs of leading Bolsheviks and leaders of the White movement. Maintained by Brian Basgen and hosted by the Marxists Internet Archive.

From Marx to Mao

http://gate.cruzio.com/~marx2mao/

An online archive of English translations of works by leading Socialist thinkers, from Marx and Engels to Mao Zedong. The material related to Russian history is featured in the online collection of works, arranged chronologically, by Lenin and Stalin. The works are mostly sources from the English editions published by the Foreign Languages Publishing House in Moscow in the 1950s and 1960s. Hosted by Santa Cruz County, California.

Marxist Writers

http://csf.Colorado.EDU/psn/marx/Other/

This site provides English translations of selected works of important Marxist theorists, both Russian and non-Russian. The Russian Marxists include Lenin,

Stalin, Anatoly Lunacharsky, and Leon Trotsky. Archives of Lenin and Stalin also contain a number of digitized photographs. Maintained by the Syber-Marx International and hosted by the University of Colorado under the auspices of the Communications for a Sustainable Future project.

Modern Customs and Ancient Laws in Russia

http://www.socsci.mcmaster.ca/~econ/ugcm/3ll3/kovalevsky/

A series of six lectures on the ancient laws of Russian society and their influence on nineteenth-century Russian customs, delivered in 1891 by Maksim Kovalevsky, a prominent Russian thinker in the field. Maintained and hosted by the Faculty of Social Sciences, McMaster University, Ontario, Canada.

Modern History Sourcebook: Catherine the Great

http://www.fordham.edu/halsall/mod/18catherine.html

A selection of materials in English translation related to Catherine the Great. Includes the characterization of Catherine by Baron de Breteuil, the French diplomat in Moscow, Catherine's proposals for the Russian law code, and an excerpt of her decree on the serfs. Maintained by Paul Halsall and hosted by Fordham University, New York.

Moscow Trials 1936: Court Proceedings

http://art-bin.com/art/omoscowtoc.html

An online version of the official transcript of the 1936 trial of Zinoviev and others accused of belonging to the so-called Trotskyite-Zinovievite United Terrorist Center. This was one of the first large show trials in the Stalinist Soviet Union, and it led to the execution of Zinoviev, Kamenev, and other members of the Left Opposition. Maintained and hosted by *Art Bin* online magazine, Sweden.

Patriotic History

http://www.lants.tellur.ru/history/index.htm

This Russian-language site has a wealth of information on Russian history. The highlights of the archive, however, are the online versions of the classic works of Russian history, including *Lectures* by V.O. Kliuchevskii and *The History of Russia from the Earliest Times* by S.M. Soloviev. Maintained by Oleg Lantsov and hosted by Tellur Network Technologies, Moscow.

The Peace Treaty of Brest-Litovsk

http://www.lib.byu.edu/~rdh/wwi/1918/brestlitovsk.html

A complete text of the peace treaty of Brest-Litovsk, which took Russia out of World War I, set the stage for invasion by various powers, and was a starting point for the Russian Civil War. Maintained by Jane Plotke as a part of the World War I Document Archive and hosted by the Brigham Young University Library.

Russian History Home Page

http://www.dur.ac.uk/~dml0www/Russhist.HTML

An important and useful online archive providing Russian historical texts in English. A wide chronological and thematic range of documents is provided, from medieval Russian chronicles describing the founding of the city of Kiev to documents on the trials of Soviet dissidents in the 1960s. Maintained by John Slatter and hosted by the University of Durham, United Kingdom.

Russian History on the Internet

http://www.ucr.edu/history/seaman/

This site is significant for its collection of photographs of Bukharin, Lenin, Stalin, and Trotsky, the key figures in the Russian Revolution and the Bolshevik movement. An AVI movie clip of Lenin is also included. A significant bibliography of sources related to Russian and Soviet history is available, but still under construction. Maintained by James Seaman, History Department, University of California, Riverside.

Russian Philosophy on the Intelnet

http://www.cc.emory.edu/INTELNET/rus_philosophy_home.html

An archive of material connected with Russian philosophers and the history of Russian philosophy of the nineteenth and twentieth centuries. Features an overview of the history of Russian philosophy, the major ideas of four Russian thinkers—Vladimir Solovyov, Nikolai Fedorov, Vasily Rozanov, and Nikolai Berdiaev, a portrait gallery, related links, and a number of other works. Maintained by Mikhail N. Epstein, associate professor, Department of Russian, Eurasian, and East Asian Languages and Cultures, Emory University.

The Song of Igor's Campaign

http://lib.ru/NABOKOW/slovo.txt

A translation of the *Song of Igor's Campaign (Slovo o polku Igoreve)*. This epic poem is an important primary source of early medieval Russian history. The poem is translated by Vladimir Nabakov, and the site contains a link to the original text.

VENONA Home Page

http://www.nsa.gov/docs/venona/

VENONA was the code name used for the U.S. Signals Intelligence effort to collect and decrypt the text of Soviet KGB and GRU messages from the 1940s. These messages provided extraordinary insight into Soviet attempts to infiltrate the highest levels of the United States government. The site features the images of the VENONA documents, the chronology of the project, and the document release monographs. Maintained and hosted by the National Security Agency, Fort Meade, Maryland.

Accounts and Opinions

Armenia-Azerbaijan Conflict

http://www.azembassy.com/confl/browse.htm

A selection of official views and supporting diplomatic documents on the Armenia-Azerbaijan conflict from the Azerbaijan embassy in Washington, D.C. Historical background to the conflict is featured on a separate page, where the conflict between the two peoples is traced to the official policies of the Russian Empire from the early 1700s onward, in which the Armenians with their Christian religion were allegedly favored over the Moslem Azeris. Maintained and hosted by the Embassy of the Republic of Azerbaijan in Washington, D.C.

Azerbaijan's History

http://www-scf.usc.edu/~baguirov/azeri/azerbaijan4.htm

A short history of Azerbaijan and the Azeri people in a brief, encyclopedic format. History material spans from the pre-Islamic period, beginning with the ninth century B.C.E., to modern days. Hyperlinks to modern and historical maps of Azerbaijan. Maintained by Adil Baguirov as a part of the Virtual Azerbaijan site and hosted by University of South California Student Computing Facility.

The Cossack Page

http://artiom.home.mindspring.com/cossacks/kazaki.htm

A very informative history of the Cossack movement in Russia, from its beginnings in late medieval Russia to its revival in the post-Soviet Russian Federation. The main section is divided into seven parts, and there are also links to subpages within the site.

Did Lenin Lead to Stalin?

http://www.geocities.com/CapitolHill/2419/lensta.html

An analysis of Lenin and his connection to Stalin from an anarchist perspective. Argues that Lenin actively pursued policies that eventually became the hallmarks of Stalinism, namely socialism in one country, one-party rule, and totalitarianism. Maintained by Andrew Flood and hosted by the Capitol Hill server of GeoCities.

The Establishment of the Kiev Rus'

http://xyz.org.ua/russian/win/discussion/hold_rus.rus.html

An online article in Russian (the Ukrainian version is available as well) by Sergei Datsyuk tracing the establishment, the rise, and the eventual demise of the Kievan Rus' and the lessons that can be learned from this medieval state by the modern Ukrainian state in its economic, social, and cultural policies. Maintained and hosted by *XYZ Online Magazine*, Ukraine.

Estonia Country Guide: History

http://www.ciesin.ee/ESTCG/HISTORY/

A concise historical overview of the history of Estonia from prehistoric times to current days. The country's history is portrayed from a distinctly nationalist point of view, with the interwar independence (1920–1940) portrayed in greatest detail and as the country's best period. World War II Estonia is portrayed as the victim of double aggression from the Soviet Union and Nazi Germany. Hyperlinks to other materials in the Estonia Country Guide site. Maintained by Toomas Mölder and hosted by CIESIN Baltics Regional Node WWW in Estonia.

Estonian History

http://www.einst.ee/history.htm

This is a collection of materials on the history of Estonia. The site contains articles describing various aspects of Estonian history, including its churches and manor houses. There are also links to the Estonian National Museum and the Estonian Historical Archives.

Factory Committees in the Russian Revolution

http://flag.blackened.net/revolt/talks/russia_fac.html

A discussion by Ray Cunningham of the factory committees' role in establishing the eight-hour day and other improvements to workers' conditions following the February Revolution of 1917. Maintained by Workers Solidarity Movement, an Irish anarchist group, and hosted by Flag.Blackened.Net server.

Funet Russian Archive Directory

http://www.funet.fi/pub/culture/russian/history/

This site contains an online version of *A Brief History of Russia and the Soviet Union* (1971), which was used to train American military personnel. It also contains a detailed chronology of Russia with relevant links and numerous miscellaneous accounts of different periods in Russian history. Maintained and hosted by Timo Hamalainen.

History and Culture of Russia

http://www.interknowledge.com/russia/rushis01.htm

An overview of the history of Russia, in which the authors aim to go beyond the usual "compendium of hazy legends and sensationalist rumors." Throughout the text there are hyperlinks to other Russian material. Maintained by the Russian National Tourist Office and hosted by InterKnowledge Corporation.

History of Belarus (Great Litva)

http://jurix.jura.uni-sb.de/~serko/history/history.html

A history of Belarus from the sixth century c.e. to modern days. Includes a chronology of Belarus, followed by a number of documents excerpted from recent works, dealing with such sensitive areas as the Stalinist repression and executions of Belarussians in the 1930s. Links to other Belarus and Lithuania related sites. Maintained by Aliaksiej Sierka and hosted by the Institute for Computers and Law, University of Saarland, Germany.

History of Kazakstan

http://members.tripod.com/~kz2000/history/

This page, part of a more general Kazakstan Online site, deals with the history of Kazakhstan and especially the origins of the various ethnic groups that populated the country throughout the ages. More modern historical events connected with Kazakhstan are dealt with in the chronology of Kazakhstan. Maintained by Yerzhan Yerkin-uly and hosted by Tripod, Inc.

History of Modern Russia

http://mars.acnet.wnec.edu/~grempel/courses/russia/

This site features, among other things, a complete set of forty-eight course lectures by Professor Gerhard Rempel. These lectures deal with a wide variety of topics in Russian history, from the democratic tradition in medieval Russia to the 1989 revolutions in Eastern Europe. Maintained by Professor Rempel and hosted by Western New England College, Springfield, Massachusetts.

A History of Russia

http://palimpsest.lss.wisc.edu/~creeca/

Online versions of lectures on the history of Russia from 800 to 1917, delivered in 1987 by Michael Petrovich, professor of Balkan and Russian history at the University of Wisconsin, Madison. The lectures are in RealAudio format, with maps and images displayed. Maintained and hosted by the Center for Russia, East Europe and Central Asia, University of Wisconsin, Madison.

The History of Russian Navy

http://www.neva.ru/EXPO96/book/book-cont.html

An online version of the book by the same name, which gives a detailed overview of the history of the Russian navy from the times of Kievan Rus to the Bolshevik Revolution. Illustrated, but no references are provided. Maintained and hosted by RUSNet, St. Petersburg, as part of the Russian Pavilion in the 1996 Internet World Exhibition.

An Inquiry into a Scandinavian Homeland for the Rus'

http://www.geocities.com/Athens/9529/scanrus.htm

Online version of "An Inquiry into a Scandinavian Homeland for the Rus'," a paper by Hugh R. Whinfrey, in which the author examines the Scandinavian origins of the founders of Russia. Well written and extensively footnoted, with a large bibliography. Maintained by Hugh R. Whinfrey and hosted by GeoCities.

The Kronstadt Uprising 1921

http://www.islandnet.com/~citizenx/kronstadt.html

An online account and analysis of the Kronstadt Uprising in Soviet Russia's Baltic Fleet in 1921, written by Brian R. Train. Examines the events that led to the uprising, its causes and effects, and the connection between the uprising and other events in Soviet history at the time. Bibliography included.

Moldova

http://www.moldova.org

An informational site on all aspects of Moldova, including brief accounts of the history of the country. A chronology of important historical events connected with Moldova and its historical predecessors is also published.

Republic of Azerbaijan

http://www.president.az/azerbaijan/azerbaijan.htm

An official WWW site of Azerbaijan from the Office of the President of the Republic, featuring a brief historical outline. In keeping with the official viewpoint of the site, the responsibility for the conflict is placed jointly on the Soviet central authorities and the then Armenian SSR and subsequently the independent Armenian state. Maintained and hosted by the Office of the President of the Republic of Azerbaijan.

Russia.Net History

http://www.russianet.ru/~oldrn/history.html

A well-written outline of Russian history, from the early Slavs and Kiev Rus to a detailed account of the August 1991 coup and the collapse of the Soviet Union. Maintained and hosted by Russia.Net, a U.S.-based Russian server, with a mirror site in Russia.

The Russian Post-Emancipation Household

http://www.uib.no/hi/herdis/HerdisKolle.html

This master's thesis in history by Herdis Kolle of University of Bergen examines Russian peasant households in two villages in the Moscow area following the emancipation of the serfs in 1861. Covers demography, family life, and the occupations pursued by the freed peasants. Maintained by the Department of History, University of Bergen, Norway.

Eastern Europe

Reference Sites

APAP Recommendations

http://www.informatics.sunysb.edu/apap/recomm/index.html

Bibliographies on all aspects of Polish history and society. History-related topics include general Polish history, Polish military history, and Holocaust/Polish-Jewish relations. Maintained by John Radzilowski on behalf of the Association of Polish-American Professionals and hosted by the Department of Informatics at the State University of New York, Stony Brook.

Historical Text Archive: Europe

http://historicaltextarchive.com/sections.php?op=listarticles&secid=12

This section contains extensive links to Web sites about European history. While not exclusively focused on Eastern Europe, there are links to information about Russia, Yugoslavia, Hungary, and other countries. Each link notes the number of visitors.

Hungarian History Page

http://www2.4dcomm.com/millenia/dates.htm

A collection of materials, in English and Hungarian, relating to the history of Hungary and Hungarian people from 5000 B.C.E. to modern days. Text, digitized maps, and links to other Hungarian history sites are included. The site is still under construction. Maintained as a part of the Hungarian Heritage Homepage site and hosted by Global Internet Services, 4D Communications, Inc.

Hungary: Battles for Freedom 1848–49

http://hungary.ciw.edu/1848–49/index.html

This reference source provides a day-by-day account of the Revolution of 1848 in Hungary and the role of various figures in it, including Louis Kossuth, the military and political leader of the Hungarian Revolution of 1848–1849. Materials include text, illustrations, and an 1890 recording of Louis Kossuth. Includes a photo gallery of Kossuth and the memorials in the United States and Hungary connected with him.

Hungary in 1848–1849

http://h-net2.msu.edu/~habsweb/sourcetexts/hungsources.html

This strong selection of documents, from 1848 to 1852, including communications between King Ferdinand and the Hungarian Diet, and the Hungarian Declaration of Independence, April 14, 1849, focuses on the impact of the revolutions on Hungary.

The Imperial House of Hapsburg

http://www.hapsburg.com/

This site on the Hapsburg monarchy is hosted by Juraj Liöiak, of McGill University, Montreal, Canada. While difficult to navigate, it contains worthwhile information on the origins of the dynasty, its symbols, the Holy Roman Empire, and the achievements of the Hapsburgs. However, it does not develop the history of the dynasty as comprehensively as it might.

New Sources on the 1968 Soviet Invasion of Czechoslovakia

http://www.gwu.edu/~nsarchiv/CWIHP/BULLETINS/b2a4.htm
http://www.gwu.edu/~nsarchiv/CWIHP/BULLETINS/b3a3.htm

A historiographical essay by Mark Kramer on the new sources of the 1968 Soviet invasion of Czechoslovakia that became available since the late 1980s and the collapse of the Eastern bloc and the Soviet Union. Maintained by the Cold War International History Project and hosted by the School of Engineering and Applied Science, George Washington University.

Polish Kings

http://projects.edte.utwente.nl/masters/spizewsk/pl_kings/pl_kings.htm

A well-designed reference site dealing with the Polish monarchy from 960 C.E. to 1795 and the partition of Poland between Russia and Prussia. Features sections on Polish royal dynasties, a timeline of Polish monarchy, and an alphabetical listing of all Polish kings, among other things. The site is intended as a teaching resource for setting up lessons about rulers in Poland. Maintained by Justyna Lanzing-Spizewska and hosted by the University of Twente in Enschede, The Netherlands.

Romania

http://risc.ici.ro/docs/romania.html

A comprehensive reference site dealing with various periods of Romanian history, from the late Middle Ages to modern days. One of the aims of this site is to debunk the commonly held myths about Romanian history. Much of the site is divided into geographical areas roughly corresponding to what the compilers of the site see as traditional Romanian regions, most of which have historical material. The site is still under construction. Maintained and hosted by the Research Institute for Informatics, Bucharest.

Online Archives

Hungarian Electronic Library (MEK)

http://www.mek.iif.hu/

The Hungarian Electronic Library (MEK) was established in 1993 and currently consists of some 2,500 documents. The history collection is significant, covering the general history of Hungary, local and regional history, the history of neighboring countries, and related subjects. Texts are mainly in Hungarian, but a significant number of English texts are available as well. Maintained by Moldován István and Drótos László, and hosted by the National Information Infrastructure Development Program of the government of Hungary. Best viewed with Central European character set.

Hungarian History

http://www.net.hu/corvinus/

A collection of digitized texts on Hungarian history from the Corvinus Library in Hungary. American and Hungarian (translated) historical texts are presented, as are important memoirs of the witnesses to various periods in Hungarian history. The texts can be read online or downloaded as Microsoft Word files. The site includes links to other Hungarian sites. Maintained and hosted by Hungary.Network.

The Wolf Lewkowicz Collection

http://web.mit.edu/maz/wolf/

Between 1922 and 1939, Wolf Lewkowicz of Poland engaged in a lengthy and intimate correspondence in Yiddish with his nephew Sol J. Zissman. This correspondence consists of 179 letters that document various aspects of life in the

Jewish community in Poland, culminating with the Holocaust, which took the lives of Wolf Lewkowicz and most of his family. The letters are translated from Yiddish. Family photographs and recordings of excerpts of some of the letters are included here. Maintained by Marc Zissman and hosted by WWW Server, Massachusetts Institute of Technology.

Accounts and Opinions

AIPC: Polish History

http://www.ampolinstitute.org

Currently under reconstruction, this Polish history site features a brief history of Poland, including portraits of all Polish kings, and the chronology of Polish history from 966 C.E. to the present. Maintained and hosted by The American Institute of Polish Culture, Miami, Florida.

Backward Through the Looking Glass: The Yugoslav Labyrinth in Perspective

http://www.demog.berkeley.edu/~gene/looking.glass.html

This is an extensive, detailed academic essay by E.A. Hammell (University of California, Berkeley) about the deep-seated roots of the ethnic conflicts in the Yugoslav area, from the Roman Empire to the modern conflict.

Brief History of Hungary

http://www.users.zetnet.co.uk/spalffy/h_hist.htm

By the author's own admission, this is a "broad outline" of the history of Hungary. Arranged in reverse chronological order, going back to the tenth century, it includes links to downloadable texts and books and to online archives on Hungarian history. Maintained by Stephen Pálffy and hosted by Zetnet Internet Service, United Kingdom.

Bulgaria.com: History of Bulgaria

http://www.bulgaria.com/history/index.html

This section of the Bulgaria.com site is divided into two parts. The first provides a chronological account of the country's history, from prehistoric antiquity to 1944, and the second provides biographies of Bulgarian rulers, from pre-Christian Khan Kubrat to post-Communist President Zhelyu Zhelev. Both sections are well translated and illustrated. Maintained and hosted by Bulgaria.com, Santa Clara, California.

Bulgarian History and Politics

http://www.b-info.com/places/Bulgaria/ref/05HIST.shtml

The Bulgarian History and Politics site contains a bibliography for Bulgarian history from medieval times to the present. Each source listed in the bibliography is fully described, and there are accompanying pictures.

Columbus and the Age of Discovery

http://marauder.millersv.edu/~columbus/mainmenu.html

This project is a massive database system offering access to over 1,100 articles from magazines, journals, newspapers, speeches, official calendars, and other sources relating to various encounter themes. The site, a joint effort of the History Department and Academic Computing Services at the University of Pennsylvania, Millersville, was awarded the status of an "Official Project" by the U.S. Christopher Columbus Quincentenary Jubilee commission, Spain 1992, and the Pennsylvania Historical and Museum Commission.

The Czech Republic: History

http://www.travel.cz/travel/history.asp

A detailed chronology of Czechoslovakia, its predecessor and successor states, and the peoples living in the territory from prehistory to current days. Well written and illustrated. Maintained by Gabriela Beranova and hosted by Tom's Travel, Prague.

Documents on Bosnia

http://www.mtholyoke.edu/acad/intrel/bosnia.htm

A substantive list of documents, texts, and contemporary material on Bosnia, hosted by Vincent Ferraro, professor of International Politics at Mount Holyoke University.

The Hungarian Revolution of 1956 and How It Affected the World

http://www.cserkeszek.org/scouts/webpages/zoltan/1956.html

Zoltán Csipke examines the causes of the Hungarian Revolution of 1956 in relation to the independence struggle of the Hungarian people, the events of the revolution, and its effects throughout Hungarian society and the world in general. Privately maintained by Csipke and hosted by Cserkeszek Online, the official site of the Hungarian scout troops 8 and 49 in the Los Angeles area.

Hungary: Essential Facts, Figures and Pictures

http://www.mti.hu/hungary/default.htm

An online version of the book by the same name published by the Hungarian News Agency (MTI). An historical overview from the Magyar settlement to the present day is featured, with some of the sections still under construction.

Intermarium

http://www.columbia.edu/cu/sipa/REGIONAL/ECE/intermar.html

This online journal provides an electronic medium for noteworthy scholarship and provocative thinking about the history and politics of Central and Eastern Europe following World War II. Jointly maintained by Andrzej Paczkowski, Institute for Political Studies, Polish Academy of Sciences, and John S. Micgiel, Institute on East Central Europe, Columbia University. Hosted by the School of International and Public Affairs, Columbia University.

Jews in Poland

http://www.cyberroad.com/poland/jews.html

This site outlines the history of Poland's Jewish community from 965 to the outbreak of World War II in 1939 and discusses Jews in Poland during the war and at the present day. Maintained by LNT Poland and hosted by Cyberville Webworks.

The Magyars of Conquest-Period Hungary

http://www.net.hu/Magyar/hungq/no141/p3.html

In this article for the *Hungarian Quarterly*, Gyula László, a retired professor of Eötvös University, examines Byzantine and Arabic sources on the arrival of Magyars in present-day Hungary, in support for his argument that the Magyars arrived in two separate waves, centuries apart. Maintained and hosted by Hungary.Network Ltd.

Romania: History

http://home.sol.no/~romemb/history.htm

A detailed outline of Romanian history from Roman times to modern days. Illustrated with images of historical landmarks, artifacts, and portraits and photographs of Romanian rulers and statesmen. Maintained by the Romanian Embassy, Oslo, Norway, and hosted by Scandinavia Online.

Twenty-Five Lectures on Modern Balkan History

http://www.lib.msu.edu/sowards/balkan/

This series of online lectures deals with the turbulent history of the modern Balkans from 1500 to the present. While most of the lectures deal with the Balkans proper, they also examine the Eastern European states of Hungary and Romania. Compiled and maintained by Steven W. Sowards and hosted by Michigan State University Libraries.

The Warsaw Uprising

http://www.princeton.edu/~poland/uprising/

An account of the Warsaw Uprising of 1944 by the Polish Resistance (AK). An overview of the situation before the uprising, followed by accounts of the events of August and September 1944, and the aftermath. Maps and photographs of the uprising and the key people involved are also provided. The page is still under construction. Maintained by Marcin Porwit and hosted by the Department of Computer Science, Princeton University.

French History

Charles H. MacKay and Dennis A. Trinkle

Metasites

Dr. Zoë Schneider's French History Web Links ✓

http://www.georgetown.edu/faculty/schneidz/web.html

Created and maintained by Dr. Zoë Schneider of Georgetown University, this site features an extensive but selective categorized list of links relating to all fields of French history.

Archives and Libraries

Archives du service historique de l'Armée
Archives du service historique de la Marine

http://www.culture.fr/culture/nllefce/fr/rep_ress/an_00481.htm

http://www.culture.fr/culture/nllefce/fr/rep_ress/an_00300.htm

French army and naval archives with contact information. Both under construction.

Archives et documentation du Ministère des affaires étrangères

http://www.culture.fr/culture/nllefce/fr/rep_ress/an_75351.htm

General listing of holdings, along with contact information.

Bibliothèque nationale de France

http://www.bnf.fr/index.htm

Home page for France's National Library. Contains lists of collections, updates, practical information, hours of operation, contacts, a virtual tour of the new facility, special exhibits, and several limited searchable online catalogs. A limited English version is available, including the online catalogs.

Centre d'accueil et de recherche des Archives nationales (CARAN)

http://www.archivesnationales.culture.gouv.fr/chan/

Home page for France's National Archives. Practical information on hours of operation, contacts, general description of holdings, information on obtaining catalogs, temporary holdings and exhibits. Includes links to the Centre des archives d'outre-mer, Centre des archives du monde du travail, and Centre des archives contemporaines.

La Nouvelle France

http://www.culture.fr/culture/nllefce/fr/indlieux.htm

Hot links to many of France's archival institutions, including the Archives Nationales, other archives of the state (army, navy, foreign affairs, etc.), many departmental and communal archives, and archives from chambers of commerce, various associations, the Bibliothèque Nationale, other libraries (including Arsenal, National Assembly, Senate, Marine, and the Institute of France), centers of study, and museums. All contain basic contact information and some idea of their holdings.

Le Ministère de la culture et de la communication

http://www.bnf.fr/index.htm

Home page for the French Minister of Culture and Communication. Virtual exhibits, links, and searchable lists for art, architecture, archeology, dance, literature, music, photography, among other subjects. France's National Archives falls under the jurisdiction of the Minister of Culture (see separate entry).

Premedieval History

GIS and Remote Sensing for Archeology: Burgundy, France

http://www.informatics.org/france/france.html

This site shows how mapping technology and satellite imagery can be used in historical research. It offers an evolving presentation of aerial photography and survey data that reveals long-term interactions between cultures and the physical environment.

Paleolithic Cave Paintings in France

http://www.culture.gouv.fr/culture/arcnat/chauvet/en/

This site discusses the paintings and engravings dating from the Paleolithic Age that have been found in the caves of southern France. The material is in both French and English and includes excellent images of the cave paintings along with historical descriptions.

Medieval History

The Age of King Charles V (1338–1380)

http://www.bnf.fr/enluminures/aaccueil.htm

One of many exhibits sponsored by the Bibliothèque Nationale. This site features 1,000 images of illuminated text. The quality of the reproductions is high and the site is available in English or French. The site is organized around five themes—history, religion, science and technology, sports and entertainment, and miscellaneous—with more refined subcategories under each. Viewers can chose any of these themes to access a thumbnail gallery of images falling under the subcategory.

Early Modern and Old Regime History

Château de Versailles ✓

http://www.chateauversailles.com/

Official site for Versailles. A rich, well-written, and well-illustrated site with an interactive map, thousands of images including Marie Antoinette's Hamlet, several 360-degree panoramic views, descriptions, practical information and contacts, and resources for French students. English version available.

Eighteenth-Century Resources

http://andromeda.rutgers.edu/~jlynch/18th/

Site dedicated to scholarly resources online. Eighteenth-Century Resources is not limited to France or even Europe nor is it limited to the study of history. Other disciplines include art, architecture, literature (and electronic texts), music, philosophy, religion and theology, and science and mathematics.

French 208: *Introduction à la littérature du XVIIIe siècle*

http://tuna.uchicago.edu/homes/jack/course.materials.html

Prepared for the American and French Research on the Treasury of the French Language (ARTFL) Project at the University of Chicago, this site is a thorough and well-organized course packet for students. It includes links to electronic sources, hundreds of images of maps, architecture, and art, chronologies, and texts on authors, philosophes, and artists.

Modern Editions of Early Modern French Sources Translated into English Compiled by Jeffrey Merrick and David A. Bell

http://jhunix.hcf.jhu.edu/~dabell/sources.html

Impressive bibliography of primary and secondary sources for the Early Modern period. Works are organized topically, including sections on art, colonialism, correspondence, crime, economic thought, education, several enlightenment groupings, literature, memoirs, politics, revolution, science, travel, witchcraft, women, and others.

The National Huguenot Society

http://huguenot.netnation.com/

Site dedicated to the study of French Huguenots. Operates like similar Scottish clan Web pages. Contains information on Huguenot history, an adequate bibliography particularly for primary sources, and links to other Huguenot-related sites and resources.

French Revolution and First Empire

The Era of the French Revolution

http://mason.gmu.edu/~gbrown6/french-rev.htm

Part of a course syllabus by Gregory S. Brown placed online, this site has a brief selection of online documents and maps as well as an excellent link list to an extensive array of Web sites on the French Revolution.

French Revolutionary Pamphlets

http://humanities.uchicago.edu/homes/mark/fr_rev.html

Another ARTFL project from the University of Chicago, this site contains three full-text pamphlets.

Images of the French Revolution ✓

http://chnm.gmu.edu/revolution/index.html

Lynn A. Hunt and Jack Censer edit this site, sponsored by the American Social History Project and the Center for History and New Media of the Department of History at George Mason University and supported by grants from the National Endowment for the Humanities and the Florence Gould Foundation. It is the companion site for their stellar new book and CD-ROM collection of the same title on the French Revolution (Penn State Press). This is the best digital collection for historians and students of the Revolution.

Napoléon

http://www.napoleon.org/

Site includes a library section with basic textual information, images, primary material, and bibliographies, a museum with a comprehensive section on Napoleonic caricatures, and links to other resources.

Napoleonic Literature

http://napoleonic-literature.simplenet.com/

Contains full-text translations of nine prominent works, including the contemporary memoirs and the military maxims of Napoleon. Has links to various art images of the period.

The Napoleon Series

http://www.napoleonseries.org/

Comprehensive site with information (in many cases images) about treaties, music, art, videos, civilian and military maps, and a vast set of links to other Napoleonic and military history sites. The best starting point for information about the First Empire.

Proctor Jones Publishing

http://www.napoleonfirst.com/

Online catalog of works published by the Proctor Jones Publishing Company. Of particular interest is the book *An Intimate Account of the Years of Supremacy*, which includes 300 color and 200 black-and-white art images.

Nineteenth Century

Encyclopedia of 1848 Revolutions

http://www.ohiou.edu/~Chastain/

An online encyclopedia of the 1848 revolutions with close to seventy contributing scholars and over 180 entries. Although the 1848 Revolutions site is not specific to France (Poland is very well represented, for instance), there are many entries on France's role in the revolutions. Site includes entries on biographies, events, institutions, and concepts. Most entries include a current bibliography.

Georgetown University Centennial Conference, February 1998: The Dreyfus Case: Human Rights vs. Prejudice, Intolerance and Demonization

http://www.georgetown.edu/guieu/colqtop.htm

Web page of a one-day interdisciplinary conference on the historical aspects of the Dreyfus case. Speakers included French and American historians, political scientists, linguists, and religious studies intellectuals. In addition to the conference poster and contact information, the site includes full-text versions of many of the papers presented and the statement by President Jacques Chirac on the centennial of Émile Zola's *J'Accuse!* The host, Jean-Max Guieu, has links to his home page, which includes links to other Dreyfus sites.

The Siege and Commune of Paris, 1870–1871 ✓

http://www.library.nwu.edu/spec/siege/index.html

This page contains more than 1,200 digitized photographs and images drawn from the Northwestern University Library's Siege and Commune Collection.

Twentieth Century

Be Realistic—Demand the Impossible! Posters from the Revolution, Paris, May 1968

http://burn.ucsd.edu/paristab.htm

Collection of twenty-nine posters and accompanying text from the Paris Revolution of 1968. Quality of the posters is good, and French captions have been translated into English.

Images de la France d'autrefois

http://www.atalante-models.com/divers/top8/france.htm

Collection of 80,000 black-and-white postcards of France, organized by traditional regions. One can search for specific departments or by size of settlement (small, medium, large). Most photographs date from the turn of the twentieth century.

Paris Libéré!

http://www.paris.org/Expos/Liberation/

Created for the fiftieth anniversary of the Liberation of Paris. Contains a timeline; photo archive; map of the attack; text on the attack, its leaders, the surrender, and prisoners; an index; and a bibliography.

The World War I Document Archive

http://www.lib.byu.edu/~rdh/wwi/

Assembled by members of H-Net's WWI Military History List, this site is organized into several categories: Conventions, Treaties, and Official Papers, Documents by Year, Memorials, Personal Reminiscences, WWI Biographical Dictionary, WWI Image Archive, Special Topics and Commentary Articles, and WWI Sites: Links to Other Resources. The picture archive is well organized and contains 1,072 images. The content, production, and quality are excellent.

General, Documents, and Reference

History of France: Primary Documents

http://library.byu.edu/~rdh/eurodocs/france.html

A rich, eclectic collection of hundreds of primary documents in French, German, Spanish, and English covering France from medieval through modern times. Many documents have been expertly photoreproduced from the Bibliothèque Nationale and other archives, and the quality of the selections and their reproduction is high. A considerable number of documents have been translated. The selections include *Les très riches heures du Duc de Berry*, the Declaration of the Rights of Man and of the Citizen, Émile Zola's *J'accuse!*, and an impressive section on World War I, World War II, and the Liberation of France.

Internet Modern History Sourcebook

http://www.fordham.edu/halsall/mod/modsbook.html

An indispensable library of documents from the Early Modern Period to the present. Hundreds of primary source documents are reproduced here, and the site contains valuable links to similar sites, visual resources, and printed reference sources. Other sites in the same series (but not referenced here) include Ancient, Medieval, African, East Asian, Indian, Islamic, Jewish, Women's, Global, Science, and Lesbian, Gay, Bisexual, and Transgendered People.

La France à travers les âges

http://www.as.wvu.edu/mlastinger/

An interesting encyclopedic potpourri of images and text covering all aspects of French culture from prehistory to the present. Numerous links and other resources.

Le Louvre: Official Web Page

http://mistral.culture.fr/louvre/

Official Web page of the Louvre. Contains hours of operation, contacts, and information about temporary exhibitions, holdings, and upcoming events. Site is available in English as well as several other languages.

Musée d'Orsay

http://www.musee-orsay.fr:8081/ORSAY/orsaygb/HTML.NSF/By+Filename/mosimple+index?OpenDocument

Official Web page of the Musée d'Orsay, which houses many nineteenth-century masterpieces. Contains hours of operation, contacts, information about temporary exhibitions, holdings, and upcoming events, and an online gift shop.

Paris Maps ✓

http://www.columbia.edu/cu/arthistory/courses/parismaps/

Paris Maps houses 100 full-color historical maps of eighteenth-century and nineteenth-century Paris.

Project for American and French Research on the Treasury of the French Language, University of Chicago (ARTFL)

http://humanities.uchicago.edu/ARTFL/ARTFL.html

ARTFL contains electronic versions of nearly 2,000 texts, ranging from classic works of French literature to nonfiction prose to technical writing. The subjects covered include literary criticism, biology, history, economics, and philosophy. The database is available only to members of universities that are associated with the ARTFL project, but those with access can perform an impressive variety of intratextual and comparative textual searches.

Treasures from the Bibliotèque Nationale de France: Creating French Culture

http://lcweb.loc.gov/exhibits/bnf/bnf0001.html

Sponsored in part by the Library of Congress, this exhibit traces the relationship between power and culture in France from Charlemagne to Charles de Gaulle by using images from manuscripts and books from the French National Library. This site is available in English or French.

German History
Claire Gabriel and Alexander Zukas

Metasites

DINO: Wissenschaft: Geschichte
http://www.dino-online.de/seiten/go14h.htm
Of the various German-language search engines, DINO (Deutsches InterNet-Organisationssystem) offers the most convenient and extensive listing of history-oriented sites. The DINO history section is divided into subcategories by time period and special interest.

German History
http://www.phil.uni-erlangen.de/~p1ges/heidelberg/gh/gh.html
This section of the WWW Virtual Library is a directory of resources arranged by epoch and historical subfield. Although the sections are uneven, it is a useful starting point for exploration.

HABSBURG Home Page
http://www2.h-net.msu.edu/~habsweb/

H-GERMAN Home Page
http://www2.h-net.msu.edu/~german/
Both of these sites, which are sponsored by the H-Net group of electronic discussion lists, provide a variety of resources, including archives of discussion threads, book reviews, news about professional conferences and meetings, teaching materials, and selected links to other sites of historical interest. H-GERMAN focuses on the scholarly study of German history of all time periods. HABSBURG is devoted "to the history and culture of the former Habsburg lands and peoples from about 1500 until this century." (HABSBURG welcome). Material provided by these sites may be in English or German.

Nachrichtendienst für Historiker

http://www.crispinius.com/nfh3/index.shtml

A site crammed with information for anyone interested in history, but somewhat difficult to navigate. Provides information on and links to—among other subjects—German television programs, news articles, research institutes, conferences, and meetings. Also included are a chatroom and a newsboard.

General Sites

Archive in der Bundesrepublik Deutschland

http://my.bawue.de/~hanacek/info/darchive.htm

Archives in Deutschland

http://www.uni-marburg.de/archivschule/deuarch.html

This site is a directory of links to individual archival repositories on the Web, arranged by category: governmental, religious, literary, political, and so on. Sponsored by the Archivschule Marburg.

Archive in Österreich/Archives in Austria

http://my.bawue.de/~hanacek/info/aarchive.htm

These sites, compiled by Andreas Hanacek, are directories of German and Austrian archives by type: governmental, religious, military, and so on. Contact information and hours are provided, along with citations to guides or articles about archival collections. With some exceptions, this site does not provide links to home pages of archives on the Web. In German and English.

Dachau Concentration Camp Memorial Site/ KZ-Gedenkstaette Dachau

http://www.infospace.de/gedenkstaette/index.html

English version is at http://www.cc-memorial-site-dachau.org/gedenkstaette/english/index.html

This site, run by the Dachau Concentration Camp Memorial Museum, is in German and English. It contains short, vivid articles on the history of the concentration camp, maps, prisoners, slave labor, suffering and death in the camp, the last months of the camp, and liberation. The site opens with a quote from

Eugen Kogon: "Dachau—the significance of this name will never be erased from German history. It stands for all concentration camps which the Nazis established in their territory."

Data Bank on the Revolution in Baden 1848/49/ *Das Informationssystem zur Revolution von 1848/49*

http://www.ruf.uni-freiburg.de/histsem/badrev/

This site contains a wealth of primary information on the Revolution of 1848–49, especially in Baden. There are collective biographies and documents, drawing on the resources of the *Erinnerungsstätte für die Freiheitsbewegungen in der deutschen Geschichte* (Memorial Foundation for Movements of Liberty in German History) at the Rastatt division of the Federal German Archives. You can search for information by communities or towns, individuals, and themes. There is also a lexicon of terms. The site is in German and maintained by a project team at the University of Freiburg.

Deutschland: Könige, Kaiser, Staatschefs

http://userpage.chemie.fu-berlin.de/diverse/bib/de-kks.html

This reference site provides birth and death dates and period of rule for German leaders from Charlemagne to Gerhard Schroeder. Compiled by Burkhard Kirste of the Freie Universitat, Berlin.

Die Körpermassaker im deutschen Bauernkrieg von 1525

http://www.ng.fak09.uni-muenchen.de/gfn/fwarb_de.html

Florian Welle writes an interesting history of the Peasant War by focusing on the body, the bodies of peasants and the bodies of the nobility and knights, and how these distinct bodies made a difference to the outcome of the struggle. She treats psychological issues as well as issues of bodily nutrition, training, and protection. The topic of the body is a new and growing research area in history, and this Web site makes a valuable contribution to that discourse.

Encyclopedia of 1848 Revolutions

http://www.cats.ohiou.edu/~Chastain/index.htm

On this comprehensive Web site, authors from around the world have contributed articles to the only complete history of all the 1848 revolutions. Organized by James Chastain of the University of Ohio, this encyclopedia covers every aspect, personality, and region of the world in which a popular revolt occurred in 1848. Germany and France are particularly well represented. The authors of the article are well-known historians of the era.

The Example of Dachau/*Zum Beispiel Dachau*

http://members.aol.com/zbdachau/index.htm

The infamous concentration camp at Dachau, outside Munich, is represented by the official site above and by this one created by the Study Group for the Investigation of the Contemporary History of Dachau. It is in German and English. Some citizens of Dachau (former camp inmates) founded the group, and later the Web site, to protest the selective memory of their fellow citizens of Dachau and demonstrate that the past was neither forgotten nor dead in Dachau. They researched the history of the city to uncover the cause and the structures that once made possible a totalitarian regime in Germany. They seek insight into the daily lives and the suffering of the inmates of the concentration camp at the hands of the SS. This is a valuable site for lessons in civic-inspired history.

The First World War

http://www.dhm.de/lemo/html/wk1/index.html

This outstanding site by the German Historical Museum contains a wealth of information on Germany during World War I. The site investigates the conduct of the war, internal politics, industrial output and control, economic life, research, war propaganda, art, and daily life. It also hosts recordings of speeches by Kaiser Wilhelm II. The site is in German.

Fredericus Rex: Prussia's King Frederick the Great

http://www.ursulashistoryweb.f2s.com/king.html

Ursula Grosser Dixon, a novice historian, has compiled a wonderful and very readable site on Frederick the Great and his contribution to German history. She discusses his military campaigns, his daily life, his social and political reforms, his "enlightened despotism," and his relations with Voltaire. This site is a good place to start understanding the life and times of this important Hohenzollern monarch.

Friedrich der Grosse

http://ibhistory.tripod.com/friedrich.html

This is an extensive article in German about the life and reign of Frederick the Great. The author, Alexander Renneberg, discusses Frederick's role in elevating Prussia to Great Power status in Europe and laying the foundations for the future German state.

German, Austrian, Swiss Cultural History

http://webcampus3.stthomas.edu/paschons/language_http/German/culthist.html

This site has several useful components: a bibliographical dictionary of several hundred prominent persons from German-speaking Europe (in German); a chronology of important events in German and world history; and a calendar of significant events in the German-speaking countries, arranged by month and date (in English). Created by Paul A. Schons of the University of St. Thomas, Minnesota.

Deutsches Historisches Museum, Berlin/ German Historical Museum, Berlin

http://www.dhm.de/

An overview of the museum founded amid some controversy in 1987 and devoted to the history of the German nation. The site provides general information about the aims and organization of the museum as well as its collections and exhibitions. In addition, descriptions and images of selected items from the permanent collections and from previous exhibitions are available. In German and English.

Der Bauernkrieg von 1525: The German Peasants' Revolt

http://www.geocities.com/Vienna/Strasse/9298/zuefallig/bauernkrieg.htm

The Peasant War was a major event in sixteenth-century Germany. This Web site provides a general overview of the conflict, its origins, place in the agrarian crisis of the age, conduct, revolutionary nature, dispersion across southern Germany, and outcome.

Haus der Geschichte der Bundesrepublik Deutschlands

http://www.hdg.de/

Haus der Geschichte der BRD presents the history of the two postwar German states—the Federal Republic of Germany and the German Democratic Republic—with particular emphasis on the development of political institutions. In German and English.

History of Austria, Austro-Hungarian Empire: Primary Documents

http://library.byu.edu/~rdh/eurodocs/austria.html

History of Germany: Primary Documents

http://library.byu.edu/~rdh/eurodocs/

The EuroDocs site at Brigham Young University is the most comprehensive resource for primary documents in German and Austrian history. Documents may be in a variety of formats and in German or English. The time period covered spans from the end of the classical period to the present. Highlights include the Works of Marx and Engels and the World War I Document Archive. Compiled by Richard Hacken.

Martin Luther Historical Site

http://www.luther.de/

This site is a good source of information about the life and times of Germany's most famous religious reformer. It includes a detailed biography, discussion of the historical background, and legends associated with Martin Luther's life. In German and English.

The Marx/Engels Archive

http://csf.colorado.edu/psn/marx/index.html

This is an extraordinary collection of the major works, as well as lesser-known publications, of two famous Germans, Karl Marx and Friedrich Engels, hosted at the University of Colorado. Of particular interest to historians of Germany beyond the well-known classics of Marxist literature also hosted at this site are: *The German Ideology*, articles by Marx in *Rheinische Zeitung*, *Critique of Hegel's Philosophy of Right*, *Deutsche-Französische Jahrbücher*, Engels's *The Peasants' War in Germany*, *Revolution and Counter-Revolution in Germany*, *The Prussian Military Question and the German Workers' Party*, *Critique of the Gotha Program*, *Reformists in Germany's Social-Democratic Party*, and *The Peasant Question in France and Germany*.

Österreichische Historische Bibliographie

http://www.uni-klu.ac.at/groups/his/his_oehb/

This searchable database corresponds to annual printed volumes, beginning in 1945, that report professional publications in Austrian history. Books, periodical articles, conference proceedings, dissertations, and essay collections are included. Produced at the Institut für Geschichte an der Universität Klagenfurt. For scholars only.

Philipp Melanchthon

http://www.melanchthon.de/

An online exhibition commemorating the 500th anniversary of the birth of the reformer and humanist. The site details Melanchthon's life and involvement in the Protestant Reformation. In German and English. The Kommunale Datenverarbeitungsgesellschaft Wittenberg created this site and the site on Martin Luther.

The Protestant Reformation

http://history.hanover.edu/early/prot.html

The Internet Archive of Texts and Documents, which organized this site on the Reformation, is a creation of faculty and students in the History Department of Hanover College. The principal goal of the archive is to make primary texts and secondary sources on the Internet available to students and faculty for use in history and humanity classes. This site hosts primary texts from the Lutheran Reformations, Reformed Reformations, Radical Reformations, the English Reformation, and the Scottish Reformation. Secondary sources and links to scholarly sites on the Reformation are included on the site.

The Radical Reformation: Thomas Münzer

http://www.slip.net/%7Eknabb/rexroth/communalism3.htm

Thomas Münzer has been closely associated with the Peasant Revolt in Germany. A Protestant dissenter, he broke with Martin Luther and became a religious radical of the Reformation. The site places him within the context of Reformation beliefs and politics and the Peasant Revolt.

Resources for Reformation History on the Internet

http://www.st-andrews.ac.uk/~www_rsi/refresou.htm

This gateway site at St. Andrews University in Scotland lists Internet resources that have attracted the attention of the site editor as being potentially useful. The sites are uneven. Some are very specific to the topic (Swiss Reformation History Institute Homepage) while others are more general (American Historical Society). Still, many of the sites are valuable and provide a fine place to start researching the Reformation on the Internet.

Das Kaiserreich (Second German Empire)

http://www.dhm.de/lemo/html/kaiserreich/index.html

The German Historical Museum has created a monumental and scholarly site where students of the German Empire from 1871 to 1918 can explore issues surrounding foreign policy, domestic policy, industrial economics, science, education, art, culture, daily life, and anti-Semitism. The site has a chronology of events for each year from 1900 to 1914. The site is richly illustrated, has some videos, and is in German.

The Thirty-Years' War

http://mars.acnet.wnec.edu/~grempel/courses/wc2/lectures/30yearswar.html

The Thirty Years' War (1618–1648) was a general European war that was fought mainly in Germany. The war devastated Germany; it took almost 200 years for the German territories to recover from its effects. Professor Gerhard Rempel of Western New England College maintains this Web page, providing an excellent overview of the war, its causes, course, and impact on Europe and on Germany in particular.

The Thirty Years' War, 1618–1648

http://www-geschichte.fb15.uni-dortmund.de/fnz/thirty.html

Stephanie Marra of the University of Dortmund maintains this Virtual Library page on the Thirty Years' War with extensive links to primary and secondary resources and essays. The page provides links to a museum presentation of the war, biographies, chronologies, the Peace of Westphalia, and a well-developed presentation of the history of the Thirty Years' War by Christopher Atkinson.

Virtual Library: *Geschichte "Drittes Reich"*

http://www.hco.hagen.de/history/index.html

This page devoted to the Third Reich, compiled by Ralf Blank of the Ruhr-Universität, Bochum, is one of the standouts of the German History section of the WWW Virtual Library. It offers information about various aspects of the Nazi regime, including *Politik*, *Wirtschaft*, and *Widerstand*.

Virtual Library: History: German History, 19th Century

http://www.phil.uni-erlangen.de/~p1ges/heidelberg/gh/e6.html

The Virtual Library carries dozens of links to important Web sites on nineteenth-century German history, including the Napoleonic Wars, the Congress of

Vienna, *Vormärz*, the Revolutions of 1848–1849, the Wars of Unification and the Second Reich, and Bismarck. This is the place to start investigating nineteenth-century Germany on the Web.

WebMuseen: Museen und Ausstellungen im deutschsprachigen Raum

http://webmuseen.de/

This site provides information and links for museums of all types in Germany, Austria, and Switzerland. The *Themen* option allows a search for historical museums.

The Weimar Republic

http://www.dhm.de/lemo/html/weimar/index.html

This German Historical Museum site maintains the museum's high scholarly standards and accessibility. Beginning with an explanation of the Revolution of 1918, the site investigates the formation of the Republic, domestic policy, foreign policy, industrial developments and economic troubles, intellectual life, art and culture, daily life, anti-Semitism, and the forerunners of Nazism. The site has a chronology of events for each year of the Republic, from 1918 to 1933, and is in German.

Willkommen bei der Bundesregierung Deutschlands

http://www.bundesregierung.de/

Auswäertiges Amt

http://www.auswaertiges-amt.de/

Der Bundespraesident

http://www.bundespraesident.de/

Deutscher Bundestag

http://www.bundestag.de/index.htm

These official sites of the German federal government are good starting points for recent history and political events. Of particular historical interest is the site of the Auswäertiges Amt (Foreign Ministry), with information about its organization, history, and publications.

The Witch Hunt

http://www.zpr.uni-koeln.de/~nix/hexen/e-index.htm

This is a very well-developed site housed at the University of Cologne. Germany was the center of witch-hunts in the Early Modern period, and this site tries to explain who were accused of witchcraft, the geographic dispersion of the persecutions, the fluctuation in persecutions, who were the hunters, the responsibility of the Church, the manner of trial, and why the hunts ended in Germany and elsewhere in Europe. Interested users may download classics of witch-hunting literature, including *The Hammer of Witches* (written by two German Dominican theologians in the late fifteenth century), *The Witches Bull*, and *The Discovery of Witches*.

Modern Greek History
deTraci Regula

Panayotis D. Cangelaris

http://www.cangelaris.com/index.htm

Extensive information on the Greek diplomat and collector, presently the Deputy Director of the Department of Expediting and Diplomatic Mail, Ministry of Foreign Affairs, Athens.

Hellenic Army General Staff

http://www.army.gr/html/EN_Army/index.htm

Thorough, official site covering everything from the history of the army and the chain of command to the equipment, the military schools, uniforms, and medals, broken down by period.

Konstantinos Karamanlis

http://www.ana.gr/en/biogr/Karamanlis.html

President of New Democracy—(then) leader of the opposition.

Nikolaos Konstantopoulos

http://www.ana.gr/en/biogr/Konstadopoulos.html

President of the Coalition of the Left.

Alexandra Papariga

http://www.ana.gr/en/biogr/Papariga.html

Brief c.v. of the secretary-general of the Communist Party of Greece.

Antonis Samaras

http://www.ana.gr/en/biogr/Samaras.html

Brief biographical information about the president of Political Spring.

Dimitrios Tsovolas

http://www.ana.gr/en/biogr/Tsovolas.html

President of the Democratic Social Movement (DHKKI).

Makis Voridis

http://members.tripod.com/~metopo_athens1/athens5voridisbio.html

Leader of the Hellenic Front (*Elliniko Metopo*), Makis Voridis has been the leader of the modern Nationalistic Hellenic Party since 1995. Available in Greek only.

Books, Journals, and Magazines

Greek University Library Catalogs Online

http://galaxy.einet.net/hytelnet/GR000.html

From Modern Greek Studies Association (MGSA), quick access to many Greek libraries, with instant search capability.

Hellenic Bookspace

http://book.culture.gr/

Site devoted to modern literature and books of all types.

Hellenism and Modern Greece

http://weber.u.washington.edu/~egkioule/books/greece_today/

Listing of books in Greek and English, with links to bibliographical information.

Journal of Modern Greek Studies

http://jhupress.jhu.edu/press/journals/titles/mgs.html

Online editions are available for subscribers. General information only here.

Modern Greek History Resources

http://www.webexpert.net/vasilios/history/history.htm

Excellent selection of Greek and English-language materials on all aspects of modern Greek history.

National Book Centre of Greece

http://book.culture.gr/2/nbc.html

Government-sponsored archive and program provider for Greek books. Includes bibliographies of folklore, lists of political books written under the dictatorship, events, links to literary journals, and a searchable bibliographical index.

Newsletters, Journals and Magazines

http://www.nyu.edu/pages/onassis/other/magz.html

Listing of English- and Greek-language periodicals pertaining to Hellenic studies.

Synthesis: Review of Modern Greek Studies

http://www.lse.ac.uk/depts/european/synthesis/

Home page for this Greek journal. This site contains a link to the U.S.-based mirror site.

Current Events

Athens News Agency

http://www.ana.gr/

Streaming headlines, daily news, and a photo of the day. A great quick look at news in Greece from the major English-language news agency.

eKathimerini

http://www.eKathimerini.com/news/news.asp

English edition of the daily paper, distributed in print form with the *International Herald Tribune.*

Macedonian Press Agency

http://www.mpa.gr/index.html?page=english

Daily online news agency based in northern Greece, available in Greek, English, and Russian.

Ministry of Foreign Affairs: What's New

http://www.mfa.gr/whatnew/

Constantly updated list of material relating to current events. Many entries only in Greek; users can scroll down for more English-language listings.

Defense Industry

Greek Defense Industry Directory

http://www.deloscomm.gr/defenc98.htm

Information on annual volume published about the Greek defense industry, listing more than 5,000 organizations.

Hellenic Defense Industries Internet Catalog

http://www.heldic.com/menu.htm

Collection of different industrial providers based in Greece. Includes aerospace, weapons systems, metalworking, electrical equipment, and virtually every industry involved in any way with the military.

Government and Military Sites

Hellenic Ministries

http://www.fossnet.com/mneng.htm

Listing of all the government ministries.

Hellenic Parliament

http://www.parliament.gr/en/today/uk/

Includes listing of members, a constitutional history, and photos.

Ministry of Culture

http://www.culture.gr/

Includes: The Identity of the Ministry; Museums, Monuments and Archaeological Sites of Hellas; Modern and Contemporary Cultural Creation; Cultural Organizations; Cultural Events; Selected Cultural Events; Special Issues; Announcements—Press Releases; Guide to the Internet.

Ministry of Foreign Affairs

http://www.mfa.gr

USA mirror site: http://www.hri.org/MFA/

The Hellenic Republic's official office of foreign affairs, with abundant links to documents pertaining to foreign policy and current events.

General Information

Ministry of Foreign Affairs: Brief on Greece

http://www.mfa.gr/aboutgr/brief_on_greece.htm

Barebones details about the geography, climate, and politics of Greece.

Greek Language Tools

Download Greek Fonts

http://www.ana.gr/gr/greek.html

Selection of fonts available for different operating systems, including Windows, Macintosh, and others.

Fonts and Tools for Greek

http://www.nyu.edu/pages/onassis/top-level/tools.html

Links to fonts and other tools for reading Greek on the Internet.

Greek Alphabet

http://sunsite.unc.edu/koine/greek/lessons/alphabet.html

From Little Greek 101, this is a great quick introduction to reading and writing the Greek alphabet. Pronunciations are Erasmian rather than Modern, but it is a good place to start.

Greek-English and English-Greek Dictionary

http://www.kypros.org/cgi-bin/lexicon

Enter any common word and find its translation.

Greek Spell Checker

http://www.kypros.org/Orthographic/

In Greek. Users can copy Greek-font text into the spell check window for a quick confirmation of spelling.

Modern Greek and Hellenic Study Programs

College Year in Athens

http://www.cyathens.org/html/about.html

General information on this program, which allows students from many universities and colleges to earn credit for study in Greece.

Modern Greek Programs

http://www.hnet.uci.edu/classics/MGSA/programs2.html

Easy-to-use finder, from Modern Greek Studies Association (MGSA), for university programs for modern Greek. Users can enter their region (United States or Canada only) to find what is offered.

Modern Greek Studies Association Information

http://www.hnet.uci.edu/classics/MGSA/

All about this organization, including its journal, prizes, programs, and publications.

MGSA Jobs Listings

http://www.hnet.uci.edu/classics/MGSA/jobs.html

Available positions in modern Greek studies and related fields.

Onassis Program in Hellenic Studies

http://www.nyu.edu/pages/onassis/

Starting point for information about this NYU-based program.

Princeton: Program in Hellenic Studies

http://www.princeton.edu:80/~hellenic/acad.html

Information on this graduate program, including committee members, faculty, general focus, required courses.

Speros Basil Vryonis Center for the Study of Hellenism

http://www.glavx.org/index.html

Information about the center and library devoted to Hellenic culture.

University of Manitoba Centre for Hellenic Studies

http://www.umanitoba.ca/faculties/arts/classics/chc/index.html

Information on this program, originally funded by the Hellenic Ministry of Culture.

Cyprus Question

Lobby for Cyprus Homepage

http://www.lobbyforcyprus.org/

Well-organized, award-winning page promoting the solution of the Cyprus problem from the Greek perspective.

Documents

Greece–FYROM Dispute

http://www.hri.org/docs/fyrom/

From the Hellenic Resource Network, various online documents pertaining to the conflicts between Greece and the former Yugoslavian Republic.

History of Modern Greece: Primary Documents

http://library.byu.edu/~rdh/eurodocs/greece.html

Extensive online collection of key documents, including the Greek Constitution, World War II, the Aegean dispute, and much more. Webmastered by Richard Hacken, European Studies Bibliographer, Brigham Young University, Provo, Utah.

Ministry of Foreign Affairs: European Union

http://www.mfa.gr/foreign/euro_union/

Links to documents and statements pertaining to Greece's participation in the E.U. Includes: Memorandum—For a European Union with Political and Social Content; Greece's Contribution to the 1996 Intergovernmental Conference; Declaration adopted by the fifteen Ministers of Foreign Affairs of the E.U. at the last General Affairs Council on July 15, 1996; Resolution on the political situation following the UN-sponsored talks on Cyprus; and the European Commission, Representation in Greece.

Ministry of Foreign Affairs: Foreign Policy: Greece and Turkey

http://www.mfa.gr/foreign/bilateral/

Includes the following official statements (among many others): Chronology of Turkish actions and claims against Greece; Turkish claims in the Aegean; The Imia Crisis; Turkish foreign policy and practice as evidenced by the recent Turkish claims to the Imia rocks; Greek and the European Union scientific and ecological programs concerning the Imia islets; Map of Imia rocks; Agreements between Italy and Turkey of 1932 (in French); Turkey's most recent aggression against Greece: the island of Gavdos; The Cyprus Issue; A revealing fact of the situation in Northern Cyprus—increasing numbers of Turkish-Cypriots seek asylum in the United Kingdom; Greek Minority of Turkey.

Ministry of Foreign Affairs: International Organizations

http://www.mfa.gr/foreign/organizations/

Includes: Greece and the Organization for Security and Cooperation in Europe (OSCE), and Greece and the Council of Europe.

Ministry of Foreign Affairs: Relations between Greece, the United States, Canada and the Latin American Countries

http://www.mfa.gr/foreign/usaen.htm

Policy statements on political relationships in the Western Hemisphere.

Treaties and Conventions

http://www.mfa.gr/foreign/treaties/

From the Hellenic Ministry of Foreign Affairs, numerous online documents pertaining to Greece.

Macedonia

Chronology of Main Crimes Against Humanity

http://www.geocities.com/Pentagon/7360/chro.e.html

Detailed listing of the alleged crimes by the Turks, from a Greek perspective. A personal home page.

The Truth about Macedonia

http://members.tripod.com/~macedonia_gr/

Page alleging to solve the debate and thwart Slavic propaganda about this dispute. Includes historic quotes and excerpts from "other points of view" that support the basic premise of the page.

World War II

German Campaign in the Balkans: Greece

http://www.army.mil/cmh-pg/books/wwii/balkan/20_260_3.htm

Account of Operation Marita and some of Italy's attacks on Greece, from documents posted by the U.S. Army via the Center of Military History. Includes maps. The lack of link-backs conceals the identity of the author and other details.

Greece: 1821–1897

http://www.fhw.gr/chronos/12/en/index.html

Information on the foundation of the Hellenic State, including the declaration of the Greek war of independence, the sortie from Missolonghi, the Battle of Navarino, the Constitution, and many other key events from this period.

Greece: 1923–1945

http://www.fhw.gr/chronos/index_en.html

From the Foundation of the Hellenic World, excellent information on the inter-war period and World War II.

Maritime History

http://holidays-in-greece.com/cyclades/myk/aegean/history.htm

An abundantly detailed history of ships and seafaring in the Aegean, focusing on Delos and Rhodes.

Museums and Societies

Historical and Ethnological Society of Greece

http://www.fhw.gr/projects/vouli/en/museum/society.html

Information about this organization devoted to the study of middle and modern Greek history and literature.

Institute of International Economic Relations

http://idec.gr/iier/aims.htm

Industry group presenting conferences, seminars, and publishing materials related to Greek economic involvement.

Messimvria and Nea Messimvria: An Ethnographic Exhibition

http://botsalo.physics.auth.gr/Messimvria/

Overview of the migration of Greeks, presented by Georgios Agelopoulos, Eleftheria Deltsou, and Aigli Brouskou. Includes photos and bibliography.

National Historical Museum: Greece

http://www.fhw.gr/projects/vouli/en/museum/museum.htm

Virtual tour of museum devoted to the history of modern Greece.

The Speros Basil Vryonis Society for the Study of Hellenism

http://www.glavx.org/

Organization devoted to the promotion of Hellenistic studies.

Religion

Ecclesia

http://www.ecclesia.gr/English/EnIndex.html

The official Web site of the Church of Greece, with the calendar, information on the Holy Synod, the Archbishop and Archdiocese of Athens, and monasteries and shrines.

Greek Orthodox Chat and Bulletin Boards

http://ww2.goarch.org/scripts/chat.exe

Messages and live chat on various subjects pertaining to Orthodoxy. Includes Ask Father, different dioceses, and so on.

Greek Orthodox Observer Home Page

http://www.goarch.org/goa/observer/

Online version of the U.S.-based *Observer*, including extensive searchable archives. Requires Adobe Acrobat viewer.

Search Engines

FORTHnet

http://dir.forthnet.gr/index-0–en.html

Greek Web site index in both English and Greek.

Phantis

http://www.phantis.com

Well-organized and regularly maintained search site, with good coverage of sites within Greece. Many Greek entries, but enough English-language ones to make a visit worthwhile even if Greek is a challenge.

RoBBy: The Greek (Hellenic) Search Engine

http://www.robby.gr/

Well-categorized search engine focusing entirely on sites pertaining to Greece. The main page also offers daily links to international exchange rates and news in Greece. Strong coverage of politically oriented sites.

Thea: Complete Greek Indexer

http://www.thea.gr/

Thorough general search machine for Greek and Greek-related sites worldwide.

Irish History

Patrick Callan

About Local Ireland: 1798 Rebellions

http://www.local.ie/history/1798/

This is a clear, illuminating site, a good introduction to the topic; it gives a clear sense of the context (back to 1601), the military background, the armies and the soldiers, and the aftermath, as well as five helpful maps.

Aspects of Ulster

http://ourworld.compuserve.com/homepages/martin_sloan/

This site by Martin Sloan features a timeline related to events in Ulster from prehistoric to modern times. While taking a longitudinal perspective to the conflict, it is often slipshod in judgment.

A to Z of Ancient Ireland

http://www2.one.net.au/~silverback/ireland/a_to_z_of_ancient_ireland.htm

This extensive glossary of terms associated with Celtic Ireland runs the gamut from *airbre druad* (or "druid's hedge") to "yew sticks" used by magicians. It is based on a text, *Ancient Ireland: The Users' Guide*, by Conan Kennedy, and provides a substantial context for the study of pre-Christian Ireland. There is a wry sense of humor throughout, as well as references to other contemporary European civilization and religions.

The Battle of Antrim

http://www.antrim.gov.uk/battle/index.html

The author deals with the background of the 1798 rebellion in Antrim, the principal participants, the battle of Antrim, and its aftermath. Outlines of the battle are supplemented by artwork, contemporary pictures, and maps. The links don't work.

The Battle of the Boyne

http://www.grandorange.org.uk/

Hosted by the Orange Order, the site contains pictures of the protagonists and the battlefield, as well as paintings by Van Wyck, and the Boyne battle plan. A description of the battle is supplemented by the account of the eminent historian Froude. The site also includes material on other events associated with the Orange Order—for example, its stand against Home Rule from 1886 to 1921.

The Battle of the Boyne Day Pages

http://www.bcpl.net/~cbladey/orange.html

The Orange Order commemorates the Battle of the Boyne at its annual July 12 parades. Conrad Bladey's site includes a substantial account of the battle, information about the armies and soldiers, and songs of the Orangemen. Contemporary illustrations give a strong visual sense. The site puts forward an impassioned defense of the Orange tradition, for example, that William III's victory brought about the "defeat of James II, an Absolutist monarch rejected by England, by a tolerant ruler subject to the rule of Parliament."

Bawnboy Workhouse

http://www.cavannet.ie/history/archeo/sites/work-hse.htm

Photographs of the remains of a typical workhouse give a flavor of the scale of these publicly funded buildings.

George Berkeley, Philosopher

http://www.maths.tcd.ie/pub/HistMath/People/Berkeley/

David Wilkins, of Trinity College, Dublin, authors this site on Ireland's most eminent philosopher. There are biographical guides (short and long ones!), lectures and essays on his philosophy, and selections from his works, including "A Treatise concerning the Principles of Human Knowledge" and "A Defence of Free Thinking in Mathematics."

CAIN Web Service✓

http://cain.ulst.ac.uk/

CAIN (Conflict Archive on the Internet) is the most comprehensive and scholarly site dealing with Northern Ireland. It provides background information on the conflict; information and source material on significant events and issues; bibliographies, databases, and other electronic services; and background information on society in Northern Ireland. It covers themes such as discrimination, housing, law and order, and women and the conflict. The section on Bloody Sunday gives an indication of the quality of the site, which is administered by Dr. Martin Melaugh.

CELT: Corpus of Electronic Texts

http://www.ucc.ie/celt/

This provides the full text of the debates that took place in Dublin in the First Debate on the Treaty between Great Britain and Ireland. An understanding of the Treaty debate is essential for any student of contemporary Irish history. The host site (Corpus of Electronic Texts) also contains primary materials on the history of the early twentieth century, including six books by James Connolly,

The Path to Freedom by Michael Collins, *Ireland in the New Century* by Horace Plunkett, and the works of Patrick Pearse and Oscar Wilde.

Celtic Ireland

http://www.unc.edu/courses/art111/celtic/

A collection of pictures, maps, timelines, a glossary, and quizzes. The site includes the crosses at Monasterboice and Castledermot, links to other crosses, a speculative look at how Celtic high crosses might have been colored, the Gallarus Oratory on the Dingle Peninsula, St. Kevin's Kitchen, and the grounds of Glendalough.

Celtic Ireland: Encyclopedia

http://celt.net/Celtic/menu.html

This general collection of material relating to the Celtic people and culture includes an informative encyclopedia of Celtic terms, manuscripts and texts, commentary on gods and myths, heroes and history, and artisans.

Chronicon: An Electronic Journal

http://www.ucc.ie/ucc/chronicon/right1.htm

This electronic journal provides scholarly articles on Irish history, high-quality postgraduate reports, and a historians' forum.

Chronology of Ireland

http://homepage.eircom.net/~chronology/

Chronology of Ireland claims to be the largest resource of its kind on the Internet, presenting information on people and events connected to Ireland. Compiled from respected reference books on Ireland, it is most thorough on modern Ireland. Hosted by Brendan O'Brien, it is a very instructive site.

Michael Collins

http://www2.cruzio.com/~sbarrett/mcollins.htm

Suzanne Barrett's biography is brief, well written, and includes a bibliography relating to Collins.

The "Confessio" of Saint Patrick

http://www.robotwisdom.com/jaj/patrick.html

Kidnapped at sixteen years of age and sold into slavery in Ireland, St. Patrick went on to convert the Irish to Christianity. His *Confessio*, originally written in Latin, offer a clear and enthralling view of life in the British Isles.

Michael Davitt: Mayo's Most Famous Son

http://www.mayo-Ireland.ie/Mayo/News/ConnTel/CTHistry/MlDavitt.htm

Davitt died in Dublin in 1906. By the time of his death at the age of sixty, "land for the people" had largely become a reality, prison reform had begun, and he himself had become an international champion of liberty.

Discovering the Bronze Age

http://www.discoveryireland.com

This site is hosted by the Discovery Programme, an archaeological research institution dedicated to investigating Ireland's past from earliest times and presenting the results to as wide an audience as possible. The site gives an illuminating outline of the main characteristics of the Bronze Age in Ireland, with color line drawings, including ritual and religion, trade, mining, clothing, jewelry, homes and settlements, farming, food, and cooking.

Famine Records

http://www.nationalarchives.ie/famine.html

This article is an attempt to bring to the attention of those interested in famine research—whether at the local or national level—collections in the National Archives that span the famine period. There is a searchable index of the relief commission papers from 1845 to 1847.

The Famine: "The Times" and Donegal

http://www.vidicator.ca/history/famine/timesDonegal.asp

Thomas Campbell Foster's very detailed reports from County Donegal provide excellent material on the local famine. Published originally in *The Times* (London) in 1845–1846, they are edited here by John Ward of County Donegal.

Forgotten Man of Irish History

http://www.mayo-Ireland.ie/Mayo/News/ConnTel/CTHistry/JDaly.htm

The year 1879 proved to be a busy and fruitful year for James Daly. He was first elected chairman of the historic Westport meeting addressed by Charles Stuart Parnell. On August 16 of the same year, he became vice president of the Land League of Mayo in Castlebar. He was also elected to the committee of the Irish National Land League founded in Dublin on October 21, 1879.

The Great War, 1914 to 1918: Commemorations

http://www.irishsoldier.org/ulster_division.html

The site of the Somme Heritage Center commemorates the involvement of the 36th (Ulster) and 16th (Irish) Divisions in the Battle of the Somme and the 10th in Gallipoli, Salonika, and Palestine. Included is a brief history of the 36th Division.

The Great War, 1914 to 1918: General Context

http://www.tcd.ie/General/Fusiliers/

Developed by four undergraduate students at Trinity College, Dublin, this site has many relevant features from Ireland's history during the Great War, dealing with the Home Rule Bill, the National Volunteers, living conditions in Dublin, the history of the Dublin Fusiliers regiment, its main battles, and some of its soldiers (such as poet Francis Ledwidge).

The Great War, 1914 to 1918: Kildare Region

http://kildare.ie/hospitality/historyandheritage/athyheritage/ww1.htm

Showing the Great War's impact on Ireland, this site provides extensive text of articles from the *Kildare Observer* for 1914 and 1915, with a comprehensive list of casualties from the Kildare area. This innovative site shows the importance of the Internet for bringing primary material to public attention.

The Great War, 1914 to 1918: Royal Dublin Fusiliers

http://www.greatwar.ie/

This very comprehensive site is hosted by the Royal Dublin Fusilier Association. It includes information on Irish battalions in the British army, Ireland's experience in World War I (including the 1916 rising), individual stories of Irishmen who enlisted in this regiment of the British Army, and a section on war monuments and how to trace a war grave. Tom Burke wrote the script. This site is a good starting point for research on this conflict, which in many ways has become a forgotten war.

The Great War, 1914 to 1918: 16th (Irish) Division

http://homepage.ntlworld.com/sh.keays/new16th.html

This site on the 16th (Irish) Division, seen as the nationalist counterpart to the 36th (Ulster) Division in the Great War, features a history, material about its famous chaplain, Father William Doyle, reproductions of photographs, illustrations, and other information from the 16th (Irish) Division scrapbook.

The Great War, 1914 to 1918: 36th (Ulster) Division

http://dnausers.d-n-a.net/dnetDkjs/36art01.htm

This site offers a brief outline of the military experiences of the 36th (Ulster) Division, which become an important symbolic element of Ulster unionism after the war.

History of Dublin ✓

http://indigo.ie/~kfinlay/

Ken Finlay's site on Dublin may seem too particular to be of benefit to general readers, but it is an engrossing and rewarding site with a richness of content that goes beyond the history of Dublin. Finlay includes a chronology of Dublin; reproduces in full many out-of-copyright books, such as P.W. Joyce's *The Neighbourhood of Dublin* and F.E. Ball's *History of Dublin*; and provides information on James Joyce, memoirs of society figures such as Buck Whaley, and politicians such as Tim Healy.

History of Ireland's National Police Force

http://www.geocities.com/CapitolHill/7900/

The Garda Síochána Historical Society has excellent material on the history of Irish policing from 1770 to 1922 and many modern controversies.

Introduction to Irish History

http://www.local.ie/history/

This is a brief introduction to Irish history, from prehistory to the modern conflict in Northern Ireland.

Ireland: History in Maps ✓

http://www.fortunecity.com/bally/kilkenny/2/iremaps.htm

A series of twenty-four maps of Ireland, ranging from the earliest habitation through the Celts and Normans, Plantations, up until the 1840s. Each map is complemented by an explanatory text and links. For instance, the map on the famine period is accompanied by a substantive text outlining literacy figures, a table relating the decline of population between 1841 and 1851 by county, links to Web sites on the Great Irish Famine, and a demographic map (1991).

Ireland's Ancient Stone Monuments ✓

http://www.stonepages.com/

This multinational site has a magnificent section on Ireland's court and passage tombs, stone circles, dolmens, standing stones, cairns, and hill forts. Navigation is very easy. The site includes a helpful glossary and an active map that locates monuments and brings you to the individual pages. Each location has at least one photograph, which can be enlarged. Monuments such as Newgrange and Tara are illuminated by outstanding commentaries.

Ireland's Pirate Queen

http://www.maths.tcd.ie/~jaymin/sca/Granuail.htm

An interesting outline of the life of Ireland's pirate queen, Granuail, feted for her daring and courage, and resurrected in recent years by Anne Chambers as part of the rediscovery of the role of independent women in Irish history.

Irish Architecture ✓

http://www.irish-architecture.com/

Archéire (Architecture Ireland) has a diverse collection of historical architectural buildings, such as Dublin Castle. The jewel of the site is Architectural Dublin, a historically based introduction to Dublin's architecture. The text is easily accessible, with a range of contemporary and historical photographs.

Irish Committee of Historical Sciences

http://www.historians.ie/

The Web site of the Irish Committee of Historical Sciences presents information about its activities and members. The site provides many useful contact points for those interested in Irish history. It also hosts pages for affiliated organizations.

The Irish Constitution

http://www.maths.tcd.ie/pub/Constitution/index.html

A copy of the 1937 constitution, introduced by De Valera, which provides the touchstone for many contemporary debates in Ireland today.

Irish Diaspora

http://www.irishknowledge.com/

Subtitled the Irish Studies Network, this very thorough site takes a very broad view of Irish studies. There are almost 1,700 reviewed sites, ranging from archaeology, Celtic history, church history, economic history, Irish diaspora, social history, nationalism, to Northern Ireland.

Irish Diaspora Studies

http://www.brad.ac.uk/acad/diaspora/

Irish Diaspora Studies is the name given to the worldwide, scholarly, interdisciplinary study of Irish emigration and its social, linguistic, economic, cultural, and political causes and consequences. The site is modest in content, but very valuable in terms of insight and scholarship, focusing on reviews, discussion papers, and notes and queries. The Irish diaspora list provides an e-mail discussion forum dealing with social, economic, linguistic, cultural, and political aspects.

Irish Famine: Blight

http://www.cavannet.ie/nature/spuds.htm

This site describes the nature of the disease that hit the Irish potato crop; uniquely, it includes color photographs of healthy leaves that then become infected by the blight.

Irish Famine, 1845–50 ✓

http://avery.med.virginia.edu/~eas5e/Irish/Famine.html

This Virginia University site features superb graphic material showing scenes from the famine, mainly drawn from the *Illustrated London News*. It has excellent selections from reports of *The Times* (London), including the paper's own index on the famine articles. Topics range from requests for outdoor relief in 1846 to reports of alleged cannibalism in June 1849. Thomas Campbell Foster's reports from County Donegal can also be viewed. The site includes a useful bibliography and a link to other Internet sources on the famine.

Irish History: Discussion Site ✓

http://www2.h-net.msu.edu/~albion/

H-Albion is a discussion network for British and Irish History. Enter "Ireland" into the search box, and you will be met with a superb range of opinions and articles. The range of topics and the expertise of the list contributors make this an essential site for those interested in researching Irish history.

Irish History: Educational Site

http://www.scoilnet.ie

This site is targeted at primary and secondary levels in Ireland; the search feature will yield much curriculum material, suitable for use in schools, on a multitude of historical topics.

Irish History: General Sites

http://bubl.ac.uk/link/i/irishhistory.htm

This is a quality site, recommending sound links with plenty of history content and variety. Interestingly, sites are cataloged by subject, as well as by Dewey Classification. An exceptional introductory site.

Irish History: General Sites

http://www.ocf.berkeley.edu/~stonerjw/eire_his.html

This is a list of WWW resources selected by John Stoner for the study of Irish history. It includes a list of metasites, genealogical resources, primary sources, bibliographical information, discussion lists, online publications, and catalogs.

Irish History: Introductory Sites

http://www.leavingcert.net/

The history section covers the gamut of ten main topics dealt with in the current Irish Leaving Certificate examination, taken by Irish students at the end of their high school education. The topics include Home Rule, the land question at the end of the nineteenth century, the growth of cultural nationalism, the labor movement, Sinn Fein, the struggle for independence, the early governments of Cumann na nGaedhael and Fianna Fail, Ireland in the 1950s, and Northern Ireland. A brief introduction to each topic is followed by a listing of relevant Web sites—a sensible introduction for those new to modern Irish history.

Irish History on the Web

http://wwwvms.utexas.edu/~jdana/irehist.html

Jacqueline Dana, M.A. in history (Irish and American) from the University of Missouri, Columbia, hosts this very useful general site, which is regularly updated, with links to genealogy and history, timelines and famine sites. This site lacks some of the traditional academic efforts at objectivity, according to Berkeley historian John Stoner.

The Irish Times

http://www.ireland.com/

The Irish Times hosts this site, which frequently features special supplements on items of historical interest, with items relevant to Northern Ireland's recent history under the heading Path to Peace.

Labor History

http://flag.blackened.net/revolt/ireland_history.html

This index of articles from the alternative perspective of labor history covers topics from the 1798 rebellion, the Irish famine, the Catholic Church, and the 1916 rising to the history of the IRA.

Local History

http://www.local.ie/general/map/

This site brings surfers to each of the thirty-two counties in Ireland, each of which has a history element. The quality is uneven, but can reward a visit.

National Archives of Ireland

http://www.nationalarchives.ie/

This Web site provides general information about the National Archives, such as the range of holdings and the main sources of material available, and features some searchable databases. The potential of the site has been limited by the very small scale of documentation available online. The site includes seventeen facsimiles related to the 1798 rebellion, with introductory and explanatory information. It briefly covers topics such as foreign affairs, agriculture, and law, with a selection of research guides on subjects including the Irish famine, and information about the transportation of Irish emigrants to Australia between 1791 and 1868.

Navan at Armagh

http://www.navan.com/

Navan Fort, the ancient Emain Macha of Irish history and legend, was the earliest capital of Ulster, the royal seat of the kings of Ulster, and the setting for the tales of Macha, Cú Chulainn, and the heroes of the Red Branch. Today, Navan is a premier archaeological monument and one of Europe's most important Celtic centers. The site, hosted by the Navan Interpretative Centre, contains clear outlines of the history of Navan Fort; dynamic, interactive displays bring the mystery and mythology of Emain Macha to life.

Newgrange Monuments

http://www.knowth.com

This site features excellent images and descriptions of the tombs in the Newgrange area.

Nineteenth-Century Ireland

http://www.qub.ac.uk/english/socs/ssnci.html

This site by the Society for the Study of Nineteenth-Century Ireland lists information about its activities and members, but also hosts a links segment on nineteenth-century history that is very rewarding.

Northern Ireland Election Results

http://www.explorers.whyte.com/

Nicholas Whyte, a Ph.D. from Queen's University of Belfast (QUB), posted this well-moderated text on the history of Westminster parliamentary elections and constituencies, providing links to local political parties.

Nuzhound News Archive ✓

http://www.nuzhound.com

This site allows surfers to access a special index of Irish history articles published in Irish newspapers during the previous few years, giving an indication of many controversies and anniversaries in Irish historiography.

Primary Sources

http://library.byu.edu/~rdh/eurodocs/ireland.html

Part of the Eurodocs site, this site contains Irish documents ranging from the Bull of Pope Adrian IV in 1155 to the 1999 report of the Independent Commission on Policing for Northern Ireland (the Patten Report).

Princess Grace Irish Library, Monaco ✓

http://www.pgil-eirdata.org/

This is the most comprehensive and accessible site on Irish Studies. Intended as a "scholars' notebook," it has the capacity to become a site of first resort for people looking for meaningful information on Irish history, although the ambit of the site is much wider. The PGIL Author Dataset contains comprehensive biographical and bibliographical information on 4,500 Irish writers, with extracts from their works and commentaries upon them. As an example, a search for "D.P. Moran," one of the formidable figures associated with the Irish Ireland movement, found over 8,000 hits, including quotations, commentaries, criticism, biography, and references. Digital versions of some classic Irish texts by Swift, Goldsmith, and Bram Stoker (*Dracula*) are highlights, along with many other notable features on this first-class site.

Proclamation of 1916

http://homepages.iol.ie/~dluby/proclaim.htm

The text and facsimile of this seminal document, rarely read but cited regularly in legitimacy arguments.

The Red Flag: The Song, the Man, the Monument

http://www.dcu.ie/~comms/hsheehan/connell.htm

Jim Connell wrote "The Red Flag" in 1889. Dr. Helena Sheehan's site provides substantial information on labor songs in general.

Reinterpreting the 1798 Rebellion in County Wexford

http://www.iol.ie/~pressecw/whelan.htm

Kevin Whelan, a reputable historian, contends that the 1790s was a pivotal decade in the evolution of modern Ireland. It witnessed the emergence of popular republicanism and loyalism, of separatism, of the Orange Order, and of Maynooth College and culminated in the 1798 Rebellion and the Act of Union of 1800, which defined subsequent relations between Ireland and Britain.

1798 Rebellion: Biographies

http://www.unet.univie.ac.at/~a8700035/biograph.htm

A brief introduction by Stiofan MacAmhalghaidh to the upheaval in Irish history caused by the 1798 rising, the Act of Union of 1800, and the 1803 rising. The site presents eleven biographies, including those of Emmet, Grattan, Tone, and O'Connell.

Time Line of Irish History, 1916 to 1923

http://www.irishancestors.com/celticorigins/dateline.html

This is a detailed timeline of Irish history, 1916 to 1923, which complements a biographical treatment of Michael Collins. It gives a clear indication of the ferment in Irish society during those turbulent years.

Unionist View of Northern Ireland

http://www.cruithni.org.uk/index.html#overview

This brief overview of Ulster history reflects a unionist perspective and is a useful reciprocal to the many sites reflecting nationalist or republican sentiment on the Internet.

A View of the Present State of Ireland

http://darkwing.uoregon.edu/~rbear/veue1.html

Author of the well-known poetry classic *The Faerie Queen*, Edmund Spenser penned an acerbic memoir, *A View of the Present State of Ireland*, in 1596, reflecting the gulf between the English overlords and the native Irish that is obvious from the first paragraph of this Renascence Edition text: "I wounder that no course is taken for the tourning therof to good uses, and reducing that salvage nation to better goverment and civillity." It establishes the context for the Englishing of Ireland over the following centuries. Richard Bar of the University of Oregon, who admits that he "cheered on the Irish the whole time," prepared the edition.

Views of the Famine

http://vassun.vassar.edu/~sttaylor/FAMINE/

This site contains many contemporary illustrations from publications including the famous *Illustrated London News* and *Punch*. The graphics show laborers, their cabins, beggars, landlords, evictions, funerals, and emigration to America. The site also has an excellent article from *The Irish Times* on the artist responsible for the artwork in the *Illustrated London News*.

The Wild Geese Today: Erin's Far Flung Exiles

http://www.thewildgeese.com

This comprehensive guide to over 450 Irish Web sites has a general bibliography. The eclecticism of its authors makes it a curio with many nuggets, including substantial information on the role of the Irish in the American Civil War, a register of American "living history" associations, Irish genealogy, language,· literature, and music.

Workhouse Famine Records

http://www.magma.ca/~jward/workhouse1.html

A local history group drew up this material on workhouse famine records. It deals extensively with the experience of famine as exemplified through the records of the regionally funded workhouses, the numbers admitted, the diet administered, and the attempts to alleviate the suffering in some of the poorest areas of Ireland.

Workhouse Living Conditions

http://www.iol.ie/~gartlan/fampt1.htm

This Web site features a poem written by M.J. McManus, a desolate tale about the distressing conditions in the Carrick-on-Shannon workhouse where he was born.

Italian History

Richard Wojtowicz

Metasites

Art History Resources on the Web

http://witcombe.sbc.edu/ARTHLinks.html

Italian art history sources appear at prehistoric art, ancient Greece and Rome, art of the Middle Ages, fifteenth-century Renaissance art, sixteenth-century Renaissance art, seventeenth-century Baroque art, eighteenth-century art, nineteenth-century art, twentieth-century art, and museums and galleries.

Brigham Young University Italian Index

http://humanities.byu.edu/classes/ital420/

Index of links to all areas of Italian history including Paleolithic, Etruscans, ancient Rome, the Middle Ages, humanism, the Renaissance, late Renaissance, Baroque, the 1700s, romanticism, the Risorgimento, and contemporary themes. Subcategories include art, literature, and music; biographies; countries and economy; cultural anthropology; history and philosophy; indexes and bibliographies; science and techniques; and urbanism.

BUBL LINK / 5:15 Catalogue of Internet Resources: Italian History

http://bubl.ac.uk/link/I/italianhistory.htm

List of resources including Archaeological Resource Guide for Europe Geographical Index, Futurism, Italian Life Under Fascism, Leaning Tower of Pisa, Medici Archive, Renaissance and Baroque Architecture, Studyweb: History of Italy, and Windows on Italy.

DMOZ Open Directory Project

http://dmoz.org/Regional/Europe/Italy/Society_and_Culture/History/

Sites on ancient Rome, archaeology, architecture, wars, Queen Adelaide, catacombs, Etruscans, bookkeeping and merchant skills, military service, and Normans in Italy (in Italian).

History of Italy: Primary Documents

http://www.lib.byu.edu/~rdh/eurodocs/italy.html

Offers links to selected sites and documents. Does not cover all periods or aspects of Italian history.

H-Italy Italian History

http://www2.h-net.msu.edu/~italy/

A member of H-Net Humanities and Social Sciences Online, H-Italy offers scholars information on Italian history. The site provides links to announcements for conferences and seminars, calls for papers and grant opportunities, jobs, discussion, literature reviews, resources, arts and architecture, Italian literature, museums and exhibitions, and other assorted links at H-Italy Links. A search facility allows the user to search H-Italy for keywords or all H-Net logs.

Hyperwar European Theater of Operations: The Mediterranean

http://www.ibiblio.org/hyperwar/ETO/Med/index.html

Materials on World War II operations in Italy from U.S. Army sites.

Internet Ancient History Sourcebook: Rome

http://www.fordham.edu/halsall/ancient/asbook09.html

Texts of Roman historians, Etruscans, foundations, republican institutions, Carthaginian war, imperialism, civil war and revolution, the Principate, law, military, empire and provinces, literature, art and architecture, education, economics, slavery, daily life, religion, gender and sexuality, and modern perspectives.

Italian History: A Guide to Resources and Research on the Web

http://web.uccs.edu/history/index/italy.html

From the University of Colorado, Colorado Springs, this site provides links to general resources, which run from the Art of Renaissance Science to Windows on Italy, and sources on the Roman Empire, from the ruins of Rome to its 2,750th anniversary.

Medieval Italy

http://www.georgetown.edu/labyrinth/subjects/italy/italy.html

Provides connections to Web resources on Italian culture, Italy and Italian language. The Labyrinth Library Italian Bookcase accesses some live sites for Boccacio's *Decameron*, but Dante has some dead links. Suggested paths include pages on Boccaccio, the Dante Exhibition, Florence tax data (1427–1429), Spello art and architecture, Botticelli, medieval Italian history, Normans in Italy, medieval culture and language, manuscripts, churches, Torrione Castle, and the Vatican Library exhibit, Rome Reborn.

The World Wide Web Virtual Library Italian History Index

http://www.iue.it/LIB/SISSCO//VL/hist-italy/Index.html

Provides links on Italian history in English, Italian, and other languages. Categories include Reference, Geographical, Chronological, Topical, and Other.

General Sites

Bellarmine's 1615 Letter on Galileo's Theories

http://www.fordham.edu/halsall/mod/1615bellarmine-letter.html

Cardinal Robert Bellarmine, in 1615, addressed whether or not Galileo's theories clashed with scripture. This site also includes some notes on later actions by the church.

Robert Cardinal Bellarmine (1542–1621)

http://es.rice.edu/ES/humsoc/Galileo//People/bellarmine.html

Biography of Bellarmine, admonisher of Galileo.

Byzantines in Renaissance Italy

http://historymedren.about.com/homework/historymedren/gi/dynamic/
offsite.htm?site=http%3A%2F%2Forb.rhodes.edu%2Fencyclop%2Flate%2
Flaterbyz%2Fharris-ren.html

Jonathan Harris's "Byzantines in Renaissance Italy" with bibliography.

A Biography of Charlemagne

http://www.chronique.com/Library/MedHistory/charlemagne.htm

Charlemagne the King from Will Durant's *Story of Civilization*, 1950.

Charlemagne

http://www.newadvent.org/cathen/03610c.htm

This *Catholic Encyclopedia* entry includes Charlemagne's involvement with Italy.

De Imperatoribus Romanis

http://www.roman-emperors.org/indexx.htm

This Online Encyclopedia of Roman Emperors provides extensive information on the emperors and empresses of Rome, with hyperlinks to other related names, bibliographies, and maps.

Encyclopedia of 1848 Revolutions: Papal States

http://www.ohio.edu/~chastain/ip/papalsta.htm

Overview from *Encyclopedia of 1848 Revolutions*.

Fascism in Italy

http://ftp.bbc.co.uk/education/modern/fascism/fascihtm.htm

This site, from the BBC network, discusses fascism under Mussolini.

Galileo Galilei

http://www.fordham.edu/halsall/mod/galileo-tuscany.html

Letter to the Grand Duchess Christina of Tuscany, 1615.

Garibaldi

http://www.fordham.edu/halsall/mod/1860garibaldi.html

Report on the Conquest of Naples, 1860.

Guide to Western Composers and Their Music

http://www.ipl.org/exhibit/mushist/

Part of the Internet Public Library, this site covers composers from the Middle Ages to the present day, including Italian, with RealAudio samples of their music.

The Italian Front in World War I

http://www.worldwar1.com/itafront/

La Grande Guerra's "The Italian Front, 1915–1918," gives information on weapons and equipment, battles, casualties, geography, diplomacy and operations, and who's who on the front.

Italian Unification

http://www.fordham.edu/halsall/mod/1861italianunif.html

Documents of Italian unification, 1846–1861.

Italy: A Timeline

http://pirate.shu.edu/~connelwi/Timeline.htm

Seton Hall students and interested visitors have compiled a more complete timeline at this site.

Italy: Culture and History

http://www.defusco.ch/en2_italy.html

Overview of culture and history from early to postwar Italy. Includes a short bibliography.

Lombards

http://www.bartleby.org/65/lo/Lombards.html

Columbia Encyclopedia article discusses these Germanic people in Italy, including sections on the Lombards' origins, their conquest of Italy, and the Lombard Kingdom.

Medieval Sourcebook: Edward Gibbon

http://www.fordham.edu/halsall/source/gibbon-fall.html

General Observations on the Fall of the Roman Empire in the West.

Medieval Sourcebook: Giorgio Vasari

http://www.fordham.edu/halsall/source/vasari1.html

Life of Leonardo da Vinci, 1550.

Benito Mussolini

http://www.fordham.edu/halsall/mod/mussolini-fascism.html

"What Is Fascism?" 1932.

The Ostrogoths

http://campus.northpark.edu/history/WebChron/WestEurope/Ostrogoths.html

Short essay on Ostrogoth relationship to Rome.

The Ostrogoths and Theodoric

http://www.btinternet.com/~mark.furnival/ostgoth.htm

Discussions of Theodoric and the Kingdom of Italy.

Otto I

http://www.newadvent.org/cathen/11354a.htm

Otto I, the Great, of Germany, from the *Catholic Encyclopedia*.

Otto II

http://www.newadvent.org/cathen/11355a.htm

Otto II, from the *Catholic Encyclopedia*.

Papal States

http://www.encyclopedia.com/articles/09805.html

Article in five sections: Papal States, Accumulation of Land, Control of the Territories, Dissolution and Resolution, and Bibliography.

Prehistoric Italy

http://myron.sjsu.edu/romeweb/GLOSSARY/timeln/t03.htm

One-page essay on prehistoric peoples of the Italian peninsula, with links to other periods and issues of Roman history.

The Renaissance in Italy

http://www.ibiblio.org/wm/paint/glo/renaissance/it.html

Essay on the Italian Renaissance provides further links to the work of specific artists, such as Giotto de Bondone, Sandro Botticelli, Andrea Mantegna, Giovanni Bellini, Leonardo da Vinci, Michelangelo, Raphael, and Titian.

Renaissance Italy

http://www.idbsu.edu/courses/hy309/docs/burckhardt/burckhardt.html

Online version of the 1878 translation of Jacob Burkhardt's six-part book, *The Civilization of the Renaissance in Italy.* Information on despots, dynasties, republics, papacy, individualism, antiquity, humanism, universities, literature, science, aesthetics, society, morality, and religion.

Southern Italy in the Early Middle Ages

http://www.maxwell.syr.edu/maxpages/faculty/penningk/Naples/LectureTwo/EarlyMiddleAges.htm

Provides a timeline and maps concerning the Moslems, Normans, and Byzantines in Southern Italy.

Timeline of Italian History

http://www.fiu.edu/~honors/italy/timeline.htm

Three thousand years of Italian history from pre-Etruscan Italic tribes to the Italian Republic.

King Victor Emmanuel

http://www.fordham.edu/halsall/mod/1871victoremm.html

Address to Parliament, Rome, 1871.

Windows on Italy: The History

http://www.mi.cnr.it/WOI/deagosti/history/0welcome.html

From the Web site of the National Research Council of Italy (*Consiglio Nationale delle Recerche*), this site offers short descriptions of the prehistoric, tribal, medieval, Renaissance, Napoleonic, Risorgimento, interwar, Republican, and present-day periods.

World War I

http://www.lib.byu.edu/~rdh/wwi/1915/italydec.html

Italian Premier Antonio Salandra's Declaration for the Allies, May 23, 1915.

Nordic (Scandinavian) History

Mary Anne Hansen

Metasites

CultureNet Sweden

http://www.kultur.nu/

This site provides almost 1,500 links to various types of resources: archives, libraries, museums, and other cultural institutions. Researchers can access English-language text either by clicking on the "in English" link at the lower right-hand corner of the page or by using the following URL: http://www.kultur.nu/index.asp?language=1&version=gfx. The Swedish Ministry of Culture sponsors CultureNet Sweden.

Finnish History Index from the World Wide Web Virtual Library

http://www.iue.it/LIB/SISSCO/VL/hist-finland/Index.html

This site provides an extensive gateway to Finnish and Scandinavian history Web resources. Researchers would benefit from exploring other country indexes within the WWW Virtual Library when doing Scandinavian history research, as well as research in a vast array of areas.

Medieval Scandinavia

http://www.medsca.org

This site provides information about the history of Norway; history of general interest throughout all of Scandinavia, Europe, and North America; and general genealogical information regarding Norwegian immigration to Canada and the United States.

Medieval Studies

http://www.hist.uib.no/middelalder/eng.htm

This site is a gateway to medieval source material, articles, and Internet discussion. Created by the Department of History at the University of Bergen, it is intended for university faculty and students, researchers and teachers in the fields of Scandinavian and European medieval history.

General Sites

Antique Maps of Iceland

http://egla.bok.hi.is/kort/english.html

All antique maps of Iceland, created prior to 1900, that are in the collection of the National and University Library of Iceland have been converted to digital format and are accessible at this site.

Bombs and Babies

http://www.hist.uib.no/bomb/

The Bombs and Babies—Oral History on the Web site aims to introduce students to the value of oral history as a tool for understanding the past. Included are information about students' work on the project, an oral history bibliography, and links to five other oral history Web sites. A page of teaching material is also included, but it is in Norwegian. This is a collaborative project between the departments of history at the University of Bergen and University College, London.

Danish Data Archives

http://www.dda.dk/

The Danish Data Archives, an independent unit within the group of Danish State Archives, is a national data bank for researchers and students in Denmark and abroad. Researchers have online access to demographic and social data through this site.

Database of Wall Paintings in Danish Churches

http://www.kalkmalerier.dk/english/default.htm

The Department of History at the University of Copenhagen has created an online database containing 5,320 high-quality images of wall paintings from Danish churches. The site also offers statistical data, articles, and literature on art and related topics.

The Demographic Data Base

http://www.ddb.umu.se/index_eng.html

The Demographic Data Base is responsible for ensuring that historical data from parish registers and parish statistics are easily available for researchers from both Sweden and abroad. The DDB's research activities include method development, service for researchers, provision of guest research posts, seminars, conferences, and more. The University of Umeå hosts the site.

The Documentation Project

http://www.dokpro.uio.no/engelsk/index.html

This project is an extensive information system of digitized materials on Norwegian language and culture, from numerous museums and archival collections throughout Norway. The site has searchable databases on a number of historical sources, including the *Diplomatarium Norvegicum*, a large collection of Norwegian official documents prior to 1570. The materials are in the original language (Norse or Latin), with a Norwegian abstract. The work of collecting and registration of the documents started 150 years ago; the digital collection contains over 90,000 documents today.

Dutch Electronic Subject Service

http://www.kb.nl/dutchess/index.html

The DutchESS site provides access to a collection of high-quality resources in all disciplines that are in the public domain and freely available on the Internet.

The resources are evaluated and selected by the subject specialists of the Dutch National Library and a number of Dutch academic libraries. The primary user group is the Dutch academic community: researchers, students, and teachers in higher education. The European and international academic community in general is also considered part of the DutchESS audience.

Edlund Medievalist

http://www.edlund.anglo.co.uk/index.htm

Though much of this site is under construction, it is a useful resource for research on medieval history, including medieval Scandinavian history. The Early Scandinavia page provides links to resources in a number of areas: texts and translations; linguistic resources; literary resources; historical resources; archaeological resources; ships; runology; academic organizations; online journals; and mailing lists.

Emigration from Norway: The Solem and Swiggum Ship Index

http://www.museumsnett.no/mka/ssa/index.htm

This site contains the names of ships known to have left Norway for America between 1825 and 1925, along with transcribed passenger lists from more than 100 ships; others will be added regularly as they are transcribed. Links to related discussion lists and sites of interests are included.

Facts about Genealogy in Denmark

http://www.genealogi.dk/factwors.htm

Written by Hans H. Worsoe in 1970, this article offers basic information for anyone wishing to do genealogical research in Denmark. Links to numerous helpful sites, such as museums, archives, and so on, are also provided.

How to Trace Your Ancestors in Norway

http://www.ide-as.com/fndb/howto.html

Published by the Royal Norwegian Ministry of Foreign Affairs, this site provides detailed information for commencing genealogical research in Norway and beyond. Numerous links to relevant sites are provided, such as genealogical societies and national archives for several countries.

H-Skand: The Electronic Network for Scandinavian History and Culture

http://www.hum.ou.dk/projekter/h-skand/

H-Skand is a daily Internet discussion forum focused on scholarly topics in Scandinavian history as well as the national histories of the Scandinavian countries. Its focus is on research and teaching interests, new scholarship in the field, discussions of Scandinavian historiography, and the sharing of knowledge and experience about the teaching of Scandinavian history, including posting and discussion of course syllabi and reading lists. Additionally, H-Skand welcomes announcements from scholarly and professional societies or other organizations about their journals, conferences, fellowships, and funding opportunities.

Iceland

http://www.iceland.org/index.html

This is the official site of the Icelandic Foreign Service. Researchers will find a wealth of information about Iceland and Icelandic nature, history, people, culture and science, travel and leisure, business and economy, and foreign policy. Links for numerous related subjects are included.

The National Archive of Norway

http://www.hist.uib.no/arkivverket/index-en.htm

This site includes the Digital Archive, a result of cooperation between the Department of History at the University of Bergen and the Regional State Archives of Bergen, part of the National State Archives. The archive holds a large collection of online and searchable nominative records from censuses, parish registers, emigration lists, and military records of Norway.

The Ninety-Two Medieval Churches of Gotland

http://www.guteinfo.com/dj_eng.htm

This site describes ninety-two medieval churches in Gotland, Sweden. You can click on a map to locate a church or click on the name of a town for a photograph and details about a church. Gotland is an island situated in the middle of the Baltic Sea.

The Norwegian Historical Data Centre (NHDC)

http://www.rhd.uit.no/indexeng.html

NHDC's goal is to computerize the Norwegian censuses from 1865 onward, together with parish registers and other sources from the eighteenth and nineteenth centuries, resulting in a national population register for the period, primarily for research purposes, but also for the benefit of schools, genealogists, local historians, and many more groups. Products include printed editions with alphabetical indexes, digital versions on diskettes, and statistical tabulations via the Internet.

The Online Medieval and Classical Library (OMACL)

http://sunsite.berkeley.edu/OMACL/

The Online Medieval and Classical Library (OMACL) is a collection of important literary works of classical and medieval civilization, created by Douglas B. Killings and hosted by the Berkeley Digital Library SUNSITE. This collection contains Scandinavian texts in English translation.

Project Runeberg

http://www.lysator.liu.se/runeberg/

Coordinated by Linköping University in Sweden, Project Runeberg is an initiative to publish free electronic editions of Nordic literature. This site contains over 200 texts.

The Rook Family's Home Page

http://www.rook.org/index6.html

Earl Rook created this private site, Our Cultural and Historical Inheritance: A Heritage Index, for his own family's genealogical research, but it is a valuable tool for almost anyone doing genealogical research. Numerous links are provided for historical and genealogical sites.

Royal Danish Ministry of Foreign Affairs

http://www.um.dk/english/

This site provides comprehensive information about Denmark: history, government, travel, and more. The site includes a valuable online publication, *Denmark*, published by The Royal Danish Ministry of Foreign Affairs in cooperation with the editors of the *Danish National Encyclopedia*. The chapters, written by leading Danish experts, give an in-depth description of Denmark.

The Saami: People of the Sun and Wind

http://www.sametinget.se/english/

This is a useful site for finding information about the Saamis, the indigenous people of northern Scandinavia, and their homeland, Sápmi or Samiland. Links are provided for the history, culture, religion, and modern government of the Saamis.

A Selection of Events and Documents on the History of Finland

http://www.pp.clinet.fi/~pkr01/historia/history.html

Created and maintained by Pauli Kruhse, an administrator with the Finnish government, this site contains numerous primary sources on Finnish history from 1200 to 1944. Although the site is abundant in resources and arranged chronologically, the lack of spacing between items makes the site somewhat difficult to use.

Statistics Norway

http://www.ssb.no/en/

Statistics Norway is a government agency under the auspices of the Norwegian Ministry of Finance. Researchers can search the site by subject, by the previous fourteen days, and by an alphabetic guide. Some English paper publications are published regularly on the Web as PDF or HTML files, including discussion papers, reports, and statistical analyses. Statistics Norway also publishes the *Statistical Yearbook of Norway* online: 575 tables and 65 graphs and maps providing information about Norwegian society. New data are added daily.

Swedish Institute

http://www.si.se/E_FirstPage.cs?dirid=1445

SI is a public agency entrusted with disseminating knowledge abroad about Sweden and organizing exchanges with other countries in the spheres of culture, education, research, and public life in general. SI publishes a multitude of information in many languages, much of which is posted on the Web, including such items as an overview of Swedish history and a description of the Saami people of Sweden.

Virtual Finland

http://virtual.finland.fi/

An official Finnish Web site produced by the Ministry for Foreign Affairs of Finland, this site provides information on a wide range of topics. Click on FINFO Directory to get to a useful list of links to topics including history, general information, society and institutions, and more.

A Web History of Finland

http://ky.hkkk.fi/~k21206/finhist.html

This site was compiled by Pasi Kuoppamäki, an amateur historian, to help foreign visitors and researchers learn basic Finnish history. It provides a detailed history of Finland and numerous links to other resources for further exploration.

The World of the Vikings

http://www.pastforward.co.uk/vikings/index.html

Calling itself "the definitive guide to Viking resources on the Internet," this site provides a multitude of links to such topics as academic information, museums, mead, ships, sagas, and runes.

Chapter 12

Latin American History

H. Micheal Tarver

Metasites

H-LatAm

http://www2.h-net.msu.edu/~latam/

This site is the home page of the Latin American section of the H-Net, Humanities and Social Sciences Online project, hosted by Michigan State University. Included in the site are links to H-LatAm's discussion lists, announcements, reviews, resources, and Internet links. A good place to start an inquiry into all aspects of Latin American studies.

Internet Resources for Latin America

http://lib.nmsu.edu/subject/bord/laguia/

This site provides information and links to Internet resources. This outstanding site contains links to a variety of sources, including Latin American news sources, additional metasites, and various databases containing Latin American content. Another good place to start an inquiry into all aspects of Latin American studies. Compiled by Milly E. Molloy at New Mexico State University.

Latin American Country Links

http://www.unites.uqam.ca/gric/pays.htm

Selected links for various Latin American countries. The University of Quebec at Montreal maintains the site, although the links include English-language sites as well as French and Spanish.

Latin American Links

http://www.ozemail.com.au/~ecuapita/latam.html

This site contains links to several locations with resources relating to Latin American culture and news. There are a variety of themes, countries, and formats. Has link for expanded Spanish-language version.

Latin American Network Information Center (LANIC)

http://www.lanic.utexas.edu

Perhaps the most comprehensive Internet site for information on Latin America. The best site around to start any project dealing with Latin America.

Latin American Studies Links

http://www.unl.edu/LatAmHis/LatAmLinks.html

Numerous links to sites of concern to Latin America, including specific country resources. The site was created and maintained by DeeAnna Manning, Department of History at the University of Nebraska, Lincoln.

Latin American Subject Resources

http://www-personal.si.umich.edu/~rlwls/andes.html

This site provides information and links to various Latin American subject-based resources, ranging from bibliographies to weather. Designed to serve as a point of reference, this excellent site will direct the user to more specific sites. Compiled by Rita Wilson.

General History

The Council on Hemispheric Affairs

http://www.coha.org/

Home page of the Council on Hemispheric Affairs, an independent and nonpartisan research and information organization.

Handbook of Latin American Studies Online

http://lcweb2.loc.gov/hlas/

This is an online, searchable version of the *Handbook for Latin American Studies*, a comprehensive annotated bibliography of selected works in the social sciences and humanities. Updated monthly by the Hispanic Division of the U.S. Library of Congress. It provides abstracts and complete bibliographic information for published materials from and about Latin America on a wide range of topics in the humanities and social sciences, covering more than sixty years of scholarly literature in Latin American Studies.

Historical Text Archive

http://historicaltextarchive.com/

This site provides access to various historical documents. From the main page there are links provided for additional Web links and documents.

Latin American and Caribbean Government Documents Project

http://www.library.cornell.edu/colldev/

This excellent site, hosted by Cornell University, contains links to various Latin American sites. Topics include both government documents and statistical resources.

Latin America and the Caribbean

http://info.usaid.gov/regions/lac/

Site at the United States Agency for International Development for Latin American and Caribbean affairs. Includes links for specific countries.

Latin America Database

http://ladb.unm.edu

Provides selected newsletters, economic data on Latin America, and information about the LADB fee-based news service. Also provides access to sites for secondary educators and resources for teaching about the Americas. According to the information presented on the site, the Latin America Database is the first Internet-based news service in English about Latin America, publishing in-depth coverage of Latin American affairs since 1986. The service's professional journalists produce three weekly news bulletins about Mexico, Central America, the Caribbean, and South America. These are available on the Web site or by e-mail with a subscription.

Latin American Library, Tulane University

http://www.tulane.edu/~latinlib/lalhome.html

http://www.tulane.edu/~latinlib/revistas.html

http://www.tulane.edu/~latinlib/igc.html

These sites contain limited access and links to selected original materials from one of the premier Latin American collections in the United States. There are excellent links to electronic journals relating to Latin America, including links to the library collections of the Latin American Studies–Southeast Region Consortium.

Perry-Castañeda Library Map Collection: Maps of the Americas

http://www.lib.utexas.edu/maps/

This site provides digitized maps of the Americas, both contemporary and historical. Historical maps for Central America date as far back as the sixteenth century. The maps, which are not copyrighted, can be downloaded and copied for individual or classroom use. The University of Texas at Austin maintains the collection.

Rey L. Pratt Center

http://kennedy.byu.edu/pratt/

This site provides invaluable links to sites of interest and importance to the study of Latin America, including, but not limited to, links to over 150 Latin American newspapers and periodicals, links to other Centers for Latin American Studies worldwide, and links to course syllabi. The Rey L. Pratt Center is affiliated with the Brigham Young University History Department.

RETAnet: Resources for Teaching About the Americas

http://ladb.unm.edu/www/retanet

A Web site for secondary educators, produced by the Latin America Database at the University of New Mexico and funded by the U.S. Department of Education.

Society for Latin American Studies (UK)

http://www.slas.org.uk/

Home page of the Society for Latin American Studies with links to related Web sites.

United States Department of State: Bureau of Western Hemispheric Affairs

http://www.state.gov/p/wha/

Site of the Bureau of Western Hemispheric Affairs, which advises the secretary of state and guides the operation of the U.S. diplomatic establishment in Latin America, the Caribbean, and Canada. It includes links to press statements, country information, briefings, and current issues in the news.

Zona Latina

http://www.zonalatina.com/

This site is geared toward Latin American media and marketing. According to its headline, the site has the most extensive collection of Web resources, including newspaper links, magazine links, radio links, and television links. Updated daily.

Argentina

The sites listed below should be consulted in addition to the General Latin American History links listed above. Where especially crucial, specific pages within the general sites have been noted below.

Argentine History: General

http://www.historiadelpais.com.ar/

Rather detailed general history of Argentina. Divided into chronological segments. In Spanish only.

Argentine Ministry of Economy

http://www.mecon.gov.ar/default.htm

Home page of the ministry with links to additional important sites and databases.

Argentine Newspapers

See the News and Newspapers section of the LANIC site, http://www.lanic.utexas.edu/la/argentina/

Latin American Network Information Center: Argentina

http://www.lanic.utexas.edu/la/argentina/

Extensive listing of links dealing with Argentina. See especially the link for Academic Research Resources.

Brazil

The sites listed below should be consulted in addition to the General Latin American History links listed above. Where especially crucial, specific pages within the general sites have been noted below.

The Brazilian Institute of Geography and Statistics (IBGE)

http://www1.ibge.gov.br/english/

English version of the home page for IBGE. According to the Web site, the mission of the IBGE includes the identification and analysis of the national territory, population, economy, labor, and production.

Brazilian National Government

http://www.brasil.gov.br/

Home page of the national government of Brazil. In Portuguese.

Brazilian Newspapers

See the News and Newspapers section of the LANIC site, http://www.lanic.utexas.edu/la/brazil/

Latin American Network Information Center: Brazil

http://www.lanic.utexas.edu/la/brazil/

Extensive listing of links dealing with Brazil. See especially the link for Academic Research Resources.

Political Databases of the Americas: Brazil

http://cfdev.georgetown.edu/pdba/Countries/countries.cfm?ID=43

Link to the resources at Georgetown University relating to Brazilian politics.

Caribbean

The sites listed below should be consulted in addition to the General Latin American History links listed above. Where especially crucial, specific pages within the general sites have been noted below.

Association of Caribbean States (ACS)

http://www.acs-aec.org/

Home page of the association, with various links for additional information on the region and the association's member states. In English, Spanish, and French.

Caribbean Community and Common Market (CARICOM)

http://www.caricom.org/

Home page of the association, with various links for additional information on the association's members.

Latin American Network Information Center: Caribbean Nations

http://lanic.utexas.edu/region/caribbean.html

This site, from the University of Texas Latin American Network Information Center, provides links to specific Web sites for information on the various Caribbean nations.

Latin American Network Information Center: Caribbean Regional Resources

http://lanic.utexas.edu/la/region/caribe/

Links to Web sites for additional information on the Caribbean region, as a whole, from the University of Texas Latin American Network Information Center.

United Nations Economic Commission for Latin America and the Caribbean (CEPAL)

http://www.eclac.cl/

Home page for CEPAL, one of the five regional commissions of the United Nations.

Chile

The sites listed below should be consulted in addition to the General Latin American History links listed above. Where especially crucial, specific pages within the general sites have been noted below.

Chilean National Library of Congress

http://www.bcn.cl/

Chilean Newspapers

See the News section of the LANIC site, http://www.lanic.utexas.edu/la/chile/

Latin American Network Information Center: Chile

http://www.lanic.utexas.edu/la/chile/

Extensive listing of links dealing with Chile. See especially the link for Education and Academic Research.

National Institute of Statistics

http://www.ine.cl/

Good source of statistical information concerning Chile.

Mexico

The sites listed below should be consulted in addition to the General Latin American History links listed above. Where especially crucial, specific pages within the general sites have been noted below.

Documents on Mexican Politics

http://www.cs.unb.ca/~alopez-o/polind.html

H-Mexico Home Page

http://www.h-mexico.unam.mx/

This site is the home page of H-Mexico, a mailing list hosted by the Universidad Nacional Autónoma de Mexico. The list is an affiliate of H-Net, the Humanities and Social Sciences Online project at Michigan State University.

Latin American Network Information Center: Mexico

http://www.lanic.utexas.edu/la/mexico/

Extensive listing of links dealing with Mexico. See especially the link for Academic Research Resources.

Mexican Archives Project

http://www.lib.utexas.edu/benson/Mex_Archives/Collection_list.html

List of collections processed by the Mexican Archives Project within the Rare Books and Manuscripts Department of the Benson Latin American Collection (University of Texas) for which finding aids exist on the Web.

Mexican Ministry of Finance: Documents and Reports on Economic Policy

http://www.shcp.gob.mx/english/docs/

Various government publications from the Mexican Ministry of Finance.

Mexican Newspapers

See the News and Newspapers section of http://www.lanic.utexas.edu/la/mexico/

Mexico Connect: History Timeline

http://www.mexconnect.com/mex_/history.html

Mexico Online: History

http://www.mexonline.com/history.html

This site is the history portion of Mexico Online. The site contains information on the Mexican government, famous battles, constitutions, documents, and culture. The page also contains a link to pre-Columbian Mexican Web sites.

World Policy Institute: Recent Articles on Mexico

http://worldpolicy.org/americas/mexico/mexico.html

Selected Library Catalogs with Major Latin American Holdings

Biblioteca Nacional: Argentina

http://www.bibnal.edu.ar/

Biblioteca Nacional: Brazil

http://www.bn.br/

Biblioteca Nacional: Chile

http://www.bibliotecanacional.cl/

Biblioteca Nacional: Honduras

http://ns.sdnhon.org.hn/miembros/cultura/binah/index.htm

Biblioteca Nacional de Antropología e Historia: Mexico

http://www.arts-history.mx/biblioteca/menu.html

Biblioteca Nacional: Panama

http://www.binal.ac.pa/

Biblioteca Nacional: Peru

http://www.binape.gob.pe/

Biblioteca Nacional: Portugal
http://www.biblioteca-nacional.pt/

Biblioteca Nacional: Spain
http://www.bne.es/

Biblioteca Nacional: Venezuela
http://www.bnv.bib.ve

Duke University Libraries
http://www.lib.duke.edu/

Stanford University Libraries: Latin American and Iberian Collections
http://www-sul.stanford.edu/depts/hasrg/latinam/latamint.html

Tulane University Latin American Library
http://www.tulane.edu/~latinlib/lalhome.html

University of California at Berkeley Library
http://www.lib.berkeley.edu/

University of Florida Library
http://www.uflib.ufl.edu/

University of Illinois Latin American and Caribbean Library
http://www.library.uiuc.edu/lat/

University of Miami Library
http://www.library.miami.edu/

University of North Carolina at Chapel Hill Libraries
http://www.lib.unc.edu/

University of Texas Library Online
http://www.lib.utexas.edu/

Vanderbilt University Library
http://www.library.vanderbilt.edu/

Chapter 13

United States History

General History

Ken Kempcke

Metasites

Academic Info: United States History

http://www.academicinfo.net/histus.html

A subject directory of Internet resources tailored to a college or advanced high school audience.

American and British History Resources on the Internet

http://www.libraries.rutgers.edu/rul/rr_gateway/research_guides/history/history.shtml

Produced at Rutgers University, this site provides a structured index of scholarly resources available online. Its contents include Reference Resources, History Gateways and Text Sites, Titles by Historic Period, and Archival and Manuscript Guides.

The Digital Librarian: History ✓

http://www.digital-librarian.com/history.html

Maintained by Margaret Vail Anderson, a librarian in Cortland, New York, this page provides links to hundreds of fascinating Web resources on American history.

Index of Resources for United States History

http://www.ukans.edu/history/VL/USA/index.html

This Web page from the University of Kansas offers links to over 1,200 sites of interest to students of United States history.

Internet Public Library: United States Resources ✓

http://www.ipl.org/ref/RR/static/hum30.55.85.html

Site hosted by the University of Michigan School of Information.

Links for the History Profession

http://www.oah.org/announce/links.html

This site, maintained by the Organization of American Historians, furnishes a wide variety of links to professional societies, associations, centers, and resources.

The TimePage: American History Sites

http://www.seanet.com/Users/pamur/ahistory.html#us

A general directory with links to hundreds of U.S. history sites.

United States History ✓

http://www.tntech.edu/www/acad/hist/usa.html

A list of links to history sites arranged chronologically and by subject from the History Department at Tennessee Technological University.

Voice of the Shuttle: American History Page

http://vos.ucsb.edu/shuttle/history.html#us

Constructed by Alan Liu at the University of California, Santa Barbara, this site provides links to U.S. history resources, academic departments, conferences, journals, discussion lists, and newsgroups.

Yahoo: U.S. History

http://dir.yahoo.com/Arts/Humanities/History/U_S__History

The well-known Web directory's list of American history sites categorized by region, subject, and time period.

Regular Sites

About.com: American History

http://americanhistory.about.com/homework/americanhistory/

A guide for American history, with feature articles, Web site links, and discussion forums. Topics covered include the Civil War, colonial America, government, immigration, biographies, and more.

An Abridged History of the United States ✓

http://www.us-history.info/home.html

An online textbook produced by William M. Brinton. The text includes photographs and hypertext links to various court cases and other historical documents.

AMDOCS: Documents for the Study of American History ✓

http://history.cc.ukans.edu/carrie/docs/amdocs_index.html

Part of the Electronic Library at the University of Kansas, this site provides access to hundreds of important documents vital to the study of American history. The materials date from the fifteenth century to the present.

American History Online ✓

http://longman.awl.com/history/default.htm

From Longman Publishing Company, this bank of resources includes interactive practice tests, downloadable maps, primary sources, Web activities, and reference links.

American Memory ✓

http://lcweb2.loc.gov/ammem

American Memory is the online resource compiled by the Library of Congress's National Digital Library Program. With the participation of other libraries and archives, the program provides a gateway to rich primary source materials relating to the history and cultural developments of the United States. The site provides multimedia collections of digitized documents, photographs, maps, recorded sound, and moving pictures.

The American Presidency

http://www.grolier.com/presidents/preshome.html

A history of presidents, the presidency, politics, and related subjects. Provides the full text of articles from the *Academic American Encyclopedia* and includes an online exhibit hall, historical election results, presidential links, and a trivia quiz.

American Studies Electronic Crossroads

http://www.georgetown.edu/crossroads

Maintained at Georgetown University, ASEC contains pedagogical, scholarly, and institutional information for the international American Studies community. Includes a collection of resources and tools for use by teachers, administrators, and students as well as indexes to online courses and projects.

A Chronology of U.S. Historical Documents

http://www.law.ou.edu/ushist.html

Provides hundreds of important documents related to American history from pre-Colonial times to the present. From the University of Oklahoma Law Center.

Douglass: Archives of American Public Address ✓

http://douglass.speech.nwu.edu

Douglass is an electronic archive of American oratory and related documents. It is intended to serve general scholarship and courses in American rhetorical history at Northwestern University.

Historic Audio Archives

http://www.webcorp.com/sounds/index.htm

Audio files containing the voices of famous Americans.

Historical Text Archive

http://historicaltextarchive.com/links.php?op=viewlink&cid=6

The Historical Text Archive provides links to Native American history, U.S. historical documents, the Colonial period, the Revolution, the early republic, the nineteenth and twentieth centuries, U.S. wars, and more.

History Buff's Home Page

http://www.discovery.com/guides/history/historybuff/historybuff.html

Produced by the Newspaper Collectors Society of America, this site is devoted to press coverage of events in American history. It includes an extensive, searchable library with the categories Civil War, Baseball, Engravings, Journalism Hoaxes, Old West including Billy the Kid, Jesse James, Crime Figures such as Bonnie and Clyde and Lizzie Borden, and over a dozen other categories. The Presidential Library includes the inaugural addresses of all U.S. presidents. There is also a primer and price guide for historic newspapers.

History Matters: The U.S. [History] Survey Course on the Web ✓

http://historymatters.gmu.edu

Designed for high school and college teachers of U.S. History survey courses, this site serves as a gateway to Web resources and offers unique teaching materials, first-person primary documents, and threaded discussions on teaching U.S. history. From the American Social History Project/Center for History and the New Media.

The History Net

http://www.thehistorynet.com

Provides access to discussion forums and hundreds of full-text articles on American history from selected journals. Also includes a picture gallery and a list of events and exhibits taking place around the United States. Produced by the National Historical Society.

History's Best on PBS

http://www.pbs.org/history/american.html

Links to American history programs that have appeared on public television.

A Hypertext on American History: From the Colonial Period until Modern Times

http://odur.let.rug.nl/~usa

The main body of this hypertext comes from a number of United States Information Agency publications: *An Outline of American History*, *An Outline of the American Economy*, *An Outline of American Government*, and *An Outline of*

American Literature. The text is enriched with hypertext links to relevant documents, original essays, other Internet sites, and to other *Outlines*.

Making of America

http://www.umdl.umich.edu/moa

Making of America (MOA) is a digital library of primary sources in American social history from the antebellum period through Reconstruction. The collection is particularly strong in the subject areas of education, psychology, American history, sociology, religion, and science and technology. The collection contains approximately 1,600 books and 50,000 journal articles with nineteenth-century imprints.

The National Archives and Records Administration

http://www.nara.gov

The NARA site furnishes electronic access to historical records of government agencies, as well as an online exhibit hall, digital classroom, and genealogy page. The site also includes multimedia exhibits, research tools, and NARA publications.

The National Portrait Gallery

http://www.npg.si.edu

A searchable site that contains photographs, portraits, and biographical information on thousands of prominent Americans.

An Outline of American History

http://usinfo.state.gov/products/pubs/history/toc.htm

A book-style outline produced by the U.S. Information Agency.

Presidents of the United States

http://www.ipl.org/ref/POTUS

This resource contains background information, election results, cabinet members, notable events, and some points of interest on each of the presidents.

Links to biographies, historical documents, audio and video files, and other presidential sites are also included to enrich this site. From the Internet Public Library at the University of Michigan.

The Smithsonian Institution ✓

http://www.si.edu

The Smithsonian Institution's Web page provides access to a fascinating array of historical resources in many subject areas. Its offerings include Smithsonian collections, exhibits, photographs, and publications, as well as links to sites hosted by the institution's museums and organizations. The Smithsonian's Online Research Information System allows browsers to search the institution's various online catalogs.

Talking History

http://www.talkinghistory.org/

This site provides audio files of the weekly radio program *Talking History*, a coproduction of the History Department of the State University of New York at Albany, the History Department of Creighton University (Omaha, Nebraska), and WRPI-FM, Troy, New York.

United States Historical Census Browser ✓

http://fisher.lib.Virginia.EDU/census

The data presented here describe the people and the economy of the United States for each state and county from 1790 to 1970.

United States History

http://www.usahistory.com

Information on presidents, history trivia, statistics, wars, states, the Constitution, and more.

U.S. Diplomatic History Resources Index

http://faculty.tamu-commerce.edu/sarantakes/stuff.html

Created by Nicholas Evan Sarantakes, a professor at Texas A&M University, Commerce, this Web page is an index of resources available to historians of U.S. foreign policy. Geared toward scholars in history, political science, economics, area studies, international relations, and journalism, it provides an extensive list of historical archives and papers indexed alphabetically and by subject.

African-American History

Mary Anne Hansen

Metasites

Academic Info: African-American History: An Annotated Resource of Internet Resources on Black History

http://academicinfo.net/africanam.html

This resource links to numerous categories of quality sites on African-American history for researchers, university students, and teachers; categories include Digital Library, Important Men and Women, Civil Rights, Teaching Materials, and more. This is a valuable site for locating primary materials. The directory is created and kept updated by Academic Info, a private organization compiling subject indexes for respected Web sites on a wide range of topics.

African-American Civil War Memorial

http://afroamcivilwar.org/

The African-American Civil War Memorial site links to a variety of informative resources, including the database of soldiers and sailors created by the United States National Park Service and the Civil War Soldiers and Sailors.

African-American Literature

http://curry.edschool.virginia.edu/go/multicultural/sites/aframdocs.html

Created as part of the Multicultural Paths Project at the University of Virginia, this resource links to numerous classic African-American documents, some of which are historical in nature, and some literary.

African-American West

http://www.wsu.edu:8080/~amerstu/mw/af_ap.html#afam

Created and maintained by the American Studies Program at Washington State University, this metasite links to a variety of resources dealing with blacks in the history of the American West.

American Identities: African-American

http://xroads.virginia.edu/~YP/ethnic.html

One of several valuable African-American history sites created and maintained by the University of Virginia's American Studies Program, with links to numerous other sites, some of which are historical.

A-Z of African Studies on the Internet

http://docker.library.uwa.edu.au/~plimb/az.html

This resource lists a vast array of links to African and African-American sites. Dr. Peter Limb of the University of Western Australia, who has a Ph.D. in African Studies, created and maintains it.

Historical Text Archive: African-American History

http://historicaltextarchive.com/

This metasite, created by Don Mabry, a professor at Mississippi State University, provides links to sites in several categories: Africa, African-American, genealogy, and teaching materials, to name a few. Although Mississippi State University hosts this site, the institution takes no responsibility for it.

Social Studies School Services: Black History

http://www.socialstudies.com

This commercial site offers a variety of helpful resources, such as lesson plans, student exercises, RealVideo clips of products for sale, and product catalogs. It also offers reviews of other sites and links. A helpful site for historical information, as well as for purchasing teaching materials.

General Sites

Aboard the Underground Railroad

http://www.cr.nps.gov/nr/travel/underground/

This site introduces travelers, researchers, historians, and preservationists, to the people and places associated with the Underground Railroad. Descriptions and photographs of fifty historic places listed in the National Park Service's National Register of Historic Places are included, along with a map of the most common directions of escape taken on the Underground Railroad and maps of individual states marking the location of the historic properties.

African-American Census Schedules Online

http://www.prairiebluff.com/

A private project, this site is a compilation of the special slave and free black manuscript census data compiled by the U.S. government before the Civil War. Twenty-eight states are represented, with the rest to be added in the future. A valuable resource for genealogical research.

African-American Heritage: Our Shared History

http://www.cr.nps.gov/aahistory/

This National Park Service resource lists an extensive array of sites for learning about individual African-Americans and significant places in African-American History. Photographic archives are included.

African-American Heritage Preservation Foundation, Inc.

http://www.preservenet.cornell.edu/aahpf/homepage.htm

Created by the AAHPF, a nonprofit foundation dedicated to the preservation of African-American history, this site provides information, photographs, and archaeological reports on preservation projects with which the organization is involved.

African-American Mosaic: A Library of Congress Resource Guide for the Study of Black History and Culture

http://lcweb.loc.gov/exhibits/african/intro.html

This Library of Congress Resource Guide was created to bring the study of black history and culture to the Web community. The site includes comprehensive text and images from nearly 500 years of the black experience in the Western Hemisphere. Coverage of a variety of topics is included: Liberia, abolitionists, western migration, and documents from the Works Progress Administration, the Federal Writers Project, and the Daniel Murray Pamphlet collection, to name a few.

African-American Resources at the University of Virginia

http://etext.lib.virginia.edu/rbs/rbs16-95.html

Assembled by the Rare Books Division of the University of Virginia, this site provides the transcribed text of documents and images relating to slavery.

African-American Web Connection

http://www.aawc.com

A private hobbyist's project, this site is a gateway to Afrocentric resources for the African-American Web community and others seeking to learn about the black Web experience.

Africans in America: America's Journey through Slavery

http://www.pbs.org/wgbh/aia/home.html

A PBS production, this resource is presented in four parts, or eras: The Terrible Transformation, Revolution, Brotherly Love, and Judgment Day. Each section offers a Narrative, a Resource Bank of images, documents, stories, biographies, and commentaries, and a Teacher's Guide for using the content of the Web site and television series in U.S. history courses. This resource is problematic with regard to authority; although it was compiled in collaboration with a panel of scholars, there is scant indication of the authorship of the various writings so users may have difficulty placing the various materials in historical context.

Afro-American Sources in Virginia: A Guide to Manuscripts

http://rock.village.virginia.edu/plunkett/

Part of the Carter G. Woodson Institute Series in Black Studies, this site was jointly produced by Michael Plunkett, the University Press of Virginia, and the University of Virginia's Electronic Text Center. It allows users to search the collections of twenty-four institutions of higher education, museums, and institutes.

American Slave Narratives: An On-Line Anthology

http://xroads.virginia.edu/~hyper/wpa/wpahome.html

From 1936 to 1938, over 2,300 former slaves from across the American South were interviewed under the aegis of the Works Progress Administration. Another creation of the University of Virginia, this site provides a sample of these narratives, as well as some of the photographs taken at the time of the interviews.

Archives of African-American Music and Culture

http://www.indiana.edu/~aaamc/index.html

The AAAMC is a repository of materials covering various musical idioms and cultural expressions from the post-World War II era. A project of the Department of Afro-American Studies at Indiana University, this site gives the details of the vast collections of the AAAMC. An extensive list of links provides a jumping-off point on a variety of topics: the African diaspora, black culture and history, various musical genres, etc. An online reference service is also offered to researchers utilizing this site. A holdings search feature is slated to be added.

The Atlantic Monthly: Black History, American History

http://www.theatlantic.com/unbound/flashbks/black/blahisin.htm

The Atlantic Monthly Web site offers online access to some of the seminal essays by black writers who published in this magazine, including "Reconstruction" by Frederick Douglass and "The Strivings of the Negro People" by W.E.B. Du Bois.

Avery Research Center for African-American History and Culture

http://www.cofc.edu/~averyrsc/

The mission of the Avery Research Center for African-American History and Culture is to collect, preserve, and document the history and culture of African-Americans in Charleston and the South Carolina Low Country. Its site lists its collections, programs, and a calendar of events.

Birmingham Civil Rights Institute

http://bcri.bham.al.us/

This institute is a cultural and educational research center that promotes a comprehensive understanding of·civil rights developments in Birmingham, Alabama. The site includes exhibit information, guides to the institute archives, and information about education and public programs.

Black Pioneers of the Pacific Northwest

http://www.teleport.com/~eotic/histhome.html

Part of the Oregon Trail History Library, this site provides historical information about blacks in the Pacific Northwest, including a timeline, biographies and photographs, discussion of the state's exclusion laws, slavery, and a bibliography of recommended reading.

Charlotte Hawkins Brown Memorial

http://www.ah.dcr.state.nc.us/sections/hs/chb/chb.htm

Created by the North Carolina Division of Archives and History, this extensive site provides a history of this founder of the Palmer Memorial Institute, including online texts of documents by and about her. Comprehensive bibliographies provide references to manuscript collections, theses, and primary material about the institute, as well as the history of blacks in the South in general.

The Charlotte-Mecklenburg Story

http://www.cmstory.org/

This site is a project of the Public Library of Charlotte and Mecklenburg County, North Carolina. Numerous photographs and historical information about African-American history are available for perusal.

Civil Rights Oral Histories from Mississippi

http://www-dept.usm.edu/~mcrohb/

This site makes available online the oral histories collected by staff at the University of Southern Mississippi's Center for Oral History and Cultural Heritage and at the Tougaloo College Archives. The online texts of interviews are searchable in a variety of ways, and a bibliography is provided. The Mississippi State Legislature, the Mississippi Department of Archives and History, and the Mississippi Humanities Council funded the project.

A Deeper Shade of Black

http://www.seditionists.org/black/shade.html

A Deeper Shade of Black is one of the premier resources on African-American history, film, and literature. Created and maintained by Charles Isbell of MIT, it is an excellent resource for biographies, with well-developed accounts of figures such as Thurgood Marshall and Paul Robeson. Isbell is also the author of a related site: This Week in Black History (http://www.seditionists.org/black/thisweek.html).

Desegregation of the Armed Forces: Project Whistlestop: Harry S. Truman Digital Archives

http://www.whistlestop.org/study_collections/desegregation/large/desegregation.htm

The Truman Presidential Library has digitized Truman's Executive Order 9981 calling for desegregation, as well as other documents from the study leading up to this decision. A chronology of the Truman administration and the desegregation of the armed forces is included, along with teaching materials.

Digital Classroom of The National Archives and Records Administration (NARA)

http://www.nara.gov/education/teaching/teaching.html

This site contains reproducible copies of primary documents from the holdings of the National Archives of the United States, teaching activities correlated to the National History Standards and National Standards for Civics and Government, and cross-curricular connections. Topics available include the *Amistad* Case, Black Soldiers in the Civil War, and Jackie Robinson. Researchers can locate other historical materials about African-Americans by searching the National Archives Digital Library.

Documenting the American South

http://docsouth.unc.edu/

DAS is an electronic collection sponsored by the Academic Affairs Library at the University of North Carolina at Chapel Hill, providing access to digitized primary materials offering southern perspectives on American history and culture. Intended for researchers, teachers, and students at every educational level, the site provides a wide array of titles. DAS offers five digitization projects, including slave narratives, first-person narratives, southern literature, Confederate imprints, and materials related to the church in the black community. Books, pamphlets, and broadsides written by fugitive and former slaves prior to 1920 are being collected and posted online. It is a project funded by the National Endowment for the Humanities.

W.E.B. Du Bois Virtual University

http://members.tripod.com/~DuBois/

Created and maintained by an African-American/African Studies historian, Jennifer Wager, this extensive site details aspects of Du Bois studies: his life, legacy, and works. It provides links to online texts by and about Du Bois, a bibliography of articles and dissertations in print by and about Du Bois, and a list of Du Bois scholars.

Electronic Text Center: African-American Resources

http://etext.lib.virginia.edu/speccol.html

This site provides online access to a vast collection of original documents about nineteenth-century African-American issues, as well as numerous historical letters from the Special Collections at the University of Virginia Library. A valuable resource for primary research materials.

Exploring *Amistad* at Mystic Seaport: Race and the Boundaries of Freedom in Antebellum Maritime America

http://amistad.mysticseaport.org/main/welcome.html

This Mystic Seaport Museum site explores the *Amistad* Revolt of 1839–1842. Included are a brief narrative, a timeline, and links to other sites. Online historical documents available at the site relate to the capture of the ship and its occupants. A teacher's guide presents numerous activities to be used in the classroom; the site is a powerful teaching resource.

Faces of Science: African-Americans in the Sciences

http://www.princeton.edu/~mcbrown/display/faces.html

This site profiles African-American men and women who have contributed to the advancement of science and engineering; included is a discussion of the present and future of African-Americans in the sciences. The biographies are grouped by scientific discipline and accompanied by an examination of the percentages of doctorates granted to African-Americans in each area of the sciences. Statistical and demographic data from the National Science Foundation are included in easy-to-read graphical format. Researchers will also find links to other related sites.

John Hope Franklin Collection of African and African-American Documentation

http://scriptorium.lib.duke.edu/franklin/collections.html

This site provides online finding aids, subject guides, and digitized materials from selected collections of the Rare Book, Manuscript, and Special Collections Library at Duke University.

Freedmen and Southern Society Project

http://www.inform.umd.edu/ARHU/Depts/History/Freedman/home.html

The editors of this project have selected over 50,000 documents from the National Archives of the United States that they are presently transcribing, organizing, annotating, and presenting online to explain the transition of blacks from slavery to freedom between the beginning of the Civil War in 1861 and the beginning of Radical Reconstruction in 1867. The project is supported by the University of Maryland and by grants from the National Historical Publications and Records Commission and the National Endowment for the Humanities.

Harlem 1900–1940: An African American Community

http://www.si.umich.edu/CHICO/Harlem

Created at the School of Information at the University of Michigan as part of its Cultural Heritage Initiatives for Community Outreach, this site is based on *Harlem: 1900–1940* originally published in 1991 by the Schomburg Center for Research in Black Culture at the New York Public Library. It includes digitized texts and photographs, along with suggestions for teachers using the materials and links to related sites.

Inventory of African-American Historical and Cultural Resources in Maryland

http://www.sailor.lib.md.us/docs/af_am/af_am.html

This site lists by count the structures, historical sites, and collections of materials in Maryland that relate to African-American history. The Maryland Commission on African-American History and Culture supports the project.

The King Center

http://www.thekingcenter.com

The official MLK historical site, this resource provides information both on Martin Luther King, Jr. and on Coretta Scott King, who established the center in 1968 as a living memorial dedicated to the preservation and advancement of the work of her late husband.

Martin Luther King, Jr.

http://www.seattletimes.com/mlk/index.html

Produced by the *Seattle Times*, this site includes editorials, interviews, news columns, and photographs from the newspaper. King is presented in historical context; included are photographs from the civil rights movement. The Study Guide is intended to prompt further discussion about King's life and legacy, in particular how society has or has not changed because of civil rights.

Martin Luther King, Jr. Papers Project of Stanford University

http://www.stanford.edu/group/King/

This project is an effort to assemble and disseminate historical information concerning Martin Luther King, Jr. and the social movements in which he participated. Begun by the King Center for Nonviolent Social Change, the King Papers Project is one of only a few major research ventures that focuses on an individual African-American. Coretta Scott King, founder and president of the King Center, invited Stanford University historian Clayborne Carson to become the project's director and senior editor in 1985. As a result, the project became a cooperative venture of Stanford University, the King Center, and the King estate.

Library Catalogs of African-American Collections

http://www.library.cornell.edu/africana/Library/Catalogs.html

Cornell University Library provides this selected list of libraries that have separate Black Studies collections. In addition to the separate collections, these institutions also maintain integrated general collections that include Black Studies materials.

Montgomery Bus Boycott Home Page

http://socsci.colorado.edu/~jonesem/montgomery.html

Created by a graduate student at the University of Colorado at Boulder, this site provides a chronology and summary of the Montgomery bus boycott, a plan for teaching about the boycott, and numerous essays and links to related sites.

Museum of African Slavery

http://jhunix.hcf.jhu.edu/~plarson/smuseum/welcome.htm

The Museum of African Slavery was created primarily by Pier M. Larson, a professor of African history at The Johns Hopkins University, for primary and secondary students and their teachers. The museum's focus is on the experiences of enslavement in the Atlantic system, Africa and the Americas.

Museum of Afro-American History, Boston

http://www.afroammuseum.org/

This site provides links to historical resources in the Boston area and beyond, including links to numerous other African-American museums, exhibits, and organizations.

National Civil Rights Museum

http://sevier.net/civilrights/

This site's purpose is to support the National Civil Rights Museum's mission to educate and preserve the history of the civil rights movement. Located at the Lorraine Motel, where Dr. Martin Luther King, Jr. was assassinated, the museum houses interactive exhibits that trace the beginnings of the civil rights struggle.

Negro League Baseball Archive

http://www.negroleaguebaseball.com/

This commercial site includes a multitude of information on the history of the Negro Leagues, including team histories and player profiles.

Resources in Black Studies

http://www.library.ucsb.edu/subj/black.html

Created and maintained by the University of California Santa Barbara Library, this site provides links to numerous historical texts and documents, other research institutions focusing on Black Studies, discussion forums, and more.

Schomberg Collection of New York Public Library

http://digital.nypl.org/browse.htm

The New York Public Library's Schomberg Collection is a major research institution for the study of the history and culture of peoples of African descent. This site provides links to digitized collections of photographs and other materials and finding aids to the various collections.

This Is Our War

http://www.afroam.org/history/OurWar/intro.html

Part of the Afro-Americ@ site, this page presents articles written by black war correspondents during World War II for the *Baltimore Afro-American*. Other significant historical resources can also be found at the Afro-Americ@ site (http://www.afroam.org/).

Voices of the Civil Rights Era

http://www.webcorp.com/civilrights/index.htm

Voices of the Civil Rights Era is an audio archive sponsored by Webcorp. It includes speeches made by a variety of historical figures: Malcolm X, Martin Luther King, Jr., and John F. Kennedy.

John H. White: Portrait of Black Chicago

http://www.nara.gov/exhall/americanimage/chicago/white1.html

This National Archives and Records Administration exhibit chronicles photographer John H. White's work photographing Chicago, especially the city's African-American community. White took the photographs for the Environmental Protection Agency's DOCUMERICA project in 1973 and 1974.

Women and Social Movements in the United States

http://womhist.binghamton.edu/index.html

This University of New York, Binghamton, site contains about twenty sets of historical documents dealing with African-American women. Compiled for secondary and higher education studies, this site contains materials by and about black women seldom found elsewhere. The National Endowment for the Humanities funded this project.

Writing Black

http://www.keele.ac.uk/depts/as/Literature/amlit.black.html

Created and maintained at the School of American Studies, Keele University, U.K., Writing Black links to essays, books, and poems about African-American history and culture in the United States up to the present day. Prominent writers include W.E.B. Du Bois, Booker T. Washington, Toni Morrison, and Maya Angelou, to name a few.

Native American History
J. Kelly Robison

General Sites

American Indian Studies

http://www.csulb.edu/projects/ais/

Created by Troy Johnson at California State University, Long Beach. Johnson maintains a useful list of links to Native American sites. Also contains a large number of images of Native Americans from precontact to the present.

Bureau of Indian Affairs, U.S. Department of the Interior

http://www.doi.gov/bureau-indian-affairs.html

The Bureau of Indian Affairs has information on the tribes, tribal governments, some history, treaties, and documents on current affairs in Native America. The documents make this site important for researchers and teachers delving into the current situation among Native Americans.

First Nations Site

http://www.dickshovel.com/www.html

A very political site maintained by Jordan S. Dill. However, the list of offsite links makes this site a good resource. The onsite links are more generally rants against the system than anything of value.

Images of Native America: From Columbus to Carlisle

http://www.lehigh.edu/~ejg1/natmain.html

Professor Edward J. Gallagher's students at Lehigh University created a series of online essays on how Europeans and Euro-Americans imagined native peoples. The essays are nicely written and contain links to related sites.

MAPS: GIS Windows on Native Lands, Current Places, and History

http://indy4.fdl.cc.mn.us/~isk/maps/mapmenu.html

Paula Giese's site that uses client-side image maps as the gateway to articles on Native American history and culture from precontact to the present. A nice resource for K-12.

Native American Documents Project

http://www.csusm.edu/projects/nadp/nadp.htm

Located at California State University at San Marcos, this site contains primary material related to Allotment, Indian Commissioner Reports of 1871, and the Rogue River War and Siletz Reservation.

Native American Sites

http://www.nativeculture.com/lisamitten/indians.html

A very nice list of sites pertaining to Native America. The topically categorized list contains links to Indian nation Web sites, organizations, and upcoming events. Maintained by Lisa Mitten at the University of Pittsburgh.

NativeWeb

http://www.nativeweb.org/

An extensive collection of links and articles—not just historical, but also political, legal, and social—both for and about indigenous peoples in the Americas. Includes search engines, message boards, and lists of Native events. An excellent site from which to begin research.

On This Date in North American Indian History

http://americanindian.net/

Phil Konstantine's Native American history and culture Web site seems, at first glance, an amateurish attempt by a history buff to have something on the Web. However, despite the somewhat cheesy "Moons," On This Date pages, and other such things, Konstantine has an incredible links page with over 8,000 links. Even On This Date is well worth clicking through.

Perspectives of the Smithsonian: Native American Resources

http://www.si.edu/resource/faq/nmai/start.htm

An excellent starting place for information on Native American history and culture. Includes online Smithsonian exhibits, resources for teachers, parents and students, and an extensive list of readings for various topics. No links, but this site in itself is worth looking into.

Topical Sites

The Avalon Project: Relations Between the United States and Native Americans

http://www.yale.edu/lawweb/avalon/natamer.htm

A superb collection of primary documents relating to Native peoples compiled and digitized by the Yale Law School Avalon Project. The main focus of this site is treaties between the United States government and Native groups. The site also includes statutes, presidential addresses, and a few court cases involving Natives.

The Aztec Calendar

http://www.azteccalendar.com

Done by Rene Voorburg, this nicely done site examines the Aztec calendar. The opening screen depicts the current date in Aztec glyphs. Also contains a calculator that converts any date to its Aztec equivalent. The introduction is a brief but thorough essay on the calendar and its meaning.

Cahokia Mounds State Historic Site

http://medicine.wustl.edu/~mckinney/cahokia/cahokia.html

Run by the Illinois Historic Preservation Agency, Cahokia is the location of a pre-European city across the river from St. Louis, Missouri. The site lists upcoming events at the park and some information on the archaeology and history of Cahokia. This site seems to be a continual work in progress since it has very few new items posted within the past two years.

Native American Authors

http://www.ipl.org/ref/native/

Part of the Internet Public Library, this section of the larger site can be browsed by author, title, or tribal affiliation. There is no search engine or subject browsing, however. Individual title "cards" contain only basic bibliographic information.

Sipapu: The Anasazi Emergence into the Cyber World

http://sipapu.ucsb.edu/

This site not only begs the reader to explore Anasazi architecture and archeology, but also asks for contributions. The research section contains a database of Chaco outliers and a bibliography of related print works. It also links to several scholarly papers on the Anasazi. One interesting item is a wonderful little toy that allows 360-degree viewing of the Great Kiva of Chetro Ketl at Chaco Canyon National Monument. Created by John Kanter at the University of California at Santa Barbara.

Colonial American History

Edward Ragan, Scott A. Merriman, and Dennis A. Trinkle

Metasites

From Revolution to Reconstruction ✓

http://odur.let.rug.nl/~usa/usa.htm

This metasite, maintained by the Arts Faculty of the University of Groningen, Netherlands, is a massive resource for all aspects of American history. The site is divided into five general sections: outlines, essays, documents, biographies, and presidents. This site is organized around several United States Information Agency publications: *An Outline of American History*, *An Outline of the American Economy*, *An Outline of American Government*, and *An Outline of American Literature*. While the text of these *Outlines* has not been changed, they have been enriched with hypertext links to relevant documents, original essays, and other Internet sites. Currently this site contains over 3,000 relevant HTML documents.

Museums, Libraries, Historical Societies, and Online Organizations

Colonial Williamsburg

http://www.history.org/

The official Web site for Colonial Williamsburg, one of the most extensive historical reconstructions in the United States. The well-illustrated site offers tourist information; educational resources; a Colonial dateline; a historical glossary of names, places, and events in Colonial Williamsburg; photos of buildings and people; articles from the *Colonial Williamsburg Journal*, and an extensive section on Colonial lifestyles.

Common-place ✓

http://www.common-place.org/

Common-place is sponsored by the American Antiquarian Society and the Gilder Lehrman Institute of American History. It bills itself as a "common place for exploring and exchanging ideas about early American history and culture" in a way that is "a bit friendlier than a scholarly journal, a bit more scholarly than a popular magazine." Published quarterly, this online journal includes essays, books reviews, roundtable discussions, and an open forum for commenting on articles that appear in *Common-place*.

H-OIEACH Discussion Network

http://www.h-net.msu.edu/~ieahcweb/

This is the Web site of the H-OIEACH discussion list, which is sponsored by the Omohundro Institute of Early American History and Culture (OIEACH). Affiliated with H-Net, this group focuses on Colonial and Early American history. Its Web pages contain information about the discussion list and allow one to subscribe. They also include calls for papers, conference announcements, bibliographies, book reviews, articles, and links to related sites, including the Omohundro Institute.

Jamestown Rediscovery Project

http://www.apva.org/jr.html

The Jamestown Rediscovery Project, sponsored by the Association for the Preservation of Virginia Antiquities (APVA), is a ten-year comprehensive excavation of Jamestown that began in 1994. This site offers photographs and progress reports on the project to date, two online exhibits, and plans for the future.

The Library of Virginia Digital Library Program ✓

http://www.lva.lib.va.us/dlp/index.htm

The Library of Virginia's Digital Library Program is an internationally recognized effort to preserve, digitize, and provide access to significant archival and library collections. Users can search court records (indexes and guides); births, deaths, marriages, wills, and Bible records; genealogy and biography databases; Virginia military records; newspaper and periodical databases and indexes; photograph collections; business records; and maps, gazetteers, and geographical resources. Perhaps the most stunning accomplishment is the Land Office Patents and Grants Database, which is searchable by keyword and provides links to scanned copies of the original Virginia land patents. To date, the Digital Library Program has "digitized more than 2.2 million original documents, photographs, and maps, and produced more than 80 fully-searchable databases, indexes, and electronic finding aids." All in all, this is a remarkable tool for Virginia historians and genealogists.

Plimoth-on-Web: Plimoth Plantation's Web Site

http://www.plimoth.org/Museum/Pilgrim_Village/1627.htm

The official Web site for the living history museum of seventeenth-century Plymouth. Like the living history museum, the Web site brings 1627 Plimoth back to life.

Society of Early Americanists (SEA) Home Page

http://www.hnet.uci.edu/mclark/seapage.htm

The SEA aims to further the exchange of ideas and information among scholars of various disciplines who study the literature and culture of America up to approximately 1800. The society publishes a newsletter, operates an electronic bulletin board, and maintains the Web site, which contains an excellent list of links on Colonial and Early American history.

Topical Histories

1492: An Ongoing Voyage

http://metalab.unc.edu/expo/1492.exhibit/Intro.html

1492: An Ongoing Voyage is an electronic exhibit of the Library of Congress. The site weaves images and text to explore what life was like in pre- and post-Columbian Europe, Africa, and the Americas. The site examines the effect that the discovery of America had on each continent and stresses the dark elements of colonization. There are excellent maps, documents, artwork, and supporting text.

Iroquois Oral Traditions

http://www.indians.org/welker/iroqoral.htm

This Web site is part of the American Indian Heritage Foundation's Indigenous Peoples Literature page. The tradition of De-Ka-Nah-Wi-Da and Hiawatha is recounted here along with over twenty other Iroquoian stories about the people of the longhouse and their place in the world. Many of these stories were translated into English and recorded in the late nineteenth and early twentieth centuries.

Salem Witch Museum

http://www.salemwitchmuseum.com/

This site primarily presents travel information, but it also offers an interactive FAQ section on witch trials and local history. Other resources are being added rapidly.

1755: The French and Indian War Home Page

http://web.syr.edu/~laroux/

Created by Larry Laroux, a professional writer, this site serves as a prologue to Laroux's forthcoming book *White Coats*, which will examine the soldiers who fought in the French and Indian War of 1755. The site is presently under construction, but Laroux eventually aims to include histories of important battles, a list of French soldiers who fought in the war, and other statistical records. The site already contains a brief narrative account of the war, along with some interesting information and trivia.

The Thanksgiving Tradition

http://www.plimoth.org/Library/Thanksgiving/thanksgi.htm

The research, education, and public relations departments at Plimouth Plantation's Living History Museum of 17th-Century Plymouth present a cornucopia of information on the American Thanksgiving tradition. Included at this site are relevant primary documents, essays, a sample menu, and a list of alternate claimants for the "first Thanksgiving."

Virtual Jamestown: Jamestown and the Virginia Experiment

http://www.iath.virginia.edu/vcdh/jamestown/

Created by Crandal Shifflett, professor of history at Virginia Tech, the "Virtual Jamestown Archive is a digital research, teaching, and learning project that explores the legacies of the Jamestown settlement." Included are links to primary documents; digitized, 360-degree reconstructions of the fort; discussion of Indian, African, and English life around Jamestown; and timelines that trace the history of the New World. This site has been selected as a top humanities site and included in the NEH EDSITEment Project. If you cannot go to Jamestown in person, this is the next best thing.

Walking Tour of Plymouth Plantation

http://archnet.uconn.edu/topical/historic/plimoth/plimoth.html

This site includes photographs and a narrative description of the living museum at Plymouth Plantation. It addresses many different aspects of early seventeenth-century life in New England, such as housing, cooking, clothing, and tools.

Wampum: Treaties, Sacred Records

http://www.kstrom.net/isk/art/beads/wampum.html

This site offers information on the construction and meaning of wampum to native America. Included are images and descriptions along with links that provide more detail.

Documents and Images

American Colonist's Library: A Treasury of Primary Documents ✓

http://www.universitylake.org/primarysources.html

Compiled by Richard Gardiner, a history instructor at University Lake School (Hartland, Wisconsin), the American Colonist's Library is a comprehensive gateway to the early American primary source documents that are currently available online. Included in the list are links to historical sources that influenced American colonists, online collections of the work of major early American political leaders, the text of the Acts of Parliament concerning the American Colonies, numerous American Revolution military documents, and much more. The hundreds of documents are grouped chronologically from 500 B.C.E. to 1800 C.E. As the site boasts, "if it isn't here, it probably is not available online anywhere."

American Historical Images on File: The Native American Experience

http://www.csulb.edu/projects/ais/nae/

Professor Troy Johnson of California State University, Long Beach, developed this collection of historical images of native peoples. The images span the chronological range of native America, from paleo-Indians to the present. They are presented here with full permission of Facts on File, Inc., but take note of the copyright details before you use them for your own purposes.

A Briefe and True Report of the New Found Land of Virginia

http://wsrv.clas.virginia.edu/~msk5d/hariot/main.html

This Web site includes both facsimiles and transcriptions of the 1588 quarto edition and the 1590 folio edition of Thomas Hariot's *A Briefe and True Report of the New Found Land of Virginia*, "the first original book in English relating to what is now America, written by one of the first Englishmen to attempt new world colonization." Only six copies of the 1588 edition are known to exist, so this site is an important resource for those interested in early English settlement of North America.

Columbus and the Age of Discovery ✓

http://columbus.millersv.edu/~columbus

A searchable database of over 1,100 text articles pertaining to Columbus and themes of discovery and encounter. The site, which has unrestricted access, was built by the History Department of Millersville University of Pennsylvania in conjunction with the U.S. Christopher Columbus Quincentenary Jubilee Commission of 1992.

Theodore De Bry Copper Plate Engravings

http://www.csulb.edu/projects/ais/woodcuts/

This collection of historical images of native peoples is the digitized versions of copper plate engravings made by the Flemish engraver and publisher Theodore de Bry. The engravings are based on the watercolor paintings of the sixteenth-century English explorer John White. Professor Troy Johnson of California State University, Long Beach, developed the site.

Early America

http://earlyamerica.com/earlyamerica/index.html

The focus of Early America is primary source material from eighteenth century America. The site is the public access branch of the commercial American Digital Library <http://www.earlyamerica.com/digital-library/>, which sells reproductions of hundreds of early American documents from the Keigwin and Mathews Collection of eighteenth- and nineteenth-century historical documents, as well as images, maps, and other materials.

The Jesuit Relations and Allied Documents: 1610 to 1791

http://puffin.creighton.edu/jesuit/relations/

This impressive undertaking is the work of Rev. Raymond A. Bucko, a Jesuit priest and professor of anthropology at Creighton University, and Thom Mentrak, a historical interpreter at the Ste. Marie Among the Iroquois Museum in Syracuse, New York. This site contains the scanned and transcribed version of the seventy-one-volume edition edited by Reuben Gold Thwait in the late nineteenth century. *The Jesuit Relations* began as private reports between the Jesuit missionaries in New France and their superiors in Paris. The Jesuits made extensive reports on the native peoples they encountered, making this source a must for serious research into Huron and Iroquoian culture in the seventeenth century.

The Leslie Brock Center for the Study of Colonial Currency

http://www.virginia.edu/~econ/brock.html

This Web site takes some of the confusion out of understanding and working with Colonial currencies. Included here are eighteenth-century pamphlets and other contemporary writings that relate to currency, as well as more recent articles on the various colonies and currencies and links to additional resources covering currency rates and monetary history.

Notes on the State of Virginia

http://etext.lib.virginia.edu/toc/modeng/public/JefVirg.html

Constructed as a series of answers to questions posed by foreign observers, Jefferson's *Notes*, first published in 1787, provide a unique description of the natural and human landscapes of Virginia in the late eighteenth century. This e-text version is sponsored by the University of Virginia Library Electronic Text Center.

The Plymouth Colony Archive Project at the University of Virginia

http://www.people.virginia.edu/~jfd3a/

The Plymouth Colony Archive presents a collection of searchable texts, including seminar analysis of various topics, biographical profiles of selected colonists, probate inventories, wills, *Glossary and Notes on Plymouth Colony*, and *Vernacular House Forms in Seventeenth-Century Plymouth Colony: An Analysis of Evidence from the Plymouth Colony Room-by-Room Probate Inventories 1633–85*, by Patricia E. Scott Deetz and James Deetz. The site itself is maintained by the Deetzes, pioneers in material culture studies.

American Revolution

Robert M.S. McDonald

Metasites

The American Revolution: National Discussions of Our Revolutionary Origins

http://revolution.h-net.msu.edu/intro.html

This metasite, hosted by the NEH-sponsored H-NET, makes available authoritative essays, archives of interesting discussions, and a bibliography of printed sources on the Revolution. For an extensive array of external links, refer to the section entitled Resources.

Eighteenth-Century Resources

http://andromeda.rutgers.edu/~jlynch/18th

Compiled by Rutgers University English professor Jack Lynch, this metasite of links to Web pages "that focus on the (very long) eighteenth century" and home pages of scholars researching eighteenth-century topics enables students of the American Revolutionary era to view it from a global (and especially trans-Atlantic Enlightenment) perspective. General categories include art and architecture, history, music, philosophy, religion and theology, science and mathematics, and professional journals.

HistoryOnline: American Revolution

http://www.jacksonesd.k12.or.us/k12projects/jimperry/revolution.html

Maintained by the Jackson (Oregon) Education Service District, this metasite provides more than two dozen links. The emphasis here is on colorful sites geared toward students and the general public.

General Sites

American Revolutionary War Timeline: People, Events, Documents

http://www.ilt.columbia.edu/k12/history/timeline.html

Here, Columbia University's Institute for Learning Technologies provides internal links to biographical sketches, historical narratives, and important documents (such as the Albany Plan of Union, the Stamp Act Congress Resolutions, and John Adams's *Thoughts on Government*). Intended for K-12 teachers and students, this site supplies a wealth of information useful to everyone.

The Avalon Project at the Yale Law School: 18th Century Documents

http://www.yale.edu/lawweb/avalon/18th.htm

This reliable, user-friendly site provides unabridged transcriptions of dozens of important Revolutionary era documents, including Colonial charters, state constitutions, Indian treaties, and the Virginia Declaration of Rights. There is also a keyword-searchable version of *The Federalist Papers*. This site is an extraordinary resource for scholars of early American statecraft.

Battles of the American Revolutionary War

http://www.ilt.columbia.edu/k12/history/aha/battles.html

Maintained by Columbia University's Institute for Learning Technologies, this site links users to information on battles and fortifications that figured prominently in the War for Independence. Brief descriptions place these flash points within the context of larger campaigns, describe strategy and important maneuvers, and estimate casualties. Historic illustrations round out the presentations. This site should aid instructors who seek abbreviated but competent descriptions of the military conflict.

Boston National Historical Park: The Freedom Trail

http://www.nps.gov/bost/ftrail.htm

For decades tourists have flocked to Boston's Freedom Trail, the three-mile stretch of historic sites from the Massachusetts State House to Bunker Hill. Now surfers of the Web can also enjoy an enlightening foray into America's Revolutionary past. Valuable information about the significance of the Old South Meeting House, Faneuil Hall, the Old North Church, and the *USS Constitution* gives depth to any student's understanding of the heady, early days of the War for Independence and hints at how urban areas constitute especially fertile fields for political unrest.

Center for Military History: War of American Independence

http://www.army.mil/cmh-pg/online/WAI.htm

This site features several useful resources. Among them is Robert K. Wright, Jr.'s *The Continental Army*, a workmanlike text that recounts the contributions of nonmilitia, nonregular state troops. This site also includes bibliographies and traces the lineages of the units of the Continental Army.

Colonial Williamsburg

http://www.history.org

The official home page of Colonial Williamsburg provides teachers and students with a vivid introduction to the recreated eighteenth-century Virginia capital and the world of imperial Anglo-America. The site offers information on Colonial and Revolutionary Williamsburg's most notable people, places, and events. Teachers will find information on electronic field trips, the Colonial Williamsburg Teacher Institute, and lesson plans for topics such as "Colonial Reaction to the Stamp Act" and "Travel in the 18th Century."

Declaring Independence: Drafting the Documents

http://lcweb.loc.gov/exhibits/declara/declara1.html

An online exhibit on the creation of the Declaration of Independence, this Library of Congress–sponsored site features photographs and transcriptions of Thomas Jefferson's drafts of the 1776 document. In addition, it showcases eighteenth-century printed versions of the text and historic illustrations of its creation and ratification. Brief introductions provide context for these materials. Composition teachers will join history instructors in making use of this site, for it provides a compelling case study of the process of writing and revision.

Documents from the Continental Congress and the Constitutional Convention, 1774–1789

http://lcweb2.loc.gov/ammem/bdsds/bdsdhome.html

Sponsored by the Library of Congress, this invaluable page contains 274 keyword-searchable documents relating to the Continental Congress and the ratification of the Constitution. The texts include treaties, resolutions, committee reports, and extracts from the Congress's journals. This site greatly expedites serious research on Revolutionary era politics.

The Early America Review

http://earlyamerica.com/review

This online historical journal, published since 1996, includes both book reviews and articles (such as "Jefferson and His Daughters," "The Enigma of Benedict Arnold," and "A Conversation with Alan Taylor"). The essays, most of which are footnoted, should interest wide audiences. Accessible and elegantly presented, this is a worthwhile site.

The Heath Anthology of American Literature

http://www.georgetown.edu/bassr/heath/index.html

The Syllabus Builder, listed under Instructor Resources, provides writings by Mercy Otis Warren, Benjamin Franklin, J. Hector St. John de Crèvecoeur, Thomas Paine, John Adams, Thomas Jefferson, Philip Freneau, Timothy Dwight, Phillis Wheatley, Joel Barlow, and other Independence era literati. This virtual library of essential texts, which should ably bolster the resources available to educators at smaller institutions, puts early American classics within reach of everyone.

Historic Mount Vernon: The Home of Our First President, George Washington

http://www.mountvernon.org

Maintained by the curators of George Washington's Potomac River estate, this site provides information about the man who commanded the Continental Army and served as the first U.S. president; in addition, it situates his house within the context of a slave-based plantation labor system. Students of the Revolution will appreciate the authoritative biographical information on Washington, along with the virtual tour of the grounds of Mount Vernon, the pages on George Washington and Slavery, and the narrated image gallery of paintings relating to Washington. A rudimentary George Washington Quiz will challenge children in the primary grades.

Thomas Jefferson: A Film by Ken Burns

http://www.pbs.org/jefferson

The Public Broadcasting System inaugurated this Web site to complement its landmark 1997 documentary series *Thomas Jefferson*, a three-hour televised account (now available on videotape) produced by Ken Burns. Like the film, this site chronicles the multifaceted life of the author of the Declaration of

Independence. Student study sheets on political, religious, social, intellectual, and personal freedom and an archive of Jefferson's writings will especially interest educators, as will "Does Jefferson Matter?," an online forum of noted scholars who assess the role of Jefferson (and other "great men") in shaping history.

Thomas Jefferson Online Resources at the University of Virginia

http://etext.virginia.edu/jefferson

The University of Virginia's Electronic Text Center sponsors this extraordinarily useful site concerning its venerable founder. More than 1,700 documents written by Jefferson are accessible, all of them keyword searchable. In addition, electronic versions of Frank Shuffelton's invaluable annotated bibliographies of books and articles about Jefferson (*Thomas Jefferson: A Comprehensive, Annotated Bibliography of Writings about Him, 1826–1980* [New York: Garland Publishing, 1983] and *Thomas Jefferson, 1981–1990: An Annotated Bibliography* [New York: Garland Publishing, 1992]) are also available, sources that truly supersede their printed versions because they, too, are keyword searchable. This is the essential site for individuals seeking to start research on a Jefferson topic.

Liberty! The American Revolution

http://www.pbs.org/ktca/liberty

This Web site accompanied the 1997 televised PBS documentary (now available on videotape) *Liberty!*, a six-hour account of the causes, course, and consequences of the American Revolution. One especially useful feature is the Chronicle of the Revolution, an illustrated narrative of the independence movement's signal events. This chronological account, which provides a good overview of the era, is supplemented by a number of internal links that give readers more in-depth information about selected topics (such as the Boston Tea Party and Thomas Hutchinson). A timeline, bibliography, index, and listing of external links round out the very useful presentation.

Loyalist, British Songs and Poetry of the American Revolution

http://www.erols.com/candidus/music.htm

The texts of one dozen Loyalist songs and poems, many of them quite obscure, appear on this attractive page. A number of links to other sites focusing on Loyalism can be found here as well.

Monticello: The Home of Thomas Jefferson

http://www.monticello.org

Sponsored by the Thomas Jefferson Memorial Foundation, this exceptional, award-winning site focuses on America's third president and life at his mountaintop home, Monticello. Notable features include A Day in the Life, a richly illustrated narrative, complete with fascinating internal links, of Jefferson's waking moments during a typical day at his plantation. The site includes a clickable index of reports on various subjects prepared by Monticello's research staff; Ask Thomas Jefferson invites youngsters to correspond with the famous Virginian (students' questions and the replies of "Jefferson" are posted on a topically indexed archive). The site also features fresh information on Sally Hemings, the slave with whom—recent DNA testing suggests—Jefferson fathered at least one child. A chronicle of interviews with descendants of Monticello slaves provides a glimpse into the lives of members of Jefferson's extended plantation "family." Teachers will discover online lesson plans that provide technical and pedagogical suggestions for optimizing classroom use of the site.

National Archives and Records Administration: Charters of Freedom

http://www.nara.gov/exhall/charters/charters.html

This online exhibit features materials relating to the Declaration of Independence, the Constitution, and the Bill of Rights. Sponsored by the National Archives, the custodian for these seminal documents, this site enables visitors to view exceptionally clear images of these texts' early manuscript and printed versions; it also includes authoritative essays that consider them in various contexts. See, for example, "The Declaration of Independence: A History," which discusses the drafting and ratification of the Declaration, as well as how different generations treated the physical document as it evolved from state paper to national icon.

Omohundro Institute of Early American History and Culture

http://www.wm.edu/oieahc

Cosponsored by the College of William and Mary and the Colonial Williamsburg Foundation, the Omohundro Institute of Early American History and Culture publishes the highly regarded *William and Mary Quarterly (WMQ)*, a journal of American history prior to 1815. Here, on its official Web site, individuals may browse recent tables of contents from the *WMQ*, see news of upcoming conferences and colloquia, and read *Uncommon Sense*, the institute's newsletter.

Thomas Paine National Historical Association

http://www.mediapro.net/cdadesign/paine

The home page of the Thomas Paine National Historical Association is a good starting point for basic research on the important trans-Atlantic radical whose 1776 *Common Sense* pushed American colonists toward revolution. The site includes information about his life and his New Rochelle, New York home (where the association is based), as well as links to full-text versions of his writings and other Paine-related Web pages.

Philadelphia's Historic Mile

http://www.ushistory.org/tour/index.html

Maintained by the Independence Hall Association, this site allows people in far-flung locales to tour Philadelphia's most historic Revolutionary landmarks. Stops include the old Pennsylvania State House (Independence Hall), where the Continental Congress and Constitutional Convention met; City Tavern; the first and second Bank of the United States; the Liberty Bell; Christ Church; and Franklin Court. Richly illustrated and competently narrated, the tour provides a tantalizing glimpse of not only a young nation's political life but also an old city's streetscape.

From Revolution to Reconstruction: A Hypertext on American History

http://odur.let.rug.nl/~usa/usa.htm

This extraordinarily useful site provides a wealth of reliable information on the American Revolutionary period. Hosted by the University of Groningen in the Netherlands, this page features numerous full-text documents, including thirty written between the 1763 Peace of Paris and the 1783 Treaty of Paris. Internal links to brief biographies of important contributors to the Independence movement appear here as well. While the documents, supplied by the U.S. Information Agency, are reliably transcribed, a few of the biographical sketches, authored by nonnative English speakers, contain spelling and grammatical errors. Quibbles aside, students and teachers of early American history will frequently resort to this massive resource.

Betsy Ross Home Page

http://www.ushistory.org/betsy/index.html

This interesting Web site, sponsored by Philadelphia's Betsy Ross House and the Independence Hall Association, includes a picture gallery of historic American flags, a brief biography of upholsterer/flagmaker Betsy Ross, and information about flag trivia and etiquette. It also includes a section, arranged in a point-counterpoint format, arguing that the story of Ross sewing the first U.S. flag (described by some as a myth) is, in reality, accurate. As a result, this site might be used as a springboard for a discussion on standards of historical evidence and the development of historical memory.

U.S. Army Military History Institute

http://carlisle-www.army.mil/usamhi

Sponsored by the U.S. Army War College at Carlisle, Pennsylvania, the Military History Institute allows historians of the Revolution to use electronic bibliographical databases to search, with keywords, a variety of important primary and secondary sources.

Virtual Marching Tour of the American Revolution

http://www.ushistory.org/march/people.htm

Maintained by Philadelphia's Independence Hall Association, this site, still under construction, currently focuses on the Philadelphia Campaign of 1777. From the landing of British troops at Head of Elk, Maryland, to Brandywine, Germantown, Fort Mifflin, and Valley Forge, this virtual marching tour includes a reliable narrative of events. Photographs, illustrations, and music supplement the text. Several dozen links connect to authoritative, mostly professionally maintained Web pages, from the National Trust for Historic Preservation and the Maryland State Archives to the Friends of the Saratoga Battlefield.

George Washington Papers Home Page

http://www.virginia.edu/gwpapers

The official home page of *The Papers of George Washington*, a documentary editing project based for thirty years at the University of Virginia, makes selected documents relating to Washington's long public career available as keyword-searchable electronic texts. Internal links also provide information about the Washington papers project and staff.

The World of Benjamin Franklin

http://sln.fi.edu/franklin

Sponsored by the Franklin Institute, this site provides a fascinating introduction to Benjamin Franklin for elementary school students. A brief biography and discussions of Franklin as scientist, inventor, statesman, printer, musician, and economist offer an interesting portrayal of this multifaceted individual. Enrichment activities on the Constitution, Franklin's epitaphs, and other subjects supplement traditional lesson plans.

Early American History (1783–1860)

Edward Ragan

Metasites

From Revolution to Reconstruction

http://odur.let.rug.nl/~usa/usa.htm

This metasite, maintained by the Arts Faculty of the University of Groningen, Netherlands, is a massive resource for all aspects of American history. The site is divided into five general sections: outlines, essays, documents, biographies, and presidents. This site is organized around several United States Information Agency publications: *An Outline of American History, An Outline of the American Economy, An Outline of American Government*, and *An Outline of American Literature*. While the text of these *Outlines* has not been changed, they have been enriched with hypertext links to relevant documents, original essays, and other Internet sites. Currently this site contains over 3,000 relevant HTML documents.

The Making of America ✓

http://www.umdl.umich.edu/moa/

The Making of America is a digital library of primary sources in American social history from the antebellum period through Reconstruction. Contained in this collection are approximately 8,500 books and 50,000 journal articles on subjects as far-ranging as education, psychology, American history, sociology, religion, and science and technology. The project, sponsored by the University of Michigan, "represents a major collaborative endeavor in preservation and electronic access to historical texts." These texts are searchable by keyword with links to digitized copies of the nineteenth-century imprints. This is an outstanding site for those who need access to nineteenth-century documents.

Nineteenth Century Documents Project

http://www.furman.edu/~benson/docs/

Lloyd Benson has prepared an extensive collection of primary documents. The period is categorized topically, and all topics seem to emphasize increased sectional differences and the coming of the Civil War. The documents are grouped under the following headings: Early National Politics, Slavery and Sectionalism, the Nebraska Bill, the Sumner Caning, the Dred Scott Decision, John Brown's raid on Harpers Ferry, 1850s Statistical Almanac, the 1860 Election, Secession and War, and the post–Civil War era.

Museums, Libraries, Historical Societies, and Online Organizations

American Treasures of the Library of Congress

http://lcweb.loc.gov/exhibits/treasures/

This is a substantial virtual exhibit from the Library of Congress collections of a variety of items, including letters by Thomas Jefferson and John Quincy Adams's notes from the *Amistad* case. Substantial detail and historical context are provided for each component of the collection. Thomas Jefferson, whose personal library became the core of the Library of Congress, arranged his books into three types of knowledge, corresponding to three faculties of the mind: memory (history), reason (philosophy), and imagination (fine arts).

Amistad: Race and the Boundaries of Freedom in Antebellum Maritime America

http://amistad.mysticseaport.org/main/welcome.html

This site is part of the Mystic Seaport Museum. It contains information on the *Amistad* slave ship, the revolt of its cargo, and the Supreme Court trial of its slave mutineers. The focus of this site is living history. A timeline of events is provided, as are classroom lessons for teachers.

The Early America Review

http://www.earlyamerica.com/review/

Don Vitale edits this electronic "Journal of Fact and Opinion on the People, Issues and Events of 18th Century America." The journal contains wide-ranging articles about the social, political, and military developments of this period. An excellent example of the ways in which modern scholarship seeks to combine traditional formats with technology.

Historic Mount Vernon: The Home of Our First President, George Washington

http://www.mountvernon.org

Visitors to the official Mount Vernon Web site will find information designed to meet a variety of needs. In addition to a virtual tour of the house and grounds, this site contains a biography of Washington written at the fifth-grade level with teaching aids such as quizzes and an electronic image collection.

The Gerrit Smith Virtual Museum

http://www.NYHistory.com/gerritsmith/index.htm

The New York History Net has detailed information about the abolitionist leader. Includes a biographical essay, bibliography, and portrait gallery of Smith and his family. This site was developed in cooperation with the Syracuse University Library Department of Special Collections and Hamilton College, both of whom hold substantial portions of Gerrit Smith's papers.

Topical Histories

Abolition

http://www.loc.gov/exhibits/african/abol.html

The Library of Congress provides information on the history of the antislavery movement in America that led to the formation, in 1833, of the American Anti-Slavery Society. Includes references to Library of Congress holdings such as abolitionist publications, minutes of antislavery meetings, handbills, advertisements, songs, and appeals to women. Demonstrates the tradition of the abolition movement in America before 1833.

African Canadian Heritage Tour

http://www.ciaccess.com/~jdnewby/heritage/african.htm

The African Canadian Heritage Tour celebrates the history of those who made the arduous journey to freedom in Canada via the Underground Railroad. This site is the central Internet presence for a collection of five historical locations that provide information about the Underground Railroad and the African-Canadian settlement of southwestern Ontario: the Buxton Historical Site and Museum, the North American Black Historical Museum, the Sandwich Baptist Church, the Uncle Tom's Cabin–Josiah Henson Interpretive Site, and the Woodstock Institute Sertoma Help Centre.

The American Whig Party (1834–1856)

http://odur.let.rug.nl/~usa/E/uswhig/whigsxx.htm

Essay by Hal Morris that describes the rise of the American Whig Party as an opposition to President Andrew Jackson's king-like tendencies. Included is a history of the Whig Party and links to biographies of Whig presidents and political leaders in America.

John Brown

http://www.pbs.org/weta/thewest/people/a_c/brown.htm

This PBS-sponsored site contains a biography of the radical abolitionist John Brown.

James Fenimore Cooper (1789–1851)

http://odur.let.rug.nl/~usa/LIT/cooper.htm

Kathryn VanSpanckeren has authored this literary biography that evaluates Cooper's role in the development of the American novel. Traces the familial and cultural influences that led Cooper to create Natty Bumppo, his chief protagonist.

Democracy in America: De Tocqueville ✓

http://xroads.virginia.edu/~HYPER/DETOC/home.html

The American Studies program at the University of Virginia maintains this site that explores American democracy in the 1830s, when De Tocqueville traveled across the United States. UVA has combined his itinerary, letters, and journal entries with cultural artifacts from the period to provide a glimpse of American democracy and culture in the early nineteenth century. Among other topics, this site examines issues of gender, race, and religion.

The Donner Party

http://members.home.net/mhaller6/donnerparty.htm

Mike Haller provides a history of the ill-fated Donner Party, which was stranded on its trek across the American West during the winter of 1846–47.

The Founding Fathers

http://www.nara.gov/exhall/charters/constitution/confath.html

The National Archives and Records Administration has compiled biographies of the delegates to the Constitutional Convention of 1787. This is an excellent place to start when studying the U.S. Constitution and the Founding Fathers.

Benjamin Franklin: A Documentary History

http://www.english.udel.edu/lemay/franklin/

J.A. Leo Lemay, the Henry Francis du Pont Winterthur Professor of Colonial American Literature at the University of Delaware, gives visitors a peek into the research that he is doing for a Franklin biography. He offers a detailed chronology of Franklin's life that is divided into three stages: early life, professional interests, and political career. Each event in Franklin's life is verified with citations that are connected to a bibliography of primary documents.

Benjamin Franklin: Glimpses of the Man

http://www.fi.edu/franklin/rotten.html

The Franklin Institute maintains this site, which celebrates the life and work of Benjamin Franklin. It emphasizes his work as a statesman, a printer, a scientist, a philosopher, a musician, an economist, and an inventor.

Horace Greeley (1811–1872)

http://www.honors.unr.edu/~fenimore/greeley.html

David H. Fenimore of the University of Nevada, Reno, offers a detailed biography of Greeley complete with photographs, quotations, a bibliography, and links to related information.

Sarah Grimké, Angelina Grimké

http://www.gale.com/freresrc/womenhst/bio/grimkes.htm

Gale Publishing has created these biographies of Sarah Grimké and Angelina Grimké that focus on their work for abolition and women's suffrage.

Thomas Jefferson: A Film by Ken Burns

http://www.pbs.org/jefferson/

This PBS-sponsored site is the online version of Ken Burns's documentary about Thomas Jefferson. It features selections of Jefferson's writings used in the film, the transcripts of interviews conducted for the film, tips for educators on teaching about Jefferson, and classroom activities for students.

The Thomas Jefferson Memorial Foundation

http://www.monticello.org

The Thomas Jefferson Memorial Foundation has prepared a virtual tour of life at Monticello to demonstrate how Jefferson spent an average day. Included here is a discussion about Jefferson's interests, inventions, family, slaves, and grounds. Lengthy essays seek to explain Jefferson's world to the twentieth-century student. Links connect the reader to additional information about Monticello, its owner, inhabitants, and visitors. "The Jefferson-Hemings DNA Testing: An On-Line Resource" is a valuable link for understanding the current controversy about Jefferson's legacy.

Lewis and Clark ✓

http://www.pbs.org/lewisandclark/

This is the PBS-sponsored online companion to Ken Burns's documentary series on the Lewis and Clark expedition. The site includes biographies for all members of the Corps of Discovery along with equipment lists, timelines, maps, and excerpts from the journals kept. Also included are short histories of the native American tribes that were encountered on the journey. Burns discusses the making of the series, and PBS provides teaching resources. Overall, this is an excellent site.

Manifest Destiny

http://odur.let.rug.nl/~usa/E/manifest/manifxx.htm

This essay by Michael Lubragge traces the history of this concept in America.

Methods of Resistance to Slavery

http://dolphin.upenn.edu/~vision/vis/Mar-95/8677.html

This brief essay by Colette Lamothe examines slaves' responses to slavery, oppression, and exploitation. Lamothe uses a comparative method to explore African slavery in the Caribbean, Latin America, and the United States from the fifteenth to the nineteenth century.

The Mexican-American War (1846–1848)

http://www.pbs.org/kera/usmexicanwar/

This PBS-sponsored site is the online companion to the television documentary. The site provides a detailed analysis of the war from both sides, with the perspective that "there are many valid points of view about a historical event." The war is placed in its larger context as a war for North America. Also included here are a bibliography, a teacher's guide, a timeline of events, historical analysis by experts, and information on the making of the documentary. This site is available in Spanish and English.

The Mexican-American War, 1846–1848

http://www.dmwv.org/mexwar/mexwar.htm

Sponsored by the Descendants of Mexican War Veterans, this site offers a history of the war with sections on the countdown to war, the various conflicts fought across Mexico and California, and the peace that followed. Also provided are maps, documents, images, and links to related resources.

The Mexican-American War Memorial Homepage

http://sunsite.dcaa.unam.mx/revistas/1847/

The Universidad Nacional Autónoma de Mexico sponsors this site. It includes documents, paintings, and a narrative history, presenting the Mexican-American War (1846–1848) from the perspective of participants and observers. The pages are available in English and in Spanish.

Mountain Men and the Fur Trade: Sources of the History of the Fur Trade in the Rocky Mountain West

http://www.xmission.com/~drudy/amm.html

This site is devoted to the mountain men of the Rocky Mountains through 1850. It includes digitized personal and public records and a bibliography for further reading.

New Perspectives on the West ✓

http://www.pbs.org/weta/thewest/

This is the PBS-sponsored online companion to the eight-episode documentary on the American West produced by Ken Burns and Stephen Ives. Burns and Ives introduce the production and provide a timeline with relevant biographies of key figures. Also included are sample primary source documents that were used to create the series and links to related sites.

Orphan Trains of Kansas

http://www.ukans.edu/carrie/kancoll/articles/orphans/

Connie Dipasquale and Susan Stafford present their research about children brought to Kansas from New York on "orphan trains." This site includes first-hand accounts, a timeline, newspaper descriptions, and partial name lists of children on the orphan trains.

Peabody Museum: The Ethnography of Lewis and Clark

http://www.peabody.harvard.edu/Lewis&Clark/

The Peabody Museum of Archaeology and Ethnology at Harvard University has developed this site to examine the cultural implications of the Lewis and Clark expedition. Included here are Native American artifacts (with detailed descriptions), route maps, and a resources page with links.

Politics and Sectionalism in the 1850s

http://odur.let.rug.nl/~usa/E/1850s/polixx.htm

Stephen Demkin has written this essay examining the major political issues of 1850s, such as the Compromise of 1850, the Kansas-Nebraska Act, and the Dred Scott decision. Also included are links to related sites.

Presidents of the United States

http://www.whitehouse.gov/history/presidents/index.html

The official White House Web site provides excellent biographies for each president, along with links to relevant documents and biographies of the first ladies.

Presidents of the United States

http://www.ipl.org/ref/POTUS/index.html

The Internet Public Library has produced a useful collection of presidential Web sites. Sections contain presidential election results, cabinet members, notable events, and links to Internet biographies. The information here is laid out in a very accessible format.

A Roadmap to the U.S. Constitution

http://library.thinkquest.org/11572/?tqskip=1

Jonathan Chin and Alan Stern of ThinkQuest have developed this site on the U.S. Constitution, re-creating the milieu out of which the Constitution emerged. This site provides an annotated copy of the Constitution, explores its origins, examines constitutional "crises" and the relevant Supreme Court decisions, and provides a discussion board for users with specific questions.

Chronology of the Secession Crisis

http://members.aol.com/jfepperson/secesh.html

James F. Epperson charts the chronology of events that culminated with the firing upon Fort Sumter, South Carolina. The site includes links to relevant documents.

The Star Spangled Banner

http://odur.let.rug.nl/~usa/E/banner/bannerxx.htm

Amato F. Mongelluzzo offers an essay that relates the events and dispels several myths surrounding the creation of this poem that became the national anthem.

Henry David Thoreau Home Page

http://www.walden.org/thoreau/

This site, sponsored by the Walden Woods Project, the Thoreau Society, and the Thoreau Institute, is the essential Thoreau site. Emphasized here are Thoreau's biography, images, electronic texts, and scholarly analysis of Thoreau's work.

To the Western Ocean: Planning the Lewis and Clark Expedition

http://www.lib.virginia.edu/exhibits/lewis_clark/ch4.html

The site is part of a map exhibition at the Tracy W. McGregor Room, Alderman Library, University of Virginia. To the Western Ocean is the fourth chapter of a

larger exploration of nation building and mapmaking. This site is valuable because it places the Lewis and Clark expedition into a larger historical context.

Two Bloody Days at Buena Vista

http://www.thehistorynet.com/MilitaryHistory/articles/1997/
02972_cover.htm

This article, by Robert Benjamin Smith, details Major General Zachary Taylor's
actions at the Battle of Buena Vista in 1847. It includes a full account of the
events of the battle along with a map.

Uncle Sam: An American Autobiography

http://xroads.virginia.edu/~CAP/SAM/home.htm

The American Studies program at the University of Virginia has created this
site to discuss the origin of this American icon. The forgotten origin of Uncle
Sam during the War of 1812 is placed alongside his evolution as a symbol and
national icon, including his official adoption and standardization by the U.S.
State Department in the 1950s.

The Valley of the Shadow ✓

http://jefferson.village.Virginia.EDU/vshadow2/

Edward L. Ayers, the Hugh P. Kelley Professor of History at the University of
Virginia, has developed this massive archive of primary sources that concern
the experiences of Franklin County, Pennsylvania, and Augusta County, Virginia, in the years just preceding the Civil War. These two counties were "sepa-
rated by several hundred miles and the Mason-Dixon line." The document
archive includes newspapers, letters, diaries, photographs, maps, church records,
population census, agricultural census, and military records. Students can research and write their own histories from the documents provided. The project
is primarily intended for secondary schools, community colleges, libraries, and
universities. This research is available in CD-ROM form from W.W. Norton
Publishers <http://www.wwnorton.com>.

War of 1812

http://www.army.mil/cmh-pg/books/amh/amh-06.htm

This is a discussion of the War of 1812 from *American Military History* (chapter 6). This e-text is sponsored by the Army Historical Series, Office of the
Chief of Military History, United States Army. The war is presented as an out-

growth of the Napoleonic Wars. The major battles are narrated in detail, as are comparisons of American and British military capabilities and strategies.

Woman of Iron

http://www.thehistorynet.com/AmericanHistory/articles/0495_text.htm

"In 1825 Rebecca Lukens took over her late husband's iron mill. The company still thrives—a testament to the management abilities of this pioneering woman CEO." The History Net sponsors this article by Joseph Gustaitis.

Documents and Images

"Across the Plains in 1844"

http://www.pbs.org/weta/thewest/resources/archives/two/sager1.htm

Catherine Sager Pringle wrote this account circa 1860. It is reprinted here from S.A. Clarke's *Pioneer Days in Oregon History*, Vol. II (1905).

Across the Plains with the Donner Party

http://www.teleport.com/~mhaller/Primary/VReed/VReed1.html

Mike Haller edited this book of reminiscences by Virginia Reed Murphy about her travel with the Donner party.

The *Amistad* Case

http://www.nara.gov/education/teaching/amistad/home.html

The National Archives and Records Administration provides all documents related to the *Amistad* slave mutiny. This site also includes teaching ideas based on the National Standards for History and the National Standards for Civics and Government.

The Annapolis Convention

http://www.yale.edu/lawweb/avalon/annapoli.htm

The Annapolis Convention assembled to discuss economic issues faced by the states under the Articles of Confederation. It resolved to explore alternatives to the Articles. This site contains the report of the commissioners from the states on September 14, 1786, and links to the Articles of Confederation, the Madison Debates, the *Federalist Papers*, and the U.S. Constitution.

The Articles of Confederation

http://www.yale.edu/lawweb/avalon/artconf.htm

The Articles of Confederation established a central government for the thirteen colonies after the American Revolution. It was a weak system in which the separate states held the balance of power. This site contains a full-text copy of the Articles and links to the Annapolis Convention, the Madison Debates, the *Federalist Papers*, and the U.S. Constitution.

The Bill of Rights

http://www.nara.gov/exhall/charters/billrights/billmain.html

The National Archives and Records Administration provides coverage of the Bill of Rights, including a high-resolution image of the document.

Boundaries of the United States and the Several States

http://www.ac.wwu.edu/~stephan/48states.html

Ed Stephan of Western Washington University has created a charming animated map that depicts the territorial growth of the United States. This site allows students to visualize how national, territorial, and state boundaries changed over time.

Cherokee Nation v. Georgia

http://www.pbs.org/weta/thewest/resources/archives/two/cherokee.htm

This is a full-text copy of the decision handed down by Supreme Court Chief Justice John Marshall in 1831.

The Confessions of Nat Turner

http://docsouth.unc.edu/turner/turner.html

This is the complete text of *The Confessions of Nat Turner* (1831).

The Constitution of the United States

http://www.nara.gov/exhall/charters/constitution/conmain.html

The National Archives and Records Administration maintain this site, where users can read a transcription of the complete text of the Constitution. The

Founding Fathers page features the biographies of the fifty-five delegates to the Constitutional Convention and links to biographies of each of the thirty-nine delegates who signed the Constitution. The article "A More Perfect Union" is an in-depth look at the Constitutional Convention and the ratification process. A quiz section gives visitors the chance to test their knowledge.

The *Federalist Papers*

http://www.yale.edu/lawweb/avalon/federal/fed.htm

John Jay, Alexander Hamilton, and James Madison authored these essays, first published in 1787–1788, arguing in favor of constitutional ratification. The collection is searchable by keyword and linked to relevant documents such as the Articles of Confederation, the Annapolis Convention, the Madison Debates, and the U.S. Constitution.

The *Federalist Papers*

http://www.law.emory.edu/FEDERAL/federalist/

The *Federalist Papers* serve as bold statements of American political theory, and this online version makes them more accessible than ever before.

FindLaw: U.S. Constitution

http://www.findlaw.com/casecode/constitution/

This site contains all articles and amendments to the U.S. Constitution, completely annotated with explanations and references. Through hyperlinks, users can access the full-text version of relevant Supreme Court decisions, each placed in its historical context along with pertinent theories of law and government. This is an invaluable resource for legal professionals.

First-Person Narratives of the American South

http://metalab.unc.edu/docsouth/fpn/fpn.html

This site contains an outstanding collection of electronic texts documenting the American South. It includes diaries, autobiographies, memoirs, travel accounts, and ex-slave narratives. The focus is on first-person narratives of marginalized populations: women, African-Americans, enlisted men, laborers, and Native Americans.

A Girl's Life in Virginia before the War

http://metalab.unc.edu/docsouth/burwell/menu.html

This memoir by Letitia M. Burwell describes southern plantation life before the Civil War. It was originally published in 1895.

Godey's Lady's Book

http://www.history.rochester.edu/godeys/

This site includes selections from the popular nineteenth-century women's magazine *Godey's Lady's Book*. Issues from the 1850s include "For the Home," "Nor Just for Ladies," and "Fashion Corner" sections. Visitors to this site will find an informative glimpse into the daily life of the mid-nineteenth-century middle class.

A Grandmother's Recollections of Dixie

http://metalab.unc.edu/docsouth/bryan/menu.html

This is a collection of letters from Mary Norcott Bryan to her grandchildren describing life on a southern plantation before the Civil War. It was published in 1912.

Historical Maps of the United States

http://mahogany.lib.utexas.edu/Libs/PCL/Map_collection/united_states.html

The University of Texas at Austin has digitized the Perry-Castañeda Library Map Collection. This is an excellent source for digitized copies of rare maps.

History of the Donner Party

http://www.teleport.com/~mhaller/Secondary/McGlashan/McGlashanTOC.html

Mike Haller has edited this book by C.F. McGlashan (1879) about the Donner Party.

"The Hypocrisy of American Slavery"

http://www.historyplace.com/speeches/douglass.htm

Frederick Douglass gave this speech on July 4, 1852, in Rochester, New York See elsewhere in this section, Douglass's speech made the following day entitled, "What to the Slave Is the Fourth of July?"

The Jay Treaty

http://odur.let.rug.nl/~usa/D/1776–1800/foreignpolicy/jay.htm

This treaty between Great Britain and the United States, proclaimed in February 1796, was the most controversial issue of George Washington's presidency. Its real significance was that it represented Britain's recognition of American nationality.

Thomas Jefferson on Politics and Government: Quotations from the Writings of Thomas Jefferson

http://etext.virginia.edu/jefferson/quotations/

This site, sponsored by the University of Virginia, contains an extensive collection of Jefferson quotations. The stated goal of this site is to constitute a "fair statement of the complete political philosophy of Thomas Jefferson." Also included are a brief biography of Jefferson and links to related sites.

John Brown: An Address by Frederick Douglass

http://lcweb2.loc.gov/cgi-bin/query/r?ammem/
murray:@field(FLD001+07012896+):@@@ REF

This speech by Frederick Douglass at the Library of Congress Web site is a tribute to John Brown, a radical abolitionist who, in 1859, raided the federal arsenal at Harpers Ferry, Virginia, in a mad attempt to foment a slave revolt, for which Virginia authorities hanged Brown. His last words were: "I, John Brown, am now quite certain that the crimes of this guilty land will never be purged away but with blood." Douglass memorialized Brown as a true hero of the abolitionist cause.

"A Journey to the Seaboard States" (1856)

http://odur.let.rug.nl/~usa/D/1851–1875/olmsted/jourxx.htm

This essay by Frederick Law Olmsted focuses on slavery and the plantation system. It was written in 1856 while Olmsted was on a journalistic assignment for the *New York Daily Times*. Olmsted is critical of slavery as both cruel and inefficient.

Kentucky Resolution (1799)

http://odur.let.rug.nl/~usa/D/1776–1800/constitution/kent1799.htm

This was Thomas Jefferson's republican response to the Federalists' Alien and Sedition Acts. The resolution advanced the state compact theory and argued that states retained the right to notify Congress when it had exceeded its authority.

The Louisiana Purchase Treaty

http://www.nara.gov/exhall/originals/loupurch.html

This online exhibit by the National Archives presents images of the document that was signed in Paris in 1803, along with a transcription of the text.

The Madison Debates

http://www.yale.edu/lawweb/avalon/debates/debcont.htm

The Debates in the Federal Convention of 1787 was created from notes taken by James Madison during the Constitutional Convention held in Philadelphia between May 14 and September 17, 1787. The debates are searchable by keyword or can be accessed according to specific dates. Also contained here are links to the Articles of Confederation, the Annapolis Convention, the *Federalist Papers*, and the U.S. Constitution.

John Marshall

http://odur.let.rug.nl/~usa/D/1801–1825/marshallcases/marxx.htm

Here are the major decisions written by Chief Justice John Marshall, including *Marbury v. Madison* and *Cherokee Nation v. Georgia*. Also included is a biography of Marshall.

The Monroe Doctrine

http://odur.let.rug.nl/~usa/D/1801–1825/jmdoc.htm

The Monroe Doctrine was an early statement on American foreign policy, presented in President Monroe's annual message to Congress on December 2, 1823.

North American Slave Narratives ✓

http://metalab.unc.edu/docsouth/neh/neh.html

This large collection of American slave narratives is part of the Documenting the American South project sponsored by the University of North Carolina at Chapel Hill. This is an excellent resource for better understanding the slaves' world in the antebellum South.

The Prairie Traveler: A Hand-book for Overland Expeditions

http://www.ukans.edu/carrie/kancoll/books/marcy/

This survival guide/handbook, written by Captain Randolph B. Marcy, U.S. Army, was published in 1859.

The Proclamation of Neutrality (1793)

http://odur.let.rug.nl/~usa/D/1776–1800/foreignpolicy/neutr.htm

President George Washington proclaimed American neutrality during the wars of the French Revolution.

Scanned Originals of Early American Documents

http://www.law.emory.edu/FEDERAL/conpict.html

This site includes scanned originals of the Constitution, the Bill of Rights, and the Declaration of Independence.

The Sedition Act of July 14, 1798

http://www.ukans.edu/carrie/docs/texts/sedact.htm

Congress passed this act on July 14, 1798.

"Slavery a Positive Good"

http://douglass.speech.nwu.edu/calh_a59.htm

John C. Calhoun delivered this speech on the floor of the U.S. Senate in 1837.

Treaty of Greenville (1795)

http://odur.let.rug.nl/~usa/D/1776–1800/indians/green.htm

This is the complete text of the American Indian treaty that formally opened the Northwest Territory for settlement.

Uncle Tom's Cabin

http://xroads.virginia.edu/~HYPER/STOWE/stowe.html

The American Studies program at the University of Virginia provides an e-text of Harriet Beecher Stowe's 1852 novel.

Virginia Resolution (1798)

http://www.yale.edu/lawweb/avalon/virres.htm

This was James Madison's republican response to the Federalists' Alien and Sedition Acts. It advanced the state compact theory, which argued that the federal government could operate only within its constitutionally defined limits.

Virginia Statute for Religious Freedom (1786)

http://www.freethought-web.org/ctrl/jefferson_vsrf.html

Thomas Jefferson drafted this act in 1777. An amended version passed the Virginia legislature in 1786. It served as the precedent for the religious freedom article in the Bill of Rights.

"What to the Slave Is the Fourth of July?"

http://douglass.speech.nwu.edu/doug_a10.htm

Frederick Douglass delivered this speech on July 5, 1852. See, elsewhere in this section, Douglass's speech made the day before in Rochester, New York, entitled, "The Hypocrisy of American Slavery."

The Civil War

James E. Jolly

Metasites

The American Civil War

http://www.homepages.dsu.edu/jankej/civilwar/civilwar.htm

Created by Jim Janke of Dakota State University, this site is an excellent place to begin a search for American Civil War materials. The page is extremely well organized into a wide variety of categories and subcategories that are frequently updated.

The American Civil War, 1861–1865: World Wide Web Information Archive

http://users.iamdigex.net/bdboyle/cw.html

This site contains links to a wide variety of Civil War–related materials such as books, documents, orders of battle, reenactment groups and other historic preservation groups, and e-text versions of Lincoln's First and Second Inaugural Addresses.

The American Civil War Home Page

http://sunsite.utk.edu/civil-war/

The American Civil War Home Page is another excellent place to begin research. It contains links to photographic collections, regimental histories, reenactors, and a host of other materials.

The United States Civil War Center

http://www.cwc.lsu.edu/

The United States Civil War Center, located at Louisiana State University, is dedicated to promoting the study of the Civil War. It has assembled an impressive collection of over 2,400 links to Civil War sites. In addition, the page contains online documents, tips for tracing one's Civil War ancestors, and links to reenactors and vendors.

General Sites

African-American Civil War Memorial

http://www.afroamcivilwar.org/

This site contains a host of information about the design and location of the African-American Civil War Memorial, a photo gallery of the project, and links to African-American Civil War sites.

American Civil War

http://spec.lib.vt.edu/civwar/

Created by the Special Collections Department of the Virginia Libraries at Virginia Tech, this page offers access to a wide variety of letters and diaries of both Union and Confederate soldiers.

Battlefield Medicine in the American Civil War

http://members.aol.com/cwsurgeon0/indexJ.html

Battlefield Medicine in the American Civil War contains a wide variety of information related to medicine in the Civil War. Copies of battlefield reports, eyewitness accounts, and even a copy of General Orders No. 147, which organized the Ambulance Corps in 1862, are included.

Battle Summaries

http://www2.cr.nps.gov/abpp/battles/tvii.htm#sums

Organized by either state or campaign, this site provides Civil War battle summaries, preservation information, and links to the National Park Service.

Captain Richard W. Burt's Civil War Letters from the 76th Ohio Volunteer Infantry

http://my.ohio.voyager.net/~lstevens/burt/

This site, managed by Larry Stevens, includes the letters, poems, and songs of Richard W. Burt of the 76th Ohio Volunteer Infantry, as well as a copy of the 76th's recruiting ad.

Civil War Diaries at Augustana College Library

http://sparc5.augustana.edu/library/civil.html

This page contains two diaries from Illinois soldiers during the Civil War.

Civil War Diary and Letters of David Humphrey Blair

http://netnow.micron.net/~rbparker/diary/index.html

This site, managed by Robert B. Parker, consists of the diary and letters of David Humphrey Blair, a soldier with Company D of the 45th Ohio Volunteers.

Civil War Diary of Bingham Findley Junkin

http://www.iwaynet.net/~lsci/junkin/

This site contains the diary entries of Private Bingham Findley Junkin of the 100th Pennsylvania Volunteer Infantry from March 1864 to June 1865.

The Civil War History of John Ritland

http://members.home.net/jritland1/

This page consists of the narrative of the life of John Ritland, who served with the 32nd Iowa Infantry from 1862 until 1865.

Civil War Letters

http://home.pacbell.net/dunton/SSDletters.html

This site includes a well-indexed collection of twelve letters written by Private Samuel S. Dunton of the 114th New York Infantry between 1862 and 1865.

Civil War Live

http://library.thinkquest.org/2873/data/ref/

This page presents a timeline, an essay outlining causes of the Civil War, and biographical sketches of both Union and Confederate generals.

Civil War Manuscripts at the Southern Historical Collection

http://www.unc.edu/lib/mssinv/exhibits/civilwar/civilwar.html

This site contains a small collection of eleven Union and Confederate letters written between 1861 and 1865. With two exceptions, all the letters come from the eastern theater of the war.

Civil War Resources: Virginia Military Institute Archives

http://www.vmi.edu/~archtml/cwsource.html

Virginia Military Institute's Civil War Resources page includes twenty-three different online manuscript collections. The two most famous are the Stonewall Jackson Papers and the Matthew Fontaine Maury Papers. Maury was an oceanographer, a Confederate States navy commander, and faculty member at VMI. In addition to his Civil War service, topics include his career at the National Observatory in Washington, D.C., his colonization efforts in Mexico, and his professorship at VMI.

Civil War Sites in the Shenandoah Valley of Virginia

http://www2.cr.nps.gov/abpp/shenandoah/svs0–1.html

This site provides a comprehensive study of the battlefields in the Shenandoah Valley. In addition to summaries, the site contains information on the historical context, preservation, and heritage tourism.

Civil War Soldiers and Sailors System

http://www.itd.nps.gov/cwss/

This project is an attempt to build a database of basic information about all those who served in the war.

Civil War Women

http://odyssey.lib.duke.edu/collections/civil-war-women.html

This page offers online information about an archival collection at the Special Collections Library at Duke University. The collection consists of the Rosie O'Neal Greenlow Papers, the Alice Williamson Diary, and the Sarah E. Thompson Papers. It also contains links to other sites containing primary sources related to women and the Civil War.

Dwight Henry Cory Letters and Diary

http://homepages.rootsweb.com/~lovelace/cory.htm

This site contains a collection of letters written by Dwight Henry Cory of the 6th Ohio Volunteer Cavalry.

The John Freeman Diary

http://www.public.usit.net/mruddy/freeman.htm

This site contains the diary of John Henderson Freeman, who served with Company I of the 34th Mississippi Volunteers.

Edward G. Gerdes Civil War Home Page

http://www.couchgenweb.com/civilwar/

This is a good resource for those interested in Arkansas during the Civil War. It includes lists of Confederate cemeteries, burial lists, regimental rosters, and Cherokee Confederate units.

H-Civwar

http://h-net2.msu.edu/~civwar

This site, part of H-Net, contains a discussion list of the Civil War and links to other sites. Eventually the page will also offer links to conferences, grants, and bibliographies.

The Iowa Civil War Site

http://www.iowa-counties.com/civilwar/

The Iowa Civil War Site discusses Iowa in the Civil War. It includes letters, diaries, unit histories, and photos.

Letters from an Iowa Soldier in the Civil War

http://bob.ucsc.edu/civil-war-letters/home.html

This page, by Bill Proudfoot, contains some letters of Private Newton Robert Scott of the 36th Infantry, Iowa Volunteers.

Letters of the Civil War

http://www.letterscivilwar.com/

This site presents a variety of letters from many different sources. Individuals are encouraged to submit letters that they might have for posting to the site. It also contains photos and diaries.

Overall Family Civil War Letters

http://www.geocities.com/Heartland/Acres/1574/

Presented at this site are letters of Isaac Overall, a private with Company I of the 36th Ohio Volunteer Infantry, written between 1862 and his death in 1863.

Pearce Civil War Documents Collection

http://www.nav.cc.tx.us/lrc/Homepg2.htm

Navarro College houses this Web site, which consists of a variety of letters, documents, and diaries.

Poetry and Music of the War Between the States

http://www.erols.com/kfraser/

This site contains wartime and postwar poetry and music from both Union and Confederate sources.

Secession Era Editorials Project

http://history.furman.edu/~benson/docs/

The Secession Era Editorials Project is sponsored by Furman University in South Carolina. Currently, the project provides editorials related to four pre–Civil War events: the Nebraska Bill, the Dred Scott case, Harpers Ferry, and the caning of Charles Sumner. Eventually the project plans to include a complete run of editorials from the major political parties.

Selected Civil War Photographs

http://memory.loc.gov/ammem/cwphtml/cwphome.html

Part of the American Memory project of the Library of Congress, this site presents over 1,100 photographs, most of which were taken by Matthew Brady. It includes a searchable database, a subject index, and links explaining more about Civil War photography.

The Shenandoah 1863 Civil War Museum

http://www.fortunecity.com/victorian/museum/63/index.html

This page contains profiles of Civil War leaders, pictures of battle flags, campaign and battlefield maps, and a list of sources for further research.

Ulysses S. Grant Association

http://www.lib.siu.edu/projects/usgrant/

This site, supported by Southern Illinois University, presents information on Grant's military service, an online version of his personal memoirs, and photographs.

Valley of the Shadow Project

http://jefferson.village.virginia.edu/vshadow2/

A Virginia Center for Digital History project, the original Valley of the Shadow Project, has now been released on CD-ROM. Currently the project is in its second phase, adding to its original collection of primary documents, images, sounds, and discussions. Part One of the Valley of the Shadow Project is titled The Eve of War. Part Two deals with the same communities but concerns itself with The War Years.

Vermont in the Civil War

http://vermontcivilwar.org/index.shtml

This site attempts to document Vermont's participation in the conflict. It contains an index of over 32,000 names of those who served in the war, letters, brief biographies of individuals who served, and a cemetery database of over 3,000 names.

The Gilded Age and Progressive Era

Kenneth R. Dvorak

Metasites

American Memory

http://memory.loc.gov/ammem/amhome.html

Established by the Library of Congress, this excellent Web research site provides a wealth of information on all topics related to American history. Containing nearly 7 million digital artifacts, the American Memory collection provides search features on print, film, and photographic indexes on all topics of special interest to students and researchers.

The Gilded Age Webquest: Documentating Industrialization in America

http://www.oswego.org/staff/tcaswell/wq/gildedage/student.htm

This award-winning Web site is an excellent resource for K-12 social science teachers looking for innovative and interactive ways to immerse their students in how industrialization transformed American society and culture during the Gilded Age. Students become part of a documentary film crew charged with the responsibility of creating a film about the Gilded Age.

Gilded and Progressive Era Resources

http://www.tntech.edu/www/acad/hist/gilprog.html

This exhaustive Web resource highlights topics central to understanding the Gilded and Progressive Eras. Produced by the History Department at Tennessee Technological University, this Web site should attract anyone interested in learning more about these two important eras in American history.

Populism

http://history.smsu.edu/wrmiller/Populism/Texts/populism.htm

Authored by historian Worth Robert Miller of Southwest Missouri State University, this comprehensive Web resource site offers several gateways for study of the Populist movement. The site contains topical, biographical, and political links that examine the rise of Populism and its appeal to Americans living in the nineteenth century.

The World of 1898: The Spanish-American War

http://www.loc.gov/rr/hispanic/1898/

This Library of Congress Web site titled The World of 1898 provides excellent resources and documents about the Spanish-American War, the period before the war, and some of the fascinating people who participated in the fighting or commented about it. Information about Cuba, Guam, the Philippines, Puerto Rico, Spain, and the United States is provided in chronologies, bibliographies, and a variety of pictorial and textual material from bilingual sources.

The World's Columbian Exposition: Idea, Experience, Aftermath

http://xroads.virginia.edu/~MA96/WCE/title.html

The 1893 World's Columbian Exposition, held in Chicago, Illinois, was the signature event of the decade. This very professional Web research site, created by Julie K. Rose of the University of Virginia, presents the exposition and its importance in an exciting virtual format. This site provides a history of the fair, a virtual tour, written reactions by visitors to the fair, the exposition's historical and cultural legacy, and an extensive bibliographic resource page.

World's Columbian Exposition: Interactive Guide

http://users.vnet.net/schulman/Columbian/columbian.html

Created and maintained by Bruce R. Schulman, this award-winning Web site details the architectural history of the 1893 Chicago World's Columbian Exposition. Divided into four areas of research, the site describes the background, exhibits, art, and architecture of the "white city."

Historical Figures

Presidents of the Gilded Age and Progressive Era

Chester A. Arthur, 1881–85

http://www.whitehouse.gov/history/presidents/ca21.html

Arthur was described by Counterpoise as looking "Presidential"—find out why.

Grover Cleveland, 1885–89 and 1893–97

http://www.rain.org/~turnpike/grover/Main.html

The Grover Cleveland Web resource page provides a complete picture of Cleveland as private citizen and president. Josh Smith of Dos Pueblos High School in Santa Barbara, California, has maintained this site since 1999. Individuals can examine photographs, speeches, family history, and bibliographic sources about Cleveland, including additional links for Cleveland and the tumultuous era in which he lived.

James A. Garfield, 1881

http://www.whitehouse.gov/history/presidents/jg20.html

Did you know that James A. Garfield was the second president shot while in office?

Ulysses S. Grant, 1869–77

http://www.mscomm.com/~ulysses/

This is an exceptional Web resource created by Webmaster Candace Scott. It contains a wealth of information about our eighteenth president, including Grant's family history, his early childhood, and his life as a private citizen, father, husband, soldier, general, and president. This is an extremely important historical resource on a very controversial historical figure.

Benjamin Harrison, 1889–93

http://www.whitehouse.gov/history/presidents/bh23.html

This Web site provides essential information about Benjamin Harrison and his presidency.

Rutherford B. Hayes, 1877–81

http://www.rbhayes.org/

The Rutherford B. Hayes Presidential Center, the first presidential library in the United States, is located in Fremont, Ohio. This Web resource site provides information on Hayes's military career during the Civil War, his personal papers, diaries, and presidential papers. The Hayes Presidential Center, which also contains information on Ohio Civil War soldiers, is sponsored in part by the Ohio Historical Society.

William McKinley, 1897–1901

http://www.cohums.ohio-state.edu/history/projects/McKinley/

One of most outstanding Web resources on the era of William McKinley is this site produced and maintained by Ohio State's history department. This extensive analysis of William McKinley is particularly well suited for students seeking information on Ohio politicians, such as Mark Hanna, McKinley's infamous political campaign manager. The site also contains information on McKinley as president, the Spanish-American War of 1898, and political cartoons and photographs of the period.

White House

http://www.whitehouse.gov/

This site specifically deals with information concerning the presidents of the United States. Managed by the Executive Office staff of the president, this excellent Web resource contains full-text inaugural speeches, information about individual presidential libraries, First Ladies, and links to other relevant historical sites.

Creating Industrial America

American Memory

http://memory.loc.gov/ammem/amhome.html

Andrew Carnegie, 1885–1919

http://www.pbs.org/wgbh/amex/carnegie/
http://www.clpgh.org/exhibit/carnegie.html

The first Web site based on the PBS film documentary *The Richest Man in the World*, provides extensive materials on industrialist and philanthropist Andrew Carnegie and his personal philosophies, timelines, and an in-depth analysis of the Homestead steel strike. The second, Andrew Carnegie: A Tribute, is an excellent Web resource on Carnegie's true-life rags-to-riches story. Sponsored by the Carnegie Library of Pittsburgh, this ambitious Web resource site contains photographs and audio links honoring Pittsburgh's most famous citizen.

J. Pierpont Morgan, 1837–1913

http://www.jpmorgan.com/CorpInfo/History/overview.html
http://www.nyyc.org/Images/Heritage%20Series/Morgan.htm

Morgan is perhaps the most admired, hated, and despised figure in American financial history. His firm, J.P. Morgan and Company, became the most influential financial center in America, helping to finance the capital needed for the burgeoning post–Civil War economy. The first site, sponsored by the J.P. Morgan Company, provides a brief history of the firm and its founder. The second Web site, sponsored by the New York Yacht Club, showcases J.P. Morgan enjoying one of his many private pursuits.

John D. Rockefeller, 1839–1937

http://www.rockefeller.edu/archive.ctr/bibliog.html#RFB2

The most intriguing Web resource on John D. Rockefeller is this exhaustive bibliographic listing of Rockefeller's family history, sponsored by the Rockefeller Archive Center. This resource also contains a complete listing of published works about John D. Rockefeller.

Industrial Conflict in an Industrializing Age

Coal Mining in the Gilded Age and Progressive Era

http://www.cohums.ohio-state.edu/history/projects/Lessons_US/Gilded_Age/Coal_Mining/default.htm

This extensive Web research site contains valuable information on coal mining in the late nineteenth and early twentieth centuries. Included are photographs, reprinted period articles, and a discussion of the dangers associated with coal mining.

Haymarket Square, 1886

http://www.chicagohs.org/dramas/

The Dramas of the Haymarket earned the 2001 American Association for History and Computing (AAHC) Multimedia Prize for Web Sites. The content is first-rate, well written, and engaging. The resources are well documented and the design includes a nice balance of images and text as well as a consistent layout throughout. The material is expertly arranged. The site is an excellent resource for all audiences from high school to the university to the casual observer interested in Chicago history.

Homestead, Pennsylvania, 1892

http://www.cohums.ohio-state.edu/history/projects/HomesteadStrike1892/
PennMilitiaInField/pennmilitiainfield.htm
http://www.history.ohio-state.edu/projects/HomesteadStrike1892/

The first Web resource site examines the role that the Pennsylvania state militia played in quelling the Homestead steel strike. The second Web resource provides a collection of historical documents pertaining to the strike and the reaction it caused throughout the country.

Inventors for a New Age

Alexander Graham Bell, 1847–1922

http://memory.loc.gov/ammem/bellhtml/bellhome.html

This outstanding Web site maintained by the Library of Congress and its American Memory division contains a multitude of research materials covering the entire life of Alexander Graham Bell, including his written correspondence, photographic images, and a detailed discussion of his invention of the telephone.

Thomas A. Edison, 1847–1931

http://www.hfmgv.org/exhibits/edison/tae.html

Sponsored by the Henry Ford Museum and Greenfield Village, this exciting research site lends itself to revealing the complexities of Edison's personality. Titled Thomas A. Edison and the Menlo Park Laboratory, this site chronicle the efforts by Greenfield Village to preserve and showcase the tremendous accomplishments of Edison.

John Wanamaker, 1838–1922

http://www.srmason-sj.org/council/journal/3-mar/quender.html
http://www.wanamakerorgan.com/

Providing a thorough narrative of the life and times of Philadelphian John Wanamaker, known as "America's Greatest Merchant," this interesting first Web site, produced by *Scottish Rite Journal*, includes photographs and testimonials to America's first successful major retailer. The second site connects with the "Friends of the Wanamaker Organ, Inc.," a historical preservation group interested in preserving the style and substance of Wanamaker's lavish turn-of-the-century department stores.

Frank Lloyd Wright, 1867–1959

http://www.prairiestyles.com/wright.htm

Considered one of America's greatest architects, Wright became world renowned for his stunning private residences and dramatic public buildings. This excellent Web resource provides extensive knowledge of Wright's life, work, and legacy to American architecture.

Writers, Philosophers, and Social Activists

Jane Addams, 1860–1935

http://www.uic.edu/jaddams/hull/hull_house.html

Produced by the University of Chicago Hull House Museum, this excellent narrative essay chronicles the life of social reformer Jane Addams. This Web resource site contains an extensive bibliography and informational links for those wishing to learn more about this famous settlement house pioneer.

Susan B. Anthony, 1820–1906

http://www.susanbanthonyhouse.org/

Susan B. Anthony, regarded as the foremost leader in the early women's rights movement in the United States, advocated that women be given the right to vote and stressed the importance of economic independence for women as a means toward emancipation. The Susan B. Anthony House Web site offers a complete background on this remarkable woman, including a virtual tour of Anthony's residence in Rochester, New York.

William Jennings Bryan, 1860–1925

http://iberia.vassar.edu/1896/1896home.html

Under the rubric "Presidential Election of 1896," Web authors Rebecca Edwards and Sarah DeFeo have created an interesting and through Web resource covering the presidential election of 1896. Here the researcher will find links to topics pertinent to this pivotal national election, including a list of all the key political players and Bryan's famous "Cross of Gold" speech delivered to the Democratic National Convention in July 1896 in Chicago.

Eugene Debs, 1855–1926

http://www.eugenevdebs.com/

Eugene Debs, labor organizer and socialist, worked tirelessly on behalf of American laborers. Long a leader of the American Railroad Union, he led the strike against the Pullman Company of Chicago in 1893, resulting in his arrest and imprisonment for union organizing. This Web site, created by the Eugene V. Debs Foundation, seeks to inform today's audiences of the importance of this nineteenth- and twentieth-century social reformer.

W.E.B. Du Bois, 1868–1963

http://historymatters.gmu.edu/text/1642d-WEB.html

W.E.B Du Bois is considered the leading African-American intellectual of the twentieth century and a man consumed with seeking economic, social, and political justice for African-Americans. He wrote tirelessly about the African Diaspora, especially in his book *Souls of Black Folk* (1903). This Web site features Du Bois's attack on the racial accommodation and gradualism advocated by Booker T. Washington.

Sarah Orne Jewett, 1849–1909

http://www.public.coe.edu/~theller/soj/sj-index.htm

Known as a "regionalist" because her writings captured the flavor of her native New England, Sarah Orne Jewett is most remembered for her book of stories, *The Country of the Pointed Firs* (1896). This excellent Web site is produced by Terry Heller of Coe College and contains an exhaustive collection of Jewett's writings.

Mary Harris (Mother) Jones, 1837–1930

http://www.kentlaw.edu/ilhs/majones.htm

Mother Jones was an enigmatic individual and tireless labor organizer working on behalf of the United Mine Workers of America. She was a free-ranging spirit speaking out against social and political injustices that she felt were damaging to American society. This Web site sponsored by the Illinois Labor History Society provides an excellent narrative of Mother Jones's life.

John Muir, 1838–1914

http://www.yosemite.ca.us/john_muir_exhibit/writings/

John Muir became America's first conservationist and activist for the preservation of wildlife and forest areas, both revered and reviled for his efforts. This informative Web site explores the life of John Muir and provides extensive links chronicling his life and professional contributions.

Frederick Jackson Turner, 1861–1932

http://www.theatlantic.com/issues/qgsep/ets/turn.htm

The American historian Frederick Jackson Turner presented his "frontier thesis" at the American Historical Association's 1893 meeting at the Chicago World's Columbian Exposition, thereby setting the stage for a rethinking of America's historical beginnings. Turner's thesis influenced an entire generation of historians, but most importantly how Americans came to view themselves and their past. This Web site, provided by the *Atlantic Monthly*, reprints an 1896 article by Turner titled "The Problem of the West."

Mark Twain, 1835–1910

http://etext.lib.virginia.edu/railton/index2.html

This excellent Web site, produced by Stephen Railton and the University of Virginia Library, introduces the Web reader to the experience of encountering "Mark Twain in His Times." Featured are online texts of Twain's writings, lesson plans, student projects, archived texts, bibliographies, and featured Mark Twain links.

Walt Whitman, 1819–92

http://memory.loc.gov/ammem/wwhome.html

Author of *Leaves of Grass* (1855), Whitman is best known for a remarkable collection of observations about American life, history, politics, geography, occupations, and speech. The American Memory Web page is an excellent source of information concerning the enigmatic Whitman, his life, and his writings.

Frances Willard, 1839–98

http://www.library.wisc.edu/etext/WIReader/Contents/Pioneer.html

Frances Willard was another of the dynamic women living and working during the Gilded Age. Long a champion of women's rights, she dedicated her life to elevating the status of women. She was one of the founding members of the Women's Christian Temperance Union. This Web site, sponsored by the University of Wisconsin, Madison Library System and the State Historical Society of Wisconsin, is an excellent source of regional Wisconsin history.

American Expansionism in the Gilded Age: Manifest Destiny and the Spanish-American War

The Age of Imperialism

http://www.smplanet.com/imperialism/toc.html

Historians have characterized the actions of the United States during the Spanish-American War as one of overt expansionism fueled by racism. This online history resource of the period examines United States interest in the Pacific Rim especially the Philippines, the Boxer Rebellion in China, and the Spanish-American War of 1898.

Historical Museum of Southern Florida: The Spanish-American War

http://www.historical-museum.org/history/war/war.htm

Florida, lying only sixty miles from Cuba, became a central staging point for American military forces embarking on their invasion of Cuba. This web site pays homage to the Cuban heritage in Florida and for those who fought for independence from Spain.

The Spanish-American War Centennial Web Site

http://www.spanamwar.com/

The Spanish-American War Centennial Web Site is an ambitious site detailing the American military campaigns against the Spanish. This extensive collection of materials includes a chronology of the war; bibliographic sources; background of the Cuban Revolution of 1895–98; eyewitness reports written by protagonists on both sides; the role of the American press in promoting the war; music written about the war; and links to events, exhibits, and Rough Rider activities.

The Spanish-American War in Motion Pictures

http://memory.loc.gov/ammem/sawhtml/sawhome.html

The Spanish-American War was the first war chronicled in the new medium of motion pictures. This Library of Congress Web site contains sixty-eight motion pictures produced by Edison Manufacturing Company and the American Mutoscope and Biograph Company, whose owner was the inventor Thomas Edison. Many of the films were shot on location in the United States, Cuba, and the Philippines, depicting soldiers, important personalities, and military parades. This is a highly recommended resource for those incorporating new materials into the study of the Spanish-American War.

The World of 1898: The Spanish-American War

http://www.loc.gov/rr/hispanic/1898/

This Library of Congress Web site provides excellent source materials, especially documenting the people and places that factored into the fighting of the war.

Topical Issues

African-Americans and the U.S. Navy

http://www.history.navy.mil/photos/prs-tpic/af-amer/afam-usn.htm

Produced by the Naval Historical Center in conjunction with the United States Navy, this interesting Web site contains a wide array of historical documents on the contributions of African-Americans serving as sailors in the U.S. Navy. Complete with a wide array of downloadable photographs, this Web site is highly recommended for high school history courses.

Americans of Asian Indian Origin

http://www-users.cs.umn.edu/~seetala/India/Articles/article001.html
http://www.hist.umn.edu/~erikalee/aahist.html

Produced and written by Srirajasekhar Bobby Koritala, this first Web resource traces the origins of individuals of Asian Indian origin and their arrival in North America. Arriving in the United States as a student, the author states that his intention was to "get a great education" and then return to India. A change in plans led to this splendid Web site devoted to the history of Asian Indian traders and immigrants to North America. The second URL is a Web resource on Asian-American history created by assistant professor of history Erika Lee at the University of Minnesota. This site contains a wealth of information surrounding Asian immigration to North America.

Blackface, Blackeye, Racist Images of African-Americans 1890–1940

http://www.authentichistory.com/images/blackface.html

Part of an expansive Web site supported by the Authentic History Center, Primary Sources from American Culture, this selection on racist images found in American advertisements, postcards, and musical sheet music targeting African-Americans is an important resource for cultural historians. Collections include images, collected speeches, and music downloads from antebellum America to the new millennium.

Cartoons of the Gilded Age and Progressive Era

http://www.history.ohio-state.edu/projects/uscartoons/GAPECartoons.htm

Sponsored by the Ohio State History Department, this excellent resource provides some of the best critique of these two eras.

Scott Joplin, 1868–1917

http://www.lsjunction.com/people/joplin.htm

Considered the Father of Ragtime Music, Joplin was a popular figure within the African-American community. This Web site traces the rise of Joplin's career and the continuing popularity of ragtime music.

Native Americans

http://www.americanwest.com/pages/indians.htm

An extensive collection of Native American Web resource links is part of this award-winning Web site supported by The American West organization, which celebrates the heritage and culture of the American West.

Supreme Court: *Plessy v. Ferguson,* 1896

http://www.sgs-austin.org/schoollife/8a/index.htm

In 1892 Homer Plessy, an African-American, refused to sit in a separate railroad car as mandated by the state of Louisiana, which in 1890 had adopted a law proclaiming "equal but separate accommodations for the white and colored races." Created by the eighth-grade Language Arts and Social Studies students at Saint Gabriel's Catholic School in Austin, Texas, this exuberant Web site contains valuable information on the struggle of African-Americans to achieve their equitable share of the American Dream.

Vaudeville

http://memory.loc.gov/ammem/vshtml/vshome.html

Before television, radio, and movies there was vaudeville! This American Memory Web site hosted by the Library of Congress contains a wealth of information on this popular turn-of-the-century entertainment medium. Included are sound recordings, motion picture clips, theater playbills and programs, and much more.

Westward the Empire: Omaha's World Fair of 1898

http://www.unotv.unomaha.edu/wte.html

This interesting Web site, the result of a television documentary produced by the UNO Television Network in conjunction with the Nebraska ETV Network, chronicles the Trans-Mississippi and International Exposition, which debuted on June 1, 1898, in Omaha, Nebraska. This interesting Web narrative explores the celebration of the West's economic and cultural development as seen appropriately enough through personalities such as William Jennings Bryan.

The Age of Roosevelt

Andrew Kersten and Anne Rothfeld

Metasites

American Memory

http://lcweb2.loc.gov/ammem

This Web site is maintained by the Library of Congress and ought to be the first site visited by anyone interested in American history.

New Deal Network

http://newdeal.feri.org

The Franklin and Eleanor Roosevelt Institute sponsors this Web site, which is the starting point for all issues, historical figures, and events about the Age of Roosevelt.

Historical Figures

Herbert C. Hoover

Herbert C. Hoover Presidential Library and Museum

http://www.hoover.nara.gov

The Hoover Presidential Library and Museum constructed this Web site, which contains information on Hoover's presidency, education modules, and research guides to both the Hoover Presidential Papers and the papers of Rose Wilder

Lane and her mother Laura Ingalls Wilder. Rose Wilder wrote one of the first biographies of Hoover, published in 1919. This site, the best place to start for topics on Hoover, is updated weekly and has links to related sites.

White House: Herbert Hoover

http://www.whitehouse.gov/history/presidents/hh31.html

Maintained by the White House staff, this page has biographies of President Hoover and the First Lady, Lou Henry Hoover, with links to the text of Hoover's inaugural address and to the Hoover Presidential Library.

Huey P. Long

Every Man a King: Excerpts from Huey Long's Autobiography

http://www.ssa.gov./history/huey.html

Constructed by the Social Security Administration, this site contains excerpts from Long's autobiography, *Every Man a King*, published in 1933.

My First Days in the White House: Excerpts from Huey Long's "Second Autobiography"

http://www.ssa.gov./history/hueywhouse.html

The Social Security Administration also maintains this page, in which one can find excerpts from all eight chapters of Long's 1935 book, *My First Days in the White House*.

Anna Eleanor Roosevelt

Eleanor Roosevelt: The American Woman

http://www.geocities.com/CollegePark/Library/4142/index.html

Created by Deborah K. Girkin, this excellent site contains extensive biographical and bibliographical information, documents, pictures, cartoons, and links to other sites on ER. A good place to start a search on Eleanor Roosevelt.

Eleanor Roosevelt Center at Val-Kill

http://www.ervk.org

Val-Kill was Eleanor Roosevelt's cottage along the Hudson River. The Val-Kill Center's purpose is "to preserve Eleanor Roosevelt's home as a vibrant living memorial, a center for the exchange of significant ideas and a catalyst for change and for the betterment of the human condition." The center's Web page provides information, photographs, and an extensive list of useful links to topics and issues concerning her.

Eleanor Roosevelt Resource Page

http://personalweb.smcvt.edu/smahady/ercover.htm

This is a wonderful place to start any Internet search relating to ER. The site, authored by Sherry S. Mahady, contains biographical and bibliographical information, quotes from scholars and peers, documents from ER's newspaper column, newspaper articles, letters from her papers and the National Archives, video clips, and links to other sites with information, pictures, and documents pertaining to Eleanor Roosevelt.

Franklin D. Roosevelt

FDR Cartoon Collection Database

http://www.nisk.k12.ny.us/fdr

At this award-winning site, constructed by Paul Bachorz of Niskayuna High School in Niskayuna, New York, one can find an extensive collection of over 30,000 FDR cartoons taken from newspapers and magazines during the 1930s and 1940s. There are also links to other Web sites, suggestions for school teachers, and Roosevelt's inaugural addresses.

Franklin D. Roosevelt Library and Museum

http://www.academic.marist.edu/fdr

Created by the staff of the Roosevelt Presidential Library, this site provides short biographies of the president and the First Lady. Additionally, the site contains several guides to the collections at the Roosevelt Presidential Library. Increasingly the library is putting documents online. Now accessible is a collection of several thousand documents from the White House safe files during the Roosevelt years. Finally, there is an exceptional, copyright-free, online photograph database.

White House: Franklin D. Roosevelt

http://www.whitehouse.gov/history/presidents/fr32.html

The White House staff maintains this site, which contains short biographies of Franklin and Eleanor Roosevelt. There are links to the texts of FDR's inaugural addresses.

The Great Depression

African-Americans and the New Deal
http://newdeal.feri.org/texts/subject.htm

This location, part of the New Deal Network, contains dozens of documents relating to blacks and the New Deal.

American Memory: FSA-OWI Photographs
http://lcweb2.loc.gov/ammem/fsowhome.html

American Memory, maintained by the Library of Congress, is a wonderful Web site for all topics in American history, with thousands of primary sources that relate to the Age of Roosevelt. This particular location contains over 50,000 (including 1,600 in color) Farm Security Administration and Office of War Information photographs covering the years 1935 to 1945.

The Shenandoah Chapter of the Civilian Conservation Corps
http://pages.prodigy.com/reunion/ccc.htm

The Shenandoah Chapter of the CCC, an organization of former agency workers, scholars, and interested people, maintains this site, which contains pictures, stories, poetry, and links to other sites concerning the CCC.

Dust Bowl Refugees in California
http://www.sfmuseum.org/hist8/ok.html

The Museum of the City of San Francisco maintains a Web page on California history that has this section on Dust Bowl refugees. It contains primary sources and photographs.

The Voices from the Dust Bowl: The Charles L. Todd and Robert Sonkin Migrant Worker Collection, 1940–1941
http://lcweb2.loc.gov/ammem/afctshtml/tshome.html

This page, part of American Memory, contains oral histories, photographs, and dozens of other primary documents relating to the Dust Bowl.

New Deal Art in South Carolina

http://people.clemson.edu/~hiotts/index.htm

This online exhibit of New Deal art in South Carolina, maintained by Susan Giaimo Hiott, has art from the state and links to New Deal art in other states, topics about the Age of Roosevelt, and exhibits from other libraries and museums. A visit to this page is worthwhile even if South Carolinian art is not one's primary topic.

A New Deal for the Arts

http://www.nara.gov/exhall/newdeal/newdeal.html

The National Archives and Records Administration maintains a Web version of this exhibit. The page has several good examples of New Deal art in various forms, including painting, photographs, and posters.

The Trials of the Scottsboro Boys

http://www.law.umkc.edu/faculty/projects/FTrials/scottsboro/scottsb.htm

This location is part of the larger Famous American Trials Web site created by Doug Linder. The page on the Scottsboro boys contains a short history, bio-graphical and bibliographical information, photographs, and trial documents.

Social Security Administration Online History

http://www.ssa.gov/history

The United States Social Security Administration built this page, which con-tains oral histories, video and audio clips, documents, photographs, brief biog-raphies, and guides to the Social Security Administration archives.

Supreme Court Decisions (Legal Information Institute)

http://supct.law.cornell.edu:8080/supct/

The Legal Information Institute and Cornell University sponsor this Supreme Court decisions Web site, which is an excellent place to gain quick access to decisions from the Wagner Act to Japanese Relocation. The site also contains general information on the Supreme Court.

Works Progress (later Projects) Administration (WPA) Folklore Project and Federal Writers Project

http://lcweb.loc.gov/ammem/wpaintro/

This American Memory site has several thousand WPA folklore and federal writers projects representing over 300 authors from twenty-four states.

WPA's California Gold: Northern California Folk Music from the Thirties

http://lcweb2.loc.gov/ammem/afccchtml/cowhome.html

This American Memory Web site includes sound recordings, still photographs, drawings, and written documents from a variety of European ethnic and English- and Spanish-speaking communities in Northern California. The collection comprises thirty-five hours of folk music recorded in twelve languages representing numerous ethnic groups and 185 musicians. This collection is well documented and easy to use.

WPA Murals and Artwork from Lane Technical High School Collection

http://www.lanehs.com/art.htm

Maintained by Flora Doody, the director of Lane Technical High School's Artwork Restoration Project, this site has lots of WPA artwork, including eleven frescoes, two oil on canvas murals, an oil on steel fire curtain, two carved mahogany murals, and two cast concrete fountain statues. The site also contains artwork created for the General Motors Exhibition at The Century of Progress, Chicago's World Fair (1933–34).

World War II Home Front

Anne Rothfeld and Alexander Zukas

German Prisoners of War in Clinton, Mississippi

http://www2.netdoor.com/~allardma/powcamp2.html

Mike Allard's site has minimal text but some interesting pictures of German prisoners at the Clinton, Mississippi, POW camp.

The Homefront During World War II

http://www.gettysburg.edu/~mbirkner/fys120/homefront.html

Professor Michael Birkner of Gettysburg College created this Web site for his first-year seminar class. The site hosts oral histories of the residents of Adams County, Pennsylvania, a photo gallery of Gettysburg College during the war, advertising from the war years, and excerpts from the *Gettysburg Times* concerning everyday life on the home front. The site clarifies how the war affected small-town America.

The Japanese-American Internment

http://www.geocities.com/Athens/8420/main.html
http://www.oz.net/~cyu/internment/main.html (mirror site)

This is a rich and very developed site concerning the internment of Japanese-Americans during World War II. Included are sections on prewar intelligence reports on the loyalty of Japanese-Americans, the politics of internment, the state of mind and intentions of policy makers, life in the camps, the impact of the camps on those detained, and firsthand accounts by survivors. The site, maintained and regularly updated by C. John Yu, contains a large number of links to other Web sites exploring issues surrounding the internment of Japanese-Americans.

Japanese-American Internment (Resource Page for Teachers)

http://www.umass.edu/history/institute_dir/internment.html

The History Institute at the University of Massachusetts at Amherst sponsors this site, which is perhaps the best place to start searching for material on the internment of Japanese-Americans. Well organized and with dozens of Web links to documents, pictures, and related camp information, this site, designed for K-12 teachers, provides rich primary sources for classroom curricula.

Japanese-American Internment and San Francisco

http://www.sfmuseum.org/war/evactxt.html

This site, maintained by the Museum of the City of San Francisco, contain dozens of newspaper articles about Japanese-American removal, photographs (including those by Dorothea Lange), contemporary accounts, and related information about internment.

Japanese-American Internment at Harmony

http://www.lib.washington.edu/exhibits/harmony/Exhibit/default.html

The University of Washington Libraries created this Web page, which contains primary source material including letters, the camp newspaper, drawings, pictures, and other documents. It is a useful place to begin an Internet search about internment; researchers should consult the other sites on internment in this section in order to compare Harmony with other camps.

Japanese American Internment in Arizona

http://dizzy.library.arizona.edu/images/jpamer/wraintro.html

This exhibit, directed by Roger Myers of the University of Arizona, has maps, photographs, primary documents, such as the text of Executive Order 9066, and poetry.

Japanese Internment Camps During the Second World War

http://www.lib.utah.edu/spc/photo/9066/9066.htm

This online photograph exhibit, sponsored by the University of Utah Special Collections Department, displays a sampling of the library's collections concerning the internment of Japanese-Americans, particularly at the Topaz and Tule Lake camps.

The Lions' History: Researching World War II Images of African-Americans

http://www.nara.gov/publications/prologue/burger.html

Barbara Lewis Burger of the National Archives gathered this remarkable series of photos after immersing herself in African-American military history and researching life on the home front in the 1940s. Her intent was to produce a publication that both fills a visual documentation void and stimulates interest in both black history and the holdings of the National Archives. This Web site does achieve both goals.

OWI Photographs

http://lcweb2.loc.gov/ammem/fsowhome.html

This site contains thousands of photographs of the home front taken for the Office of War Information during the war years. It is part of the American Memory project maintained by the Library of Congress.

Pictures of World War II

http://www.nara.gov/nara/nn/nns/ww2photo.html

The National Archives has a treasure-trove of images from World War II. The war was documented on a huge scale by thousands of photographers and artists who created millions of pictures. American military photographers representing all the armed services covered battlefronts around the world. Every activity of the war was photographed. On the home front, the many federal war agencies produced and collected pictures, posters, and cartoons on such subjects as war production, rationing, and civilian relocation. Among the areas covered in this photo ensemble are Leaders, The Home Front, Supply and Support, Rest and Relaxation, Aid and Comfort, and Victory and Peace. If a picture is worth a thousand words, then little more needs to be said.

Rosie the Riveter and Other Women: World War II Heroes

http://www.u.arizona.edu/~kari/rosie.htm

This site contains short vignettes about women's roles in World War II, when women were factory workers, nurses, doctors, soldiers, journalists, prostitutes, and subjects of propaganda art. The site provides a different perspective on the war and some little-known information. A number of World War II propaganda posters illustrate the points in the texts.

Rutgers Oral History Archives of World War II

http://fas-history.rutgers.edu/oralhistory/orlhom.htm

The Rutgers World War II oral history project was funded by the Rutgers class of 1942 and directed by Sandra Stewart Holyoak. Several dozen oral histories from veterans and civilians are available for download (in Adobe Acrobat format).

San Francisco During World War II

http://www.sfmuseum.org/1906/ww2.html

This site, maintained by the Museum of the City of San Francisco, contains information about San Francisco during the war years. Most of the primary sources on this site come from the *San Francisco News*.

Topaz Camp

http://www.millardcounty.com/topazcamp.html

Millard County, Utah, hosts this site, which provides a brief overview of Topaz, a Japanese-American "relocation camp" located in Millard County during World War II. The site explains the background of the relocation of Japanese-Americans, life in the camp, and conditions in the desert. The site also boasts picture postcards of the camp.

What Did You Do in the War, Grandma? Rhode Island Women During World War II

http://www.stg.brown.edu/projects/WWII_Women/tocCS.html

An oral history of Rhode Island women during World War II, written by students in the Honors English Program at South Kingstown High School, this site provides not only information about lesser-known aspects of the war, but also a good model of action for teachers interested in using the Internet for class projects.

World War II Posters: Powers of Persuasion

http://www.nara.gov/exhall/powers/powers.html

The National Archives and Records Administration maintains this page, which has thirty-three war posters and one sound file. The page is divided into two categories representing the two psychological approaches used in rallying public support for the war.

World War II Poster Collection

http://www.library.nwu.edu/govpub/collections/wwii-posters/

The Northwestern University Library's Government Publications division maintains this site. It has a searchable database of 300 wartime posters.

World War II Military History

Alexander Zukas

A-Bomb WWW Museum

http://www.csi.ad.jp/ABOMB/

This online project is a Japanese-hosted Web site designed to inform visitors about the effects of atomic weapons on Hiroshima and Nagasaki and to encourage discussions about world peace. Produced by the Hiroshima City University Department of Computer Science, the site gives a different perspective on the dropping of atomic weapons on Japan from that usually found in the United States. The creators of the Web site state, "The website is neither meant to condemn nor condone the bombing, but is meant as a way for people to express their views on how to achieve peace, on what peace is, and other thoughts about peace." Although the site is a somewhat random collection of material, it will stimulate student discussion of the issues surrounding the use of atomic weapons at the end of World War II and the cultural legacy of the bomb.

Achtung Panzer

http://www.achtungpanzer.com/panzer.htm

One of the many enthusiast sites dedicated to German armor. This one features many illustrations, tables of technical data, and a large number of links to other World War II sites.

Atomic Bomb Decision

http://www.dannen.com/decision/index.html

This site contains full-text documents on the arguments for and against the use of atomic weapons on human targets in the months leading up to the dropping of the atomic bomb on Hiroshima. Most of the originals are in the U.S. National Archives.

The Battle of Britain

http://www.raf.mod.uk/bob1940/bobhome.html

This is a detailed and extensive Web site about the aerial battle over Great Britain in 1940. Hosted by the Royal Air Force, it contains the official reports and a day-by-day account of the four-month battle.

China Defensive, 1942–1945: The China Theater of Operations

http://www2.army.mil/cmh-pg/brochures/72-38/72-38.htm

This account of World War II in China was prepared in the U.S. Army Center of Military History by Mark D. Sherry. In it he explains the differences between the Chinese, European, and Pacific war fronts, what the United States hoped to achieve in China, and the ultimate result of U.S. interventions, supplies, and strategic intentions. The site helps fill out the picture of World War II in this major theatre of the war.

Codebreaking and Secret Weapons in World War II

http://home.earthlink.net/~nbrass1/enigma.htm

This site deals with some of the secret weapons developed by the combatants in World War II and how the Allies found out about the ones the Axis had developed. The site provides a window on the clandestine but militarily significant aspects of the war.

Dad's War: Finding and Telling Your Father's World War II Story

http://members.aol.com/dadswar/index.htm

If you can tolerate the small promotional effort for his works on writing personal history, Wes Johnson has done a service with this index of personal histories and initial instructions for writing your own history for a family member who served in World War II (and, by extension, any war).

East Anglia: The Air War

http://www.stable.demon.co.uk/

Contains a series of informative essays with illustrations concerning various air forces and the aircraft flown during World War II. The site also provides an excellent index of links to related Web pages and a bibliography of print reference works.

Feldgrau.com: A German Military History Research Site 1919–1945

http://www.feldgrau.com/

A detailed Web site developed by an independent scholar working on a number of projects related to German World War II military history. It covers "the history of the units and formations of the various military, paramilitary, and auxiliary forces from 1933–45." Includes discussions of various battles and a bibliography of nearly five hundred titles.

504th World War II Home Page

http://www.geocities.com/~the 504thpir/index.html

An example of the many sites dedicated to military units, this one chronicles the experiences of the 504th Parachute Infantry Regiment during World War II.

Guadalcanal Online

http://www.geocities.com/Heartland/Plains/6672/canal_index.html

Detailed discussion of the first major American offensive in the war in the Pacific.

Hyperwar: A Hypertext History of the Second World War

http://www.ibiblio.org/hyperwar/

A linked anthology of articles related to World War II, many of them discussing specific battles in detail, along with links to other sources.

Imperial Japanese Navy Page

http://www.combinedfleet.com/

Enthusiast Jon Parshall has created a detailed index to links about the Japanese navy during World War II, including detailed histories of individual vessels.

The Luftwaffe Home Page

http://www.ww2.dk/

This site provides data on the *Luftwaffe* and an index of links to *Luftwaffe*-related Web pages.

A Marine Diary: My Experiences on Guadalcanal

http://www.gnt.net/~jrube/index2.html

Entries from the diary of a marine who served at Guadalcanal, with a large set of links to related World War II resources on the Internet.

Midway

http://www.history.navy.mil/photos/events/wwii-pac/midway/midway.htm

This Department of the Navy Naval Historical Center site contains a detailed narrative and excellent photographs of the battle. This is a good place to start gathering information about this important battle, often considered the turning point of the war in the Pacific. The site contains a FAQ section and a list of related resources.

Nanjing Massacre Archive

http://www.cnd.org/njmassacre/index.html

The *China News Digest* hosts this extensive site on the famous Nanjing Massacre in 1937–38 in China, including the war crimes testimony and trial after the war.

Naval Air War in the Pacific

http://www.ixpres.com/ag1caf/navalwar

Photos and paintings of American air combat during World War II.

Normandy: 1944

http://normandy.eb.com/

The *Encyclopedia Britannica*'s multimedia examination of the Normandy invasion.

The Pacific War: The U.S. Navy

http://www.microworks.net/pacific/

This page, a conscious complement and counterpoint to the Imperial Japanese Navy page above, informs visitors of the U.S. Navy's contribution to the overall victory that ended World War II with as much awesome detail as can be mustered. Comparing the information on both Web sites will give the student of World War II naval warfare an excellent overview of the military strength and tactics of these two major Pacific powers. The sites also contain short profiles of naval leaders and personal histories of veterans.

A People at War

http://www.nara.gov/exhall/people/people.html

This site, an online exhibition by the National Archives, focuses much more on the people who served than on a traditional history of the war. It includes a brief discussion of events leading up to the war and links to related sites.

Propaganda Leaflets of the Second World War

http://www.cobweb.nl/jmoonen/

Most of the propaganda shown in these pages is anti-Nazi (airdropped by the U.K./U.S. Allied Air Forces). The Nazis used the same weapon of propaganda and these Nazi leaflets are shown here also. The Web site's author warns that the images and texts of the Nazi propaganda leaflets can be disturbing and offensive on religious, racial, or ethnic grounds. The material, which is produced exactly from the originals, provides visitors with good comparisons on the use of symbols and propaganda during the war.

Red Steel

http://www.algonet.se/~toriert/

Enthusiast Thorleif Olsson's extensive Web site on Russian tanks and armored vehicles.

Return to Midway

http://www.nationalgeographic.com/features/98/midway/

National Geographic has created this multimedia site featuring images and streaming video of the wrecks of the carriers sunk at the Battle of Midway.

The Russian Campaign, 1941–1945: A Photo Diary

http://www.geipelnet.com/war_albums/otto/ow_011.html

This site is the diary of a German soldier along with pictures he took of his experiences on the Russian front with an antitank battalion. It covers the whole span of the Russian campaign and provides an on-the-ground look at the fortunes of German troops and rare scenes of the fighting between German and Russian forces.

U-Boat Net

http://uboat.net/

A comprehensive study of the German U-boat, including maps, technology, and profiles of more than 1,100 German submarines employed during World War II.

Women Come to the Front: Journalists, Photographers, and Broadcasters During World War II

http://lcweb.loc.gov/exhibits/wcf/wcf0001.html

This Library of Congress site documents the work of eight female war correspondents, most of whom worked overseas while a few documented the home front. The site provides some corrective to the male-dominated discussions of World War II life at the front while documenting continued male prerogative in the periodical business.

The Women's Army Corps

http://www.army.mil/cmh-pg/brochures/wac/wac.htm

The United States Army has developed this online article about the Women's Army Corps during World War II.

The World at War

http://www.euronet.nl/users/wilfried/ww2/ww2.htm

Wilfried Braakhuis has created an extremely detailed timeline of the war, with illustrations, statistics, and a very large number of links, organized by relevant dates. This graphic-intensive site takes a while to load, but is worth looking at.

World War Two in Europe

http://www.historyplace.com/worldwar2/timeline/ww2time.htm

Part of The History Place, a large Web site dedicated to assisting students and educators, this is a World War II timeline with links to illustrations and short articles on specific events.

World War II on the Web

http://www.geocities.com/Athens/Oracle/2691/welcome.htm

An index to more than 400 Web sites concerned with World War II, many of them highly specialized.

World War II Propaganda Posters (U.S.)

http://www.openstore.com/posters/index.html

This is an interesting collection of World War II posters from the United States. They range from recruiting posters to those exhorting greater patriotism, sacrifice, and secrecy. The posters provide an excellent window on wartime culture, at least as officially propagated by the U.S. government.

World War II Resources

http://metalab.unc.edu/pha/index.html

An extensive collection of historical documents from World War II based at the University of North Carolina, Chapel Hill.

World War II Seminar

http://ac.acusd.edu/History/classes/ww2/175.html

Class materials for a World War II history course from the University of San Diego, including an extended bibliography and several timelines created by students.

World War II Sites

http://www.geocities.com/dboals.geo/a-art1a.html#WORLD%20WAR%20II

This is an excellent directory to over 200 Web sites on all aspects of World War II. The major purpose of this directory is to encourage the use of the World Wide Web as a tool for learning and teaching and to provide some help for teachers in locating and using the resources of the Internet in the classroom. This directory is a superb place to start searching for Web sites on World War II.

The World War II Sounds and Pictures Page

http://www.earthstation1.com/wwii.html

Sounds, video, and images of aircraft, warships, propaganda posters, and many other items related to World War II.

The World War II Study: North Africa

http://www.topedge.com/panels/ww2/na/index.html

In this site, many issues regarding the North Africa campaign of the Allies from 1940 to 1943 receive a fresh look. The author examines the importance of North Africa to the Allies and Axis and dispels myths about the campaigns and personalities of the North African theater. He provides a timeline of the conflict and discusses supply issues, troop levels, weaponry, commanders, tactics, and high-command disputes.

World War II Timeline

http://history.acusd.edu/gen/WW2Timeline/start.html

A fairly good and general timeline for World War II that includes a very valuable list of additional links, interesting pictures, maps, and documents, and a good bibliography. Includes some student pages. A first-rate site by Steve Schoenherr of the University of San Diego's History Department.

The Cold War

Margaret M. Manchester and Alexander Zukas

American Experience: Race for the Superbomb

http://www.pbs.org/wgbh/pages/amex/bomb

This PBS companion site explores a top secret U.S. Cold War program to build a weapon more powerful than the atomic bomb dropped on Japan. The site includes audio clips, a timeline, primary documents, and other educational materials.

The Avalon Project: Documents in Law, History, and Diplomacy

http://www.yale.edu/lawweb/avalon/coldwar.htm

Maintained by the Yale University Law School, this site contains basic documents relating to American Foreign Policy 1941–49; the United States Atomic Energy Commission proceedings in the Matter of J. Robert Oppenheimer; The Warsaw Security Pact: May 14, 1955; State Department Papers Relating to the Foreign Relations of the United States, Vol. X, Part 1, 1958–60; the U-2 Incident: 1960; the RB-47 Airplane Incident: July–September 1960; and the Cuban Missile Crisis.

The Berlin Airlift

http://www.wpafb.af.mil/museum/history/postwwii/ba.htm

This Web site is part of the larger online exhibit entitled U.S. Air Force Museum, Post–World War II History Gallery 1946–50s. The focus is primarily military. The site is a good source of information and images of the aircraft used to airlift provisions to the inhabitants of Berlin.

Chronology of Russian History: The Soviet Period

http://www.departments.bucknell.edu/russian/chrono3.html

The Bucknell University History Department maintains this chronology of Soviet history from 1917 to 1991. The chronology contains numerous links to primary and secondary source materials that provide further information and background.

CIA and Assassinations: The Guatemala 1954 Documents

http://www.gwu.edu/~nsarchiv/NSAEBB/NSAEBB4/index.html

The National Security Archive is an independent, nongovernmental research institute and library located at George Washington University in Washington, D.C. The archive collects and publishes declassified documents acquired through the Freedom of Information Act. On May 23, 1997, the CIA released several hundred records verifying the CIA's involvement in the infamous 1954 coup in Guatemala at the height of the Cold War politics of "brinkmanship." Some of these documents, including an instructional guide on assassination found among the training files of the CIA's covert "Operation PBSUCCESS," are stored on this site.

CNN: Cold War

http://cnn.com/SPECIALS/cold.war/

This Web site was created to accompany the twelve-part series on the Cold War airing on CNN in the winter and spring of 1998–99. The Web site is a valuable resource because it provides an extraordinary diversity of materials, including multimedia and audio clips, interactive maps, primary documents, newspaper and journal coverage of the events, and transcripts of interviews that formed the basis for the series.

Cold War Hot Links: Web Resources Relating to the Cold War

http://www.stmartin.edu/~dprice/cold.war.html

David Price, an anthropologist at St. Martin's College in Lacey, Washington, has compiled an impressive list of links to Web sites that contain primary sources as well as essays and analyses examining the impact of the Cold War on American culture.

Cold War International History Project

http://cwihp.si.edu/default.htm

The Cold War International History Project (CWIHP) Web site was established at the Woodrow Wilson International Center for Scholars in Washington, D.C., in 1991. The project supports the full and prompt release of historical materials by governments on all sides of the Cold War. In addition to Western sources, the project has provided translations of documents from Eastern European archives that have been released since the collapse of communism in the late 1980s. Users may join discussion groups and download issues of the *Bulletin* issued by CWIHP.

The Cold War Museum

http://www.coldwar.org/

In 1996, Francis Gary Powers, Jr. and John C. Welch founded the Cold War Museum to preserve Cold War history and honor Cold War veterans. The Cold War Museum, a Smithsonian Affiliate Museum, endeavors to maintain a historically accurate record of the people, places, and events of the Cold War that will enable visitors to reflect upon the global geopolitical climate of that period (1940s to 1990s). On its Web site, the museum displays artifacts and memorabilia associated with various Cold War-related events, such as the Marshall Plan, the Berlin airlift, the Korean War, the building of the Berlin Wall, the U-2 incident, the Cuban Missile Crisis, the Vietnam War, President Gorbachev's glasnost, the fall of the Berlin Wall, and the collapse of the Soviet Union.

A Concrete Curtain: The Life and Death of the Berlin Wall

http://www.wall-berlin.org/gb/berlin.htm

This site contains a detailed history of the Berlin Wall from its creation to its destruction. Originally it was part of an exhibition comprising a hundred photographs for the Deutsches Historisches Museum in Berlin; this is a good place to start examining the historical and cultural significance of "The Wall."

The Costs of the Manhattan Project

http://www.brook.edu/FP/PROJECTS/NUCWCOST/MANHATTN.HTM

These estimates were prepared by the Brookings Institute and are part of the larger U.S. Nuclear Weapons Cost Study Project.

The Cuban Missile Crisis

http://www.personal.psu.edu/staff/r/x/rxb297/CUBA/MAIN.HTML

This site contains excellent links to primary and secondary source materials on the Cuban Missile Crisis, including the Library of Congress, the Federation of American Scientists, the State Department, the National Security Archive, and Khrushchev's memoirs. The site provides an overview of the crisis and discusses its causes, U.N. and Turkish involvement, and its outcome.

The Cuban Missile Crisis, 1962

http://www.state.gov/www/about_state/history/frusXI/index.html

This is the site for Volume XI of *Foreign Relations of the United States*, the official U.S. Department of State volume of documents dealing with the Cuban Missile Crisis. The entire volume or excerpts can be read online. A very important source for the official documents dealing with this crisis.

The Cuban Missile Crisis, 1962

http://www.fas.org/irp/imint/cuba.htm

The FAS, the intelligence resource program of the Federation of American Scientists, maintains this metasite. It contains links to online State Department documentation, analysis of Kennedy's advisers, the photographic evidence, transcripts of ExComm deliberations, and photographic evidence of the Soviet presence in Cuba until the 1980s.

The Cuban Missile Crisis, October 18–29, 1962

http://www.hpol.org/jfk/cuban/

This Web site contains audio files of a set of tape recordings released by the John F. Kennedy Library in October 1996. These recordings, made in the Oval Office, include President Kennedy's personal recollections of discussions, conversations with his advisers, and meetings with the Joint Chiefs of Staff and members of the president's executive committee. Transcripts of the audio files are included. A rich source of information on the American perspective of the crisis.

Documents Relating to American Foreign Policy: The Cold War

http://www.mtholyoke.edu/acad/intrel/coldwar.htm

The International Relations Program at Mount Holyoke College maintains this Web site. Arranged on a yearly basis from pre-1945 to recent retrospectives on the meaning and significance of the Cold War, this site contains hundreds of links to both primary and secondary source material—especially useful to students and researchers because of the variety of sources available.

Documents Relating to American Foreign Policy: Cuban Missile Crisis

http://www.mtholyoke.edu/acad/intrel/cuba.htm

This collection of links allows researchers and students access to newspaper coverage of the crisis, information relating to Soviet and Cuban perspectives, and essays and books by the most influential historians of this crisis.

Famous American Trials: Rosenbergs Trial, 1951

http://www.law.umkc.edu/faculty/projects/ftrials/rosenb/ROSENB.HTM

Created by Professor Douglas Linder of the University of Missouri, Kansas City School of Law, this Web site contains links to a wealth of firsthand materials, including excerpts from the trial transcript, the judge's sentencing statement, excerpts from appellate court decisions, images, the Rosenbergs' final letter to their sons, and a link to the Perlin Papers, a collection of about 250,000 pages related to the investigation, trial, and execution of Julius and Ethel Rosenberg. The papers were declassified in the 1970s.

Fifty Years from Trinity

http://www.seattletimes.com/trinity/supplement/internet.html

The *Seattle Times* compiled this list of Internet resources relating to the development of the atomic bomb and nuclear energy.

For European Recovery: The Fiftieth Anniversary of the Marshall Plan

http://lcweb.loc.gov/exhibits/marshall

An excellent online exhibit prepared by the Library of Congress, containing primary and secondary source materials on the Marshall Plan and links developed by the Koninklijke Bibliotheek (the National Library of the Netherlands) and other European libraries.

Harvard Project on Cold War Studies

http://www.fas.harvard.edu/~hpcws/

This annotated set of links relating to the study of the Cold War is prepared and maintained by the Davis Center for Russian Studies at Harvard University. The project intends to build on the achievements of the Cold War International History Project and the National Security Archive. The site also contains links to Harvard University's new *Journal of Cold War Studies*.

A History of the Berlin Wall in Text and Pictures

http://members.aol.com/johball/berlinwl.htm

This site was an entry in the Connecticut state competition for National History Day on May 10, 1997. It is a great resource for K-12 students to explore the history of the wall.

The Hungarian Revolution, 1956

http://www.osa.ceu.hu/archives/rip/1956/index.htm

Links are provided to both English-language and Hungarian resources, both primary and secondary.

An Introduction to National Archives Records Relating to the Cold War

http://www.nara.gov/publications/rip/rip107/rip107.html

Hosted by the National Archives, this metasite was compiled by Tim Wehrkamp. It identifies several representative series and data sets of textual, electronic, still picture, and motion picture records that document U.S. government policies, programs, and actions during the Cold War. The compilers have chosen records that illustrate the range and content of National

Archives and Records Administration (NARA) holdings relating to this period. These records by no means represent all NARA-held documentation concerning the topic. The intended audience for this publication is graduate students and other researchers new to the field of Cold War history and unfamiliar with NARA records. It would be a good place for them to begin their research.

The National Security Archive Homepage

http://www.gwu.edu/~nsarchiv/

The National Security Archive is an independent, nongovernmental research institute and library located at George Washington University in Washington, D.C. The archive collects and publishes declassified documents gathered through the Freedom of Information Act (FOIA). The archive boasts the world's largest nongovernmental library of declassified documents, including thousands of documents relating to nuclear history, U.S.-Japanese relations, the Cuban Missile Crisis, and other crises of the 1960s and 1970s.

1948: The Alger Hiss Spy Case

http://www.thehistorynet.com/AmericanHistory/articles/1998/698_cover.htm

This site links to a June 1998 *American History* article by James Thomas Gay that examines the Alger Hiss case and the issues that still remain unresolved fifty years later.

The Real Thirteen Days: The Hidden History of the Cuban Missile Crisis

http://www.gwu.edu/~nsarchiv/nsa/cuba_mis_cri/

The National Security Archive has created an extensive Web site on the Cuban Missile Crisis. It includes the essays "Turning History on Its Head" by Philip Brenner, "The Declassified Documents" by Peter Kornbluh and Laurence Chang, "The Most Dangerous Moment in the Crisis" by Jim Hershberg, and "Annals of Blinksmanship" by Thomas Blanton. Visitors can hear audio clips of White House meetings, read the documents exchanged between the White House and the Kremlin, see the U-2 surveillance photos of Russian missile installations, and read a detailed chronology of events relating to the crisis from 1959 to 1992. The site is revisionist and dedicated to dispelling myths about the crisis, especially the myth of calibrated brinkmanship—the belief that if you stand tough you win and that nuclear superiority made the difference in moments of crisis.

Secrets of War

http://www.secretsofwar.com/

This is the companion site to the History Channel's twenty-six-part documentary series entitled *Sworn to Secrecy: Secrets of War*, which was aired in 1998. The site contains transcripts, links to maps, images, and other information relating to the history of espionage.

A Select Bibliography of the U-2 Incident

http://redbud.lbjlib.utexas.edu/eisenhower/u2.htm

This brief bibliography is located at the Dwight D. Eisenhower Presidential Library.

Senator Joe McCarthy: A Multimedia Celebration

http://webcorp.com/mccarthy/

This archive contains film and audio clips from Senator Joseph McCarthy's speeches and appearances on television.

Soviet Archives Exhibit

http://metalab.unc.edu/expo/soviet.exhibit/entrance.html#tour

The Library of Congress developed this online exhibit. Visitors to this site may browse images of documents from the Soviet archives. The two main sections of this exhibit are the Internal Workings of the Soviet System and The Soviet Union and the United States. The section on postwar estrangement includes commentary on Soviet perspectives on the Cold War and the Cuban Missile Crisis.

A Trip Through the Cold War

http://www.bishops.ntc.nf.ca/socstud/coldwar/index.htm

This multimedia project is a product of the History 3201 classes at Bishops College, an urban high school in eastern Canada. The Web site provides an overview of significant people and events of the Cold War era. Its creators hope that students from all over the world will participate in the project. The site includes student essays on various topics of the Cold War, such as the Berlin airlift, the Berlin Wall, the Cuban Missile Crisis, the Korean War, and the Vietnam War, with photos and links to other sites on the Internet. The site provides an imaginative use of the Web for beginning, publishing, and archiving high school history projects.

The U-2 Incident 1960

http://www.yale.edu/lawweb/avalon/u2.htm

The Avalon Project at Yale University developed this Web site, a useful starting place for finding the basic diplomatic documents, including the exchange of notes between the U.S. and Soviet governments, public statements by State Department officials, and the documentation maintained by the State Department in the Foreign Relations of the United States Series.

The VENONA Project

http://www.nsa.gov/docs/venona/index.html

VENONA was the codename used for the U.S. Signals Intelligence effort to collect and decrypt the text of Soviet KGB and GRU messages from the 1940s. These messages provided extraordinary insight into Soviet attempts to infiltrate the highest levels of the U.S. government. The National Security Agency has declassified over 3,000 messages related to VENONA and made them available at its home page.

Twentieth-Century American History

Scott A. Merriman and Dennis A. Trinkle

The American Experience: America 1900

http://www.pbs.org/wgbh/pages/amex/1900/index.html

This site looks at the PBS program of the same title, which detailed what life was like in 1900. The site includes a detailed description of the program, a teacher's guide, and a timeline.

American Memory Collection

http://memory.loc.gov/ammem/ammemhome.html

Over fifty collections and one million items are now online. Collections in twentieth-century history range from Baseball Cards to Voices from the Dust Bowl to Mapping the National Parks. Includes a FAQ section and a Today in History section, which has links to related collections and sites. Includes information on future initiatives. A must-see for all interested in American history.

American Temperance and Prohibition

http://www.history.ohio-state.edu/projects/prohibition/

A good overview of the move toward prohibition in America. Includes biographies of key figures, an outline of developments, tables of data for alcohol consumption and beer production, and an excellent collection of cartoons.

Anti-Imperialism in the United States, 1898–1935

http://www.boondocksnet.com/ail98–35.html

This site looks at a variety of issues concerned with American imperialism in the first third of the twentieth century. Presents many writings, including Rudyard Kipling's *The White Man's Burden*, and numerous period cartoons. The U.S. intervention in Haiti and the Philippines, along with many writings on related subjects by William Jennings Bryan, are featured. A good site both for people interested in the period and for teachers.

Apollo Lunar Surface Journal

http://www.hq.nasa.gov/office/pao/History/alsj/frame.html

This site examines the lunar landings of the Apollo missions. It includes many photographs and video clips, summaries of the missions, checklists, crew lists, and crew biographies.

Broadcasting in Chicago, 1921–1989

http://www.mcs.net/~richsam/home.html

This site looks at sixty-eight years of broadcasting in America's Second City. Includes an examination of many of the programs aired in Chicago, including *Amos n' Andy*, and *Fibber McGee and Molly*. A virtual tour of the studio facilities is also available.

CIA and Assassinations: The Guatemala 1954 Documents

http://www.gwu.edu/~nsarchiv/NSAEBB/NSAEBB4/index.html

This site reproduces several primary sources dealing with the CIA's involvement in the 1954 coup in Guatemala, including the CIA's plan for assassination. A useful series of documents focusing on the darker side of our nation's past.

Coal Mining in the Gilded Age and Progressive Era

http://www.history.ohio-state.edu/projects/Lessons_US/Gilded_Age/
Coal_Mining/default.htm

This site looks at coal mining in the late nineteenth and early twentieth centuries. It includes many pictures and reprints of stories from the period and a discussion of the dangers of coal mining. A good site for those interested in coal mining of the period.

Coney Island

http://naid.sppsr.ucla.edu/coneyisland/

An engaging popular culture/history site done by a history buff trained in engineering. It discusses the amusement park and presents articles about its history, a timeline, links to related sites, and maps.

Detroit Photos Home Page from the Library of Congress

http://lcweb2.loc.gov/detroit/

This site, part of the American Memory collection, looks at a collection of 25,000 glass negatives and transparencies, taken by the Detroit Photographic Company, that show life at the turn of the century. Includes information on how to order reprints.

Digger Archives

http://www.diggers.org/

This site presents the story of this anarchist counterculture group of the Sixties. Among its activities, centered in San Francisco, were street theater and free stores. The site presents the activities of the organization, pictures, and links to current related groups. An interesting look at an interesting group.

The Digital Classroom

http://www.nara.gov/education/

Presents classroom lessons utilizing resources available in the National Archives. Includes a documentary analysis sheet that helps users analyze and work with documents—a vital resource. Also presents information about summer development workshops for educators. The heart of the site is a set of units, ten on the twentieth century alone, that use primary documents as teaching tools.

Documents from the Women's Liberation Movement

http://scriptorium.lib.duke.edu/wlm/

This site includes a large number of primary source materials on the women's liberation movement. Organized into categories, but also searchable by keyword. Includes links to related resources.

Early Motion Pictures, 1897–1920

http://memory.loc.gov/cgi-bin/query/r?ammem/collections:@FIELD (SUBJ+@band(Motion+pictures++United+States.)):heading= Subjects%3a+Motion+pictures—United+States.

A large collection from the Library of Congress's American Memory project. An excellent and very engaging site. Includes films of San Francisco around the time of the Great Earthquake and Fire of 1906, and films of New York around the turn of the century.

Edsitement

http://edsitement.neh.fed.us/

A good resource for teachers. Includes a large number of lesson plans for teaching any century of American history by using Web resources. Also provided are simple directions for those unfamiliar with the Web, including a glossary, commentary on the pluses and minuses of the Internet, and "Tips for Better Browsing." A very useful site.

Famous Trials of the Twentieth Century

http://www.law.umkc.edu/faculty/projects/ftrials/ftrials.htm

This site looks at many famous trials in the twentieth century, including the trials of the Rosenbergs, Leopold and Loeb, and the Scottsboro Boys. It also includes a few from before the twentieth century, including the *Amistad* case, the Salem Witch trials, and the Johnson impeachment. A set of very well-done, very informative pages.

The Fifties

http://www.fiftiesweb.com/fifties.htm

Slightly celebratory look at the Fifties. Aimed at the Boomer generation (this site even includes a claim to be "Boomer Enhanced" and thus have no small print), it includes music, TV, and a list of Burma-Shave slogans. An illuminating example of Fifties culture, though not very analytical.

Films: Research and Resources

http://www.gen.umn.edu/faculty_staff/yahnke/film/cinema.htm

This site contains a great number of resources to learn more about film. It includes a list of the top films of each decade with a commentary; a list of good recent films; a list (in the site author's opinion) of the best fifty-five films of all time; and a discussion of intergenerational issues. Although film is not commonly thought of as traditional history, this site provides an interesting look at another side of history.

For European Recovery: The Fiftieth Anniversary of the Marshall Plan

http://lcweb.loc.gov/exhibits/marshall/

This site, presented by the Library of Congress, discusses the Marshall Plan that rebuilt Europe after World War II. It presents a detailed chronology of the plan, explains the reasoning behind it, and provides excerpts from the book *The Marshall Plan and the Future of U.S. European Relations*, which contains documents from the twenty-fifth anniversary of the Marshall Plan.

The Emma Goldman Papers

http://sunsite.Berkeley.EDU/Goldman/

A good example of how a Web site can promote both primary research and general learning. This site presents an online exhibit about Goldman, a late nineteenth/early twentieth-century radical, along with a discussion of the holdings of the Emma Goldman papers. Includes examples from the collection, images, moving pictures, and other materials to help students learn about Goldman. This is what an archive collection site should look like.

Guide to the Supreme Court

http://www.nytimes.com/library/politics/scotus/index-scotus.html

This site, from the *New York Times*, provides a good overview of the Supreme Court at the present time. Includes a list and short description of the "top ten" cases ever decided by the Court, and articles about the justices currently on the court, as well as excerpts from recent decisions.

A History of the White House

http://www.whitehouse.gov/history/index.html

This site, a subsite of the official White House site, contains biographies of every president, First Lady, and family that has lived in the White House. Also contains a history of the building and a virtual tour.

Kennedy Assassination Home Page

http://mcadams.posc.mu.edu/home.htm

The Kennedy Assassination Home Page is the most balanced and extensive online resource for exploring John F. Kennedy's death. It is maintained by John McAdams, a professor of political science at Marquette University. McAdams's list of links on the Kennedy assassination also offers the best gateway to serious and reliable materials.

Little Rock Central High School Fortieth Anniversary

http://www.centralhigh57.org/1957–58.htm

This site examines the integration of Little Rock Central High School in 1957. Provides pictures and videos, a timeline of events, and a look at the fortieth anniversary celebration in 1997.

Lower East Side Tenement Museum

http://www.wnet.org/archive/tenement/

An interesting museum housed in a restored Lower East Side tenement in New York City. This building had been sealed off for fifty years and now is exactly the way it was in 1935. The site also presents unique dollhouse diorama dramatizations of life at the time, complete with descriptions and explanations. It also includes two Quick Time movies of rooms in the tenements as they might have been in the 1870s and 1930s.

NAACP Home Page

http://www.naacp.org/

This site primarily offers information about the modern NAACP currently, but it also explores the NAACP's past and the struggles it has been involved in.

National Archives

http://www.nara.gov/

Everything you wanted to know about the National Archives and Records Administration. Includes the National Archives Archival Information Locator (NAIL), which allows users to search for records. Also has an online exhibit hall with examples of NARA records including the Declaration of Independence, portraits of black Chicago, and gifts given to presidents from Hoover to Clinton. A necessary stop for all wanting to ride the research train. Includes general information on grants, research facilities, records management, and the Federal Register. It must be noted that only a very small percentage of NARA's 4 billion records are online, so this is a good place both to *find* material and to *find* how to *find* material.

National Civil Rights Museum

http://216.157.9.6/civilrights/main.htm

This is the Web site of the National Civil Rights Museum, located in Memphis, Tennessee. The site discusses the museum, gives hours and other basic information, summarizes the exhibits currently portrayed, and includes an in-depth interactive tour of the museum.

Oyez, Oyez, Oyez

http://oyez.nwu.edu/

This site includes hours of audio of arguments before the Supreme Court of the United States. Site also includes pictures and short biographies of each Supreme Court justice, both past and present, and, for some justices, presents links to related resources, transcripts of decisions, and lists of selected cases they participated in.

The Population Bomb

http://www.pbs.org/kqed/population_bomb/

A look at Paul Ehrlich's book *The Population Bomb* and a PBS show based on the book. The book argues that the world's population is exploding at an unsustainable rate and that more developed countries put an overly large strain on the resource base. This site is a favorable look at one of the more important ecology books of the twentieth century. Includes a population timeline.

Presidential Elections, 1860–1996

http://fisher.lib.virginia.edu/elections/maps/

Contains popular and electoral returns for every election between 1860 and 1996. Includes links to related sites.

Presidential Libraries

http://www.nara.gov/nara/president/address.html

A very useful site for users doing research concerning twentieth-century presidents. All presidents from Hoover to Clinton have (or will have) presidential libraries, and this site contains addresses; phone, fax, and e-mail information; and links to specific sites for each library. Includes a very informative overview of the presidential libraries that explains the background of the system and answers basic questions.

Presidential Speeches

http://odur.let.rug.nl/~usa/P/

In addition to presidential speeches, particularly State of the Union and inaugural addresses, this site includes brief presidential biographies and links to other resources. A good starting point to look for presidential addresses.

Project Whistlestop

http://www.whistlestop.org/index.htm

An online examination of President Truman's actions. Includes a discussion of the Truman Doctrine, the Marshall Plan, and the Berlin airlift.

Retro

http://www.retroactive.com/

Web magazine discussing a variety of subjects, including politics, fashion, and music. Includes feature articles, links to related Web sites, a community discussion board, and a vintage postcard depot, where one can send vintage postcards to a friend.

Redstone Arsenal Historical Information

http://www.redstone.army.mil/history/welcome.html

A site dealing with all aspects of the U.S. Army's aviation and missile command. Includes oral histories, information on specific weapons programs, and chronologies of this command's history. Also presents declassified documents and a history of Warner von Braun.

Jonas Salk, Biography

http://www.achievement.org/autodoc/page/sal0bio-1

The site presents the biography of the developer of the polio vaccine, complete with pictures and the transcript of an oral interview with Salk.

Scopes Monkey Trial

http://www.law.umkc.edu/faculty/projects/ftrials/scopes/scopes.htm

This site relates to the 1925 trial in Dayton, Tennessee, of John Scopes for teaching evolution. The trial loosely became the model for the play and movie *Inherit the Wind*. Cartoons, part of the textbook used by John Scopes, and a discussion of *Inherit the Wind* are included in this very balanced and in-depth look at the case.

The Sixties

http://www.bbhq.com/sixties.htm

This is the Sixties section of the Baby Boomer Headquarters. It includes a quiz to test your knowledge of the Sixties, a list of the events of the Sixties, a gallery of Sixties music, and reflections from a baby boomer.

The Sixties

http://www.geocities.com/SoHo/Studios/2914/

This is a general site on the Sixties. Includes biographies of some of the leading counterculture figures, quotations, the full text of Martin Luther King's "I Have a Dream" speech, and an in-depth timeline for the decade.

Skylighters

http://www.skylighters.org/

This is the official site of the 225th AAA Searchlight Battalion. Although the site is still under construction, it is a great starting point for World War II resources. Includes a chronology of World War II, related links, and oral histories.

The *Time* 100

http://cgi.pathfinder.com/time/time100/index.html

This is a list of the 100 most influential people of the century as decided by *Time* magazine. It presents biographies of the 100 with links to related sites.

The Trial of the Century: The Lindbergh Case

http://www.lindberghtrial.com/index.htm

This site reminds us that the O.J. Simpson trial was not the trial of the century. This site presents an outline of the kidnapping, recaps the events of the trial, and includes a timeline to manifest historical context. It contains a wealth of pictures, both of people connected with the trial and with the period. Finally, it discusses what has happened since the trial and some of the main principles involved. Also contains links to related sites.

Trinity Atomic Web Site

http://nuketesting.enviroweb.org/

This site presents a history of the development of atomic weapons, mostly focusing on the United States. It presents documents, movies, quotations, an annotated bibliography, and links to related sites.

Votes for Women

http://www.huntington.org/vfw/

A very good, comprehensive site on the women's suffrage movement presented by the Huntington Library. Includes biographies of important individuals, descriptions of the important organizations involved, a breakdown of the various eras in the movement, and a long list of related links.

Watergate

http://www.washingtonpost.com/wp-srv/national/longterm/watergate/splash1a.htm

This site, sponsored by the *Washington Post*, looks at the controversy and scandal that toppled President Richard Nixon. Includes a timeline, an examination of where key figures in the scandal are now, and speculation on the identity of "Deep Throat," a key source for the reporters.

Women and Social Movements in the United States, 1830–1930

http://womhist.binghamton.edu/

While not wholly on the twentieth century, this is still a good site to explore for this issue. The codirectors of this project include Kathryn Kish Sklar. The site presents undergraduate and graduate student work and includes related links.

Projects of relevance for the twentieth century include Workers and Allies in the New York City Shirtwaist Strike, 1909–1910; Women's International League for Peace and Freedom; and Right-Wing Attacks, 1923–1931. An interesting example of student work posted to the Web.

Writers and Their Works

http://www.pitt.edu/~englweb/weblinks/writers.html

This site examines some of the top nonfiction writers of the postwar era, including Hunter Thompson, Truman Capote, and Joan Didion. Includes links to related sites.

The American West

J. Kelly Robison

The American West is generally thought of as the region of the United States west of the Mississippi River, though sometimes as the area west of the ninety-eighth meridian. Yet historians also study westward expansion, which brings in that area between the Appalachian Mountains and the Mississippi River. In practice, Western American history encompasses a wide scope of place and time. Chronologically, Western History embraces the entirety of human history of the West, from the beginnings in the Neolithic era to the present day. Additionally, historians who study Native American history are usually classified as Western historians, which brings an even larger geographic area and chronological era into the fold. The study of the America West is a diverse field, and the following sites reflect that diversity.

General Sites

America's West: Development and History

http://www.americanwest.com/

Though at first glance this site seems hokey and interested in the much-mythologized "Old West," it does contain useful articles, some images, and links to other sites.

New Perspectives on the West

http://www3.pbs.org/weta/thewest/

The Web site for the PBS special on the American West produced by Ken Burns. An extensive site with links to a wide range of primary documents, articles on various Western topics, and biographies of Western figures.

Sources for the Study of the Southwest

http://www2.smu.edu/swcenter/links.htm

A well-thought-out and well-organized list of links to sites of interest to those studying the Southwest. Link topics range from the cattle industry to the archaeology of the Southwest. Created by Bob Skinner of Southern Methodist University.

WestWeb: Western History Resources

http://www.library.csi.cuny.edu/westweb/

A growing collection of topically organized links to Western history resources. Created and maintained by Catherine Lavendar of the City University of New York. The site is broken down into thirty-one different chapters, each of which contains numerous links to sites that specialize in that topic. Some of the topic chapters also contain image thumbnails linked to National Archives photographs. The site is also indexed. This site should be the first place anyone interested in Western history sites on the Web should go.

Topical Sites

Borders/*Fronteras*

http://www.si.edu/folklife/vfest/frontera/start.htm

The Smithsonian Institution's online exhibit on the southern U.S. border. Contains essays on music (samples in au form), art, language, and culture, as well as a discussion on what is a border. Also available in Spanish.

California Heritage Collection

http://sunsite.Berkeley.EDU/calheritage/

From the Bancroft Library, this site is a collection of over 30,000 images of California's history and culture. Includes resources for K-12 instructors.

California Mission Studies Association

http://www.ca-missions.org/

Dedicated to the study and preservation of California's missions, this organization's Web site contains articles on the missions, a nice glossary of mission-related terms, and some wonderful photographs. The site also maintains both annotated and unannotated links pages.

Crossing the Frontier: Photographs of the Developing West, 1849 to Present

http://WWW.CalHum.ORG/sfmoma-crossing/

An online version of a traveling exhibition developed by the San Francisco Museum of Modern Art. The site itself contains fifty of the three hundred images in the exhibit, several articles on the West, and teachers' resources. The server is slow, so have patience.

General George A. Custer Home Page

http://www.garryowen.com/

A site dedicated to the study of Custer and the Plains Indian Wars. Contains a plethora of information, including short articles, primary data, and photographs. The site itself is poorly designed and the chosen links are often of dubious quality.

Gallery of the Open Frontier

http://gallery.unl.edu/

In development by the University of Nebraska Press, this site contains a searchable image collection, most of which is derived from the National Archives. Although the Gallery has been around for at least four years, it is still in the demonstration stage.

The Interactive Santa Fe Trail (SFT) Homepage

http://raven.cc.ukans.edu/heritage/research/sft/index.html

Created by Nancy Sween for Kansas Heritage, this site's most interesting feature is its extensive list of other sites related to the Santa Fe Trail. The site takes a long time to load, despite relatively few images.

The Japanese-American Internment

http://www.geocities.com/Athens/8420/main.html

Contains a timeline of the Japanese-American internment, basic information on the camps, and remembrances of internees. Numerous links to other Web sites and to primary documents are also available on this site by John Yu.

Klondike Ho! 1897–1997

http://www.kokogiak.com/klon/

Visually impressive site with basic information on the Klondike gold rush. The site was created by Alan Taylor to commemorate the centennial of the gold rush.

The Lewis and Clark Expedition

http://www.pbs.org/lewisandclark/

The Ken Burns PBS production companion site. Contains excerpts from the Corps of Discovery journals, a timeline of the journey, maps of the expedition, interviews with authorities on the expedition, classroom resources for teachers, and numerous other related materials.

Mormon History Resource Page

http://www.indirect.com/www/crockett/history.html

Dave Crockett's site breaks the history of the Mormon Church into several historical periods, including the trek west and the early days in Utah. The site lists many links and also contains original articles by Crockett.

Mountain Men and the Fur Trade: Sources of the History of the Fur Trade in the Rocky Mountain West

http://www.xmission.com/%7Edrudy/amm.html

This nicely done site contains transcripted primary documents from the fur trade era, digitized business records of the fur trade, and a nice collection of digitized images of period artifacts and art.

Multicultural American West

http://www.wsu.edu:8080/~amerstu/mw/

Essentially an online, annotated bibliography of sites relevant to the study of the American West. As the site's name implies, most of the resources and links are related to ethnicity in the West. Designed by the Washington State University American Studies program.

New Mexico Ghost Towns

http://www.vivanewmexico.com/ghosts/ghosts.html

David Pike's compendium of New Mexican ghost towns has a list of most of the depopulated urban areas in the state. His ranking system (which could also be used simply as a list of the ghost towns in New Mexico) is nicely done. Surprisingly, some of the ghost towns on the list still have residents. The individual ghost town pages contain few pictures, but provide information on the towns and short essays by Pike.

The Overland Trail

http://www.over-land.com/

A site dedicated to Ben Holladay's Overland Trail, created by Elizabeth Larson. Contains a large amount of information, including a clickable map to articles that describe the route itself, stopovers, Indian problems along the route, and other topics. Links to other sites are categorized by topic and include brief descriptions.

The Silent Westerns: Early Movie Myths of the American West

http://xroads.virginia.edu/~HYPER/HNS/Westfilm/west.html

Mary Halnon's site devoted to the portrayal of the West in silent film includes excellent essays on the early film industry and the mythologized elements in Western movies.

Vigilantes of Montana: Secret Trials and Midnight Hangings

http://montana-vigilantes.org/

This site, maintained by Louis Schmittroth, contains a wealth of information on the Montana Vigilantes. The site contains online books and articles by well-known Montana historians. The politics of the site are apparent, but the information contained within is well worth perusing.

Who Killed William Robinson?

http://web.uvic.ca/history-robinson/

A wonderful resource for teachers, this site by Ruth Sandwell and John Lutz takes the reader through a historical mystery to determine the identity of a murderer. Contains primary documents and asks pertinent questions dealing with race, politics, and settlement.

Women Artists of the American West, Past and Present

http://www.sla.purdue.edu/waaw/

Created by Susan Ressler of Purdue University and Jerrold Maddox of Penn State, this online exhibit of female artists provides essays on those artists and on particular groups of artists.

Yukon and Alaska History

http://arcticculture.miningco.com/library/blYAindex.htm

A subsite within the Mining Company, a commercial Web indexer. Contains articles on Yukon and Alaskan history and culture, covering early pioneers and mining in the region with an emphasis on the Klondike gold rush.

Chapter 14

Women's History

Tracy Penny Light

About.com: Women's History

http://womenshistory.about.com

This site includes Web links on women's history topics, original articles, an index of news stories on women's history, an index of recent book reviews, women's quotes, an online forum, and occasional chats.

African-American Women

http://scriptorium.lib.duke.edu/collections/african-american-women.html

Part of the Special Collections Library at Duke University, this site includes manuscripts and texts by African-American women, focusing on the slave experience.

African-American Women Writers of the Nineteenth Century

http://digital.nypl.org/schomburg/writers_aa19/

The New York Public Library's index of online books by and about African-American women, searchable by author, title, or category.

American Women's History: A Research Guide

http://frank.mtsu.edu/~kmiddlet/history/women.html

This rich and well-updated resource includes bibliographies of print and Internet materials, helpful information for researchers, a subject index to research sources, and links to electronic discussion lists.

Anthony, Susan B.: Anthony's Rochester Home

http://www.susanbanthonyhouse.org/

This site includes information on Susan B. Anthony's Rochester, New York, home, now a National Historic Landmark, and biographical information on one of the best-known American women.

Bible Passages on Women

gopher://dept.english.upenn.edu/11/Courses/Lynch3/Bible

This site contains Bible passages on the role and status of women, mostly from the Christian New Testament, some from Hebrew Scriptures.

Bryant, Emma Spaulding (Letters)

http://scriptorium.lib.duke.edu/bryant/

Part of the Special Collections Library at Duke University, this collection of letters written by Bryant to her husband, John Emory Bryant, in summer 1873 recounts her visit to relatives in Illinois and Ohio while her husband tended to his political affairs in Georgia. Because these letters are unusually frank for this time period, they reveal much about the relationships between husbands and wives in this era and about medical practices that were often kept private.

Celebrating Women's Achievements

http://www.nlc-bnc.ca/2/12/index-e.html

A series of portraits that highlight the achievements of women from Canada's past in sports, activism, the book trade, politics, librarianship and bibliography, society, music, and literature. Each woman's life and achievements are described, followed by a list of suggested readings. The National Library adds a new theme to this site every year to celebrate Women's History Month.

Celebration of Women Writers

http://digital.library.upenn.edu/women/

Extensive collection of links to biographies of and online books by women writers, including many international writers. Lists names and birth/death years for authors whose works and biography are not (yet?) online.

Civil War Women

http://odyssey.lib.duke.edu/collections/civil-war-women.html

Part of the Special Collections Library at Duke University, this site includes primary sources for studying the lives of women during the American Civil War.

Diotima: Materials for the Study of Women and Gender in the Ancient World

http://www.stoa.org/diotima/

One of the Web's best examples of how to make resources available online. Contains an extensive range of topics; primary sources, some in translation; secondary sources, including essays from a variety of other sites; and some graphic images. Includes Biblical studies.

Distinguished Women of Past and Present

http://www.DistinguishedWomen.com/

Danuta Bois's collection of short, basic biographies of women, most of which include a short bibliography for more information. Includes searches by name and field of endeavor.

Documents from the Women's Liberation Movement

http://scriptorium.lib.duke.edu/wlm/

Part of the Special Collections Library at Duke University, this site includes texts and scanned images and documents from the 1969–1974 U.S. women's liberation movement. Flyers, pamphlets, and booklets provide a view into that energetic period of women's history.

The Emma Goldman Papers

http://sunsite.berkeley.edu/Goldman/

Since 1980, the Emma Goldman Papers Project has collected, organized, and edited tens of thousands of documents by and about Goldman, an anarchist and feminist, from around the world. Electronic resources include a sampling of photographs and primary historical documents, biographical and bibliographical essays and finding aids, and samples from a number of publications about Emma Goldman.

Famous American Women

http://www.plgrm.com/history/women/

A helpful index to notable women—no content here, just formatted search engine links.

Feminist Collections: A Quarterly of Women's Studies Resources

http://www.library.wisc.edu/libraries/WomensStudies/fcmain.htm

Online essays often include Web site reviews and information on how to study women's issues using Web resources.

4,000 Years of Women in Science

http://www.astr.ua.edu/4000WS/4000WS.html

This site provides a brief introduction to the history of women in science. It contains a large collection of biographies, photographs, and references and can be searched alphabetically, by field, or by the time in which the scientist completed the bulk of her work.

Gage, Matilda Joslyn

http://www.pinn.net/~sunshine/gage/mjg.html

This site contains information about the life and writings of Matilda Joslyn Gage, the nineteenth-century women's rights leader (and mother-in-law of *Oz* author Frank Baum). The site also provides information and links on other women in the nineteenth century and on early feminists, a Gage newsletter, and conferences.

Gifts of Speech

http://gos.sbc.edu/

Archive of women's speeches from around the world that have influenced history or were given by famous women.

Godey's Lady's Book Online

http://www.history.rochester.edu/godeys/

Godey's Lady's Book was a popular nineteenth-century women's magazine whose articles and fashions helped shape the middle-class American woman. A good resource for fashions, lifestyle research, and the articles and poetry.

Guide to Uncovering Women's History in Archival Collections

http://www.lib.utsa.edu/Archives/links.htm

A geographical listing of libraries with archival collections relating to women's history. Heavy on the United States but also includes international collections, mostly in English-speaking countries.

Hawaii Women's Heritage

http://www.soc.hawaii.edu/hwhp/

Exhibits on the life of women in the history of Hawaii.

Hearts at Home: Southern Women in the Civil War

http://www.lib.virginia.edu/exhibits/hearts/

Images of manuscripts, letters, journals, and other documents, showing the many aspects of life for Southern women. Topics range from music, poetry, and religion to slavery, hard times, and war work.

Herstory: An Exhibition

http://library.usask.ca/herstory/

This retrospective exhibition is an attempt to capture the flavor of twenty years of work on a unique feminist project to honor the history of Canadian women. It samples the pages of *Herstory: The Canadian Women's Calendar* from 1974 to 1995 and reflects on the process and the people that created them.

History of Women's Suffrage

http://www.rochester.edu/SBA/history.html

From the University of Rochester's Susan B. Anthony Center for Women's Leadership, this site provides a brief history of women's suffrage in America, including a bibliography and links.

H-Minerva

http://www.h-net.msu.edu/~minerva/

Focused on the study of women and war and women in the military in many eras. Site hosts a moderated discussion list, archives of discussions, conference and call-for-papers announcements, and book reviews.

H-Women

http://www.h-net.msu.edu/~women/

Directed to researchers, teachers, and librarians, this site hosts a moderated discussion list, archives of women's history syllabi, book reviews, bibliographies, and discussion threads.

Images of Women in Prints from the Renaissance to the Present

http://www.lib.virginia.edu/dic/bayly/women/docs/home.html

This online exhibit from the Bayly Art Museum shows how women have been seen in history, through prints and contemporary writing.

International Alliance for Women in Music Home Page

http://music.acu.edu/www/iawm/

Resources for women in music. Includes extensive modern resources and links to resources on historical women composers.

Jewish Women's Archive

http://www.JWA.org/main.htm

The mission of the Jewish Women's Archive is to uncover, chronicle, and transmit the rich legacy of Jewish women and their contributions to our families and communities, to our people and our world. Included is the Virtual Archive database, which consists of 500 archival images and the records of over 200 women, from collections held in repositories in the United States and Canada. The archive is searchable by subject, occupation, and genre of the primary source material (i.e., oral histories, diaries, personal papers). The site also contains access to a discussion forum and a place to share stories.

Lesbian History Project

http://www-lib.usc.edu/~retter/main.html

Annotated links to print and Web resources for studying lesbian history. Many eras represented; also includes links for studying lesbians of color.

Living the Legacy: The Women's Rights Movement, 1848–1998

http://www.legacy98.org/

This site was designed for the 150th anniversary of the Women's Rights Convention at Seneca Falls, New York. The resources on this valuable site include teaching and activism ideas and an overview of 150 years of women's rights.

Madam C.J. Walker (1867–1919)

http://www.madamcjwalker.com/

Although this site mainly serves as an advertisement for the work of Walker biographer A'Lelia Bundles, this site does offer a brief biography, photos, and bibliography of Walker, an African-American millionaire, inventor, and social activist.

Matrix: Resources for the Study of Women's Religious Communities

http://matrix.bc.edu/

A scholarly resource for the study of women's religious communities from 400 to 1600 C.E., this site provides profiles of individuals and communities ("monasticon"), an image library, a glossary, an index of secondary sources, and a bibliography.

Medieval Women

http://www.georgetown.edu/labyrinth/subjects/women/women.html

Georgetown's Labyrinth project lists key links for researching medieval women, including Hildegard of Bingen, Joan of Arc, and Julian of Norwich. It also points to good bibliographies.

Medieval Women Web Sites

http://www.library.wisc.edu/libraries/WomensStudies/fc/fcwebho.htm

Cynthia Ho, Amelia Washburn, and Tim Gauthier suggest and review key Web sites for studying medieval women's history.

National First Ladies' Library

http://www.firstladies.org/

This Web site launched by Hillary Rodham Clinton on February 22, 1998, is devoted to the history and legacy of America's First Ladies. The Web site contains 40,000 selected books, manuscripts, journals, newspaper articles, and other materials.

National Women's Hall of Fame

http://www.greatwomen.org/

This Seneca Falls, New York, museum Web site honors a woman each month and includes information on visiting the museum, a history of the museum, classroom educational activities, and an online catalog of books and gifts.

National Women's History Museum

http://www.nmwh.org

This U.S. women's history project presents online exhibits while working toward a building of its own. Exhibits include Political Culture and the Imagery of American Suffrage and Motherhood, Social Service, and Political Reform: Political Culture and Imagery of American Woman Suffrage.

National Women's History Project

http://www.nwhp.org/

The organization behind Women's History Month, this site includes classroom ideas, suggested ways to honor women's history in local communities, a listing of events nationwide, membership information, links, and more. The materials are particularly aimed at the middle and high school levels. Includes an online catalog of educational and promotional materials.

New York Public Library: Women's Studies/History Research Guide

http://www.nypl.org/research/chss/grd/resguides/women/womhist.html

A list of books available at the New York Public Library (and, usually, other libraries as well) on topics in women's history.

9,000 Years of Anatolian Woman

http://www.arzu.com/turknet/ninethousand/index.html

Gunsel Renda's online illustrated exhibit of artifacts spanning 9,000 years of history tells the story of the Anatolian woman, illustrating woman's creativity, productivity, and prominence in all the civilizations that have flourished in the peninsula from ancient times to modern.

The Ninety-Nines: International Organization of Women Pilots

http://www.ninety-nines.org/index.html

Women in aviation, including astronauts who made history or are making it. The site includes the stories of women who have made a significant contribution to aviation as well as information on the history of women in aviation generally.

Notable Women Ancestors

http://www.rootsweb.com/~nwa/

Genealogical information on researching women ancestors. Site includes contributed essays on women, both famous and not.

Notable Women with Liberal Religious Connections

http://www.geocities.com/Wellesley/Garden/1101/

List of women with Unitarian, Universalist, Ethical Culture, and Free Religion connections, plus an annotated bibliography for those doing research on the topic.

The Shadow Story of the Millennium

http://www.nytimes.com/library/magazine/millennium/m2/index.html

Articles, images, audio, and forums: key issues in women's history in the last 1,000 years. Note that users must fill out a subscription form to access this site (subscription is free).

Social Studies: Women's History

http://www.socialstudies.com/c/@0/Pages/womenindex.html

Products, mostly for purchase, for teaching women's history from kindergarten through 12th grade. Some essays and some curriculum units (with reproducible master) are available without charge on the site.

Sources for Women's Studies in the Methodist Archives

http://rylibweb.man.ac.uk/data1/dg/methodist/methfem.html

A bibliographic essay on women in Methodist history and sources found at the Methodist Archives.

Suffragists Oral History Project

http://library.berkeley.edu/BANC/ROHO/ohonline/suffragists.html

Online transcripts of interviews, taped in the 1970s, with twelve leaders and participants in the U.S. suffrage movement.

University Publications of America: Women's Studies

http://www.lexisnexis.com/academic/2upa/Aws/Womens%20Studies.htm

These guides to manuscript collections and other resources detail historical information on aspects of women's history.

Victorian Women Writers Project

http://www.indiana.edu/~letrs/vwwp/vwwp-links.html

This site is a collection of links to journals, online projects on individual authors and related topics, syllabi, and information related to Victorian women writers and society.

Voice of the Shuttle: Gender Studies

http://vos.ucsb.edu/shuttle/gender.html

Extensive Webliography, including much of current as well as historical interest.

Votes for Women: Selections from the National American Woman Suffrage Association Collection, 1848–1921

http://lcweb2.loc.gov/ammem/naw/nawshome.html

From the Library of Congress, letters and other writings plus images from the collection donated by Carrie Chapman Catt.

What Did You Do In the War, Grandma?

http://www.stg.brown.edu/projects/WWII_Women/tocCS.html

High school students' oral history project, documenting women's roles in World War II. Excellent both as an information resource and as a model for a student project in women's history.

What's New in Women's History?

http://xroads.virginia.edu/g/DRBR/gordon.html

Linda Gordon, women's historian, on the history and purpose of women's history.

Witch Craze Links

http://shanmonster.lilsproutz.com/witch/links/index.html

Resources on the witch craze in seventeenth-century America and in Europe, along with a host of other sites in related genres.

Women and Social Movements in the United States, 1830–1930

http://womhist.binghamton.edu

The history of women in the United States is connected to the history of the social movements they founded and in which women developed and applied leadership skills. Student essays on a broad range of topics.

Women at MBL: The Early Years

http://hermes.mbl.edu/women_of_science/women.html

The Marine Biology Laboratory at Woods Hole, Massachusetts, was one of the earliest schools to accept female science students. A number of those students between 1850 and 1930 are profiled on this page, which includes photographs.

Women Come to the Front

http://lcweb.loc.gov/exhibits/wcf/wcf0001.html

Women journalists and photographers at the front in World War II. Primary sources include newspaper and magazine articles and photographs from the Library of Congress.

Women in America, 1820–1842

http://xroads.virginia.edu/~hyper/detoc/fem/home.htm

Selections from writings (letters, journals, books) of notable European travelers to early nineteenth-century America, excerpted to highlight their observations on women's lives.

Women in World History.com

http://www.womeninworldhistory.com/

This commercial site contains an extensive collection of curriculum materials on women in world history. Some sample lesson plans are free, and the essays and other materials will interest many researchers who are not teachers.

Women Mathematicians

http://www.agnesscott.edu/lriddle/women/women.htm

More than 100 biographies, with bibliographies of print and Web resources. Many have photographs.

Women Nobel Laureates

http://www.almaz.com/nobel/women.html

Women who have won the Nobel Prize for their contributions to science, peace, and literature.

Women's Early Music, Art, Poetry

http://music.acu.edu/www/iawm/pages/index.html

This extensive site from Abilene Christian University contains essays and links on a wide array of information related to women and the arts, including Early Spirituality; Eastern Music, Arts, and Poetry; and Women and Geometry, which focuses on quilting.

Women's History

http://www.thehistorynet.com/WomensHistory/

Every month features a different issue of *Women's History* magazine with interesting articles and photographs on all aspects of women in history.

Women's Internet Information Network (WiiN)

http://www.undelete.org/

This site by Irene Stuber, Director of (WiiN), includes more than 20,000 profiles of notable women.

Women's Legal History Biography Project

http://www.stanford.edu/group/WLHP

Biographies of more than 100 American women lawyers and judges.

Women's Studies Programs, Departments and Research Centers

http://research.umbc.edu/~korenman/wmst/programs.html

From the University of Maryland, Baltimore County, Joan Korenman, Director of the Center for Women and Information Technology, provides this extensive list of women's studies programs. About half of the programs are in the United States, and the other half are in other countries. Includes links to several other lists of such programs.

Women Veterans

http://userpages.aug.com/captbarb/

"Captain Critical" presents a large collection of online material on women in the military. Documents the role of women in American wars from the Revolution through today's news.

Chapter 15

World History

David Koeller

The academic study of world history is a rapidly evolving field, and the Web sites devoted to world history reflect this reality. In choosing Web sites for inclusion in this list, I have focused on sites that are global or interregional in scope and especially on those that focus on the interactions among regions of the world.

Metasites

Academic Info: World History Gateway

http://www.academicinfo.net/hist.html

This metasite presents links to a variety of history resources, including world history resources. The site is operated by Academic Info and maintained by Mike Madin.

NM's Creative Impulse

http://history.evansville.net/index.html

This is one of the best—if not the best—sites for the study of world history. While it is concerned mostly with the histories of various cultures, rather than with their interactions, this site provides links to many important resources on the Web. Of special note are the links for cultural resources, such as poetry, music, and drama, not just politics, religion, or philosophy. Also of interest is a set of links entitled "History of . . . ," as in History of Bowling and History of the Toaster. Maintained by Nancy Mantz for Harrison High School, Evansville, Indiana, and for the University of Evansville.

World Culture

http://sun.kent.wednet.edu/curriculum/soc_studies/text/gr7.html

Maintained by Diana Eggers of the Kent School District, Kent, Washington, this site provides links to material for a seventh-grade world cultures course. The geographic distribution is quite good—it even includes material for Australia and Polynesia.

The World History Compass

http://www.worldhistorycompass.com/index.htm

This is not, strictly speaking, a world history Web site since it is organized by region and nation, rather than interregionally or globally. Nevertheless, this metasite has such an extensive collection of links on such a wide range of subjects that anyone teaching or studying world history will find it useful. The site is maintained by Schiller Computing and serves as a way to draw customers to their online bookstore.

WWW-VL World Central Catalogue

http://history.cc.ukans.edu/history/VL/index.html

An incredible collection of links to hundreds of articles on most aspects of history. There are, however, few references that are specifically world history. This would be a good place to research a comparative history project, however. Lynn H. Nelson at the University of Kansas maintains this site.

General Sites

Fleet Gazelle

http://www.ojo.com/

Fleet Gazelle publishes a number of educational CD-ROMs and has three Web sites to advertise them. The first, and most relevant for the study of world history, is cultures.com [http://www.cultures.com/], which features several short

multimedia pieces mostly on preurban societies. The second, MesoWeb [http:/
/www.mesoweb.com/], is dedicated to the study of Mesoamerican cultures. Finally, MythWeb [http://www.mythweb.com/] is devoted to Greek mythology,
with some resources for teaching mythology. All three sites feature impressive
graphics, animations, and extensive teacher guides.

History of the World

http://www.camelotintl.com/world/index.html

Camelot International is a British accommodation representation company that
maintains this site as a service to its customers. This site is similar in construction to the WebChron site, but without the nesting of the chronologies. The
articles linked to the chronologies are unsigned but appear to be of good quality.

H-World Homepage

http://www2.h-net.msu.edu/~world/

This is the Web site for the H-World online discussion group. This group, sponsored by the National Endowment for the Humanities and Michigan State University, is composed of those who have a teaching or research interest in world
history, including leaders in the field of world history. This site is both an archive
of the group's discussions and a resource for world historians. The list's postings
are arranged both chronologically and by thread. A search engine is also available. Besides the discussion archives, the site includes course syllabi for teaching world history at the secondary, college, and graduate levels, bibliographies
on many world history topics, reviews of recent scholarship, and teaching aids,
most drawn from the list's discussions.

Hyper History

http://hyperhistory.com/online_n2/History_n2/a.html

This site shows the real potential for the Internet for teaching and studying
history. The site consists of an image-mapped chronology of world history from
prehistory to the present. The events listed on the chronology are then
hyperlinked to very brief descriptions. The site is very good for visualizing the
temporal relations between events in different parts of the world.

The Internet Global History Sourcebook

http://www.fordham.edu/halsall/global/globalsbook.html

One of the series of sourcebooks developed by Paul Halsall. This site focuses
on the interaction among cultures. This site is under construction, but has a
number of significant sources.

The Journal of World History

http://muse.jhu.edu/journals/jwh/

The *Journal of World History* is the foremost academic world history periodical. This site offers for a fee access to HTML or PDF editions of recent articles from the journal.

The Journal of World-Systems Research

http://csf.colorado.edu/jwsr/

The *Journal of World-Systems Research* is an electronic journal distributed free over the Internet. As the name suggests, it is "dedicated to scholarly research on the modern world-system and earlier, smaller intersocietal networks." World-system theory is one of the important approaches to the study of world history, and this Web site and journal are an important resource for learning of the latest scholarship in this field.

National Center for History in the Schools

http://www.sscnet.ucla.edu/nchs/

The National Center for History in the Schools has developed standards for world history in grades 5–12. This site provides an online version of those standards. In addition, the center also has samples from its sourcebook, *Bring History Alive!*, to help teachers meet these standards.

Dr. Silvestri's World History Resources

http://www.drhitory.org/

This site was designed for use in a ninth-grade world history course. The site consists of the instructor's lecture notes and supporting materials. As of this moment, the supporting material is still largely under construction. The lectures notes, however, are complete and provide some useful information. The graphics and layout of the page are quite well done.

Frank Smitha's World History

http://www.fsmitha.com/index.html

Frank Smitha is an amateur historian who has developed a very impressive online world history interpretive essay that could be profitably used as a world history textbook. It covers world history from antiquity to the present with a gap for the nineteenth century, which is still under construction. The essay is impressive not only for its scope, but also for its balance and emphasis on the interconnectedness of history. Also included at the site are excellent map and image collections.

United Nations Organization: Cyber School Bus

http://www.un.org/Pubs/CyberSchoolBus/index.html

This site presents student and teacher resources for ages ten to eighteen, including information on U.N. member states, quizzes, and curriculum modules on global poverty, human rights, and other issues. Although focused on contemporary events, the site offers some material for those interested in comparative world cultures.

WebChron: The Web Chronology Project

http://www.campus.northpark.edu/history/WebChron/index.html

While there are many Web sites of chronologies, WebChron is unique in that it attempts to present a global chronology, using hyperlinks to "nest" more detailed chronologies "inside" more general chronologies and describing many of the events using articles written by students. This "nesting" provides a sense of how one period relates to another and how events in one region of the world correspond to events in other regions of the world. Because the articles are student projects their quality is uneven, but many are excellent.

World Cultures: An Internet Classroom and Anthology

http://www.wsu.edu:8080/%7Edee/WORLD.HTM

One is first struck by the very suberb graphic presentation at this site. Then one is pleasantly surprised that the content is as good as the presentation. Developed by Richard Hooker of Washington State University for a course for first-year college students, the site integrates a world cultures text, written principally by Hooker, with primary source readings and links to other Web resources. While very impressive in its treatment of the cultures represented, the focus of the course and of the site is the development of these cultures and not on their interaction. Nevertheless, this site is quite notable.

World History Archives

http://www.hartford-hwp.com/archives/index.html

"A collection of documents for teaching and learning about world history from a working-class perspective." The site, administered by Haines Brown, contains both primary and secondary sources for the study of contemporary world history.

The World History Association

http://www.woodrow.org/teachers/world-history/

The official Web site of the World History Association, the leading organization for world historians. It contains a series of links to many of the resources listed here as well as a series of links to teaching resources, including course syllabi.

The World History Center at Northeastern University

http://www.whc.neu.edu/

The World History Center at Northeastern University is a "uniquely comprehensive institution, supporting basic and applied research, curriculum development, and institutional growth in world history." As a result of this broad mission, the center's Web site is an important resource for the study of world history. Among the resources are a series of bibliographies for secondary, college, and graduate study in history, reviews of world history textbooks, and the course syllabi used by the instructors at the center.

The World History Reader

http://www.wsu.edu:8080/~wldciv/world_civ_reader/

An advertisement for a now out-of-print world history reader, this site nevertheless has some useful excerpts from primary sources. The editor of the anthology is Paul Brians of Washington State University. While the translators are often mentioned by name, we are given little other information about the source of the translations. Many of the sources are taken from older translations, but some appear to have been done specifically for this anthology.

Specific Aspects

BBC Online: Modern World History

http://www.bbc.co.uk/education/modern/

A very impressive site. To fully use the site's resources, you must have a Shockwave-enabled browser. The site is focused primarily on Europe.

Exploring Ancient World Cultures

http://eawc.evansville.edu/

This site provides links to essays, texts, and images of the ancient world. This is not a true world history site since there is little on the comparison or interaction of these societies, but there is good information for study and the foundation for comparison. This site is under the general editorship of Anthony F. Beavers and is housed at the University of Evansville.

Studies in the World History of Slavery, Abolition and Emancipation

http://www.h-net.msu.edu/~slavery/

This is an electronic journal for the global study of slavery, edited by Patrick Manning, Northeastern University, and John Saillant, Massachusetts Institute of Technology.

Women in World History Curriculum

http://www.womeninworldhistory.com/

This site, developed by Lyn Reese to advertise her Women in World History Curriculum, provides some very useful resources for teaching about women in world history. Especially impressive is a page devoted to the role of women in the industrial revolution, which shows through the use of primary source material the differences and inequities of the roles of men and women.

Chapter 16

Agricultural History and Rural Studies

Leo E. Landis

Agricultural Engineering Historic Landmarks

http://asae.org/awards/histcomm.html

The American Society of Agricultural Engineers has designated a number of significant places and machines, and this site includes summaries of these landmarks.

Agricultural History

http://www.public.iastate.edu/~history_info/aghistry.htm

This is the site for the editorial office of the academic journal *Agricultural History*. The site is updated quarterly and contains selected book reviews from the current and past volumes.

Agripedia

http://www.ca.uky.edu/agripedia/

This is a good glossary of agricultural terminology for novices. The site is part of a larger agricultural site developed by the University of Kentucky.

Appleton's *Cyclopedia* of Applied Mechanics

http://www.history.rochester.edu/appleton/a/agmac-m.html

A limited version of Appleton's *Cyclopedia* from the late nineteenth century is presented here; the links offer primary source descriptions and images of selected agricultural machinery.

Books of The Kansas Collection

http://www.ukans.edu/carrie/kancoll/books

The site includes a number of public domain full-text documents relevant to agriculture of the Midwest and Great Plains.

Breeds of Livestock: Oklahoma State University Department of Animal Science

http://www.ansi.okstate.edu/breeds/

This site is based at the Oklahoma State University's Animal Science Department. It contains a directory of common breeds of livestock in the United States, including historical background and images.

Conner Prairie Rural History Project

http://www.ruralhistoryproject.com/

The Rural History Project is a community documentation and heritage preservation effort undertaken by Conner Prairie to study and preserve the history of rural life in Hamilton County, Indiana, from 1875 to the present.

Directory of Rural Studies Scholars and Educators

http://www.nal.usda.gov/ric/ricpubs/scholars.html

Although not updated since the mid-1990s, this page is an excellent listing of more than 800 scholars with interests in American agriculture and rural studies. The site contains a subject and regional directory at the conclusion of the page.

"The Farmer's Wife"

http://www.pbs.org/wgbh/pages/frontline/shows/farmerswife/

This *Frontline* program explored the life of the Boeschkoetter family and their struggle to maintain their marriage and their Nebraska farm in the late 1990s. The site contains a number of links related to American agricultural issues in the late twentieth century.

Glidden's Patent Application for Barbed Wire

http://www.nara.gov/education/teaching/glidden/wire.html

Part of the National Archives' initiative "Teaching With Documents," this site blends the history of technology and agricultural history in order to correlate with National Education Standards.

A History of American Agriculture, 1776–1990

http://www.usda.gov/history2/back.htm

This site, an online version of a U.S. Department of Agriculture poster, has been updated through the 1990s. The topics include milestones from U.S. agricultural history in the following categories: Economic Cycles, Farm Economy, Farmers and the Land, Farm Machinery and Technology, Crops and Livestock, Transportation, Agricultural Trade and Development, Life on the Farm, Farm Organizations and Movements, Agricultural Education and Extension, and Government Programs and Policy.

McCormick–International Harvester Company Collection

http://www.shsw.wisc.edu/archives/ihc/index.html

Nicely designed, although somewhat light on content, this site offers an introduction to one of the more significant archival collections for American agriculture.

National Agricultural Library

http://www.nalusda.gov/speccoll/

The National Agricultural Library holds volumes of significant materials. The Web site provides information on the research collections and visitor information. The Special Collections page and the homestead and steward links hold a selection of images.

North Carolina Agricultural History

http://www.agr.state.nc.us/state/history/history.htm

The best, and maybe the only, state agricultural history on the Web. This site offers an excellent overview of agriculture in the upper American South, although it has little flexibility in navigation.

The Northern Great Plains, 1880–1920: Images from the Fred Hulstrand and F.A. Pazandak Photograph Collections

http://lcweb2.loc.gov/ammem/award97/ndfahtml/

The collections on this site offer unparalleled photographic documentation of rural life in North Dakota. The holdings are from the Institute for Regional Studies at North Dakota State University. The site is now part of the American Memory project of the Library of Congress. The pages contain about 900 photographs, are well designed, and load quickly. Visitors can also explore links that contain background and bibliographic information.

The Rice Museum, Georgetown, South Carolina

http://www.ego.net/us/sc/myr/rice

An informative Web site on an often-ignored American agricultural crop. The site contains a brief history of rice culture in the Low Country and a bibliography on Low Country life.

The Road I Grew Up On

http://www.lib.iastate.edu/spcl/road/summary.html

A local history project based on a county in northwest Iowa. The site contains a good selection of photographs from 1900 to 1995.

A Rural Studies Bibliography: U.S. Department of Agriculture

http://www.nal.usda.gov/ric/ricpubs/ruralbib.html

An online version of a 1994 publication from the USDA, the site is an extensive bibliography of 216 sources compiled by the National Rural Studies Committee. The annotated citations range from classics in agricultural history, such as Paul Gates's *The Farmer's Age: Agriculture, 1815–1860*, to sociological studies of rural America.

Smithsonian: Agriculture and Horticulture

http://www.si.edu/resources/faq/nmah/agriculture.htm

A brief collection of links related to agriculture and horticulture sponsored by the Smithsonian Institution.

The Sunshine Harvester Works Web Site

·http://www.museum.vic.gov.au/sunshine/

Though often overlooked, the Sunshine Harvester Works produced an excellent combine from the late nineteenth until the mid-twentieth century. The archives, which are held at the Museum Victoria in Australia, contain magnificent photographic materials.

Surviving the Dust Bowl

http://www.pbs.org/wgbh/amex/dustbowl/index.html

The Web site for the PBS program *American Experience.* The site contains audio oral histories, teacher's guides, bibliographies, and other resources for educators.

Troublesome Creek

http://www.pbs.org/wgbh/amex/trouble/

The Web site for this Sundance Film Festival award-winning documentary, which was broadcast on the PBS program *American Experience.* The site contains photographs dating to the late nineteenth century and lesson plans based on the program.

University of Saskatchewan, College of Agriculture: History of Agriculture

http://www.ag.usask.ca/exhibits/walkway/plains/history.html

A Canadian site from the University of Saskatchewan that offers a brief timeline and narrative for agriculture on the Canadian prairie.

Chapter 17

History of Computers

Kenneth R. Dvorak

A Brief History of Computing

http://www.ox.compsoc.net/~swhite/history.html

Created by Stephan White, a math and computation student at Keble College, Oxford, this interesting Web site offers a great variety of informational materials on the evolution of the computer. Included are a timeline, related links, bibliography, hardware history, a history of the Internet, and a history of WIMPS (windowing systems).

Generations Through the History of Computing

http://www.dg.com/about/html/generations.html

Do you remember the first computer you used? This fascinating virtual tour sponsored by Data General, a division of EMC, takes users back in computer history to relive those glory days of the IBM 360 and the Apple II. This site is recommended for computing geeks and historians alike.

The History of Computing

http://ei.cs.vt.edu/~history/

Maintained by the Computer Science Department at Virginia Tech, this award-winning Web research site is an excellent source for those interested in the history of computers. Sponsored in part by the National Science Foundation (NSF), the site contains a comprehensive index of computer-related topics and subjects.

History of Computing Information

http://ftp.arl.mil/~mike/comphist/

Created by Mike Muuss, this Web resource celebrates the invention of the computer and the central role the U.S. Army had in its development. This Web site contains articles from the Army Research Lab and from the home of ENIAC. Included is an extensive list of related web links that further explores the history of the computer.

i-MB: Resources and Information

http://www.imb.f2s.com/index.htm

Sponsored by MB Solutions, this informative Web site for professional designers showcases the latest news affecting the computer industry, a timeline of computer history, CAD history, software information, and a thorough list of useful Web links.

Jones Telecommunications and Multimedia Encyclopedia

http://www.digitalcentury.com/encyclo/update/comp_hd.html

As the introductory page of this extremely resourceful Web site states, whether we view computers as the harbingers of the future or the destruction of humankind, they have infiltrated into every aspect of our existence. Sponsored by Jones International, this informative Web resource offers insightful commentary on the history of the computer.

National Archive for the History of Computing

http://www.man.ac.uk/Science_Engineering/CHSTM/nahc.htm

According to the National Archive opening page, "Computing, in its many ramifications, was central to technological and social change in the 20th century, and a major factor in the 21st. Britain played an important role in the development of this technology. However the artefacts and the historical records are fast disappearing. The National Archive for the History of Computing opened in 1987 to provide a repository for the documents and images of computer history, and a centre to encourage its study. A rich collection is now available to scholars." This Web resource is devoted to providing scholars interested in the history of computers and computing with archival documents and illustrations.

Resources on the History of Computing

http://www.cbi.umn.edu/resources/index.html

Sponsored by the Charles Babbage Institute of Information Technology, this thorough Web resource provides an interesting glimpse into the history of computing. The Web site includes a link that explains how to donate old computer hardware and a Hollywood film list that details the love/hate relationship the American film industry has had with "good" and "bad" computers.

The Virtual Museum of Computing (VMoC)

http://vmoc.museophile.sbu.ac.uk/

Jonathan Bowen of the Virtual Library Museums, supported by the International Council of Museums, maintains this exciting collection of WWW sites devoted to the history of computing. This Web resource contains a wealth of information past and present concerning articles, conferences, and computer-related exhibits around the world.

Chapter 18

History of Science

Scott A. Merriman and Kalpana Shankar

General Directories and Indexes

ECHO Virtual Center: Science and Technology

http://echo.gmu.edu/center/index.html

The Center for History and New Media maintains this site, which focuses on science and technology. One can survey sites in a number of areas or perform a keyword search. This site also links to other sites that allow users to record recollections of scientific events such as the New York City blackout or electric vehicles. This is a good place to begin research.

E-mail Forums and Web Sites

http://www.shef.ac.uk/~psysc/hpsss.html

This Web site, maintained by the library at the Center for Psychotherapeutic Studies at Sheffield University in the United Kingdom, contains subscription information for a number of listservs in the history of science; science as culture; science, technology, and society studies; and the history and philosophy of the social sciences. The rest of the page contains many Web sites of interest, but they are not well organized or annotated.

H-SCI-MED-TECH

http://www.h-net.msu.edu/~smt/

H-SCI-MED-TECH is a moderated and active listserv on all aspects of history of science, medicine, and technology. To subscribe to the History of Medicine, Science, and Technology listserv, follow the directions at: http://www.h-net.msu.edu/~smt/.

History of Science on the WWW

http://www.ou.edu/cas/hsci/rel-site.htm

This Web site is the work of the History of Science Department at the University of Oklahoma. It contains links to many of the other resources listed here, as well as to other libraries, archives, and research centers of note. However, there is no annotation or order to the list, apart from some very general top-level categories, although the list is small enough to scroll through. This site is useful for the number of links to subject indexes on the history of various scientific disciplines.

Horus' Web Links to History Resources

http://www.ucr.edu/h-gig/horuslinks.html

Horus is maintained and sponsored by the faculty of the History Department of the University of California at Riverside. The areas of specialization to date include history of science, technology, medicine, mathematics, public health, and technology. Numerous subdivisions within each category contain links to online texts, academic departments, and collections of resources. Despite this Web site's lack of annotation, this is a good place to begin research.

Internet History of Science Sourcebook

http://www.fordham.edu/halsall/science/sciencesbook.html#Islam

This page and other Internet History sourcebooks have been created and are maintained by Paul Halsall of Fordham University. Organized chronologically, the site provides teachers with links to public domain texts, commentaries, and other Web sites. Halsall's sections on Greco-Roman scientific philosophy and culture, science in Latin Christendom, and Islamic science are particularly strong; however, non-Western scientific topics are not well represented, and there is little annotation. Nevertheless, this is a useful resource for undergraduate educators.

History of Astronomy

The Galileo Project

http://es.rice.edu:80/ES/humsoc/Galileo/

The Galileo Project is a hypertext source of information on the life and work of Galileo Galilei (1564–1642) and the science of his time. The Office of the Vice President of Computing of Rice University supports the project, which represents the collective efforts of Dr. Albert Van Helden and Dr. Elizabeth Burr and their students.

The History of Astronomy Home Page

http://www.astro.uni-bonn.de/~pbrosche/astoria.html

This is the most extensive metasite for the history of astronomy. It is maintained on behalf of Commission 41 (History of Astronomy) of the International Astronomical Union and the Working Group for the History of Astronomy in the Astronomische Gesellschaft, Germany.

History of Biology

CADUCEUS-L

CADUCEUS-L is a moderated electronic discussion list that provides a forum for exchanging information on any aspect of the history of the health sciences. To subscribe: Send the command sub caduceus-l [your name] to listproc@list.ab.umd.edu

History of Biomedicine

http://www.mic.ki.se/History.html

This site, maintained at the Karolinska Institute in Sweden, is extremely thorough. Links are divided by categories, including extensive sections on traditional Indian, Chinese, and Islamic biomedicine. There are also links to resources on ethnobotany and pharmacognosy. Many of the links are extremely general (links to the *Mahabharata*, for example). The site does not have a search feature.

History of Medicine Division: National Library of Medicine

http://www.nlm.nih.gov/hmd/hmd.html

The National Library of Medicine, a division of the National Institutes of Health, maintains this Web site. The most important resource is HISTLINE, NLM's bibliographic index to literature published since 1965 in the history of medicine and related topics. It currently contains about 150,000 citations and is updated weekly. Another major resource is the searchable database of nearly 60,000 images from NLM's print and photo collection. These images are digitized, but one can order high-resolution prints from NLM.

Natural History Caucus, Special Libraries Association

http://www.lib.washington.edu/sla/

The home page of the SLA Natural History Caucus is aimed at special librarians working in natural history museums and repositories, but it contains useful resources for the historian as well. The site includes a hyperlinked, alphabetical list of natural history libraries around the world (unfortunately, these are not annotated); a similar list of natural history museums around the world, organized by geographical region; and hyperlinked lists of annotated bibliographies and other resources that are oriented to scientists.

History of Chemistry

CHEM-HIST

CHEM-HIST seeks to promote information and communication among historians of chemistry and of the chemical industry. To join, send mail to MAISER@LISTSERV.NGATE.UNI-REGENSBURG.DE with the following command in the body of your message: subscribe CHEM-HIST.

Classic Papers in Chemistry

http://dbhs.wvusd.k12.ca.us/Chem-History/Classic-Papers-Menu.html

This Web site is maintained by ChemTeam and John L. Park, a high school chemistry teacher. Although many of the chemistry resources are aimed at educators and students, the Classic Papers section contains a growing list of historical works in chemistry (mostly excerpted). Unfortunately, it is not clear which papers have been excerpted and which sections have been removed.

Selected Classic Papers from the History of Chemistry

http://webserver.lemoyne.edu/faculty/giunta/papers.html

This page, maintained by Carmen Giunta at Le Moyne College, is a companion Web page to the ChemTeam's Classic Papers in Chemistry site listed above. There are more papers (although some links point to the ChemTeam site) and more annotations. The papers are divided by subject category, but there is no searchable index. Giunta notes when papers are excerpted. This Web site contains an extensive collection of papers, but there are some links that are unique to the ChemTeam Web site and are not cross-linked here.

History of Geology

GeoClio: Webserver for the History of Geology and the Geosciences

http://geoclio.st.usm.edu/

This Web site was created at the University of Southern Mississippi in fall 1995 with the assistance of a grant from the National Science Foundation. The list of links is small and not annotated. Many of the links are quite broadly historical or scientific, but contain some resources of relevance to the history of geology.

History of Mathematics

L-MATH

L-MATH is a mailing list on the history and philosophy of mathematics and probability. To subscribe, send a message to l-math-request@math.uio.no

The MacTutor History of Mathematics Archive

http://www-history.mcs.st-and.ac.uk/~history/index.html

This searchable Web site, maintained at the University of St. Andrews in Scotland, contains biographies of mathematicians of note (accessible chronologically or alphabetically), images, references, information on Famous Curves, bibliographies, and links to other resources. The generally informal tone and the lack of primary references make this site more suitable for teaching purposes than for research.

Women in Mathematics

http://www.scottlan.edu/lriddle/women/women.htm

This Web site is part of an ongoing project of mathematics students at Agnes Scott College in Atlanta, Georgia. This resource is best for teachers and students in K-12. The brief biographical essays contain some references and photographs.

History of the Physical Sciences

AIP Center for History of Physics

http://www.aip.org/history/

The American Institute of Physics has had a long history of promoting study of the history of physics. Its semiannual newsletter since 1994 is online and contains articles, announcements, reports on archival materials, bibliographies, and funding and conference opportunities. The Niels Bohr Library catalog, finding aids to various archival collections, the Emilio Segrè Visual Archives photo collection catalog, online exhibits, and an extensive list of related links make this collection useful to scholars, teachers, and others.

Contributions of Twentieth-Century Women to Physics

http://www.physics.ucla.edu/~cwp/

Sponsored by the American Physical Society, this Web site is maintained by physicist Dr. Nina Byers at the University of California, Los Angeles. The site contains a searchable archive of biographies, indexed by subfield of physics. Although the research for the biographies is verified by working physicists around the world, the information may be more useful as an educational tool than as a research tool, as there are almost no links to primary resources or mention of archival collections related to each scientist.

History of Oceanic and Atmospheric Science Locator

http://www.lib.noaa.gov/docs/windandsea4.html#HistoryOceanic

Although this site is only part of a much larger Web page, there are no other metasites that deal with this subject. The page points to biographical information and other National Oceanic and Atmospheric Administration resources. The resources that are mentioned are not hyperlinked, however.

Map History/History of Cartography

http://www.ihrinfo.ac.uk/maps

Tony Campbell, the map librarian at the British Museum in London, maintains this exceptional Web site. An extensive and extremely well-organized collection of resources for both the scholar and the amateur, it contains links to both paper and electronic resources, including reference books, map listservs, grants, societies, and commercial venues. This list is not searchable, however.

National Oceanic and Atmospheric Administration History

http://www.history.noaa.gov/

This site makes available many of the historical resources of the National Oceanic and Atmospheric Administration. The site contains a catalog (with low resolution images that can be printed to a plotter in higher resolution) of the entire map and chart collection of the Office of Coast Survey, as well as biographical sketches of important persons (drawn from official newsletters), an extensive photo library, and stories and poems.

History of Psychology

History and Philosophy of Psychology Web Resources

http://www.psych.yorku.ca/orgs/resource.htm

This site is maintained by Christopher D. Green at York University in Canada and is shared by several divisions of the American Psychological Association, the Canadian Psychological Association, and other international professional organizations. It contains links to relevant professional organizations, archives and manuscript collections, full-text documents, and translated versions of important texts and papers in psychology. The classic papers section is searchable by keyword, but the rest of the site is not.

Resource Guide: History of Psychology

http://www.slu.edu/colleges/AS/PSY/510Guide.html

Miriam E. Joseph of the University of St. Louis compiled this library guide, a good resource for students and teachers interested in the history of psychology. It contains annotations to relevant and useful books, reference works, overviews, journals, citation indexes, manuscript collections, and Web sites.

Miscellaneous Resources

Catalog of the Scientific Community in the Sixteenth and Seventeenth Centuries

http://es.rice.edu/ES/humsoc/Galileo/Catalog/catalog.html

This catalog, compiled by the late Dr. Richard S. Westfall of the Department of History and Philosophy of Science at Indiana University, contains extensive biographical profiles of sixteenth- and seventeenth-century scientific person-alities. The database can be searched by any of twenty fields, including means of support, religion, and nationality. In addition to biographical information, Dr. Westfall included known references to the scientist. One shortcoming is that there is no way to browse the list of scientists.

The Faces of Science: African-Americans in the Sciences

http://www.princeton.edu/~mcbrown/display/faces.html

This Web site is maintained by Princeton University. In addition to biographi-cal profiles of numerous African-American scientists, inventors, and doctors, the Web site contains links to electronic conferences on this topic, historical data on doctoral degrees awarded to African-Americans, and bibliographies. This site is probably best suited to teachers, both university and K-12, who are interested in the historical role of African-Americans in science.

The Medieval Science Page

http://members.aol.com/mcnelis/medsci_index.html

This Web site is maintained by James McNelis, the editor-in-chief of *Envoi: A Review Journal of Medieval Literature*. Although the list does not appear to have been updated in several months, the site contains a large amount of infor-mation. Annotated links are organized by topic and include links to scholarly listservs, full-text documents, classic texts, and other materials. The list is not searchable, but instead is organized in linear fashion. Included are links to

WISE: Archives of Women in Science and Engineering

http://www.lib.iastate.edu/spcl/wise/miss.html

This Web site is the informational page of Iowa State's collection of records and papers of women in science, one of the largest in the United States. Although there are some K-12 resources, virtual exhibits, and bibliographies, this Web site is primarily useful for its collection list.

International History of Science and Medicine

ASAPWeb: Australian Science Archives Project

http://www.asap.unimelb.edu.au/

ASAP is an organization that is working to identify and preserve scientific records of enduring value, both those from the past and those that are being created today. One feature on the Web site is Bright Sparcs, a searchable database of biographical information on Australian scientists in history. Where appropriate, there are links to information on archival repositories that house information on the scientist. Other important resources include a biographical and bibliographic database of Australian physicists to 1945, and information on Australian archival repositories.

Chi Med: History of Chinese Medicine Web Page

http://www.albion.edu/history/chimed/

This Web site is maintained at Albion College. In addition to an international list of scholars working in the field, this Web site has links to numerous online resources, bibliographies, syllabi, conference and grant listings, and research institutions. The Web site is still fairly small, but growing. There is also subscription information for a listserv devoted to junior faculty and graduate students researching this area.

Historical Health Information Locator Service (Canada)

http://www.fis.utoronto.ca/research/ams/hilscan/

This service is, according to the Web site, "a national research service dedicated to expanding awareness of, and access to, the wealth of historical resources relating to Canadian health care and medicine." This site serves researchers, archivists, and custodians of Canadian health care collections. The service will assist in finding sources of information and records. The site contains a list of Internet resources and contact information.

WWW Virtual Guide to the History of Russian and Soviet Science and Technology

http://web.mit.edu/slava/guide

This guide was established and is maintained by Dr. Slava Gerovitch, a lecturer in the Science, Technology, and Society program at MIT University. There is an extensive list of archival collections, journals, scholars, relevant Russian institutions, and course syllabi. The site is fairly easy to navigate, but does not have search capability. This unique site would be useful for both research and teaching.

Chapter 19

History of Technology

Leo E. Landis and Eric G. Swedin

Metasites

H-GIG Technology

http://www.ucr.edu/h-gig/hist-science/techn.html

One of the finest collections of history of technology links on the Web. Produced by the Department of History at University of California, Riverside.

History of Technology Resources Available on the Internet via ICE

http://www.englib.cornell.edu/ice/lists/historytechnology/
historytechnology.html

List of history of technology sites, including e-mail lists, and a short bibliography; provided by the Internet Connections for Engineering project at Cornell University.

H-Sci-Med-Tech Links Page

http://www2.h-net.msu.edu/~smt/web-links.html

H-Sci-Med-Tech is the H-Net discussion list and Web site intended for scholars who study science, medicine, and technology. This page presents a list of related links.

Media History Project

http://www.mediahistory.com/

The site's slogan is "promoting the study of media history from petroglyphs to pixels." Includes an extensive timeline and well-organized links to related sites.

Technology History

http://www.refstar.com/techhist/index.html

An "annotated collection of links" to Web sites in the history of technology, "including little-known subsites buried on many well-known commercial sites."

World History Compass: History of Science, Medicine, and Technology

http://www.worldhistorycompass.com/science.htm

Contains a short catalog of history of technology sites.

WWW Virtual Library for the History of Science, Technology, and Medicine

http://www.asap.unimelb.edu.au/hstm/hstm_technology.htm

Excellent list of links to other history of technology sites, including summaries of each site.

WWW Virtual Library for the History of Science, Technology, and Medicine (Biographical Sources)

http://www.asap.unimelb.edu.au/hstm/hstm_bio.htm

Links to online biographies of many important scholars, scientists, engineers, and inventors.

General Sites

A-Bomb WWW Museum

http://www.csi.ad.jp/ABOMB/

An activist site based in Japan, with English and Japanese versions.

All About The Internet: History of the Internet

http://www.isoc.org/internet-history/

Sponsored by the Internet Society (ISOC); includes many links to documents and other sites concerning the founding of the Internet, plus a historical narrative written by the founders of the Internet themselves.

Ancient Metallurgy Research Group

http://www.brad.ac.uk/acad/archsci/depart/resgrp/amrg/amrginfo.html

Part of the Department of Archaeological Sciences at the University of Bradford, England, this site describes the group's efforts and provides links to other archaeometallurgy sites.

Aquae Urbis Romae: The Waters of the City of Rome

http://www.iath.virginia.edu/waters/

Created by the Institute for Advanced Technology in the Humanities at the University of Virginia, this cartographic study uses graphics, QuickTime movies, and interactive maps to survey the 2,800-year history of water in Rome. Includes a timeline and bibliography. This ambitious site is currently incomplete.

Charles Babbage Institute of Computer History

http://www.cbi.umn.edu/

Based at the University of Minnesota, the Babbage Institute is an archive for the history of computing that also sponsors research in the field. Some excellent sections illuminate various aspects of computing. An extensive list of sites related to the history of information processing is also provided.

Alexander Graham Bell's Path to the Telephone

http://jefferson.village.virginia.edu/albell/homepage.html

Describes Bell's invention of the telephone; includes reproductions of Bell's lab notebooks in the form of images and transcripts.

Caltech Archives

http://www.caltech.edu/archives/

Archives of the California Institute of Technology, including descriptions of manuscript holdings and an online archive of 3,000 photographs and other visual materials.

Centre for the History of Defense Electronics: History of Technology Research Unit

http://chide.museum.org.uk/

Sponsored by School of Conservation Sciences at Bournemouth University in the United Kingdom, this virtual museum contains narratives, exhibit photos, and links to similar sites.

Discovery Online, Feature Stories: The Unkindest Cut

http://www.discovery.com/stories/history/panama/panama.html

Discovery Channel often creates Web sites to supplement the material in its television programs. This site features the building of the Panama Canal, including an interactive timeline, audio recordings, and videos.

Epact

http://www.mhs.ox.ac.uk/epact/introduction.asp

Epact is an electronic catalog of medieval and renaissance scientific instruments from four European museums: the Museum of the History of Science in Oxford, the Istituto e Museo di Storia della Scienza in Florence, the British Museum in London, and the Museum Boerhaave in Leiden.

Firearms History

http://www.rrnotes.co.uk/

Includes primary documents on the history of firearms and links to similar sites.

Hagley Museum and Library

http://www.hagley.lib.de.us/

Web site for the Wilmington, Delaware, museum and library. Hagley's "mission is to promote the understanding of American business and technological history."

Henry Ford Museum and Greenfield Village

http://www.hfmgv.org/

This site, which has received many Web awards for its comprehensive content, is a worthy companion to the impressive museum and village in Dearborn, Michigan. It includes inventor biographies, many pictures, and a virtual tour of the museum.

History of Australian Science and Technology

http://www.asap.unimelb.edu.au/hast/asaphast.htm

Starting point for exploring the Australian contributions to science and technology.

The History of Chemical Engineering

http://www.cems.umn.edu/~aiche_ug/history/h_intro.html

Overview of chemical engineering, including "its conceptual origins in Great Britain, subsequent struggle for survival in the United States, and . . . a cornucopia of contributions made in this century." This site includes a lengthy timeline, numerous graphs, and a large bibliography.

History of Computing

http://ei.cs.vt.edu/~history/

Large collection of primary materials related to the history of computing.

H-Sci-Med-Tech

http://www2.h-net.msu.edu/~smt/

H-Sci-Med-Tech is the H-Net discussion list and Web site intended for scholars who study science, medicine, and technology.

ICOHTEC: International Committee for the History of Technology

http://www.icohtec.org/

The international equivalent of the American-dominated Society for the History of Technology (SHOT); includes the full text of newsletters and the tables of contents of *Icon*, the committee's annual journal.

IEEE History Center

http://www.ieee.org/organizations/history_center/

History of the Institute of Electrical and Electronics Engineers (IEEE), with additional material on electrical and radio engineering.

Inventure Place: National Inventors Hall of Fame

http://www.invent.org/

Contains dozens of short biographies of inductees into the National Inventors Hall of Fame, located in Akron, Ohio. Various programs and exhibits are also described.

Issues in Science and Technology Home Page

http://www.nap.edu/issues/

Web site for the *Issues in Science and Technology* quarterly, "published by the Cecil and Ida Green Center for the Study of Science and Society at the University of Texas at Dallas in cooperation with the National Academy of Sciences." The site includes the full content of back issues.

Jerome and Dorothy Lemelson Center for the Study of Invention and Innovation

http://www.si.edu/lemelson/index.html

The Lemelson Center is part of the Smithsonian Institution's National Museum of American History. By sponsoring research and education, the center seeks to "foster an appreciation for the central role invention and innovation play in the history of the United States." Extensive site with a featured inventor on the home page.

The Museum of Science and Industry in Manchester

http://www.msim.org.uk/

Web site for the museum, located in Manchester, England. Includes hands-on games and extensive information on the exhibitions and resources of the museum.

NASA History Office

http://www.hq.nasa.gov/office/pao/History/index.html

Comprehensive history of the National Aeronautics and Space Administration, including a catalog of publications, a timeline, a reference guide, and links to other sites.

Oral History on Space, Science, and Technology

http://www.nasm.edu/nasm/dsh/

Excellent example of providing primary historical material on the Web. This NASA site contains the complete transcripts of "over 850 hours of oral history interviews with more than two hundred interviewees" involved in the space industry from World War II to the present. A summary and a table of contents are provided for each interview.

Psychology of Invention

http://hawaii.psychology.msstate.edu/invent/invention.html

By examining the invention of the airplane and telephone, this site explores the psychology behind the practice of inventing. Includes extensive text, diagrams, short videos, bibliography, and links to similar sites.

Science and Technology In the Making

http://sloan.stanford.edu/

An ambitious effort, funded by the Alfred P. Sloan Foundation, to "establish a network of history of technology Web sites." The five completed projects are: History of Electric Vehicle Owners and Drivers, History of Human Computer Interaction, History of the Invention of Polymerase Chain Reaction, History of the New York City Blackouts of 1965 and 1977, and History of Scheme Z and the Building of the Boston Central Artery. Includes primary and secondary material.

A Science Odyssey

http://www.pbs.org/wgbh/aso/

A PBS site chronicling scientific discoveries and achievements from 1900 to about 1995.

SHOT: The Society for the History of Technology

http://shot.press.jhu.edu/associations/shot/index.html

This official site of the leading history of technology academic organization includes sample syllabi, an archive of society newsletters, job opportunities, and other announcements.

STS Links

http://www2.ncsu.edu/ncsu/chass/mds/stslinks.html

Large list of links provided by the North Carolina State Program on Science, Technology, and Society.

Technology and Culture

http://shot.press.jhu.edu/associations/shot/tc.html

This site for the journal of the Society for the History of Technology (SHOT) includes notes for contributors, sample articles, the current journal index, and subscription information.

Technology Review

http://www.techreview.com/

Web site for MIT's "Magazine of Innovation," including sample articles from each issue. The magazine often publishes articles of historical interest.

"To Fly is Everything . . . "

http://invention.psychology.msstate.edus

This comprehensive site is a "A Virtual Museum covering the Invention of the Airplane."

Totalizator (Totalisator) History: A World's First

http://www.ozemail.com.au/~bconlon/

A patriotic ode to Australian inventor Sir George Julius, who in 1913 invented the automatic totalisator, an early form of mechanical computer.

Transistorized!

http://www.pbs.org/transistor/

The companion site to the PBS program on the development of the transistor and its importance in the electronic age.

Van Gogh Museum Light Exhibition

http://www.vangoghmuseum.nl/light/english/index.html

An elegant site, though it takes a while to learn to navigate it, analyzing the history of light from 1750 to 1900.

Eli Whitney Armory Site

http://www.yale.edu/ewhitney/

Extensive report by Yale University on the continuing archaeological excavations at the site of Eli Whitney's arms factory.

Whole Cloth: Discovering Science and Technology Through American Textile History

http://www.si.edu/lemelson/centerpieces/whole_cloth

Extensive site developed by the Society for the History of Technology (SHOT) and the Lemelson Center of the Smithsonian Institution to assist teachers in American survey courses. Both high school and college instructors will find a wealth of information. Among the instruction modules are such topics as Early Industrialization, True Colors, and Synthetic Fibers. Lesson plans, documents, glossaries, bibliographies, and samples essays are included. A model to emulate of how to create an instructional site offering curriculum materials.

Robert C. Williams American Museum of Papermaking

http://www.ipst.edu/amp/

Includes a virtual tour of the Atlanta, Georgia, museum that covers the entire history of papermaking.

Chapter 20

Holocaust Studies

Solomon Davidoff and Anne Rothfeld

AMCHA

http://www.amcha.org/

AMCHA is the support organization of Israeli centers for Holocaust survivors and the children of survivors.

Anne Frank Center USA

http://www.annefrank.com/

The site for the Anne Frank Center USA, with educational information for teachers and students, information on the center's traveling exhibit and activities.

Anne Frank House

http://www.annefrank.nl/

The Web site for the Anne Frank House, this site gives viewing and exhibition information, a keyword and book list, and photos of her famous diary.

Bulgarian Jews During World War II

http://www.b-info.com/places/Bulgaria/Jewish/

An archive of articles, letters, and other documents that attempts to explain the experience of Jews in Bulgaria, and why not a single Bulgarian Jew was deported to the Nazi death camps during World War II. Also includes a bibliography and link section.

Cybrary of the Holocaust

http://remember.org

An impressive resource for both teachers and students of the Jewish Holocaust. This site includes a wide variety of both text and artwork, including discussion forums, eyewitness accounts, poetry, photos, and bibliographies, with all content donated by user/participants.

The Desert Holocaust Memorial

http://www.palmsprings.com/points/holocaust/

A photo and information page for a memorial in Rancho Mirage, California, that has an impressive number of Holocaust related links.

The Forgotten Camps

http://www.jewishweb.org/ForgottenCamps

An extensive site devoted to several of the lesser known concentration camps, work camps, police camps, transit camps, and similar facilities. This site, created by Vincent Chatel, son of a survivor, and Chuck Ferree, a witness and camp liberator, is also accessible in a French version.

H-Holocaust

http://www.h-net.msu.edu/~holoweb/

The Web location for the Humanities and Social Science Online Initiative's Holocaust discussion list. Includes an opportunity to join the list, as well as scholarly reviews, academic announcements, course syllabi, and an entire log of H-Holocaust messages. Other related listservs include H-German, H-Judaic, and H-Antisemitism.

Holocaust Education Resources for Teachers

http://www.Holocaust-trc.org/

Sponsored by the Holocaust Education Foundation, this site offers lesson plans, curricula, essays and publications, bibliographies, and a vast array of information and locations for those intending to teach about the Holocaust.

The Holocaust History Project

http://www.holocaust-history.org/

An archive of documents, photographs, recordings, book reproductions, and essays regarding the Holocaust, with a focus on direct refutation of Holocaust denial.

Holocaust Memorial Center: Illuminating the Past, Enlightening the Future

http://www.holocaustcenter.com/

The Web site of the first American Holocaust memorial, in West Bloomfield, Michigan, contains exhibits, an archive of documents and artifacts, and an oral history archive. An interesting addition is the Lifechance exhibit, an interactive role-playing scenario wherein you make choices that determine whether you would have lived or died during the Holocaust.

Holocaust: Non-Jewish Victims

http://www.holocaustforgotten.com/

A site dedicated and devoted to the more than 5 million people, other than Jews, who were slaughtered during the Holocaust.

Holocaust Pictures Exhibition

http://fmv.ulg.ac.be/schmitz/holocaust.html

A collection of thirty-seven photos with documentation and commentary. Also available in French.

The Holocaust Ring

http://www.pgonline.com/electriczen/holoring.html

A list of Web pages that contribute to Holocaust understanding, study, or research.

Holocaust Understanding and Prevention by Alexander Kimel

http://users.systec.com/kimel/

Informative site, recommended by The History Channel, created by Holocaust survivor Alexander Kimel. Contains a wide variety of documents, memoirs, and poetry by Holocaust survivors; an online magazine on Holocaust issues; and an excellent collection of links to other sites.

KZ Mauthausen-GUSEN Info-Pages

http://linz.orf.at/orf/gusen/

An archive of documentation and information about the Mauthausen-GUSEN death camps, considered the worst of all the camps that existed.

L'Chaim: A Holocaust Web Project

http://www.charm.net/~rbennett/l'chaim.html

Another educational site project, containing a virtual tour of Dachau, a glossary and link section, two photo essays, and the story of survivor Ingrid Griffin.

Louisiana Holocaust Survivors

http://www.tulane.edu/~so-inst/laholsur.html

With space contributed by The Southern Institute for Education and Research, this is a Web-based archive of the stories of Louisiana residents who survived the Holocaust.

Mauthausen Concentration Camp Memorial

http://www.mauthausen-memorial.gv.at/engl/index.html

This Web site for the Mauthausen camp memorial contains documentation and information about the camp.

The Nizkor Holocaust Educational Resource

http://www2.ca.nizkor.org/index.html

The Nizkor Project Web site is the home page of an international multimedia effort, spearheaded by Canada-based archivist Ken McVay (http://veritas.nizkor.org/~kmcvay/), that aims to counter those who deny the Holocaust. This extremely well-documented and rich resource, containing over 4,000 documents, is the world's largest collection of Holocaust-related materials online.

Rescuers during the Holocaust

http://www.cs.cmu.edu/afs/cs.cmu.edu/user/mmbt/www/rescuers.html

A bibliography of works in English that discuss the lives and actions of rescuers during the Holocaust.

To Save A Life: Stories of Jewish Rescue

http://www.humboldt.edu/~rescuers/index.html

The text from a previously unpublished work by Ellen Land-Weber that tells the stories of nine Jews who were rescued from the Holocaust and of the six people who saved them.

The Simon Wiesenthal Center

http://www.wiesenthal.com/

The Simon Wiesenthal Center in Los Angeles is dedicated to chronicling the history of human rights and the Holocaust. The center's online site contains exhibits, glossaries, articles, information on the center's activities, and more.

Survivors of the Shoah Visual History Foundation

http://www.vhf.org/

Founded by Steven Spielburg in 1994, this nonprofit foundation is dedicated to videotaping and archiving interviews of Holocaust survivors all over the world, using the latest technology. The site offers information on the project, repositories, and production status.

Teaching the Holocaust

http://www.socialstudies.com/c/@c0kc44xusXy6Y/Pages/holo.html

A collection of links to resources and materials for teaching about the Holocaust.

Teaching the Holocaust Through Stamps, Pictures and Text

http://mofetsrv.mofet.macam98.ac.il/~ochayo/einvert.htm

An interdisciplinary, computer-based resource for teaching about the Holocaust through stamps, pictures, texts, and paintings by children who suffered in the Holocaust. This site, which offers a complete teacher's guide, dictionary, and teaching unit, is also available in a Hebrew version.

The United States Holocaust Museum

http://www.ushmm.org/

This official site of the United States Holocaust Museum offers information on the museum's exhibits and activities, as well as an array of documents and contact information. The museum, a memorial to everyone who perished in the Holocaust, focuses on photographic and cinematic exhibits.

The Wolf Lewkowicz Collection

http://web.mit.edu/maz/wolf/

The Wolf Lewkowicz Collection is made up of 178 letters translated into English (the original Yiddish is also available) from a man in Poland to his nephew in the United States, written between 1922 and 1939. Lewkowicz was later sent to Treblinka, where he died. Photos, sound recordings, a list of names, and a chronology of the letters are included.

Women and the Holocaust: A Cyberspace of Their Own

http://www.interlog.com/~mighty/

A collection of essays, tributes, bibliographies, poetry, and personal reflections that focus on women's experiences during the Holocaust.

Yad Vashem: The Holocaust Martyrs and Heroes Remembrance Authority

http://www.yadvashem.org/

Yad Vashem is the Jerusalem-based Holocaust memorial, established in 1953. The site consists of online exhibits, information about the center and its research, its vast collection of publications (now available online), calls for papers, and more.

Chapter 21

Law, Civil Liberties, and Civil Rights

Richard P. Mulcahy

Law

The *Amistad* Case

http://www.nara.gov/education/teaching/amistad/home.html

This interesting and worthwhile National Archives site examines the *Amistad* case. It offers excellent graphics, presenting images of several of the important handwritten documents involved in their entirety, such as the Supreme Court's order of release.

The Avalon Project

http://www.Yale.edu/lawweb/avalon/avalon.htm

This site offers access to a wide variety of documents relating to American legal history. The documents included are in plain text, presented in their entirety, arranged according to period, and are cross-referenced according to subject matter. Selections include The *Mayflower* Compact (complete with the names of its signatories), Thomas Paine's *American Crisis*, Lincoln's Gettysburg

Address, and the Yalta Accords. The site features a section for e-mail comments, a bibliography, a help desk, and a link to Project DIANA, which is listed as "An Online Human Rights Archive." This very thorough site is a valuable resource for both advanced scholars and students alike.

The Bill of Rights

http://www.nara.gov/exhall/charters/billrights/

This informative and well-thought-out National Archives site makes important documents in America's legal history available. It features the Preamble to the Constitution, the Bill of Rights itself, and Amendments Eleven through Twenty-Seven. The site also features informational items, such as the article "A More Perfect Union," which gives an overview of the Constitutional Convention.

Connections

http://www.law.pitt.edu/hibbitts/connect.htm

This site is maintained by the University of Pittsburgh's School of Law. Although designed primarily for use by law students, it features sections on American Legal History, Ancient Law, and English Legal History. Interested students can access such diverse items as decisions of the United States Supreme Court, slave narratives, and a chronology of the Salem witch trials. The Ancient Law section provides access to Roman law, the Cicero Home Page, Aristotle's *Athenian Constitution*, and similar topics, making the site useful not only to historians, but to classicists as well. The site is linked to various law journals currently available on the WWW.

Famous American Trials

http://www.law.umkc.edu/faculty/projects/ftrials/ftrials.htm

This site, maintained by the University of Missouri, Kansas City School of Law, is probably one of the most extensive and informative, dealing with American court cases. It offers detailed coverage of many major cases, including Leopold and Loeb, the Scopes Monkey Trial, the Rosenberg case, the Chicago Seven, and the My-Lai courts martial. This highly recommended site features full narratives, original documents, and graphics of the people and evidence involved.

Guide to Legal History Resources on the Web

http://www.law.utexas.edu/rare/legalhis.htm

Maintained by the Jamail Center for Legal Research of the University of Texas's Tarlton Law Library, this site should be a first stop for all students and scholars doing research in this field. The site is divided into five subject headings: General Sources, Court Records, Academic Libraries, Research Libraries, and Full-Text Sources. Each section is a treasure-trove of information. For example, in the General Sources section, the user can choose from a host of sites ranging from the Ames Foundation to Roman law. Particularly helpful are the annotations that appear with each listing. Well organized and thoughtfully laid out, this site is highly recommended.

Civil Liberties

American Radicalism

http://digital.lib.msu.edu/Exhibits/
Collection.cfm?ID=1&SectionID=1&DBaseID=1

Maintained by Michigan State University, this site offers access to digital reproductions of various writings and pamphlets dealing with American radicalism. The subjects covered include the Hollywood Ten, the Scottsboro Boys, the Rosenberg case, the IWW, the Sacco-Vanzetti case, and others. Although the quality of the individual selections varies widely, each is valuable in providing insight into the time it was written, as well as the mentality of the audience it was attempting to reach. All in all, a site recommended for anyone interested in studying radical movements.

Banned Books Online

http://digital.library.upenn.edu/books/banned-books.html

This page offers information on past and recent efforts to ban various works, including James Joyce's *Ulysses*, Charles Darwin's *Origin of Species*, and Mark Twain's *Tom Sawyer*. For example, the site reports on a 1996 effort by a New Hampshire school board to ban Shakespeare's *Twelfth Night*. The site includes complete texts of the works. The information it presents makes it a useful resource for anyone interested in freedom of thought.

Blacklisted: Resources and Links

http://www.weisbroth.com/blacklisted/resources.html

This is the "resources" subsite for the audio drama *Blacklisted*, which deals with the Hollywood blacklist during McCarthyism. The subsite offers links for serious researchers, including two essays by Professor Ellen Shrecker: "The Impact of McCarthyism" and "Interpreting McCarthyism: A Bibliographic Essay."

Encyclopedia of USA History: McCarthyism

http://www.spartacus.schoolnet.co.uk/USAred.htm

This site is part of Britain's Spartacus Online Encyclopedia. This is a beginner's site for anyone interested in McCarthyism, civil liberties, or the Cold War, offering basic information on a number of interrelated topics, including the Hollywood Ten, Elizabeth Bentley, a former Communist spy, and Alger Hiss.

The File Room

http://www.thefileroom.org

This site offers access to information about censorship efforts worldwide, not just in the United States.

Literature and Culture of the American 1950s

http://Dept.English.upenn.edu/~afilreis/50s/home.html

This site, maintained by the University of Pennsylvania's Department of English, focuses on McCarthyism and the Cold War. Stated simply, this site offers an "embarrassment of riches." Among the highlights are Justice Hugo Black's dissenting opinion in *Dennis v. U.S.* (the 1951 treason trial of the leadership of the Communist Party of the United States of America under the Smith Act), a guide to FBI files available under the Freedom of Information Act, and information on the House Un-American Activities Committee (HUAC). The site is highly recommended for all users.

McCarthy

http://Webcorp.com/mccarthy/

This site offers audio and video clips of some of the major figures of the McCarthy era, including Senator Joseph R. McCarthy, President Dwight David Eisenhower, and Vice President Richard Nixon. Featured video clips include Nixon's "Checkers" speech and the Army McCarthy hearings of 1954. However, the most interesting piece the site offers is a twenty-minute audio clip of a speech McCarthy made during the height of his influence, in which he makes his oft-repeated charge that communism had enslaved more people in the course of the twentieth century than Christianity had converted in 2,000 years. This site manages to be both amusing and informative.

Paul Robeson

http://www.founders.howard.edu/robeson.htm

Interest in Paul Robeson was rekindled by his centennial birthday on April 9, 1998. Regardless of his failings, the man, through his myriad accomplishments, forced this nation to reassess its attitudes about race relations. This site, established by Howard University Libraries, provides the user with an extensive series of links to other sites about Robeson, from his films to his personal papers.

Civil Rights

Americans United for Affirmative Action

http://www.auaa.org

This site, maintained by Americans United for Affirmative Action, includes a library of full-text primary documents dealing with race relations. In addition to the Declaration of Independence, the Constitution, and the Emancipation Proclamation, the site covers *Dred Scott v. Sanford*, *Plessy v. Ferguson*, *Brown v. Board of Education*, *U.C. Regents v. Bakke*, and other materials.

Anti-Defamation League Holocaust Resources

http://www.adl.org/main_holocaust.asp

This site deals with the Holocaust and related issues, such as Holocaust deniers, the "hidden children," and the Lipstadt case (where historian Debra Lipstadt won a libel case filed against her by David Irving.) As for the hidden children, the site offers a great deal of information, especially personal narratives. This site is highly recommended for anyone interested in the Holocaust and the toll it continues to take.

Civil Rights Documentation Project

http://www-dept.usm.edu/~mcrohb/

This site, maintained by the Mississippi Humanities Council and the Mississippi Department of Archives and History, includes the Civil Rights Oral History Bibliography, which provides access to oral history interviews on the civil rights movement in Mississippi from the early 1960s through the 1970s. The site lists the names of all people who were interviewed and provides complete online transcripts, some featuring audio enhancement, for a number of the interviews. The transcripts list the subject matters discussed and include biographical sketches of the interviewees, including movement activists who went to Mississippi to take part in the Freedom Rides and Freedom Schools, and those who were born and raised in Mississippi. This site is an important tool for the serious educator and researcher.

Civnet

http://www.civnet.org

Civnet is maintained by Civitas, which describes itself as "an international, non-governmental organization dedicated to promoting civic education and civil society." Among the documents included here are the Virginia Declaration of Rights, the French Declaration of the Rights of Man, *The Federalist Papers*, and Thomas Paine's *The Rights of Man*. These documents, combined with its coverage of recent political issues, makes the site an invaluable tool for the study of democratic government and its workings.

Greensboro Sit-Ins: Launch of a Civil Rights Movement

http://www.sitins.com

This site deals with the so-called Greensboro Four who, on February 1, 1960, sat at a "white only" lunch counter at a Woolworth's in Greensboro, North Carolina, and demanded to be served. Credited with being the first sit-in, the tactic became a staple in the arsenal of nonviolent protest against institutional racism. The site includes a bibliography on the civil rights movement, biographical sketches of the four original protestors, and an extensive timeline on civil rights, dating from 1865 to the present. A multimedia section features an extensive collection of photographs relating to the Greensboro Four, video and audio selections, and links to the National Civil Rights Museum and the NAACP home page.

National Civil Rights Museum

http://www.civilrightsmuseum.org

The single most important contribution this site makes is the virtual tour it offers of the National Civil Rights Museum. It also presents a useful narrative about the civil rights struggle, dating back to Independence; basic information on such figures as Frederick Douglass, Harriet Tubman, and William Lloyd Garrison; and pictures of several of the museum's exhibits, including a city bus from the Montgomery, Alabama, bus boycott. All in all, the site offers a good basic introduction to the history of the civil rights movement.

Chapter 22

Modern Military History

Mark Gellis

General Resources

African-American Military History

http://www.coax.net/people/lwf/aa_mh.htm

Bennie J. McRae Jr. has provided this valuable set of indexes to links on the history of black Americans during armed conflict from the Revolution to the Vietnam War as part of his "Lest We Forget" project.

Air Force Historical Research Agency

http://www.au.af.mil/au/afhra/

The United States Air Force's historical agency provides links to various resources on military aviation history.

American History: Wars of the Twentieth Century

http://www.geocities.com/Athens/Academy/6617/wars.html

A short but useful index of military history sites on the Internet.

American Merchant Marine

http://www.USMM.org/

The home page of the United States Merchant Marine includes extensive resources on the history of merchant marine efforts during wartime.

American Wars, Military History, and Military Affairs

http://www.hist.unt.edu/09w-ame4.htm

Professor Lee E. Huddleston has developed a large index of Web sites related to military history, including separate subindexes dedicated to each of the World Wars and another providing links on military affairs and archives.

Article Index

http://www.thehistorynet.com/general/articleindex.htm

Historynet's article index features more than 500 online articles, many of them dealing with various aspects of military history.

BUBL: Military History

http://bubl.ac.uk/link/m/militaryhistory.htm

This index of links, provided by BUBL (BUlletin Board for Libraries) Information Service, includes links to the Battle of Britain History Site and a site dedicated to Britain's small military conflicts during the Cold War.

The Center of Military History

http://www.army.mil/cmh-pg/

The United States Army's Center of Military History provides access to many resources, including a large number of online articles, photographs, and artwork. In addition, one can view and order from the center's catalog of publications on military history.

DefenseLINK

http://www.defenselink.mil/

Offers numerous links to military-related Web sites (including some with sections on military history) and news on defense-related issues—in effect, American military history as it happens.

Department of Defense Dictionary of Military Terms

http://www.dtic.mil/doctrine/jel/doddict/

An online dictionary of military terminology.

Federation of American Scientists

http://www.fas.org/index.html

This remarkable resource, one of the best on the Internet for those interested in military history, provides an enormous set of detailed Web pages with links to military and intelligence operations of the past and present, weapons and military vehicles, arms sales, and related subjects.

Haze Gray and Underway

http://www.hazegray.org

This is one of the best Internet sites in the world for those interested in modern naval warfare. The site includes the World Navies Today page, which provides detailed information on virtually every navy in the world, including the Russian and Chinese navies, and an online version of *The Dictionary of American Naval Fighting Ships*.

The History Guy: Military History

http://www.historyguy.com/Militarylinks.html

Provides links to various Web pages on military history.

History, Reference, and Preservation

http://www.usni.org/hrp/hrp.html

Historical and reference links at the United States Naval Institute's Web site.

Homework Center: Wars and World History

http://www.multnomah.lib.or.us/lib/homework/warwldhc.html

The Homework Center, developed by the Multnomah County Library (Oregon), provides an index of sites oriented around the needs of students learning about military history.

Military History Museums

http://dir.yahoo.com/Arts/Humanities/History/By_Subject/Military_History/
Museums_and_Memorials/

A Yahoo! index of museums dedicated to military history.

Military History Webrings

http://F.webring.com/hub?ring-militaryhistory

Lists Web rings and categories of Web rings dedicated to military history.

Navy Historical Center

http://www.history.navy.mil/

This United States Navy provides this page as a starting point leading to a very large number of links related to naval history. Links include everything from underwater archaeology and information about available research grants to online encyclopedias of naval history and navy ships.

Redstone Arsenal Historical Information

http://www.redstone.army.mil/history/welcome.html

An index to many military history sites, many of them dedicated to the role of missilery in military history.

Responses to War: An Intellectual and Cultural History

http://chomsky.arts.adelaide.edu.au/person/DHart/ResponsesToWar/

David Hart has developed an extensive set of bibliographies and other online resources for students, teachers, and historians.

Twentieth-Century Documents

http://www.yale.edu/lawweb/avalon/20th.htm

Part of the Avalon Project at the Yale University Law School, this index provides links to many online copies of historical documents related to the conflicts of the twentieth century.

Veterans Affairs Canada

http://www.vac-acc.gc.ca/general/

Offers an extensive section—click the history link—on Canada's participation in the conflicts of the twentieth century.

War, Peace and Security WWW Server

http://www.cfcsc.dnd.ca/index.html

This Canadian site, provided by the Information Resource Centre at the Canadian Forces College, offers an extensive list of resources on military history, current conflicts, and modern armed forces.

Warships of the World

http://warships1.com/

A large and very detailed site providing historical and technical data for warships and their weapons, past and present, from virtually every naval power of the modern era.

Wars of the Twentieth Century

http://militaryhistory.about.com/homework/militaryhistory/cs/
wars20thcentury/index.htm

Another index of Web sites, this one offers indexes of various topics, including military societies, naval warfare, military aircraft, and modern conflicts like Vietnam and the Gulf War.

The World at War

http://www.fas.org/man/dod-101/ops/war/index.html

Provides an index of links on various contemporary and recent military conflicts.

Conflicts at the Turn of the Century

Anglo-Boer War Centenary

http://www.icon.co.za/~dup42/war.htm

A useful set of links on the Boer War.

Boer War Index

http://users.netconnect.com.au/~ianmac/boermain.html

The Boer War is the focus of this site.

Border Revolution

http://ac.acusd.edu/History/projects/border/page01.html

An illustrated online explication of the Mexican Revolution.

Mexican Revolution

http://www.mexconnect.com/mex_/history/jtuck/jtrevolution11.html

Author Jim Tuck provides an illustrated summary of the Mexican Revolution.

The Philippine-American War Centennial

http://www.phil-am-war.org/

An detailed examination of this conflict, with charts, timelines, illustrated articles, and historical editorial cartoons and quotations.

The Philippine-American War (1899–1902) from Filipino-Americans.com

http://www.filipino-americans.com/filamwar.html

A detailed summary of the conflict, including numerous excerpts from accounts by participants.

The Russo-Japanese War

http://www.navy.ru/history/hrn10-e.htm

Summary of the Russo-Japanese War from a Web site dedicated to the history of the Russian navy.

Russo-Japanese War Research Society

http://www.russojapan.com/

Provides a summary of the war, an image gallery, and other resources.

South African War Virtual Library

http://www.bowlerhat.com.au/sawvl/index.html

Historian Robert Wotton has developed an extensive virtual archive that contains research data related to the Second South African War (1899–1902).

Spanish-American War Page

http://www.ecsis.net/~jrwilobe/

A useful set of links on the Spanish-American War.

The World of 1898: The Spanish-American War Home Page

http://www.loc.gov/rr/hispanic/1898/

A Library of Congress Web site dedicated to the Spanish-American War.

World War I and Its Aftermath

The Aerodrome

http://www.theaerodrome.com/

Provides information on the aces and aircraft of World War I.

America's Secret War

http://secretwar.hhsweb.com/

Amateur historian Dan Leifheit's useful Web site, with government documents and a large collection of images, on American's intervention during the Russian Civil War (1918–1920).

The Australian Light Horse Association

http://www.lighthorse.org.au/

This site contains both historical and current information on famous Australian regiments and battles during the Boer War and World War I.

The First World War

http://www.spartacus.schoolnet.co.uk/FWW.htm

Spartacus, an educational publishing company, is committed to providing free informational resources for the Internet community. This large, illustrated hypertext encyclopedia is dedicated to World War I.

The Great War Series

http://www.wtj.com/wars/greatwar/

A list of links to online books and articles on World War I, including a memoir of the war written by Manfred von Richthofen—the Red Baron—shortly before his death.

The Great War Society

http://www.worldwar1.com/tgws/

This site, from a historical society dedicated to the study of World War I and its effects on human history, includes a list of more than 300 Web sites related to World War I.

History of the British Army in the Great War

http://www.geocities.com/Athens/Acropolis/2354/index.html

Historian and reenactor Jason Griffeth has developed this set of Web pages and list of links on the British Army during World War I.

The Russian Civil War

http://mars.acnet.wnec.edu/~grempel/courses/stalin/lectures/CivilWar.html

One of several lectures placed online by Professor Gerhard Rempel, this one outlines the events of the Russian Civil War that followed the 1917 Revolution.

World War I

http://historicaltextarchive.com/sections.php?op=listarticles&secid=7

Part of the Historical Text Archives Project, this page provides links to articles and multimedia resources about World War I, including a detailed examination of its effects on small European nations and on Arabs.

The World War I Document Archive

http://www.lib.byu.edu/~rdh/wwi/

Developed by scholars at Brigham Young University, this page provides links to a wide range of historical documents related to World War I, ranging from treaties and government proclamations to personal memoirs. The site also includes a biographical dictionary and an image archive.

World War I: Trenches on the Web

http://www.worldwar1.com/

Another Web site providing several links to historical documents and multimedia files.

The Spanish Civil War

Spanish Civil War

http://ac.acusd.edu/History/WW2Timeline/Prelude07.html

Part of a larger project on the history of World War II, this site contains a timeline and links to an image archive.

Spanish Civil War

http://lcweb2.loc.gov/cgi-bin/query/r?frd/cstdy:@field(DOCID+es0031)

A brief summary of the war from a Federal Research Division Country Study of Spain.

The Spanish Revolution and Civil War

http://www.geocities.com/CapitolHill/9820/

Eugene W. Plawiuk's site offers an index of Web resources related to the Spanish Civil War.

World War II

Achtung Panzer

http://www.achtungpanzer.com/panzer.htm

One of many enthusiast sites dedicated to German armor. This one features many illustrations, tables of technical data, and a large number of links to other World War II sites.

The Battle of Britain Historical Society

http://www.battleofbritain.net/bobhsoc/

A detailed site dedicated to the aerial battle over Great Britain in 1940.

Dad's War: Finding and Telling Your Father's World War II Story

http://members.aol.com/dadswar/index.htm

Wes Johnson has done a service with this index of personal histories and initial instructions on writing your own history for a family member who served in World War II (and, by extension, any war).

East Anglia: The Air War

http://www.stable.demon.co.uk/

Contains a series of informative essays with illustrations concerning various air forces and the aircraft flown during World War II. The site also provides a useful index of links to related Web pages and a bibliography of print reference works.

504th WWII Home Page

http://www.geocities.com/~the504thpir/index.html

An example of the many sites dedicated to specific military units, this one chronicles the experiences of the 504th Parachute Infantry Regiment during World War II.

German Armed Forces: 1919–1945

http://www.feldgrau.com/

A detailed Web site covering the German armed forces from the end of World War I until the end of World War II.

Guadalcanal: The First Offensive

http://www.army.mil/cmh-pg/books/wwii/GuadC/GC-fm.htm

A book-length study of this offensive, including maps and charts, one of the many resources provided by the United States Army Center of Military History.

Hyperwar: A Hypertext History of the Second World War

http://metalab.unc.edu/hyperwar/

A linked anthology of articles related to World War II, many of them discussing specific battles in detail, along with links to other sources.

Imperial Japanese Navy Page

http://www.combinedfleet.com/

Another example of the many sites on World War II created by enthusiasts and amateur historians. This one, by Jon Parshall, covers the Japanese navy and provides details about its ships and top officers, along with a useful bibliography of print sources.

The *Luftwaffe* Homepage

http://www.ww2.dk

This site provides data on the *Luftwaffe* and an index of links to *Luftwaffe*-related Web pages.

A Marine Diary: My Experiences on Guadalcanal

http://www.gnt.net/~jrube/indx2.html

Entries from the diary of a marine who served at Guadalcanal, with a large set of links to related World War II resources on the Internet.

Marines at Midway

http://metalab.unc.edu/hyperwar/USMC/USMC-M-Midway.html

Part of the Hyperwar project, this is a detailed, illustrated examination of the Battle of Midway, written by Lieutenant Colonel R.D. Heinl, Jr., USMC.

Naval Air War in the Pacific

http://www.ixpres.com/ag1caf/navalwar/

Photos and paintings of American air combat during World War II.

Normandy: 1944

http://normandy.eb.com/

Encyclopedia Britannica's multimedia examination of the Normandy invasion.

Red Steel

http://www.algonet.se/~toriert/

Enthusiast Thorleif Olsson's extensive Web site on Russian tanks and armored vehicles.

Return to Midway

http://www.nationalgeographic.com/features/98/midway/

National Geographic has created this multimedia site featuring images and streaming video of the wrecks of the carriers sunk at the Battle of Midway.

U-Boat Net

http://uboat.net/

A comprehensive study of the German U-boat, including maps, technology, and profiles of more than 1,100 German submarines employed during World War II.

What Did You Do in the War, Grandma?

http://www.stg.brown.edu/projects/WWII_Women/tocCS.html

An oral history of Rhode Island women during World War II, written by students in the Honors English Program at South Kingstown High School, this site provides not only information about lesser known aspects of the war, but also a good model of action for teachers interested in using the Internet for class projects.

The Women's Army Corps

http://www.army.mil/cmh-pg/brochures/wac/wac.htm

The United States Army has developed this online article about the Women's Army Corps during World War II.

World War II in Europe

http://www.historyplace.com/worldwar2/timeline/ww2time.htm

Part of The History Place, a large Web site dedicated to assisting students and educators, this is a World War II timeline with links to illustrations and short articles on specific events.

World War II in the Pacific's Webring

http://www.geocities.com/guy_conquest/webrings.html

Amateur historian Brian Smith has provided a large and useful index of links on World War II in the Pacific.

World War II Resources

http://www.ibiblio.org/pha/index.html

A large collection of historical documents from World War II.

World War II Seminar

http://ac.acusd.edu/History/classes/ww2/175.html

Class materials for a World War II history course from the University of San Diego, including an extended bibliography and several timelines created by students.

World War II Webring

http://nav.webring.yahoo.com/hub?ring=ww2&list

More than 700 Web pages are listed on this Web ring.

World War II Website Association

http://www.ww2wa.com/

Provides links to various Web pages on aspects of World War II.

The Korean War

Korea

http://tlc.ai.org/korea.htm

This educational site on Korea features an index of links to the Web sites on the Korean War.

The Korean War Museum

http://www.theforgottenvictory.org./

This home page provides an index of links to Internet sites on the Korean War; it also provides information on the museum and its newsletter.

The Korean War Project

http://www.koreanwar.org/

An index to a large set of links (particularly in the Reference section), including other Web sites, articles, images, and maps.

The Korean War Veteran Association

http://www.kwva.org/

This organization's home page provides information on and for veterans of the Korean War.

The Vietnam War

Images of My War

http://www.ionet.net/~uheller/vnbktoc.shtml

One of many personal accounts of Vietnam veterans, this one is a detailed autobiography of a U.S. Army Ranger, focusing on his experiences during the conflict.

Tonkin Gulf Yacht Club

http://nav.webring.yahoo.com/hub?ring=gtyc&list

Large list of Web sites on the naval history of the Vietnam conflict.

U.S. POW/MIAs in Southeast Asia

http://www.wtvi.com/wesley/powmia/powmia.html

An index of online resources related to POW/MIA issues.

Vietnam War Bibliography

http://hubcap.clemson.edu/~eemoise/bibliography.html

Professor Edwin Moïse of Clemson University has developed a large bibliography of print and other sources on the Vietnam conflict.

Vietnam War Internet Project

http://www.lbjlib.utexas.edu/shwv/vwiphome.html

This online project, housed on the Lyndon Baines Johnson Library Web server at the University of Texas, provides links to an extensive list of resources, including bibliographies, images, personal memoirs, documents related to the war, and a complete archive of the Soc.History.War.Vietnam newsgroup.

Vietnam War Webring

http://nav.webring.yahoo.com/hub?ring=vwhring&list

Small but select list of Web sites on the Vietnam War.

Vietnam: Yesterday and Today

http://servercc.oakton.edu/~wittman/

Designed for students and teachers, this site includes a timeline of the war and a large set of related links.

The Wars for Vietnam

http://students.vassar.edu/~vietnam/

This site, developed at Vassar College, provides a historical overview of the war, with links to historical documents and other Vietnam-related Web pages.

Other Cold War Resources

Cold War Hot Links

http://www.stmartin.edu/~dprice/cold.war.html

Professor David Price offers a detailed index of Web resources, mostly articles but some multimedia, on the leading figures and events of the Cold War.

Documents Relating to American Foreign Policy: The Cold War

http://www.mtholyoke.edu/acad/intrel/coldwar.htm

A large list of documents related to the Cold War.

Military History: The Cold War and the Marshall Plan

http://www.nara.gov/alic/milrsrcs/coldwar.html

A list of links related to the Cold War, including online historical texts and bibliographies.

The Israeli-Arab Wars

Arab-Israeli Conflict in Maps

http://www.jajz-ed.org.il/100/maps/

A list of maps detailing the various Arab-Israeli conflicts during the last century.

The Battle of Latakia

http://www.us-israel.org/jsource/History/latakia.html

An online article discussing the historic naval battle—the first involving missile boats—between Israeli and Syrian forces in 1973.

The Battle of Latakia

http://www.geocities.com/SoHo/Coffeehouse/2981/latakia.htm

Another online article on this historic battle, with many photographs of the various types of ships involved.

History of the Israeli Defense Force (IDF)

http://www.idf.il/english/history/history.stm

Detailed historical essays by the Israeli Defense Force outlining the activities of the IDF during the War of Independence, the Six-Day War, and other operations.

Israel

gopher://gopher.umsl.edu:70/11/library/govdocs/armyahbs/aahb6

An Army Area Handbook on Israel, this online book includes discussions of the Arab-Israeli conflicts.

Jewish Virtual Library: Wars

http://www.us-israel.org/jsource/History/wartoc.html

Part of a larger Web site on Jewish history and culture, this is a table of contents for a large set of detailed online articles about the various Arab-Israeli conflicts.

Maps of the Arab-Israeli War

http://www.dean.usma.edu/history/dhistorymaps/Arab-Israel%20Pages/aitoc.htm

Another list of maps showing Arab-Israeli conflicts.

Young Warrior

http://tetrad.stanford.edu/eli/YoungWarrior.html

Memoir of an Israeli soldier fighting in the 1948–1949 war, with many pictures.

The Falklands War

The Falklands Island Conflict

http://met.open.ac.uk/group/cpv/falkland.htm

This site features a data library on military vessels and aircraft, a QuickTime video library, and links to other Falklands-related sites.

Falklands Remembered

http://www.thenews.co.uk/news/falklands/menu.htm

This site, developed by an online Portsmouth, U.K. newspaper, covers many aspects of the Falklands war. The site includes a timeline and a large number of short articles and photographs.

Falklands War

http://www.naval-history.net/NAVAL1982FALKLANDS.htm

Detailed explanation of the 1982 conflict, with maps, photographs, and summaries of the forces involved in the various operations of the war.

The Gulf War

Desert-Storm.com

http://www.desert-storm.com/

An index of sites related to operations Desert Shield, Desert Storm, and Desert Fox.

807th MASH: Operation Desert Shield and Operation Desert Storm

http://www.iglou.com/law/mash.htm

An online account of the experiences of a mobile army surgical hospital's staff during the Gulf War.

Fog of War

http://www.washingtonpost.com/wp-srv/inatl/longterm/fogofwar/fogofwar.htm

Resources on the Gulf War developed by the *Washington Post*, including government documents, images, and video clips.

Operation Desert Storm

http://www.fas.org/man/dod-101/ops/desert_storm.htm

This site provides a brief summary of the Gulf War and a large set of links to articles about the conflict and other military resources.

Persian Gulf War/Operation Desert Storm

http://historicaltextarchive.com/sections.php?op=listarticles&secid=16

This page offers a list of documents related to the Gulf War, including the diaries of an Israeli woman and an Iraqi soldier.

Ronald A. Hoskinson's Gulf War Photo Gallery

http://www.hoskinson.net/gulfwar/

Images and a detailed personal account from a field artillery captain who served in the Gulf War.

Other Recent Conflicts

Blackhawk Down

http://www.philly.com/packages/somalia/sitemap.asp

A Web site detailing one of the battles during American operations in Somalia in 1993.

Conflict Between Ecuador and Peru

http://www.ccm.net/~jsruiz/conflicto.htm

A discussion of the 1995 war, written from an Ecuadorian perspective.

The 1971 India-Pakistan War

http://freeindia.org/1971war/

A detailed online history, from an Indian perspective, of the short but brutal conflict between India and Pakistan in 1971.

Operation El Dorado Canyon

http://www.fas.org/man/dod-101/ops/el_dorado_canyon.htm

A Federation of American Scientists (FAS) Web page on the U.S. attack on Libya in 1986.

Operation Just Cause

http://www.fas.org/man/dod-101/ops/just_cause.htm

A Federation of American Scientists (FAS) Web page on Operation Just Cause, the American invasion of Panama in 1989.

Operation Just Cause

http://www.army.mil/cmh-pg/documents/panama/just.htm

Supplemental documents from the United States Army on Operation Just Cause.

Operation Safe Border

http://www.fas.org/man/dod-101/ops/safe_border.htm

A Federation of American Scientists (FAS) Web page listing Web resources on the Ecuador-Peru conflict of 1995.

Operation Urgent Fury

http://www.specialoperations.com/Operations/grenada.html

This site provides links to Web sites related to the American invasion of Grenada, including a detailed discussion of SEAL operations during the invasion, a bibliography of printed sources, and a video clip of President Ronald Reagan announcing the invasion.

The Soviet Invasion of Afghanistan

http://www.afghan-politics.org/Reference/Soviet_Invasion/soviet_invasion_main.htm

Provides a list of links on the Soviet invasion of Afghanistan.

U.S. Special Operations

http://www.specialoperations.com/Operations/default.html

An index of Web sites on U.S. Special Operations, providing information on many of the conflicts of the last fifty years.

Organizations, International Military Services, and Other Military History Sites

The Australian War Memorial

http://www.awm.gov.au/

Covers the Australian experience in war and includes an online encyclopedia and search engines for exploring the memorial's large collections of war-related photographs and documents.

The Battleship Page

http://www.battleship.org/

This page, hosted by the Iowa Class Preservation Association, a nonprofit organization dedicated to preserving this aspect of America's heritage, provides links to a large number of pages related to the role of the battleship in modern military history.

Institute for the Advanced Study of Information Warfare

http://www.psycom.net/iwar.1.html

Provides links to sites and articles related to the gathering and use of information in warfare.

Military Aircraft Database

http://www.csd.uwo.ca/~pettypi/elevon/gustin_military/

An online encyclopedia dedicated to past and present military aircraft of the world.

Military Woman Home Page

http://www.MilitaryWoman.org/homepage.htm

An index of resources related to issues facing women who serve in the military or who are married to those who serve. Useful for those investigating the history of private lives.

The South African Military History Society

http://rapidttp.com/milhist/

Home page for the organization with various links, including a journal with online articles related to the Boer War and other subjects.

Three-Four-Nine: The Ultimate Reference for the Ultimate F-16 Enthusiast

http://www.f-16.net/index.html

A detailed online encyclopedia dedicated to the F-16 Falcon, one of the most widely exported combat aircraft in the world.

United States Naval and Shipbuilding Museum

http://www.uss-salem.org/

Dedicated to the USS *Salem* (CA-139), the world's only preserved heavy cruiser, and related topics.

Chapter 23

Psychohistory

Lloyd deMause

Deutsche Psychohistorische Gesellschaft

http://www.isppm.de/psychohistorie

Web site of the German branch of the Institute for Psychohistory.

Digital Archive of Psychohistory Articles and Texts

http://members.nbci.com/_XOOM/childhistory/index.htm

Over 100 articles and seven books on psychohistory, complete with references.

Free Online Course in Psychohistory

http://www.topica.com/lists/onlinetrain/read

Twenty course assignments in psychohistory given free, with readings all online and easily accessible, and a Certificate of Graduation given by the Institute for Psychohistory.

The Institute for Psychohistory ✓

http://www.psychohistory.com

A rich site of complete articles and books on psychohistory, the study of historical motivations. Includes articles from *The Journal of Psychohistory*, a subject index to the journal, complete contents (including scholarly references) of three psychohistory books, and links to psychohistorical sites.

The International Psychohistorical Association and the Profession of Psychohistory

http://www.geocities.com/Athens/Acropolis/8623

The activities of the International Psychohistorical Association, its yearly convention, and an outline of the profession of psychohistory.

Psychohistory Online Discussion Group

http://www.topica.com/lists/psychohistory

A discussion list on psychohistory for hundreds of scholars, psychotherapists, and students, intended as a forum for scholarly discussions of current and past political group fantasies, the history of childhood, and bibliographic resources. You can join by sending a blank e-mail to psychohistory-subscribe@topica.com.

Chapter 24

Historiography

Guido Abbattista

Metasites and General Historical Methodology

Historiology

http://www.cannylink.com/historyhistoriology.htm

A short index of sites on historical methodology at the Cannylink Internet Guide.

History and Historiography, Carnegie Mellon University

http://eng.hss.cmu.edu/history/

A valuable collection of links to historical resources.

The History Index at the University of Kansas

http://www.ukans.edu/history/VL/

This site provides an extensive list of links to historical sites on all the relevant subdivisions of historical research.

Voice of the Shuttle

http://vos.ucsb.edu/shuttle/history.html#historiography

On the history page of this well-known metaindex, under the category Historiography, there is a choice of the best sites of historiographical interest.

Yahoo!: Index of History Resources

http://dir.yahoo.com/Arts/Humanities/History/Historiology/

This index enumerates several sites of historical interest: It is worth browsing in search of materials of a more definitely historiographical-methodological character.

Electronic Libraries and Historiographical Texts

American Hypertexts

http://xroads.virginia.edu/~HYPER/hypertex.html

A large collection of textual resources on American history, including *The Federalist Papers*, Tocqueville's *Democracy in America*, and works by Francis Parkman and Frederick Jackson Turner.

Aragonese Historiography

http://eng.hss.cmu.edu/history/aragonese-historiography.txt

An online essay on the essentials of Aragonese historiography, this resource is part of the English Server at the Carnegie Mellon University.

Fernand Braudel Center

http://fbc.binghamton.edu/

The French historian Fernand Braudel made a profound impact on how historians view and practice their discipline. He played a leading role in the articulation of social history and interdisciplinary studies. This Web site at Binghamton University, State University of New York, provides a wealth of resources relating to Braudel. Among the members of its scientific board is Immanuel Wallerstein.

CHPE: Centre d'histoire de la pensée économique: Bibliothèque virtuelle de la pensée économique

http://panoramix.univ-paris1.fr/CHPE/textes.html

Located at the Université de Paris-I, this virtual library gives access to rich materials on the history of economic thought, as well as the history of historiography and methodology in modern Europe—for example, texts by Giovanni Botero, Matthew Hale, Lord Bolingbroke, Jean-Jacques Rousseau, Adam Ferguson, Thomas Malthus, Frederic Maitland, and Benedetto Croce.

Crusade Historiography

http://www.uni-heidelberg.de/subject/hd/fak7/hist/o1/logs/mt/
t7/940901–051/

At this Web location, users concerned with historical narratives of the Crusades can read a series of mails belonging to a thread of discussion on the theme of Crusade historiography. More mails on different aspects of the history of historiography, methodology, and philosophy of history (for example, philosophies of history and contemporary historical research on the Middle Age; definitions of "medieval") can be read at the same site under the URL http://www.uni-heidelberg.de/subject/hd/fak7/hist/o1/logs/mt/t7/.

Eliohs: Electronic Library of Modern Historiography

http://www.eliohs.unifi.it/

An electronic and virtual library of texts concerning modern (mainly seventeenth- to eighteenth-century) historiography, philosophy of history, and methodology. This is the only resource born out of a project expressly devoted to the history of historiography, and it led to the creation of the electronic journal *Cromohs* (see below). Its catalog includes electronic editions of historical, methodological, and philosophico-historical works from the sixteenth to the twentieth century produced by Eliohs and includes links to texts of the same kind electronically published elsewhere on the Net.

Gallica (Bibliothèque Nationale de France)

http://gallica.bnf.fr/

The French national library offers online versions of many nineteenth-century French historians's most important works.

Historians and Philosophers

http://www.scholiast.org/history/histphil.html

This site by P. Rasmussen consists of a biographical dictionary of historians and philosophers (arranged in four sections: ancient, medieval, early modern, and modern period), in the form of original or linked biographical profiles, (sometimes) bibliography, and external links to electronic editions of main works. The biographies, are very unequal in content and value. A useful reference site for history of historiography, but still heavily under construction.

The Historian Underground: Making History Relevant for Life

http://www.geocities.com/SoHo/Cafe/8579/under.htm

A voice from outside the academic world. This site is designed to provide views about the object of history that challenge the normal aims of the historian's craft. It is based on the presupposition that normal academic historical method has lost touch with the importance of history for people's lives. This site's editors, therefore, attempt to gather articles that question traditional ways of thinking and stir up a bit of controversy. These pages go deep into an examination of the relation of history, philosophy, and literature as well as evaluating education and its role.

The Hume Archives

http://www.utm.edu/research/hume/

This very important site, maintained by Jim Fieser, includes Hume's writings, commentaries, eighteenth-century reviews of Hume's works, and early biographies. Also available are some writings by the Scottish philosopher documenting his ideas on history and his historical treatment of such subjects as man's religious sentiments.

The Internet Classics Archive at the Massachusetts Institute of Technology

http://classics.mit.edu/index.html

Offers full texts of works by Greek, Jewish, Roman, Persian, and other historians, such as Herodotus, Thucydides, Strabo, Xenophon, Josephus, Plutarch, Julius Caesar, Livy, Tacitus, Firdousi, and Lao-tzu. Texts are translated into English and available for free downloading in text-only format. This site, on the Internet since 1994, is sponsored in part by the MIT Program in Writing and Humanistic Studies.

Internet Public Library Online Texts

http://readroom.ipl.org/bin/ipl/ipl.books-idx.pl?type=deweystem&q1=901

Classic texts of interest for the methodology of history and general views of the historical process are present in this remarkable electronic library at the University of Michigan. Among the collection are writings by Francis Bacon, John Milton, James Dunbar, John Millar, Constantin-François Volney, T.B. Macaulay, Charles Babbage, Edwin Seligman, Antonio Labriola, Joel Salit, and Charles Kingsley.

Labyrinth

http://www.georgetown.edu/labyrinth/

This project from Georgetown University hosts a selection of contemporary sources on Medieval history arranged on a linguistic basis. Each Labyrinth Library section (e.g., *Auctores et fontes*) does not give direct access to digital editions, but provides a small choice of external sites loosely referring to several areas of European medieval history. Among these, users may find important electronic editions of relevant sources, but may frequently be disappointed to be offered heterogeneous links not critically selected.

Liber Liber

http://www.liberliber.it/biblioteca/index.htm

An excellent, multidisciplinary, searchable collection of mainly Italian, but also foreign texts, books, articles, documents, theses, and reviews. Every text is accompanied by information about the author and a short introduction. Works by Italian early modern and modern historians can be found here: Dino Compagni, Giovanni Villani, Niccolò Machiavelli, Francesco Guicciardini, Giambattista Vico, Vincenzo Cuoco, Francesco de Sanctis, and Antonio Labriola. This site, part of Progetto Manuzio, is hosted at the University of Milan.

Philosophy of History Archive

http://www.nsu.ru/filf/pha/

This Russian site introduces itself as follows: "The International Philosophy of History Archive (PHA) administered by Prof. Nikolai S. Rozov is a Web node that indexes links and materials related to the Philosophy of History and Theoretical History (PH and TH) on the Internet. It aims to serve those whose research interests include the rational theoretical explanatory approaches to World History and Modernity, the scientific predictions of global future trends, and the application of philosophical and scientific research results to Global Praxis." The site contains a list of internal and external links to e-texts and sites related to philosophy of history and theoretical history.

The Scriptorium: Center for Biblical Antiquities

http://www.scriptorium.org/

The Scriptorium: Center for Biblical Antiquities is a nonsectarian research center working in conjunction with the Van Kampen Foundation, which serves as the repository for the Van Kampen Collection of ancient artifacts, manuscripts, and rare printed materials. The collection consists primarily of biblical texts in all representative forms and is supplemented by secondary resources and the personal library of Eberhard Nestle, a leading nineteenth-century German biblical scholar. The scriptorium sponsors various academic initiatives reflecting the faculty's commitment to public education, scholarly research, and innovative pedagogy.

Giambattista Vico Home Page

http://www.connix.com/~gapinton/

This site, maintained by Giorgio A. Pinton, offers a biography and chronology of the life of one of the most important eighteenth-century European philosophers of history, plus bibliographies relating to his major works.

Voltaire: *Oeuvres diverses*

http://perso.wanadoo.fr/dboudin/Voltind.htm

This electronic library of works by Voltaire includes some historical works.

Voltaire Page

http://www.geocities.com/Athens/7308/

A site compiled by F. DeVenuto and expressly devoted to one of the most outstanding Enlightenment historians, with links to related sites.

Voltaire Society of America: Web Sites on Voltaire

http://humanities.uchicago.edu/homes/VSA/websites.html

More sites on the great Enlightenment philosopher and historian.

World History Archives

http://www.hartford-hwp.com/archives/10/index.html

World History Archives provides a selection of materials from Hartford Web Publishing. This site hosts a collection of essays, excerpts from classics of historiography, messages, dialogues, shorter essays on interpretative aspects of world history (e.g., the peculiarity of world history, Eurocentrism, the limits and divisions of history, the world systems approach). This material has been mainly selected from the H-Net list for world history. It is an interesting collection of ideas and insights expressed through the medium of a discussion list.

Electronic Journals

Cromohs

http://www.unifi.it/riviste/cromohs/

This electronic journal, founded in 1995, is expressly devoted to the history, theory, and methodology of historiography. It publishes in yearly issues original articles, review essays, and short reviews. Among its services are a very useful current bibliography of monographs and periodical literature and a list of relevant events. It was born as both a journal and an electronic library of sources. The library, called Eliohs (q.v.), has grown so much as to acquire a distinct identity. Chief editors and initiators of both *Cromohs* and Eliohs are Guido Abbattista and Rolando Minuti.

Histos: The Electronic Journal of Ancient Historiography

http://www.dur.ac.uk/Classics/histos/about.html

This journal, founded in 1997, is published at the Durham Classics Department and contains articles, essays, reviews, notices on research projects, and conferences on all aspects of ancient historiography.

Reviews in American History

http://muse.jhu.edu/journals/reviews_in_american_history/toc/rahv026.html

An invaluable tool for an up-to-date survey of contemporary historiographical production and debates, this electronic journal covers both general theoretical and methodological topics and, in particular, American history research.

Print Journals with Web Sites

History and Theory

http://www.wesleyan.edu/histjrnl/hthome.htm

This is the site of the well-known journal of historical methodology and philosophy of history established in 1960, which represents the main reference for contemporary research and debate on these topics.

Storia della Storiografia

http://www.cisi.unito.it/stor/home.htm

Storia della Storiografia—History of Historiography—Histoire de l'Historiographie—Geschichte der Geschichtsschreibung is a journal founded in 1982 by the International Commission for the History of Historiography. It publishes in four languages articles on all relevant aspects of the history and theory of historiography and the historical profession. Its Web site provides general information on the journal's activity and complete indexes of past, current, and forthcoming issues with an archive of contributors.

Teaching History: A Journal of Methods

http://www.emporia.edu/socsci/journal/main.htm

This is the Web site of a journal whose aim is to give general information and indexes of current and past issues. Designed for history teachers at all levels who wish to read about, or contribute to, innovative methods of teaching history, it is edited by Samuel Dicks and maintained by Michael Handley at the Division of Social Sciences of Emporia State University.

Didactic Resources

Internet Modern History Sourcebook: Studying History

http://www.fordham.edu/halsall/mod/modsbook.html

http://www.fordham.edu/halsall/mod/modsbook01.html

A first-rate didactic project devoted to a full presentation of the problem of historiographical research, knowledge, and methodology and of theories of history in the modern age. The site includes excerpts from primary sources and a rich library of essays, pages of important works on the subject, and lectures, being collectively a large anthology of class materials. Many of these materials are not locally produced, but just linked on the Net.

National Standards for World History

http://www.iac.net/~pfilio/part1.html

The electronic text of one of the most controversial documents on the reform of history teaching in the United States.

Ten Commandments of Good Historical Writing

http://www.bluffton.edu/~schlabachg/courses/10commnd.htm

This site, by Theron F. Schlabach, contains a list of practical, common-sense (but at times controvertible) suggestions from a teacher to beginning or amateur historians. Schlabach's views of what a historian-to-be's work ought to be are interesting but better considered as provocative suggestions than as mandatory commandments.

Chapter 25

Historical Population Databases

Gunnar Thorvaldsen

Population databases contain information on the inhabitants of a certain region, most notably whole countries, enabling users to do statistical studies or find information on individuals or groups of persons. Some data sets are statistical, typically the number of men and women or the number of births and deaths, based on censuses, ministerial records, or longitudinal population registers. The tables or data extracts requested can be stored in static formats or be created dynamically to the user's specifications on the basis of individual level information in a database interacting with specially designed software. Alternatively or complementarily, such microdata may be presented for downloading or inspection online. Historical population databases often contain contemporary data, but we have omitted from this overview those mostly containing data sets assembled during the last couple of decades.

The Canadian Families Project

http://web.uvic.ca/hrd/cfp/

The project team is completing a 5 percent national sample of the 1901 Census of Canada employing the same methods for sampling and standardization as the Integrated Public Use Microdata Series (IPUMS) project in the United States. No data sets are presently available online, but the nationally representative sample with 50,943 dwellings and 265,286 persons will be made available to researchers as a public use sample in 2001. The Canadian Families Project is based at the University of Victoria, but is a collaborative research project by eleven scholars at five Canadian universities.

Census Data for the United States 1790–1970

http://fisher.lib.virginia.edu/census/

The statistical data presented here describe the people and the economy of the United States for each state and county based on all the decennial censuses from 1790 to 1970. The data sets, provided by the Inter-university Consortium for Political and Social Research (ICPSR), can be browsed online with software provided by the Instructional Computing Group of Harvard University.

The Danish Demographic Database

http://ddd.sa.dk/DDD_EN.HTM

Here the 1787 to 1911 censuses for selected districts in Denmark and the Danish emigrant database for 1868 to 1900 can be searched free of charge for information on individuals and their families. The latter database is considered to be more complete than the U.S. immigration registers. This site is a cooperative effort of the Danish Data Archives, the Danish Emigration Archives, and the Centre of Microfilming in the Danish Provincial Archives.

The Demographic Data Base

http://www.ddb.umu.se/index_eng.html

The DDB holds transcripts of nineteenth-century catechismal records for seven selected parishes and three regions in Sweden. A demonstration sample can be searched free of charge via the Internet, but researchers must contact the DDB to order data extracts. Historical population statistics for Swedish localities and provinces are also available. The DDB is a permanent part of Umeå University and cooperates closely with its Centre for Population Studies.

The Digital Archive

http://www.hist.uib.no/arkivverket/introduc.htm

The National Archives of Norway have made major parts of the 1865 and 1900 censuses available for online data retrieval via the Internet, together with various other kinds of source material, such as emigration records and probate registers. The University of Bergen hosts the databases, also making available the

1801 census for all of Norway. Some statistical functions like filtering and cross tabulations, are available for the censuses.

Historical Microdata around the World

http://draug.rhd.isv.uit.no/nhdc/micro.html

The main section of this metapage lists links to significant sites with information on the individual level, e.g., transcriptions from censuses or church records. "Significant" excludes sites with data stemming from individual research projects. Some of these are listed in an auxiliary section called "other databases for historical research." This metapage is maintained by the Norwegian Historical Data Centre at the University of Tromsø in Norway.

The Historical Sample of the Netherlands

http://www.iisg.nl/~hsn/

This site presents a longitudinal and representative sample of about 80,000 people born in the Netherlands from 1812 to 1922, built on information from certificates of births, deaths, and marriages, records from the population registers, and other historical sources. Occupations, locations, and other information have been encoded for statistical analyses. A provisional data set from the Utrecht pilot project can be ordered at a nominal price. The database is hosted by the International Institute of Social History in Amsterdam.

The History Data Service

http://hds.essex.ac.uk/

The HDS aims to take into custody data sets from historical projects and provide possibilities for reuse in future research. The organization provides access to manuscript census records, primarily the 1881 census of Great Britain. At present no data sets are available online, but the register of archival holdings can be searched in the database Biron. The HDS is located at and integrated with the Data Archive at the University of Essex, the national social science data archive for the United Kingdom.

IPUMS: Integrated Public Use Microdata Series

http://156.40.88.3/about/cpr/dbs/res_integrated.htm

The IPUMS project integrates representative samples from thirteen U.S. censuses covering the period 1850 to 1990 in the world's largest historical database (currently IPUMS-98). The samples enable researchers to study the American population by combining variables such as race and occupation on the individual or household level. Sample densities vary from one in 760 (1900 census) to one in twenty (1980 and 1990 censuses), the aim being to have at least one percent samples for every census. With the exception of group quarters, the entire household is kept intact when sampling. For 1970 to 1990 there exist several samples based on different densities and strategies. Two nominative censuses are not available: the 1890 census returns were burned in a fire, and for 1930 data entry is pending.

While the samples stem from different sources, the IPUMS project has molded them into the same form, using record and variable formats with a uniform layout, so that, for example, occupational coding schemes are compatible over the whole series of censuses. A number of auxiliary variables make explicit the location of family members such as fathers and mothers within the household. The original work with the census returns, the data entry process, and the IPUMS group's data integration are documented in three volumes, the content of which is available for inspection or downloading in Acrobat Reader format via the Web pages. All the samples (25GB uncompressed) can be downloaded individually with FTP. A better method is to use the online data extraction system via the button "Get IPUMS data" to order subsets of whatever censuses, sample densities, variables, and geographic areas are of interest in a particular research project. Afterward, the tailor-made data set can be downloaded free of charge. Genealogists should be warned that samples from after 1920 contain no names, and that earlier samples, having a density of one percent or less, give little chance of identifying particular individuals. IPUMS is based in the Department of History at the University of Minnesota.

IREP: *L'Institut interuniversitaire de recherches sur les populations*

http://www.uqac.uquebec.ca/decsr/irep.html

The Interuniversity Institute for Population Research bases many of its activities on the database BALSAC, mainly containing parish records for parts of the Quebec Province from 1838 up to 1971. Various other records, for example, economic or cultural, have been added to the relational database for specific research purposes. In order to protect privacy and economize resources, the data sets are made available to researchers only after an evaluation of the ethical character and scientific significance of each project. The IREP now consists of researchers from seven universities and other institutions in Quebec, mainly dealing with demographic and genetic aspects of the population's history.

The Norwegian Historical Data Centre

http://www.isv.uit.no/seksjon/rhd/indexeng.htm

The NHDC computerizes historical microdata such as censuses and ministerial records from selected municipalities. Full-text and encoded versions are available as books, on microfiche, as computer files, and on the Web for research, teaching, and genealogical purposes. Significant parts of the 1865, 1875, and 1900 censuses are available free of charge for retrieval via an interactive HTML interface. Another major data set available in this way is the 1886 tax assessment list covering all registered Norwegian farms and farmers. Encoded individual-level versions of the censuses can be ordered for downloading into major statistical packages. Upon application, the NHDC will computerize historical material from the original sources for research projects meeting certain standards. The Norwegian Historical Data Centre is a permanent part of the University of Tromsø.

The Research Archive *(Forskningsarkivet)*

http://www.foark.umu.se/

This is another part of Umeå University holding various types of archival resources. Most notably, significant parts of the 1890 census for Sweden are searchable through a Web interface. There is currently only a Swedish version of these pages.

The Stockholm Historical Database

http://www.ssa.stockholm.se/texter/shd.htm

This database covers the central parts of the Swedish capital during the period 1878 to 1926 with records on each move made by the inhabitants. It is probably the best resource in the world for studying historic gross migration longitudinally. There is no online interface, and the Web page is in Swedish only, so Agneta.Geschwind@ssa.stockholm.se should be contacted for further information, for example, on its CD-ROM and microfiche products.

U.S. Census Bureau

http://www.census.gov/

Here users can find the complete results from the 2000 United States Census. Most information is provided in both ASCII text and PDF format. The State and County Quickfacts link allows users to quickly locate a specific area. Census tract outline maps are available in PDF format. Some files from the 1990 census can be located in PDF format in various places in the database.

Chapter 26

Historic Preservation and Conservation

Charlene Mires and Anne Rothfeld

Advisory Council on Historic Preservation

http://www.achp.gov

Created by the independent federal agency that advises the president and Congress on historic preservation issues, this site offers links to historic preservation officers throughout the United States and information about the National Historic Preservation Act of 1966.

American Institute for Conservation of Historic and Artistic Works

http://aic.stanford.edu/

This organization of professional conservators shares its expertise on how to care for prized possessions from paintings and photographs to home videotapes. The site also offers advice on how to locate and select a professional conservator.

Built in America: Historic American Buildings Survey/ Historic American Engineering Record, 1933–Present

http://memory.loc.gov/ammem/hhhtml/hhhome.html

As part of its American Memory project, the Library of Congress has begun digitizing the vast documentation of American architecture, engineering, and design collected by the Historic American Buildings Survey and the Historic American Engineering Record. As the records go online, they can be searched by keyword, subject, and geographic area.

CoOL: Conservation Online

http://palimpsest.stanford.edu

From Stanford University Libraries, information on a wide range of conservation topics of interest to libraries and their users, including digital imaging and the conservation and use of electronic records.

Council on Library and Information Resources

http://www.clir.org/home.html

Offers online publications related to current issues in the preservation of library materials.

Heritage Conservation and Historic Preservation

http://home.vicnet.net.au/~conserv/hp-hc.htm

The State Library of Victoria in Australia has assembled this online library about conservation issues. International in scope, the many topics addressed by articles and accompanying Web links include information about caring for cultural objects such as books and paper, film and photography, and sound and magnetic materials.

Keeping Our Word: Preserving Information Across the Ages

http://www.lib.uiowa.edu/ref/exhibit

This virtual version of an exhibit by the University of Iowa Libraries addresses the issues of preserving materials from cave paintings and clay tablets to electronic media. The exhibit includes links for doing further research on preservation issues.

National Archives and Records Administration: Archives and Preservation Resources

http://www.nara.gov/nara/preserva

From the experts at the National Archives, information about preserving documents and photographs.

National Center for Preservation Technology and Training

http://www.ncptt.nps.gov

This project within the National Park Service includes an extensive, annotated database of online resources in archaeology, history, historic architecture and landscapes, and conservation of materials and objects. The database includes links for subscribing to listservs related to preservation and conservation.

Links to the Past: National Park Service Cultural Resources

http://www.cr.nps.gov

A site of great scope and depth, this project of the National Park Service is the place to start for information about visiting historic sites throughout the national parks system, teaching with historic places, and volunteering at historic sites. Online exhibits cover topics such as the life of Frederick Douglass and camp life at Gettysburg, and virtual tours take Web visitors to historic places in Detroit, Seattle, and other regions of the country. The site also serves as the gateway to programs such as Tools for Teaching (http://www.cr.nps.gov/toolsfor.htm), the Historic American Buildings Survey/Historic American Engineering Record (http://www.cr.nps.gov/habshaer) and the National Register of Historic Places (http://www.cr.nps.gov/nr).

National Preservation Institute

http://www.npi.org

This organization offers online registration for its numerous training seminars in historic preservation and cultural resources management.

National Trust for Historic Preservation

http://www.nthp.org

This private, nonprofit organization dedicated to saving historic buildings, neighborhoods, and landscapes offers a site with information about the group's mission and many projects, including its annual list of the nation's most endangered places. A link to its *Preservation* magazine offers tables of contents, book reviews, and excerpts. A link to the National Trust's Main Street Center (http://www.mainst.org), which works to revitalize historic and traditional commercial areas, provides information about the history and preservation of Main Street communities and advice for organizing a Main Street revitalization project.

Northern States Conservation Center

http://www.collectioncare.org

Northern States Conservation Center of Saint Paul, Minnesota, here offers numerous articles about the management and preservation of museum collections, including advice about museums' use of the World Wide Web.

PreserveNet

http://www.preservenet.cornell.edu

Incorporating the PreserveNet Information Service and the PreserveNet Law Service, this site at Cornell University includes extensive links to preservation organizations, education programs, conferences and events, and job and internship opportunities. The Law Service offers texts of major state and federal preservation legislation and models for preservation ordinances. This is also the host site for the Guide to the African-American Heritage Preservation Foundation, Inc. (http://www.preservenet.cornell.edu/aahpf/homepage.htm).

RLG DigiNews

http://www.rlg.org/preserv/diginews

Online newsletter by the Research Libraries Group in cooperation with the Cornell University Library Department of Preservation and Conservation, focusing on preservation through digital imaging.

The Society of Architectural Historians

http://www.sah.org

This organization's collection of Internet resources includes links to collections of images of historic buildings.

State Historic Preservation Legislation Database

http://www.ncsl.org/programs/arts/statehist_intro.htm

The National Conference of State Legislatures offers this database of state legislation and constitution articles governing historic sites, archaeological sites and materials, and significant unmarked burial sites.

World Heritage

http://www.unesco.org/whc/nwhc/pages/home/pages/homepage.htm

Home page for the UNESCO project that encourages the preservation of cultural and natural heritage sites around the world. This site includes information about more than 500 World Heritage sites, including those considered endangered.

World Monuments Fund

http://www.worldmonuments.org

The site of this private, nonprofit organization working to safeguard works of art and architecture includes information about the fund's international list of 100 most endangered sites.

Chapter 27

Urban History

Martin V. Minner

Metasites

H-URBAN Web Links

http://www2.h-net.msu.edu/~urban/weblinks/index.htm

H-URBAN'S links page, an exhaustive collection of Web sites, is the indispensable place to start when looking for online urban history resources. The site is compiled and annotated by Clay McShane, professor in the History Department at Northeastern University. It gives users the option of displaying links by title, subject, or location and provides alphabetical listings for international and U.S. locations.

Perry-Castañeda Map Collection: City Map Sites

http://www.lib.utexas.edu/maps/map_sites/cities_sites.html

Provides links to hundreds of contemporary city maps listed alphabetically by city name. Also includes links to useful map sites and collections.

Bibliographies

American Studies Serial Bibliography Project

http://www.inform.umd.edu/EdRes/Colleges/ARHU/Depts/AmericanStudies/
serial/histurb.html

An annotated bibliography of journals covering urban and planning history. Part of a larger American Studies bibliographic project at the University of Maryland.

The Urban Past: An International Urban History Bibliography

http://www.uoguelph.ca/history/urban/citybib.html

An excellent bibliography compiled by Gilbert Stelter, professor emeritus at the University of Guelph. Especially useful because of its broad chronological scope and global perspective.

Urban Planning, 1794–1918: An International Anthology of Articles, Conference Papers, and Reports

http://www.library.cornell.edu/Reps/DOCS/homepage.htm

An online anthology of planning history documents compiled and annotated by historian John W. Reps. Also provides a lengthy bibliography of sources not included in the anthology.

Urban Transportation Resource List

http://www.upa.pdx.edu/MB/transportsources.htm

An extensive bibliography on urban transportation, including historical works as well as recent material on policy.

Journals and Organizations

H-URBAN

http://www2.h-net.msu.edu/~urban/

The H-URBAN discussion network is an electronic forum for scholars of urban history. Its site provides announcements, reviews, a job guide, teaching resources, Web links, and information on joining the e-mail list.

Journal of Urban History

http://www.sagepub.com/

Provides subscription information, submission guidelines, and a list of editorial board members.

Société Française d'Histoire Urbaine

http://www.sfhu.msh-paris.fr/home.htm

The site for the French Society of Urban History provides information about the organization and includes a list of recent French works in the field.

Society for American City and Regional Planning History

http://www.urban.uiuc.edu/sacrph/index.html

Provides membership information, a newsletter, and announcements of conferences and publications.

Urban Affairs Association

http://www.udel.edu/uaa/

Membership information, meeting announcements, and information on the *Journal of Urban Affairs.*

Urban History

http://www.journals.cup.org/owa_dba/owa/
ISSUES_IN_JOURNAL?JID=UHY

Provides abstracts of the contents of recent issues of the British journal *Urban History.*

Urban History Association

http://www.unl.edu/uha/assoc.html

A newsletter, membership information, conference and award announcements, and a page of urban history links.

Urban History Review/Revue d'histoire urbaine

http://www.science.mcmaster.ca/Geography/urbanhis.html

Offers abstracts in English and French for the current issue of this journal of Canadian urban history. Also provides a list of the contents of back issues and an illustrated history of the journal.

Selected Sites

The Ancient City of Athens

http://www.indiana.edu/~kglowack/athens/

A photographic tour of ancient Athens, intended primarily for students and teachers.

Aquae Urbis Romae: The Waters of the City of Rome

http://www.iath.virginia.edu/waters/

An interactive cartographic project dealing with the impact of water systems on the development of Rome since 753 B.C.E. Visitors can build their own maps by choosing elements such as aqueducts, sewers, and fountains, and can examine the city's topography in three dimensions.

Building the Washington Metro: An Online Exhibition

http://chnm.gmu.edu/metro/

A history of the Washington, D.C., Metro in text and images, with sections on planning, engineering, architecture, construction, and operation. Researched and written by Zachary M. Schrag, a Ph.D. candidate in U.S. history at Columbia University.

Centennial Exhibition Digital Collection: Philadelphia 1876

http://libwww.library.phila.gov/CenCol/index.htm

A history of the Centennial Exhibition of 1876, with many photographs and maps. Includes teaching resources.

Centre for Metropolitan History

http://ihr.sas.ac.uk/cmh/cmh.main.html

A useful site on London history, including links to research projects, publications, and archives.

Chicago Historical Society

http://www.chicagohs.org/

A significant urban history site providing access to the Chicago Historical Society's exhibits, research collections, and online projects. Two of the site's many noteworthy projects are The Dramas of Haymarket, a history of the Haymarket bombing and executions, and The Great Chicago Fire and the Web of Memory, an exhibit focusing on the ways in which the 1871 fire has been remembered.

Chicago Imagebase

http://tigger.uic.edu/depts/ahaa/imagebase/

Based at the University of Illinois at Chicago, the Imagebase provides an impressive collection of digitized images pertaining to Chicago's built environment.

City Directories of the United States

http://www.citydirectories.psmedia.com/

A full-text, searchable collection of U.S. city directories. This commercial site offers free use of several selected directories but requires a subscription for access to the full collection.

City Sites: Multimedia Essays on New York and Chicago, 1870s–1930s

http://artsweb.bham.ac.uk/citysites/

An electronic book examining the visual and literary cultures of New York and Chicago from a multidisciplinary perspective. A collaborative effort by scholars in Europe and the United States, this site is part of the 3 Cities project based at the Universities of Birmingham and Nottingham.

The Encyclopedia of Cleveland History

http://ech.cwru.edu/

Contains all of the articles from *The Encyclopedia of Cleveland History* and *The Dictionary of Cleveland Biography*, additional articles not included in the print editions, and high-resolution photographs.

Greenwood's Map of London 1827

http://www.bathspa.ac.uk/greenwood/home.html

Based entirely on a detailed 1827 map of the city of London, this site allows visitors to zoom in on a selected portion of the city. Provides links to present-day maps and aerial photographs to permit comparison with the city of 1827.

Harlem: Mecca of the New Negro

http://etext.lib.virginia.edu/harlem/

A digital version of *Survey Graphic* magazine's special issue in March 1925 devoted to the Harlem Renaissance. Provides the issue's entire contents in text and JPEG formats.

Harlem, 1900–1940: An African-American Community

http://www.si.umich.edu/CHICO/Harlem/index.html

An exhibition by the Schomburg Center for Research in Black Culture at the New York Public Library. Includes text, photographs, and teaching resources.

Historic Pittsburgh

http://digital.library.pitt.edu/pittsburgh/mainpage.html

Intended primarily for researchers and students, this site provides access to digitized books, plat maps, and U.S. Census schedules. Also provides finding aids to manuscripts held by the University of Pittsburgh and the Historical Society of Western Pennsylvania.

History of Mumbai

http://theory.tifr.res.in/bombay/history/

An introduction to the history of Mumbai (Bombay).

Integrated Digital Archive of Los Angeles

http://www.usc.edu/isd/locations/cst/idala/

Described as a "regional meta-collection," the IDA-LA is a major project that provides digital access to a number of collections dealing with the Southern California metropolitan area. Includes photographs, manuscripts, records, texts, newspapers, documents, and maps. At present the site includes collections of the Automobile Club of Southern California, the Chinese Historical Society of Southern California, the Dunbar Economic Development Foundation, the Huntington Library, the Korean American Digital Archive, the Los Angeles City Archives, and the University of Southern California.

Jerusalem: Life Throughout the Ages in a Holy City

http://www.biu.ac.il/JS/rennert/

A history of Jerusalem created for a course at the Ingeborg Rennert Center for Jerusalem Studies at Bar-Ilan University, Israel.

La Guardia and Wagner Archives

http://www.laguardiawagnerarchive.lagcc.cuny.edu/defaulta.htm

Provides finding aids and a searchable database for the collections of New York mayors Fiorello La Guardia, Robert Wagner, Abraham Beame, and Edward Koch. Many photographs from the collections are available online.

Levittown: Documents of an Ideal American Suburb

http://tigger.uic.edu/~pbhales/Levittown.html

Produced by photographic historian Peter B. Hales, this site offers family and commercial photographs of Levittown along with a primer on Levittown history.

The Living City

http://156.145.78.54/htm/home.htm

A new site dealing with public health in New York from 1865 to 1929. Includes a searchable database of historical documents in PDF format, an annotated timeline, and several exhibits and essays.

Monuments and Dust: The Culture of Victorian London

http://www.iath.virginia.edu/mhc/

A collaborative effort by scholars in England and the United States, this site brings together visual, statistical, and textual sources on Victorian London.

Lewis Mumford Center for Comparative Urban and Regional Research

http://www.albany.edu/mumford/census/

Analyzes changes in the racial and ethnic composition of metropolitan areas over the last ten years and examines diversity in local neighborhoods.

Museum of the City of New York

http://www.mcny.org

The museum's project New York Before the War provides access to photographs taken under the auspices of the Works Projects Administration's Federal Arts Project. Other valuable exhibitions are Looking North: Upper Manhattan in Photographs, 1896–1939; Gotham Comes of Age: New York Through the Lens of the Byron Company, 1892–1942; and Berenice Abbott: Changing New York.

Museum of the City of San Francisco

http://www.sfmuseum.org/

Offers numerous interesting online exhibitions ranging from the 1849 gold rush to 1960s rock music.

New York Public Library

http://www.nypl.org/research/chss/spe/art/photo/photo.html#online

Provides online access to the exhibition Berenice Abbott: Changing New York, 1935–1938 and to two projects on Lewis Hine: Work Portraits, 1920–1939 and Construction of the Empire State Building, 1930–1931. The library's exhibition Small Town America: Stereoscopic Views from the Robert Dennis Collection presents digitized versions of 12,000 stereographic images from New York, New Jersey, and Connecticut.

Places in Time: Historical Documentation of Place in Greater Philadelphia

http://www.brynmawr.edu/iconog/frdr.html

The collaborative effort of several organizations, this site brings together a broad collection of images, documents, and links on the five-county Philadelphia area. Among the sources available are photographs, panoramic views, postcards, paintings, prints, and atlases.

San Diego History

http://www.sandiegohistory.org/index.html

Includes a photo gallery, online exhibitions, and articles from the *Journal of San Diego History*. Online tours of San Diego's 1915 and 1935–36 expositions feature maps, stereographic views, and postcards.

The Siege and Commune of Paris, 1870–1871

http://www.library.northwestern.edu/spec/siege/

The Charles Deering McCormick Library of Special Collections at Northwestern University has digitized more than 1,200 photographs and images from the Siege and Commune of Paris. The images can be browsed by category or searched by keyword.

Social Life of Cities

http://www.yale.edu/socdept/slc/

A collection of photographs assembled by Joseph Soares, professor in the Department of Sociology at Yale University, dealing with public space, collective memory, urban design, and architecture. Includes photographs of Boston, New Haven, New York, London, Paris, and medieval German towns.

The Urban Landscape

http://scriptorium.lib.duke.edu/diap/

A searchable database of 1,000 images from the Rare Book, Manuscript, and Special Collections Library at Duke University on the theme "The Urban Landscape."

Virtual Greenbelt

http://www.otal.umd.edu/~vg/

Created by the Department of American Studies at the University of Maryland, Virtual Greenbelt provides images, oral history interviews, and other sources pertaining to the New Deal-era planned suburban community of Greenbelt.

John H. White: Photographing Black Chicago

http://www.nara.gov/exhall/americanimage/chicago/white1.html

A collection of photographs of Chicago's African-American community taken in 1973–1974 by John H. White, then a photographer for the *Chicago Daily News*, for a federal documentary project.

Chapter 28

Living History and Historic Reenactment

Bambi L. Dingman

Metasites

Histreenact: The Historical Reenactment Web Site

http://www.montacute.net/histrenact/welcome.htm

Links to general suppliers and craftsmen, historical information, online reenactment information, and societies that re-create different time periods.

Living History Online

http://www.LivingHistoryOnline.com/

An online magazine that serves as a reference source for all historical periods. This site contains excellent articles, an events calendar, bibliographies, and a search capability.

Reenactor's WebMall

http://rampages.onramp.net/~lawsonda/mall/

A comprehensive source for reenacting information, including a sutlers list, arranged by time period.

U.S. Regular Army Reenacting Unit Directory

http://www.halcyon.com/strandjr/Regs/

A huge index of reenacting units, sorted by time period. Some organizations have links to their Web pages, while others have e-mail contact information.

General Sites

The Alliance of Early American Interpreters

http://members.xoom.com/AEAI/index.html

The Alliance of Early American Interpreters is dedicated to re-creating the lives of civilian colonists in America in the period 1750 to 1790. Its Web site has membership information, an events calendar, recipes, and related sites.

American Longrifle Association

http://www.liming.org/alra/

A period trekking group and umbrella organization spanning the years 1750 to 1850. A calendar of events can be found online, as well as photographs and a bibliography.

Angelcynn

http://www.angelcynn.org.uk/

All content is related to Anglo-Saxon living history representing the period 400 to 900 C.E.: clothing and appearance of the early Christian Anglo-Saxons, weapons and armor, history, and related links.

Association for Living History, Farm and Agricultural Museums (ALHFAM)

http://www.alhfam.org/

Home of the Association for Living History, Farm and Agricultural Museums. The association's Web page has conference information, employment classifieds for living history specialists, planning tips for living history sites, and extensive links to living history organizations throughout the world.

Buckskins and Black Powder

http://www.geocities.com/Yosemite/Gorge/7186/index.htm

This excellent site has links to a variety of black powder and buckskinning sites on the Web. Also includes information about black powder clubs, the fur trade era, and re-creating history.

Butler's Rangers

http://iaw.on.ca/~awoolley/brang/brang.html

This corps of rangers served in the American Revolution and is re-created at living history events today. Information about the rangers, both past and present, can be found on this site, as well as historical source material and other information.

C & D Jarnagin Company

http://www.jarnaginco.com/

A provider of fine wares for the period 1750 through 1865, with a full complement of uniforms and equipment for American troops.

Camp Chase Gazette

http://www.campchase.com/

A well-known publication devoted to American Civil War re-creation. The online edition contains informative articles, a virtual roster of Civil War reenactors, upcoming events, and other relevant information.

Camp Life

http://www.cr.nps.gov/csd/gettex/

Gettysburg National Park holds the largest Civil War collection in the National Park System, with more than 40,000 cataloged items. A unique aspect of the collection is that many of the pieces are common, everyday items that allow us a glimpse into the lives of the soldiers who owned them. Now a portion of the collection can be viewed online in this virtual museum of photographs and artifacts devoted to everyday camp life.

Castle Keep Ltd.

http://www.reenact.com

Living history information and supplies for reenactors, categorized by period of interest, from medieval times to the twentieth century.

The Civil War Artillery Page

http://www.cwartillery.org/artillery.html

Information about organization and drill, weapons, ammunition, equipment, history, and reenactment of field and foot artillery units of the American Civil War.

Clothing of the Ancient Celts

http://www47.pair.com/lindo/Textiles_Page.htm

The primary focus of this Web page is prehistoric and classical Celtic culture and costuming, with a wealth of information about hair, jewelry, dyes, and textiles and links to other Celtic sites.

Compagnie Franche de la Marine du Detroit

http://www.richnet.net/~kamoore/

A volunteer living history interpretation organization devoted to all Detroit impressions, including marine, militia, Native American and civilian, c. 1754–1760. The company Web page has original and current unit history.

Company of Saint George

http://www.chronique.com/george.htm

Fostering the spirit of chivalry by portraying a tournament company of the fourteenth and fifteenth century, this site offers ceremony information, upcoming events, and a discussion about the role of historic interpreters.

Coon 'n Crockett Muzzleloaders

http://www.coon-n-crockett.org/

This page is loaded with information about the club, the muzzleloading hobby, photos, upcoming events, and more.

The Costume Page

http://members.aol.com/nebula5/tcpsupp.html

This is the definitive source for costuming information on the Web, conveniently sorted by period of interest. Links to costume suppliers, accessories, and patterns for every time period.

Digital History Ltd.

http://digitalhistory.org

A comprehensive site for everything related to the French and Indian War, including well-written accounts of the battles, forts, and participants, as well as links to groups that are currently re-creating colonial North American history.

Elizabethan Fencing and the Art of Defence

http://jan.ucc.nau.edu/~wew/fencing.html

An interesting page related to the art of fencing and swordplay. Topics include period masters, terminology, types of blades, and links to other fencing sites on the Web.

Elizabethan Period Costumes

http://www.resort.com/~banshee/Faire/Costume/index.html

A complete source of information on Elizabethan clothing, patterns, and footwear.

Fall Creek Sutlery

http://fcsutler.com/

Supplies for Civil War reenactors and Victorian era enthusiasts.

Flintlock FAQ

http://www.aye.net/~bspen/flintlockfaq.html

A beginner's guide to flintlock shooting with a concise history of flintlock weapons and answers to questions about flintlock performance.

French and Indian War Magazine Online

http://members.aol.com/fiwar/home.html

An electronic magazine that will interest French and Indian War reenactors. This informative site has a great listing of reenactment groups and other topics related to the war, such as British and French forts, music, and clothing.

GI Journal

http://www.militaria.com

Articles of interest to World War I and World War II reenactors and links to division Web pages, reproduction uniforms, and military history magazines.

The Gunfighter Zone

http://www.gunfighter.com

A Web site for reenactors of the Old West and Cowboy Action Shooting groups, with links to discussion boards, suppliers, books, magazines, and informative articles.

The Historical Maritime Society

http://www.hms.org.uk/

Re-creates British Navy life from 1793 to 1815 (Napoleonic War period).

Historical Reenactors

http://novaroma.org/via_romana/reenactments/index.html

Costuming information, reenactment guidelines, and a listing of reenactment groups portraying military and civilian life during the Roman era, compiled and presented by Nova Roma, an organization dedicated to the study and restoration of ancient Roman culture.

Historic Arms and Armour

http://www.historicenterprises.com/

Specializes in highly accurate handmade replicas of museum pieces. Although this is a commercial site, it includes a great deal of historical information and interesting photos of the company's work.

Hudson's Bay Company Digital Collection

http://collections.ic.gc.ca/

A digital collection of artifacts from the fur trade era, presented by the Manitoba Museum of Man and Nature.

19th Indiana Volunteer Infantry, Company A

http://www.19thindiana.com/

Civil War reenactors and nineteenth-century civilian impressionists. The Web page has an event schedule, company newsletter, and historical information.

Jas. Townsend & Son

http://www.jastown.com/

A mail order company specializing in historic clothing, camp gear, tents, books, music, knives, tomahawks, oak kegs, and other assorted items for the period 1750 to 1840.

1st Kansas Volunteer Infantry and Kansas Women's Relief Corps

http://www.cs.twsu.edu/~crgrier/1stks.html

A great company Web page.

King's Arms Press and Bindery

http://www.kingspress.com/

Specialized reprints of eighteenth-century books and pamphlets, including drill books and regulations, as well as military treatises.

Knighthood, Chivalry and Tournaments Resource Library

http://www.chronique.com/

Information on books, battle accounts, codes of conduct, armoring techniques, and more. Also includes a lengthy index of sites related to chivalry, armor, and reenactment groups.

Le Poulet Gauche

http://www.lepg.org/

A compendium of information on the history, daily life, and culture of sixteenth-century France. This site re-creates Le Poulet Gauche, a sixteenth-century alehouse, and offers information on food, drink, gaming, clothing, fencing, tradesmen, and suppliers.

Links to the Past

http://www.cr.nps.gov/colherit.htm

An amazing Web page from the National Park Service with online archives for many historic sites, as well as battle summaries, battlefield information, national landmarks, online exhibits, and much more.

Longshot's Rendezvous

http://members.aol.com/lodgepole/longshot.html

A source of rendezvous information for mountain men, buckskinners, and muzzleloaders of Missouri and Illinois. Also includes a guide to getting started in rendezvous and links to other sources.

28th Massachusetts Volunteer Infantry, Company A, C, and H

http://www.28thmass.org/

A well-designed Web page with information for historical research and reenacting.

Medieval/Renaissance Food Homepage

http://www.pbm.com/~lindahl/food.html

A comprehensive site containing recipes, primary sources, clip art, medieval cooking articles, and food publications.

Milieux: The Costume Site

http://www.milieux.com/costume/

A comprehensive list of links to costuming sites with diversified themes, such as medieval costuming, armor, Civil War uniforms, colonial garb, and modern accessories.

Morningside Books

http://www.morningsidebooks.com

Noted for its Civil War collection and as a recognized dealer of Don Troiani artwork.

Mountain Men and the Fur Trade

http://www.xmission.com/~drudy/amm.html

An online research center devoted to the history and traditions of trappers, explorers, and traders, with a digital collection, a bibliography, an archive of trade records, and links to Web sites related to the fur trade era.

.National Renaissance Faire Directory

http://Renaissance-Faire.com/Locations.htm

A listing of Renaissance Faires around the country, with links to Web pages and event information.

NetSerf

http://www.netserf.org/

A huge index arranged by subject matter with links to all things medieval—religion, culture, art, and literature, etc.

47th New York State Volunteers: "Washington Grays"

http://www.awod.com/gallery/probono/cwchas/47ny.html

A federal reenacting unit. Its Web page has an extensive unit history and reenactment information.

5th New York Volunteer Infantry, Company A: Duryée's Zouaves

http://www.zouave.org/

An excellent company Web page with a detailed history, roster, and extensive photo gallery.

North/South Alliance

http://www.nsalliance.org/

Information on the First Confederate and First Federal Divisions in the American Civil War and an event listing.

The Northwest Territory Alliance

http://www.nwta.com/

This group strives to re-create the lifestyle, culture, and arts of the Revolutionary War era with an accurate representation of uniforms, weaponry and battlefield tactics. This Web site offers forms and documents useful to reenactors, an event schedule, a chronology of events in the War for Independence, pattern lists, publications, and more.

Oakhill Enterprises

http://www.frontiernet.net./~oakhill

Guns, clothing, and accessories for the period 1640 to 1840.

The Patriots of Fort McHenry

http://www.bcpl.lib.md.us/~etowner/patriots.html

This organization hopes to preserve the historical legacy of the patriots who defended Baltimore in 1814. Fort McHenry is best known as the scene of the battle which Francis Scott Key witnessed and wrote about in the "Star Spangled Banner."

Plimoth Plantation

http://www.plimoth.org/

Plimoth Plantation's Pilgrim Village brings to life the Plymouth of 1627. This Web site provides information about the village and also includes educational information for reenactors.

Pre-1840's Buckskinning

http://www.geocities.com/Yosemite/2839/index.html

Contains a lengthy list of rendezvous groups around the United States, publications, trader events, and buckskinning classifieds.

Proper Elizabethan Accents

http://www.resort.com/~banshee/Faire/Language/index.html

Pronunciation guide, drills, and vocabulary to perfect your accent for the Faire.

Rationed Fashion

http://www.geocities.com/SoHo/coffeehouse/6727/rationed_fashion.html

American fashion during World War II with style descriptions, designers, images, and sources.

Reenacting.com

http://www.dstylus.com/victorianlady/index.html

An online guide to civilian impressions of the Civil War, with helpful tips for creating interesting female impressions for both the Union and Confederacy.

Reenactor Net

http://www.reenactor.net/

A list of links to reenactor Web sites, categorized by time period.

Reenactors Page

http://www2.tsixroads.com/~rodbond/reenacting.html

This Web site offers photos, history, trivia, event reviews, and related links for reenactors and Civil War enthusiasts.

Regia Anglorum

http://www.regia.org/

A society with a vast number of resources available for portraying the British people as they were 100 years before the Norman conquest. The Web site has membership and contact information.

64th Regiment of Foot

http://freenet.vcu.edu/sigs/reg64/

Members of the 64th Regiment portray British infantry soldiers from the time of the Revolutionary War. Their Web page has information on the British army, regimental colors, the Brown Bess, women and the army, and plenty of primary reference material.

Renaissance Faire Overview

http://www.resort.com/~banshee/Faire/General/faire.html

An introduction to attending Faires and a description of what to expect.

Renaissance Magazine

http://www.renaissancemagazine.com

Well-known to reenactors as an informative print magazine, the online version is packed with useful information as well. Includes past features on books, music, movies, and products, with links to related Web sites.

The Rolls Ethereal

http://www.waks.org/rolls/

This is an online directory of members of the Society for Creative Anachronism, with hundreds of searchable listings.

Roman Life

http://www.dl.ket.org/latin1/things/romanlife/

This site contains historical information on Roman life and directions for making your own Roman-style costumes.

Roman Orgy

http://www.diax.ch/users/julien.courtois/orgy/

An excellent site with information about the art of Roman cooking, recipes, historical documents, and links to related sites.

The 42nd Royal Highland Regiment: "The Black Watch"

http://www.42ndrhr.org/index.php

This well-designed site is a terrific source of information on period music, dancing, uniforms, and everything related to the Black Watch of the late 1700s in North America.

SCA (Society for Creative Anachronism) Music and Dance Homepage

http://www.pbm.com/~lindahl/music_and_dance.html

Links to primary sources, articles, and sound files related to Renaissance music and dance.

SCRIBE's History Archives

http://www.faire.net/SCRIBE/archives/History.Htm

These pages contain hundreds of text files related to the history of the Renaissance and the Middle Ages, including listings of Renaissance Faire participants, guilds, groups, song lyrics, and events around the country. Images and articles related to period crafts, such as Celtic knotwork, heraldic crests, brewing, cooking, blacksmithing, and textiles can also be found at this site.

Second Panzer Division

http://www.panzerdivision.org

The largest and best-equipped German reenacting unit in North America. Its Web site has information about equipment and tactics, a bibliography, and links to World War II reenactors.

Shadows of the Past

http://www.sptddog.com/sotp.html

This organization's guide to reenacting the Old West contains articles, historical resources, photographs, literature, and links to related sites.

Society for Creative Anachronism (SCA)

http://www.sca.org/

This site, dedicated to researching and re-creating pre-seventeenth-century European history, has a huge amount of information on topics related to medieval history, such as the art of combat, including official documents, events, and more.

1st South Carolina Artillery, C.S.A.

http://www.awod.com/gallery/probono/cwchas/1scart.html

Reenacts the history of the men who manned the artillery of the Confederate defenses of the South Carolina coast during the American Civil War. This Web site has history, photos, and a bibliography.

A Stitch Out of Time

http://home.flash.net/~wymarc/

Medieval embroidery techniques from the ninth through sixteenth centuries.

Trans-Mississippi Rifles Infantry

http://members.aol.com/rlhtmr

This Web site has membership information, an events listing, and extensive links to Civil War reenacting groups for both Union and Confederate soldiers.

Trev's Rendezvous Down Under

http://www.geocities.com/Yosemite/Trails/1878/

This site has contact information for many groups who have only e-mail, as well as for organizations that are already on the Internet.

U.S. Civil War Center

http://www.cwc.lsu.edu/cwc/civlink.htm

The Civil War Center is an attempt to index all the Civil War sites on the Web, including national parks, battlefields, roundtables, reenacting groups, and events. This should be one of the first stops for users interested in re-creating the American Civil War.

4th U.S. Infantry Regiment, Company C

http://www.halcyon.com/strandjr/4thUS_Inf/

Information about Civil War arms and equipment, regimental insignia, and the Army of the Potomac.

The Viking Home Page

http://www.control.chalmers.se/vikings/indexframe.html

Reenactors and organizations interested in Viking culture will want to bookmark this page, which has information about sagas, eddas, runes, Viking ships, culture, exhibitions, and links to groups that are interpreting this time period.

42nd Virginia Volunteer Infantry

http://www.erols.com/va42nd/present.html

A helpful introduction to reenacting, an authenticity code, reference room, and related information.

Welcome to Fort Erie and the War of 1812

http://www.iaw.on.ca/~jsek/

Great information about the Fort Erie siege and the War of 1812 reenactment units.

White Oak Society, Inc.

http://www.whiteoak.org/

This Web site has a wealth of information about rendezvous and the fur trade era, from interpreters who portray authentic characters of the eighteenth century.

World War I Trenches on the Web

http://www.worldwar1.com/index.html

A compendium of information for the World War I reenactor. This history of the Great War has a reference library, World War I poster reproductions, interesting articles, and reenactor photographs.

Chapter 29

Genealogy

Samuel E. Dicks

Genealogists have created many Internet sites, publications, and other research tools that are also of use to biographers, social historians, military historians, and others. Probate, military, census, immigration, and land records are among the many kinds of materials most familiar to genealogists. Many sources can be accessed only by visiting a location or arranging for a local researcher, but the Internet makes it easy to find out the kinds of materials available before a trip is planned, make contact with others working on the same family lines, discover sources more easily, and, in some cases, obtain detailed genealogical information by the Internet or by mail. Religious and fraternal organizations, and many other groups, often have materials of value; some of these can be located in Cyndi's List and RootsWeb (see below) or by using search engines and published reference works. The single most useful reference work is *The Source: A Guidebook of American Genealogy*, published by Ancestry.com (see below) and available at most public libraries.

Most Useful Sites

American Family Immigration History Center (Ellis Island Records)

http://www.ellisislandrecords.org/

More than 22 million people entered the United States through Ellis Island from 1892 to 1924. The ships' manifest records ordinarily include the immigrants' given name and surname, ethnicity, last place of residence, name of ship and departure port, arrival date, age, gender, and marital status, along with the location of their name on the manifest. Numerous other Web sites provide background on the Ellis Island experience, including Ancestry.com and RootsWeb.com. This is a new Web site that plans to add additional information in the future. Interest has been high—try again later if you are unable to access it or try this alternative site—http://sites.netscape.net/stephenpmorse/ellis.html. If you are searching for passenger records before 1892, try the Immigrant Ships Transcribers Guild, which is compiling a list of earlier ship passengers (http://istg.rootsweb.com/).

Ancestry.com

http://ancestry.com/

Ancestry.com, a publisher of genealogy books, is also a highly popular, low-cost subscription library of genealogical databases. Most newly added databases are free for ten days, and many sites are permanently free. Free sites include several noted columnists, genealogy lessons, and the SSDI or Social Security Death Index, which lists millions of deceased people and provides instructions on gaining additional information. Thousands of other invaluable sites are available to subscribers, including on-screen original pages of most federal censuses and the genealogy periodical index of the Allen County Public Library of Fort Wayne, Indiana, which includes over a million articles. Ancestry has a free daily newsletter that notes new sites, links, and other useful information and also publishers several basic books and magazines for genealogists.

Cyndi's List of Genealogy Sites on the Internet

http://www.cyndislist.com/

Cyndi Howells's Web site is the best-known and most comprehensive genealogy site, with 100,000 links to states, counties, provinces, nations, military sites, ethnic sites, and other sites too numerous to note. The United States site is at http://www.cyndislist.com/genusa.htm. Browse through Cyndi's List slowly over several days. There is a great deal here worth exploring. The site is also available in book form.

Family History Library (LDS Church, Salt Lake City)

http://familysearch.org/

The Church of Jesus Christ of Latter-Day Saints maintains the world largest family history library; information from these holdings continues to be added to this Web site. The International Genealogical Index (IGI) is one of the most commonly used sites. Local Family History Centers, commonly operated by volunteers in many Mormon churches, can provide additional information and arrange for the borrowing of microfilm. Church records from overseas and local government records are among the many holdings that may accessed online or, in some cases, only by visiting a local center. As with all sites, information provided should be verified by other sources. Personal Ancestral File (PAF), a widely used free genealogy software program, may be downloaded free; numerous databases on CD-ROM are also available at minimal cost. Freedmen's Bank Records, a major African-American database, is among the more important low-cost sources available on CD-ROM. This unique Web site has numerous avenues which should be explored over many days.

The Genealogy Page: National Archives and Records Administration

http://www.nara.gov/genealogy/genindex.html

The National Archives is one of the most user-friendly sites provided by the federal government. Census schedules, immigration and naturalization records, ship passenger records, military and military pension records, and Native American records are among the sources most commonly used by genealogists. Many of the microfilmed materials, including the census schedules and military pension indexes, are also in the thirteen regional branches of NARA, which may also be accessed from this site. This site provides information on the holdings in each regional branch and how one may receive copies of materials or additional information. Among the useful links from this site are Clues in Census Records, 1850–1920 (http://www.nara.gov/genealogy/cenclues.html) and The Soundex Machine (http://www.nara.gov/genealogy/soundex/soundex.html). Soundex is a system originally developed in the 1930s for Social Security applicants who were born before birth certificates were common and who needed to prove their date of birth. It provides a code that takes into account different spellings and acts as an index to most census schedules since 1880. Another Soundex converter that allows you to list several soundex numbers at once is http://www.bradandkathy.com/genealogy/yasc.html.

RootsWeb

http://www.rootsweb.com/

Rootsweb is the oldest and largest genealogy site. One of its best-known features is the Rootsweb Surname List (RSL) which is a sort of international bulletin board where one can connect with others pursuing the same surnames (http://rsl.rootsweb.com/). The site also includes a list of resources for each state (http://www.rootsweb.com/roots-l/usa.html#Statelist). Rootsweb deserves several hours or days of exploring, and a good place for beginners to start is at http://www.rootsweb.com/~rwguide/. Rootsweb also has free e-mail newsletters that provide information on new sites and on problems or experiences encountered by others.

State Historical Societies and Archives

http://www.ohiohistory.org/links/arch_hs.html

Most states have a state historical society and a state archive. The historical society will probably include microfilm copies of newspapers and census records, private papers donated to the society, early state and local histories, and other publications relating to the region. A state archive is ordinarily the custodian of official state government papers, such as those of the governor or adjutant general. In some states the state archive and state historical society are a single institution, usually in the state capital. Elsewhere they are separate organizations and may even be in different cities. Newspapers or other materials may also be in a state library or a state historical library. The Ohio Historical Society provides links to most state historical societies and archives; other state societies, archives, and libraries can be located at the Cyndi's List or RootsWeb sites (see above). State archives may also be found at http://aagsnc.org/library/archives.html or at http://ils.unc.edu/archives/archive7.html.

USGenWeb

http://www.usgenweb.org/

The USGenWeb Project, manned by volunteers, is one of the most useful sites for quickly accessing states and counties. The site provides a map which one can click to access states and counties (http://www.usgenweb.org/statelinks.html), plus other projects and links.

Additional Sites

African-American Genealogy: Christine's Genealogy Website

http://ccharity.com/

This provides information and links to most other sites that deal with African-American genealogy. Also see the African-American page on Cyndi's List (http://www.CyndisList.com/african.htm).

British Information for Genealogists

http://www.pro.gov.uk/readers/genealogists/default.htm

The British Public Record Office provides information and links for those researching families from the British Isles. Users can go to Resources for Genealogists to access numerous other links. Cyndi's List, above, provides additional links for the United Kingdom and for other parts of the world.

Center for Life Stories Preservation

http://www.storypreservation.com/home.html

This unusual site provides many memoirs and life stories of slaves, veterans, pioneers, and others. It includes information for students and teachers who wish to use oral history and other techniques to understand and preserve early family experiences.

The Civil War Soldiers and Sailors System

http://www.itd.nps.gov/cwss/

The National Park Service, in conjunction with the National Archives and Records Administration, the Genealogical Society of Utah (LDS Church), the Federation of Genealogical Societies, the United Daughters of the Confederacy, and numerous other military and genealogy organizations, is developing a computerized database of all soldiers and sailors of the Civil War, both Union and Confederate. The Web site is also available at numerous military cemeteries. Individuals not yet listed here may be located at state or local Web sites—users can check county historical and genealogical sites, state archives, and historical societies. Also, indexes to pension files are available through the National Archives branches and other locations with the use of Soundex. These may also be located at Ancestry.com (fee based).

The Commonwealth War Graves Commission

http://www.cwgc.org/

Personal and service details of the 1.7 million soldiers of the British Commonwealth who died in World War I or World War II. Also includes civilian casualties and other information.

Family Tree Maker Online

http://www.familytreemaker.com/

Broderbund's Family Tree Maker has one of the largest software programs for genealogists. It also provides much free information on its Web site.

Federation of East European Family History Societies (FEEFHS)

http://feefhs.org/

A basic Web site for Central and Eastern European countries, including Switzerland and Germany. Indexes connect with related Web sites from all parts of the world.

The Genealogical Database

http://www.gentree.com/gentree.html

This site contains links to all known databases on the Web. Family sites are included only if a database is available for searching. An index lists most, but not all, of the databases on the site.

Helm's Genealogy Toolbox

http://genealogy.tbox.com/

Matthew L. Helm's site is one of the oldest and best-known sites for a wide variety of information and links. There is information on genealogy software and other topics.

International Black Sheep Society of Genealogists

http://homepages.rootsweb.com/~blksheep/

An organization for those with horse thieves or other scoundrels among their ancestors; the site has many interesting stories and useful links.

JewishGen

http://www.jewishgen.org/

JewishGen is the primary Internet source for those engaged in Jewish genealogy. It connects with numerous databases, including JewishGen Family Finder, which connects people searching the same ancestral towns and surnames. For locating Holocaust survivors, see Missing Identity (http://www.jewishgen.org/missing-identity/).

Korean War and Vietnam War Casualties

http://www.nara.gov/nara/electronic/kcashr.html
http://www.nara.gov/nara/electronic/vcasal.html

These sites contain the National Archives' lists, by state, of the casualties of the Korean War and of the Vietnam War.

Native American Genealogy: The Cherokee Genealogy Page

http://www.allthingscherokee.com

Users can scroll down past the Cherokee sites to other Native American genealogy sites and to other sites useful to historians. Also see Cyndi's List (http://www.CyndisList.com/native.htm).

Public Libraries

http://www.publiclibraries.com/

Local public libraries often have genealogical holdings for their communities; large metropolitan libraries usually have extensive holdings. Public libraries or local historical and genealogical societies generally have basic reference works, as well as such local resources as community histories, church records, obituaries, city directories, and compilations of area cemetery, birth, marriage, and death records. If a public library cannot be found here, use a search engine, such as www.dogpile.com, to find local communities and libraries. For state libraries, go to http://www.publiclibraries.com/state_library.htm.

The 10,000 Year Calendar

http://calendarhome.com/tyc/

This is a site of great practical use to historians and genealogists. It provides a calendar for any month of any year desired, information on calendar changes, Mayan and Chinese calendars, and other information. For a simpler calendar of any month and year, go to http://alabanza.com/kabacoff/Inter-Links/cgi/cal.cgi.

USGS National Mapping Information Query Form

http://geonames.usgs.gov/pls/gnis/web_query.gnis_web_query_form

For those doing genealogical research, this U.S. Geological Survey Query Form is useful for locating obscure places, cemeteries, and other sites in the United States. In most cases, one is able to gain the coordinates and also maps indicating the locations. Many Canadian sites may be located at http://geonames.nrcan.gc.ca/english/cgndb.html and at http://atlas.gc.ca/english/index.html. Maps for other places in the world are available at http://uk2.multimap.com/. For British locations, see http://www.geog.port.ac.uk/gbhgis/ and http://www.streetmap.co.uk/.

U.S. Immigration and Naturalization Service

http://www.ins.usdoj.gov/graphics/aboutins/history/index.htm

This site, titled "INS, Genealogy, and Education," contains considerable information on immigration history and laws, much of it designed for classroom use. For INS forms and fees, go to http://www.ins.usdoj.gov/graphics/formsfee/index.htm.

U.S. Surname Distribution

http://www.hamrick.com/names/index.html

The 1850, 1880, and 1920 U.S. Census and 1990s phone books are used to show the distribution of surnames by states at these four different times. Use the arrow next to the "Display" button and go to "All Periods" for quick comparisons. Hamrick software also has programs to facilitate the use of photographs in compiling a genealogy.

U.S. Vital Records Information

http://vitalrec.com/index.html

Modern state and territory sites for finding birth, marriage, divorce, and death records are available here. Some earlier records are available at local, rather than centralized state offices; some of the earlier records are available online. Go to "Related Links" provided for each state and territory for many additional useful sites.

Chapter 30

State Historical Societies

Leo E. Landis, Scott A. Merriman, and Dennis A. Trinkle

Metasite

National Council on Public History (NCPH) Page of Historical Societies
http://www.iupui.edu/~ncph/societies.html

Canada

Canada's National History Society
http://www.historysociety.ca/

United States

Alabama Department of Archives and History
http://www.archives.state.al.us/

Alaska Historical Society
http://www.alaska.net/~ahs/ahsinfo.htm

Arizona Historical Society
http://www.tempe.gov/ahs/ (Central Division)

http://www.infomagic.net/~ahsnad/index.html (Northern Division)

http://w3.arizona.edu/~azhist/rio.htm (Rio Colorado Division)

http://w3.arizona.edu/~azhist/index.html (Southern Division)

California Historical Society, San Francisco
http://www.calhist.org/

Colorado Historical Society
http://coloradohistory.org/home.htm

Connecticut Historical Society
http://www.chs.org/

The Historical Society of Delaware
http://www.hsd.org/

Florida Historical Society
http://florida-historical-soc.org/

Georgia Historical Society
http://www.georgiahistory.com/

Historical/Genealogical Societies in Georgia
http://widow.mindspring.com/~bevr/bevrgen.html

The Hawaiian Historical Society

http://www.hawaiianhistory.org/index.html

Idaho State Historical Society

http://www2.state.id.us/ishs/index.html

Illinois State Historical Society

http://www.prairienet.org/ishs/

Indiana Historical Society

http://www.indianahistory.org/

State Historical Society of Iowa

http://www.iowahistory.org/

The Kansas State Historical Society

http://www.kshs.org/

Kentucky Historical Society

http://www.des.state.ky.us/agencies/khs/

Louisiana Historical Society

http://www.louisianahistoricalsociety.org

Louisiana State Museum

http://lsm.crt.state.la.us/

The Center for Maine History

http://www.mainehistory.org/

Maryland Historical Society

http://www.mdhs.org/

Maryland Historical Trust

http://www.marylandhistoricaltrust.net

The Massachusetts Historical Society

http://www.masshist.org/

Michigan Historical Center

http://www.sos.state.mi.us/history/history.html

Minnesota Historical Society

http://www.mnhs.org/

Mississippi Historical Society

http://mshistory.k12.ms.us/mshistsociety.html (magazine)

http://www.mdah.state.ms.us/admin/mhistsoc.html (membership)

Missouri Historical Society

http://www.mohistory.org

The Montana Historical Society

http://his.state.mt.us/index.html

Nebraska State Historical Society

http://www.nebraskahistory.org/

Nevada Historical Society

http://dmla.clan.lib.nv.us/docs/museums/reno/his-soc.htm

New Hampshire Historical Society

http://www.nhhistory.org/index.html

New Jersey Historical Commission

http://www.state.nj.us/state/history/hisidx.html

New Jersey Historical Society

http://www.eventworksnj.com/njhist/njhistorical.html

New Mexico State Records Center and Archives

http://www.state.nm.us/cpr/

New York Historical Society

http://www.nyhistory.org/

New York State Historical Association

http://www.nysha.org

North Carolina Division of Archives and History

http://www.ah.dcr.state.nc.us/

State Library of North Carolina

http://prioris.dcr.state.nc.us/ncslhome.htm

The State Historical Society of North Dakota

http://www.state.nd.us/hist/

The Ohio Historical Society

http://www.ohiohistory.org/

Oklahoma Historical Society
http://www.ok-history.mus.ok.us/

Oregon Historical Society
http://www.ohs.org/

The Historical Society of Pennsylvania
http://www.hsp.org/

The Rhode Island Historical Society
http://www.rihs.org

South Carolina Historical Society
http://www.schistory.org/

South Dakota State Historical Society/Office of History
http://www.sdhistory.org/

East Tennessee Historical Society
http://www.east-tennessee-history.org/

West Tennessee Historical Society
http://www.wths.tn.org/

Texas Historical Commission
http://www.tsl.state.tx.us/

Texas State Historical Association
http://www.tsha.utexas.edu/

The Utah State Historical Society
http://www.dced.state.ut.us/history/

Vermont Historical Society
http://www.state.vt.us/vhs/

Virginia Historical Society
http://www.vahistorical.org/index.htm

Washington State Historical Society
http://www.wshs.org/

West Virginia Division of Culture and History
http://www.wvculture.org/

West Virginia State Archives
http://www.wvculture.org/history/

State Historical Society of Wisconsin, Archives Division
http://www.shsw.wisc.edu/index.html

Wyoming State Historical Society
http://wyshs.org/

Chapter 31

History Books on the Internet

Susanna Betzel

Book Search Networks

The Internet has brought about one of the greatest changes—and advances—in the out-of-print/rare book trade in decades. With the advent of Internet search networks, which can search the inventories of thousands of dealers worldwide in seconds, it has suddenly become far easier to hunt down that elusive out-of-print (or, for that matter, in-print) book and to compare prices among dealers offering it. The following networks are leaders in the field:

Advanced Book Exchange

http://www.abebooks.com

Used, out-of-print, and rare books. Especially recommended.

Alibris

http://www.alibris.com/home.cfm

Used, out-of-print, and rare books.

Amazon.com

http://www.amazon.com

New books. Also does searches for rare books.

Antiqbook

http://www.antiqbook.com/

Includes a larger percentage of rare/antiquarian book dealers, especially European.

Barnes and Noble

http://www.barnesandnoble.com/

New books. Also does searches for rare books.

Bibliofind

http://www.bibliofind.com

Used, out-of-print, and rare books. Especially recommended; the fastest and most efficient of the networks.

Bookfinder

http://www.bookfinder.com

Simultaneously searches most of the above networks and displays the results on a single page. Bookfinder also searches the in-print databases at Amazon.com (see above) and Powell's Books (see below).

Books and Book Collecting

http://www.trussel.com/f_books.htm

This is a fabulously useful site for all facets of out-of-print book buying and collecting. It includes SetMaker, a free search/sell forum for odd volumes from multivolume sets; BookSeek, links to the online catalogs of many dealers who are not members of the large networks; and direct links to major library catalogs, the search networks, and many large individual book dealers worldwide who have their own searchable sites.

Individual Book Dealers

The following is just a sampling of book dealers and bookstores worldwide who specialize in history books (new, remaindered, and/or out-of-print) or who have strong history sections, and who have a presence on the Internet, either as members of one of the networks or with their own Web sites and online catalogs. Owner or proprietor is listed at the beginning of each description.

Note: Credit cards: AE = American Express; D = Discover; MC = MasterCard; V = Visa.

Alden Books, Inc.

Email: aldenbks@cdt.infi.net

Web site: http://www.aldenbooks.com

Karen and Steve Deutsch and Maria and Charles Melchioris. Specialty: General history, scholarly. Number of history books: 2,500. Credit cards: AE MC V. Location: USA.

Antiquariat Hohmann

Email: antiquariat-hohmann@t-online.de

Wilhelm Hohmann. Specialty: Economic and business history. Number of history books: 5,000; fifty percent of total stock is history books. Credit cards: No; foreign checks accepted. Location: Germany.

Archer's Used and Rare Books, Inc.

Email: archers@megsinet.net

Paul Bauer. Specialty: General history, Americana. Number of history books: 1,000. Founded 1986. Credit cards: MC V. Location: USA.

The Avid Reader Used and Rare Books, Inc.

Email: avid@avidreader.com

Web site: http://www.avidreader.com

Barry Jones. Specialty: General, American, scholarly, American regional, Southern, genealogy. Number of history books: 15,000; fifty percent of total stock is history books. Credit cards: D MC V. Location: USA.

Beulahland Books

Email: beulahland@coslink.net

William Tompkins. Specialty: General history. Number of history books: 4,000. Founded 1980. Credit cards: D MC V. Location: USA.

Book CloseOuts, Inc.

Email: als@bookcloseouts.com

Web site: http://www.bookcloseouts.com

Al Siebring, Customer Service. Specialty: General history. Number of history books: 3,000. Founded 1982. Credit cards: MC V. Location: USA.

Book House in Dinkytown

Email: bookhous@pro-ns.net

Kristen Eide-Tollefson. Specialty: General history. Number of history books: "40 cases." Founded 1976. Credit cards: AE D MC V; foreign checks accepted. Location: USA.

Books Unlimited

Email: otierney@booksunlimited.com

Web site: http://www.booksunlimited.com

Joseph, Barbara, and Owen Tierney. Specialty: General history, American. Number of history books: 10,000. Founded 1988. Credit cards: D MC V. Location: USA.

Calhoun Book Store

Email: calhounbk@aol.com

Virginia Lou Seay. Specialty: General history, university press. Number of history books: 6,000. Founded 1961. Credit cards: No; foreign checks accepted with surcharge. Location: USA.

Chameleon

Email: afrank@uswest.net

Web site: http://www.abebooks.com/home/chameleon/

Alan D. Frank. Specialty: General history, Native and Western American, African, African-American, history of medicine, art history. Number of history books: 8,000. Credit cards: MC V. Location: USA.

Clifton Books

Email: jhodgk9942@aol.com

Web site: http://www.bibliofind.com/cliftonbooks.html

John Hodgkins. Specialty: General history, British history since 1600. Number of history books: 4,500 listed on the Web; 25,000 in stock; all of the stock is history books. Founded 1969. Credit cards: AE MC V Access; U.S. dollars and checks accepted. Location: UK.

Comenius-Antiquariat

Email: shess@access.ch

Web site: http://www.comenius-antiquariat.com

Samuel Hess and Joerg Zoller. Specialty: General history, Swiss, social history, anarchism. Number of history books: 6,000. Credit cards: MC V; foreign checks accepted with surcharge. Location: Switzerland.

Ed Conroy, Bookseller

Email: edconroy@wizvax.net

Edward Conroy. Specialty: Russian, military, political/social science, university press. Number of history books: 36,000; 90 percent of total stock is history books. Founded 1987. Credit cards: MC V; U.S. and British checks accepted. Location: USA.

D.K. Publishers Distributors Ltd.

Email: dkpd@del3.vsnl.net.in

Web site: http://www.dkpdindia.com

Parmil Mittal. Specialty: Asian. Number of history books: 7,000. Founded 1974. Credit cards: No; foreign checks accepted. Location: India.

Editions

Email: nleditions@aol.com

Web site: http://www.nleditions.com

Norman and Joan Levine. Specialty: General history. Number of history books: 20,000. Founded 1948. Credit cards: D MC V. Location: USA.

Expatriate Bookshop of Denmark

Email: expatbks@post11.tele.dk

John Jackson. Specialty: General history, South Asia. Number of history books: 2,000. Credit cards: No; foreign checks accepted. Location: Denmark.

Franklin's Old Book Shop

Email: oldbooks@usit.net

Web Site: http://www.auldbooks.com/biblio/clients/franklin (under construction)

Ed Franklin. Specialty: General history. Number of history books: 4,000. Credit cards: yes. Location: USA.

Great Northwest Bookstore

Email: gnw@greatnorthwestbooks.com

Web site: http://www.greatnorthwestbooks.com

Phil Wikelun, John Henley, and Grace Pastine. Specialty: General, American West, prehistory. Number of history books: 85,000; fifty percent of total stock is history books. Founded 1977. Credit cards: AE D MC V; foreign checks accepted. Location: USA.

Greenfield Books

Email: greenfld@escape.ca

Web site: http://www.greenfieldbooks.com/

Specialty: General history, military, nautical, Canadian, polar exploration. Number of history books: 8,000. Credit cards: AE MC V; U.S. and Canadian checks accepted. Location: Canada.

Ground Zero Books, Ltd.

Email: gzbooksltd@aol.com

R. Alan Lewis. Specialty: Military history, world wars, Vietnam, American Civil War. Number of history books: 50,000; entire stock is military history books. Founded 1978 and operated by trained historians. Credit cards: AE D MC V. Location: USA.

Gutenberg Holdings

Email: gutenbrg@ziplink.net

Web site: http://gutenbergholdings.com

Rhett Moran. Specialty: General history, American. Number of history books: 13,000. Credit cards: AE D MC V. Location: USA.

Peter J. Hadley: Bookseller

Email: books@hadley.co.uk

Web site: http://www.hadley.co.uk

Peter J. Hadley. Specialty: General history, English history. Number of history books: 1,200; fifty percent of total stock is history books. Founded 1984. Credit cards: MC V Switch; checks in U.S. dollars accepted. Location: UK.

Caroline Hartley Books

Email: Hartleybk@clara.net

Caroline Hartley. Specialty: General history, British. Number of history books: 3,500. Founded 1983. Credit cards: MC V. Location: UK.

History to Go

Email: old_stuff@bigfoot.com

Lance Sprung. Specialty: Historic documents, letters, autographs, signed books, newspapers, broadsides, manuscripts, diaries, from the Middle Ages to the present. Number of documents: about 3,500. Not a book dealer per se, but certainly of interest to historians; entire stock is historical items. Plans to issue catalogs. Credit cards: MC V (in shop only). Location: USA.

R.R. Knott Bookseller

Email: rrknott@cyberus.ca

Web site: http://www.cyberus.ca/~rrknott

R.R. Knott. Specialty: Medieval, Canadian, military, ancient. Number of history books: 6,000; fifty percent of total stock is history books. Founded 1980. Credit cards: MC V; foreign checks accepted. Location: Canada.

Labyrinth Books

Email: books@labyrinthbooks.com

Web site: http://www.labyrinthbooks.com/

Specialty: General history, scholarly/university press. Number of history books: Thousands—new and remaindered. Credit cards: AE MC V. Location: USA.

David M. Lesser, Fine Antiquarian Books LLC

Email: dmlesser@lesserbooks.com

Web site: http://www.lesserbooks.com

David Lesser. Specialty: Americana. Number of history books: 10,000; ninety-five percent of total stock is history books. Credit cards: MC V. Location: USA.

McDermott Books

Email: mcdermottbooks@gdinet.com

Patrick McDermott. Specialty: General history. Number of history books: 10,000. Credit cards: D MC V. Location: USA.

O and I Books

Email: oibooks@sprint.ca

Web site: http://www.oibooks.com

Juan M. Ormaechea. Specialty: General history, Hispanic. Number of history books: 1,000. Credit cards: V; checks accepted in all major currencies. Location: Canada.

The Old Bookroom

Email: books@OldBookroom.com

Web site: http://www.OldBookroom.com

Sally and Barbara Burdon. Specialty: Asia, Africa, Middle East, Australia. Number of history books: 15,000. Founded 1969. Credit cards: AE MC V Diners. Location: Australia.

The Owl at the Bridge

Email: owlbridge@home.com

Samuel and Penelope Hough. Specialty: General history, medieval, Italian Renaissance. Number of history books: 4,000. Founded 1981. Credit cards: MC V; foreign checks accepted with surcharge. Location: USA.

Parmer Books

Email: parmerbook@aol.com

Web site: http://www.stairway.org/parmer/index.html

Jean Marie Parmer. Specialty: Voyages, exploration, discovery, Western Americana. Number of history books: 3,000; ninety-five percent of total stock is history books. Founded 1983. Credit cards: yes; foreign checks accepted with surcharge. Location: USA.

The Personal Navigator

Email: persnav@shore.net

Web site: http://www1.shore.net/~persnav/books1.htm

Samuel W. Coulbourn. Specialty: American, nineteenth-century diaries, journals, and autograph books. Number of history books: 500. Credit cards: MC V. Location: USA.

Mark Post, Bookseller

Email: markpost@att.net

Mark Post. Specialty: American, European, medieval, colonial Africa, historical fiction. Number of history books: 1,200. Credit cards: MC V. Location: USA.

Powell's Books

Email: powellschicago@MSN.com

Web site: http://www.powells.com/

Specialty: General scholarly. Number of history books: Probably in the tens of thousands; Powell's is a vast warehouse dealer of remaindered and out-of-print university press books. Credit cards: yes. Location: USA.

Prairie Reader Bookstore

Email: praireader@ctos.com

Hans Knoop. Specialty: General history, western U.S., U.S. presidents, Colorado history. Number of history books: 15,000; fifty percent of total stock is history books. Credit cards: AE D MC V. Location: USA.

Priceless Books

Email: priceless@net66.com

Web site: http://www.abebooks.com/home/priceless

William Thornhill, Michael Vaillancourt, and Leslie Troutman. Specialty: General history. Number of history books: 3,000. Credit cards: D MC V. Location: USA.

John William Pye Rare Books

Email: pyebooks@tiac.net

John William Pye. Specialty: Ancient, ancient Egypt, Egyptology. Number of history books: 3,000; ninety percent of total stock is history books. Credit cards: MC V. Location: USA.

Gaston Renard Fine and Rare Books (Books Australasia)

Email: booksaus@ozemail.com.au

Web site: http://bibliocity.com/dealers/renard

Julien Renard. Specialty: General, Australian, Pacific Rim, exploration/discovery/voyages. Number of history books: 10,000. Founded 1945. Credit cards: AE MC V Bankcard; checks accepted in Australian dollars, U.S. dollars, British sterling. Location: Australia.

Richard Owen Roberts Booksellers and Publishers

Email: roberts@safeplace.net

Web site: http://www.abebooks.com/home/RORoberts/

Richard Owen Roberts. Specialty: General history, Church history. Number of history books: 15,000. Founded 1961. Credit cards: MC V. Location: USA.

Serendipity Books

Email: serendip@merriweb.com.au

Web site: http://members.iinet.net.au/~serendip/

Ilonka and David McGill. Specialty: Australia, the Pacific, Southeast Asia, university press/academic books. Number of history books: 11,000; fifty percent of total stock is history books. Founded 1974. Credit cards: AE MC V Bankcard; U.S. and British checks accepted with surcharge for conversion. Location: Australia.

Neil Shillington: Bookseller

Email: neilsbks@bellsouth.net

Neil Shillington. Specialty: European, American, historical biography, Jewish, history related to theology. Number of history books: 3,000. Founded 1980. Credit cards: pending; foreign checks accepted. Location: USA.

Strand Book Store, Inc.

Email: strand@strandbooks.com

Specialty: General history. Number of history books: 30,000. No searchable Web site or online catalog, and not a member of a network, but as the largest used bookstore in New York City, the Strand cannot be ignored. Credit cards: AE MC V. Location: USA.

Naomi Symes Books

Email: naomi@symes.demon.co.uk

Web site: http://www.naomisymes.com/

Naomi Symes. Specialty: Social history, women's history, British, Victorian, eighteenth century. Number of history books: 1,200. Credit cards: MC V; foreign checks accepted with surcharge for conversion. Location: UK.

Time and Again Books

Email: mcurtis@inetport.com

Web site: http://www.abebooks.com/home/mcurtis

Michael S. Curtis. Specialty: American. Number of history books: 2,000. Credit cards: yes. Location: USA.

Tomes of Glory Books

Email: ppodolick@aol.com

Web site: http://www.abebooks.com/home/TMSFGLRY/

Phillip A. Podolick. Specialty: Military, American, American Civil War. Number of history books: 7,500; ninety percent of total stock is history books. Credit cards: AE MC V. Location: USA.

Tricolor Books

Email: tricolor@mhonline.net

Web site: http://www.angelfire.com/ny/tricolorbks

Susanna Betzel. Specialty: French history, eighteenth/nineteenth-century British and European history, French Revolution. Number of history books: 3,000; entire stock is history books. Credit cards: No; foreign checks accepted with a three-dollar surcharge for conversion. Location: USA.

Triple A Books

Email: tripleabks@aol.com

Web site: http://www.abebooks.com/home/aaaalways

David A. Katz. Specialty: American, Russian, American presidential biography. Number of history books: 8,000; seventy-five percent of total stock is history books. Credit cards: MC V. Location: USA.

Valley Books

Email: orders@valleybooks.com

Web site: http://www.valleybooks.com

Lawrence and Charmagne Pruner. Specialty: General history, New England. Number of history books: 4,000. Founded 1975. Credit cards: AE MC V. Location: USA.

Vintage Books

Email: vintageb@teleport.com

B. Milner. Specialty: General history, regional (Washington state), history of crime, transportation history, sports history. Number of history books: 10,000. Founded 1975. Credit cards: AE D MC V. Location: USA.

Volk and Iiams, Booksellers

Email: christ@vibooks.com

Web site: http://www.abebooks.com/home/vibooks/

Christine Volk and Shep Iiams. Specialty: African-American, women's. Number of history books: 3,000. Credit cards: MC V. Location: USA.

Webster's Bookstore Cafe

Email: usedbook@vicon.net

Web site: http://www.abebooks.com/home/zeppelin

Elaine Meder and Fred Ramsey. Specialty: General history, British, British Commonwealth, American presidential, Russian/Soviet. Number of history books: 10,000. Founded 1974. Credit cards: AE D MC V. Location: USA.

Winghale Books

Email: winghale@enterprise.net

Web site: http://www.abebooks.com/home/JOHNSTON/

Irwin and Hilary Johnston. Specialty: European, American, British, classical, medieval (all scholarly). Number of history books: 10,000; self-described as the leading dealer in academic history books in the U.K. Founded 1985. Issues snailmail catalogs. Credit cards: AE MC V; U.S. checks accepted with surcharge. Location: UK.

Wolf's Head Books

Email: wolfhead@aug.com

Web site: http://wolfsheadbooks.com

Harvey Wolf and Barbara Nailler. Specialty: Americana, military, Florida, American Civil War, World War I and II. Number of history books: 10,000. Founded 1980. Credit cards: AE D MC V. Location: USA.

Woodland Park Bookstore

Email: woodbook@lex.infi.net

Diana Turnbull. Specialty: General history. Number of history books: 12,000; fifty percent of total stock is history books. Founded 1985. Credit cards: yes; foreign checks accepted. Location: USA.

Xerxes Fine and Rare Books and Documents

Email: catra@xerxesbooks.com

Web site: http://xerxesbooks.com

Carol Travis. Specialty: General history. Number of history books: 2,500. Founded 1980. Credit cards: AE MC V. Location: USA.

Chapter 32

History and Social Studies Organizations

Scott A. Merriman and Dennis A. Trinkle

American Historical Association

http://www.theaha.org

The home page for the American Historical Association provides information
on the AHA and more than 100 affiliated societies, selected articles from the
newsletter *Perspectives*, a calendar of historical events, and a "primer" on how
the AHA serves K-12 teachers in history.

The History Cooperative

http://www.historycooperative.org

Although technically not an "organization," the History Cooperative provides
online connections to the journals of several professional associations, including the *American Historical Review* and the *Journal of American History*. This
service is a cooperative venture of the American Historical Association, the
Organization of American Historians, the University of Illinois Press, and the
National Academy Press. Users can access electronic versions of articles in
current issues if they are members of the AHA or OAH or if their institutions
have subscriptions to print versions of the journals.

H-NCC—National Coordinating Committee for the Promotion of History

http://www.h-net.msu.edu/~ncc

Operated through the H-Net group out of Michigan State University, H-NCC is "the official electronic voice" of the National Coordinating Committee for the Promotion of History, which supports history and historians in the political circles of Washington, D.C., and the American states. Included at the site is a connection to past issues of *Washington Updates* that describe the work of NCC and its lobbying successes. A keyword search mechanism allows easy use of materials in the H-NCC site.

National Council for History Education

http://www.history.org/nche

The NCHE Web site is more useful than many organizational sites because it goes well beyond descriptions of NCHE and its programs. For example, History Links sends a user to a diverse mix of sites: Web sites for historical organizations, history education sites, links of interest to social studies educators, and repositories of primary sources, which get promoted as "a listing of over 3000 Web sites . . . for the research scholar."

NCSS Online: National Council for the Social Studies

http://www.ncss.org

NCSS Online offers Web-based information services for the National Council for the Social Studies, the largest "umbrella organization" for social studies educators. This site promotes NCSS, which is to be expected, but it also provides links for professional development, standards and curriculum, and teaching resources.

Organization of American Historians

http://www.oah.org/

The Organization of American Historians is the premier professional association for United States history. But beyond its service to college and university teachers and researchers, OAH serves precollegiate history teachers through such means as the *OAH Magazine of History* and outreach programs, which are described at this site. A link to History Teaching Units introduces lesson plans for grades 6 to 12 based on primary documents developed by the OAH in concert with the National Center for History in the Schools at UCLA.

Society for History Education/*The History Teacher*

http://www.csulb.edu/~histeach/

This site features the Society for History Education, which publishes *The History Teacher*. The two entities are linked together through the Web server at California State University at Long Beach, where the journal is housed. The Web site provides a current table of contents as well as past issues of *The History Teacher*, links to related organizations, and contact information for the society and the journal.

Chapter 33

Maps and Images

Martin V. Minner

Maps

Metasites

Cartography: Calendar of Exhibitions

http://users.supernet.com/pages/jdocktor/exhibit.htm

A worldwide compendium of exhibits on the history of cartography.

Mercator's World

http://www.mercatormag.com/links.html

The online version of *Mercator's World: The Magazine of Maps, Exploration and Discovery* provides a useful set of links divided by subject area. The most helpful for historians are in the areas of cartography, history, libraries and collections, and museums. A section on education provides handy links for teachers.

Odden's Bookmarks

http://oddens.geog.uu.nl/index.html

An extensive site at Utrecht University providing a searchable list of more than 13,000 links to cartographic sites, map collections, and other map resources.

Perry-Castañeda Map Collection: Historical Map Web Sites

http://www.lib.utexas.edu/Libs/PCL/Map_collection/map_sites/
hist_sites.html

Compiled by the Perry-Castañeda Library at the University of Texas, this site offers an extensive list of links to historical map Web sites. Useful for world history as well as United States and European history.

Exhibits and Collections

Color Landform Atlas of the United States

http://fermi.jhuapl.edu/states/

Provides a variety of maps for each of the fifty states, including shaded topographical maps, satellite images, county maps, and scans from an 1895 Rand McNally atlas.

Cultural Maps

http://xroads.virginia.edu/~MAP/map_hp.html

An American Studies project at the University of Virginia, this site seeks to create an American historical atlas examining the physical landscape as well as mapmakers' mental and cultural terrain. At present the site includes U.S. territorial maps from 1775 to 1920, excerpts from an essay on the South by John Shelton Reed, and links to a number of useful exhibits and collections.

The Earth and the Heavens: The Art of the Mapmaker

http://www.bl.uk/exhibitions/maps/

This is the online version of a British Library exhibition that explored attempts to represent the earth and the cosmos. Online images range from a world map by Ptolemy to a world geological map from 1849.

1895 U.S. Atlas

http://www.livgenmi.com/1895.htm

Created by genealogist Pam Rietsch, this site provides scans of U.S. state maps from an 1895 atlas. The site also offers detailed scans at the county level.

Exploring the West from Monticello

http://www.lib.virginia.edu/exhibits/lewis_clark/home.html

Based on an exhibit at the University of Virginia's Alderman Library, this site examines the planning of the Lewis and Clark expedition and the history of North American cartography from Columbus to Jefferson.

Greenwood's Map of London 1827

http://www.bathspa.ac.uk/greenwood/home.html

This site is based entirely on a detailed 1827 map of the city of London and allows visitors to zoom in on a selected portion of the city. The site provides links to present-day maps and aerial photographs to permit comparison with the city of 1827.

University of Georgia Rare Map Collection

http://scarlett.libs.uga.edu/darchive/hargrett/maps/maps.html

The University of Georgia's Hargrett Rare Book and Manuscript Library provides online images of many historical maps from its collection, with an emphasis on maps of Georgia.

Library of Congress Geography and Maps: An Illustrated Guide

http://www.loc.gov/rr/geogmap/guide/

This site, an introduction to the Library of Congress's cartographic collections, features selected images in a variety of subject areas.

Map Collections: 1500–1999

http://lcweb2.loc.gov/ammem/gmdhtml/gmdhome.html

Part of the Library of Congress's American Memory project, this site provides online images in the following subject areas: cities and towns, conservation and the environment, discovery and exploration, cultural landscapes, military battles and campaigns, transportation, and general maps.

MapHist

http://www.maphist.nl/

The MapHist e-mail discussion group for map historians maintains an online archive of maps that have been discussed on the list.

Maps of the Pimería: Early Cartography of the Southwest

http://www.library.arizona.edu/pimeria/welcome.html

Based on maps from the University of Arizona Library Map Collection, this exhibit examines the cartographic history of the region of New Spain formerly known as Pimería, encompassing what is now southern Arizona and northern Sonora. Online images cover the period from 1556 to 1854.

National Geographic: Maps

http://www.nationalgeographic.com/maps/

The online version of *National Geographic* provides a variety of map resources including MapMachine, an easy-to-use feature that lets users point-and-click to zoom in on the map of their choice. The Historical Maps section includes panoramic maps, railroads, explorations, battles, and general maps.

The Newberry Library: Maps and History of Cartography Collections

http://www.newberry.org/nl/collections/L3cover.html

The Newberry Library's site includes bibliographic material on the library's Maps and History of Cartography Collections. A link to the Hermon Dunlap Smith Center for the History of Cartography leads to information about teaching with historical maps.

Osher Map Library

http://www.usm.maine.edu/~maps/

This site provides online versions of exhibits that have appeared at the Osher Map Library and Smith Center for Cartographic Education at the University of Southern Maine. Among the exhibits available online are Road Maps: The American Way, Charting Neptune's Realm: From Classical Mythology to Satellite Imagery, and The "Percy Map": The Cartographic Image of New England and Strategic Planning During the American Revolution.

The U.S. Civil War Center

http://www.cwc.lsu.edu/links/links3.htm#Maps

The U.S. Civil War Center, a division of Louisiana State University Libraries Special Collections, has compiled an extensive list of links to Civil War maps.

Images

Metasites

Australian National University
http://rubens.anu.edu.au/

The Australian National University's ArtServe site provides links to worldwide art and architecture sites, primarily emphasizing the Mediterranean Basin.

The Daguerreian Society: Links
http://daguerre.org/resource/links.html

The Daguerreian Society maintains an excellent list of links to sites that feature daguerreotype images. The site also provides links to sites on photographic history in general.

Massachusetts Institute of Technology: Rotch Visual Collections
http://libraries.mit.edu/rvc/imgcolls/imgcoll1.html

The Rotch Visual Collections at Massachusetts offer an excellent page of links to image collections on the Web organized by subject area, such as anthropology and archaeology, art, photography, and urban design.

Mother of All Art History Links Pages
http://www.umich.edu/~hartspc/histart/mother/

An extensive annotated collection of links to visual resources, image collections, online exhibitions, and museums. Sections on Africa, Asia, and Islam, as well as on Europe and the Americas, make this metasite a valuable resource for world history.

NM's Creative Impulse: The Artist's View of World History and Western Civilization
http://history.evansville.net/

Compiled by Nancy B. Mautz, a teacher in Evansville, Indiana, this award-winning metasite provides a rich collection of links organized around a two-semester high school course on world history. Emphasizing art as a way to study world history, the site offers links to many images of use to teachers.

Exhibits and Collections

American Memory

http://memory.loc.gov/ammem/amtitle.html

The American Memory site, produced by the National Digital Library Project of the Library of Congress, provides access to more than 7 million digitized primary source items on U.S. history and culture. Collections available online include advertising, baseball cards, maps, motion pictures, music, photographs, and posters.

American Museum of Photography

http://www.photographymuseum.com

A virtual museum drawing from the private collection of William B. Becker. Several current galleries of historical interest deal with slavery, spirit photography, and daguerreotypes made by the firm of Southworth & Hawes.

The Center for Creative Photography

http://www.library.arizona.edu/branches/ccp/ccphome.html

Offers an index of the center's collection of more than 60,000 photographs as well as selected online images. The center maintains more than 100 collections of papers, manuscripts, and artifacts pertaining to photographers and photographic organizations and provides an archive list and finding aid in PDF format.

The Center for Documentary Studies

http://cds.aas.duke.edu/index.html

The Center for Documentary Studies promotes documentary work encompassing photography, filmmaking, oral history, folklore, and writing. Recent online exhibits featuring photography are Behind the Veil: Documenting African American Life in the Jim Crow South and Indivisible: Stories of American Community.

City-Gallery.com

http://www.city-gallery.com/

A genealogy site emphasizing photographic research and preservation. Members can upload family photos to an online album, contribute to message boards, or create a digital family album. The site provides access to PhotoGen, an e-mail discussion list on family photography and genealogy.

Collected Visions

http://cvisions.nyu.edu/mantle/index

Although not historical, the Collected Visions project offers a provocative perspective on how photographic images shape personal memory. The site invites visitors to submit photographs and to create photo essays from their own photographs or from other visitors' submissions.

The Daguerreian Society

http://www.daguerre.org/home.html

The Daguerreian Society's excellent site features a selection of digitized daguerreotype images and informative explanatory text. Galleries deal with the American vision in the daguerreotype era, images of California gold mining, and scenic daguerreotypes. The site's resource page offers a history of the daguerreotype, nineteenth- and twentieth-century published sources, a bibliography, and information on the daguerreotype process. One very helpful feature is the Tips for Best Viewing page.

Denver Public Library Photography Collection

http://gowest.coalliance.org/

This site features exhibits based on the photography collection in the Denver Public Library's Western History/Genealogy Department. Galleries cover the history of flight, Native American women, urban beautification, Fourth of July celebrations, and an elite World War II Army division that trained in the Rockies.

Digitizing Medieval Manuscripts: Creating a Scholarly Resource

http://medieval.mse.jhu.edu/

Created in conjunction with a Johns Hopkins University colloquium on digitizing medieval manuscripts, this site provides links to several noteworthy digitization projects.

George Eastman House International Museum of Photography and Film

http://www.eastman.org/home.htm

The George Eastman House, an important resource for research in the history of photography, does not provide online access to its collections but offers selected images in four areas: daguerreotypes, nineteenth-century British and French photography on paper, American nineteenth-century holdings, and important photography from the late nineteenth and early twentieth centuries. A downloadable video clip shows photographs taken with banquet and panoramic cameras.

Images from the History of Medicine

http://wwwihm.nlm.nih.gov/

Provides online access to more than 60,000 images in the prints and photographs collection of the History of Medicine Division of the U.S. National Library of Medicine. Offers keyword searching and a browsing function. This valuable collection includes portraits, caricatures, drawings, and a variety of other media.

Images of African-Americans from the 19th Century

http://digital.nypl.org/schomburg/images_aa19/

A valuable selection of images from the Schomburg Center for Research in Black Culture of the New York Public Library. The archive can be searched by keyword or subject area.

I.N. Phelps Stokes Collection of American Historical Prints

http://www.nypl.org/research/chss/spe/art/print/stokes/stokes.htm

Provides selected images from the New York Public Library's I.N. Phelps Stokes Collection of American Historical Prints. The collection consists largely of town views, historical scenes, and some maps.

John H. White: Photographing Black Chicago

http://www.nara.gov/exhall/americanimage/chicago/white1.html

A collection of photographs of Chicago's African-American community taken in 1973–74 by John H. White, then a photographer for the *Chicago Daily News*, for a federal documentary project.

Lester S. Levy Sheet Music Collection

http://levysheetmusic.mse.jhu.edu

Part of the special collections at the Milton S. Eisenhower Library at Johns Hopkins University, this collection contains more than 29,000 pieces of music and focuses on American popular music from 1780 to 1960. All are indexed on the site and many, including illustrated covers, are available online.

LIFE Online

http://www.lifemag.com/Life/features/index.html

All *LIFE* front covers from 1936 to 1972, the period when the magazine was published weekly, can be browsed online or searched by keyword or date. The site's Features section offers exhibits of archival photos in areas such as war, space, civil rights, and politics. A section on *LIFE* master photographers features Larry Burrows's Vietnam coverage, W. Eugene Smith's 1946 photo essay "Country Doctor," and a fifty-year retrospective on Alfred Eisenstaedt.

Living Landscapes

http://royal.okanagan.bc.ca/histphoto/index.html

A searchable archive of photographs from the Thompson/Okanagan region of British Columbia, Canada. Sponsored by the Royal British Columbia Museum and Okanagan University College.

Motion Picture and Television Reading Room

http://lcweb.loc.gov/rr/mopic/

The Library of Congress offers many early motion pictures online in QuickTime, MPG, and Real Media formats. Subject areas and periods range from popular entertainment in the 1870s to the consumer economy of the 1920s. The site also provides access to sound recordings in Real Player, MP3, and WAV formats.

Museum of the City of New York: Prints and Photographs Collection

http://www.mcny.org

The museum's exhibitions on New York history make excellent use of images. One noteworthy project, New York Before the War, provides access to photographs taken under the auspices of the Works Projects Administration's Federal Arts Project. Other valuable photographic exhibitions of historical interest are

Looking North: Upper Manhattan in Photographs, 1896–1939; Gotham Comes of Age: New York Through the Lens of the Byron Company, 1892–1942, and Berenice Abbott: Changing New York.

NASA Multimedia Gallery

http://www.nasa.gov/gallery/index.html

The National Aeronautics and Space Administration's multimedia gallery features a searchable archive of hundreds of thousands of still images. The gallery also provides access to NASA-related audio, video, and works of art.

National Archives Online Exhibit Hall

http://www.nara.gov/exhall/exhibits.html

The showpieces of the National Archives and Records Administration's site are online images of the Declaration of Independence, Constitution, Bill of Rights, and many other important historical documents. The site also features several excellent exhibitions of historical images: Picturing the Century, a photographic retrospective of the twentieth century; Powers of Persuasion, a collection of thirty-three World War II propaganda posters; and Portrait of Black Chicago, an exhibition of photographs of 1970s Chicago.

National Museum of Photography, Film and Television

http://www.nmpft.org.uk/home.asp

Provides an introduction to the museum's collections and selected images.

New York Public Library

http://www.nypl.org/research/chss/spe/art/photo/photo.html#online

The New York Public Library's Photography Collection provides online access to its exhibition Berenice Abbott: Changing New York, 1935–1938 and to two projects on Lewis Hine: Work Portraits, 1920–1939 and Construction of the Empire State Building, 1930–1931. The library's exhibition Small Town America: Stereoscopic Views from the Robert Dennis Collection presents digitized versions of 12,000 stereographic images from New York, New Jersey, and Connecticut from the 1850s to the 1910s.

Panoramic Photographs

http://www.nara.gov/exhall/americanimage/panorama/panoram1.html

An excellent selection of high-resolution panoramic photographs from the National Archives and Records Administration's Still Picture Branch. The photographs date from approximately 1864 to 1921 and include the wreck of the U.S.S. *Maine*, the San Francisco earthquake, World War I images, and many other subjects.

Princeton University: Seeley G. Mudd Manuscript Library

http://www.princeton.edu/~mudd/

Features recent exhibits from the Mudd Library including photographs and audiovisual items. Among recent exhibits are A Voice of Conscience: The Legacy of Adlai Stevenson, which includes video clips of interviews, speeches, and campaign commercials.

Royal Photographic Society

http://www.rps.org/index.html

The Royal Photographic Society's site offers an archive of recent exhibitions held at the society's Octagon Galleries in Bath. Of particular interest is Faces of the Century, an exhibition of 100 prints representing the last 100 years of British history.

The Samuel Putnam Avery Collection

http://www.nypl.org/research/chss/spe/art/print/collections/avery/ avery.htm.bak

Provides a selection of images from the collection formed by New York art dealer Samuel Putnam Avery and donated to the New York Public Library in 1900. The collection is made up of more than 17,000 etchings and lithographs from the late nineteenth century.

The Siege and Commune of Paris, 1870–1871

http://www.library.northwestern.edu/spec/siege/

The Charles Deering McCormick Library of Special Collections at Northwestern University has digitized more than 1,200 photographs and images from the Siege and Commune of Paris. Visitors can browse through categorized lists of images or use the site's online search feature.

Small Towns, Black Lives

http://www.blacktowns.org

Created by Wendel White, professor of art at Richard Stockton State College of New Jersey, this project presents documentary images of historically African-

American communities in southern New Jersey. The project includes contemporary and historical photographs, historical documents, and QuickTime video clips. White also uses panoramic images to give visitors a 360–degree view of selected communities and historic sites.

Smithsonian Institution

http://photo2.si.edu/

Offers numerous online exhibitions and a searchable database of images in the Smithsonian collections. A few of the projects of historical interest are: The Presidential Inaugural, Magic Lanterns, Magic Mirrors: A Centennial Salute to Cinema, and Reflections on the Wall: The Vietnam Veterans Memorial.

Temple of Liberty: Building the Capitol for a New Nation

http://lcweb.loc.gov/exhibits/us.capitol/s0.html

A Library of Congress exhibit on the history and meaning of the U.S. Capitol, including many maps, prints, architectural drawings, and photographs from the eighteenth to the twentieth century. Of particular interest is the discussion of visual symbols of the nation.

They Still Draw Pictures

http://orpheus-1.ucsd.edu/speccoll/tsdp/

An impressive collection of more than 600 drawings made during the Spanish Civil War by schoolchildren in Spain and in French refugee centers. Each drawing is accompanied by a caption identifying the artist by name, age, and location, as well as notes found on the front and back of the artwork. The images are from the Southworth Spanish Civil War Collection at the University of California, San Diego.

UCR/California Museum of Photography

http://www.cmp.ucr.edu/

An excellent site based on the museum's collection of historical and contemporary images. One of the site's strengths is a project drawn from the hundreds of thousands of stereographic images in the museum's Keystone Mast Collection. By using three-dimensional red/blue glasses, visitors to the site can see the images in a format that simulates the effect of a stereographic viewer. The site also features a searchable database of Ansel Adams photographs and galleries on a variety of photographic topics.

United Nations Photo

http://www.un.org/av/photo/

The United Nations Photo site provides a selection of some of the approximately 200,000 images in the United Nations Photo Library. The site's U.N. Pictorial History section includes a timeline of images from the League of Nations to the present.

The U.S. Civil War Center

http://www.cwc.lsu.edu/cwc/links/links3.htm#Images

This site provides links to many Civil War images including photographs, prints, paintings, and cartoons. The project is the work of the U.S. Civil War Center, a division of the Louisiana State University Libraries Special Collections.

Virtual Greenbelt

http://www.otal.umd.edu/~vg/

Created by the Department of American Studies at the University of Maryland, Virtual Greenbelt provides images, oral history interviews, and other sources pertaining to the New Deal-era planned suburban community of Greenbelt. Images range from planning and construction under the Roosevelt administration to recent community life.

Women Come to the Front

http://lcweb.loc.gov/exhibits/wcf/wcf0001.html

An excellent Library of Congress exhibit that focuses on women who served as journalists, photographers, and broadcasters in World War II. Includes photographs, posters, newspaper clippings, and introductory essays.

Frank Lloyd Wright: Designs for an American Landscape, 1922–1932

http://lcweb.loc.gov/exhibits/flw/flw.html

The online version of a 1996–1997 exhibit at the Library of Congress, this site integrates many of Wright's drawings into a helpful essay on his work from 1922 to 1932. David G. DeLong, professor of architecture at the University of Pennsylvania, served as guest curator. The project includes images of five hypothetical study models created for the exhibit on the basis of Wright's drawings.

Chapter 34

Resources for Teachers of History: K-12 and College

Stephen Kneeshaw

Metasites

Academic Info

http://www.academicinfo.net/table.html

Academic Info is a subject directory designed for college-level use that provides both annotated listings of Internet sites and gateways to specialized materials. The site offers metaindexes, general directories, and teaching materials. Especially useful is the section on U.S. history—Academic Info United States History—at http://www.academicinfo.net/histus.html, with an annotated directory of Internet resources in American history.

Index of Resources for Historians

http://www.ukans.edu/history/VL

Maintained by the University of Kansas and *Lehrstuhl für altere Deutsche* at the University of Regensburg in Germany, the Index of Resources for Historians is an exceptional metasite with more than 3,000 connections arranged alphabetically by subject and name. There are no annotations, but subject breakdowns make this an easily usable site. The list emphasizes college and university-level history, but some sites are geared specifically to K-12 audiences. Designed originally as a lynx site accessible by Telnet, with text rather than graphics, the index is effective with text-to-speech and text-to-Braille, making it friendly to the visually handicapped.

Lesson Plans and Resources for Social Studies Teachers

http://www.csun.edu/~hcedu013/index.html

This site, maintained by Marty Levine, Professor Emeritus of secondary education at California State University, Northridge, should be the first gateway accessed by elementary and secondary history teachers who want to sample the wealth of the World Wide Web. A clickable table of contents on the opening page leads to nine areas, such as Lesson Plans and Teaching Strategies, Other Social Studies Resources (including government and museum sites), Teaching Current Events, and Newsgroups and Mailing Lists. The lengthy lists of links are alphabetized and annotated for a quick reading of contents.

The Best Sites: Ten From the List

American Memory

http://rs6.loc.gov

The rich collections of the Library of Congress come to life in words and pictures in American Memory. This rapidly growing site, now with forty-two collections online, includes documents, maps, photos and prints, motion pictures, and sound recordings. An easy-to-use search engine and a list of entries alphabetized by both keywords and titles provide entry to topics ranging from baseball cards, Civil War photographs, and the conservation movement (one of my favorites) to presidents and First Ladies, the Spanish-American War, and Voices from the Dust Bowl.

The Digital Classroom

http://www.nara.gov/education

The Digital Classroom, from the National Archives and Records Administration (NARA), encourages teachers at all levels to use documents in their classrooms. This is NARA's complement to American Memory from the Library of Congress. The site delivers documentary materials from the National Archives, lesson plans, and suggested methods for teaching with primary documents. The topics already available online span a wide range, from the *Amistad* case to the Zimmerman Telegram to FDR's court-packing scheme. NARA also provides a reproducible set of document analysis worksheets for written documents, photographs, cartoons, posters, maps, artifacts, sound recordings, and motion pictures that history teachers will find easy to use and attractive for their students.

Digital Librarian: A Librarian's Choice of the Best of the Web: History

http://www.digital-librarian.com/history.htm

Self-described as "a librarian's choice of the best of the Web" (and run by Margaret Vail Anderson of Cortland, New York), the Digital Librarian covers virtually every academic discipline, many of which are linked to the History page. This site provides an entry point for such diverse topics as the ancient world, genealogy, Judaica, Latin America, the Middle East, and women's resources. For elementary teachers, there are useful connections to children's literature and resources. Lists are alphabetized and annotated briefly, but there is no internal search mechanism.

History Matters

http://historymatters.gmu.edu

Designed for secondary and college teachers in American history, History Matters combines the efforts of the American Social History Project at the City University of New York and the Center for History and New Media at George Mason University. With an express "focus on the lives of ordinary Americans," this site offers teaching materials, first-person documents (from the Knights of Labor to Sacco and Vanzetti), interactive exercises, electronic essays, "syllabus central," and threaded discussions on teaching history. The current focus is on the years from 1876 to 1946, but eventually the site will grow to cover all of the American experience. A keyword search option allows users easy access to materials in the site.

History/Social Studies Web Site for K-12 Teachers

http://www.execpc.com/~dboals/boals.html

As the name suggests, this site focuses on the needs of K-12 classroom teachers in locating and using the resources of the Internet. A clickable table opens a wide range of topics, including K-12 resources, archaeology, genealogy, geography, American history, and non-Western history. This site provides a gateway to some 600 locations, including lesson, commercial, project, and general sites. The one downside is that the lists are not alphabetized, although they do provide brief but useful annotations.

Learning Space: Social Studies for Washington Students and Teachers

http://www.learningspace.org/socialstudies

The Learning Space provides many links specific to a single state, here Washington state, but the site has great value for all history teachers, with links for history, geography, museums, Holocaust resources, K-12 education, and much more. Each connection provides lengthy alphabetized and annotated lists of Web sites for history teachers at all levels everywhere.

Kathy Schrock's Guide for Educators

http://school.discovery.com/schrockguide

Kathy Schrock, identified as "the Administrator for Technology" for a school district on Cape Cod, Massachusetts," created and maintains one of the best-known Web sites for educators. This "categorized list of sites on the Internet," which Schrock updates daily, covers the whole span of academic subjects. She promises that users will get "search strategies, evaluation of Internet information, copyright issues, and use of the computer as a tool to support instruction." Clicking the link for history and social studies opens connections to American and world history, general history, and social studies sites.

SCORE History–Social Science

http://score.rims.k12.ca.us

This site, designed primarily for K-12 teachers, comes from Schools of California Online Resources for Education (SCORE). Links include resources and lessons by grade level, resources by theme and topic, virtual projects, and field trips. Although one objective of SCORE is to link WWW resources to California's curriculum, this site will be useful to teachers in all states. All of the materials have been evaluated and rated for accuracy, grade appropriateness, depth, and variety on a 1–5 scale by a team of educators.

Studying and Teaching History

http://www.tntech.edu/www/acad/hist/study.html

This fine Web site from Tennessee Technological University aims to create a database of syllabi and suggestions for history teachers and students. Currently available are study guides for history classes from several universities, reference works, guides for research and writing, and links for oral history, maps and audiovisual materials, portfolios, living history and reenactments, studying and teaching history at K-12 levels, and graduate schools.

Teaching History: A Journal of Methods

http://www.emporia.edu/socsci/journal/main.htm

Designed and maintained at Emporia State University by the publication team for the journal *Teaching History*, this site reflects the main objective of the journal, to provide teachers at all academic levels "with the best and newest teaching ideas for their classrooms." Besides information on the journal, this site provides links to a rich list of resources in ten history-related categories, from American and world history to genealogy, maps, writing and editing, and teaching resources.

Resources for History Teachers

Agents of Social Change

http://www.smith.edu/libraries/ssc/curriculum/index.html

Working with a grant from the National Endowment for the Humanities, Smith College processed eight manuscript collections that centered around the major theme of "agents for social change." Reaching "beyond the traditional community of archival users—beyond senior scholars, graduate students and undergraduates," Smith designed lesson plans for middle and high school students, on such diverse topics as the fight for civil rights, for urban reform, and for women's rights from the 1930s into the 1980s.

AskERIC Virtual Library

http://ericir.syr.edu/virtual

The AskERIC Virtual Library archives hundreds of lesson plans in a variety of disciplines, informational guides on topics of interest to K-12 educators, links to the searchable databases of ERIC Digests (brief reports on educational issues), information on using the Internet in the classroom, and links to other

Internet sites. Under both American and world history, AskERIC offers descriptive and adaptable lesson plans for grades 1–12. Especially interesting is the section titled "Crossroads: A K-16 American History Curriculum," accessible via http://askeric.org/cgi-bin/printlessons.cgi/Virtual/Lessons/Social_Studies/US_History/crossroads.html, which includes specific materials for elementary, middle school, high school, and postsecondary curricula.

Association for Academic Computing: History Links

http://odur.let.rug.nl/ahc/histlink

This Web site delivers an eclectic mix of links to many countries (alphabetical by continents), from general historical sites and computing in the humanities to e-magazines. For example, in the list of sites in the United States, you can link to such disparate individuals as Anne Frank, Emma Goldman, and John Muir. Ironically, this site, based in the Netherlands, offers one of the best collections of materials on American presidents on the Web, including full texts of inaugural addresses and State of the Union speeches (http://odur.let.rug.nl/usa/P).

The Avalon Project: Documents in Law, History, and Diplomacy

http://www.yale.edu/lawweb/avalon/avalon.htm

History teachers frequently use documents to enrich lesson plans and illustrate key ideas. The Avalon Project from the Yale Law School provides connections to a wealth of documents from before the eighteenth century through the twentieth century. An alphabetic author and title list and a search engine make this user-friendly Web site accessible for all grade levels.

Awesome Library: K-12 Education Directory

http://www.neat-schoolhouse.org/awesome.html

Awesome Library "for teachers, students, and parents" gives users links to all teaching fields. Under the social studies link, you can click into history and lesson plans or connect to more specialized history-related fields such as current events, ecology, holidays, and multicultural resources.

Biographical Dictionary

http://www.s9.com/biography

Biographical Dictionary offers biographies of more than 25,000 men and women "who have shaped our world from ancient times to the present." Users can search the list by names, birth or death years, professions, literary and artistic works, and other keywords, making these men and women easily accessible for students and teachers.

Biography.Com

http://www.biography.com

This Web site is the gateway to the popular Arts and Entertainment television series *Biography*. The Biography.com Store currently stocks more than 1,500 videos that have run on the cable network. For teachers who use videos to supplement class presentations, this site will be quite valuable.

Center for the Liberal Arts at the University of Virginia

http://www.virginia.edu/cla/home.html

This Web site is dedicated to "opportunities for continuing content education for K-12 educators," although many of the materials are appropriate for college and university levels as well. Clicking on the History link takes the user to a wonderful collection of Web sites on American history, current events, geography, government, world history, and Virginia state history, which, of course, is rich in early American and Civil War–related topics.

Chronicle of Higher Education

http://chronicle.com

This Web site provides online access to some of the materials delivered in print each week by the *Chronicle of Higher Education*. The clickable links include topics such as today's news in education, information technology, government and politics, grants, and job announcements.

CIT Infobits

http://www.unc.edu/cit/infobits/index.html

CIT Infobits is an electronic service of the University of North Carolina at Chapel Hill that provides brief notes on information technology and instructional technology sources. Besides the summaries, the site gives hot links to Web resources mentioned in the summaries and brief book notes. Subscriptions to CIT Infobits are free.

Clip Art Resources for History

http://library.hilton.kzn.school.za/history/history.htm

For teachers who use clip art and art images to enrich their teaching materials—Web pages, lectures, handouts, overhead projections, and such—this site will be extremely valuable. Maintained by Hilton College in South Africa, it provides a clickable map to access clip art image search engines, directories of clip art sites, and clip art sites. There is also an alphabetized category list of clip art and icons.

CLNET History Resources

http://latino.sscnet.ucla.edu/research/history.html

This Web site from UCLA provides a gateway (with annotations) to more than thirty sites on Chicano/a and Latino/a history. The list of diverse resources links the user to topics such as historical documents, Hispanics in the American Revolution, the Chicano movement in history, and the Mexican-American civil rights movement in the United States.

Core Documents of U.S. Democracy

http://www.access.gpo.gov/su_docs/locators/coredocs/index.html

This Web site from the Government Printing Office delivers more than the title suggests. Beyond such "core documents" as the Declaration of Independence, Constitution, Bill of Rights, and Supreme Court decisions, users get a statistical abstract of the United States, a weekly compilation of presidential documents, and more. This site will be useful for history teachers who bring current events into their classrooms.

Ditto.Com

http://www.ditto.com

For teachers wanting to liven up PowerPoint and lecture presentations by bringing more visuals into their classrooms, Ditto.com provides "a visual mechanism to search the web using pictures instead of texts." Ditto.com's search engine is fast and user-friendly, and it provides so many suggestions that any teacher will be satisfied with the results—but perhaps overwhelmed with the number of choices. For example, a search on the word "Vietnam" brought up more than 3,000 hits (i.e., pictures to use); a search on "Yellowstone" yielded more than 800; and "Civil War" provided some 4,300 images. Descriptive information about each picture and source information to assure proper citations are provided.

Documents for the Study of American History

http://history.cc.ukans.edu/carrie/docs/amdocs_index.html

This Web site, managed at the University of Kansas, provides users with one of the richest lists of documents on American history available on the Web. Running from the fifteenth century through the twentieth century, the documents range from Columbus's letter to Ferdinand and Isabella in 1494 to Bill Clinton's inaugural address in 1993. The list is strongest in the eighteenth and twentieth centuries, but the whole of U.S. history gets good coverage. This kind of Web site removes the need to buy documents collections for the classroom when such good materials are available at a click.

Edsitement

http://www.edsitement.neh.fed.us

Edsitement provides subject-based connections to top humanities sites in four different fields: literature and language arts, foreign languages, art and culture, and history and social studies. All of the sites have been "peer-reviewed for outstanding intellectual quality, superior design, and educational impact." The materials are set into grade-specific categories from K-2 through 9–12, with many of the 9–12 materials suitable for college and university classrooms. A clickable map provides quick jumps to lesson plans, at-home activities for students, and "additional learning activities." In history and social studies, Web sites run the gamut from African-American women to photographs from the Depression.

Folkmusic.org

http://www.folkmusic.org

Folkmusic.org links users to "the human resources in the folk and acoustic music community." For teachers who want to include music resources in their history curriculum, this site includes biographies, discographies, pictures, lyrics, and sound bytes.

FREE: Federal Resources for Educational Excellence

http://www.ed.gov/free/index.html

FREE is the result of a "partnership" of teachers and federal agencies to develop Internet-based learning modules and learning communities. The agencies include the CIA, FBI, National Park Service, Library of Congress (American Memory), NARA (Digital Classroom), and White House. A "site map" provides connections to various topic areas, including the social studies. Topics are arranged alphabetically with the sponsoring agency identified. There are no annotations, but the descriptive titles give good direction for users.

Great American Speeches

http://www.pbs.org/greatspeeches

This fine PBS-created Web site provides links to speech archives, pop-up trivia (good stuff for the MTV generation of students), ideas for teachers, and more. The speech collection starts before 1900 (e.g., Booker T. Washington at the Atlanta Exposition and William Jennings Bryan's "cross of gold") and runs through the twentieth century, finishing with Bill Clinton and Elie Weisel (on "the perils of indifference"). Full texts of the speeches appear in pop-up boxes, and for some there is an audio component.

Helping Your Child Learn History

http://www.ed.gov/pubs/parents/History/

This Web site, aimed primarily at parents, offers suggestions to bring history to life for children aged four through eleven. The suggestions, of course, are equally pertinent for lower-grade teachers. Topics include History Education Begins at Home (e.g., "history is a habit"), History as Story (e.g., "cooking up history"), and History as Time (e.g., "put time in a bottle").

The Heritage Education Network (THEN)

http://www.mtsu.edu/~then

Many students who turn away from history turn on to the discipline when teachers introduce family and local history into the classroom. THEN—The Heritage Education Network—provides a nice mix of resources for teachers who want to make "nearby history" part of their curriculum. As the Web site notes, "Heritage Education is the use of local cultural and historic resources for teaching the required curricula of grades K-12." In fact, it can work at the college level too. Operated through Middle Tennessee State University, THEN spotlights such diverse resources as family history, historic buildings and structures, cemeteries, farms, and photographs. THEN also provides a list of contacts in each of the fifty states, including local historical societies, state agencies, and others who can assist in program development.

The History Channel

http://www.historychannel.com

This Web site provides an easy gateway into the video materials of the cable network, The History Channel. The History Store is the place to order videos, but this is more than just a commercial site. Traveler introduces historic sites and Great Speeches provides clips of "the words that changed the world," from such diverse characters as Franklin D. Roosevelt, Malcolm X, Martin Luther King, Jr., Babe Ruth, and Casey Stengel. Classroom materials are available online to accompany videos, including vocabulary terms, discussion questions, and extended activities.

History Departments Around the World

http://chnm.gmu.edu/history/depts

Maintained by George Mason University, this site provides an index of links to all history departments around the world that have an online presence. An in-site search engine allows a search for departments or a searcher can browse the entire list.

History Happens

http://www.ushistory.com

History Happens is a commercial site that advertises and sells music video materials for the classroom. Self-described as mirroring the old ABC television series *School House Rocks*, History Happens aims at a primary audience of teachers and parents of children aged from eight to fifteen.

The History Net: Where History Lives on the Web

http://www.thehistorynet.com

The History Net provides links to published articles from journals such as *Civil War Times*, *Military History*, *Vietnam*, *British Heritage*, *Wild West*, and *American History*. For an interesting sidebar, the History Net also provides a link to materials on "alternate history," that is, the history that might have been if events had run differently.

History on Public Television

http://www.current.org/history/index.html

Drawing from *Current*, a biweekly newspaper on public television and radio in the United States, this site provides a guide to history programming on PBS, access to stories from back issues of *Current*, and links to various media sites. Teachers will find useful materials to supplement classroom videos that aired originally on PBS.

The History Place

http://www.historyplace.com/index.html

The History Place provides a variety of links that will be useful to history teachers, especially at the secondary level. At this point, the site emphasizes American history, but there are some strong sections on Hitler and the Holocaust, with an annotated bibliography on Hitler's Germany. Other European topics are listed "in progress." Users will find timelines (e.g., the Civil War through quotations), photographs, and "points of view," which are reviews and reflections from established writers and historians. The site also offers an annotated list of Great History Videos.

H-Net Teaching

http://www.h-net.msu.edu/teaching

H-Net Teaching provides a gateway to an extensive number of sites on teaching maintained by the H-Net system (Humanities and Social Science Online) out of Michigan State University. Each of these sites includes edited, threaded discussions on topics of interest to list subscribers and archives, complete with search mechanisms, on previous discussions. H-Net Teaching includes the following:

> EDTECH, on educational technology
>
> H-AfrTeach, teaching African history and studies
>
> H-High-S, teaching high school history and social studies (an indispensable site for secondary history teachers)
>
> H-HistoryDay, a forum for high school teachers "to share methodological and thematic ideas, approaches, and problems" related to National History Day
>
> H-Mmedia, high-tech teaching, multimedia, CD-ROM
>
> H-Survey, teaching United States history survey courses (a must-see site for college-level American survey teachers)
>
> H-Teach, teaching history at all levels (my personal favorite of the H-Net sites), with enlightening discussions on a wide range of important topics for history teachers
>
> H-W-Civ, teaching Western Civilization courses (a companion to H-Survey).

IBM K-12 Education

http://www.solutions.ibm.com/k12

This site, designed and maintained by IBM, does much more than promote the products designed and sold by "Big Blue." Users will find links to various social studies topics such as American history, baseball, holidays, inventions, maps and mapping, Native Americans, and multicultural education, as well as teacher resources.

InforMNs: Internet for Minnesota Schools

http://informns.k12.mn.us

Here is another site designed with the needs of teachers in a specific state—here Minnesota—as the primary focus. But as with the Learning Space (Washington) and SCORE (California) sites (described above), InforMNs delivers information and links useful to a much wider audience. The site also allows quick jumps to search engines, metasearch engines, subject directories, and topical directories through a link to TIES (Technology and Information Educational Services).

Internet Archive of Texts and Documents

http://history.hanover.edu/texts.html

This internet archive from Hanover College delivers a variety of primary texts and documents on United States and European history, all from the public domain. The site promises additions for Latin America, Africa, the Middle East, and Asia. Some of the documents come through the Hanover Historical Texts Project; others arrive via links to other repositories.

Internet for Educators: History and Social Studies Resources

http://www.speakeasy.org/educators/history.html

This site provides a large database of links for K-12 teachers in history, with a clickable chart that allows easy moves into other disciplines that have value in the history classroom, such as arts resources and diversity resources. The list of sites now available in history is small but useful.

Internet Modern History Sourcebook: History and Music

http://www.fordham.edu/halsall/mod/modmusic.html

As this site notes, it does not provide a history of music. Instead, this section of the Internet Modern History Sourcebook links the user to musical texts and sounds (lyrics and/or music) that illustrate selected topics, such as nineteenth-century nationalism and imperialism, and periods, from the Reformation to in modern history. The United States gets some play, but most materials apply to European history. Some songs get "streamed" over the Internet through RealAudio.

K-12 History on the Internet Resource Guide

http://www.xs4all.nl/~swanson/history

This K-12 site, run by two teachers from the Netherlands, provides a series of valuable links for history teachers. Clicking on "general information sources," users enter into a section called "charting the unknown," where a variety of navigational tools and information resources introduce connections to history-related sites around the world.

The Library in the Sky

http://www.nwrel.org/sky/index.asp

Run by the Northwest Regional Educational Laboratory in Portland, Oregon, the Library in the Sky offers more than 1,400 links to educational resources in every field of study for teachers, librarians, students, and parents. History and the social studies get enough attention to make this a useful site for the K-12 community.

Multimedia/Hypermedia

http://eng.hss.cmu.edu/multimedia

This site offers a sizable collection of media and hypertext materials through the English Server at Carnegie Mellon University and other servers across the Internet. Includes ASCII art, audio, public-domain clip art, hypermedia, maps, soundtracks, and videos (using QuickTime technology).

National Center for History in the Schools

http://www.sscnet.ucla.edu/nchs

The National Center for History in the Schools, located at UCLA, publishes online the National Standards for United States History, K-4 and 5–12, the National Standards for World History, and the Revised Standards for History. In addition, "Bring History Alive" introduces sourcebooks for U.S. and world history, grades 5–12, with more than 1,200 activities arranged by grade level and keyed to the revised standards.

National Portrait Gallery

http://www.npg.si.edu

The National Portrait Gallery, a branch of the Smithsonian Institution, provides online access to many of its collections that teachers and students can tap for PowerPoint and lecture presentations. This will be the only way to get to National Portrait Gallery collections during a four-year renovation (from January 2000 to fall 2004). The Web site includes twenty virtual past exhibitions and the permanent collection of the NPG, including the Hall of Presidents. For some of the special exhibitions, teacher resources packets are available.

ParkNet: National Park Service

http://www.nps.gov

The National Park Service, through ParkNet, delivers one of the best Web sites maintained by a U.S. government agency. Links to the Past sends users to "tools for teaching" (archaeology, historic landscapes, structures, and more) and "teaching with historic places" (which gets a full description below). Visit Your Parks opens links for all NPS properties. Some of these—Olympic National Park in Washington state, for example—have expanded Web sites that provide attractive resources, such as lesson plans, that teachers can pick up and use with ease.

Presidential Letters: U.S. Postal Service

http://www.usps.gov/letters/volume2/pres-main.html

Organized by the U.S. Postal Service, this site provides a series of letters that show the "hopes, dreams, [and] passions" of America's executive leaders. With letters from fifteen different presidents, from Washington to Reagan, the purpose is "to humanize the men we have chosen to lead our nation." These letters will provide nice supplements for lectures, class projects, and research assignments, especially for secondary level courses.

Project Gutenberg

http://www.promo.net/pg

One of the best-known early WWW sites, Project Gutenberg brings hundreds of classic works in world history and literature into the classroom as electronic texts at the click of a mouse. An in-site search engine allow users to find e-texts by checking alphabetical lists of authors and titles, which can be downloaded via FTP or the Web.

Smithsonian Institution Social Studies Lesson Plans

http://educate.si.edu

The Smithsonian Center for Education and Museum Studies provides detailed information on "Field Trips: Learning and Resources" that are available through the Smithsonian Institution. From the main page a user can jump quickly to lesson plans, a resources bank, and an internal search engine, making the site easy to navigate. The site provides information on a variety of disciplines, including social studies, arts, language arts, and sciences.

Social Studies Resources

http://www.kent.wednet.edu/curriculum/soc_studies/soc_studies.html

This Web site from the Kent School District in Washington state provides a variety of lesson plans in all disciplines, including social studies, where teachers can make connections in history, state history, family history, and more. The lesson plans are broken into grade levels K-3, 4–6, junior high, and high school; the resources area—with outline lessons, project ideas, and minilessons—includes separate sections for every grade level K-12.

Social Studies School Service

http://catalog.socialstudies.com

This commercial site advertises the wares of the Social Studies School Service in Culver City, California. Here users can bypass printed catalogs to locate and order CD-ROMs, laserdisks, maps and globes, videos, simulations, reproducibles, and books. Different mechanisms allow searches by grade level, by reading level, or by author, title, and subject.

Teachers Helping Teachers

http://www.pacificnet.net/~mandel/index.html

Teachers Helping Teachers opened in 1995 under the direction of Scott Mandel, a middle school English and history teacher in Pacoima, California, who updates the site each week during the school year. Now with more than one million hits—testimony to its value for teachers—the site provides lesson plans (all submitted by teachers and easily adaptable to a variety of teaching situations) for K-12 grade levels, a teacher chat room, and links to educational resources on the Web, alphabetized by subject.

Teaching with Historic Places

http://www.cr.nps.gov/nr/twhp/index.htm

This site, from the National Park Service, focuses on the teaching opportunities presented by properties on the National Register of Historic Places. The purpose is to "turn students into historians as they study primary sources, historical and contemporary photographs and maps, and other documents, and then search for the history around them in their own communities." The NPS provides lesson plans, education kits, and workshops to facilitate the integration of historic places into the curriculum. In a nice invitation to get teachers to add new materials, the NPS also provides an Author's Packet to "help [teachers] create materials to convey the meaning and importance of these places to students from upper elementary to high school."

Teachnet.Com

http://www.teachnet.com

Opening with the "brainstorm of the day"—actually several ideas introduced in one paragraph each—this attractive site packages a mix of materials and ideas that teachers will enjoy and use. Some of the more useful links are "lesson ideas," "teacher-2–teacher," and "how-to" ideas that include everything from classroom decor to classroom management.

THOMAS

http://thomas.loc.gov/#thomas

THOMAS bills itself as "legislative information on the Internet." Maintained by the Library of Congress, THOMAS follows the work of the United States Senate and House of Representatives, providing summaries, status reports, and full texts of congressional legislation. The site also provides directories for members of Congress, making it a critical tool for teachers who use current events in their classrooms.

UCLA's Social Sciences Division

http://www.sscnet.ucla.edu

The UCLA Social Sciences Web site, is a fine starting point for social studies links, contains connections to social science departments, institutes, and resources at UCLA. By working through several layers in some program descriptions, notably the American Indian Studies Center, users will get to a series of useful links to other WWW resources.

United States Department of Education

http://www.ed.gov

This official home page of the U.S. Department of Education contains federal educational initiatives, policy documents, and links to related sites, e.g., FREE (described above).

Virtual Field Trips Site

http://www.field-guides.com/

This Web site provides a way for teachers to take their students around the world without leaving their classroom. They can start with field trips to Deserts, Fierce Creatures, Hurricanes, Natural Wonders of the World, Oceans, Salt Marshes, Sharks, Tornadoes, and Volcanoes. The site also provides links, using a second Web window, to other field trips, including Antarctica Field Trip, Dinosaurs, Endangered Species, Insects and Minibeasts, Iditarod, Rainforest, Temperate Forest Biomes, and Wildfires. At the individual field trip sites, users will find terms to learn, concepts, and teacher's resources.

Web66: A K-12 World Wide Web Project

http://web66.coled.umn.edu

For most teachers, the greatest value of Web66 is its ability to link users to most American elementary and secondary schools with a Web presence, encouraging all kinds of exchanges between teachers across cities, states, and country. Web66 also provides access to Mustang, a "Web cruising vehicle" that helps teachers "cruise" rather than "surf" the Web. And the site provides links to many Web resources in history and the social studies that make it particularly suited to the needs of history teachers.

Words and Deeds in American History

http://lcweb2.loc.gov/ammem/mcchtml/corhome.html

This site from the Library of Congress, actually an offshoot of American Memory (described above), gives a condensed collection of manuscript materials (some ninety "representative documents") that can enrich the teaching and study of history. The site provides a detailed description of each document and links to related resources in the library's collection.

Chapter 35

Discussion Lists

Keith C. Trinkle

Discussion lists are one of the most beneficial and useful resources on the Internet. Many organizations and associations now sponsor lists for their fields, and the number of lists is climbing rapidly. There is also a large consortium sponsoring history discussion lists called H-Net—the Humanities Online Initiative. H-Net is funded by the National Endowment for the Humanities and Michigan State University. It supports more than one hundred discussion groups covering a wide range of historical topics. The list below outlines the major discussion lists, but there also are hundreds of smaller, less active groups that are not listed. The best online guide to these lists is the Directory of Scholarly and Professional E-Conferences at http://www.kovacs.com/.

As mentioned in Chapter 1, you must subscribe to a discussion list in order to participate. To subscribe, it is necessary to send what is called a "subscribe message" to the address listed below. A subscribe message simply contains the word "Subscribe," the name of the discussion list, and your full name. For example,

Subscribe H-France Michael Garrison

Chapter 1 describes the process of subscribing to discussion lists in more detail. The following information gives the addresses of the listservers to which subscription messages should be sent.

H-Net Lists

A current directory of available lists is provided at http://www2.h-net.msu.edu/. For the following lists, send a subscribe message to

listserv@h-net.msu.edu

APSA-CIVED, civic education for the next century
EDTECH, educational technology
HABSBURG, culture and history of the Central European Habsburg monarchy and its successor states, 1500–present
H-AfrArts, African expressive culture
H-AfResearch, primary sources in African studies
H-Africa, African history and culture
H-AfrLitCine, teaching and study of African literature and cinema
H-Afro-Am, African-American Studies
H-AfrPol, current African Politics
H-AfrTeach, teaching African history and studies
H-AHC, Association for History and Computing
H-Albion, British and Irish history
H-AmIndian, American Indian history and culture
H-AmRel, American religious history
H-Amstdy, American studies
H-Announce, H-Net academic announcements
H-Antisemitism, antisemitism
H-ANZAU, history of Aotearoa / New Zealand and Australia
H-Appalachia, Appalachian history and studies
H-Arete, sports literature
H-ArtHist, art history
H-Asia, Asian studies and history
H-Atlantic, H-Net Network on Atlantic history
H-Bahai, culture and history of the Baha'i Faith
H-Business, history of business and commerce
H-California, history and culture of California
H-Canada, Canadian history and studies
H-Caribbean, H-Net network on Caribbean studies
H-Catholic, history and culture of Catholicism
H-Cervantes, life, times, and work of Cervantes
H-Childhood, history of childhood and youth

H-CivWar, U.S. Civil War history
H-CLC, computers and literary studies
H-Communal-Societies, study and preservation of historic communal sites
H-DC, Washington, D.C. history and culture
H-Demog, demographic history
H-Diplo, diplomatic history and international affairs
H-Disability, H-Net network on history of disability
H-Dritter-Sektor, European nonprofit sector
H-Education, history of education
H-Environment, environmental history
H-Ethnic, ethnic and immigration history
H-Film, cinema history; uses of the media
H-Francais, *H-Net liste des Clionautes, sur l'histoire et la géographie en France*
H-France, French history and culture
H-Frauen-L, women and gender in early modern Europe
H-GAGCS, German-American and German-Canadian studies
H-Genocide, history, theory and analysis of genocide
H-German, German history
H-Grad, for graduate students only
H-High-S, teaching high school history and social studies
H-HistBibl, study and practice of history librarianship
H-HistMajor, undergraduate history major
H-History-and-Theory, philosophy of history
H-HistoryDay, National History Day forum
H-Holocaust, Holocaust studies
H-Ideas, intellectual history
H-Indiana, Indiana history and culture
H-Islamart, history of Islamic art and architecture
H-Italy, Italian history and culture
H-ItAm, Italian-American history and culture
H-Japan, Japanese history and culture
H-Judaic, Judaica, Jewish history
H-Labor, Labor history
H-LatAm, Latin American history
H-Law, legal and constitutional history
H-Levant, history and culture of the Eastern Mediterranean (from ca. 1500)
H-LIS, history of library and information science
H-Local, state and local history; museums
H-Mac, history and Macintosh society
H-Maryland, Maryland history and culture
H-Michigan, history and culture of Michigan
H-Mideast-Medieval, Islamic lands of the Medieval period

H-Minerva, women in war and women and the military
H-Mmedia, high-tech teaching, multimedia, CD-ROM
H-MusTxt, musico-textual studies
H-NCC, National Coordinating Committee for the Promotion of History
H-NewMexico, culture and history of New Mexico
H-NEXA, The Science-Humanities Convergence Forum
H-Nilas, nature in legend and story
H-Ohio, history and culture of the state of Ohio
H-OIEAHC, colonial and early American history
H-Oralhist, studies related to oral history
H-PCAACA, Popular Culture Association and the American Culture Association
H-Pol, United States political history
H-Polmeth, H-NET/APSA list for political methodology
H-Psychohistory, research, theory, and teaching in psychohistory
H-Public, public history
H-Quilts, quilting research and documentation
H-Radhist, history, theory, politics from a radical perspective
H-Review, H-Net book reviews (reviews only, no discussion)
H-Rhetor, history of rhetoric and communications
H-Rural, rural and agricultural history
H-Russia, Russian history
H-SAE, Society for the Anthropology of Europe
H-Safrica, South African history
H-SAWH, women and gender in the U.S. South
H-Scholar, independent scholars and scholarship
H-Sci-Med-Tech, history of science, medicine, and technology
H-SEASIA, South East Asia
H-SHEAR, early American Republic
H-SHGAPE, Society for Historians of the Gilded Age and the Progressive Era
H-Skand, Scandinavian history
H-South, history of the United States South
H-Soz-u-Kult, *Methoden, Theorie, und Ergebnisse neuerer Sozial- und Kulturgeschichte*
H-State, history of the welfare state, "putting the state back in."
H-Survey, teaching united states history survey courses
H-Teach, teaching college history
H-Teachpol, teaching political science (postsecondary)
H-Tennessee, Tennessee history and culture
H-Texas, history and culture of Texas
H-Turk, Turkish studies
H-UCLEA, labor studies
H-Urban, urban history

H-USA, international study of the U.S.A.
H-US-Japan, U.S.-Japan relations
H-US1918–45, American history and culture, 1918–1945
H-War, military history
H-W-Civ, teaching Western Civilization courses
H-West, history and culture of the North American West and frontiers
H-West-Africa, West African history and culture
H-Women, women's history
H-World, world history
Jhistory, list for discussion of history of journalism and mass communication
PSRT-L, H-Net/APSA political science teaching and research

For H-Pol, send a subscribe message to listserv@ksuvm.ksu.edu
H-Pol, United States political history

For EH.Eastbloc, go to http://eh.net/lists/subscribe.php?l=eastbloc
EH.Eastbloc, economic history of Eastern Europe

For EH.NEWS, go to http://eh.net/lists/subscribe.php?l=news
EH.News, economic history news, announcements

For EH.Res, go to http://eh.net/lists/subscribe.php?l=res
EH.Res, economic history research ideas

For EH.Teach, go to http://eh.net/lists/subscribe.php?l=teach
EH.Teach, teaching economic history

For HES, send a subscribe message to lists@eh.net
HES, history of economics/economic thought, announcements, discussion

For H-Mexico, go to http://www2.h-net.msu.edu/lists/subscribe.cgi?list=H-Mexico
H-Mexico, Mexican history and mexican studies

For LPBR-L, send a subscribe message to listserv@unt.edu
LPBR-L, law and politics book review (reviews only, no discussion)

For OZNZ.Society, send a subscribe message to lists@eh.net
OZNZ.Society, Australia and New Zealand economic history research, announcements

Other Discussion Lists

AERA-F, educational history and historiography
Send a "subscribe AERA-F" message to listserv@lists.asu.edu

AEROSP-L, aeronautical and aerospace history
Send a "subscribe AEROSP-L" message to listserv@sivm.si.edu

AMERCATH, history of American Catholicism
Send a "subscribe AMERCATH" message to listserv@lsv.uky.edu

ANCIEN-L, ancient history
Send a "subscribe ANCIEN-L" message to listserv@listserv.louisville.edu

ASTR-L, theater history
Send a "subscribe ASTR-L" message to listserv@postoffice.cso.uiuc.edu

AZTLAN, pre-Columbian history
Send a "scripe AZTLAN" message to listserv@listserv.louisville.edu

C18–L, eighteenth-century interdisciplinary studies
Send a "subscribe C18–L" message to listserv@lists.psu.edu

CHEIRON, Society for the History of the Social and Behavioral Sciences
Send a "subscribe CHEIRON" message to listserv@yorku.ca

EARLYSCIENCE-L, History of Science Society, Early Science Interest Group
Send a "subscribe EARLYSCIENCE-L" message to listserv@listserv.vt.edu

ELIAS-I, figurational studies in social science, history and psychology
Send a "subscribe ELIAS-I" message to listserv@nic.surfnet.nl

ETHNOHIS, ethnology and history
Send a "subscribe ETHNOHIS" message to listserv@nic.surfnet.nl

HASTRO-L, history of astronomy
Send a "subscribe HASTRO-L" message to listserv@wvnvm.wvnet.edu

HISLAW-L, legal history
Send a "subscribe HISLAW-L" message to listserv@listserv.louisville.edu

HISTORY-OF-GEOG, history of geography and geographical thought
Send a "subscribe HISTORY-OF-GEOG" message to listserv@lsv.uky.edu

HOPOS-L, history of the philosophy of science
Send a "subscribe HOPOS-L" message to listserv@listserv.nd.edu

HPSST-L, history and philosophy of science and science teaching
Send a "subscribe HPSST-L" message to listserv@post.queensu.ca

HTECH-L, history of technology
Send a "subscribe HTECH-L" message to listserv@sivm.si.edu

INDIAN-ROOTS-L, Native American history and genealogy discussion
Send a "subscribe INDIAN-ROOTS-L" message to listserv@listserv.indiana.edu

ISLAM-L, history of Islam
Send a "subscribe ISLAM-L" message to listserv@listserv.louisville.edu

KYROOTS, Kentucky genealogy and history discussions
Send a "subscribe KYROOTS" message to Listserv@lsv.uky.edu

MEDART-L, medieval art history
Send a "subscribe MEDART-L" message to listserv@listserv.utoronto.ca

MEH, media history
Send a "subscribe MEH" message to listserv@frodo.carfax.co.uk

MENA-H, history of the Middle East and North Africa
Send a "subscribe MENA-H" message to listserv@listserv.louisville.edu

NORTHEAST-ROOTS, genealogy and history in the New England area
Send a "subscribe NORTHEAST-ROOTS" message to listserv@listserv.indiana.edu

PHILOFHI, philosophy of history
Send a "subscribe PHILOFHI-L" message to listserv@yorku.ca

PSYHX, psychology history archive
Send a "subscribe PSYHX" message to listserv@maelstrom.stjohns.edu

PUBLHIST, public history
Send a "subscribe PUBLHIST" message to listserv@listserv.iupui.edu

RENAIS-L, Renaissance history
Send a "subscribe RENAIS-L" message to listserv@listserv.louisville.edu

RUSHIST, Russia History
Send a "subscribe SAH-L" message to listserv@VM.USC.EDU

SHARP-L, Society for the History of Authorship, Reading and Publishing
Send a "subscribe SHARP-L" message to listserv@listserv.indiana.edu

SISTER-L, history of female Catholic religious
Send a "subscribe SISTER-L" message to listserv@listserv.syr.edu

SLAVERY, history of slavery
Send a "subscribe SLAVERY" message to listserv@listserv.uh.edu

SOCHIS-L, social history of medicine
Send a "subscribe SOCHIS-L" message to listserv@webber.oup.co.uk

SPORTHIST, sports history
Send a "subscribe SPORTHIST" message to listserv@pdomain.uwindsor.ca

STUDIUM, university history
Send a "subscribe STUDIUM" message to listserv@cc1.kuleuven.ac.be

TAMHA, teaching American history
Send a "subscribe TAMHA" message to listserv@lists.wayne.edu

WHIRL, women's history in rhetoric and language
Send a "subscribe WHIRL" message to listserv@lists.psu.edu

WOMENSHISTORYFORUM, women's history
Send a "subscribe WOMENSHISTORYFORUM" message to listserv@ashp.
listserv.cuny.edu

Chapter 36

Newsgroups (Usenet Groups)

Keith C. Trinkle

Like discussion lists, newsgroups are an interesting and enjoyable way to engage in a discussion or learn about your favorite historical topics. The addresses of newsgroups are simple to remember. They are the name of the group plus the tag news://. For example, to have your browser bring up the soc.history.living group, you would type news://soc.history.living. A complete list of the more than 10,000 newsgroups is accessible online at

UseNet News Groups: Comprehensive Directory

http://www.tile.net/tile/news/index.html.

The following groups are likely to be of particular interest to readers of *The History Highway 3.0*:

alt.history.future
alt.history.living, history and reenactments
alt.history.ocean-liners.titanic, history of ocean liners
alt.history.what-if, what-if scenarios in history
alt.war.vietnam
soc.college, a general forum on college issues

soc.college.teaching-asst, issues affecting TAs
soc.history, a wide array of historical topics
soc.history.living, living history and reenactment
soc.history.medieval, medieval topics
soc.history.moderated, all aspects of history
soc.history.science, history of science
soc.history.war, all wars and military history
soc.history.war.misc, military history
soc.history.war.us-civil-war, aspects of the U.S. Civil War
soc.history.war.vietnam, the Vietnam War
soc.history.war.world-war-ii, World War II and the Holocaust
soc.libraries, library issues

Chapter 37

Electronic Journals

Todd Larson, Scott A. Merriman, and Dennis A. Trinkle

Directories

The History Journals Guide

http://www.history-journals.de/index.html

This guide, compiled by Stefan Blaschke of the German *Nachrichtendienst für HistorikerInnen* (News Service for Historians Project), includes a comprehensive listing of print and electronic journals. Blaschke updates the section on e-journals frequently, making this the best starting point for efficiently locating online history journals.

NewJour

http://gort.ucsd.edu/newjour/

NewJour is a frequently updated database which lists new online journals and their addresses as they appear. It is a place to watch for new journals on topics that interest you.

Project Muse

http://muse.jhu.edu/

Project Muse is a project sponsored by The National Endowment for the Humanities to make the Johns Hopkins journals available online. At present, the full text of more than forty journals in the humanities and sciences are online, including *Eighteenth-Century Studies*, *Bulletin of the History of Medicine*, *French Historical Studies*, *Modernism/Modernity*, *New Literary History* and *Reviews in American History*. Access to the full-text issues is limited to those affiliated with subscribed institutions, but bibliographic material and tables of contents are freely accessible for all the journals.

Scholarly Journals Distributed Via the World-Wide Web

http://info.lib.uh.edu/wj/webjour.html

This directory provides links to established Web-based scholarly journals that offer access to English-language article files without requiring user registration or fees.

E-Journals

Arachnion: A Journal of Literature and Ancient History on the Web

http://www.cisi.unito.it/arachne/arachne.html

Published in Italy at the University of Bologna, *Arachnion* is an online journal that features articles and forums on the ancient world. There are also announcements and many useful links to related sites.

The Bryn Mawr Classical Review

http://ccat.sas.upenn.edu/bmcr

The Bryn Mawr Classical Review is a monthly journal published jointly by Bryn Mawr College and the University of Pennsylvania. It contains reviews of books on Greek and Latin literature and history and has occasional notices (e.g., about conferences). It has an excellent archive of past articles and reviews that is searchable by author, reviewer, or book title. It has been online since 1990.

Chronicon

http://www.ucc.ie/chronicon/

Chronicon is an electronic journal of international history published by the Department of History at University College, Cork, Ireland. It is published annually and is freely available on the Internet. Each volume appears at the start of the calendar year and remains open for that year. As new articles are received, they are added to the current volume.

Classics Ireland

http://www.ucd.ie/~classics/ClassicsIreland.html

Classics Ireland, the official journal of the Classical Association of Ireland, publishes articles and reviews on the classics, ancient history, and archaeology. Like *Chronicon*, it appears as an annual register.

Clio en Afrique: L'histoire africaine en langue française

http://www.up.univ-mrs.fr/~wclio-af/

Clio en Afrique is a French-language journal dedicated to African history. It is published triennially under the auspices of the Université de Provence African Studies program.

Comitatus: A Journal of Medieval and Renaissance Studies

http://www.humnet.ucla.edu/humnet/cmrs/publications/comitatus/
comitatu.htm

Published under the auspices of the UCLA Center for Medieval and Renaissance Studies, *Comitatus* is devoted to publishing articles by new scholars, either working toward doctoral degrees or having completed such work within the previous three years. It also maintains a tradition of gathering work from across disciplines, with a special interest in articles that have an interdisciplinary scope.

The Concord Review

http://www.tcr.org/

The Concord Review was founded in March 1987 to recognize and to publish exemplary history essays by high school students in the English-speaking world. With the forty-seventh issue (Fall 2001), 517 research papers have been published from authors in thirty-seven states and twenty-four countries. According to its home page, *The Concord Review* remains the only quarterly journal in the world to publish the academic work of secondary students.

Connections: American History and Culture in an International Perspective

http://www.indiana.edu/~oah/connections/

Connections is an international announcements newsletter distributed monthly on e-mail and quarterly in print to over 100 countries. The newsletter, supported by the Organization of American Historians, provides a concise digest of information for students, scholars, and professionals who wish to develop international contacts with others interested in the transnational study of American history and culture.

Cromohs: Cyber Review of Modern Historiography

http://www.unifi.it/riviste/cromohs/

Cromohs is the first electronic review of history of modern historiography and its aim is the establishment of a particularly effective online resource for studies and research relating to modern historical culture (historiography, erudition, philosophies of history, methodologies of historical research, didactics of history). The term "modern historical culture" is intended to refer to a period from the end of the fifteenth century to the contemporary age, the assumption being that the links between the earlier period and our times are an important element in determining a consciousness and a cultural and civic responsibility for scholars, and particularly for historians, that ought not to be neglected.

Electronic Antiquity: Communicating the Classics

http://scholar.lib.vt.edu/ejournals/ElAnt/

Published out of the University of Tasmania, Australia, this is a monthly refereed, international journal that publishes scholarly articles and reviews on ancient history and archaeology, as well as "kite-flying" papers seeking feedback and items of interest (announcements of conferences and vacant positions) to the wider classics community.

Electronic Journal of Australian and New Zealand History

http://www.jcu.edu.au/aff/history/

The Electronic Journal of Australian and New Zealand History is an initiative of the School of Humanities, James Cook University, the Centre for

Cross-Cultural Research, Australian National University, and the Tasmanian School of Nursing, University of Tasmania.

Electronic Newsletter for the History of Astronomy

http://www.astro.uni-bonn.de/~pbrosche/aa/enha/

The Electronic Newsletter for the History of Astronomy is published monthly by the Working Group for the History of Astronomy.

Essays in History

http://etext.lib.virginia.edu/journals/EH/

Essays in History is a refereed journal published annually for the past thirty-five years by graduate students of the Corcoran Department of History at the University of Virginia. Online since 1994, it now appears only in electronic form. Each issue has six to eight scholarly journal articles in a wide variety of fields.

49th Parallel: An Interdisciplinary Journal of North American Studies

http://artsweb.bham.ac.uk/49thparallel/

49th Parallel is a quarterly electronic journal published by the Department of American and Canadian Studies at the University of Birmingham, England. The journal promotes interdisciplinary study of the North American continent in the nineteenth and twentieth centuries. The editors seek contributions from disciplines including history, politics, international relations, cultural studies, literature, cultural geography, media studies, and sociology. Run by postgraduate students, the journal aims to promote the work of postgraduates alongside that of more established scholars.

Heritage Post Interactive

http://heritage.excite.sfu.ca/hpost_e/ipost1/editors_desk/default.html

Published in full color in a tabloid-size format, the bilingual *Heritage Post* tells stories from Canada's past and raises questions about issues in Canadian history. Stories in the *Post* are suggested by commemorative stamps from Canada Post Corporation and Heritage Minutes, one-minute dramatizations that appear on television and in movie theaters. The Web site presents the full contents of the print journal.

Intermarium: The Online Journal of East Central European Postwar History and Politics

http://www.columbia.edu/cu/sipa/REGIONAL/ECE/intermar.html

Intermarium provides an electronic medium for noteworthy scholarship and provocative thinking about the history and politics of Central and Eastern Europe following World War II. The journal is meant to broaden the discourse on aspects of national histories that are undergoing change thanks to the availability of new documentation from recently opened archives. Its name, *Intermarium*, reflects East Central Europe's geographic location between the seas: Baltic, Adriatic, and Black. It is a project of the Institute of Political Studies of the Polish Academy of Sciences and Columbia University's Institute on East Central Europe.

IOUDAIOS Review

http://listserv.lehigh.edu/lists/ioudaios-review/

IOUDAIOS Review, a quarterly journal for professional scholars of early Judaism and related fields, was spawned by the listserv discussion group IOUDAIOS-L. Some knowledge of classical Hebrew and Hellenistic Greek is assumed. The journal disseminates information on conferences and publishes reviews of pertinent literature. The site includes is an archive of all past issues with a fully cross-referenced bibliographic index, a guide that gives instructions for contributors, and transliteration tables for Greek and Hebrew text.

The Journal for Multimedia History

http://www.albany.edu/jmmh/

The *JMMH* is supported by the History Department at the University at Albany, SUNY. The journal is dedicated to presenting and reviewing historical scholarship focusing on all periods and all nations.

Journal of Online Genealogy

http://www.onlinegenealogy.com/

The *Journal of Online Genealogy* carries articles and notices intended to help the genealogical community.

Journal of the Association for History and Computing

http://mcel.pacificu.edu/JAHC/jahcindex.htm

This journal is sponsored by the American Association for History and Computing, which aspires to promote and develop interest in the use of computers in all types of historical study at every level, in both teaching and research. Intended for a general audience of teachers, students, and researchers, the journal publishes articles dealing with the creative application of computers to particular problems in history and reviews relevant research in the field, appropriate software, and related Internet resources. It is published quarterly, though individual issues will be continually updated for a period of one year via interactive devices before being archived. Those wishing to be notified by e-mail as each volume of the journal is published can contact Ken Dvorak at kdvorak@lansing.cc.mi.us; in the subject heading, enter: "Notification JAHC."

Journal of World-Systems Research

http://csf.colorado.edu/jwsr/

The *Journal of World-Systems Research* is an electronic journal dedicated to scholarly research on the modern world-system and earlier, smaller intersocietal networks. It is interdisciplinary in focus. *JWSR* is published under the sponsorship of the Program in Comparative International Development in the Sociology Department at Johns Hopkins University.

KMT: A Modern Journal of Ancient Egypt

http://www.egyptology.com/kmt/

Created in 1990, *KMT* is an English-language journal published quarterly in Egypt. The title of the journal is an abbreviation of *Kemet*, meaning "Black Country," which is what the ancient Egyptians called their homeland. Readers can find the full text of *KMT*'s articles, announcements, reports, and reviews online.

Media History Monographs

http://www.scripps.ohiou.edu/mediahistory/mhminfo.htm

Media History Monographs is a quarterly online journal devoted to publishing historical scholarly works that are too long for regular journal articles and too short for books. All articles are peer-reviewed and all methodologies are welcome. MHM was created to accommodate the increased study of history in the field of mass communications. The journal is sponsored by the cooperative efforts of the School of Journalism at Ohio University and the Mass Communication Department at Emory and Henry College.

The Medieval Review

http://www.hti.umich.edu/b/bmr/tmr.html

The Medieval Review is based at the Medieval Institute at Western Michigan University in conjunction with Bryn Mawr College. It publishes timely reviews of current work in all areas of medieval studies, a field it interprets as broadly as possible (chronologically, geographically, and culturally). The editorial board consists of influential scholars in the field, including Patrick Geary (UCLA) and Robert Stacey (University of Washington).

MERGER: Newsletter of the Migration and Ethnic Relations Group for European Research

http://www.ercomer.org/merger/index.html

MERGER is published three times a year, and the online version contains the full text of the newsletter.

Old World Archaeology Newsletter

http://www.wesleyan.edu/classics/OWAN.html

The *Old World Archaeology Newsletter* (*OWAN*) is published three times a year by the Department of Classical Studies at Wesleyan University, Middletown, Connecticut.

Perspectives Online

http://www.theaha.org/perspectives/

Perspectives Online is the electronic newsletter of the American Historical Association. It is published monthly except during the summer recess.

Postmodern Culture Journal

http://jefferson.village.virginia.edu/pmc/

Postmodern Culture is an interdisciplinary e-journal produced under the auspices of the University of Virginia and the Institute for Advanced Technology in the Humanities. Unlike other journals, it is published and revised in a free-flowing, experimental manner. It contains articles, musings, and other types of imaginative scholarly exchange. A truly postmodern journal of cultural studies.

Renaissance Forum

http://www.hull.ac.uk/Hull/EL_Web/renforum/

Renaissance Forum is an interdisciplinary refereed journal specializing in early modern English literary and historical scholarship and in the critical methodologies of these fields. The journal is published biannually by an editorial board based in the Departments of English and History at the University of Hull.

Slavic Review

http://www.econ.uiuc.edu/~slavrev/

Published quarterly by the University of Pennsylvania's Center for Eastern European and Russian scholars, *The Slavic Review* has been online since 1994, making it one of the first Internet journals.

Southern Register

http://www.olemiss.edu/depts/south/register/index.htm

The Southern Register is the official newsletter of the Center for the Study of Southern Culture at the University of Mississippi. Published four times a year, the online version contains the full contents of the print journal, including articles, reviews, forums, and announcements.

War Times Journal

http://www.wtj.com/

The *WTJ* is a popular journal devoted to all areas of military history.

Chapter 38

Libraries

Laura Winninghoff and Jessie Bishop Powell

Library of Congress

Library of Congress

http://www.loc.gov

Arguably one of this country's premier collections, the Library of Congress collects in all areas *except* medicine and technical agriculture. Items are in many formats (books, periodicals, maps, music, prints, photographs, recorded sound, and videos), and most items are available through interlibrary loan. On the Web site, one can search the library's holdings, including some links to digitized materials, but the catalog is available only during limited hours:

> Monday–Friday: 4:40 a.m.–9:30 p.m.
> Saturday: 8:00 a.m.–5:00 p.m.
> Sunday: 11:35 a.m.–5:00 p.m.
> (Eastern Time)

There are two search options: a word search or browse. Browsing is a much more general search, and most records used in this type of search are available at any time Monday through Friday; they give an indication of the library's holdings in a certain area, but not call numbers for specific works. A word search is more specific and available only during the hours stated above, and the types of materials one can search are also limited (e.g., most pre-1975 *cataloged* items are not available). Note: all inquiries by author or title and Boolean searches for subject, name, series, notes, and so on are considered "word" searches.

The library also makes available its *experimental* search system, which has only 10 percent of the library's holdings entered. Two major improvements over the current catalog are the possibility of browsing a shelf (or section) without being in the library and performing a search for "related" materials. This latter improvement is a very good way to determine the correct Library of Congress Subject Heading (LCSH) once you have narrowed your topic. These Subject Headings, the basis of entry in most library catalogs, are not always intuitive terms or phrases.

Other Libraries and Collections

American Memory: Historical Collections of the National Digital Library

http://memory.loc.gov/ammem/ammemhome.html

American Memory is the collective term for those items deemed by the Library of Congress important to the cultural history of the United States. The level of cataloging varies with the collection and depends partly on the format, its age, and its acquisition date. Most collections are searchable and many have finding aids such as subject and author lists.

The Bancroft Library (UC, Berkeley)

http://sunsite2.berkeley.edu/oac/

Access to the Bancroft Library's collections, via the Online Archive of California, including access to UC, Berkeley Finding Aids and the California Heritage Digital Image Access Database.

The Beinecke Library

http://www.library.yale.edu/orbis/

Yale's library of rare books and manuscripts is searchable through ORBIS, Yale's online catalog.

Bibliothèque Nationale de France

http://www.bnf.fr/web-bnf/catalog/index.htm

Catalog of the French National Library, in French, with an English gateway under construction. The above link is to the summary page for all four catalogs, including GALLICA, an effort to chronicle nineteenth-century France through digitized images and sound.

British Library Public Catalog

http://opac97.bl.uk/

British Library Public Catalog provides access to the major catalogs of the British Library in London and Boston Spa. Presently, individual collections have separate catalogs but all can be searched using the form given on the Web page. The collections include humanities, social science, hard science, technology, and business collections cataloged from 1975 to the present, all music cataloged from 1980 to the present, and all reference materials cataloged before 1975 (including the archives and materials of the former India Office and colonial Africa). In the older reference materials, please note that the "D-" before items means that the original was destroyed during World War II and has since been replaced. Finally, all serials from 1700 to the present are included in the catalog.

Hours of operation: Monday–Saturday: 4 a.m.–midnight (GMT)

The Center for Research Libraries

http://wwwcrl.uchicago.edu OR Telnet crlcatalog.uchicago.edu (login as "guest" at prompt)

The Center for Research Libraries is a consortium of college and university libraries from all over the United States. The center holds materials deemed by many libraries important but too obscure to take up valuable shelf space in their own institution. Through membership in the CRL, libraries take advantage of these materials and their patrons have fairly quick access to them. Currently, 98 percent of the nearly 5 million entries in the CRL's catalog are available online, including books, newspapers, serials, microforms, archival collections, and other research materials. There is a handbook on the Web page describing the holdings in certain areas; a name authority file is also available.

EuroDocs: Primary Historical Documents from Western Europe

http://www.lib.byu.edu/~rdh/eurodocs/

Compiled by Richard Hacken, a librarian at Brigham Young University, this list of links connects to Western European (mainly primary) historical documents that are transcribed, reproduced, and, in some cases, translated.

The Getty Research Institute for the History of Art and the Humanities

http://opac.pub.getty.edu

Collections include Western art, archaeology, and architecture from the Bronze Age to the present, with a special strength in French, German, Russian, Italian, and American avant-garde materials. There are also extensive collections on the conservation of cultural heritage and historic preservation and an unparalleled auction catalog collection with more than 110,000 volumes of materials from the late seventeenth century to the present. Included in the Special Collections are artists' journals and sketchbooks, albums, architectural drawings, early guidebooks, emblem books, prints, and drawings. The Getty collection's strengths are in Futurism, Dada, Surrealism, the Bauhaus, Russian Constructivism, and Fluxus. Many items from the research library are available for interlibrary loan.

The Hagley Library

http://www.hagley.lib.de.us/library.htm

The Hagley Museum and Library's focus is American Business and Technological History. As of this writing, the catalog is under construction.

The Kinsey Institute for Research in Sex, Gender and Reproduction

http://www.indiana.edu/~kinsey/

Collections at the Kinsey Institute are searchable via KICAT, at Telnet infogate.ucs.indiana.edu. Login as "guest" and when prompted to choose a catalog, type KICAT. The catalog is also available at http://www.iucat.iu.edu/uhtbin/cgisirsi/tn31OJYmdl/28779029/60/69.

KICAT does not contain records for all items in the library, nor does it contain records for the Institute's art and archival collections. Records are continually being added to the online catalog as part of the library's retrospective conversion project. Information on other materials is available only through onsite finding aids and published book catalogs (citations available on the Web site).

For help in using the library's holdings of sex-related magazines, films and videos, newspapers and tabloids, pulp fiction, and books still cataloged in Dr. Kinsey's system of categories, users must consult with library staff. Records for these materials will be entered into the online catalog as quickly as legal restrictions and resources permit. Until then, access is limited to information available through in-house files, lists, and databases. E-mail libknsy@indiana.edu or call (812) 855-3058 for more information about the library.

Labriola National American Indian Data Center at Arizona State University

http://www.asu.edu/lib/archives/labriola.htm

The Labriola National American Indian Data Center, part of the ASU Libraries, brings together current and historic information on government, culture, religion and worldview, social life and customs, tribal history, individuals from the United States, Canada, and Sonora and Chihuahua, Mexico. All materials held by the center are searchable via ASU's online catalog (http://catalog.lib.asu.edu/).

The Lilly Library

http://www.indiana.edu/%7eliblilly/

At present, the Lilly Library's online resources include searchable indexes of the manuscript collections, chapbook collection, and French Revolution docu-ments. The library's holdings are searchable via Indiana University's catalog, IUCAT (Telnet infogate.ucs.indiana.edu. Login as "guest," and when prompted enter IUCAT). This is a command-driven catalog. Users can also reach the IU catalog on the Web at http://iucat.iu.edu/index_main.html.

The National Library of China

http://www.nlc.gov.cn/etext.htm

Non-Chinese-speaking visitors to this site submit questions to librarians who then search for the information, so this site is most useful if researchers have a specific question or request. The catalog is searchable by those whose comput-ers register Chinese characters.

The Newberry Library

http://www.newberry.org/nl/collections/virtua.html

The Newberry is slowly adding to its Web-based catalog, but currently only 15 percent of collections are searchable. Where available, OCLC has the complete holdings of the Newberry already as part of its database. Bibliographic guides are available on the Web site for beginning researchers.

The New York Public Library

http://catnyp.nypl.org/

CATNYP is the online catalog of The Research Libraries of The New York Public Library. This catalog includes materials added to the collections after 1971, as well as some materials acquired before 1971. At this time, however, the best place to search the libraries' holdings is the 800–volume *Dictionary Catalog of The Research Libraries*, published by G.K. Hall. Copies of this catalog are available at many research institutions and all NYPL Research Libraries. There is a link on the Web page to a global list of libraries that own a copy of the *Catalog*.

OhioLink

http://www.ohiolink.edu

This is the communal catalog for all libraries (public, private, college, and university) in Ohio.

OLIS (Oxford University Libraries' Online Catalog): Oxford's Bodleian Library, University of Oxford

telnet://library.ox.ac.uk

Without a password from Oxford you may not search any other Oxford library (although all are listed). This is a command-driven search, and most materials are available for interlibrary loan.

Oriental Institute Research Archives

http://www-oi.uchicago.edu/OI/DEPT/RA/ABZU/ABZU.HTML

This is a guide to resources for the study of the ancient Near East consisting of primary and secondary indexes of information, available on the Internet. The guide is compiled and updated by Charles E. Jones, research archivist at the Oriental Institute Research Archives at the University of Chicago.

The Library Company of Philadelphia

http://www.librarycompany.org/

Founded in 1731 by Benjamin Franklin, the Library Company of Philadelphia has over half a million items covering American history and culture from the seventeenth to the nineteenth century. The online catalog, WolfPAC, currently includes about 20 percent of the collection, with more added daily. However, this online catalog also includes records from the Union catalog of the Philadelphia Area Consortium of Special Collections Libraries (PACSCL): the Academy of Natural Sciences, the Balch Institute for Ethnic Studies, Saint Charles Borromeo Seminary, and the Philadelphia Museum of Art. Joining in the near future are the Rosenbach Museum and Library, the Presbyterian Historical Society, the Athenaeum, and the Historical Society of Pennsylvania. Several other PACSCL member libraries have, or will soon have, catalogs available through the PACSCL Web site, or through their individual institution's Web site. These include the American Philosophical Society, the Free Library of Philadelphia, the University of Pennsylvania, Winterthur, The Hagley Museum and Library, Temple University, the College of Physicians of Philadelphia, the Wagner Free Institute of Science, Bryn Mawr, Haverford, and Swarthmore.

Public Records Office–UK

http://www.pro.gov.uk/finding/catalogue/default.htm

At present, the catalog of the PRO (United Kingdom) contains references only to selected policy records of twentieth-century British government departments.

The Schlesinger Library

http://www.radcliffe.edu/schles/

(Searchable via Harvard's online catalog at Telnet://hollis.harvard.edu)

The Schlesinger Library at Radcliffe College is the foremost library on the history of women in America. Its holdings of audiovisual materials, books, ephemera, manuscripts, oral histories, periodicals, and photographs document the social history of women in the United States, primarily during the nineteenth and twentieth centuries.

Schomburg Center for Research in Black Culture

http://www.nypl.org/research/sc/sc.html

(Holdings searchable via CATNYP, the New York Public Library catalog, http://catnyp.nypl.org)

The Schomburg Center for Research in Black Culture is a national research library devoted to collecting, preserving, and providing access to resources documenting the experiences of peoples of African descent throughout the world. The center provides access to, and professional reference assistance in, the use of its collections to the scholarly community and the general public through five research divisions. The center's collections include art objects, audio and videotapes, books, manuscripts, motion picture films, newspapers, periodicals, photographs, prints, recorded music discs, and sheet music.

University of Oklahoma Western History Collections

http://libraries.ou.edu/depts/westhistory/

This collections' aim is to provide opportunities for research into the development of the Trans-Mississippi West and Native American cultures. Catalog information for many of the materials within the Western History Collections may be accessed through the University of Oklahoma Libraries online catalog, OLIN. Catalog information for Western History Collections material is divided as follows: choose "OU Catalog" from the Libraries menu to search for books held by the Western History Collections, or choose "Archives" from the Libraries menu to search for manuscript and photo collections of the Western History Collections.

Top Ten Research Libraries in the United States*

1. Harvard University

http://hollisweb.harvard.edu/

telnet://hollis.harvard.edu

Excellent instructions on searching strategies for HOLLIS (Harvard Online Library Information System) and other command-driven search systems are available at http://www.radcliffe.edu/schles/libcolls/search/index.htm.

Digest of Education Statistics, U.S. Department of Education, National Center for Education Statistics, 1997, page 464, table 417.

2. Yale University

http://www.library.yale.edu/orbis/

ORBIS is available in a Web-based or Telnet platform, with links to both appearing on this page.

3. University of Illinois at Urbana-Champaign

http://www.library.uiuc.edu/

This gateway provides access to search systems for library materials and serials. The catalog is, as of this writing, Telnet accessible, with an experimental Web catalog available for users as well.

4. University of Texas at Austin

http://dpweb1.dp.utexas.edu/lib/utnetcat/

5. University of Michigan

http://www.lib.umich.edu/libhome/mirlyn/mirlynpage.html

6. University of California at Berkeley

http://www.lib.berkeley.edu/Catalogs/guide.html

UC Berkeley provides multiple options in searching its collections, and this page lists all of them, along with a chart indicating which system to use for specific searches. Pathfinder is the Berkeley-specific catalog, MELVYL (Web or Telnet) contains the holdings of all nine campus libraries of the University of California, and GLADIS is the technical services catalog.

7. Columbia University

http://www.columbia.edu/cu/libraries/indexes/resource_type_10.html

CLIO (Columbia Libraries Information Online) and all other New York City area libraries have links on this page. Each library at Columbia has its own catalog (e.g., Law School, Medical School, Teacher's College), necessitating many searches to get a complete picture of the holdings on most subjects.

8. Stanford University

http://www-sul.stanford.edu/search/socii/

Socrates II, the Web-based catalog for Stanford, is only available to those with a Stanford ID. The general public can, however, access the older, Telnet-based and command-driven Socrates from this page.

9. University of California at Los Angeles

http://www.library.ucla.edu/

10. The University of Chicago

http://webpac.lib.uchicago.edu/webpac-bin/wgbroker?new+-access+top

Chapter 39

Archives and Manuscript Collections

Susan Ferentinos

Information for Researchers

Primary historical research can be intimidating for the beginner. The following sites provide background for new researchers that will make the structure of archives seem less daunting.

Introduction to Archives

http://www.umich.edu/~bhl/bhl/refhome/refintro.htm

This essay, part of the Web site of the Bentley Historical Library of the University of Michigan, details the ways in which archives differ from libraries in their collecting focus and their organization.

Library Research Using Primary Sources

http://www.lib.berkeley.edu/TeachingLib/Guides/PrimarySources.html

The library at the University of California, Berkeley, offers this step-by-step guide to primary research. It elaborates the difference between primary and secondary resources and suggests multiple avenues for tracking down primary material.

Primary Sources Research Colloquium

http://www.library.yale.edu/ref/err/primsrcs.htm

Designed to complement a Yale University course in primary research, this site supplies introductory information on using primary documents in historical research. It discusses various types of sources and provides definitions of words such as *records*, *finding aids*, and *manuscripts*. Although some parts of the site deal specifically with Yale University resources, overall it contains valuable resources for beginning researchers.

Using Archives: A Practical Guide for Researchers

http://www.archives.ca/04/0416_e.html

Maintained by the National Archives of Canada, this online essay is geared toward first-time users of archives. It discusses research strategies, what to expect from an archive, and how to locate desired material.

Information for Archivists

For those interested in learning more about the profession of collecting, organizing, and preserving historical documents, the following sites are good starting points.

Archives of the Archivist Listserv

http://listserv.muohio.edu/archives/archives.html

This page offers information on the major archivist listserv. Through links, visitors can join the list, review past postings, and search the listserv's archives for specific topics or authors.

Archives Resource Center

http://www.coshrc.org/arc/index.htm

A cooperative effort of the Council of State Historical Records Coordinators, the American Association of State and Local History, and the Society of American Archivists, the Archives Resource Center strives to be a gateway to Web-based information for archivists. The site includes links to professional organizations, lists of professional development opportunities, and descriptions of professional standards.

Conservation OnLine (CoOL)

http://palimpsest.stanford.edu/

Maintained by Stanford University Libraries, Conservation OnLine is a clearinghouse of information on the conservation of manuscript material. Visitors can access online articles on a wide range of conservation topics, such as pest management or digital imaging. Lists of conservation professionals and organizations throughout the world (though mostly in English-speaking countries) are also provided, and the entire site is searchable.

Encoded Archival Description (EAD) Official Web Site

http://lcweb.loc.gov/ead/

Encoded Archival Description promises to make collection finding aids widely available on the Web. The Library of Congress maintains the EAD Official Web Site, which contains an introduction to the format, relevant links, and application guidelines.

Society of American Archivists (SAA)

http://www.archivists.org/

The Society of American Archivists is the major American professional organization for archivists. Its Web site provides information about the organization, position papers, job postings, professional development opportunities, and a list of SAA publications.

Archives, Manuscripts, and Special Collections

With such a wealth of historic documents available, it can be difficult to know where to begin. The following list includes information on locating sources, along with the Web sites of repositories particularly well known in their area of specialty. Most repositories affiliated with larger institutions (such as universities or national governments) enable the user to search catalogs through their Web sites; however, a significant portion of collections have not been electronically cataloged. Researchers should contact the reference staff of the repository to ensure that they have not missed valuable sources.

The institutions in North America and Western Europe generally maintain more sophisticated Web sites than those in other regions. In an effort to include multiple historical fields, I have included sites from throughout the world that are distinctive within their region, though they may appear somewhat basic to North American eyes. All sites are in English unless otherwise noted.

Metasites

(Lists for a specific country or genre are located under the appropriate subheading.)

Gabriel: National Libraries of Europe

http://www.konbib.nl/gabriel/en/countries.html

This site provides address, phone number, e-mail address, major collections, operating hours, and mission for the national libraries of over thirty-five nations in Eastern and Western Europe. It also provides links to the individual servers of each library.

Guide to the Archives of Intergovernmental Organizations

http://www.unesco.org/archives/guide/uk/index.html

A joint project between the United Nations Educational, Scientific, and Cultural Organization (UNESCO) and the International Council on Archives, Section of Archivists of International Organizations (ICS/SIO), this guide provides the general history of approximately eighty intergovernmental organizations, along with information on accessing the archives of each group.

Ready, 'Net, Go! Archival Internet Resources ✓

http://www.tulane.edu/~lmiller/ArchivesResources.html

Describing itself as an "archival meta-index," this site has compiled lists of major archival resources around the globe. Master lists of archives and archival search engines allow researchers to quickly access clearinghouses of information, such as multirepository catalogs. The site's Professional Resources and Tools for Archivists sections point users to resources of particular interest to archivists.

Repositories of Primary Sources ✓

http://www.uidaho.edu/special_collections/Other.Repositories.html

The University of Idaho maintains this international listing of over 4,600 repositories. It is as close to a comprehensive list as is available, and using the links on this site is one of the quickest ways to locate a specific library. The list is arranged by region and also includes a section of links to additional lists.

UNESCO Archives Portal ✓

http://www.unesco.org/webworld/portal_archives/Archives/

This site includes links to archival repositories around the world, online primary sources, and professional information for archivists. Searchable lists of archives are arranged by both topic and country.

Africa

Africa Research Central: A Clearinghouse of African Primary Sources

http://www.africa_research.org/

Africa Research Central provides information on manuscript repositories with holdings of Africana. African, European, and North American libraries are included. For African repositories, users can search a database to find institutions in specific countries or with particular types of holdings (such as business records or government archives). The database lists contact information, use restrictions, Web address, and published inventories for each institution, though some of the data is incomplete. For European and North American repositories, the site provides direct links to home pages. The clearinghouse also offers information on the preservation crisis facing manuscripts in Africa.

Africa South of the Sahara: Libraries and Archives

http://garamond.stanford.edu/depts/ssrg/africa/libs.html

Stanford University's list of resources in African studies includes links to Africana collections around the world, bibliographies, and digitization projects.

Archives in South Africa

http://www.archives.org.za/archivesa.html

Compiled by the South African Society of Archivists, this page provides links to archival repositories in South Africa.

Electronic Journal of Africana Bibliography

http://sdrc.lib.uiowa.edu/ejab/1/

This issue of *Africana Bibliography* carries the subtitle *Guides, Collections and Ancillary Materials to African Archival Resources in the United States.* It provides a bibliography of archival resources on the history of Africa that are available in the United States through print or microfilm. Selections are grouped by country, region, and language. The site is similar to a print resource in that it provides few hypertext links.

Repositories of Primary Sources: Africa and the Near East

http://www.uidaho.edu/special-collections/africa.html

Part of the comprehensive University of Idaho list of primary source repositories, this page links to manuscript collections throughout Africa and the Near East. The sources are divided by country and include sites in a variety of languages.

African-Americans

African-American Archives, Manuscripts and Special Collections: A Guide to Resources

http://www2.lib.udel.edu/subj/blks/internet/afamarc.htm

The University of Delaware library has compiled this guide to resources in African-American history. The list of links is divided into repositories, subject guides, and the finding aids of particular collections housed throughout the United States.

Amistad Research Center

http://www.tulane.edu/~amistad/

The Amistad Research Center, an independent library housed at Tulane University, holds one of the preeminent groupings of manuscript material pertaining to African-American history. The center's mission is to enable "the study of ethnic history and culture and race relations in the United States"; about 90 percent of its materials pertain to African-Americans. Its Web site contains lists of manuscript collections, arranged both alphabetically and by major subject, and a growing collection of digitized images from its collections. The site devotes an entire section to the *Amistad* slave ship uprising, including historical essays and descriptions of the center's resources on this topic.

Moorland-Spingarn Research Center, Howard University

http://www.founders.howard.edu/moorland_spingarn/

The Moorland-Spingarn is a research center devoted to the study of people of African descent in Africa and the Americas, with a particular emphasis on black "families, organizations, institutions, social and religious consciousness, and the continuing struggle for civil rights and human justice." Its manuscripts department reflects this mission with its offering of oral history projects, personal and organizational papers, a special music collection, and prints. The center's Web site provides brief biographies of interviewees in the Black Military History and Civil Rights Documentation oral history projects, digital samples of historic photographs, descriptions of manuscript holdings, and a special bibliography of library resources in African-American women's history.

Schomburg Center for Research in Black Culture

http://www.nypl.org/research/sc/sc.html

The Web site of the Schomburg, a research branch of the New York Public Library, carries many of the features of its parent organization's site: multiple digital resources, clear logistical information, and extensive description of its holdings. The center is devoted to the study of the African diaspora, and its strength lies in twentieth-century history, literature, and the performing arts. Its site provides access to online exhibits, a "multimedia sampler" (utilizing video and sound technology), and digitized examples of its holdings.

Asia and the Pacific

Directory of Archives in Australia

http://www.asap.unimelb.edu.au/asa/directory/

Maintained by the Australian Society of Archivists, this site offers contact information, hours, collecting focus, and Web links to the major repositories of Australia. Visitors can search the site by subject.

National Archives of Japan

http://www8.cao.go.jp/koubunsho/index_e.html

The English language pages of the Japanese National Archives offer descriptions of major holdings, a guide for users, and a list containing the contact information of the archives of Japanese prefectures and some Japanese cities.

National Archives of Singapore

http://www.museum.org.sg/NAS/nas.shtml

Singapore's National Archives has a wide collection of materials documenting the country's heritage, including oral histories, photographs, and public records. The site contains information on the holdings, as well as samples of material held in the collections.

Register of Australian Archives and Manuscripts (RAAM)

http://www.nla.gov.au/raam/

This searchable catalog of manuscript collections held in Australia contains more than 37,000 thousand documents.

Repositories of Primary Sources: Asia and the Pacific

http://www.uidaho.edu/special-collections/asia.html

Part of the comprehensive University of Idaho list of primary source repositories, this page links to manuscript collections throughout Asia and the Pacific. The sources are divided by country.

Canada

Canadian Archival Resources on the Internet

http://www.usask.ca/archives/menu.html

Indexed by name, location, and repository type, this online guide provides links to the home pages of Canadian archives.

National Archives of Canada

http://www.archives.ca/08/08_e.html

The National Archives of Canada Web site offers a variety of paths into the Canadian past. Visitors can click on particular topics to access a variety of digitized collections; a genealogy page describes the archive's many family history resources; and ArchiviaNet, the archive's online research tool, serves as a portal into various catalogs and finding aids.

National Library of Canada

http://www.nlc_bnc.ca/index_e.html

The mission of the National Library of Canada is to collect and preserve Canada's published heritage. Available from this site are the Canada National Library catalog, digital collections, and research guides on specific aspects of Canadian history.

Europe—Eastern

Levéltárak (Archives): Hungary

http://www.lib.uni_miskolc.hu/lib/archive/kapcsolat/ukanIndex/h4levtar.htm

This site provides a list of archives in Hungary; however, this page and most of the archival sites it links to are in Hungarian, with no translation available.

PIASA Archival Information Center

http://www.piasa.org/archives.html

The Polish Institute of Arts and Sciences of America (PIASA) provides this electronic guide to archival collections concerning Poland and the Polish-American community. Resources are divided into those in Poland and those in North America.

Slavic and East European Collections at UC, Berkeley

http://www.lib.berkeley.edu/Collections/Slavic/collect.html

The University of California, Berkeley, collects widely in materials on Slavic and East European countries, including the former Soviet Union. Included in the Special Collections department is an array of modern (post-1989) independent Russian periodicals, an extensive arrangement of materials from the Czech Republic, and information pertaining to writers and literature in this region.

Slovene Archives

http://www.pokarh_mb.si/today.html

This site provides a listing of archives in the Republic of Slovenia. For each institution that does not have its own Web site, the Slovene Archives site gives contact information along with a preliminary description of its collections. The site supplies links to those repositories that maintain their own Web pages. While the Slovene Archives page is in English, some of the links connect to pages in Slovene.

State Archives in Poland

http://www.archiwa.gov.pl/index.eng.html

This site not only details the holdings of the Polish State Archives, it also answers FAQs about Polish archives in general and provides links to other Polish repositories. While the major pages of the site have been translated into English, some links from the main page lead to information available only in Polish.

Europe—Western

ARCHIESPA: Índice de páginas Web sobre archivos de España: Spain

http://rayuela.uc3m.es/~pirio/archiespa/

ARCHIESPA is a metasite providing links to hundreds of resources on archives in Spain. Links are available to various archives, Spanish archival organizations, online articles about Spain's repositories, digital manuscripts, directories to other libraries in Europe, and links to additional lists of resources. Users should be aware that this site does lack some currency, so some links are no longer accurate. The site is in Spanish.

Archives Hub: United Kingdom

http://www.archiveshub.ac.uk/

This gateway catalog allows users to search for archival collections held in colleges and universities in the United Kingdom. Searches by repository, subject, document type, and personal name are possible, and the advanced search form enables full-text searching. Search results include a description of the collection's contents.

Archives in Germany

http://www.bawue.de/~hanacek/info/earchive.htm

The bulk of this site is in German; however, the initial page is in English and provides a glossary of German words frequently used on the subsequent pages (as well as on other German archival sites). The home page lists German archives divided by type (church, state, private, etc.). Following the link on a particular repository leads to a page (in German) providing introductory information on the institution.

Archivos Estatales: Spain

http://www.mcu.es/lab/archivos/index.html

Spain's Ministry of Education and Culture maintains this site, which provides an overview of state libraries and archives. Users can search a bibliography of Spanish archives, access information on specific repositories, and read a general description on the organization and policies of the libraries within this system. The site is in Spanish.

ARCHON: Archives Online: United Kingdom

http://www.hmc.gov.uk/archon/archon.htm

ARCHON is a clearinghouse of information for users of British archives and manuscripts. It offers a list, with links, of all repositories in the United Kingdom, along with information on British history and resources for those in both the history and archival professions. The site also contains a register of ongoing, planned, or completed archival projects.

Bodleian Library, University of Oxford: United Kingdom

http://www.rsl.ox.ac.uk/

One of the most famous libraries in the world, the Bodleian houses an extensive array of Western manuscripts, reaching back into ancient times. The library's Web site allows access to multiple catalogs of holdings, some online finding aids, and general library information. In addition, numerous digital library projects, such as an online collection of medieval manuscripts, are available for viewing.

Bundesarchiv Online: Germany

http://www.bundesarchiv.de/index.html

Visitors to the National Archives of Germany Web site can access a timeline of the library's history, descriptions and indexes of its major holdings, and a list of the library's publications. The site is entirely in German.

Les Centres de Ressources Documentaires: France

http://mistral.culture.fr/culture/sedocum/ceresdoc.htm

This list, maintained by the French Ministry of Culture, provides access to the major repositories of France, grouped by subject area. Users can access data regarding address, hours of operation, major holdings, and library history. The site is completely in French.

Latin America

Benson Latin American Collection, University of Texas at Austin

http://www.lib.utexas.edu/benson/index.html

The Benson Collection contains over 2 million pages of manuscripts on Mexico, Central America, the Caribbean, South America, and the American Southwest during the period it was part of Mexico and the Spanish Empire. In addition, it houses one of the largest collections of secondary material on this region. Archival collection descriptions, bibliographies, online exhibits, and information about visiting the library are available through the library's home page.

Biblioteca Nacional de México

http://biblional.bibliog.unam.mx/bib01.html

This site gives visitors information on Mexico's National Library and its holdings. The repository owns over 2 million items, including rare books and manuscripts, all of which pertain to Mexican history. Currently, this site is available only in Spanish.

Biblioteca Nacional del Perú

http://www.binape.gob.pe/

Peru's National Library has created multiple avenues of exploration on its Web site. Visitors can search library catalogs, view online historical photographs, peruse a listing of the library's publications, and access information on other branches of Peru's national library system. The site is entirely in Spanish.

H-LatAm Archives

http://www2.h_net.msu.edu/~latam/archives/

The H-Net listserv for Latin American history maintains this resource of information on archives in Latin America. Researchers who have physically visited a repository complete a questionnaire, which is then posted to this site. Details include contact information, access requirements, information on collections, descriptions of the facilities, and tips for visiting the repository, such as nearby hotels, restaurants, and public transportation. Users of the site should be aware, however, that descriptions are up to five years old and so might be outdated.

Latin American Library: Tulane University

http://www.tulane.edu/~latinlib/lalhome.html

Tulane's Latin American Library is comprised of both secondary and primary sources, as well as an extensive collection of Latin American rare books. Primary sources include historical newspapers, photographs, and manuscripts. This site contains information on the library's holdings, summaries of recent Latin American exhibits, a bibliography of dissertation research, and links to related sites. Also included are digital representations of Mayan rubbings and other "treasures of the collection."

Military History and Peace Collections

Hoover Institution: Library and Archives

http://www_hoover.stanford.edu/homepage/library.html

The Hoover Institution on War, Revolution, and Peace at Stanford University boasts collections from throughout the world. The library has particularly strong holdings on the Chinese Revolution, the Russian Revolution, the Nazis, and Italian fascism. At its Web site, visitors can find information about the Hoover Institution, descriptions of its holdings, historical essays on the collections, bibliographies, and links to related sites.

Swarthmore College Peace Collection

http://www.swarthmore.edu/Library/peace/

This research archive collects and maintains materials pertaining to nongovernmental efforts toward peace. Its holdings include manuscripts, periodicals, and extensive ephemera (such as posters, flyers, and buttons). This site provides collection descriptions, subject guides, online exhibits, and resources for the further study of peace movements.

U.S. Army Military History Institute

http://carlisle_www.army.mil/usamhi/index.html

The U.S. Army Military History Institute collects and organizes resources on American military history, including oral histories, manuscript material, photographs, and maps. Its manuscript collections include the personal papers of individuals connected to the U.S. army, as well as curriculum materials from the U.S. Army War College, dating back to the school's inception in 1901. The Web site contains collection finding aids, a large digital collection, and transcripts of dozens of oral history interviews with veterans of various twentieth-century military actions.

Virginia Military Institute Archives

http://web.vmi.edu/archives/~archtml/index.html

The Virginia Military Institute (VMI) has extensive holdings on United States military history in the nineteenth and twentieth centuries. The Web site provides genealogy information on VMI alumni, detailed information on the archives' Civil War collections, textual transcriptions of some of the Civil War material, and selections from the library's photograph collection.

Russia and the Former Soviet Union

ArcheoBiblioBase: Archives in Russia

http://www.iisg.nl/~abb/index.html

This English language resource provides information on Russian archives. The material is divided into three sections: federal archives (administered by the Rosarkhiv), major federal agencies that maintain their own records, and local state archives in Moscow and St. Petersburg. Under each category are lists of archives with contact information, previous names, major holdings, access restrictions, and the titles of any recently published guides. This resource is now searchable, though the limited information given about each repository demands that search terms remain general.

Estonian Historical Archives

http://www.eha.ee/

Previously the Estonian State Central Archives, the Estonian Historical Archives houses documents from Estonia's history, including the eras of Swedish rule, Soviet affiliation, and independent statehood. Its home page offers an essay on the history of the archives, information for researchers planning to visit the repository, and descriptions of its holdings. An English language version of the site is available.

National Library of Russia

http://www.nlr.ru:8101/eng/

This repository owns copies of every publication produced in Russia. In addition, it houses collections of Greek writings from the early Christian era, European codices (handwritten books) and manuscripts, and Eastern texts illustrating the development of writing in that region. The National Library site's English-language offerings are considerable, providing access to online exhibits and databases (although the databases themselves are in Russian).

State Archives of Latvia

http://www.arhivi.lv/engl/en-lvas-frame.htm

Collecting the documentary heritage of Latvia since 1919, the State Archives of Latvia is today a joint system of numerous collection agencies. Its Web site details major holdings and supplies information on visiting each of its branches.

Sexuality

Archiv für Sexualwissenschaft/Archive for Sexology

http://www2.hu-berlin.de/sexology/

This institute contains numerous resources for the study of sexuality and the history of sexology, most pertaining to Europe and the United States. Its Web site includes articles on the history of sexology, samples from the collection, syllabi for graduate and undergraduate courses, and descriptions of the institute's holdings.

Human Sexuality Collection, Cornell University

http://rmc.library.cornell.edu/HSC/

Cornell University's Sexuality Collection seeks to document historical shifts in attitudes toward sexuality. It has particular strengths in gay, lesbian, bisexual, and transgender history and in the politics of pornography. Its Web site describes its holdings, includes bibliographies of published sources, and features an informative guide with advice on how to research the history of sexuality.

Kinsey Institute for Research in Sex, Gender, and Reproduction

http://www.indiana.edu/~kinsey/

Dr. Alfred C. Kinsey gained worldwide attention in the 1940s with the publication of his controversial book *Sexual Behavior in the Human Male*. The Kinsey Institute, which he founded, continues his work by facilitating the study of human sexuality. The library houses materials in numerous formats (including manuscripts, periodicals, photographs, and artifacts) from throughout the world, ranging in date from 3200 B.C.E. to the present. The institute is not open to the general public, and researchers must gain approval to access the materials; the necessary steps for doing this are described on the Web site. The site also offers essays describing the life of Dr. Kinsey, the often colorful history of the institute, and the library's holdings; information on exhibits (with links to some online exhibition catalogs); a catalog of publications; a photographic history; and a list of grant opportunities. The institute's annotated list of other repositories collecting in the history of sexuality is particularly useful and can be accessed directly at http://www.indiana.edu/~kinsey/centers.html#Speclib.

Lavender Legacies: Guide to Sources in North America

http://www.archivists.org/saagroups/lagar/home.htm

Compiled by the Lesbian and Gay Archives Roundtable of the Society of American Archivists, Lavender Legacies lists manuscript repositories with significant holdings in gay and lesbian history. While the list is not searchable by keyword, it is indexed by both repository name and location.

United States

Congressional Collections at Archival Repositories

http://www.lib.udel.edu/ud/spec/c_clctns.html

While the National Archives holds the collections of many members of Congress, other collections are scattered throughout the United States in various repositories. The University of Delaware has compiled this list of the locations of congressional collections to aid researchers in finding the material they require. Many names on the list contain links to biographical essays or collection descriptions maintained by the holding institution.

The Library of Congress

http://www.loc.gov/

The Library of Congress, the largest library in the world, adds about 10,000 items to its collections each day. Its Web site is designed to assist the public in accessing this mind-boggling array of information. From its home page, users can find out more about the library's collections, search its catalog, or read answers to FAQs. America's Library, a special section for children, introduces young people to the nation's heritage; the THOMAS clearinghouse supplies information on current and past congressional bills; and the Copyright Office, affiliated with the library, provides answers to an array of copyright questions. The library's online exhibit gallery contains dozens of offerings, and the American Memory collection (discussed in more detail in the Digital Collections section below) acts as a portal into the National Digital Library Program, devoted to digitizing major collections of "historical Americana."

National Archives and Records Administration (NARA)

http://www.nara.gov/

This extensive site contains something for every historian interested in U.S. history. An online exhibit hall provides access to digital exhibitions that include a photographic journey through the twentieth century and images of the Declaration of Independence and Constitution; the Digital Classroom supplies lesson plans and teaching strategies for a variety of age levels; a genealogy page (http://www.nara.gov/genealogy/) discusses the family history resources available both at the National Archives and elsewhere on the Web. Online versions of Federal Register publications are available, and the Archives and Preservation section offers information to archivists and records managers. Of course, the site also provides a searchable catalog and collection descriptions. For more information on NARA's online documents, see the Digital Collections section below.

NUCMC Home Page (National Union Catalog for Manuscripts Collections) ✓

http://lcweb.loc.gov/coll/nucmc/nucmc.html

This online version of the National Union Catalog of Manuscripts Collections allows users to search for manuscript material located throughout the United States. Users enter a subject or keyword, and NUCMC returns a list of relevant collections and their locations. This database is a useful starting point for archival research.

Presidential Libraries

http://www.nara.gov/nara/president/address.html

At this site, the National Archives and Records Administration provides contact information and Web links to all of the U.S. presidential libraries, along with an overview of the presidential library system.

State Archives and Historical Societies

http://www.ohiohistory.org/textonly/links/arch_hs.html

In the United States, state archives provide access to the records of each state's government, and state historical societies normally contain collections of historical manuscripts pertaining to state history. This page, part of the Ohio Historical Society Web site, provides links to state archives and historical societies in the United States.

United States Immigration History

California Ethnic and Multicultural Archives (CEMA)

http://www.library.ucsb.edu/speccoll/cema.html

The University of California, Santa Barbara, administers this repository devoted to documenting the history of African-Americans, Latinos, Asian-Americans and Native Americans in California. CEMA's Web site houses lists of collections, along with explanatory essays detailing the historical significance of each major manuscript group. The archive's collecting policy is also accessible, so researchers can quickly ascertain the relevance of the library's holdings to their work.

Chicano Research Collection, Arizona State University

http://info.lib.asu.edu/lib/archives/chicano.htm

Arizona State University owns an extensive Chicano Research Collection, which documents the experience of Mexican-Americans through books, newspapers, periodicals, photographs, manuscripts, and ephemera. The collection's Web site offers information on these holdings, access to an online exhibit of Chicano history, and links to related sites.

Immigration History Research Center

http://www1.umn.edu/ihrc/

The Immigration History Research Center (IHRC) of the University of Minnesota maintains this Web site, which provides information on its holdings and mission. The collection focus is on American immigration and ethnic history, particularly as it pertains to groups from Eastern, Central, and Southern Europe and the Near East—those most involved in the immigration wave of the late nineteenth and early twentieth centuries. The site provides advice to genealogical researchers, collection descriptions, and an online catalog of publications distributed by the IHRC.

Women

Sallie Bingham Center for Women's History and Culture, Duke University

http://scriptorium.lib.duke.edu/women/

The Bingham Center at Duke University has a broad collecting focus that includes political activities, labor, Southern writers, religion, and education. The bulk of the materials pertains to women in the United States, though other countries are represented. The archive's Web site is part of Duke's award-winning Scriptorium site. Through it, researchers can access online versions of many holdings and more than fifteen Web-based bibliographies on topics pertaining to women's history. A list of links to other resources on women's history is also available (http://scriptorium.lib.duke.edu/women/article.html), as are numerous digital collections. For more information on Duke's digital collections, see the Digital Collections section of this book.

Guide to Uncovering Women's History in Archival Collections

http://www.lib.utsa.edu/Archives/links.htm

The Archives for Research on Women and Gender at the University of Texas, San Antonio, has compiled a state-by-state listing of repositories with online descriptions of their women's history collections. The list is annotated and provides a hyperlink to each institution's home page.

Schlesinger Library, Radcliffe Institute for Advanced Study at Harvard

http://www.radcliffe.edu/schles/

The Arthur and Elizabeth Schlesinger Library on the History of Women in America is one of the most respected libraries on its topic in the world—and an excellent starting point for researchers. Examples of the manuscript collections include the personal papers of Charlotte Perkins Gilman, Betty Friedan, and Harriet Beecher Stowe. Visitors to its Web site will find descriptions of the Schlesinger's collections along with eighteen bibliographies on various aspects of women's history, from women in science to culinary resources.

Sophia Smith Collection of Women's History Manuscripts, Smith College

http://www.smith.edu/libraries/ssc/

With documentary strengths in women's political activism, women working abroad, and women in the arts and professions, the Sophia Smith Collection at Smith College houses substantial primary evidence of women's historical experience. Its Web site provides logistical information, thematic subject guides, and a list of collections. The permanent online exhibit, Agents of Social Change: New Resources on Twentieth-Century Women's Activism, chronicles women's role in the major reform movements of the century, including labor, civil rights, and welfare reform.

Chapter 40

Special Collections

Anne Rothfeld and Susan Tschabrun

Metasites

Archives Around the World: UNESCO Archives Portal

http://www.unesco.org/webworld/portal-archives

Not nearly as complete as Terry Abraham's Repositories of Primary Sources (below), this UNESCO site is worth knowing about for the important role UNESCO plays in helping archives around the world. This listing of over 4,000 links covers archives in Europe, North America, Latin America, Asia, and the Pacific as well as international archival organizations, professional associations, archival training, international cooperation, and Internet resources.

ARCHON: Archives Online

http://www.hmc.gov.uk/archon/archon.htm

The main gateway to repositories with manuscript material for British history, ARCHON is a key British resource for both archivists and researchers. The Royal Commission on Historical Manuscripts maintains the site. Researchers will be most interested in the British National Register of Archives (NRA) at www.hmc.gov.uk/nra/nra.html. The NRA leads researchers to a wide variety of manuscript collections, including papers of individuals of note, estates, local authorities, and societies, located both inside and outside the United Kingdom.

Users may search the indexes by name of individual or corporate body, type of corporate body, and place name.

Repositories of Primary Sources

http://www.uidaho.edu/special-collections/Other.Repositories.html

With over 4,600 links, this Web site is by far the most complete listing of Web sites for actual (not virtual) archives and special collections departments. Updated frequently by Terry Abraham of the University of Idaho, the site arranges its links by geographical region (continent, country, state, and province). Additional Lists is a good jumping-off point for other archive and special collections metasites.

RLIN AMC Search Form

http://lcweb.loc.gov/z3950/

This important search gateway will lead the researcher to descriptions of holdings for a large number of manuscript and archival repositories, predominately, but not exclusively, in the United States. Select from one of three straightforward, fill-in-the-blank search forms. This electronic catalog derives from the print source, the National Union Catalog of Manuscript Collections, a project of the Library of Congress. Check the List of RLIN Library Identifiers on the search forms to see a list of the participating institutions.

www.archivesinfo.net

http://www.archivesinfo.net

Originating out of a University of London master's project by Simon Wilson, this site—mainly targeted at archivists—provides two important listings of archival links useful to researchers: UK Archival Repositories on the Internet and Overseas Archival Repositories on the Internet. One of the best features of these lists is the annotations prepared by the site's author that briefly indicate each site's contents.

General Sites

Africa Research Central: A Clearinghouse of African Primary Sources

http://www.africa-research.org

A collaboration between a history professor and an academic librarian at California State University, San Bernardino, this site assists researchers to locate often scarce information about archives, libraries, and museums with primary source collections related to Africa. The site focuses on repositories in Africa, but also provides information for those in Europe and North America. An important mission of the site is to alert researchers to the preservation crisis under way in many countries in Africa and to indicate ways to help.

American Memory: Historical Collections for the National Digital Library

http://lcweb2.loc.gov/ammem/

The forty-two multimedia collections of over 7 million digitized documents, photographs, recorded sound, moving pictures, and text selected from the Library of Congress's vast Americana holdings cover topics as diverse as twentieth-century architectural design and ballroom dancing. The collections may be searched by keyword or browsed by titles, topics, or collection type. A fun spin-off is Today in History, which presents people, facts, and events associated with the current day's date. Educators are particularly targeted in the Learning Page with activities, lesson ideas, and other information to help teachers use the primary source material at American Memory in their classrooms.

Annuaire des archives et des bibliothèque nationales, des bibliothèque parlementaires et des centres nationaux d'information scientifique et technique de la Francophonie

http://www.acctbief.org/publica/anuinfsc.htm

This directory, originally published in print form in 1996, has been converted into a searchable Web database by the publishers, Canadian-based BIEF (Banque internationale d'information sur les États francophones). The directory includes basic contact information for the national archives and libraries of forty-seven francophone countries. Further descriptive information about the listed institutions can often be found in a BIEF companion Web site, titled *Profis géodocumentaires des états et gouvernements membres des sommets francophones.* Together, these databases are an important source of scarce information about archives for many smaller, non-Western countries.

Archives and Knowledge Management: Scholarly Online Resource Evidence and Records

http://www.dcn.davis.ca.us/~vctinney/archives.htm

Created and maintained by V. Chris and Thomas M. Tinney Sr., retired genealogical specialists, this Web site includes links to resources of particular interest to genealogists, including a link to the Genealogy on the Web site and the Salt Lake City LDS Family History Center. The Tinney Family organizes their links to archives, libraries, and many other types of resources in a variety of categories, from Business, Community and Geography, and Religion to Surnames.

Archives in Deutschland

http://www.uni-marburg.de/archivschule/deuarch.html

This list of archival resources, maintained by Karsten Uhde of the Archivschule Marburg in Germany, brings together links of interest to both archivists and researchers. Historians and genealogists will find the following pages particularly useful: Archives in Germany, listing German archives by type (state, city, church, etc.); Archives in Europe; non-European Archives; and Genealogy.

Archives of American Art

http://artarchives.si.edu/start/htm

The Smithsonian maintains the Archives of American Art (AAA) and its Web site to provide researchers with access to "the largest collection of documents on the history of the visual arts in the United States"—13 million items, including the papers of artists, dealers, critics, art historians, museums, and art-related organizations of all kinds. The letters, sketchbooks, diaries, and other paper archives are supplemented with a large oral history interview collection and a sizable photograph collection. General collection descriptions of AAA treasures can be found in the Smithsonian online catalog (SIRIS) as well as RLIN, and the Smithsonian is beginning to make more detailed finding aids available as well.

Archives of Traditional Music at Indiana University

http://www.indiana.edu/~libarchm/

This Web site provides information about an important and unusual archive of ethnographic sound materials housed at Indiana University. The largest such university-based archive in the United States, the Archives of Traditional Music preserves commercial and field recordings of vocal and instrumental music, folktales, interviews, and oral history from the state of Indiana, the United States, and the diverse cultures of the world. Holdings can be searched using the IUCAT online catalog.

ArchivesUSA

http://archives.chadwyck.com/

Chadwyck-Healey, Inc., has developed a product that is an important tool for researchers interested in locating archival material in the United States. Although ArchivesUSA is a subscription service and therefore not available for free over the Web, it is an important resource that some libraries and archives make available to the public. ArchivesUSA integrates the entire print edition of the National Union Catalog of Manuscript Collections with other sources of information to create a more complete record for a greater number of repositories than is available through RLIN AMC (see above).

The Avalon Project at the Yale Law School: Documents in Law, History and Government

http://www.yale.edu/lawweb/avalon/avalon.htm

Directed by William C. Fray and Lisa A. Spar, the Avalon Project is a major source of digital primary source documents in the fields of law, history, economics, politics, diplomacy, and government. Access to the documents is by time period (mainly century), author/title, and subject. Major collections include the Nuremberg Trials Collection and the Native American Treaty Collection. A recent addition to the digital repository is a section on the Cuban Missile Crisis and its aftermath with over 250 documents (including editorial notes), prefatory essay, and lists of persons and abbreviations—a good example of the project's aim not simply to mount static text, but to add value.

Black Film Center/Archive

http://www.indiana.edu/~bfca/

By and about African-Americans, the historic 700 films housed at the Black Film Center/Archives at Indiana University consist of both Hollywood and independent efforts. Supplementing the films and videotapes are interviews, photographs, and other archival material. The Web site gives access to descriptions of the repository's holdings, the Frame by Frame database, and related Internet sites.

Canadian Archival Resources on the Internet

http://www.usask.ca/archives/menu.html

A comprehensive list of links to Canadian archives and associated resources on the Internet, this guide is the work of two Canadian archivists: Cheryl Avery, University of Saskatchewan Archives, and Steve Billinton, Archives of Ontario. Researchers can locate archives by name, type (provincial, university, municipal, religious, and medical), and Canadian region and find links to archival educational resources, associations, listservs, and multirepository databases.

Directory of Archives in Australia

http://www.asap.unimelb.edu.au/asa/directory/asa_dir.htm

The updated Web version of a directory originally printed in 1992, this directory of Australian archives allows researchers to browse archives alphabetically and by Australian states and to search them by keyword. There are also handy lists of links to Australian archives and finding aids on the Web.

Directory of Corporate Archives in the United States and Canada

http://www.hunterinformation.com/corporat.htm

The fifth edition of this important print directory, put out by the Society of American Archivists, Business Archives Section, has recently moved to the Web. From Amgen to Walt Disney Corporation, each corporate archive entry supplies contact information, type of business, hours of service, conditions of access, and holding information. "Corporate" is interpreted broadly, including professional associations ranging from the American Psychiatric Association to the International Longshoremen's Union. The directory may be searched by name of corporation, name of archivist, or by geographical location.

DPLS Online Data Archive

http://dpls.dacc.wisc.edu/archive.html

The Data and Program Library Service at the University of Wisconsin is creating access to a large selection of archival machine-readable datasets (raw data and documentation files) that can be downloaded for use by social science researchers. The datasets, listed in reverse chronological order or alphabetically by title, cover raw data from an extremely diverse range of historical and current topics, such as French Old Regime Bureaucrats (1661–1790), Vegetation Change in the Bahamas (1972), and the effects of the Learnfare Program (1993–1996).

EuroDocs: Primary Historical Documents from Western Europe: Selected Transcriptions, Facsimiles and Translations

http://library.byu.edu/~rdh/eurodocs/

Aiming to provide digitized documents that shed light on "key historical happenings" in political, economic, social, and cultural history, EuroDocs links to a wealth of digitized resources organized under twenty-three Western European countries from Andorra to Vatican City. Documents are also accessible from pages devoted to Medieval and Renaissance Europe and to Europe as a Supranational Region. EuroDocs is a project of Richard Hacken, the European Studies Bibliographer at the Harold B. Lee Library, Brigham Young University in Provo, Utah.

Guía preliminar de fuentes documentales etnográficas para el estudio de los pueblos indígenas de Iberoamérica

http://www.lanic.utexas.edu/project/tavera/

An important guide in the Spanish language, made available on the Web, the Guía describes the holdings related to indigenous peoples at hundreds of libraries and archives throughout Latin America, the United States, and Europe. A project of La Fundacién Histérica Tavera in Spain, the Guía is organized by country and type of archive (civil or ecclesiastical), providing contact information and holdings descriptions for all of the institutions listed.

A Guide to Uncovering Women's History in Archival Collections

http://www.lib.utsa.edu/Archives/links.htm

This guide to the archives, libraries, and other repositories on the Web with archival materials by or about women is maintained by the Archives for Research on Women and Gender Project at the University of Texas at San Antonio. Arranged by states in the United States (plus a link devoted to institutions outside of the United States), each listing includes annotations indicating which materials in a given collection may be of interest to researchers in women's history.

Historical Maps: The Perry-Castañeda Library Map Collection

http://www.lib.utexas.edu/maps

A wonderful collection of digitized historical maps from all regions of the world offered by the Libraries at the University of Texas at Austin. Maps are organized by continent (including the polar regions and oceans), and each map listing gives both publication information and file size. Although most maps are in JPEG format in the 200–300K range, some map files are much larger, so expect some slow load times. The site also includes links to other historical map collections.

International Institute of Social History

http://www.iisg.nl

Founded in 1935 in the Netherlands, IISH is one of the world's largest archival and research institutions in the field of social history, particularly labor history. Its 2,000 archival collections cover a range of topics not always well represented in traditional archives, like anarchism, revolutionary populism in nineteenth-century Eastern Europe, the French revolution and Utopian socialism, and World War II resistance movements. Collections may be identified using an online catalog, a list of archival collections, or other finding aids. Other IISH resources include the William Morris Archive on the Web; Occassio, a collection of digital social history documents; and numerous electronic publications. The institute's image collections are highlighted by virtual exhibitions such as The Chairman Smiles and Art to the People.

National Archives and Records Administration

http://www.nara.gov

NARA's Web site is a rich source of information for historians, genealogists, teachers, and students. For historians, the Research Room organizes information about historical archival records by branch of government and type of material. For genealogists, the Genealogy Page publishes practical information about using NARA's facilities nationwide, and a growing list of "quick guides" on census, military, immigration, and other types of records. Teachers and students will appreciate the Digital Classroom: Primary Sources, Activities, and Training for Educators and Students, with reproducible documents and teaching activities. The Online Exhibit Hall is a showcase for NARA treasures. Finally, NARA's searchable database, the Archival Information Locator (NAIL), contains more than 386,500 descriptions of selected NARA holdings in Washington, D.C., the regional archives, and Presidential libraries, including 106,215 digital copies of selected textual documents, photographs, maps, and sound recordings.

New York Public Library for the Performing Arts

http://www.nypl.org/research/lpa/lpa.html

"The world's most extensive combination of circulating, reference, and rare archival collections" in the performing arts, this Web site describes the library's important collections of recordings, videotapes, autograph manuscripts, correspondence, sheet music, stage designs, press clippings, programs, posters, and photographs in the areas of dance, music, and theater.

Online Archive of California

http://sunsite2.Berkeley.edu/oac

The Online Archive of California is an umbrella site bringing together information on a steadily increasing number of archival institutions in California. Its most important resource is a centralized database of 120 searchable electronic finding aids, which allows a level of precision searching for archival materials not available in more traditional online library catalogs, like RLIN AMC (above).

Portuguese Libraries, Archives and Documentation Services on the Internet

http://www.sdum.uminho.pt/bad/bibpte.htm

This simple, but useful Web site provides links to the thirty-three libraries, archives, and documentation centers in Portugal with an Internet presence. Maintained by the Working Group on Information Technologies of the *Associação Portuguesa de Bibliotecários, Arquivistas e Documentalistas.*

Social Science Data Archives: Europe

http://www.nsd.uib.no/cessda/europe.html

A map of Europe organizes links to fourteen important European social science data archives, with separate links to similar non-European institutions. Maintained by the CESSDA (Council of European Social Science Data Archives), this Web site also allows researchers to search the holdings of eleven electronic data repositories through its Integrated Data Catalogue.

Television News Archive

http://tvnews.vaderbilt.edu

Vanderbilt University holds "the world's most extensive and complete archive of television news," including 30,000 evening news broadcasts and 9,000 hours of special news-related programming. These news broadcasts have been consistently recorded and preserved by the archive since 1968. The Web site makes several searchable indexes available, including Network Television Evening News Abstracts, Special Reports and Periodic News Broadcasts, and Specialized News Collections (containing descriptive summaries of news material for major events like the Persian Gulf War of 1991). The archive is willing to loan videotapes to researchers worldwide.

United States Holocaust Memorial Museum

http://www.ushmm.org/research/collections

The Archive of the Holocaust Memorial Museum in Washington, D.C., has gathered together 13 million pages of microfilmed documents, 50,000 photo images, 200 hours of historical motion picture footage, 250 documentary or feature films, and 2,900 oral interviews related to the Holocaust, its origins, and its aftermath. The document and photographic archives may be searched individually or together using the USHMM Information Access query form available at the Web site.

USIA Declassified Historical Information

http://fbcdrom.fb10.uni-bremen.de/cd/infousa/usiaweb/usis/index.html

Pursuant to Executive Order 12958, the USIA (United States Information Agency) Declassification Unit prepares a listing of declassified documents in order to alert the general public, especially academic researchers, to information no longer classified. Researchers may do keyword searching of this listing or browse by broad topic, from Africa to Youth, to find the titles of more than 5,300 classified and unclassified one-cubic-foot boxes of records coming from the National Archives and many other document-holding federal agencies.

Chapter 41

Digital Collections

Susan Ferentinos

The World Wide Web has created the opportunity to share history with a wider audience, and more and more repositories are rising to the challenge by digitizing selections of primary documents and making them available through the Internet. The following list is comprised of prime examples of the potential of the Web to open archives to an ever wider array of people. The sites below contain extensive collections of digitized documents and/or particularly well-curated online exhibits. The sites are in English unless otherwise noted.

Metasites

Library Exhibits on the Web

http://www.sil.si.edu/SILPublications/Online-Exhibitions/

The Smithsonian Institution Libraries maintain this list of links to online exhibits curated by libraries and manuscript repositories. Only exhibits containing digital images and textual descriptions are included, and the majority have a historical theme. The list is arranged alphabetically by exhibit title; unfortunately, it is not yet searchable by keyword or subject.

Other Digital Image Sites (DL SunSITE) ✓

http://sunsite.berkeley.edu/Collections/otherimage.html

Links to dozens of digital imaging projects are available through this list maintained by the Berkeley SunSITE (see below). By following the links, users can access digitized photos, maps, sheet music, and manuscripts. It is a nice starting point for the visually inclined researcher.

Other Digital Text Sites (DL SunSITE)

http://sunsite.berkeley.edu/Collections/othertext.html

Part of the Berkeley SunSITE (see below), this list links users to dozens of digital text collections on the World Wide Web. It covers multiple topics and thus is a good site for historians who draw on other disciplines, such as literature, in their research.

General Sites

American Memory from the Library of Congress ✓

http://lcweb2.loc.gov/ammem/ammemhome.html

The American Memory Web site contains online versions of photographs, documents, sound recordings, and motion pictures from the Library of Congress Americana collections. Currently, nearly 100 collections are included in the site, which is searchable and updated frequently. New collections are added monthly, making American Memory one of the largest digital archives projects currently available.

Berkeley Digital Library SunSITE

http://sunsite.berkeley.edu/

This site offers both digital collections of archival material and resources for the development of such collections. The Catalogs and Indexes page lists databases for finding historical documents, while the Collections section links to primary documents available for perusal on the Web.

The Digital Past

http://www.digitalpast.org/

Twenty local Illinois libraries, all part of the North Suburban Library System, contributed historic collections to this digital archive. Holdings include cemetery lists, medical ledgers, newspaper clippings, photographs, and a collection of documents pertaining to the American Nazi Party's attempt to stage a demonstration in Skokie, Illinois, in 1978. Visitors can browse the collections using various criteria of selection or perform more specific keyword searches.

Digital Sources Center, Michigan State University

http://digital.lib.msu.edu/

The special collections division of the Michigan State University Library has undertaken an ambitious project to digitize its holdings on selected topics. These collections include American radicalism, cookbooks, early French writings, comics, temperance, and botany, among others. The majority of the digitized items are page scans of entire books published in the nineteenth century or earlier. Digitization work is ongoing, so offerings continue to grow.

Early Canadiana Online

http://www.canadiana.org

Maintained by the Canadian Institute for Historical Microreproductions (CIHM), this digital collection of primary sources contains thousands of books and pamphlets documenting Canadian history from European contact to the early twentieth century. The full text of each of these documents is searchable and is available in PDF format.

Gallica: France

http://gallica.bnf.fr/

This endeavor of the French National Library aims to digitize major contributions to French history and culture. The offerings, covering the period from the Middle Ages to the nineteenth century, pertain to philosophy, literature, and the sciences as well as history. To date, over 80,000 documents have been added, including text, prints, audio, and video. The site is entirely in French.

The Library of Virginia Digital Collections

http://www.lva.lib.va.us/dlp/index.htm

A gold mine for genealogists, the Library of Virginia Digital Collections site contains over eighty databases, including many digitized versions of old card catalogs. These catalogs include indexes of Virginia marital records, birth and death certificates, wills, land deeds, war pensions, and court proceedings. In addition, numerous manuscript collections have also been digitized. Most of these online documents are maps and photographs, although some family Bible records are also included.

Making of America (MOA)

http://www.umdl.umich.edu/moa/

The Making of America (MOA) project provides the text of 8,500 books and 50,000 journal articles published in the United States, primarily between 1850 and 1877. The collection includes scientific writings, religious tracts, and publications in the then-emerging fields of education and psychology. Users can access the material through specific searches or by browsing lists of holdings.

National Archives and Records Administration (NARA) Online Exhibit Hall ✓

http://www.nara.gov/exhall/exhibits.html

The Online Exhibit Hall of NARA offers numerous exhibits on United States history, as well as showcasing individual documents of great import. Two exhibits deal with different aspects of World War II, and When Nixon Met Elvis contains documents and photos surrounding this odd event that occurred in 1970. The American Originals exhibit provides access to documents of the nation's most moving events, such as the police blotter listing President Lincoln's assassination and the 1868 treaty with the Sioux Indian Nation. Additional digital documents can be accessed from the NARA Archival Information Locator (http://www.nara.gov/nara/nail.html). NARA's Digital Classroom section is a leader in the effort to bring primary documents into the nation's classrooms via the Internet.

Prints and Photographs: An Illustrated Guide

http://lcweb.loc.gov/coll/print/guide/

The Library of Congress maintains this rich resource of prints and photographs in its collections. The guide is divided into six thematic chapters: An American Gallery; Pictorial Journalism; Politics and Propaganda; Architecture, Design, and Engineering; American Landscape and Cityscape; and The World at Large (featuring depictions of other countries). Each section offers an introduction to the theme and images that illustrate the topic. Each image is accompanied by an annotation describing its significance. The site includes a chronology of the library's acquisition of substantial print and photograph collections.

Rare Book, Manuscript, and Special Collection Library at Duke University ✓

http://scriptorium.lib.duke.edu/

This site showcases Duke's award-winning Digital Scriptorium, an online collection of historical items from the library's holdings. The documents are accompanied by informational essays providing historical context, transcriptions (where applicable), and links to related information. The scriptorium's selections reflect the strengths of the library: African-Americans, women, advertising, and music. Much of Duke's impressive papyrus collection is also represented. From this site, users can access an impressive array of subject guides to Duke's collections.

San Diego Historical Society ✓

http://www.sandiegohistory.org

In addition to the usual information on upcoming events and operating hours, the San Diego Historical Society provides an extensive array of historical information on its Web site. The site includes historical postcards; numerous photographs and informational articles, particularly on the Panama-California Exposition (1915–1916) and the California Pacific Exposition (1935–1936) ; biographical sketches of dozens of past residents of San Diego; a photo gallery that includes early motorcycles, diners, and amusement parks; excerpts from oral history interviews in the society's collections (http://www.sandiegohistory.org/audio/audiofile.htm); and accounts of colorful moments in San Diego history from Rick Crawford's *Stranger than Fiction*. With an eye toward the quirky, this site is a delightful introduction to the history of San Diego.

Schoenberg Center for Electronic Text and Image, University of Pennsylvania ✓

http://www.library.upenn.edu/etext/

The Schoenberg Center for Electronic Text and Image (SCETI) allows access to digital versions of selected images and documents from the University of Pennsylvania Special Collections. The site hosts multiple online exhibits, plus an assortment of texts reflecting the library's strengths in South Asian manuscripts; sheet music; cookbooks; diaries; and artifacts about science, the occult, and religion, among other topics. The center's current focus is on creating "a major archive of virtual Shakespeareana."

Special Collections Digital Center, University of Virginia

http://www.lib.virginia.edu/speccol/scdc/scdc.html

The Special Collections Digital Center of the University of Virginia serves both as a gateway to the unique library holdings of the university and a clearinghouse of information on digitization. The Collections section of the site provides access to such treasures as Thomas Jefferson's handwritten letters, Walt Whitman's personal notebooks, photographs of early twentieth-century African-American life, and Sanborn fire insurance maps of the Charlottesville, Virginia, area. The Exhibitions section leads to nearly two dozen online exhibits. For those seeking further guidance on the process of digitization, the Information section offers links to a variety of educational sites on the topic.

Treasures from Europe's National Libraries

http://www.kb.nl/gabriel/treasures/entree.html

Part of the Gabriel site described in the Archives chapter above, this site brings together the treasures of forty libraries throughout Eastern and Western Europe. Visitors can browse the digital collection by document type, subject, country of origin, or time period, and each item is accompanied by a brief description of its significance. The presentation more resembles a museum exhibit than a research database, however, as complete multipage documents are not included.

Chapter 42

Online Reference Desk

Anne Rothfeld

Metasites

Argus Clearinghouse

http://www.clearinghouse.net

"Provides a central access point for value-added topical guides which identify, describe, and evaluate Internet based information resources."

Avalon Project at Yale Law School

http://www.yale.edu/lawweb/avalon/avalon.html

Documents in law, history, and diplomacy from the pre-eighteenth, eighteenth, nineteenth, and twentieth centuries. "The Avalon Project will mount digital documents relevant to the fields of Law, History, Economics, Politics, Diplomacy and Government. We do not intend to mount only static text but rather to add value to the text by linking to supporting documents expressly referred to in the body of the text. The Avalon Project will no doubt contain controversial documents. Their inclusion does not indicate endorsement of their contents nor sympathy with the ideology, doctrines, or means employed by their authors. They are included for balance and because in some cases they are by our definition a supporting document."

.Center for History and New Media

http://chnm.gmu.edu

"The Center produces historical works in new media, tests the effectiveness of these products in the classroom, and reflects critically on the promises and pitfalls of new media in historical practice." In addition, the center's Web pages provide electronic access to extensive directories, journals, sources, and professional discussions related to historical issues. The center's resources are designed to benefit professional historians, high school teachers, and students of history.

History Cooperative

http://www.historycooperative.org

"A project of the American Historical Association (AHA), the Organization of American Historians (OAH), the University of Illinois Press, and the National Academy Press, this site currently offers free, full-text access to recent issues of the *American Historical Review* and the *Journal of American History*. In the near future, access will be restricted to members of the AHA and OAH, and to institutions that subscribe to the print versions."

History Departments Around the World

http://chnm.gmu.edu

Sponsored by the Center for History and New Media at George Mason University. "We hope that this list will help you find ideas for creating departmental web pages, let you look in on or locate colleagues, conduct historical research, or help out with a graduate or undergraduate application."

History Resources

http://blair.library.rhodes.edu/histhtmls/histnet.html

Covering a wide range of areas and regions: general compilations; general WWW servers; electronic texts, documents, exhibits, and collections; Asian, Middle Eastern, and African history; electronic journals and listservs; North American, European, and Western history; and maps. Many links are annotated. Sponsored by Rhodes University.

H-Net Humanities and Social Sciences Online

http://www2.h-net.msu.edu

"H-Net is an international interdisciplinary organization of scholars and teachers dedicated to developing the enormous educational potential of the Internet and the World Wide Web. Our edited lists and Web sites publish peer reviewed essays, multimedia materials, and discussion for colleagues and the interested public. The computing heart of H-Net resides at MATRIX: The Center for Humane Arts, Letters, and Social Sciences OnLine, Michigan State University, but H-Net officers, editors and subscribers come from all over the globe. H-Net's hundreds of volunteer editors foster online communities in the humanities and social sciences by monitoring email-based discussion lists and associated web sites."

INFOMINE

http://infomine.ucr.edu

"INFOMINE is intended for the introduction and use of Internet/Web resources of relevance to faculty, students, and research staff at the university level. It is being offered as a comprehensive showcase, virtual library and reference tool containing highly useful Internet/Web resources including databases, electronic journals, electronic books, bulletin boards, listservs, online library card catalogs, articles and directories of researchers, among many other types of information. INFOMINE is librarian built. Over thirty University of California and other university and college librarians have contributed to building INFOMINE."

Internet Public Library (IPL), Reference Center

http://www.ipl.org/ref

Provides links to general ready reference information and to specific subject areas. Links to additional subject-related sites are subdivided and annotated. IPL is also creating subject pathfinders. Maintained by the University of Michigan School of Information.

Research-It! Your One-Stop Reference Desk

http://www.iTools.com

A metasearch site for information including dictionaries, translations, biographical, and "quotation resources, maps, and stock quotes." Each area has its own search screen. Hosted by iTools!

Scout Report for Social Sciences and Humanities

http://scout.cs.wisc.edu/report/socsci/current/index.htm

A Publication of the Internet Scout Project, Computer Sciences Department, University of Wisconsin, Madison. "The target audience of the Scout Report for Social Sciences and Humanities is faculty, students, staff, and librarians in the social sciences and humanities. Each biweekly issue offers a selective collection of Internet resources covering topics in the field that have been chosen by librarians and content specialists in the given area of study. The Scout Report for Social Sciences and Humanities is also provided via e-mail once every two weeks. Subscription information is included at the bottom of each issue."

Reference Works

Almanacs

CIA World Factbook 2001

http://www.cia.gov/cia/publications/factbook

Complete resource of statistics, maps, and facts for over 250 countries and other entities. The *Factbook* is in the public domain. Other excellent resources are linked, including Chiefs of State and Cabinet Members of Foreign Governments and selected task force reports. Prepared by the CIA with information provided by numerous federal agencies including the Bureau of the Census, Bureau of Labor Statistics, Department of State, Defense Intelligence Agency, and U.S. Board on Geographic Names.

Information Please

http://www.infoplease.com

Information Please LLC has been publishing almanacs for over fifty years. Features a daily dictionary, encyclopedia, almanac, interactive almanac, learning networks, and theme-based almanacs covering the subject areas of the world, United States, history/government, biography, sports, entertainment, and weather/climate.

PoliSci.com Headquarters

http://www.polisci.com

Some portions of this Web site are fee-based and require a password. The site covers U.S. political information: U.S. government; state and local government; political science; economics; and political history. Includes the political reference desk (fee-based); links to news centers, newspapers, and magazines; book reviews and book listings; and the political reference almanac. Maintained by Keynote Publishing Co.

Archives

ArchivesUSA: Integrated Collection and Repository Information

http://archives.chadwyck.com

Fee-based service providing information and access to primary source holdings of 5,400 repositories, indexes to 118,000 special collections, and links to over 900 online finding aids. ArchivesUSA includes three major references: Directory of Archives and Manuscript Repositories in the United States (DAMRUS); National Union Catalogue of Manuscript Collections (NUCMC); and National Inventory of Documentary Sources in the United States (NIDS). ArchivesUSA on the Web is updated quarterly.

Historical Text Archive

http://www.historicaltextarchive.com

This site is divided into two sections: articles, books, documents, and photographs, and Web links to other sites. Organized by geographical and topical subject headings, sites focus on the studying and teaching of history.

Manuscripts Catalogue

http://molcat.bl.uk/

"This site is designed to serve as a single access point to information on the catalogs of the British Library's Department of Manuscripts, which cover accessions from 1753 to the present day. Visitors may search the catalogs index (a list of those available online can be found in the About section) by name, language, year, and other modifiers."

Repositories of Primary Sources

http://www.uidaho.edu/special-collections/Other.Repositories.html

This site lists over 4,500 Web and Gopher sites describing special collections holdings in the United States, including manuscripts and photographs. Repositories are divided geographically and subdivided by states. Additional links include other history-related Web sites with an international scope and subject specialty. Comprehensive and updated monthly. Maintained at the University of Idaho Library Special Collections and Archives.

Biographies

Biographical Dictionary

http://www.s9.com/biography

A database including over 28,000 notable men and women from ancient times to the present day, searchable by name, birth year, death year, and other keywords. The site contains links to biography-related sites, arranged by subject, and tips for students and teachers on how to use this resource in the classroom. Hosted by S9 Technologies.

Biography.com

http://www.biography.com

Searchable database with over 25,000 biographical entries and 2,500 video clips. Features discussions and materials for the classroom. Site is produced by A&E.

Dictionaries and Thesauri

The Alternative Dictionaries

http://www.notam.uio.no/~hcholm/altlang

Contains over 3,100 words and phrases in 120 different languages that would not be found in a standard dictionary. Readers and users can add words to the site.

Merriam-Webster Dictionary

http://www.m-w.com/dictionary.htm

Sponsored by Merriam-Webster, Inc. Full definitions with an online thesaurus available. Features new words recently added, word of the day, and language InfoZone, a portal to additional online resources.

Oxford English Dictionary Online

http://www.oed.com/

Fee-based service. Second edition now available, updated quarterly.

Roget's Thesaurus

http://www.thesaurus.com

Print version now online.

Wordsmyth English Dictionary-Thesaurus

http://www.wordsmyth.net

Users can search for exact words or words in phrases. Search returns definition and pronunciation guides. The site provides access to additional dictionaries and words of the week. Produced by Robert Parks and the ARTFL Project at the University of Chicago.

YourDictionary.com

http://www.yourdictionary.com

A metasite linking over 1,800 multilingual dictionaries, thesauri, and other sites relating to words and phrases. Grammar guides in selected languages are also available. Its predecessor, the Web of Online Dictionaries, was launched in 1995 at Bucknell Unviersity as a linguistic tool. YourDictionary.com also includes the Endangered Language Repository (ELR) to preserve almost extinct languages.

Dissertations and Theses

Electronic Theses and Dissertations in the Humanities

http://etext.lib.virginia.edu/ETD/ETD.html

Created in 1996, Electronic Theses and Dissertations is a directory and listing of those theses and dissertations currently in progress. Contains initiatives and a bibliography documenting arguments of electronic theses and dissertations.

Networked Digital Library of Theses and Dissertations

http://www.ndltd.org

A portal for dissemination of theses and dissertations. The site's goals include "to improve graduate education," "to increase the availability of student research," and "to empower universities."

UMIs Online Dissertation Services

http://www.umi.com:8080/hp/Support/DServices

Links to published and archived dissertations and theses and those available for purchase. Maintains a comprehensive bibliography for over 1.4 million doctoral dissertations and master's theses. Listing of best-selling dissertations is also available.

Encyclopedias

Encyclopedia Britannica Online

http://www.eb.com

This is a fee-based resource. Content is taken from the print edition. The site also includes Britannica Books of the Year, Nation's of the World, Merriam-Webster's *Collegiate Dictionary*, 13,000 graphics and illustrations, and links to related Web sites.

Encyclopedia.com

http://www.encyclopedia.com

Free encyclopedia featuring more than 50,000 articles from *The Concise Columbia Electronic Encyclopedia*, third edition.

Symbols.com: Encyclopedia of Western Signs and Ideograms

http://www.symbols.com

Site contains over 2,500 Western signs with discussions of histories, uses, and meanings. Users can search using the graphic index or the word index. Online version of *Thought Signs* by Carl G. Liungman.

FAQs (Frequently Asked Questions)

Encyclopedia Smithsonian

http://www.si.edu/resource/faq

Encyclopedia Smithsonian features answers to the Smithsonian's FAQs with links to available Smithsonian resources. Topics are filed alphabetically.

FAQ Search Engine

http://www.cs.ruu.nl/cgi-bin/faqwais

This search engine allows users to search FAQs and other informative articles from a large database of newsgroups. Alphabetically indexed. From the Institute of Information and Computing Services at the University of Utrecht.

Geographic Names and Maps

Getty Thesaurus of Geographic Names

http://www.getty.edu/research/tools/vocabulary

Sponsored by the Getty Research Institute, this site currently has information for the Art and Architecture Thesaurus (AAT), the Union List of Artist Names (ULAN), and the Getty Thesaurus of Geographic Names (TGN). The TGN currently has over a million geographic names and places. Users can search by using geographic hierarchy displays, definition/description of term, other known names, and sources. AAT contains over 125,000 terms and notes for describing fine art, archival materials, and material culture. ULAN contains over 220,000 names and biographical information about artists and architects.

Perry-Castañeda Library Map Collection: Historical Map Web Sites

http://www.lib.utexas.edu/maps/Map_sites/hist_sites.html

Links to historical maps at other Web sites. Scope of site includes historical maps from Africa, Asia, the Pacific, North and South America, Europe, and the Middle East; also includes astronomical maps.

USGS (United States Geological Survey) Mapping Information: Geographic Names Information System (GNIS)

http://geonames.usgs.gov/

Contains over 2 million physical and cultural geographic features in the United States supplied by the Geographic Names Information System (GNIS) and U.S. Board on Geographic Names (BGN). Includes a search engine and links to online geographic resources.

Government and State Resources

FedStats

http://www.fedstats.gov

Statistical information gateway for over 100 federal government agencies and departments. FedStats is searchable by topics, such as demography, education, and labor. Each site provides annotated links. Includes the Statistical Abstract of the United States.

Social Statistics Briefing Room

http://www.whitehouse.gov/fsbr/ssbr.html

Access to current federal social statistics on crime, demographics, education, and health. Links are produced and provided by numerous federal agencies. Graphics are available.

THOMAS: U.S. Congress on the Internet

http://thomas.loc.gov/

Users can search for congressional bills, the Congressional Record, committee bills, and historical documents. FAQs regarding THOMAS are available. Links to other government agencies.

Indexes

Librarians' Index to the Internet

http://lii.org

Annotated directory to 7,900 Web resources arranged by subject, including over 200 history-related sites. Using the available search engine can focus a search. Produced by the Berkeley Public Library and Berkeley SunSITE.

The WWW-Virtual Library History Index

http://www.ukans.edu/history/VL

A portal to over 3,500 electronic resources arranged by different topics of history. Links also include research methods and materials, eras and epochs, and countries and regions. Users can recommend sites.

Internet Tutorials

Evaluating Internet Resources

http://library.albany.edu/internet/evaluate.html

Discusses what elements should be included in a reliable Web site and why—for example, the intended audience, the source of the content, accuracy and comprehensiveness of the content, and the style and functionality of the page.

Searching the Internet: Recommended Sites and Search Techniques

http://library.albany.edu/internet/search.html

Searching hints and tips for successful usage of subject directories and search engines within Web pages.

Libraries

The Library of Congress

http://www.loc.gov/

"The nation's oldest federal cultural institution. The Library preserves a collection of nearly 121 million items, more than two-thirds of which are in media other than books. These include the largest map, film and television collections in the world. In addition to its primary mission of serving the research needs of the U.S. Congress, the Library serves all Americans through its popular Web site and in its 22 reading rooms on Capitol Hill."

The National Agricultural Library

http://www.nal.usda.gov/

"As the Nation's primary source for agricultural information, the National Agricultural Library (NAL) has a mission to increase the availability and utilization of agricultural information for researchers, educators, policymakers, consumers of agricultural products, and the public. The Library is one of the world's largest and most accessible agricultural research libraries and plays a vital role in supporting research, education, and applied agriculture."

The National Library of Education

http://www.ed.gov/NLE/

NLE is the federal government's main resource for education information.

U.S. National Library of Medicine

http://www.nlm.nih.gov/

The World's largest biomedical library explores the uses of computer and communication technologies to improve the organization and use of biomedical information, supports a national network of local and regional medical libraries, and educates users about available sources of information.

Listservs

H-Net

http://www2.h-net.msu.edu

For historians, librarians, and archivists, H-Net hosts over 100 different topical listservs, a call for papers page, conference announcements, and employment information.

Tile.Net: The Comprehensive Internet Reference

http://tile.net

Search for discussion lists, newsgroups (Usenet), and FTP sites by entering a subject search. All of the results are linked to a page describing the listing and how to subscribe.

Quotations

Bartlett's Familiar Quotations (1901)

http://www.columbia.edu/acis/bartleby/bartlett

Sponsored by Columbia University's Bartleby Library Archive. The tenth edition, published in 1919, is available online, whereas the sixteenth edition is available in print. Includes English and French writers and wisdom from the ancients. Browse by author or search by keyword. Indexes are available to browse by author, both alphabetical and chronological.

Quotations Home Page

http://www.geocities.com/~spanoudi/quote.html

Use this home page to find quotations from twentieth-century authors and orators, arranged by topic. Provides specialized databases of quotations including Alternative Definitions, Serious Sarcasm, Childsong, Film, and Good Starts. This site contains 24,000 quotations in over thirty collections.

The Quotations Page

http://www.quotationpage.com

Users can read quotes of the day and motivational quotes of the day. This site, which can be searched, contains links to other quotation sites.

Statistics

Historical U.S. Census Data Browser

http://fisher.lib.virginia.edu/census

Descriptions of the people and the economy of the United States for each state and county from 1790 to 1970.

Statistical Abstract of the United States

http://www.census.gov/statab/www

Excellent resource for statistical information: demographics, employment, industrial production statistics, and government financial information. Online information covers data from 1995 to 2000.

Statistical Resources on the Web

http://www.lib.umich.edu/libhome/Documents.center/stats.html

A metasite of statistical information. Searchable using the indexes, including business, demographics, labor, education, and sociology. Includes annotated links to government resources on the Web. Maintained by University of Michigan Documents Center.

U.S. Census Bureau: U.S. Gazetteer

http://tiger.census.gov/cgi-bin/gazetteer

Census data on all incorporated municipalities in the United States. Maps provided.

Student and School Information

American Universities

http://www.clas.ufl.edu/CLAS/american-universities.html

A metasite listing universities and colleges in the United States.

CollegeNet

http://www.collegenet.com

A search engine allows students to find the ideal college by using such categories as region, sports, major, and tuition. The site also covers scholarships and financial aid, college Web applications, and college recruiting. Virtual tours allow users to see campuses from their desktop, with links to the schools' Web sites.

History Departments Around the World

http://chnm.gmu.edu/history/depts

Alphabetical listing of links to history departments' home pages. Maintained by the Center for History and New Media at George Mason University.

Peterson's College Search

http://www.petersons.com/ugrad/ugsector.html

Users can search for their ideal college by major, region, and size of student population. The search results provide a link to an institution's profile, not its Web site.

Peterson's Guide: Colleges, Career Information, Test Prep, and More

http://www.petersons.com

Education resource with links to colleges and universities, graduate programs, and international programs. Users can search the database by keywords and subject specialty.

U.S. News and World Report Online: Graduate School Ranking

http://www.usnews.com/usnews/edu/beyond/bcrank.htm

Users can find a graduate program meeting their requirements. Includes methodology of rankings.

U.S. News and World Report Online: Undergraduate School Ranking

http://www.usnews.com/usnews/edu/college/corank.htm

This site allows users to locate a school by using categories, from the most expensive school to one with the best marching band! Includes methodology of rankings.

Style Manuals and Usage

Citing Electronic and Print Resources

http://www.lib.ucdavis.edu/citing/

Citation information for Modern Language Association (MLA), American Psychological Association (APA), Turabian style, *Chicago Manual of Style*, Council of Biology Editors, National Library of Medicine, and government information. Includes thorough discussions and examples.

MLA Online

http://www.mla.org/

Explanations of *MLA Handbook for Writers of Research Papers* and *MLA Style Manual* and *Guide to Scholarly Publications* are available online, including information about citing electronic resources. Official site for the Modern Language Association (MLA).

Strunk's Elements of Style

http://www.columbia.edu/acis/bartleby/strunk

The 1918 print edition is now available online.

Virtual Libraries

CARRIE: A Full-Text Electronic Library and Documents Room

http://www.ukans.edu/carrie/docs_main.html

Besides an electronic reference desk, this site contains selected full-text documents on these topics: the Catholic Church, United Nations, U.S. history, world constitutions, and World War I. Sponsored by University of Kansas.

THOR: The Virtual Reference Desk

http://thorplus.lib.purdue.edu/reference

Lists dictionaries, thesauruses, zip code directories, and other useful reference sources. Sponsored by Purdue University Libraries.

Virtual Library

http://library.albany.edu/subject/history.htm

The Virtual Library includes "sites in the news," which are hot topic sites; a reference section, which is subdivided into subject areas; subject and library catalogs, which include Internet resources and research databases; electronic publications; and fee-based services. All sites are linked, some with descriptions.

Specific Topics

Acronym Finder

http://www.acronymfinder.com

This site includes 196,000 common acronyms and abbreviations with definitions, including technology, telecommunications, computer science, and military acronyms. Updated weekly, the site contains search hints and links to other acronym sites. Sponsored by Mountain Data Systems.

The Best Information on the Net (BIOTN): The Librarians' Guide to Internet Information Sources

http://www.sau.edu/internet/

A portal to resources on the Internet. Links include hot paper topics, national and international newspapers, search engines, and a job-hunting guide. Geared for librarians and useful for historians. Site is sponsored by the librarians at O'Keefe Library, St. Ambrose University.

C-Net's Shareware

http://www.sharewarenet.com

Search engine listing over 190,000 shareware computer programs and links to sites where they can be downloaded.

Corporations

http://www.internet-propsector.org/company.html

Annotated links to corporate giving, company information, corporate directories, and stock quotes and securities. Includes links to Companies Online, CorpTech, and manufacturers' profiles. Maintained by Internet Prospector, Inc.

FinAid! The Smart Student Guide to Financial Aid

http://www.finaid.org/

"One of the most comprehensive annotated collections of information about student financial aid on the web." Includes links to loans, scholarships, and military aid; information on other types of aid; and tips for applying for aid.

Find-A-Grave

http://www.findagrave.com/index.html

Locate the graves of famous and nonfamous people. Database is organized by last name and geographic location; photos of some graves are included. Searchable by name, location, claim to fame, and date. Database currently contains over 2.5 million names in over 28,000 cemeteries.

Flags of the World

http://www.fotw.ca/flags

View more than 9,800 pages about flags and over 18,000 images. Flags can be searched by country, title, maps, and keywords. Site contains news and reports posted to the site's mailing list, a glossary, and a bibliography.

The Foundation Center: Your Gateway to Philanthropy on the WWW

http://fdncenter.org

The Foundation Center site provides grant information, funding trends and analysis, libraries and locations, and Foundation Center publications. Searchable links to over 160 sources of private, commercial, and corporate funding. Ranks foundations by assets and total giving.

The HistoryNet: Where History Lives on the Web

http://www.thehistorynet.com

Contains an archive of different topical areas, including eyewitness accounts, historic travel, and people profiles. Links to history magazines on the Internet and sponsors daily quizzes and factoids. Sponsored by the Cowles History Group.

Horus' Web Links to History Resources

http://www.ucr.edu/h-gig/horuslinks.htm

This Web page is designed to experiment in Internet history teaching and research. Contents include histories of specific countries, times, and places; areas of history; online services about history; Web tools; and searching hints. Hosted and supported by the University of California, Riverside, Department of History.

HyperHistory Online

http://www.hyperhistory.com/online_n2/History_n2/a.html

A 3,000–year timeline is available to access over 2,000 files with relevant maps, biographies, and brief histories of people, places, and events. The People section reaches from 1000 B.C.E. to the present for over 800 individuals in science, culture, religion, and politics. The History section displays timelines for major civilizations. The Events section continually grows on the site, ranging from 1790 to the present.

Intellectual Property Law

http://www.cs.utexas.edu/users/ethics/prop_rights/IP.html

Connects visitors to numerous topics including patents, trademarks, copyright, general intellectual property law, other resources on the Internet, and publications.

Internet Scout Project

http://scout.cs.wisc.edu/

Published every Friday on the Web and by e-mail, this site provides valuable information about new electronic and online resources free of charge. Subject report areas include social sciences; science and engineering; business and economics; and the site's general weekly report. Librarians and educators contribute reviews of useful and not-so-useful pages. Searchable archives.

Locating U.S. Corporation Records Online: A Directory of State Web Sites and Secretaries of State Contact Information

http://www.internet-propsector.org/secstate.html

Links to state Web sites that provide information on corporations within selected states. Databases for U.S. nonprofit companies in some states are available. Links to state home pages and secretaries of state. Locator provides a search engine to browse through over one million entries.

U.S. Copyright Office

http://www.loc.gov/copyright

The purpose of the U.S. Copyright Office is to "promote the Progress of Science and useful Arts, by securing for limited Times to Authors and Inventors the exclusive Right to their respective Writings and Discoveries" (U.S. Constitution, Article I, Section 8). This site describes how to file for a copyright, what can be copyrighted and the terms of a copyright and also includes information on the Digital Millennium Copyright Act, legislation, and publications.

Chapter 43

Online Databases

Andrew Sawyer and Jean Colson

American Memory from the Library of Congress

http://lcweb2.loc.gov/

American Memory is a gateway to rich primary source materials relating to the history and culture of the United States. The site offers access to 7 million digital items from more than 100 historical collections. Despite the complexity of the site, which serves as a top level to a wide range of collections from other institutions, the search facilities work quite well.

Berkeley Digital Library SunSITE

http://sunsite.berkeley.edu/

The site provides information and support to digital library developers, via pages and links covering a range of issues such as copyright and current R&D. An important resource for those contemplating online publication of sources.

The Age of King Charles V (1338–1380)

http://www.bnf.fr/enluminures/aaccueil.htm

Part of the Bibliothèque Nationale de France's site, this site contains a thousand illustrations from illuminated manuscripts, accessed by a walkthrough introduction, by themes, or by the manuscripts in which they appeared.

Chinese Biographical Database

http://www.lcsc.edu/cbiouser/

Created and managed by Marilyn A. Levine. Containing a wealth of prosopographical information on 3,500 individuals, mainly from the nineteenth and twentieth centuries, this site is underpinned by a helpful, clear, and explicit theoretical agenda relating the database to the wider needs of history. It includes an option for Chinese language searches and output.

Civil War Soldiers and Sailors System

http://www.itd.nps.gov/cwss/info.htm

The Civil War Soldiers and Sailors System is a computerized database containing very basic facts about servicemen who served on both sides during the Civil War. The initial focus of the CWSS is the Names Index Project, a project to enter names and other basic information from 5.4 million soldier records in the National Archives. Currently, 3 million names are searchable.

Clearinghouse of Image Databases

http://www.library.arizona.edu/images/image_projects.html

The Clearinghouse of Image Databases is a major online directory, hosted by the University of Arizona Library. It is multidisciplinary in scope, "targeted at professionals working with imaging technology, librarians, archivists, metadata specialists, database administrators and others who are planning or developing databases containing digital objects."

Columbia University Digital Library Collections

http://www.columbia.edu/cu/libraries/digital/

The site includes a range of texts and images online, together with e-journals. It also has good pages listing other datasets and databases of interest to the historian. However, parts of the site are open only to faculty and staff of the university.

Other Digital Image Collections

http://sunsite.berkeley.edu/Collections/otherimage.html

Part of Berkeley's SunSITE. A superb, if eclectic, range of sources, covering many periods and subjects. Especially noteworthy, in terms of online access, are the rich collections of pictorial and audio material. The site has useful links to other resources.

Digital National Security Archive

http://nsarchive.chadwyck.com/nsaindexhome.htm

Through the Digital National Security Archive, the National Security Archive and Chadwyck-Healey have joined forces to produce the most comprehensive collection available of significant primary documents central to U.S. foreign and military policy since 1945. More than 35,000 of the most important, declassified documents—totaling more than 200,000 pages—are included in the database. Many are published now for the first time. This is a subscription site.

The Digital Sources Center of the Michigan State University Libraries

http://digital.lib.msu.edu/

As well as a range of collections on American radicalism, this site covers more general humanities subjects, including, for example, sections on comic art, the history of osteopathy, and "Shaping the Values of Youth," a selection of Sunday School books. The size of the collections varies, and their availability in different forms (JPG, GIF, PDF, HTML, SGML, and XML) reflects the most appropriate mode of display.

Other Digital Text Collections

http://sunsite.berkeley.edu/Collections/othertext.html

Part of Berkeley's SunSITE. A primary metasite with many links to online texts covering a very wide eclectic range of periods and subjects, providing the historian with insights into related disciplines such as literature and anthropology. Includes oral history sites.

De Tachtigjarige Oorlog (The Eighty Years War)

http://dutchrevolt.leidenuniv.nl/default.htm

This site has a range of useful material relating to the Dutch Revolt (1568–1648), known as the Eighty Years War, including a considerable number of key contemporary texts, mostly in Dutch. In addition, nearly fifty sources, often referring to the role of the Reformed religion in the revolt, are available in English. Some of the sources have useful commentaries.

EuroDocs: Primary Historical Documents From Western Europe

http://library.byu.edu/~rdh/eurodocs/homepage.html

These links connect to a very extensive range of Western European historical documents that are transcribed, reproduced in facsimile, or translated. No search facility is provided at the top level, but the sites are carefully organized and navigation is straightforward.

Hanover Historical Texts Project

http://history.hanover.edu/project.html

Commenced in 1995, the Project's principal aim is to make primary texts readily available to students and faculty for use in history and humanities courses. Sources are classified by: the following categories Europe (ancient, the Middle Ages, early modern, modern), United States (seventeenth century, eighteenth century, nineteenth century, twentieth century), the Americas outside the United States, Africa, the Middle East, India and South Asia, and East Asia. Full scanning and proofing attributions are provided, with a useful guide to other historical datasets.

History Data Service

http://hds.essex.ac.uk/index.asp

The History Data Service (U.K.) collects, preserves, and promotes the use of digital resources that result from or support historical research, learning, and teaching. It holds over 500 separate data collections transcribed, scanned, or compiled from historical sources. The collection covers a time period from the late tenth century to the twentieth century and, although the primary focus is on the United Kingdom, includes a significant body of cross-national and international data collections. The collection is particularly strong in nineteenth- and twentieth-century economic and social history.

Images of Early Maps on the Web

http://ihr.sas.ac.uk/maps/webimages.html

Part of Tony Campbell's excellent Map History/History of Cartography site. Given the fragmented nature of map collecting and digitization, this comprehensive and well-maintained site acts as an excellent portal to online map collections. Several hundred online collections, graded by geographic coverage and size, can be reached from this page.

Index of Christian Art

http://www.princeton.edu/~ica/indexca.html

The Index of Christian Art records without geographical limitations works of art produced from early apostolic times up to 1400 C.E. (extended in the case of the Morgan Library project to include its manuscript holdings up to the end of the sixteenth century). Over 23,000 records from the collection are now available online, with powerful search tools including ICONCLASS classification.

Library and Archival Exhibitions on the Web

http://www.sil.si.edu/SILPublications/Online-Exhibitions/

This site features online exhibitions created by libraries, archives, and historical societies, as well as museum online exhibitions with a significant focus on library and archival materials, some of which include useful sources for historians.

Library of Congress Grant

http://memory.loc.gov/ammem/award/

Three years' funding from Ameritech resulted in awards to enable institutions to create digital collections of primary sources. The results, in the form of some significant projects, are available from this site.

Making of America (MOA)

http://moa.umdl.umich.edu/

Making of America is a digital library of primary sources in American social history from the antebellum period through Reconstruction. The collection is particularly strong in the subject areas of education, psychology, American history, sociology, religion, and science and technology. The collection currently contains 8,500 books and 50,000 journal articles with nineteenth-century imprints. The site has useful search tools for its impressive collection of texts.

Lopez Martin Collection of Maps and Manuscripts

http://www.ukans.edu/carrie/ms_room/martin_coll/welcome.html

This site covers the history of Spain, Portugal, and the Netherlands, with an emphasis on trade and shipping. It includes maps, manuscripts, and useful links to other map-oriented sites. The present collection is the first step of a wider project regarding the use of the Internet to study early modern Iberian history.

New York Public Library Digital Library Collection

http://digital.nypl.org/

This site includes some fine image collections, under these headings: A Hudson River Portfolio, Surveyors of the American West, African-American Women, Writers of the Nineteenth Century, and Studies Dedicated to Fernando Ortiz (1880–1969): A Bibliography of Afro-Cuban Culture. It does not contain any finding aids for online data, but it is a useful introduction to the breadth of the library's holdings.

Prints and Photographs: An Illustrated Guide

http://www.loc.gov/rr/print/guide/

The Library of Congress has a rich collection of prints and photographs; this site provides a glimpse of the material available. This small sample can be accessed via six thematic chapters, which offers useful interpretation, or from a list ordered by appearance in the essays.

Rare Book, Manuscript, and Special Collections Library: Duke University

http://scriptorium.lib.duke.edu/

Duke University's Digital Scriptorium presents a range of mostly U.S. sources—for example, over 16,000 pages of sheet music published in the United States between 1650 and 1920. There are also strong collections on African-Americans, advertising, and women's history and some of the university's papyrus collection.

Schoenberg Center for Electronic Text and Image (SCETI)

http://www.library.upenn.edu/etext/about/index.html

Offering access to the University of Pennsylvania's Special Collections, this site has books, manuscripts, photographs, maps, broadsides, ephemera, and recorded sound covering a range of subjects, including music, South Asian manuscripts, medieval manuscripts, collections of photographs, the occult, and early science.

Smithsonian Institution Libraries

http://www.sil.si.edu/newstart.htm

A range of digital resources, including a Featured Digital Edition for the month, which includes historical topics.

University of Houston Library: History Research on the Web: Getting Started

http://info.lib.uh.edu/histwww.htm

This site has links organized into General History sites and Examples of Specialized United States and World History sites, with a brief review of each. It provides a good, broad-ranging introduction to material on the web.

Virtual Exhibitions

http://www.bnf.fr/pages/expos/usindex.htm

This is the page for the Bibliothèque Nationale de France's virtual exhibitions. Currently listed exhibitions cover comic strips, the quest for Utopia in the Occident, Persian splendours, and Marcel Proust.

Glossary

ActiveX: This is a Microsoft technology used on the Internet. ActiveX controls can be downloaded from the Internet. These controls are "activated" by the Web browser and perform a variety of different functions, allowing users to view Microsoft word documents via the Web browser, play animated graphical effects, and display interactive maps. As the name suggests, ActiveX controls make the Web page "active"; and they provide the same functions as Java Applets.

alias: A name used in place of a "real" name. Aliases are often shorter or cleverer than a person's real name.

animated GIF file: A special type of GIF File. A collection of GIFs, presented one after the other, with each picture slightly different from the previous one, gives the impression of a video.

applet: An applet is a brief program written in the Java programming language that can be used only as part of a Web page.

ASCII (American Standard Code for Information Interchange): This is a way of formatting data so that it can be read by any program, whether DOS, Windows, or Mac.

BBS (bulletin board system): This term usually refers to small, dial-up systems that local users can call directly.

bit: A bit is the smallest unit of information understood by a computer. A bit can take a value of 0 or 1. A byte is made up of eight bits, which is large enough to contain a single character. A kilobyte is equivalent to 1,024 bytes. A mega-byte is equivalent to 1,024 kilobytes. A gigabyte is equivalent to 1,024 megabytes.

browser: A program used to access the World Wide Web. The most popular browsers—Netscape and Mosaic—allow users to interact audiovisually with the World Wide Web.

client: A synonym for Web browser or browser.

DNS (Domain Name System): DNS is the system which locates addresses on the WWW. A DNS error message given by a browser means the address it is looking for cannot be found.

document: On the WWW, a document can be either a file or a set of files that can be accessed with a Web browser.

download: The process of getting a file or files from a remote computer—that is, a computer other than the one on a user's desk or local area network.

e-mail (electronic mail): Sending typed messages and attachments through an electronic mail network.

encryption: A method of converting data into "unreadable code" so that prying eyes cannot understand the content.

FAQ (frequently asked questions): A FAQ is a document that contains answers to the most frequently asked questions about a given topic.

file: A file is a collection of data stored on a disk or other storage device under a certain name.

flame: The practice of sending negative or insulting e-mail.

FTP (file transfer protocol): FTP is a tool for moving files from another computer site to a user's local service provider's computer, from which they can be downloaded.

GIF (graphic interchange format): A set of standards for compressing graphic files so that they occupy less space in a computer's memory or on a storage device. CompuServe and Unisys developed GIF.

gopher: An older method of navigating the Internet developed at the University of Minnesota (where the mascot is the Golden Gopher). It displays information and links to documents, but is not graphics-based and is more difficult to use than the World Wide Web. The World Wide Web is rapidly replacing Gopher.

hits: This is Internet slang for both the number of times a site is accessed by a user and for the number of sites found when using any Web search engine.

H-Net (The Humanities Network, or Humanities Online Initiative): H-Net is an organization dedicated to exploiting the potential of electronic media for history. It is supported by the National Endowment for the Humanities, the University of Illinois–Chicago, and Michigan State University. H-Net sponsors discussion lists, Web sites, book reviews, conferences, and other activities.

home page: A home page is the designated beginning point for accessing a WWW site.

hypermedia: Computer-generated displays that combine text, images, and sound.

hypertext: Data that provide links to other data, allowing a user to move from one resource to another.

HTML (Hypertext Markup Language): This is the computer language used to construct documents on the World Wide Web. Most home pages are written in HTML.

http (hypertext transfer protocol): This is a method of coding information that enables different computers running different software to communicate information. It permits the transfer of text, sounds, images, and other data.

icon: A graphic image that is used to represent (and usually activate) a file or program.

Internet: The Internet refers to the worldwide network of computers that is linked together using the Internet protocol TCP/IP.

Java: A programming language developed by Sun Microsystems that allows programmers to create interactive applications that can be run within Web browsers on any type of computer. Java programs are referred to as applets.

JavaScript: A programming language for developing Internet applications. A Web browser interprets JavaScript statements embedded in an HTML page to create interactivity.

JPEG (Joint Photographic Experts Group): The standard format for compressing graphic files so that they occupy less space in a computer's memory or on a storage device.

Kbps (kilobits per second): The unit used to measure how fast data is transferred between devices on a network. One kilobit is 1,024 bits.

LAN (local area network): A group of computers connected together by cable or some other means so that they can share common resources.

link: A connection point that takes a user from one document to another or from one information provider to another.

listserv: A computer that serves a discussion group by processing, distributing, and storing messages and files for all members of the list.

log in: The process of gaining access to a remote computer system or network by typing the user's login name and password.

login name: The name used for security purposes to gain access to a network or computer system.

MPEG (Moving Pictures Expert Group): The standard format for compressing video images so that they occupy less space in a computer's memory or on a storage device.

netiquette: Etiquette for the Internet.

network: A group of interconnected computers.

page: Either a single screen of information on a Web site or all of the information on a particular site.

PDF (Portable Document Format): A file type developed by Adobe Systems to allow the preservation of complex formatting and symbols.

POP (Post Office Protocol): A standard for exchanging e-mail between a user's computer and an Internet access provider.

RAM (random access memory): RAM is the memory that a computer uses to temporarily store and manipulate information. RAM does not hold information after the computer is turned off.

RealAudio: Software that allows sound files to be transmitted from the Internet back to the user's computer in streams, allowing the experience of immediate and simultaneous playing.

service provider: Any organization that provides connections to the Internet.

SLIP/PPP (serial line internet protocol/point to point protocol): This is a connection which enables a home computer to receive TCP/IP addresses. To work with the World Wide Web from home, via a modem, a SLIP or PPP connection is necessary.

SMTP (Simple Mail Transfer Protocol): An accepted standard used extensively on the Internet to allow the transfer of e-mail messages between computers.

snail mail: A term that e-mail users employ to describe the traditional mail or post office service.

spam: To send e-mails to people who did not ask to be sent that information. Spamming is usual done as bulk e-mailing to promote a product.

TCP/IP (Transfer Control Protocol/Internet Protocol): Essentially this is the most basic language on the Internet. The rules of TCP/IP govern the sending of packets of data between computers on the Internet and allow for the transmission of other protocols on the Internet, such as http and FTP.

Telnet: An Internet protocol that enables a user to log on to a remote computer.

T-1 line: A leased Internet line connection. The speed at which data can be transmitted is 1.45 megabits per second on a T-1 line.

UNIX: Like DOS or Windows, UNIX is an operating system run by most of the computers that provide access to the Internet.

URL (uniform resource locator): This is the address for an Internet site.

Usenet: A network of newsgroups dedicated to thousands of different topics.

Web bot: A search engine that obtains its information by starting at a specified Web page and visiting each Web page that has a link to it. Web bots are used by large search engines such as Yahoo! to create their database. Also called spider, bot, and robot.

Web browser: A program used to access the WWW. The most popular browsers—Netscape and Mosaic—allow users to interact audiovisually with the World Wide Web.

Winsock: A program which runs in the background on a Windows-based personal computer, allowing the user to make a SLIP/PPP connection to the Internet and to use TCP/IP.

WWW (World Wide Web): An Internet service that enables users to connect to all of the hypermedia documents on the Internet. The Web is like a network within the Internet.

Zip: Zip (or zipped) files are files that have been compressed by a software package to reduce the amount of space that the data take up. This type of file is popular on the Internet because smaller files can be sent faster. To create or open a Zip file, a user needs a special software package such as WinZip or PKUNZIP. The .zip extension indicates a Zip file.

About the Editors
and Contributors

Guido Abbattista is Full Professor of Modern History, University of Trieste, Italy. His field of research is eighteenth-century political and historical culture in Europe and North America. Among his recent publications are *La rivoluzione americana* (Roma, 1998); "*Imperium e libertas*: repubblicanesimo e ideologia imperiale all'alba dell'espansione europea in Asia, 1650–1780," in *Studi settecenteschi*, n. 20, 2000, pp. 9–49; "Risorse elettroniche e telematiche per gli studi di Storia moderna," in *Memoria e Ricerca*, n. 5, January–June 2000, pp. 205–215; and "'Quand a commencé leur sagesse'? il *Journal des Sçavans* e il dibattito su antichità e civiltà della Cina (1754–1791)," in *Saggi in onore di Antonio Rotondò*, a cura di L. Simonutti, Firenze, Olschki, 2001, pp. 593–625 (forthcoming). He is currently a member of the team working on the critical edition of G.-T. Raynal, *Histoire philosophique et politique des établissements des Européens dans les Deux Indes* (1770–1780) (Oxford, Voltaire Foundation), and is writing a book on the Europeans in Asia in the early modern age. He is coeditor of the journal *Storia della Storiografia* and founder and editor of *Cromohs*, an electronic journal of the history of modern historiography (http://www.cromohs.unifi.it) with an electronic library of historiography and methodology (http://www.eliohs.unifi.it).

Jeffrey G. Barlow is the Matsushita Chair of Asian Studies at Pacific University in Forest Grove, Oregon, and editor of the *Journal of the Association for*

History and Computing (http://mcel.pacificu.edu/JAHC/). He has written four books and a number of articles on Chinese and Chinese-American history. He is a frequent traveler to Asia and has lived in China for more than six years, one year of which he spent working on a 64K Kaypro computer with a voltage regulator somewhat smaller than a Volkswagen. He is also the President and the Webmaster for the Association of Asian Studies on the Pacific Coast (ASPAC) (http://mcel.pacificu.edu/aspac/home/aspac.html).

Susanna Betzel is a bookseller and freelance writer with a particular interest in revolutionary France. She is currently working on her second novel about the French Revolution and hopes soon to have *Keystone of the Terror*, her transla- tion of the memoirs of the executioner of Paris, published by a university press.

Patrick Callan is a Deputy Principal and Lecturer at Maynooth-National Uni- versity of Ireland. He received his B.A., M.A., and Ph.D. from University Col- lege, Dublin, and he is a frequent speaker, writer, and lecturer in Ireland on the future of education and technology.

Jean Colson researches and teaches at the nexus of humanities and informa- tion technology. As a multimedia developer, one of her many roles, she created the CD, "Chicago 1919," which won the American Association for History and Computing's prize for the best Web site for the year 2001. She is a director of Mackenzie Ward Research. Originally an anthropologist, she has always been concerned with the development of methods and tools with which to research, study, and display the myriad representations of meanings in text and image.

Solomon Davidoff is an Instructor for the Department of Ethnic Studies and a doctoral candidate in the American Culture Studies Program at Bowling Green State University, Ohio.

Christine de Matos has taught history and computing over the past nine years at the University of Sydney; the University of Technology, Sydney; and the Univer- sity of Western Sydney. She is currently a doctoral candidate at the University of Western Sydney. Her dissertation explores Australians and the Left in Japan dur- ing the Allied Occupation from 1945 to 1949. Recent publications include a pa- per on the use of computing technology in Bachelor of Arts degrees and another on the Australian Labor government's policy toward the democratization of Ja- pan from 1945 to 1949. She is currently the manager of the Web site for the Professional Historians Association (NSW), Inc. (http://www.phansw.org.au).

Lloyd deMause is the Director of the Institute for Psychohistory, New York City, and editor of the *Journal of Psychohistory*. He has written widely on psychology and psychohistory, including three books: *Foundations of Reagan's America*, *Psychohistory*, and *Childhood and History*.

Samuel E. Dicks holds a doctorate from the University of Oklahoma and has been a member of the history faculty at Emporia State University, Kansas, since 1965. He is the publication director of *Teaching History: A Journal of Methods*, and edits its Internet Web site. In addition to courses in ancient and medieval history, he also teaches historiography and an introductory class in genealogy.

Bambi L. Dingman is a freelance writer from New Jersey. She has been the French and Indian War editor for *Smoke and Fire News*, an internationally recognized living history newspaper, and has also written for *Recreating History Magazine*. She currently serves as the Regimental Adjutant for the 7th Vermont Infantry Regiment as part of the Web-based project Vermont in the Civil War.

Kenneth R. Dvorak is the Secretary-Treasurer of the American Association for History and Computing and a doctoral candidate in American culture studies at Bowling Green State University, Ohio. He is the codirector of two nationally honored Web sites—America in the 1890s and 1890s Bowling Green, Ohio, and he has written numerous articles that have appeared in the *Journal of Film and History*, the *Journal of Popular Culture*, and the *Journal of American Culture*.

TammyJo Eckhart is an assistant instructor and Ph.D. candidate in ancient history at Indiana University in Bloomington. She focuses on issues of gender and sexuality, mythology, and slavery. Her minor fields are folklore and comparative women's history. Her research has been published in *Aeon: A Journal of Myth and Science*, her book reviews appear regularly in *The Women's Classical Caucus Newsletter*, and she is a contributor to Salem Press's *Encyclopedia of the Ancient World*. She presented a paper at the Fall 2001 Classified Association of the Atlantic States (CAAS) meeting in Maryland.

Susan Ferentinos is associate editor of the *OAH Magazine of History*, published by the Organization of American Historians, and a Ph.D. candidate in U.S. history at Indiana University. She holds an M.A. in history and an M.L.S., with a concentration in special collections.

Claire Gabriel is Librarian for United States and World History at New York University and has worked previously for the Humanities and Social Sciences Library of the New York Public Library. She holds an M.L.S. from Columbia University and an M.A. in history from New York University. Past projects include a Web history tutorial designed for students at NYU and other historical researchers.

Mark Gellis is an amateur historian, with an interest in military history, and Associate Professor of Rhetoric and Professional Communication at Kettering University in Flint, Michigan.

Kathryn L. Green is an independent scholar. She received her M.A. and Ph.D. from Indiana University and has published numerous articles on African history. Her current research deals with the roles of archives and museums in civil society. She is online coeditor for two H-Net listservs, H-Africa and H-AfResearch, and is the coauthor of the Web site Africa Research Central (http://www.africa-research.org/), which continues to develop.

Mary Anne Hansen is an Assistant Professor at Montana State University Libraries. She has authored numerous articles and presented papers at several scholarly conferences, including the Association of College and Research Libraries Biennial Conference.

James E. Jolly is a doctoral student and Adjunct Professor of American History at Middle Tennessee State University.

Ken Kempcke received his M.A. in American studies from Purdue University and his M.L. S. from Indiana University. He is currently the Social Science Reference Librarian and Coordinator of Library Instruction at Montana State University, Bozeman.

Andrew E. Kersten has taught at the University of Wisconsin, Green Bay, since 1997. He earned his B.A. at the University of Wisconsin, Madison, and he received the M.A. and Ph.D. in United States history from the University of Cincinnati. He has published in the *Queen City Heritage*, *The Michigan Historical Review*, and *The Missouri Historical Review* and has contributed to several anthologies. He is currently working on a book-length study of President Franklin D. Roosevelt's Fair Employment Practice Committee.

Stephen Kneeshaw is Professor of History at College of the Ozarks in southwest Missouri. He is also involved with the teacher education program, specifically history and social studies education. He completed his B.A. in history and English at the University of Puget Sound and his M.A. and Ph.D. in American history at the University of Colorado, Boulder. Since 1972 he has been on the history faculty at College of the Ozarks, where he was named the first recipient of the college's Distinguished Faculty Award for excellence in teaching, scholarship, and service. He has held fellowships for study and research at the Newberry Library, Harvard, MIT, and the U.S. Military Academy at West Point. Steve is the founder and editor of *Teaching History: A Journal of Methods* and for several years has presented workshops on "Active Teaching and Learning" at high schools and colleges. His publications cover a wide range of topics from diplomatic history to history education, active learning, and writing to learn.

David Koeller received his M.A. and Ph.D. from the University of California, Berkeley, and is a specialist in the German Enlightenment. He is an Associate Professor of History at North Park University, where he has taught world history for many years. He also serves as a member of the World History Association and recently won a grant from the Ameritech corporation to help develop the WebChron Web Chronology Project.

Jessica Lacher-Feldman serves as the Public and Outreach Services Coordinator at the W.S. Hoole Special Collections Library at the University of Alabama. As a part of the libraries faculty, she coordinates reference services and instruction, curates archival exhibitions, arranges public events, and manages the Hoole Web site. A native of New York State, she holds a B.A. in French studies and master's degrees in history and library science (archives concentration) from the State University of New York at Albany. She is active in the American Association for History and Computing, the Society of American Archivists, and the Society of Alabama Archivists.

Leo E. Landis is Curator of Agriculture at Henry Ford Museum and Greenfield Village in Dearborn, Michigan. He launched the Web site for the editorial office of *Agricultural History* in October 1995. He often provides content for the museum's Web site (http://www.hfmgv.org) and is working toward a Ph.D. in agricultural history from Iowa State University. His research interests are Midwestern agriculture and social and cultural history. He is author of *Building Better Roads: Iowa's Contribution to Highway Engineering*.

Julia Landweber is Visiting Assistant Professor of Early Modern European History at Gettysburg College in Gettysburg, Pennsylvania. In 2001 she received her Ph.D. from Rutgers University for the dissertation "French Delight in Turkey: National Identity Construction in the Seventeenth and Eighteenth Centuries," a cultural history of the construction of national identity as revealed through France's diplomatic, political, and cultural relationship with the Ottoman Empire between the late seventeenth and mid-eighteenth centuries.

Todd E.A. Larson is a doctoral candidate in modern British history at the University of Illinois at Urbana-Champaign. He has been deeply involved in academic technologies and has held technology appointments at the National Center for Supercomputing Applications, the Division of Guided Individual Study, and the University of Illinois Provosts' Office. Currently he is the first historian to be named an associate fellow of the Merriam Laboratory for Analytic Political Research. He was a coauthor of *The History Highway* (M.E. Sharpe, 1997) and the coeditor of the forthcoming *Splendidly Victorian: Essays in Nineteenth and Twentieth Century British History in Honour of Walter L. Arnstein* (Ashgate Press, 2001).

Tracy Penny Light is a Ph.D. candidate in the Department of History at the University of Waterloo, Ontario, Canada, and currently holds a Teaching Fellowship at the University's Centre for Learning and Teaching Through Technology. Her research areas include Canadian and women's history and the improvement of student learning through the use of new instructional technologies, in the discipline of history specifically and across the disciplines generally. She teaches in these areas and also develops workshops and coordinates programs for instructors on a wide array of instructional design issues.

Charles H. MacKay is Assistant Professor of History at Morehead State University, Kentucky. He received his B.A. from the University of Arkansas and his doctorate from Florida State University. He has served on the Executive Board of the American Association for History and Computing and spoken widely on teaching and technology.

Margaret M. Manchester is Assistant Professor of History and Director of the American Studies Program at Providence College, Rhode Island.

Robert M.S. McDonald is Assistant Professor of History at the United States Military Academy, West Point. A specialist in the Revolutionary and early national periods of U.S. history, he holds degrees from the University of Virginia, Oxford University, and the University of North Carolina at Chapel Hill, where he received his Ph.D. He is currently at work on a book about Thomas Jefferson's public image between 1776 and 1826.

Scott A. Merriman is a doctoral candidate in modern American history at the University of Kentucky. He has previously taught history at the University of Cincinnati, Northern Kentucky University, and Thomas More College. He is also a coauthor of *The History Highway: A Guide to Internet Resources*, coeditor of *The History Highway 2000: A Guide to Internet Resources*, coeditor of *History.edu: Essays on Teaching with Technology*, and an associate editor for the *Journal of the Association for History and Computing*. He has contributed to the *Register of the Kentucky Historical Society*, *Historical Encyclopedia of World Slavery*, *American National Biography*, and *Buckeye Hill Country*.

Martin V. Minner is a Ph.D. candidate at Indiana University who specializes in urban history and photographic history. His current research is on civic politics and cultural memory in Newark, New Jersey. He is also a technical communication consultant and has worked in software development and computer publishing.

Charlene Mires is Assistant Professor of History at Villanova University. She received her M.A. from the University of Pennsylvania and her doctorate from Temple University. She has published widely on American culture and material culture and serves as the project coordinator for the Centennial Exhibition of 1876 Project (http://www.villanova.edu/~his2998cm/).

Richard P. Mulcahy is Associate Professor of History and Director of the Division of Social Sciences at the University of Pittsburgh, Titusville. The author of a number of refereed articles and book chapters, he just had a book published on social policy in Appalachia.

Jessie Bishop Powell is completing her M.L.S. at the University of Kentucky, where she holds an M.A. in English. Her primary research interest is the economic situation of Appalachian libraries in Eastern Kentucky.

Edward Ragan is currently a Ph.D. candidate at Syracuse University, where he is studying early American and native American history. His dissertation explores Anglo-Indian relations in Virginia. Through his research, he has become involved with Virginia's Indians in their efforts to gain federal recognition.

deTraci Regula is the author of *The Mysteries of Isis*, which explores the religion of Isis in Greece, in Ptolemaic Egypt, and in modern revivals. She has written dozens of articles on Greece, ancient and modern. She is presently the Greece for Visitors Guide at the Mining Company, http://gogreece.min ingco.com.

J. Kelly Robison is an American Studies Fellow and the Academic Computing Specialist at the Center for U.S. Studies, Martin-Luther University Halle-Wittenberg, Wittenberg, Germany. He holds a Ph.D. in American history from Oklahoma State University and an M.A. in American history from the University of Montana. His research and teaching focus is the history of the American West and Native America, with a special emphasis on the Spanish Borderlands and cross-cultural acculturation. He is also interested in the use of computer technology in teaching and researching history. He is a consulting editor for the *Journal of the Association for History and Computing* and is a member of the Executive Board of the American Association for History and Computing.

Anne Rothfeld is an Information Specialist at the University of Maryland, Baltimore. She earned her M.A. in library science from the Catholic University of America, concentrating in special collections and archives. Previously she was the Archivist Technician at the U.S. Holocaust Memorial Museum in Washington, D.C.

Andrew Sawyer is a project manager for MacKenzie Ward Research, a new media company in the United Kingdom with a strong commitment to cultural heritage publishing. His doctoral thesis examined the interface between power and imagery in the early Dutch Republic. To allow a systematic analysis of the sources, they were digitally modeled, then analyzed using Kleio Image Analysis Software.

Kalpana Shankar is a doctoral candidate in library and information science at the University of California, Los Angeles. Her particular interest is in scientific record keeping, scientific archives, and their relationship to the historiography of science.

Christopher A. Snyder is currently Acting Chair of the Department of History and Politics at Marymount University in Arlington, Virginia. He taught at Emory University and the College of William and Mary before coming to Marymount, and he is a Fellow of the Society of Antiquaries of Scotland. His books include *Sub-Roman Britain (AD 400–800): A Gazetteer of Sites* (Oxford, 1996) and *An Age of Tyrants: Britain and the Britons, AD 400–800* (Penn State, 1998).

Eric G. Swedin holds a Ph.D. in history from Case Western Reserve University. He currently works as the Webmaster at the Thiokol Propulsion Division of Cordant Technologies and as Adjunct Professor of History at Weber State University in Ogden, Utah.

H. Micheal Tarver is currently Assistant Professor of World History at McNeese State University (Lake Charles, Louisiana) and Profesor Invitado at the Centro de Estudios Históricos "Carlos Emilio Muñoz Oráa" at the Universidad de Los Andes (Mérida, Venezuela). He received his M.A. from the University of Southwestern Louisiana and his doctorate from Bowling Green State University, Ohio.

Gunnar Thorvaldsen is the Manager of Research at the Norwegian Historical Data Center, The University of Tromsoe, with a specialty in migration studies and the computerization of historical microdata. He is currently a member of a research team in the Center for Advanced Study in the Norwegian Academy of Sciences and Letters, studying the mortality decline in Norway between 1770 and 1920. He also has spent a sabbatical at the Census Projects, the University of Minnesota, and has been a guest researcher at the Demographic Database, The University of Umeå, Sweden, and at the Stockholm Historical Database.

Dennis A. Trinkle is the Tenzer University Professor in Instructional Technology and the Associate Coordinator of Information Services and Technology at DePauw University. He received his B.A. from DePauw University and his M.A. and Ph.D. from the University of Cincinnati. He also serves as the Executive Director of the American Association for History and Computing (http://www.theaahc.org). He has published broadly on technology, teaching, and history. His recent books include *The History Highway: A Guide to Internet Resources*; *Writing, Teaching, and Researching History in the Electronic Age*; *History.Edu: Essays on Teaching with Technology*; and *The History Highway 2000*.

Keith C. Trinkle is the chief financial officer for ETC: The Educational Technology Consulting Group. He majored in history at Indiana University and is a nationally recognized pioneer in the development of interactive computing environments such as bulletin boards, newsgroups, and chat sites. He is currently completing an M.B.A. at Indiana State University.

Susan Tschabrun is Reference and Electronic Resources Librarian at California State University, San Bernardino. She holds a Ph.D. in history from University of Wisconsin, Madison, and an M.L.S. from UCLA. She is currently the project director for a Getty-funded grant to catalog and digitize the holdings of the Center for the Study of Political Graphics, an educational archive of domestic and international political and protest posters in Los Angeles. Other projects include work on a set of multimedia learning modules to teach history majors information competency skills and coauthorship of the Web site Africa Research Central: A Clearinghouse of African Primary Sources.

Laura Winninghoff is the Evening Circulation Librarian at the Law Library at Indiana University, Bloomington. She has also worked in the Curatorial and Collections Departments of the Houdini Historical Center and the Children's Museum of Indianapolis and has taught history and English at Notre Dame Girls Academy in Chicago. Her research interests include the interaction of museum visitors and Web-based exhibits. She earned her M.L.S. and M.A. in history at Indiana University, Bloomington.

Richard Wojtowicz is Reference Librarian and Assistant Professor at Montana State University, Bozeman. He received his M.S. in library and information science from the University of Illinois, Urbana-Champaign (2000), his M.A. in the history of science and technology from Montana State University (1989), and his B.A. in geography from S.U.N.Y. at Buffalo (1973). In 1989, he compiled *Blacks Who Stole Themselves: Advertisements for Runaways in the Pennsylvania Gazette, 1728–1790* with Billy G. Smith. He is presently working on an environmental history of the Yellowstone River basin.

Alexander Zukas is Associate Professor of History at National University in San Diego. He received his Ph.D. in history from the University of California, Irvine, in 1991. He has written on European working-class and gender history, innovative approaches to the teaching of world history, and the use of music and theater to teach historical subject matter. His publications include the articles "Lazy, Apathetic, and Dangerous: The Social Construction of Unemployed Workers in the Late Weimar Republic," *Contemporary European History* (forthcoming); "Cyberworld: Teaching World History on the World Wide Web," *The History Teacher* (August 1999); "Age of Empire," *Radical History Review* (Winter 1997); and "Different Drummers: Using Music to Teach History," *Perspectives* (October 1996). He is currently working on articles about teaching world history courses on the Internet, the phenomenology of teaching online, Karl Korsch's Marxism, unemployed workers in the Ruhr region of Germany during the Weimar Republic, and the ecology of the Ruhr from 1850 to 1930. He serves as Director of the Institute for Community and Oral History of the Center for Cultural and Ethnic Studies at National University.

Index

I

Sipapu: The Anasazi Emergence into the
Cyber World, 259
SISTER-L, 548
Sites by T.F. Boettger, 149
Sixties (bbhq.com), 343
Sixties (geocities.com), 343
Skylighters, 343
Slavery, 548
Slavery a Positive Good, 291
Slavic and East European Collections at UC
Berkeley, 559
Slavic Review, 578
SLIP/PPP Serial Line Internet Protocol/Point
to Point Protocol, 636
Slovene Archives, 578
Small Towns, Black Lives, 520
Smitha, Frank's World History, 367
Smith, Gerrit Virtual Museum, 277
Smithsonian Institution, 244, 521
Smithsonian: Agriculture and Horticulture,
374
Smithsonian Institution Libraries, 630
Smithsonian Institution Social Studies Lesson
Plans, 537
SMTP: Simple Mail Transfer Protocol, 636
Snail Mail, 636
soc.college, 549
soc.college.teaching-asst, 550
SOCHIS-L, 550
soc.history, 550
soc.history.living, 550
soc.history.medieval, 550
soc.history.moderated, 550
soc.history.science, 550
soc.history.war, 550
soc.history.war.misc, 550
soc.history.war.us-civil-war, 550
soc.history.war.vietnam, 550
soc.history.war.world-war-ii, 550
soc.libraries, 550
Social Life of Cities, 461
Social Science Data Archives - Europe,
598
Social Security Administration online
history, 315
Social Statistics Briefing Room, 615
Social Studies Resources, 538
Social Studies School Service, 538
Social Studies School Services: Black
History, 246

Social Studies: Women's History, 360
Société Française d'Histoire Urbaine, 456
Society for American City and Regional
Planning History, 456
Society for Creative Anachronism (SCA),
474
Society for History Education:The History
Teacher, 509
Society for Latin American Studies (UK),
231
Society for Romanian Studies, 145
Society of American Archivists (SAA), 572
Society of Architectural Historians, 452
Society of Early Americanists (SEA) Home
Page, 262
Song of Igor's Campaign, 156
Sophia Smith Collection of Women's History
Manuscripts, Smith College, 589
Sources for the Study of the Southwest, 346
Sources for Women's Studies in the
Methodist Archives, 360
South African Military History Society, 432
South African Truth and Reconciliation
Commission, 95
South African War Virtual Library, 96, 417
South Asia, 105
South Carolina 1st Artillery, C.S.A, 475
South Carolina Historical Society, 491
South Dakota State Historical Society/Office
of History, 491
Southeast Asia Guide, 105
Southern Italy in the Early Middle Ages,
218
Southern Register, 559
Soviet Archives Exhibit, 334
Soviet Invasion of Afghanistan, 430
Soviet Leaders, 149
Soviet War Photography, 154
Spam, 636
Spanish-American War Centennial Web Site,
308
Spanish-American War in Motion Pictures,
308
Spanish-American War Page, 417
Spanish Civil War (geocities.com), 419
Spanish Civil War (lcweb2.loc.gov), 419
Spanish Revolution and Civil War, 419
Special Collections, 590
Special Collections Digital Center, University
of Virginia, 605

W